COUNSEL
IN THE
CREASE

COUNSEL
IN THE
CREASE
A BIG LEAGUE PLAYER
IN THE HOCKEY WARS

ROBERT O. SWADOS
FOREWORD BY SCOTTY BOWMAN

Prometheus Books

59 John Glenn Drive
Amherst, New York 14228-2197

Published 2006 by Prometheus Books

Inquiries should be addressed to
Prometheus Books
59 John Glenn Drive
Amherst, New York 14228-2197
VOICE: 716-691-0133, ext. 207
FAX: 716-564-2711
WWW.PROMETHEUSBOOKS.COM

10 09 08 07 06   5 4 3 2

Library of Congress Cataloging-in-Publication Data

Swados, Robert O.
   Counsel in the crease : a big league player in the hockey wars / by Robert O. Swados.
      p. cm.
   Includes bibliographical references and index.
   ISBN 1-59102-355-6 (hardcover : alk. paper)
   1. Swados, Robert O. 2. Hockey team owners—New York—Biography.
3. Buffalo Sabres (Hockey team). 4. Lawyers—New York (State)—Biography.
I. Title.

GV848.5.S93A3 2005
796.962'092—dc22

2005018360

Printed in the United States of America on acid-free paper

CONTENTS

3

PART 3: THE HOCKEY WARS—THE FACE-OFF

PART 4: AT THE LEAGUE'S BLUE LINE

PART 5: COUNSEL IN THE CREASE

FOREWORD

Scotty Bowman

I consider it both an honor and a privilege to write the foreword to this fascinating book, *Counsel in the Crease.*

I have known Bob Swados personally for more than twenty-five years, and I am truly amazed at his recall of events. Bob has faced and overcome many difficult challenges because of his constant determination and consistent attitude.

In *Counsel in the Crease,* Bob takes the reader through his early days as a student, his military experiences, and, finally, his legal career, which has spanned nearly sixty years. Bob's devotion to the Western New York area is clearly represented in his many attempts to bring major league baseball and hockey to Buffalo. Bob's fierce determination and passionate approach were essential to achieving the ultimate goal of acquiring an NHL franchise for the Western New York area: the Buffalo Sabres. *Counsel in the Crease* documents Bob's unwavering support for the Buffalo Sabres and the expertise he shared with the late Knox brothers, Seymour and Northrup.

Bob also served as the secretary of the NHL Board of Governors for more than fifteen years and under three leaders: Clarence Campbell, John Ziegler, and Gary Bettman. Bob's service as secretary, along with his active involvement in the labor disputes between players and owners, displays both his integrity and his intellectual insight.

Bob Swados was a pioneer in the NHL. While drafting bylaws for the NHL, Bob enacted legislation to protect teams from abandoning cities in attempts to move to more lucrative markets. This foresight had a leaguewide stabilizing effect for NHL franchises such as Edmonton, Oakland, St. Louis, and Buffalo.

Bob and I share many of the same beliefs with regard to the most recent NHL labor dispute. The agreement between owners and players that has been in place for the past ten years makes it challenging to carve out the framework for a new agreement. Bob knew what he was writing about regarding the 1994 NHL labor dispute: that the NHL came very close in 1994 to accomplishing exactly what they have had difficulty in achieving in 2005.

Bob Swados's true legacy will be remembered as his strong ability to forge new deals and to make others wonder how he had the time to wear so many hats.

Good Luck, Bob.

Scotty Bowman
May 2005

ACKNOWLEDGMENTS

To the colleens, colleagues, and comrades whose talent, intelligence, friendship, and enthusiasm over the years enabled me to produce this book:

Marcella and Jeff Whitman and Julie Schuetze and Jan Haas, and the entire staff at my law firm—Phillips Lytle;

Bill Wippert;

Steven L. Mitchell, Peggy Deemer, Meg French, and the editorial crew at Prometheus Books;

My daughter, the composer-playright Elizabeth Swados; and Eric Lerner, Ken Cohen, and David Garbus; Denise Levy, Karen Mathews, Bonnie Flickinger, Bob Rich Jr., Nellie Drew Meosky, and Gene Rudzinski; my brother, the designer Kim Edgar Swados; and Dennis and Kay Kempner;

Elaine Burzinski, Dolores Burke, and Teri Orsini;

And Jean Hough Davey and Bob, and Dorothy Hughes and Bill; and Ken Dryden and John McAllister and Brian Bellmore; and Jim Locke, and Greg Ivancic;

Jay Brett, Jack Dee, Larry Kerman, John Blair, and Dave Roach; Pat Tone, Burt Wilkinson, Bill Lutz, and Ray Stevens; and Al Mugel;

John Ziegler, Gary Bettman, and Bill Wirtz;

Scotty and Suella Bowman;

10 ACKNOWLEDGMENTS

Gerry Goldberg, Gene Warner, and the *Buffalo News* staff; the *Sports Business Journal*, and Eric Duhachek of the *Toronto Globe and Mail*; and Ed Kilgore of WGRZ-TV;

And most of all, Jean Knox, Cetta Knox, and their families, and Jean-Jacaues Boissier and the Paul and Fred Schoellkopf and George Goodyear families, who enriched my life so much and will be remembered with warmth forever.

Finally—Fran Kempner, who through some mystical error loved me and caused the gods to smile on me one more time.

Introduction

THE AUTHOR—AS FAN, COUNSEL, MOVER, AND HOCKEY MOGUL

I loved the law, not for any philosophical or jurisprudential reason, but for the range and stage it gave me. I had learned to love "the Hockey," as my Canadian friends would speak of it, not as a confirmed jock—although I'd begun to learn and breathe the elementals of the game as a kid on the frozen Delaware Park Lake (now Hoyt Lake) in Buffalo—at the hands of a former defenseman in the Montreal Canadiens' organization, who was my neighbor. But it would be years before my range in the law met the excitement on the ice. I had been a wide-swinging corporate counsel—pretty adept, and on the national legal scene, before the challenges of the National Hockey League began to consume my practice. With the usually enthusiastic ambitions of our clients, I had been at various times a tax lawyer, a defender of Western New York companies attacked in proxy fights and tender offers, a merger specialist, an expert on broadcasting and the acquisition of television stations, a New York State Commissioner of Probation, a builder in the theatrical arts and the regional theater, a conservative husbander of family assets in estate practice, and an active strategist in moves to bring Major League Baseball to the Western New York community.

With all that fancy language, what kind of lawyer was I, really? Well, I learned early in my career, after returning from World War II, that barrister roles such as those now portrayed in *Law and Order* or *The Practice* were not for me. I could handle the trials if I had to, but I couldn't sleep at night when the sessions were on. Other lawyers would come to us to represent their clients on appeals, and those I could deal with. We always insisted on first-rate research and the most current knowledge of trends and court decisions. But it was solving problems and producing results that most appealed to me and seemed to fit my talents. For those issues I could choose my timing, to some degree, and I found that in negotiations I could start early in the morning, stay awake and alert through the night, and continue, still articulate, at 5:00 AM.

But how did I end up, at age fifty—in 1969—living most of my life and career over the next thirty years in the excitement, pleasures, wins, and defeats of that bruising Canadian game hockey?

I was very lucky; I had talented associates and partners who indulged my passion for making our practice exciting, on the cutting edge of the economy, and socially productive. Our firm was large enough to take on, within limits, almost any complex legal problem; yet it was small enough so that, a principal partner most of those years, I could roam across and fire intensely at the area that needed the most attention—or satisfied my taste! If we didn't know as much as anybody else about a particular field, we would soon find out, or find somebody who did. With that flexibility, I could pander to the notion, engendered by my Harvard Law training and standing, that *any* problem could benefit from our contribution. I used to tell my juniors that one-on-one or six-on-six we could do as good a job as any New York or Washington firm. If the issue required a much larger staff, for instance, a major antitrust case, of course we might have to relinquish the lead to a larger organization. But this "controlled arrogance" attracted and held our clients, who, fortunately, were men and women of intelligence and public standing who were risk takers with an eye to the needs of their community.

Those clients' attraction for intelligence, risk, and good judgment seemed, starting in 1960, to be strongly interested in major-league professional sports—and their accompanying magnetic auras: the quick leap to local prominence with the fans, the emotional highs in the wins, the challenges of the losses, the national stage created by television. It was Reg Taylor who called on me in 1960 to make Buffalo's first try for a Major League Baseball franchise in the Continental League, formed by Branch Rickey and Bill Shea in an attempt to force the majors to grant New York City a second team to compete with the Yankees. We called on our experience in proxy fights to force the leading concessionaire in the baseball world, Sportservice, to cast its vote for the Buffalo Bisons to enter the Continental League. In the end we didn't make it—the Senate Commerce Committee made a deal with Major League Baseball to let four teams into the majors—Houston, New York (Mets), Los Angeles, and Kansas City (which moved from Washington)—leaving Toronto, Dallas, and Buffalo out in the cold. It was an exclusive but painful education in the monopoly and the political and financial practices of the major leagues. It was a frustrating and strange experience; no one was allowed to vote except the senators, who supported Bill Shea.

We tried again in 1967–1968. Van DeVries, my client and onetime general manager of Buffalo's Channel 2 (the TV station our Buffalo-Niagara Group had created) was the leader of the application, along with other former television owners and the principal political figures in the city. I have a copy of the *New York Daily News* headline announcing, with fallacious finality, that the two new franchises in the National Baseball League would go to San Diego and *Buffalo*. Fred Fleig, vice president of the National League, called me from the owners' meeting at 6:00 PM that Sunday. "Get your group together, Bob—it looks like you're going to get it!" Three hours later I got another call: "Sorry, Bob. It's gone to Montreal. . . ."[1] Bowie Kuhn, then general counsel for the league, who would later become commissioner of Major League Baseball, told me some years later that we had a unanimous vote except for San Francisco's Horace Stoneham, who refused to go along with choosing Buffalo. I have always believed that Stoneham was acting as a shill for Dodgers bigwheel Walter O'Malley, who didn't want to be seen as opposing our group, but, despite his encouraging words to us, secretly held out for his protégés, Buzzy Bavasi and John McHale, who had made connections with Montreal and San Diego.

The veto by the National League had everybody in Buffalo upset—and I was left with the reputation as "the greatest living authority on how *not* to get a major league sports franchise"!

Although baseball was the origin of my adventure in professional sports, it was a group of television owners that financed our ultimately successful entry into the major leagues. In a dramatic episode in the 1950s, a coalition headed by Paul and Fred Schoellkopf and George Goodyear won the fight for the original grant from the Federal Communications Commission for Channel 2 Buffalo, which promptly expanded its coverage across the Canadian border to Toronto, Ontario. After the expiration of a two-year contract with NBC—which was supposed to be the prize for winning the fight in the FCC for the channel—NBC pulled its contract and sought to take away its network programs by acquiring a local UHF station, leaving the group that had acquired Channel 2 with no marketable network and faced with sudden insolvency. But the Buffalo-Niagara Group responded with unusual courage and know-how, established its own network of seven television stations called Transcontinent Television Corporation, and with a display of smarts and political savvy became a power in the television industry on its own. This compelled NBC to restore its network affiliation with the Buffalo station. The multiple venture ultimately sold ten years later, in a transaction negotiated by the author, for the largest price in the history of the broadcast industry at that time. That ten-year experience educated me and my law firm on a national level and produced dollars for the investors, making them loyal and perceptive friends and clients. They came willingly to the fold as Buffalo Sabres partners in the National Hockey League in 1969, when Seymour Knox III and Northrup Knox, with my help, began the grand and exciting thirty years of major-league hockey ownership.

In this book I'll now tell the tales I've been privileged to live through as hockey counsel: of politics and economics and strikes and lockouts, of player contracts, of expansion, of the WHA, of the conflicts between Canadian law and culture and that in the United States, of talent and mediocrity, of judgment and luck, of litigation and solution, of TV ratings and hockey marketing, of finances and arena, of rules and farm teams, of drafts and trades, of free agency and "caps," of the media . . . of exhilarating wins and bitter losses—of coaches and scouts and managers—of fans and owners and the players' association and the commissioners, and the Board of Governors.

A hockey rink is configured with a space marked in front of the goal called the crease. Its shape and even its color (the paint) has changed over the years. Once intended for the protection of the goaltender, it told the players: You can't score if you're standing in that zone when you shoot the puck. Changes to that rule were sponsored by Gary Bettman in the 1999 Stanley Cup Finals, following the controversy fulminated by Brett Hull's winning "no goal," scored while he was standing in the crease, producing Dallas's tainted triumph over Buffalo. Since then the protected zone has been penetrated. But it's still the target, the place to be, to score—if you can't, maybe your teammate can. In my more than thirty years in the hockey business I've tried for my share of goals from the crease, in all the wonderful issues I've been privileged to encounter. Maybe I didn't make as many as I would have liked—but I always tried to hit the crease. As you read, you'll see . . .

Part 1

THE COUNSEL IN WAR AND PEACE

Chapter 1

WASHINGTON, DC

The Lawyer as Public Servant

THE STARS AT HARVARD

The year 1941–42 in Cambridge, Massachusetts, was a delightful experience. My marriage to Sylvia was fun. My late-blooming academic success at Harvard Law School and my appointment as faculty assistant, and then as law clerk to Chief Judge Calvert Magruder of the US Court of Appeals for the First Circuit, gave me a heady confidence. The sounds of Pearl Harbor broke into the Boston Symphony concert on December 7— so we knew the world and the war were out there, but the university community provided a mantle of protection for a while. We had tenth-row orchestra seats at the symphony for fifty cents each; an on-campus apartment—we had to stoke our own furnace—reserved for young faculty and graduate students; and a warm welcome from the faculty at occasional teas and cocktail parties—including the teaching "greats" such as James M. Landis and Paul Freund and Austin Scott and Erwin Griswold, who engaged us in sharp dialogue about law and foreign relations and politics and science as if, rookies though we were, our views were entitled to be voiced, if not accepted. I played tennis, and Sylvia, a national doubles champion at table tennis, made small change beating unbelieving arrogant male Ping-Pong players in the dorm basement. We knew that ultimately we would have to go out into the world—not to conquer it, I told Mrs. Magruder, but "to make it better."

My principal assignment at the law school was the Ames Competition—the system of moot court tournaments used to teach the students how to present a case to an appeals tribunal—including analyzing the facts, researching the laws and precedents, drafting the written presentation, and crafting the oral argument. The cases were theoretical—designed to stimulate research and logic—but in the later rounds of the competition the judges were real, drafted from the local, state, and federal courts. It was my personal responsibility to create the case and procure the judges for the finals—argued by the two teams that had emerged as the best in the third-year class. I came up with a lollapa-loser. Why not, I said to Dean Landis and Paul Freund (the distinguished professor of constitutional law), try an actual case of national import now pending in the courts? The Federal Communications Commission had recently announced new regulations restricting the number of hours the networks could impose their programs on local radio stations—"prime time"—and other measures designed to preserve local news and entertainment, and the networks had appealed to the courts, charging that the FCC rules were unreasonable, illegal, and unconstitutional. I didn't stop with the case. Why not, I asked, invite one of the Supreme Court justices to be presiding judge in the moot court? The faculty thought it was a great idea and helped me invite Justice Robert Jackson (later of Nuremberg fame), and he accepted. I used the record—simplified—as it appeared in the FCC report filed with the lower federal court.

But there was a problem. The case had not yet been heard in the Supreme Court, and NBC objected. The network's lawyers intervened, arguing to the dean that they had a right to have the Supreme Court's ear *first*. They didn't want those learned judges' first impressions to be marred or distorted by some rookie law students, whatever their competence. Dean Griswold referred the question to Felix Frankfurter (then still a part-time faculty member). The weighty Frankfurter judgment was as follows: the NBC barristers had no constitutional right to insist that the Supreme Court be ignorant of the facts or the law before they heard the case. The intervention was dismissed.

The moot court argument was exciting and intellectually first-rate; Justice Jackson said he found the occasion enjoyable and helpful. I took him to the airport—I should have delegated that to someone else—and added some unnecessary excitement when, aroused by the presence of the star justice and confused by the old Boston cobblestones, I drove the wrong way on a one-way street. But the judge took it with good humor, and I put him on his plane without injury.

The "prime time" restrictions would later become an important concept in the network-affiliate structure, continuing into the era of broadcast and cable television.

LIFE WITH THE JUDGE'S JUDGE

Calvert Magruder, my first boss in the outside world, was a wonderful man. As the most important federal judge in New England, he had prestige and power. He carried his robe with intellect, but humility; dignity, but humor. In an environment when "A" gasoline rations were a rare privilege available to federal judges, he rode the subway. When he could have had gourmet meals in the local clubs, he ate in the courthouse cafeteria—and taught me to like oyster stew.

I walked into the judicial chambers one day to see the three judges flipping coins. "What's that?" I asked his secretary. "Oh," she said, "the associate judges don't like certain cases—loser gets the patent appeal." When Judge Magruder disagreed with my recommendation in a major tax case and was unanimously reversed by the Supreme Court, he vowed "never to overrule Swados again."

With Calvert Magruder, loyalty was a principal value. A Web site raising again the issue of the guilt or innocence of Alger Hiss recently appeared on the Internet.[1] Magruder knew Hiss well—as a student at the law school and as an officer of international organizations on whose boards the judge had served as director or officer. At Hiss's second trial on the charges of communism, spying, and perjury made by Whittaker Chambers, Hiss's lawyers needed a character witness—preferably Jewish because the venue was in New York City. According to Paul Cohen—my uncle and ultimately the senior partner in my law firm—the lawyers asked Joseph Proskauer, a former New York judge and founder of the prominent New York firm that now represents the NHL, to be that witness. Paul told me, with some pride and sense of satisfaction, that he had "talked the judge out of it; it would do him no good." (Paul Cohen was Proskauer's son-in-law.) The witness who did agree to serve was Calvert Magruder. Magruder was High Episcopal, but much respected in New York circles. When I asked him about it, Judge Magruder responded laconically, "I cannot believe he is guilty."

THE LURE OF WASHINGTON

The year as Harvard assistant/Magruder clerk was intellectually, socially, and financially remarkable. (The two jobs earned me the highest pay in my law school class—about $5,000). The judge asked me to stay on, and while it was tempting, I knew the military was on the horizon. I was anxious for some practical experience before induction and wanted to participate somehow in the war effort. Henry Hart, a very decent guy and a leading authority on administrative law on the Harvard Law faculty, was moving to Washington to serve as associate general counsel of the Office of Price Administration

(OPA), and he persuaded me to join his staff as an associate price attorney. It proved to be one of the most rewarding experiences of my life: as an economics major, the thrust of the agency—controlling inflation and preventing war-bloated prices from producing unwise or unfair allocation of resources—was right up my alley. The morale of the staff was great—idealist, but practical—the caliber was terrific, recruited from top firms and top students; and the leadership was brilliant, but kind and personable. Sam Block, my boss, later founded Jenner & Block, LLP, one of the leading Chicago law firms. Sam was like a great coach—demanding, resourceful, and appreciative. It was a good feeling, working there every day. Working with talented people, on important issues implicated in the war economy, what we did counted. There was, however, a sense of the temporary: the job did not provide an exemption from military service, and for many of us there was a need to move toward the army, despite our temporary cynosures. Sam Block had poor eyesight; in the midst of a price-ceiling crisis, he would use special muscular exercises and medication from a holistic opthamologist in the hope of improving his eyesight enough to make him eligible for the service.

One of my jobs was the preparation of the Statement of Considerations, which was published when a new price regulation was issued. This was like a congressional committee report explaining the reasons for the price ceiling and its technical provisions. In litigation—and there was plenty, as not only the Roosevelt haters and the war profiteers, but irritated ordinary laissez-faire businessmen attacked the agency—it was an important defensive weapon. Sam Block strongly believed in team play; there were no observable favorites, and he delegated so that everybody got a shot at the interesting developments. One day his impartiality went a little too far. He directed me to write the statement on a new laundry and dry-cleaning regulation. I worked very hard at it, explored the pricing structure and history in the industry, invoked the gods of fairness and cost of living, and tried to write—a major goal of mine—in understandable street English rather than sophisticated legalese. The regulator became "we," the regulatee became "you," and so on. Inadvertently—I believe—Sam had given the same assignment to another lawyer. I was crushed. But Sam came through nobly. Holding up the two drafts, he said, "This is like sacred and profane love." He chose mine. Was I sacred or profane? I didn't ask.

FROM WASHINGTON POWER TO FIRING IN THE FIELD

The physical conditions of our life in DC were hardly ideal. The OPA, a new, unpopular, wartime agency, was assigned minimal quarters. We worked in Temporary Building D, a flat-roofed, one-story structure without air-conditioning. In the summer months the heat was so intense and the sweat so pervasive that we had to line up twice a day for compulsory salt pills. Sylvia and I lived first in a basement apartment on Whittier Place in the "third alphabet" (the outer rim of streets in DC). All you could see from the only windows were passing feet on the adjacent sidewalk—like the apartment in the film *My Sister Eileen*. We then moved to lodgings built cheaply, with very thin walls, in Congress Heights—Anacostia, near the military airport, Bolling Field. Our sleep was regularly interrupted every night at 1:00 AM by the sexual gyrations of our upstairs neighbors and at 5:00 AM by the aeronautical gyrations of the dawn patrol.

It was an exciting and satisfying life for a young lawyer, given intense dimension by the birth of our son. He was born in Washington, so we named him Lincoln! For a few months, it was a happy, carefree household. Sylvia had a difficult pregnancy; constantly in pain, she was confined to bed in the last months. The gynecologist continuously prescribed pain pills, and I remember the pharmacist's critical complaint, "Too many, too many, Mr. Swados. . . . Those pills'll hurt the baby!" As I recall Lincoln's future—paranoia, schizophrenia, and attempted suicide—I wonder if this was a warning I should have heeded. I relied upon the doctor, well recommended by my colleagues. Whether the medication had anything to do with it or not, my wife suddenly began to experience very high fevers, peaks and valleys that made it impossible for her to function. I couldn't afford maid service, so the ministrations to our son fell to me—which meant absence from the office. Sam Block sent messengers to find out what was happening and provided some help, and Sylvia's family came to take over for a few days. But the situation was very difficult, and when the Washington doctors could not cure, or even diagnose her condition, Sylvia asked to return to Buffalo, where her family could provide the support she needed.[2] I asked the OPA for a transfer to the Buffalo Regional Office. It was an unpleasant decision—the Washington career, with induction approaching, up in smoke. But I had no choice.

My friends and bosses in DC—Henry Hart, Sam Block, and George Galland, a fine lawyer in my section—tried to persuade me to stay, but at my insistence managed the transfer. I refocused. The Washington office had made broad economic decisions and promulgated the price ceilings and regulations. Working in the regional office would provide the interesting opportunity to see how the rules were *enforced*.

The prospects in the district job were promising. I would be dealing with people, not just paper. What I didn't expect was a sharp lesson in the realities of government service in the political environment. Things went well for a while. My direct supervisor in Buffalo was Milton Friedman, a practical, intelligent lawyer who was also seeking to be involved in the war effort and who functioned with skill, a decent acceptance of the role of the agency, and a sense of humor. The titular head of the office, the district director, was not particularly interested in OPA policy. He was a veteran politician, and his reaction to every issue enshrined public reaction as the major consideration. The idealistic war effort morale of the Washington/ Harvard price regulators had not seeped down to the local level. As the migrant from DC, I was looked upon with a certain degree of suspicion. Was I a spy, or one of the boys?

The reality hit when I didn't get paid for three months. Repeated inquiries at the finance office produced only vague responses: "The checks got fouled up somehow—it'll be straightened out." Desperate, with a sick wife and no other income, I called my friends in the general counsel's office in Washington. The word came back: "It's the local politicos. They're holding up the transfer—and your checks. They want to send you back to DC so they can give your job to one of the commoners at the trough!" My Washington friends raised a little hell, and the paychecks were delivered.

BATTLING THE REVEREND CHURCHILL

Despite the urgency of its role, the OPA was not very popular. It was inter-fering with habitual pricing and marketing practices; it was Big Brother, peeking into books and records. Its rationing of scarce gasoline and heating oil was an easy target for charges of corruption and incompetence. I believed in the fairness and sincerity of my colleagues in Washington, and it wasn't long before I was faced with a conflict between policy and politics. The price regulation scheme started with a general freeze, holding everyone covered in a regulation—such as food—at the prices in effect on a specified date. The freeze date might catch an industry in aberration or fail to take into account historical margins, such as the difference between a retail and a wholesale price. When a problem arose, after study and sometimes hear-ings, a specific price regulation would follow, tailored to the industry's par-ticular structure.

Chickens. A pretty identifiable commodity, with an easily understood structure: chicken farmer, processor, wholesaler, retailer. It happened that in the Buffalo district, one of the most prominent and successful chicken farmers was the Reverend Clinton H. Churchill, evangelist extraordinaire, with his own radio pulpit, WKBW-AM. Word came from the agency inves-tigators that the reverend was violating the price regulation. One of the churches complained that Churchill was charging it the retail price. The practice in the chicken industry on the date of the price "freeze"—and for many years prior—was to sell to institutional customers at the wholesale price, a substantial discount. The rationale was that churches, schools, and the like normally purchased in bulk and received free delivery by truck to their institution buildings. Retail sales, under the regulation, were defined so as to require not only that the buyer be a person historically paying the retail price but also that each chicken be individually wrapped.

I wrote Churchill my number one form letter, noting the price regulation and asking that the seller cease and desist from the violations. Some time passed before the investigator reported back. Churchill was still charging churches and synagogues the retail price, but with one difference—he was now wrapping each chicken sold to the institutions individually in butcher paper and asking each purchaser to accept delivery over the counter at his farm store. I wrote form letter number two, advising the seller that he was now in violation on two counts: charging the retail price to buyers entitled to the wholesale discount and eliminating the free delivery option. If the seller did not stop the violation, I threatened "appropriate legal proceedings, including an injunction and possible fines." Letter number two produced a response, all right. There descended on me an imposing delegation, consisting of Churchill, his farm manager, his lawyer (a close friend and tennis partner of my uncle, Paul Cohen), his lawyer's assistant, and, finally, to underscore the momentous character of the meeting, my local boss, the district director himself.

The director, deferential and uncertain, at least refrained from criticizing his employee in the presence of others. The lawyer first tried an intellectual argument: my interpretation of my own regulation was erroneous. When that would not budge me, he resorted to blandishments: "Bobby, you've got such a fine *academic* record, but you've got to learn to be *practical*. . . ." During a break, in a confidential tone, he asked, "And what are you doing when you leave the agency, Bob? My law firm might be interested. . . ." Churchill, short on patience and long on rhetoric, would have none of this. Speaking as if he were not only the beknighted interpreter of the gods but of Adam Smith as well, he said, "I'm telling *you*, Sir, that you are a self-righteous bureaucrat interfering with a business man's natural rights, and if you don't withdraw these charges immediately, I'm goin' on the air with my next sermon, and I'm gonna' blast you and the OPA as evil, incompetent, *fascists*! That'll be the end of the OPA in this town. . . ."

I concluded the meeting—feeling pretty powerful for a twenty-two-year-old public official—declining to terminate the charges. I had helped prepare the regulation in my Washington stint. I thought it was fair and easily understood. The violation was gross and deliberate. We had to enforce the rules, in the interest of the community and the country. When Churchill's entourage left, the director called me into his office, asking if I would reconsider. There would be a blast at all of us, and the agency was having a tough time with public relations as it was. I responded that this was an *opportunity* for the agency. Chicken was a basic commodity. Churchill was a hypocrite. Public sentiment would be on our side. Enforcement would show that even "God's messenger" was not above our law.

Milton Friedman, no friend of fakers, backed me up. Churchill's radio attack was milder than expected, and his lawyer reported that Churchill would reluctantly comply. I suspect the director agreed to look the other way. When the army took me in the winter of 1943, I ceased to worry about it. In 1957 I would be shocked to learn that Churchill had been awarded Buffalo's Channel 7 by the FCC in a comparative hearing, triumphing—doubtless because of his character and reputation—over distinguished citizens with greater influence but lesser counsel.

Chapter 2

IT ISN'T RAINING VIOLETS

THE COUNSEL WITH THE TWO LEFT FEET

At my induction physical in 1943, I had dreams of the air force or the navy—dreams that evaporated when I faced the exam for color perception. The recruiting sergeant presented me with the Ishihara color blindness test—the one that looks like a Jackson Pollock painting, with hidden numbers in its amorphous circles. The first one was easy: "67," I intoned. The next page, after some concentration and hesitation, revealed itself to me as the number "24." The third page? I began to perspire and palpitate. I couldn't see *any* number! "You're color-blind," said the sergeant. "You're crazy," I replied—my first and last defiance of the army. "I can tell chartreuse from aquamarine, red from pink. . . ." The recruiting noncom sharply interrupted—"Step aside, SOLDIER!"—and proceeded to shove the color book at the next recruit in line, who flipped the pages rapidly and sang out, at machine-gun pace—"67, 34, 76, 12, 99, 00."

"So you're in the army now, Swados," the recruiting sergeant commented in a momentary interlude of kindness. "You're probably wondering why a person of your education and experience ends up as a foot soldier. The answer is, my friend, the infantry needs *bodies*. Once in and you can show your stuff, you can always apply for Officer Candidate School. Of course," he added prophetically, "if you have two left feet . . ."

After seventeen weeks of basic training, crawling with an M-1 rifle through the red dust of Camp Croft in Spartanburg, South Carolina, I emerged as a presumptively qualified infantry soldier—classified in the army's records as a rifleman, category 745. It is a testament to the pedagogical qualities of the US Army that someone, somehow, taught this mechanical dimwit to break down a rifle, a carbine, a Browning automatic rifle, and a pistol, and reassemble each of them without losing any of the parts. I had some confidence, but not much, that I would survive—despite achieving the lowest grade in hand-to-hand combat in my company. My drill sergeant, not impressed at all with my Harvard education, held his satirical fire somewhat when it turned out on the range that I could not only carry the M-l, but shoot it.

The training was tough, but the environment was not completely unpleasant. Our wives and babies joined us, and we lived in a high-ceilinged, black-draped old building that was acceptable—except for the occasional cockroach and some dramatic noises from the top floor, where some ladies of the evening were ensconced with their transient customers. Spartanburg was dry, but we soon found a restaurant whose "speciality" of the house was dessert embellished with a sweet wine. So it was fruit-cup Saturday night for most of the seventeen weeks.

As a buck-ass private I had no transportation privileges, so my first journey to Europe was in the sixth hold of a troopship with no amenities, stale air, and crowded quarters that made me nauseous throughout the fifteen-day trip. The destination—which was not disclosed to us—turned out to be a replacement depot (a "reppledepple") near Naples, Italy. We reached the depot in a careening open truck, in which we were stacked, standing up with full field packs like loose cannons on end, along the Amalfi Drive—with the Isle of Capri across the bay, so near and yet so far. I found myself dumped, with no ceremony or orientation, into a pyramidal tent with two other rookies and seven refugees from the regimental stockade. We soon learned that we were following the 45th Infantry Division, which had already established the record for casualties, as the result of savage combat in Sicily and in Italy at Anzio and Salerno. So we knew we were not pointed for soft service and, in fact, the seven refugees—more precisely, parolees—had been released from the stockade prison on the express condition that they would serve in the front line units. The parolee buddies were engaging rogues who had been sentenced to significant terms for serious offenses, but they didn't pause at missing curfew or disappearing from the camp for bouts of dubious recreation in the city. I got to like them, and we would try to cover their lapses. I would lecture them on staying in line, to preserve their status and avoid being jailed again, or even charged with desertion. I didn't accomplish very much, but I did generate their affection, to the point where they nicknamed me "the Reverend." Except for discovering that I had a talent for sleeping anywhere—in dirt, in mud, in a ditch, in a shelter half (the half a tent a soldier carried on his back)—I didn't improve my qualifications as a soldier; but I did read good books and learned to speak a little Italian, mostly confined to "Quanto vi debbo?" (How much?) and "E troppo" (Too much).

At least while they were under my observation, none of my pyramidal mates was incarcerated again, and we speculated together on what front would claim us. The Normandy landings had started well, and then stalled. Going up the backbone of Italy would be tough—the veterans in the 45th would testify to that, but no secret information came to the enlisted men in a reppledepple. We shipped out on a beautiful night in the Mediterranean, and it was only on August 15, 1944, on deck in the light of the moon, that we learned our destination was a "second front"—southern France—part of the "soft underbelly" end-run strategy attributed to Winston Churchill. The actual site of the attack for us was Saint-Tropez, in its time a lovely resort town on the French Riviera. I have no idea what it looked like then—we were moving too fast across the beach! Our advance units had already moved on, pursuing the Germans; the fire was light and sporadic, and we were ordered to catch up in a forced march of about seventy-five kilometers with full field pack—the toughest assignment I'd received so far. We stopped for rest in a town called Carpentras and were greeted, much to my embarrassed pleasure—we had yet to be in a fire fight—as heroes. In the home to which we were sent, I received the warmest welcome and the greatest meal of my life.

I don't remember what we ate, but it was all of ten courses, each morsel cooked and served separately, honored for its essence and taste, and surrounded by gratitude and affection. It was my first use of French since college, and the ability to converse helped us all enjoy that wonderful evening. I learned that Carpentras was part of unoccupied France—unoccupied by the Germans, that is, but governed by the jackals of Vichy. It was the temporary refuge of a number of Parisian families, and I had trouble at first navigating between the soft drawl of the *Midi* farmers and the *gamouche* Brooklyn-like patois of Paris. My spoken French, my host informed me (later confirmed at NHL soirees in Quebec), honed as it was by the French professor who coached me in the part of a Gallic con man in a college play, was *classique* enough to be understood by both homesteaders and visitors.

I was later to think of this period as an extension of Hemingway's *Paris Is a Moveable Feast*. It was the last time for many months that food had any value except to keep us going. We continued north along the Loire Valley, and I got twenty-four hours' leave in the magnificent medieval town of Grenoble. I don't remember much what it looked like, except that I had to tip-toe like a tightrope walker over the single bar that remained of the bombed-out bridge across the river to meet my buddy and get back to base in time. But I do remember the meal. There was no meat available, yet the restaurant cook did wonders with mushrooms and eggplant, clothed in delicious sauces that in former times would have graced veal or tenderloin.

MIRACLE AT EPINAL

Bob Gainey, now general manager of the Monreal Canadiens, would decades later send me photographs of the lively city in the Vosges Mountains of northeastern France, where he coached a winning hockey club before returning to the NHL. But on October 2, 1944, all I could see of Epinal was the top of a bare hill, with no cover, and all I could hear were the sounds of mortars and machine guns, very loud and very close.[1]

"How close?" I asked the lieutenant who'd brought me. "About three hundred yards," he answered, adding, "Get rid of everything but a blanket and your piece [rifle]!"

I had been assigned to Company C, 157th Infantry Regiment, 45th Infantry Division—the unit that was down there to the left, taking heavy fire from the Germans. I followed the lieutenant's orders and was standing there ready—but not eager—to accept my fate, when a second jeep drove up and what looked like a GI with a major's insignia (gold leaf) jumped from the vehicle and grabbed the lieutenant before we could take off. "Let's see those cards," he said. "I've got to find somebody with some education!"

The major thumbed through the cards, muttering to himself, then louder. I tried to stand in a soldierly fashion, at near attention, craning my neck to hear. "Let's see," uttered the officer. "Harvard Law School, judge's secretary, honor graduate—looks as if this guy could do this job better than I can—S W A H D O S!!!" he shouted.

"Yes sir, YES SIR," I responded—maybe a little loud, but with as snappy a salute I had ever given at Spartanburg. The major explained calmly and quietly, as if we were in a conference room in Cambridge, not in the orbit of a fire fight in France. He had just been promoted from captain of a company in the front line to G-1 at headquarters of the division. He needed someone to help who had education and intelligence. The job involved such things as line company inventory (who's left to shoot and be shot at) investigations (which officer should get a medal), statistics, housing, billets, and so on. Could I do the job? The answer was, with appropriate vocal restraint, an emphatic ipso facto YES!

Thus my Harvard education saved my life. Ten days later Company C was ambushed in a draw, and only a third of the unit survived. One of my buddies from the Buffalo suburbs was killed in the action, and when that got back to Buffalo, with a communications blackout, my family thought I was dead. And, indeed I almost was, but for the providential intervention of God and the major.

THE GIs IN THE G-1

When I got to know Maj. Frank Glasgow well, I could see I really hit the cosmic jackpot. He was bright, optimistic, informal, kind, and real. He came out of the reserve corps in Arizona and New Mexico, and had few of the postures and prejudices of the WPPA (the caustic name for the regular army officers—the West Point Protective Association). He gave me every opportunity to use whatever talents I had, saw almost instantly that he had an asset in his section, and promoted and supported me whenever he could. Ultimately, he recommended me for a commission, promoted me to second lieutenant, and saw to my transfer to military government in the spring of 1945. He had a sweet sense of humor and would regale me with stories and word pictures of the Southwest. The still and beautiful mountains of New Mexico seemed always to be a horizon for his active remembrance and his longing to return.

When I looked closely at the G-1 section, I understood the major's concern. The workload was tremendous, and there were only four of us: the major; a veteran clerk-type regular, Jim; Arnie, a noncom handyman; and me. I had no difficulty with Arnie once I ceased to volunteer and recognized that, even for the physical and mechanical assignments he had—such as folding up and transporting the section tent—there was jurisdictional jealousy. Jim was a different problem. He had some education, but nothing that produced the sophisticated use of language and data and personnel the major employed himself and needed in his staff. It was obvious that I was there in part to make up for Jim's deficiencies. I tried to help him fill in the gaps, and he seemed outwardly appreciative, but I could see he resented my education, my

Maj. Frank Glasgow, the author's commanding officer in Germany. Photo courtesy of the author.

rapport with the major, and even my presence. Every once in a while, he would hit the bottle, come in late, oversleep, and make ugly sounds instead of friendly speech. As I had in the reppledepple in Italy, I would cover for him, sympathize, and offer my friendship.

There came a time when the division came off the line, into "rest." We were billeted in a famous resort hotel in Bains Les Bains, which we called "Bathless Baths" because none of the plumbing worked. There were no beds; you just spread your shelter half (part of your field pack) on the wood floor and went at it. We had done plenty of sleeping in the open, on the hard ground, so this was at least some rest. There was an indoor pool, still filled with warm mineral water from the belowground springs, and with no warning signs, I languished in the peripheral tubs for nearly an hour, thankful for this respite. When I emerged, I could hardly walk! The minerals had sapped up my energy and motive power. So I hit the sack early, hung my uniform on the nearest chair, covered my blanket with my shelter half, and turned off to dream of Western New York. As was his frequent custom, Jim hit the bistros. Around midnight, I was awakened by the sound of rain pelting my shelter half. But we were inside. It wasn't raining rain at all—and it wasn't raining violets. Jim, doubtless thinking he was rising from a ditch, was relieving himself with a high stream, aimed, intentionally or not, at my sleeping self!

In the morning: apologies, promises, undertakings to wash my uniform, resentment. We never did completely resolve our relationship. Yet when I returned to Buffalo in the summer of 1946, the *first* to visit me was Jim of the Indoor Rainbow.

Chapter 3

DEATH AT DACHAU

The Battle of the Bulge (November/December 1944) was a scary time, even for "rear-echelon" types like us. We were bombed, strafed, and threatened with infiltration in a war that did not stop at the forward observer or the front-line company. Word spread that the Germans were sending patrols dressed in US Army uniforms and that headquarters bases were being attacked from the rear; we were cautioned to take nothing for granted—the next contact post might be enemy in disguise. The fellows in the G-1 section of the 45th Division had moments of animal fright, but we were largely safe and emerged from this battle—the last great German offensive—secure and unharmed, with a healthy respect for the foot soldier and an active skepticism about the much-touted exploits of the tank battalions and the air force.

DOING RIGHT BY GEN. ROBERT FREDERICK

Our 45th Division was under the general command of the 7th Army, on the southern right flank of the Allied front. With the other US units to the north, we pushed on to the banks of the Rhine River and prepared to cross. It was here that I received my first lesson on the ethics and outlook of the

WPPA. (Some bias here—the 45th officers came out of the Colorado–New Mexico *reserve corps*, except for Gen. Robert Frederick himself.)

THE WEST POINT PROTECTION ASSOCIATION

The Remagen Bridge on the northern stretch of the river had been captured earlier that month, before it could be blown up, but the German resistance was still heavy and the Allies couldn't move all their forces through that small opening. We had to make our own crossing, even with no bridge. General Frederick sent a small patrol across in the early morning, led by a major—a classmate of Frederick's at West Point. Before any detailed news was received from the patrol, the general called me into his office. "I want you to get down to the river bank immediately, Swados!" he ordered. "It"—the patrol crossing—"was an incredibly brave thing to do. There may be a Silver Star, or even a DSC, in it for my friend. Find out what happened and write up a full report—you know how to do it!"

I complied with the order and interviewed the major and the sergeant on the patrol. They had climbed into a small rowboat, navigated to the narrowest point in our area, climbed the banks on the east side, keeping cover, and then spread out, checking woods and clearings in a quarter-mile circle. They found no enemy, no sounds, no weapons, and no sign of the Germans. They then climbed down to their rowboat, rowed rapidly back across the river, climbed the west bank, and headed for base. They drew no fire at any point and had nothing to report—except that the area they had scouted seemed like an appropriate spot for a company landing.

I ruefully gave my report to the general, together with my comment—which he accepted with some mumbled disappointment—that while it was undoubtedly a brave thing to do, under the circumstances, with no results, no hostile fire, and no wounded soldiers, the patrol would not support a medal. The next morning the coordinated attack across the Rhine began. Units to the north crossed the river and took the far banks without difficulty and with minimal resistance. In our sector, the force led by the major met a savage and ruthless counterattack—machine guns, mortars, and focused fire. The major's force had been seduced into a trap; the major himself was grievously wounded—he lost a leg—and sent on his way to the base hospital. The general called me back to his post. "I guess he'll get his medal now," he said. I did not disagree.

The 7th US Army, as part of the 6th Army Group, pressed on, into the heart of Germany, crossed the Rhine, crossed the Main, and headed into Aschaffenburg. The retreating German army, we were told, offered little resistance to the dashing, speeding tanks in General Patton's strike force. There was only one problem: Patton stayed only long enough in the "conquered" towns to leave his marker. By the time our infantry arrived, the Germans came out of their holes and let us have it. Aschaffenburg, supposedly a "cleared" town, was not clear at all, and we suffered heavy casualties before the city was safely secured. In that intermezzo, when we thought Aschaffenburg had been taken and we were approaching an easy victory, a delightful report came to the G-1 section: near the city was the site of a major PX store and warehouse for German officers. As the nonvolunteer with the "best" language facility (my German had good accent, no vocabulary; and my stage French didn't work too well in Upper Bavaria), I was chosen to raid the facility. Priority: fine wine, cognac, and good cigars.

As we approached the site, it was obvious that this target was no secret. Vehicles of every sort, from every direction, from every unit—Army, Division, Battalion, and Corps—were in competing lines—in star formation—for miles around, seeking to get the goodies first. If the enemy had not been regrouping—actually lying in wait in the city at the moment—we would have been clay pigeons for any foray. I had some head start, got to a narrow rear window on the ground floor, forced the latch, and found my trophies in a hurry. The problem was how to get out without dropping my booty. The latch I had broken in the entry somehow got hooked in my GIs, and I was hung in the window, for several embarrassing moments, between piracy and nudity.

Fortunately, my driver managed to rescue me and we made it back to base in that cold open jeep. It took great discipline and restraint not to consume too much of the cognac on our journey home.

LIBERATING DACHAU

The 7th Army turned south, took Nuremberg, and headed toward Munich and the "neighboring" city of Dachau, with orders to find the concentration camp. Units of my division reached the rail lines outside the Dachau complex on the morning of April 29, 1945. As reported by the colonel (later brigadier) in charge of the battalion, Felix L. Sparks, the attacking force "knew virtually nothing about Dachau except that it was a concentration camp near the city of Dachau."[1] Company C of the 157th Infantry Regiment (the same unit from which Major Glasgow had extricated me at Epinal) experienced the "atmosphere of human depravity, degradation and death. Even before entering the camp. The first evidence of the horror to come . . . about *forty* railway cars on a siding near the camp entrance. *Each car was loaded with emaciated human corpses, both men and women. A hasty search by the stunned infantry revealed no signs of life among the hundreds of still bodies. . . .*"[2]

As the Allied forces advanced rapidly into Germany, the monsters who had contrived the "Final Solution" began to fear for their own lives. There

A view inside one of the railway cars.
Photo courtesy of the United States Holocaust Museum Archives.

was too little time, even for the efficient ovens and gas chambers at Auschwitz, for the Nazis to obliterate all their living victims, and the emaciated camp inmates themselves were alarming evidence of the war crimes committed. The temporary solution: force-march the ambulant victims to rural venues—more difficult to find—and ship the ill and dying inmates, like so much detritus, in railway freight cars to the interior camps, where crematories were available.[3] The forty coal cars encountered by the 45th on the siding outside the Dachau facility were part of that macabre escape attempt to destroy the evidence. As our troops entered the camp, we learned that just three days before, about seven thousand prisoners had been forced by the SS on a six-day death march to Tegernsee, about sixty miles southeast of Dachau. As described in the *Historical Atlas* prepared by the United States Holocaust Memorial Museum, "During the six-day death march, anyone who could not keep up or could no longer continue was shot. Many others died of exposure, hunger or exhaustion."[4]

In the afternoon of April 29, 1945, we received word that the Dachau concentration camp had been secured, and the major authorized two of the four staff members of the G-1 section to visit the camp immediately; the others could go on the next tour. We drew lots, and I lost. Sergeant Barrett, a nice guy and a new member of the staff on detached service, got one of the wins, but he immediately turned to me. "Bob," he said, "you should go. It's your people. It'll mean more to you."

"No," I responded. "It's more important that you go. You're not Jewish, you'll be objective; you as a witness can do more than I to make sure what you see will never be forgotten." It was a principled decision I made, but I've sometimes had second thoughts in view of what happened. The sergeant returned, tired and depressed. "How did it go?" I asked. "Terrible, awful, unbelievable." He didn't want to talk about it any further that night.

The following morning, the major said I could take a jeep to the camp. When I reached the main gate, I was told that I could not enter. The facility was closed to all but personnel on duty. The reason given: the threat of typhus. (When the British had overrun the Bergen-Belsen camp at Celle in northwestern Germany earlier that month, some sixty thousand prisoners were found alive, but most were in critical condition because of a typhus epidemic, and more than ten thousand died of malnutrition or disease within a few weeks.)[5]

I was terribly disappointed and tried to persuade the guard to let us enter, but to no avail. But we did go around the southwest corner of the facility to the railroad siding. There, I saw the "death train." Although I had some idea of what to expect, I was stunned and overwhelmed by the scene in the open box car—death horizontal, death vertical, death crumbling; humans, made into detritus. Years later, when the Holocaust Museum opened in Washington, I climbed to the exhibit on the second floor and turned on the tape. I felt a shock throughout my brain and body. There, in front of me again, vivid, detailed, and horrible, was the movie George Stevens shot of that same box car I'd seen in Dachau in the spring of 1945.

Of course, I wanted to speak as a total *witness*, and my idealistic response to Barrett's offer prevented that. But I knew there would be other witnesses who would articulate for history the horrors and celebrations of that day. I'll quote one of them, because of its importance and spontaneity:

> It was late afternoon—about 4 PM—as the men made their way down the tracks. They knew that the camp ahead was guarded by SS troops and that they expected a hard fight. And like all men going into an attack, be they rookies or vets, these men were afraid.
>
> They picked up the clawing stink before they reached the first boxcar. They stopped and stared and the dead stared back.
>
> There were about a dozen bodies in the dirty boxcar, men and women alike. They had gone without food for so long that their dead wrists were broomsticks tipped with claws. There were the victims of a deliberate starvation diet, and they weren't pretty.
>
> The men looked, then shuffled on to the new car in silence. There were more dead eyes here staring out at the German houses not 200 yards from the tracks.

Someone broke the stillness with a curse and then with a roar the men started for the camp on the double.

"I never saw anything like it," Lieutenant Moyer later said. The men were plain fighting mad. They went down that road without any regard for cover or concealment. No one was afraid, not after those boxcars. We were just mad.[6]

I hope that both Barretts—the reporter and the sergeant—over the decades have steadfastly told the facts in the face of the psychotic Holocaust denials. The fight against the philistines is never over. A short time after my return to civilian life, I gave a speech to the Niagara Falls Bar Association. The words "Shoah" and "Holocaust" had not yet emerged in the literature as the labels for the horror and, using a book by Gerald Reitlinger as my text, I described my own experiences and the facts then known about the concentration camps and the "Final Solution." I described Bergen-Belsen, Dachau, and Auschwitz. I stressed that this was a deliberate, heinous plan to exterminate a people. One of my contemporaries, a young lawyer who had served in the US Army (I've forgotten which theater) came up to the podium. "You're kiddin' us, aren't ya', Bob?" he said.

"What do you mean?" I asked.

"Oh," he replied, "all this stuff about deliberately killing off a people."

"But it was a deliberate, intentional, planned, large-scale action to wipe out the Jews," I insisted.

"Oh hell," said the lawyer. "When we were an advance party we'd frequently take prisoners, and when we didn't have time or opportunity to send 'em back, we'd have to kill 'em. . . . But wipe out an entire people! That's unbelievable. . . . You're kiddin', aren't ya?"

BUT WHO DID LIBERATE DACHAU?

Dachau was not the first camp the Allies liberated. The British overran Bergen-Belsen in the north, the United States took Buchenwald (near Weimar, the city of Germany's temporary democratic enlightenment between the wars), and the Soviets overran the largest killing machine, Auschwitz, as early as January 1945. (In typical paranoia, with conflicting agendas, the Russians did not broadcast to the world the horrors they found at Auschwitz. I wonder whether a more outraged moral response might have influenced FDR to unleash the bombers and destroy the railroads to the camps.) But if the camp in the Munich suburb was not the first to be captured, it was the first to be established; it was the first to use crematories and other factory line techniques to turn humans into fecal matter. It was the first to stage experiments in human pain and torture. Thus, in a strange way, it became a prize to the American troops who seized it and a singular honor to the officers who commanded the liberating forces.

We didn't know it at the time (although Major Glasgow might have been aware of these developments), but April 29, 1945, produced a major controversy that has received wide treatment in the media but seems irrelevant now: Who liberated the Dachau concentration camp?

As recounted by Colonel Sparks in his report,[7] the 45th Division force, driven by their anger at the horrors in the coal cars, broke into the facility first, moving from the railway siding near the southwest corner of the *Dachau Lager*—the large facility that included the SS barracks, the crematories, and the concentration camp itself; the latter was in a separate enclosure within the *Lager*. The 45th entered over the west wall and through the road and railway gates at the southwest corner. At some point—perhaps an hour or two later, after the 45th had moved in to the *Lager*—units of the 42nd Division, which were coming in on our left flank, entered the Dachau complex through the main gate, situated on the southeasterly wall, near the southeast corner of the *Lager*. In dispute is the question of which unit entered the concentration camp itself—the interior prisoner compound, surrounded by a brick wall and a barbed-wire fence. Entry to this compound had to be made through a third gate structure, called the *Jourhaus*.

The seriocomic scene developed when Sparks received orders not to permit *anyone* to enter or leave the complex, and the commanding officer of the 42nd Division arrived—a man named General Linden—with eager reporter Marguerite Higgins in tow, to challenge his authority. Linden, apparently a fan of Eric Von Stroheim or George Patton, arrived in a motor car, but equipped with a riding crop. When Sparks refused to let the general enter, Linden, in a rage, shouted that he was taking over, superseding Sparks. When Sparks refused to budge, Linden threatened Sparks with a general court-martial and punctuated his outburst with a slash of the crop to the head of the unfortunate enlisted man who delivered the colonel's message. (Linden did, in fact, pursue the court-martial at corps headquarters, but, according to Sparks, Patton's chief of staff delighted in tossing the charges into the irreversible round file.) A Steven Spielberg documentary, charged with egregious error by representatives of the 45th, gave credit for the liberation to the 42nd and Linden. Linden had apparently screeched loudly enough to be given the honor of accepting the formal surrender of the camp. A later investigation report plays the Solomon: the 45th was the first to enter the Dachau complex, while the 42nd was the first to overrun the internal area that included the prison compound. But the Dachau scene at the Holocaust Memorial Museum displays the colors of the Thunderbird Division—the 45th!

I just know we were there! The defining moment for me, the ineffable indictment of the Nazi monsters, was that coal car of death.

A few weeks later, in May of 1945, I returned to Munich as a commissioned military government officer and was invited to dinner at a home in the Dachau suburb near the *Dachau Lager*. I said to my hostess, a charming cultured lady with facile English, "How did you deal with the camp? You must have known."

"Oh no, Herr Leutnant," she protested. "We had no idea!"

The lady's statement is not worthy of belief. The camp was situated *one kilometer* northeast of the town of Dachau. In the words of one of the 45th Division soldiers, "the clawing stink" was overwhelming, and there were hundreds of "dead eyes here staring out at the German houses not 200 yards from the tracks."[8]

Chapter 4

THE ROOKIE MILITARY JUDGE

I n May of 2000 E. Edward Herman sent me a provocative book—*Surviving the Americans*—that was very critical of the conduct of the US military government's handling of displaced persons in Germany in 1945.[1] The US forces had overrun the concentration camps in the course of their advance and had freed the concentration camp inmates, but in some cases, the book charged, they had merely converted the camps into military government holding stockades for the liberated Jews and other "displaced" beings. The book claimed that the "liberated" were neglected and no better off under the Americans than they were under the Nazis. What follows is my response to Herman.

* * *

Dear Mr. Herman:

It was very good of you to send me so quickly *Surviving the Americans*. I've given it a quick read (more detailed reaction later), and it certainly has caused me to rethink—and research—that period in my life when I served as a military government second lieutenant in Frankenthal, Erbach, Darmstadt, and, for most of '45 and '46, Wiesbaden. The curse of the Army doctrine of "need to know." Does the worker ant even get to know the existence of his Queen?

My first contact with the concentration camps was in late April '45 when my Division, 45th Infantry, was one of those that overran and liberated Dachau. I had had good access to some intelligence reports, since I worked in the G-1 section directly under the Major in charge, and did some work for our General, "Rapid Robert" Frederick. Yet I do not recall seeing any messages or memoranda warning the Division of the camps, or suggesting procedures to deal with the liberation. We were still infantry soldiers, with danger and battle ahead of us. Hence the absolute surprise and horror when some of our units entered the camp, found the skeleton-like survivors, and the boxcars with the dead Jews on their way to the ovens. (Shown vividly in the film made by George Stevens, on display at the Holocaust Museum in DC) As described in the reports filed by the Division, our units attacked and "beat up" the Germans directing and operating the camp.

I had just been commissioned, having served as a PFC in the infantry for two years, and when the European war ended, was immediately shipped, with my Harvard Law degree, into military government. I was in the vanguard, without realizing it. We were, on reviving memory, much unprepared in that period your book describes—shortly after the camps were overrun. The staffing wasn't yet available, and I, early on the scene, for a time had to act as displaced persons officer, property control officer, public relations officer, finance officer and, when time permitted, local judge.

There were policy statements, draft regulations, etc., but in my areas, few personnel to install or enforce them. My "training" for military government was perfunctory and minimal—although I was young enough and confident enough (read: arrogant) to have little doubt about my ability to handle the problems. I certainly sensed that, while the war had been won, victory and even the discovery of the camps hadn't driven anti-Semitism off the planet, either in or out of the army.

Some time after my reassignment (Hannukah/Christmas 1945), my sergeant reported that twenty-five Jews in the nearby displaced persons camp (formerly a concentration camp) had been arrested and placed in the stockade—convicted of wearing illegal badges because they refused to remove their yellow stars. My superiors were nowhere around, so I commandeered the nearest jeep, got to the camp as quickly as I could, wrote out an order rescinding the conviction and setting them free. On returning, my temporary CO—I think he was a vice-mayor somewhere in the western states, hauled me into his office and came close to threatening me with court-martial. I explained—with some trepidation, but considerable ardor as well—that the yellow stars had become important emotional and practical symbols that they felt entitled them to protection and special treatment, not harassment, and since they should be regarded as under our protection, technical violations of regulations that were designed to prevent perpetuation of the aura of Nazi authority should be ignored. He finally, but grumpily, backed off—but it was clear that he did not consider the war fought to save the Jews. Fortunately, he was transferred and my new CO was a very decent, sensitive businessman from Lake Tahoe.

I'll try to find the notes and drafts of the book I began years ago dealing with my military government experience. My recollection, however, is that in my areas, when the staff and the officers and funds finally arrived, and VE day happened, and we didn't have to prepare for firefights any more—General Frederick was ready to ship me and the whole 45th Division to Japan until peace came. I think we did a pretty good job in those early occupation days, despite the lack of preparation and experience to deal with thousands of sick, impoverished persons unable to go home and, with the hostile British shutting down their path to Palestine with no place to go.

Perhaps my understanding and direct contact with the problem was limited because, as other personnel arrived, I was assigned less and less to social and economic and administrative issues and more and more to legal matters. Stationed in Erbach, with no local lawyer or judge free enough of Nazi taint to be qualified for office, I drove all the way to Stuttgart to find an ex-judge who had moved there. He seemed to have at least non-Nazi credentials and I established him as the local German judge. Operating as the local military government judge—dealing with offenses of Germans and displaced persons against the governing military government rules and German law—I found in Erbach and Darmstadt a Berlitz school that had a cadre of women who could take testimony in shorthand in any of five languages and translate into any of the others. Since I had the naive but idealistic notion that part of my mission was to demonstrate the values of democratic justice, I would have a fairly complete record of the testimony in serious cases—like possession of a weapon or false statements on a *fragebogen* (the military government questionnaire required for employment). It turned out I had the only local trial records in all of the Gross Hesse region of the American occupation. The result: I was "promoted" and transferred to Wiesbaden to be, twenty-four-year-old second lieutenant or not, the head of the military government courts section.

The *fragebogen* cases became so numerous and I was so busy, I had to set up a specialized court at Wiesbaden to deal with them, so my contact with the camps declined. But I had a concrete handle on the pervasive lies in the face of meticulous Nazi records and the weakness of the de-Nazification system. Subject to some doubts because the *fragebogen* itself was a violation of the Anglo-American prejudice (privilege) against self-incrimination, I was determined to produce fair trials but rigorous punishment. A former president of the Medical Society of Wurtemberg-Baden was charged with falsification of his employment *fragebogen* to qualify as a practicing physician. He was represented by a German lawyer cleared by the US authorities for resuming his law practice and introduced by me to the art of advocate's cross-examination—a procedure not available in the German, Continental trial system. The doctor—son of the regional Bishop—had failed to mention, in listing his membership in Nazi organizations, that he had joined the SA in 1924! Despite the excellent character presentation by his counsel, and his loss of a leg at the hip—which some regarded as punishment enough—I sentenced the doctor to a year in jail, with forfeiture of his professional rights.

I'm sure there were many others who were dedicated, idealistic, highly competent soldiers and professionals of Jewish faith who tried conscientiously to do the job they were given to do, but wish, as do I, they had known what history has revealed; and could have somehow done more. . . .

Chapter 5

THE COUNTRY LAWYER IN THE CORPORATE BOARDROOM

The scene is a corporate raid—a hostile takeover. A giant conglomerate seeks to gobble up a successful independent company, offering a twenty-dollar premium over the share price on the NASDAQ. The managing directors think the offer is insuficient, and they want to stay independent, anyway; they propose to install a "poison pill" to kill the raider's offer. Who should make the decision—the directors or the stockholders? In Strasbourg, France, in early July 2001, the European Parliament rejected a regulation that would have *compelled* the target company to submit the offer to the shareholders. The vote actually split right down the middle—273 to 273—with Volkswagen and the Germans attacking the proposed rule and the British "invaders" seeking its adoption. The issue was with me and my firm for forty years.

CORSETS, BEER, AND PAINT

The sixties and seventies were a time when rapacious "entrepreneurs" targeted old-line companies that had gone public without retaining control. If the target company's stock was selling below its true value, or if the company had assets that were not reflected in its share price, or if a larger corporation wanted to produce a dramatic increase in its percentage of the market, the strategy of choice was not to make a public buy of the target's stock; that would merely bid up the cost and alert the management to the danger. The solution was a *raid*. The raid technique could take the form of a proxy fight, in which the aggressor would buy a substantial block of stocks surreptitiously, then attack management publicly and seek to outvote the incumbents at a stockholders' meeting; or a tender offer, in which the raider would gather his finances and make an outright public bid to buy enough stock, at a substantial premium over the market price, to give him control.

In the early days of this raider's era, a number of Western New York companies were particularly vulnerable. They had developed under the old rules of corporate prudence: keep your debt down, pay modest dividends, reinvest your earnings, and go to the stock market for capital only when absolutely necessary. The family kept control. But as years went by, the original owners became estates, which sold some of their holdings; the need for capital brought in public shareholders, and the family's grip on ownership and management began to erode. Undisturbed, a block of 20 percent of the shares outstanding would be enough to maintain control if the remaining 80 percent was held in many unrelated accounts. But to a raider, it was a juicy target. There were defenses—"white knights" and "poison pills"—but those required quick action and broad expertise.

CORSETS AND RAIDERS

My first experience in this field was, to put it mildly, ignominious. The Spirella Companies, leaders in the door-to-door sale of corsets and bras, were important clients of my Niagara Falls firm. The companies had originated in Niagara County under the management of William Wallace Kincaid in the nineteenth century and had expanded, with the introduction of other owners and other capital, to Canada, Britain, Sweden, Germany, and other countries. My firm—through Morris Cohn (the old firm's founder), Paul Cohen, and then me—had been the companies' counsel for at least seventy-five years. The law firm's first assignments may have been restricted to such matters as defending Spirella against the charge that the door-to-door saleswoman—called a "corsetiere"—had inaccurately thrust a corset bone into the customer's bosom, but as the organization expanded the problems came more into my line—corporate organization, international taxation, employment regulations, and so on. The companies were interesting clients. I use the plural intentionally because one of the interesting facets of the organization was that no one knew, from country to country, what kind of an organization it was. There were the operating companies—headquartered at Niagara Falls, New York, and Niagara Falls, Ontario; a holding company, Spirella International, organized under the laws of Delaware; the foreign operating companies in London, England, and Malmo, Sweden. We never were sure—the principals believed in the limitations of the "need to know" principle—which owned what. Then at the top there was the Spirella Board of Administration, a chameleon-like entity composed of the principals of the various companies, which changed its mission and its character to meet the conditions in whatever country in which it was required to disclose its existence. In the United States it might be as corporation; in England, a partnership; in Sweden, a joint venture; in Germany, a group of advisers; and so forth.

The managers were somewhat abashed at the failure of a highly touted new product to reach the market. Implants had not yet arrived, and the British Spirella Company had created a new "falsie" whose shape was maintained with a balloon-like inflated insert. The Brits proudly sent a model across the Atlantic wearing the new device. Unfortunately, the designers had not taken into account the air pressure at twenty-thousand feet and the bra exploded—sending the model and the product back to Britain on the next available flight.

But at the time of these events, Spirella was still profitable. Although the department and specialty stores had made serious inroads into the revenues of the US and Canadian companies, the corsetieres, like the Avon sales ladies of a later day, were still popular abroad, and the operations in Europe were still going strong. The public investors, largely on the North American continent, were receiving little in the way of dividends or interest, and the market in the stock was stagnant. Practical control was in the hands of the managers at Niagara Falls and Malmo, but legal control was iffy, with the holdings of the Kincaid family diluted long ago.

A setup for a raid? But who should appear as the raider, but our own principal personal client, Paul Schoellkopf! Paul was seduced into the adventure by his friend Charley Stephens, who will go down in my gallery as the most sophisticated dunderhead of all. Charlie proceeded, he thought, to feather his own nest first: buy a bloc of stock at a low price, oust the gray-haired in-house executives, begin proceedings to liquidate the losing North American companies, and move to take over administration of the European entities that had operated independently for so long. Charlie (with Paul in buddylike acquiescence) permitted my firm to continue to handle routine operating matters, but did not consult us on his strategy, and he paid little attention to the key question: Who owned Spirella? It was not long before Charlie was shocked with the answer. His liquidation plan had alienated staff, employees, and executives, all longtime holders of Spirella shares; they had sought counsel, secretly prepared a proxy fight, and showed up with the signed proxies—more than enough to oust Charlie and Paul and take control of the company. It was utter defeat, and so unnecessary. The Schoellkopfs produced a press release—which I had to draft—that made it sound like a voluntary sale and thus preserved a reputation for business acumen. But we lost a valuable client whose loyalties had been with us for decades. It was the last time I gave unquestioned response to a client's orders.

BEER AND PAINT

We went on in the later years of that era to protect local industries against hostile proxy fights and tender offers—china, paint, beer, and business forms were among the industries we helped to keep independent. The Spirella experience honed our expertise, confidence, and judgment.

Of course, when the raiders appeared on the corporate landscape, defenses were created. The simplest defense was to buy them off. There were risks: Was it proper to use company funds for that purpose if the object was really to keep the original owners in control? And if the buyout worked the first time, how do we handle a second semiscoundrel? Then there was the knifelike judgment required: Was the raider really seeking to take control, or was he just in it for the blackmail?

TERRY THE FOX AND STEVE THE BERG

As related in the next chapter, one of the friends who emerged from that challenging and exciting era in my firm's career was Bill Lutz, son-in-law of Alanson Deuel, the owner of the *Niagara Falls Gazette*. Bill was vice president of Pratt & Lambert, a Buffalo paint manufacturer of national prominence, known for its popularity with architects because of the special qualities of its paint and service. Like many other old-line companies that had conservative and prudent budgets, P&L had long ago diluted family control through stock distributions. Now on the American Stock Exchange, it had become vulnerable to outsiders accumulating strong market positions in the stock. One day out of the blue, Bill asked to see me, and he brought with him Burt Wilkinson, chairman of the P&L Board of Directors. Their stock transfer agent—Georgeson and Company—had warned them of a rapid rise in the number of shares held by outsiders. An investigation showed that a group headed by one Terry Fox and a Buffalo lawyer, Steven Berg, had acquired enough stock to be in sight of a threat to control, and the past history of the hostile duo suggested that they could indeed be bent on unseating the board, taking over the company, then doubtless selling and liquidating for cash. Bill and Burt had gone to their regular counsel first (a predecessor of my present firm) for help, and hadn't received much.

The local lawyer they consulted had advised a wait-and-see approach, but Burt and Bill were unwilling to surrender to disaster. They asked if there was anything they could do. My answer was, "Plenty—if you're willing to fight." We rapidly commandeered the groups of stockholders our clients could count on—their former employees and their families—made sure Georgeson was keeping a close check on every stock purchase, and began a PR campaign for the existing nonhostile shareholders, emphasizing the successes achieved by existing management in earnings and stock price (although the latter was admittedly slumbering). We enlisted the advice of experts, bearing in mind the firm's principle that's there's always somebody who knows more about this than we do. In this case it was Covington & Burling, the Washington firm that had been our legal partner in the television wars. We began to educate Burt and Bill in a program for long-term acquisitions of other companies, to broaden the base of control and make a raid more expensive and more difficult. But the danger was *now* and the necessary target was the personae of the raiders themselves. The conservative lawyer our friends had consulted apparently could not get beyond the "hornbook law," which mandated that directors had their primary duty to their shareholders, and if a shareholder wanted to elect himself to power the management could not interfere with that—even if the result was a loss of the long-term value of the company and a loss of jobs for its employees.

I had a different point of view: those long-term and employee values were entitled to protection, and the law (primarily guided by the courts of Delaware, which had jurisdiction over most national firms in the United States) developed that way with the thrust of the prudent judgment rule. That rule reinforced the right of directors to take action to control the fortunes of a company, even if it did not seem consistent with the short-term price of its shares—so it justified devices to maintain control. Since I had acted in diverse fields, I felt—and we persuaded our local courts—that a threat of job loss, liquidation, and loss of long-term benefits justified fighting off the raider with whatever legitimate resources we could muster: in proxy fights, vigorous ads, auctions, and, if need be, litigation.

Terry Fox and Steve Berg had parlayed a purchase of a company whose main asset was the patent on Angostora bitters, a popular ingredient of manhattans, old-fashioneds, and other mixed drinks, into a local brewery (Iroquois), and then proposed, by borrowing large sums against the brewery's assets, to buy enough stock in P&L to take over our client. By the time the head-to-head confrontation took place, we knew everything attainable about Terry and Steve—certainly as much as their dentists and their urologists—and we had made it clear, through our own stock purchases and maneuvers, that we were ready and able to fight.

As fate would have it, Steve Berg was my next-door neighbor. His wife, Sandy, and my children, Liz and Lincoln, were friendly neighbors and sometimes carpool associates. We lived on Nottingham Terrace, one of the great residential streets of the city. Steve had one of the biggest houses on the street, and I had the smallest, but we had one common problem: we were situated at a sharp-angled arc near the end of the avenue. Once or twice a year a car would come barreling round the angle, miss the turn, and crash into the beautiful oak tree that spanned our property line. Steve or Sandy and I would appear simultaneously at the sound of the crash, receive apologies from the driver, and then go our separate ways. The tree would be repaired, and we would hope for its escape until the next crash. Finally its roots—no doubt trying to escape its trauma—overgrew the entire lawn and drained away its leaves. I had to replace it with a sugar maple that I didn't like nearly as much—my price for saving the company!

The periodic near funerals of the big oak had at least created a semblance of friendship between Steve and me, and perhaps that led to a more gentle approach than we had expected from his reputation. I was prepared and determined to make our stance strong and unyielding. Yet I was somewhat shocked when Steve suggested a merger. "*Merger!!!*" I exclaimed. "No way! Beer and paint! It makes me nauseous."

In the face of my intransigence, backed up by the numbers of the cohorts we had lined up, Terry and Steve shifted their ground and came up with an offer to sell out. The price was above market but considerably less than our internal valuation. So I persuaded Burt and Bill, and ultimately the board, to accept their offer. "Get rid of them," I told the board. "Then set up an acquisition program of your own to improve and protect the company and its investors." After the meeting, Steve, half satirically and half with an approving stare, said, "Bob, you saved the company!"

PUMPING OUT THE STOCK

The board, under Burt Wilkinson's leadership, was glad to escape the raid and enthusiastically endorsed the acquisition program we had projected. Over the next decade we moved ownership of the company to successful small- and medium-sized paint manufacturers in Richmond, Virginia; Memphis, Tennessee; California; Alabama; and other locales. Each time, we were careful to issue shares to a small group with good contact and control, and to exclude companies greater in size than P&L, so that the acquired tail did not wag the Wilkinson-Lutz dog. Finding me too intrigued by the complex marketing of the Pratt & Lambert management, Bill Lutz took me down to the guts of the Richmond plant and showed me rows of large vats. "Which is house, which is decor, and which is environmental protection?" I asked? Said Bill: "It's all *paint*, Bob."

As the company grew in market power and asset size, its number of shareholders inevitably increased and the possibility of an attack on control persisted. (I could not use the device employed in Transcontinent Television of a special class of control stock or the equivalent of a voting trust.) We were fortunate to encounter Pierce and Stevens, a local company headed by Ray Stevens, that could, with the departure of the older executives such as Burt Wilkinson and Bill Lutz, provide younger management, related products of quality, markets that fit the P&L configuration, and, more important, had a strong stake and interest in maintaining operations in Western New York. Pierce and Stevens presented and required a larger share of the control pie than previous acquirees, but its earnings and its relative size were acceptable in the light of the management it would bring to the picture. I recognized, as did Bill and Burt, that there was nevertheless an internal drive toward increased share price—and maybe ultimately the sale of the company.

SWALLOWING THE PILL

The stock acquisitions and mergers were aggressive tactics, but they did not provide complete protection. As corporations that did not inflate their share prices, the Western New York old-line companies were still vulnerable to intruders who saw easy pickings for companies with good earnings or high-value assets with low stock prices. It wasn't long before raids, proxy fights, and tender offers drove the local entities to the hoped-for protection of the "poison pill." In its elemental form, the pill—a complex document—was a simple concept. If a hostile buyer began circling the wagons and reached a danger point—say, buying 20 percent of the outstanding shares—and thus swallowed the "pill," the pill spread its poison to make the raider's acquisition of no avail. It did this by providing in the company's documents an immediate distribution of stock to the old shareholders—so the raider's 20 percent was diluted, and his cost to acquire control essentially doubled. The pill could be triggered, under the decisions of the Delaware and other business-oriented courts, by action of the board, the very group the raider was seeking to unseat. We installed the pill, or various variations of it, in Pratt & Lambert and most other clients we considered to be vulnerable. Some hostile buyers attacked the pill, with varying success, and it ultimately turned about to be only a temporary protection. But it did provide the target time to find an alternative or more attractive buyer, and the pill became an almost essential requisite for a company seeking to further its acquisition plans. It sometimes had a reverse spin—as in the case of our important client Moore Corporation, the Canadian parent of Moore Business Forms, then a leading manufacturer in the forms industry. Moore fit the profile of the vulnerable target: it had a static share price, good earnings, and a widely dispersed shareholder list. I had trouble convincing the Moore chairman and its board to install the pill, and I was able to do so only when the provincial and federal regulators insisted that the pill could not be installed or invoked without a shareholders' vote. This messed up the timing and strength of the pill, but the chairman gave me a kind of backsided compliment when he remarked, "I knew someday, Bob, you'd get this company in trouble!" As it happened, the trouble hit in reverse. The pill protected Moore from raids for a while, but it did not protect the company from its own economic decline. Its failure to lock on to the computer industry led a later chairman to convert Moore from target to predator, and when it sought to attack a new company with markets and product it needed badly to repair its fortunes, what sent it to defeat? The target's poison pill!

THE END IN GRANADA

The decades of independence for Pratt & Lambert were bound to expire. My policy of limiting acquisitions to companies or groups smaller or less powerful than P&L was not universally or perpetually accepted. In a bullish economy, a static stock price no longer fit with the pull of family and estate consequences, and Ray Stevens finally succumbed to the pressure and accepted the acquisition of the Chicago-based United Paint Company—with an attractive entrée into Wal*Mart—that almost equaled our client in size and earnings. The company that emerged from the negotiations (from which my NHL duties excluded me) had a board equally represented by the newcomers and P&L, with me as the "swing" vote—or, since my firm did not participate, as the odd man out. It was clear that the new partners were bent on sale, and, after some short negotiations in which I helped some to encourage the auction and push up the price, Sherwin Williams swallowed up our fine company, with its local operations, its disappointed employees, and even its unique inventory of the *Saturday Evening Post* paintings of Norman Rockwell. My friend George Gregory had impelled me to invest a modest amount in the stock before I was elected to the board, so I received some benefit from the deal.

After what I thought was the closing, my wife, Bikki, and I took off to the Caribbean island of Grenada, frequented by my Canadian friends, and I immersed myself in some pleasant scuba in a reef not too deep for my expertise. As I emerged from the sea on a Saturday, late in the day, the acting manager grabbed me to say I had an urgent call from the United States. Someone had goofed slightly at the closing, and a vital document had been overlooked. They would fax it to me, and they needed my signature back in Buffalo by Monday breakfast. Problem: the only fax machine at the resort was locked in the manager's office, and he was unreachable on some outer island. It was a reminder that Pratt & Lambert and my loyal clients and friends—Ray Stevens, Jerry Castiglia, Bill Lutz, and Burt Wilkinson—would never be out of my memory. I persuaded the guide to perform a kind burglary. I forced the fax machine to work, and the document crossed the Caribbean and finally closed the agreement. Grenada was a dream island, and I dreamed a bit of the phrase on the ancient document given to me by Burt Wilkinson that graces the wall of my office:

> In the year of our Lord 1689, by the Grace of God, of England, Scotland, France, and Ireland, William and Mary, King and Queen, Defenders of the Faith.[1]

We did not become rulers of Britain and France, but they had been good years at Pratt & Lambert. We were not the king and queen of England or France, even two hundred years later, but I had defended the faith and was grateful.

Part 2

TRIUMPH IN TV, FRUSTRATION IN BASEBALL

Chapter 6

TV OR NOT TV

THE FIGHT FOR CHANNEL 2, 1953-1954

The Prize: The local NBC affiliate and the 1.5 million homes in Western New York and southern Ontario

The Judges and the Courthouse: The FCC in Washington, DC

The Target Territory: The VHF TV channels to be granted by the FCC for the Buffalo-Niagara market:

- Channel 2, the target NBC
- Channel 7, the target ABC (less valuable)
- Channel 4, already captured by CBS and the *Buffalo Evening News*

Waiting at the Courthouse: The VIPs from NBC:
- *The Long Shots.* The Buffalo owners of the UHF channels, hoping to stall the VHF channels, caught in "comparative hearings" before the FCC, long enough to capture the major networks for themselves: UHF 17 (Gary Cohen and Sherwin Grossman) and UHF 59 (Charles Diebold and Robert Millonzi)
- *The Battlers for Channel 2.* Niagara Frontier Amusement Corporation (NFAC; George Goodyear, Paul and Fred Schoellkopf, Paul Cohen, and the author), the *Niagara Falls Gazette* and radio station WHLD (Al Deuel), and WGR Radio (Leo Fitzpatrick and Ike Lounsberry)

* * *

It was 1968, and Seymour Knox III and I were in the Hot Stove League dining room at Toronto's Maple Leaf Gardens. I was making one of my most passionate, but least successful, pleas to Stafford Smythe, a principal owner of the Toronto Maple Leafs—trying to persuade him to either cast his vote in favor of an NHL expansion franchise for Buffalo or permit us to transfer the Oakland Seals to Western New York. "Why should I do that?" asked Stafford—no doubt with the voice of his associate John Bassett, owner of Toronto's Channel 9, coming in to his backside. "You'd be direct competition in our market. Your TV stations are local stations here. I might just as well hand a franchise to one of my friends to beat our ass on York Street!" No dice.

At the time we were outraged. We were convinced that we deserved a grant, that in the long run our entry would benefit the Leafs and the league. We didn't enjoy hearing veto language from the least likable member of the NHL hierarchy. (A few years later, Stafford and his partner, Harold Ballard, were convicted of embezzlement.) But as a monopolist, Smythe was right: Buffalo's TV channels 2, 4, and 7, with their North American network reach, barreled right into Toronto and its large and populous suburbs, already claiming a major percentage of the Buffalo–southern Ontario market, even without a Buffalo NHL club. It's only two hours' driving time between the two cities and seventy miles as the crow—or a VHF signal—flies. The Toronto stations (Channels 9 and 13) were also viewed as local stations in the Buffalo market, and the Leafs were completely sold out for every game, but when one has a monopoly, why should he create a competitor?

When you drove north on the Queen Elizabeth Highway in the late 1940s, as Buffalonians did frequently—to shop in Toronto, or take their kids to a Muskoka camp or a Georgian Bay fishing site—you couldn't help but notice the tall, ungraceful antennae on the roofs of most of the houses. The antennae had sprouted because the only way to get US television programming in the southern Ontario area was to boost an antenna high enough to capture the signal of WBEN-TV, Channel 4. That signal had to leap over the Niagara escarpment to reach Toronto homes. From 1948 to 1953 a freeze by the US Federal Communications Commission on channel grants enthroned the *Buffalo Evening News*'s Channel 4 as the only US network station in the Toronto-Buffalo market. It was easy, then, for Canadians to look to Buffalo TV for entertainment and advertising; and for the Canadian NHL owners, fortified by their own natural ethnocentrism, to adopt policies that would, for a long time in the future, show hostility to Buffalo's eventual NHL franchise and frustrate cooperative Leafs-Sabres proposals that could have been profitable for both teams.

At the threshold, then, television influenced the future Buffalo Sabres—and my own career and life, as well.

THE PRIZE: THE WESTERN NEW YORK–SOUTHERN ONTARIO TV MARKET

Broadcast television came to Western New York—indeed, to North America—in 1948. Just back from the war and military government in Germany, groping my way in Niagara Falls, trying to find stability and direction as a liberal young lawyer in that declining base of cheap electric power and archconservative politics, I had no idea how much the mushrooming TV industry would affect my life. It would transform my law practice, move the "eye" of my law firm from Niagara Falls to the larger Buffalo community, and change the nature—though I would hasten to say, not the quality—of its work from local to national, from routine to challenging, to intersect and compete in a new field of corporate battle. TV would prove to be the most comprehensive, intense, and profitable on-the-job training for me and my firm. It was a new industry, and, except for Washington law firms involved with the government regulators, there were relatively few experts. When the opportunity arose to be the first owners of a major TV station in the Buffalo market (what turned out to be Channel 2, WGR-TV and now WGRZ-TV), my clients and friends, led by George Goodyear and Paul and Fred Schoell-kopf, seized the day and the chase. What ensued was a hard-fought crusade in which I reveled, a journey that produced a new communications giant for the investors, Transcontinent Television Corporation, owner of seven television stations in important markets—and, for me, a continuing challenge of ten years, from 1954 to 1964, over which I still salivate—thrusting me into problems in economics, merger, taxation, on-the-air performance, unions and strikes, public relations, lobbying, politics, and finance. The Transcontinent experience fine-tuned whatever talent I had in the art of negotiation, draftsmanship, and compromise; in the confidence to think ahead and view the total picture, to use maximum resources to achieve major results, and to know and feel the rhythm of transactions and the necessary compulsion to "get there fastest with the mostest."

THE WAR FOR CHANNEL 2

The Transcontinent journey began quite routinely. George Goodyear, who would become my steadfast client and friend, came to my firm with the request that we organize a corporation to operate a television station—a task that could, under my standards, be classified as routine, and could be performed in twenty-four hours. At first we knew little of the circumstances, and could not have imagined the saga of intrigue and tension that ensued. But with the confidence in us shown by George Goodyear and Paul Schoellkopf—a longtime friend and then one of our most important personal clients—the facts began to come out on the table. The name had to obscure the purpose of the company. There were many competitors, and secrecy was paramount. It was 1953; the FCC was releasing its freeze and there would be competitive hearings for both Channel 2—which friends of George wise in the broadcast business had suggested as the more achievable and desirable target—and Channel 7. Channel 2 was regarded as more favorable than Channel 7, which had powerful locals, including the morning newspaper, the *Courier Express*, among its competing groups.

The multimillion-dollar prize was the NBC network affiliation contract. Channel 4—the only VHF station then on the air in Buffalo—had chosen CBS, and NBC was the only other extant network that could ensure profitability. With so few stations permitted to operate by the FCC, the third network, ABC, had great difficulty penetrating many markets. Its station coverage, programming, and advertising lineup were relatively weak at that stage of that network's development. Financing an ABC station could have been a problem. Bankers proved hesitant and uncertain when asked to make capital loans against an unfamiliar balance sheet profile; even major network TV stations showed very little in tangible assets, and the studio furniture and equipment and antenna stick had a relatively low cost and value. The price was almost entirely intangible based on projected earnings. Projections for an ABC affiliate were entirely speculative.

So it was of critical importance not only to get on the air but to get on the air *first*. Competition for the NBC network came not only from the other applicants for Channel 2 and Channel 7 but from three UHF stations already broadcasting in the Buffalo market as well. Very few homes in Western New York—or across the country, for that matter—were equipped to receive a decent picture in the ultra-high-frequency range, and the transmission technology was inadequate. As a result, Channel 59, for example, produced very little for most of its broadcast life except variegated snow. At a lower position on the UHF band, Channel 17, with a substantial investment in tower, antenna, and studio, had greater technical success but very little market penetration. With these handicaps, why did the UHF broadcasters enter the race? Everyone in the market knew that the FCC had so many applications for the vacant VHF channels it had ordered comparative hearings; that there were at least four applicants for Channel 2 and a similar number for Channel 7; and that it would take many months, maybe years, for the winning candidate for either channel to emerge and be approved. We were given an estimate of seven years for Channel 7, where the leading competitors, the morning newspaper and (ultimately) the controversial broadcaster-evangelist Clinton H. Churchill, seemed at indissoluble odds.[1] The chance to own a major communications unit in a significant market, even to beat the VHF applicants to affiliation with NBC, seemed a reasonable gamble—putting aside the possibility of obstruction itself as a profitable objective.

With NBC and ABC pressing the commission to open more markets, and the huge backlog of applications and hearings, the FCC, in one element of a schizoid policy, announced that it would encourage the merger of applications to reduce its backlog by providing that if, on any Wednesday, there was only one application for a channel on file, and that applicant was qualified, an immediate grant of a construction permit (the "CP," the badge of ownership) would be issued to that sole applicant. In another facet of this policy, however, it discouraged merger: when faced with the issue, the commission frowned upon, and even ordered an investigation of, the survivor paying off the departing applicant. It quickly became apparent to the leaders of our group—George Goodyear, Paul and Fred Schoellkopf, and Washington counsel Tom Dowd—that the only way to get on the air and get on first with the NBC network was to negotiate a merger with the other applicants for Channel 2, to do it quietly and quickly—and to get that single, qualified application on the commission's desk on the first Wednesday after the consolidation was accomplished.

BEGINNING THE BATTLE: THE NIAGARA FRONTIER AMUSEMENT CORPORATION

Our first task was easy. We named our group the Niagara Frontier Amusement Corporation (NFAC) to disguise its purpose, precleared the text of the certificate of incorporation in Albany, but held its filing in the secretary of state's office until we were ready to put the FCC application on the commission's desk. The merger target and timing were daunting. It reminded me of the historic cowboy movies and the search for gold: the channel applicants were the claimants with their stakes racing to the courthouse to file first; the UHF stations were setting traps for the ensnarement of the onrushing VHF stations; the commission was the sheriff, posing as the judge, not unwilling to share a whiskey now and then with one or more of the competitors; and the networks were camped at the courthouse, urging the contestants on, ready to be married—or at least engaged—to the winner.

The leaders of our group had to somehow persuade a disparate gaggle of contestants—the publisher of the *Niagara Falls Gazette*, Al Deuel; Paul Fitzpatrick and Ike Lounsberry, the owners of a leading Buffalo radio station, WGR; Victory Television, represented primarily by prominent furniture retailer Arthur Victor Jr. and other longtime supporters of the Democratic Party, including Peter Crotty (a former county chairman) and Eugene McMahon—to join in the merger effort with all deliberate speed. Moreover, if the objective was an unchallengeable single application, the NFAC group itself needed reconfiguration. The idea for the project had been generated in part by George's New York friends and associates; the final structure required more local investment and control. Seymour Knox Jr., father of the eventual founders of the Sabres, was one of the investors brought into the group, and his sons became interested observers of our progress— which would later prove important in the future fight for an NHL franchise.

It is still hard to believe that so much was accomplished with so many diverse interests in so short a time. We were lucky to have so sophisticated and effective a foursome in charge. At this stage, I was primarily a technician and draftsman; George, Paul, Fred, and my senior partner, Paul Cohen, conducted most of the negotiations.

George Goodyear

George had the contacts with the television vanguard. He also had the intellect (he was reputed to have read every page of the *Encyclopaedia Brittanica*); the legal background (Harvard Law School, to which I could not object); and magnificent contacts in finance, theater, and the arts and sciences.

I have thought from time to time how much this man has enriched my life and my experience. He got me into baseball, helped me into hockey, and began my career in television. He arranged for me to represent his father, A. Conger Goodyear, cofounder of the Museum of Modern Art, intimate advisor of Katherine Cornell, and a major contributor to what is now the Albright-Knox Art Gallery. "Moonbeam" was the semiaffectionate, semipejorative moniker I would hear from some of our colleagues, George's longtime buddies, reaching back to their juvenile disdain for the intellectual. I resented it; George apparently did not. To me, the great range of George's interests was stimulating and refreshing. We talked tennis and baseball; art and cosmology. My contacts with science had been superficial ever since I innocently caused a basic experiment in my college chemistry class to blow up in the face of the experimenters. I read Hawking and Hubble like poetry, without full understanding. Yet that did not deter George from plunging me into his effort to persuade the Buffalo Museum of Science to sell the collection called Milestones of Science. While the collection contained only copies (and rarely the only copies) of short works or extracts written by such greats as Copernicus, Kepler, and Galen, the museum needed the dollars badly, and George felt the collection had reached a market value far in excess of its intrinsic worth.

From time to time I am asked, by some hockey reporter, no doubt mistaking me for a goaltender: What was the greatest day in your career? My answer is not the day we got the construction permit for Channel 2, not the day we got the Sabres franchise, not the day we defeated the corporate raider at Pratt & Lambert. It is the day George called me and asked me to fly with him to Long Island to inventory the works of art in his father's house. A whole day with those magnificent paintings, just the two of us and the housekeepers—a beautiful primitive iron sketch in the entryway; in the hallway, a Picasso, a Burchfield, a Matisse; in the living room, Gauguin's *Manao Tupapao* and a seminal Van Gogh; at the corners of the swimming pool, sculptures by Malliol; and in the bathroom, under the towels, Conger's favorite piece, a lovely primitive twenty-two-inch figure in terra cotta, which he could feel and see. There were many more; I breathed them in all afternoon. That day changed my view of art forever.

Paul Schoellkopf

The Schoellkopf family had been principal, if not controlling, stockholders in the Niagara Falls Power Project for many years, and my law firm had been the Paul Schoellkopf family's principal counsel (Paul's was the Niagara Falls branch for decades). I think my first practical assignment from the firm was when I was sent to get the signature of Paul Schoellkopf Sr. on a document. I don't remember whether it was an affidavit, which had to be notarized and subscribed and sworn to, or an acknowledgment that had to be witnessed and notarized. I remember I was a little nervous because, frankly, despite my Harvard education, I didn't know which was which. But I accomplished this difficult task and there began an association and friendship with Paul Jr. that continued through dozens of projects, right up to today. Paul did not purport to be sophisticated, but he was a quick learner and had everyone's respect. He had power and prestige as a member of a leading family in the community; he was knowledgeable, direct, and practical. He was a fine judge of character. He could tell a faker at a thousand yards. His Niagara Falls credentials were prime and impeccable, and he was a natural for bringing Al Deuel, owner of the *Niagara Falls Gazette*, into the merger.

Fred Schoellkopf was sophisticated, president of the Schoellkopf investment company Niagara Share Corporation and ultimately president of the Marine Midland Bank, and a former pilot. A skilled negotiator, he was at home in financial board meetings or smoke-filled rooms. He was the good-humored strategist and, if need be, the manipulator. But he appreciated my approach and technique as the negotiations moved to documents. "Bob succeeds," he said once, in my presence, "because he knows to the full the law and the facts, and he tells it as it is." His death on December 7, 1969 (a suicide, for whatever reason I will never understand), was a great blow to all of us, but to me especially; he backed me in every project I brought to him.

Paul Pincus Cohen

Paul Cohen, my uncle, my mentor, my partner, was my professional idol. Harvard Law Review, Phi Beta Kappa—he had all the credentials, and, a practicing Reform Jew, he had made his way to prominence in that illiberal nineteenth-century town of Niagara Falls, with its dominance of chemical factories, electric power, environmental disdain, and tourism. He had all the negotiating skills, a disciplined grasp of when and when not to move, a grasp of economics and finance, and a love and undeniable demand for graceful, accurate, and effective language. My back still aches in memory of the hours I spent looking over his shoulder as we debated the likes of "affect" versus "effect." Most important, Paul was a fighter, a trasher of unfairness and routineers, and an advocate of the public interest.

ACTS OF INTRIGUE AND BETRAYAL

The NFAC group moved toward the FCC filing with confidence. We had the financial resources; the broadcast experience, with the *Gazette* and WGR personnel; the political know-how, at least at that stage, on the Republican side; leadership in the Buffalo community; and, through George's New York City friends, the entrée to the FCC. A late filing for a CP on Channel 2 by the Victory Group was a momentary obstacle, but their clout in the Democratic Party seemed to add strength and speed to our application. Despite some uneasiness about the Victor group's financial capabilities and the size of their demand for participation in ownership, the need for speed and the importance of being first to get NBC impelled both sides to reach an accommodation. Arthur Victor brought his colleagues into the NFAC structure.

On October 26, 1953, George met with NBC in New York and was assured that that network would be available if the NFAC got the CP. Concurrently, meetings with WGR radio's counsel in Detroit produced agreement on the sale of that station to our group and the acceptance by Al Deuel (the *Gazette*) of an option to acquire 25 percent of the NFAC—the same interest to be accepted by Victor and his partners. Word went out to the NFAC group that merger, and victory, was now possible. We were all to drive for a formal agreement and a filing with the FCC on the following Tuesday, and we were hopeful the commission would issue the grant on the following day.

Negotiations to finalize the deals and the documents went 'round the clock on Friday, October 30; Saturday, October 31; and Sunday, November 1, culminating in an eighteen-hour session in the wee hours of Monday night and Tuesday morning. Agreements were worked out, drafted, and signed—purchasing WGR radio, granting the Victory Group 25 percent equity. We added to the Deuel deal a buyout of the equipment of WBES, Channel 59, in contemplation of its cooperation in not opposing a grant of the Channel 2 CP to us. The merger agreements resulted from a full-court press and an astute deployment of resources: George on Kirk and Bliss, Paul Schoellkopf on Al Deuel, Paul Cohen on Art Victor, and so on, and Fred and both Pauls on Diebold and Millonzi, the principals in Channel 59. When the multiphased negotiations were completed and signed and the revised application finalized in the early hours of Tuesday, November 2, 1953, George was on his way to Washington with Tom Dowd, prepared to file the merged application in time to qualify for the FCC's expected Wednesday grant.

In Buffalo, I had been hard at work completing details, checking the documents into the small hours Tuesday night. I went home, exhausted but unable to sleep, and finally succumbed about 8 AM, falling asleep on the couch. Around noon my wife awakened me with words of near doom: "Sam Darlich filed for Channel 2 at 4 PM yesterday." All of the full-court press, all the dollars and stock committed to Victory and Diebold and the *Gazette* had gone for naught. There was no longer a single, cleared application for the channel, and we would be faced with further delay and obstruction—perhaps even a comparative hearing, which might take years and produce only a roll of the dice.

THE "STRIKE" APPLICATIONS

Who was Sam Darlich? What was he after? There was anger and suspicion on our side, and, with the pieces of the putative pie already given out, none of us had any desire or patience for another payoff.

Our suspicions of conspiracy were confirmed when we learned that the Darlich application (the dummy corporation was named Enterprise Transmission, Inc.) was filed almost in tandem with a similar application by a number of Democratic stalwarts in the name of Best Television, Inc., blocking a merger of the postulants on both Channel 2 and Channel 7.

When Tom Dowd read the Darlich (Enterprise) application on that dismal afternoon, he immediately concluded that it was a "strike"—obstruction—filing. He stalked the Washington counsel who filed the application and confronted him. In a natural emotional reaction of disappointment and anger—he had worked so hard and come so close—Dowd, shouting at the lawyer in the commission corridor, charged blackmail. That was bad enough, but he went further. In spite of his experience and his skillful warnings to us—and without consultation with our group—Dowd, on the emotional spike of the moment, offered the Darlich lawyer a substantial sum of money for a withdrawal. Dowd's offer was immediately rejected, and all that it had accomplished was a potential violation of FCC policy and a possible taint on the NFAC's methods and character. So the battle, and the solution, if there were one, had to shift to Buffalo. The documents contained cutoff dates for the key agreements, and with the Darlich filing the entire NFAC structure and the merger itself were in danger.

Up to this point my role had been primarily as legal technician in support of the negotiations. But with the Darlich roadblock, my role had to change.

In the small-town environment in Buffalo, it took only a few days for the story of what happened to surface. We were concerned that the Darlich application was not a bona fide claim for a Channel 2 CP—but how could we prove it and get the FCC to knock it out? And how could we work it out in time, so that our merger deals did not unravel? Art Victor, friend of Paul Cohen and me, and Gene McMahon, friend of Paul Fitzpatrick—conflicted by their loyalties to their Democratic cronies and the bet they'd made on our success—disclosed the treachery. Fitzpatrick, the former Erie County Democratic Party chairman, had a substantial interest in Channel 59. He may have inspired the creation of Art's Victory Television itself—perhaps both to delay the grant on Channel 2 to give Channel 59 a chance for the network and to provide a hedge in case Channel 59 didn't survive. When we sent word that the merger deal was go, the Victory Group felt compelled to reveal this to Fitzpatrick, and Gene McMahon was elected to make the call. He did call, and the result was outrage (Fitzpatrick could not be invited into the NFAC because his Democratic position did not fit). The outrage produced the simultaneous filing of the Darlich application to block Channel 2 and the Best Television strike filing to block Channel 7. In the subsequent negotiations to unblock our channel, Fitzpatrick actually threatened several times to have WBES file independently for Channel 2.

After conferring with Dowd, it was clear we had to attack—to come up with evidence that would persuade the FCC to strike the Darlich application. I immediately put together what amounted to an attack squad: my partner, Preston Wright; law clerks; secretaries; paralegals; and Felix Piech, executive secretary of the Schoellkopf interests. We moved in and took over Buffalo's venerable Grosvenor Public Library. There were no computers then, but the Grosvenor Library was a great depository of information. Its main reading room, with the files and indexes, was round, and made for easy access and communication among the members of our squad. We did not resist the temptation to call, if not shout, across the room with directions or to cheer major or minor finds, and the librarians may have been shocked at the way we shredded the tradition of heavy quiet. But desperation ruled the day. The main sources were the indexes and copies of the *Buffalo Evening News* and the morning *Courier Express*. But we sent out assignments to the county clerk records, the radio stations, the federal and state courts, and the banks (where inquiries had to be discreet and carefully chosen, since some of our putative enemies were officers of local lending institutions).

The result was, I say with some prejudice, the right stuff. We produced a chart that showed a damning relationship between Darlich and his cohorts in Enterprise, on the one hand, and the stockholders in Channel 59, on the other; and a similar relationship with the owners, directors, and officers of Best Television, the entity that filed the blocking application on Channel 7. (Embarrassing, but unspoken was the tie of the Darlich and Best TV groups with some of our own bedfellows in Victory Television.) Our findings might have been, technically, newspapers and hearsay, but they were good enough to raise suspicion and concern at the FCC and jump-start an investigation.

Presented passionately and professionally by Dowd, our chart, with the other evidence assembled, persuaded the commission on November 10, 1953, to set a hearing for December 10 to determine whether Enterprise had filed solely to obstruct the grant of our application. The order had some negative implications—the time involved in a hearing would blow the cutoff dates in the WBES, WGR, and *Gazette* deals and raise questions as to our paying off competitors, but it had a sharp practical effect. Sam Darlich was a wealthy man who didn't need the prospective TV income or deductions. He had filed the Enterprise claim out of loyalty to his friends and associates; but he was not well, and his loyalty did not extend to an unpleasant, protracted hearing and cross-examination for which he would receive no recompense. The commission's order enabled Paul Cohen to persuade Darlich he was in for just that. When the differences over bailing out the owners of the near-bankrupt Channel 59 were resolved, Paul, working with George and the Schoellkopfs (with some background noise from me), brought Darlich in to sign a release and a withdrawal of his application.

Sherwin Grossman and Gary Cohen, the owners of Channel 17, had done a much better job in vamping for a network or local operation: they had a better transmitter site, tower, and studios, and a more sophisticated understanding of broadcasting operations, with a lower signal, combining lower power costs with greater coverage. Outright purchase of the competing and obstructing entities might have made the acquisition of the CP for Channel 2 easier and quicker, but we were faced with an FCC policy that was at least bipolar, and certainly self-contradictory. It began with the notion that the CP should be granted to the applicant that showed the best contribution to the public interest—on the merits. This meant hearings, frequently controversial and protracted, in which each combatant presented its claim to the public interest. At the other pole, the commission was under great pressure to expand this new marvel to every community in the nation as quickly as possible. To meet this concern, when faced with a swarm of applications in many major markets, it responded with the procedural rule for the Wednesday grant to an emerging lone applicant, thus encouraging merger. Yet it had no rules regarding how these mergers could be brought about. It preferred to make judgments case by case—a "smell" test that frowned upon, but did not bar, buyouts; that occasionally, but not consistently, invoked the sanctity of its allocation plan to bar or question a transaction that accompanied the failure of another station, or where the consideration paid was just "too much." Decades later, in allocating other broadcast bands, successor commissions would abandon this pretense and grant CPs by outright auction. But in the FCC's high-and-mighty allocation plan of the 1950s, cash was tainted. Thus our group and its Washington counsel, Pierson and Dowd, had the delicate job of managing to sweep the unacceptable competitors aside, or producing their withdrawal or joinder in such a way that inducements for departure could not be seen—or characterized—as blackmail, given or received.

With the withdrawal of Darlich, the snipers were eliminated, and we thought the prize was ours. Then, on December 28, came the heavy artillery: Channel 17—owned by Grossman and Cohen and represented by an able lawyer, my friend, David Landy—filed a petition to intervene. Their cause was described frankly and eloquently: They had been pioneers in UHF, they had established a respectable station, and the development of the UHF band was in the public interest. They needed more time to become strong enough to compete with the lower channels of the VHF band, now well accepted by the viewing public and the important advertisers.

Delay, delay, and more delay. . . . Would we ever get to the courthouse and receive our prize? Fortunately, we were not the only ones getting impatient. NBC was chomping at the bit. With very few TV sets equipped to reproduce an adequate UHF signal, the network was effectively blocked out of the Western New York market so long as CBS's Channel 4 remained the only VHF station in the area. The regulators certainly observed the impatient pacing of the NBC executives in the FCC corridors, and, with an assist from the postmaster general inspired by George's friend, Russell Kirk, the commission promptly denied Channel 17's petition to intervene in January 1954. The denial led to negotiations to get Channel 17 to step back.

This time the strategists had a more difficult job. Grossman and Cohen suggested that they, too, might be interested in becoming investors in the NFAC or in being bought out, but George Goodyear effectively barred that door. "We're already being accused of bringing about the demise of two stations," he said. "We can't be tainted with a third!" The solution made business sense: WUTV would continue operations on 17, but at a lower cost, at the Channel 59 studios in the Lafayette hotel—to be purchased from WBES—and the NFAC would lease Channel 17's Barton Street facilities, which were much more desirable, with an option to purchase at the end of the lease. The lease and option terms were quite generous—so generous that George had to use all of his influence with Kirk and Bliss to get them to go along. Yet the move into the Barton Street facilities would enable Channel 2 to get on the air much more quickly and efficiently.

George's sensitivity to the importance of continued operations by Channel 17 proved of great significance when the FCC, instead of routinely approving the revised application, ordered a hearing into the payoff transactions and their effect on the NFAC's qualifications for the franchise. This called for testimony by the Schoellkopfs, George Goodyear, Paul Cohen, and even Sam Darlich himself (although this time under the eyes of friendly counsel). Our law firm was really in the middle when the Schoellkopfs announced that they would not testify. As seemed to happen often over the years, we were confronted with the ethical question that throws so many lawyers and judges: Whom did we represent? It could be viewed as bitchy and at least inconsiderate, for Paul and Fred, at the crucial moment, to shy away, ostensibly to protect their reputation and position in the investment industry. Typically, instead of making a big deal of the supposed conflict of interest—we represented the NFAC, Paul Schoellkopf and George (in some matters), as well as the Marine Trust Company (in Niagara Falls), which could be involved in financing—Paul Cohen chose to carry the ball himself. He was confident he could be fair and effective for all. The solution: Paul Cohen (with George in tandem) would testify himself and would incorporate the fact that Paul and Fred would have put forward into his own and George Goodyear's testimony. With Paul speaking for others, it was obvious hearsay, but with the wide discretion and political temper available to an administrative agency, no real objection was presented by the FCC. And there was really no opposing party, except those one or two commissioners who were wrinkling their noses. Finally, on April 7, 1954, by a vote of six to one, the CP prize was granted to the NFAC. In one of those strange aberrations that gave the FCC its vulnerable reputation in the appellate courts, the dissenting commissioner, Robert Bartley, allowed that it wasn't the Channel 17 transaction or the purchase of the WBES assets to which he objected, but the arm's-length, businesslike purchase of WGR radio!

In the consummation, WGR was purchased for about $1.6 million, the *Gazette* and the Victory Group were accepted as minority stockholders, WBES sold its equipment for its liquidation value, and the owners of Channel 17 retained their operating station. Channel 17 granted us a long-term lease, with an option to buy, at generous rental and option prices, for their tower, transmitter, and studios, enabling Channel 2 to become fully operational at a much earlier date than we had hoped.

It was the hooker in the WBUF transaction—our judgment to keep Channel 17 alive—that would become the sword of Damocles in the scramble to get a permanent network contract.

THE NETWORK TREACHERY AND THE TRANSCONTINENT COUNTERATTACK

In April 1954 things looked rosy for WGR-TV—a network affiliation, full-time and full programming with one of the two leading TV networks—the National Broadcasting Company; projections of profits and rapid penetration of the Buffalo-Toronto market, with no competition for some years in the VHF band except CBS affiliate Channel 4; and only minimal competition from the UHF band, with viewers slow to buy costly converters needed to receive UHF signals. But the network affiliation contract providing NBC programming was limited by FCC regulation (doubtless with network encouragement) to two years. Experience began to show the networks that their most profitable outlets were their "O and O's"—the stations they owned and operated themselves. O and O's owed no commissions (network compensation to local owners), so the income from productions and network and local advertising flowed directly and fully from the O and O to the network itself. At that time, each network was restricted to no more than five VHF and two UHF stations in the United States. NBC already owned six, but had one UHF slot to fill. Despite what we thought were warm relations with NBC, and its role in urging us to gobble up the opposition to get on the air fast, the network's loyalty did not last. A scan by NBC executives of the station landscape focused on Channel 17 in Buffalo—an available UHF station in a major market with owners who had already tried to sell. Without ceremony or discussion, NBC dropped the bomb. It quickly purchased Channel 17 and let it be known that our network affiliation contract would be terminated after only two years. The consequences were frightening: Channel 4 had locked up CBS; ABC had committed to the ultimate victor in the Channel 7 hearing; and with NBC operating its own station, we were indeed out in the cold. Projections dropped from a substantial profit to a miserable loss. Desperate, we launched entreaties at all ends of the broadcasting spectrum. Fred pushed hard at RCA and NBC ownership, now as a stockholder in RCA under Niagara Share. The WUTV owners were jubilant and defiant. "You blew it, Bob," said Clarence Obletz, a Channel 17 principal. "You should have knocked us out when you had the chance." I even wrote an emotional letter to my high school friend and one-time next-door neighbor, Dave Adams, then associate general counsel of NBC. To no avail, the NBC executives were obsessed with their UHF O & O plan. It was the courageous response of our leaders, however, that ultimately won the war. Said Fred, Paul, and George: We'll build our own network, and NBC will be forced to come back to us!

BUILDING THE TRANSCONTINENT CHAIN

The first step in "building our own network" was to buy a TV station—almost any station. The first venture was pretty limited—a half-interest in a VHF station in Harrisonburg, Virginia. I had trouble finding it on the map, but we were in business. The second step was to create an organization. Neither Paul nor Fred nor George desired to leave their regular corporate pursuits, including the closed investment company Niagara Share, primarily owned by the Schoellkopf families. They considered George Goodyear too nice and soft a guy, and board strategies and policies were more Paul and Fred's métier. But the company needed a front man, a nubile executive with TV and advertising contacts, and Fred and Paul came up with David Channing Moore. Moore's TV experience was almost nonexistent, but he was a handsome dog with a generous widow's peak and a wife, Hatsie, who would have been comfortable in the pages of *Harper's Bazaar*. It was not the first or the last time my clients would rescue a friend from relative oblivion (Dave had been mustered out of IBM) and install him in a position whose importance exceeded his competence. But Paul and Fred recognized Moore's limitations, and delegated—with confidence—most of the critical projects to Paul's friend Dave Forman as vice president, administration to Cliff Kirtland as chief financial officer, and to me and my firm for negotiation of acquisitions and other legal matters, with the help of Washington counsel.

Washington counsel was a key slot, and with every proposed acquisition we needed to build up multistation strength, rapidly, requiring the approval of the Federal Communications Commission. There was momentary panic in my law firm when Dave Moore began calling communication lawyers—friends of his friends. But while Dave's nominees may have known the way to the FCC clerks, Paul Cohen and I were convinced that we needed a firm with broad talent and experience and political respect, if not clout. After a brief call to Paul and Fred Schoellkopf, I was on the next flight to Washington to meet with Covington & Burling. It was a home run. Covington was Dean Acheson's firm and I had two classmates, both *Harvard Law Review*, in the partnership roster. My classmates put us directly with their FCC expert, Ernie Jennes. Jennes was good-looking, in a leonine way, medium young, beetle-browed, and very serious. He was clearly knowledgeable and practical. Perhaps what impressed me the most, as I sat listening to him adroitly handle call after call in my presence, was his ability to think and deal with multiple decisions at once. Not think on his feet, mind you—his feet were off the ground most of the time, extended to his back wall where he had his series of telephone buttons, manipulating one, two, three, sometimes four lines with his feet! I put Jennes to work immediately as Transcontinent's Washington counsel, thus preempting Dave Moore's plans and preserving control of legal matters for the Buffalo group, which ultimately bought out the New York/Detroit crowd.

Paul Schoellkopf liked Jennes immediately, and Ernie proved to be what we had hoped: not just a lobbyist or a guy with an ear of a commissioner or the private number of a network executive, but a fine, solid, imaginative lawyer with good judgment.

Over the next eight years, from 1956 to 1964, the Transcontinent team—Dave Forman in Buffalo, Ernie in Washington, and me hopping all over the country, with Paul and Fred Schoellkopf providing strategies and financial contacts—was as active as any in the broadcasting business. We bought and sold Harrisonburg; bought and ultimately sold Rochester, New York; bought a leading radio station in Cleveland; purchased a VHF station in Kansas City, Missouri; acquired through merger a leading VHF station in San Diego and successful UHF in Bakersfield, California; and combined two losing UHF operations into a successful UHF station in Scranton and Wilkes-Barre, Pennsylvania. While the original objective in organizing Transcontinent was to frustrate the effect of NBC's acquisition of Channel 17 and secure a national network for our Buffalo station, as we achieved that goal and honed our expertise, the appetite for TV transactions grew, and by 1963 we had reached the full complement of station ownership permitted by the FCC—five VHF and two UHF—spanning the continent.

We were not always successful. Before San Diego became available, word came that a VHF in Sacramento would be on the market. The station's counsel and financial advisers were in San Francisco, and Paul and Fred dispatched me to that glamorous city with instructions to "keep the pressure on the owner and stay there until a deal was made." I was cautioned to be constantly in touch—the scoop on the owner was that he had a reputation for acting quickly, even precipitously, so I'd better be ready to make our bid as soon as the auction opened. I complied: daily calls to the seller's lawyers, daily unanswered calls to the seller himself, letters, memoranda—a constant flow, I thought, of considerate, expertly crafted expressions of interest. Since I had to be continuously reachable, there wasn't much I could do except sleep and eat. The latter I did, with gusto; and after three weeks of tours of duty at the likes of Ernie's, Ondine, and L'Orangerie, I gained fifteen pounds. Unfortunately, unknown to our spies and informants, a connection lurking in the background held the right of first refusal, and my gastronomic fortnight went for naught.

Of the many transactions the team produced in this era—involving investments of more than $35 million—Rochester was the most critical; San Diego, the most valuable and most costly; and Scranton/Wilkes-Barre, the most dramatic.

In Buffalo, when NBC purchased Channel 17 and pulled its network away from WGR-TV, the situation was desperate. Without a national net-work, Channel 2 would in one quarter go from profit to deep loss. Because Channel 4 had CBS and ABC had a commitment to the eventual winner of Channel 7, any hookup in the Buffalo market with ABC—a network only partly developed at that time—would provide only temporary and partial relief. In Rochester, New York, however—a substantial and affluent market only seventy miles east—opportunity knocked: Rochester's Channel 8 was having ownership conflicts and might become available. Leverage was pos-sible. ABC was eager to reach more markets, and there were only two VHF stations then authorized and in operation in that city. So if we bought Channel 8 and waved a network affiliation contract at the ABC brass, that would encourage ABC to treat us well in Buffalo and would put pressure on NBC. We moved quickly to buy the Rochester station, and an ABC network deal for our outlets in both cities quickly followed.

In the end, it was economics and luck—luck that follows the brave, I like to think—that solved the problem. The Western New York community, used to the stronger and more reliable VHF signal, did not take kindly to NBC programming on UHF Channel 17. Before cable, television was sup-posed to be free, and conversion of a TV set to receive UHF signals was costly and something of a nuisance. After two years of slow conversions and dis-appointing ratings, the NBC executives—once so quick to discard their orig-inal undertakings to us—began to reverse course. We were now a force to be reckoned with, and, by the end of 1958, NBC abandoned Channel 17 and welcomed Channel 2 back to the NBC network, with a standard affiliation contract and normal station compensation.

SCRANTON—WHEN MINUS ONE PLUS MINUS ONE MEANT PLUS TWO

NBC's surrender to Transcontinent came about because of the inability of Channel 17 to compete, in those days of small UHF market penetration, with the standard VHF stations on the Buffalo market. But the FCC alloca-tion program had created a few UHF islands—where all the stations assigned to a market were UHF, and each UHF station was competing only against stations with the same type of signal and the same handicaps. One of those was the Scranton/Wilkes-Barre market, with four stations assigned: two making money and two losing big dollars. One of the losers was owned by the family of William W. Scranton, former governor of Pennsyl-vania. Paul and Fred Schoellkopf knew Bill Scranton socially, and as soon as we saw a potential target there, Dave Forman and I got our materials together and headed for northeastern Pennsylvania. The proposal was simple, though we had trepidations about an arbitrary response from the

FCC: the market wasn't large enough for four stations, two were deeply in the red, and there were only three national networks (giving ABC the benefit of the doubt)—so why not consolidate the two? It was a pattern Transcontinent was uniquely familiar with—we had put WGR-TV on the air in Buffalo in record time by using the equipment and personnel of the failing UHF stations in that city. Sure, it was inconsistent with the commission's august station allocation plan, and it reduced the number of stations serving the community. But, we argued successfully, the allocation concept had to yield to economic reality, and Ernie Jennes delivered the FCC approval. We had combined two losers into one winner.

Bill Scranton turned out to be a reasonable, good-humored, and practical target. He was really no problem; he immediately saw the advantage of our plan, seemed to like us, and welcomed the opportunity to trade his red ink for a share in Transcontinent's future. The owners of the Wilkes-Barre station were not so easy a sell, and I had to make trip after trip to the area to secure their approval. Getting there from Buffalo was no slam dunk. There were no convenient air routes from Western New York, and the long drive was a time waster. Only one train stopped in Scranton for three minutes on its way to New York City—at 4 AM. After several of these uncomfortable journeys, I learned to schedule all my meetings early in the morning, hoping to stay awake long enough to keep my brain working.

The lack of sleep probably added to the depression I felt in that old, senile city. Scranton had been an important community at the beginning of the twentieth century, with its coal, iron, oil, and rail connections. But it had failed to progress, lost its main industries, and seemed an ugly shell of its 1900 self. For years after my journeys to the area, I would challenge a naysayer, in my crusades on behalf of the Studio Arena or the Sabres, "Do you want to become another dead and dying Scranton?"

FINDING THE LOST LEASE

The Wilkes-Barre owners did not have Bill Scranton's glamour, but the station had a better financial record than Bill's, and they exhibited strong independence, tinged with an element of a sort of xenophobism: they didn't want the city of Wilkes-Barre to play second fiddle to the town on the other side of the mountain. Programming concerns, choice of equipment, retention of personnel (they were intensely loyal to their employees), and call letters all became the subject of extensive debate. We resolved all of those issues, and with the FCC approval, prepared to close, when an obstacle arose in the area I'd always treated as routine and beneath my attention: title to real property. We learned that the "stick" (tower and antenna) of the Scranton radio station (we were buying that, too) was on subleased mountain land. The sublease to the station had expired—and nobody could find the new lease. When a further search of the station offices turned up nothing, I asked the station manager to take me up on the mountain to the transmitter site, hoping to find a clue there. The manager, who had remained in the background throughout the negotiations, gave his unsmiling consent, and we inserted ourselves into his Porsche for the climb to the summit. Perhaps I'm investing that journey with the flavor of hindsight, but it was one of the scariest rides I've ever taken—surpassing even the Amalfi Drive in 1944, when I was jammed with forty other infantry, rifle, full field pack, and all, into an open flatbed truck that careened along the mountainous cliffs toward Naples and the Italian front.

Grim-faced throughout the journey, the manager spoke not a word and drove at frightening speed, slamming the brakes, occasionally skidding on the curves, paying no attention to my halfhearted protests. At the summit, a farmer greeted us with the key to the transmitter building—he acted more or less as house sitter. He had no information, he said, and knew nothing of the lease. I reported my frustration to Ernie Jennes, who shrugged his shoulders—"We'll just have to wait," he said. But I persisted. I was, as always, concerned that delay could unravel the deal. My suspicions had started to form from the manager's demeanor. The farmer had said nothing helpful, except to comment that the land was now owned by a family "out West"—Kansas or Missouri, he wasn't sure which. The title documents disclosed the address of the owner of title but provided no clue as to who held the lease. The break came when one of the secretaries in the station office gave me the address. It was in Indiana.

An emergency plane ride and a dusty journey by auto brought me to the owners of the land—or the holders of the lease, I was never sure which. They were an elderly couple, residing in a clean, spare farmhouse near the Missouri border. I had intimations of the famous Grant Wood painting. They were dead serious, acknowledged that they owned the land and had leased it again when the old lease expired, but could not, they insisted, tell me who the new tenant was. I argued strenuously that this made no sense. We were buying the station—the only possible user of the land. What good was the lease without a tenant? They seemed decent people, and it was obvious something untoward was afoot—why did they want to be mixed up in it? The woman seemed in charge of the response, and she was unyielding. I thanked them and had started toward my car, when the man appeared in the doorway and asked me to come back in the house. They had made a call, talked it over, and wanted to tell me the truth. The station manager was the woman's nephew; they had sympathy for him, but would not lie to protect him, would not wish to be involved in his plans, however justified. The manager was opposed to the deal with us, feeling he had been unfairly treated by the Scrantons, and had contrived this scheme as a sort of blackmail, designed to make us buy the sublease from him so that he would be compensated for the loss of his job and his prestige. My sense of unease as we took the Porsche ride up the Scranton mountain was right on. When we confronted the station manager, he collapsed. The sublease he held in his malign hand, he understood, belonged to his employer. We tore it up, negotiated a new document, and closed the acquisition.

THE TRANSCONTINENTAL CLIMAX—
THE GREAT TRANSACTION AND THE MAJOR GOOF

The Transcontinent experience taught me to navigate frustration and failure, and to be bold enough to question or influence a client's business judgment. The growth of the company from a single channel in Buffalo to stations in six other cities had not been achieved without difficulty or danger. San Diego, a major growing market, and the UHF station in Bakersfield, California, had been acquired in a semimerger by issuing stock in Transcontinent to Jack Wrather, a Texas oil entrepreneur who owned Muzak and the Lassie movies and was married to onetime movie star Bonita Granville. Ms. Granville never showed up at board meetings, but she did host a delightful formal dinner in San Diego, which I was forced to attend in a sports jacket because American Airlines lost my luggage. (The carrier ultimately bought me one-half of a new blue suit, which looked remarkably like its attendants' uniforms!) It wasn't long before the seven stations we had acquired—and the broadcast chain itself—became extremely valuable, and it wasn't long before the Wrather oil, with its ambitions for leveraged growth in the heady entertainment world, didn't mix with the conservative, old-money waters of Lake Erie. I had constructed the company and the acquisitions so that the Buffalo group retained the controlling class of stock. When a dispute over future policy of the company reached a boiling point, I received an overheated call from the nationally prominent lawyer Louis Nizer, threatening my colleagues and me with dire litigation if we didn't grant Jack Wrather equal voting power, commensurate with his investment, since the San Diego station had become relatively more valuable. In a response that later prepared me for the attempt by the Soviet Union to recapture hockey star Alexander Mogilny in 1979, I respectfully parried Nizer's challenge, reminding him that there had been full disclosure on our part and full vetting by the Wrather counsel at the time of the deal. We had great confidence in the control documents, but my clients, with a handsome profit hovering and other pursuits that interested them more, decided that the best solution was to sell the company.

My senior partner, Paul Cohen, went through the roof. To give up seven major units in a growing industry, to give up the influence and power of

Channel 2 in the Buffalo community—this was anathema. Fred and Paul Schoellkopf came to me, saying, "This involves millions and millions of dollars. The Tafts are all set to buy the company—you've got to handle the negotiations; Paul is so opposed to the deal, we're afraid he'll blow it." So I got the assignment and negotiated—over a long and complex nine months—what turned out to be, in 1964, the largest broadcast deal ever negotiated: $55 million plus assumed debt of $30 million. It took tough negotiations with three different purchasers—Time-Life, August Meyer, and, most important, Taft Broadcasting. The three deals staged negotiations in seven cities: Cincinnati, Washington, New York, Chicago, Buffalo, Bakersfield, and San Diego.

The principal issue between Taft's lawyer, Don Alexander (later commissioner of the IRS), and me was over the meaning of "net/net." I'd had first crack at the drafting and had persuaded the Tafts, with no objection from their original counsel, to sign a letter of intent that called upon Taft Broadcasting to pay an amount that, after all taxes payable by Transcontinent were deducted, would yield $55 million for our stockholders. In drafting this "net/net" concept, I was aware through my work on the Bar taxation committees that a new, draconian tax was on the horizon—depreciation recapture. A tax bill had just been passed that would require Transcontinent, on the sale of its assets, to add back to income—and pay a tax at peak rates—on all the depreciation on buildings and equipment, and all the amortization of the cost of network affiliation contracts that had been deducted on the company's tax returns for the eight years of its existence. The depreciation/amortization recapture was a big number, and if it were a burden on the sellers, it would have seriously threatened the deal. Don was aware of this development, but he came into the negotiations too late.

Don tried, in meeting after meeting, in city after city, to strike the "net/net" clause. But I would not yield. Finally, at the end of a long day, Don gave me what I prefer to recall as a tribute to my tenacity—or intransigence, depending on your point of view. I accepted a call to the men's room, and when I returned, found no place to sit. Don had removed my chair!

Don and the Tafts ultimately capitulated. My letter of intent was the law of the deal. It was a triumph for me. I had worn down Don Alexander of the Taft firm and Ernie Jennes of Covington & Burling, whose tender stomach forced him to withdraw. We had produced a handsome profit for the investors, but a goof of major proportions. Paul Cohen was right: years later, the TV properties—Buffalo, Kansas City, San Diego, Scranton/Wilkes-Barre, and Bakersfield—would have sold for more than a billion dollars.

From my personal point of view, the ten-year Transcontinent experience was a smashing success. It gave me a sense of intellectual power and judgment that could be asserted on the national scene. It provided entrée to important corporate clients in Western New York. Thus, Bill Lutz, son-in-law of *Niagara Falls Gazette* owner Al Deuel, retained me to fend off the raiders circling the well-known paint manufacturer Pratt & Lambert, of which he was vice president; Arthur Schmon brought to my firm the Ontario Paper Company, a leading Canadian manufacturer with its plant in St. Catharines, just thirty-five miles from Buffalo. And when Seymour Knox III and I began our search in 1968 and 1969 for investors in the pursuit of an NHL franchise, it was the Transcontinent stockholders who responded quickly and with generosity and confidence in our judgment. Bill Lutz, Arthur Victor, Gene McMahon, Peter Crotty, the Schoellkopfs, Dick Rupp, and George Strawbridge (through Dave Forman and Bob Rich Jr.), plus Peter and Ed Andrews, who were left out in Channel 7 as stockholders in the now-defunct *Courier Express*, all became enthusiastic and loyal supporters of the Sabres throughout the thirty years of our ownership.[2]

Chapter 7

DOIN'
THE CONTINENTAL

THE FIRST FRANCHISE FIGHT: BUFFALO AND
THE "OUTLAW" CONTINENTAL LEAGUE

I n the 1950s, when Walter O'Malley moved his Brooklyn Dodgers to the less revered but more profitable Los Angeles venue and Horace Stoneham moved his Giants in tandem to San Francisco—not just to keep O'Malley company—New York City was left, for the first time in decades, with only one Major League Baseball team. This did not suit one baseball fan of wealth, notoriety, and influence, Joan Whitney Payson, or the many non-Yankee patrons of the national game who were left stranded. With the encouragement of the city's mayor, Robert Wagner, Mrs. Payson set about to restore this grievous situation, and in 1960 she hired M. Donald Grant as her strategist and Bill Shea as her counsel to find a way to bring a new franchise to the world's number one market. Shea was an affable and able lawyer, wise in the ways of New York and Washington politics, and he played all the instruments in his attempt to do Mrs. Payson's bidding: offer to purchase and transfer an existing franchise; put pressure on the Leagues to expand; pressure Congress to force expansion; threaten to have Major League Baseball's court-created antitrust exemption annulled; plead with the commissioner. None worked. The baseball cartel remained stone-faced

and immovable. Civil means exhausted, then came the notion of war: organize a new league, with a new team in New York as its pivot and base.

The concept of a war against the establishment leagues was not a new
one. It had been tried during the World War I years with the Federal League,
when the new group hired away star players like Joe Tinker of "Tinker to
Evers to Chance" fame, only to be faced with a vicious counteroffensive by
the majors: blackballing defecting players, lockouts, lawsuits, and slander
won the day, and the Federal franchises—including Buffalo—were driven to
bankruptcy. The conduct of the majors appeared to be a clear case of violation of the Sherman and Clayton antitrust laws, which make contracts in
restraint of trade and attempts at monopolization illegal; but in his famous,
aberrational, but seminal decision of 1922, Justice Oliver Wendell Holmes
announced that baseball was a sport, not commerce, and that antitrust laws
were inapplicable, and the defeat of the Federal cities was total.

BILL SHEA'S CREATION

The new weapon to conduct the 1960 war was called the Continental
League. The cast of characters in the ensuing battle included, as principals
and supporting actors, Bill Shea, the redoubtable counsel for Mrs. Payson
and Mayor Wagner's point man in the drive to bring a second team to New
York City; Branch Rickey, the leading exponent of MLB's farm system and
the most successful and knowledgeable GM in the majors; Estes Kefauver,
the PR-conscious senator from Tennessee and chairman of the Senate Sub-
committee on Anti-Trust and Monopoly; Jack Cooke, owner of the Toronto
Maple Leafs, who would later own the Washington Redskins NFL franchise
and the NHL's Los Angeles Kings. On the Buffalo scene, the cast included
my client, Reginald B. Taylor, Shea and Rickey's target for financing a Buffalo entry into the Continental; John Stiglmeier, a local politician who had
headed a drive to save baseball in Buffalo in 1956 and served as president
of the International League Bisons; Louis M. Jacobs, head of the Jacobs
brothers' Sportservice, the worldwide concessionaire that held more than a
third of the Bisons stock and 100 percent of Offerman Stadium, the ballpark in which the Bisons played their home games; Mayor Frank Sedita of
Buffalo; and Ralph C. Wilson Jr. of Detroit, the new owner of the Buffalo
Bills, just anointed as a contingent franchise in another outlaw coalition,
the new American Football League. Finally, I must add, to complete the
cast, the author and subject of this book, a young and successful tax lawyer
who became transmuted into a professional sports mogul, then virginal in
baseball except for the proud memory of an arthritic ankle, broken in a
slide into second base, and an enlarged knuckle in my left hand, nearly pulverized in hauling down a hot liner over third.

REG TAYLOR ON THE BUFFALO FRONT

Reg Taylor had acquired the pet name "Commish" in his tour of duty as New York State probation commissioner. I say "pet name," not sobriquet or nickname, because it denotes the affection we all had for him. Reg was a small man with a square mustache and a large smile. He was sometimes difficult to read, sometimes loquacious and good humoured, and often taciturn—he loved to keep his real thoughts and objectives under his vest, secreted from even his closest associates. He was undoubtedly wealthy, assuring me he had the resources to finance the Continental franchise, but I never saw a balance sheet. He had a lovely home on Sheridan Drive in Williamsville, nestled strategically between the Park Country Club golf course on the south side and my club, Westwood, on the north, on a lot that seemed to stretch forever into the neighboring forest. He had a lovely, gracious wife named Peach, who made every meeting in their home a pleasure. Peach would draw Reg out when he was playing poker with my questions (Reg was an inveterate card player) or warn me off when afternoon cocktails had conspired to blur his laconic comments.

I finally got some grasp of Reg's true financial status when, one day, he gave me an assignment that had nothing to do with baseball. Out of the blue, Reg called to ask me if I would fly with him to Newport, Rhode Island; his mother's estate there had some problems. He was in the process of selling some of her property, and his local agent had encountered some tax and negotiation issues that Reg felt were not being handled adequately. Would I tackle them? He confidently predicted it would only take me a day. Reg had chartered a three-seater Aero Commander. This was the first time I had ever flown in that fragile little plane, and with the excitement of that first voyage and Reg's continued taciturnity, my questions were blown away by the engine noise and I arrived in Newport (after a spectacular view of its molded meadows) as inadequately prepared as possible. Reg's modus operandi was to leave me with the agent while he went off for recreational activities, confident I'd work it out. Fortunately, the agent turned out to be a decent, practical guy, eager to please and to learn, not resentful of my heavy revision of the documents and the selling structure. It was not a very complicated set of transactions, and once I recast the deals to qualify for tax purposes as installment sales, the changes and the day went smoothly.

Around 5 PM Reg showed up and announced we were heading to the "barns" for some "fun." I had no clue what he meant by "fun." The barns turned out indeed to be barns and stables—Reg and Peach were always heavy into horses—converted into delightful, well-furnished apartments. Reg climbed up to the second floor; I followed, to be greeted, with no notice from Reg and to my plagued surprise, by two ladies—obviously there by appointment. "Ladies of the evening?" I thought. I had never seen such tendencies from Reg before. I looked closer—neither bosoms nor costumes seemed consistent with that thought. I made pleasant conversation, and finally I asked Reg in hushed tones, and he responded with a sardonic smile: "We're going to play bridge, Bob." He had an oversupply of confidence in me and never inquired about my experience at auction or contract.

I protested. "Reg," I said, "I haven't played bridge since college. That was 1938—and I still play Culbertson!" I had never learned Goren or any of the sophisticated point counts, artificial bids, slam invitations, and the like. Reg would hear none of it, and he plunged me into this dangerous game—fortunately, at surprisingly minimal stakes. I consented and managed to survive; my bidding was wild, but my play and my cards were adequate. When we returned the next week, however, we were greeted with a new duo, and I was not so fortunate. One of the ladies of this evening, built like a battle-ax and with a jaw and voice to match, introduced herself right off the bat as a former Boston city champion, and my hopes plunged. It took that distressed damsel about seven minutes to expose my weaknesses and banish me from the table—much to my relief. The bridge wasn't successful, but the negotiations were; Reg and I laughed a lot, and the incident solidified our friendship.

BRANCH RICKEY AS CONTINENTAL'S GURU

On the national scene, to give the new league credibility, experience, and PR, the Continental League hired Branch Rickey, whose credentials were impeccable, to be its president. He was generally regarded as, if not the creator, certainly the most successful developer of the farm system. He had proved to be a man of guts and vision when, in 1947, as the general manager of the Brooklyn Dodgers, he had signed Jackie Robinson, the first African American to play in the modern major league. I remember vividly the excitement in Offerman Stadium when Robinson came to Buffalo in an International League series between the Montreal team and the Bisons. It didn't take a rocket scientist to see that Robinson was already a star. At the plate, running the bases, and fielding at second, he was a powerful, dominating player. I was conscious of the virulent antiblack emotion still prevalent in the majors and in the Dodgers organization itself, sometimes expressed, as in Peewee Reese's case, with public derision. Robinson was just too good, as player and teammate, and Reese and other detractors ultimately backed off, and the door opened for other black stars like Willie Mays and Curt Flood. Robinson's success was testimony to Rickey's superior courage and judgment. He served as general manager of the St. Louis Browns in the American League, and the St. Louis Cardinals, Brooklyn Dodgers, and Pittsburgh Pirates in the National League. His teams won eight National League pennants and four World Series. A graduate of the

University of Michigan Law School, he was literate and articulate. As the "Mahatma," he had no difficulty getting the attention of the press for his many pronouncements as the Continental case was argued before the media, the Continental owners, the baseball commissioner, and Congress.

The frequent meetings of the Continental owners, at which I usually pinch-hit for Reg Taylor, were a terrific experience for me. Rickey was seventy-eight years old in 1960, but his intelligence, sense of humor, and enthusiasm for the game were undiminished. At times, he seemed intimidated by the ebullient Shea and the ever-voluble Cooke, but that may have been a natural reluctance to be didactic on legal and money matters in the face of those who were to finance the new league. When the opportunity arose to talk about issues in the GM's orbit—drafts, trades, contracts, farm clubs—he was loquacious and fascinating. It was as if he wanted to use the Continental as a means to review and correct every aspect of baseball play, rules, personnel, and structure. There may have been a revival, too, of long-suppressed resentment at the establishment—his forced departure from the Dodgers organization by Walter O'Malley, the attack by Judge Kenesaw Mountain Landis on his farm system, and so on. Whatever his motives in taking on the burden of the Continentals, he was an effective spokesman for the new league and a delightful mentor for me. He would expound on the bunt, the balk, free agency, minor-league operations, pitching techniques, player salaries, the pitcher as hitter—the whole gamut of the game.

BEHIND THE SCENES: LOU JACOBS

On the local scene, the leading member of the Continental cast in my view, and certainly the one who influenced my career the most, was Lou Jacobs. I first met Jacobs through his general counsel, Ben Reisman. Ben's daughter, Irma, was the closest friend of my wife, Sylvia, so Ben had a sort of parental view of my operations. As the controversy over the Bisons and the Continental League heated up, Yankees GM George Weiss was quoted in the local press and the *New York Times* as denigrating the new league and Buffalo's proposed entry. I wrote a letter objecting to Weiss's comments and charging him with a superficial response to the situation. This enraged Ben, and he called me into his office—the relationship called for my respect—and proceeded to lecture me on my naïveté, inadequate information, and unjust criticism of Weiss. George Weiss, he informed me, was a decent man and the most knowledgeable and successful general manager in baseball. If I were to get anywhere in the business, I'd better get to know and appreciate people like Weiss. Having duly and justly chastised me, Ben, with a warning to be respectful and reasonable, then introduced me to Jacobs.

I was first struck by the efficient, inexpensive style of the offices. I was used to more sumptuous quarters—for my own rooms as a senior partner in my firm, and certainly for the CEOs I knew, manning their own corporate cloisters. The main management floor for Sportservice seemed to me to consist of rows of cubbyholes and caves, not occupied only by clerks and secretaries, but by lawyers, social workers, division heads, and underexecutives. Ben Reisman's office was a little larger, but hardly typical of the venue for a major company counsel. Lou Jacobs's office was somewhat larger, but just as spare, free of knickknacks and credentials, with a large, four-wall window. Lou's desk was situated so he could see every cave and cubbyhole on the floor. There were three chairs in the room: Lou's at the desk, one opposite him, and one near the door. Lou greeted me politely and, with a quizzical smile, asked if I was out to change the baseball world. Throughout the polite discourse—not on the Continental, but on my family, my education, and so forth—I noticed a stream of people entering the room, saying nothing, writing something on a pad, then retreating to their respective cubbyholes. I later learned that this was Lou Jacobs's appointment process. If you wanted to talk to him, you had to sign the pad: top for "urgent" matters, bottom for "routine." You had to indicate whether the meeting had to be personal or by telephone, the requested time, and so on. I was somewhat appalled and inhibited by the stream of supplicants, but I ultimately learned that this was Jacobs's way of handling and juggling the hundreds of matters his flourishing company was producing, with minimum staff and minimal delegation. The Jacobs brothers had begun by selling peanuts to the fans in the Bisons' ballpark; they were now selling concessions to the world—and all the decisions seemed to be made at this one desk, with the supplicants streaming in and out of this president's office.

The first interview closed with Jacobs's request that if I had questions, concerns, or ideas, would I please take them up with Ben (forget outside counsel) or with Lou directly. I never called him "Lou," but I did use direct contact. However, I could never bring myself to wait in a cubbyhole or to sign the appointment pad.

The relationship flourished modestly, and over the next ten years, as the Continental episode ended, as we tried to get a National Baseball League franchise in 1968, and when we finally created the Sabres in 1970, Lou Jacobs and his son, Jerry, were a constant, loyal, and effective resource in our endeavours.

A SPORTS EDUCATION AT THE FOOT—OR BOOT!— OF LOU JACOBS

That the devil is in the details—knowing and acting on that was one of the important lessons I learned at the Jacobs desk. In the sixties, the tape/dictating machine had just become a useful tool, but for Lou Jacobs it was a little too useful. I remember one night, probably in our second campaign for Major League Baseball in 1968, we had worked late at the Jacobses' office on a Sunday night. (The larger the company grew, the longer the Jacobses' work hours—Lou was still making all the major decisions.) I returned home, got a few hours of sleep, and awoke to find on my doorstep what seemed to be a verbatim transcript of whatever he or I had said. I pointed out to Jacobs that sometimes he might be creating a record of things he didn't want to cast in stone, but he was too captivated by the machine to turn it off. When I was asked, or decided on my own, to make contact with a key mover in the professional sports scene, Jacobs would cross-examine me: Are you going to write a letter, or send a telegram, or make a telephone call? Whom are you going to call: the man? his secretary? his lawyer? What time of day: breakfast? midnight? early or late? Are you going to make the call yourself, or get someone closer to the target to do it?

He would frequently deride "going through channels" and recommended going "over top" when I could satisfy him that I had the quality contact. But he also had a feel for the lower-echelon personnel who had special know-how—such as the time he insisted I meet with Montreal Canadiens GM Frank Selke on strategy in the search for an NHL franchise. He could play many roles, and he reminded me of the time, in military government in Germany in 1945, I interviewed and recommended a leading non-Nazi physician as chancellor of Heidelberg University. The doctor seemed, in his sweater vest and bow tie, the friendly, quiet, democratic intellectual we were seeking. I was shocked several months later, at the opening of the first string quartet concert after the VJ Day, to see and hear him speak, in stentorian tones, wing collar and Prussian hairdo, of the greatness of the Reich. Lou Jacobs would undergo similar metamorphoses. In his office, he would be relaxed, informal, sometimes profane and harsh. But when the occasion called for it, he could be smartly accoutered, urbane, and literate. His wife was a devout Catholic, and his children were raised in that religion. (It was rumored that this came about when Mrs. Jacobs offered to adopt the Jewish religion if Lou would go to synagogue regularly, but when his ever-increasing work hours seemed to prevent that, she elected to remain with her own faith.) Yet he did not hesitate to remind me of his own religious origins. He spoke with disdain of the seeming irresolution of our investment group, which would ultimately produce the Sabres; of our delay in securing major capital sources; and our seeming reliance on him for commitment. "These classy clients of yours," he would say, "what are they doing, coming to an old Polish Jew like me for financing?"

The years I represented Sportservice were among the most challenging, enjoyable, and educational of my early career. Lou sent me to Cincinnati to evaluate the building, the Royals NBA team, the coach, and Dave Brown, an up-and-coming GM his spies had singled out. While there, he called me to make a side sweep to the Lexington, Kentucky, River Downs racetrack, in which he had an investment and a concession agreement. My assignments were never purely legal. It was my judgment—yes, business judgment—he sought and seemed to respect. Should he buy the team? Should he fire the coach? The ultimate assignment was a survey of the overall structure, operations, and prospects of the company. Should it—could it—go public? He encouraged me to probe, with candor, every "special situation" in which Sportservice or his family was involved. He dispatched me to New York and Boston to meet with investment bankers and specialists in new issues and going public. As I recall it, I recommended that the company not attempt to go to the securities markets until these special situations were sold, cleared up, or moved into the company. (It was one of these special situations in Las Vegas that created a national embarrassment in later years.) Some were valuable but could be an encumbrance to a registration statement; some were not worth retaining. "Mr. Jacobs," I said. "You work longer and harder than anybody I know, but you can't watch everything!" To this day, the company is still privately owned.

One of the most important things I learned from Lou Jacobs was that my view of the value of my services was not necessarily equivalent to that of my client. I had a somewhat arrogant posture, created by national corporate clients such as Moore Business Forms and Pratt & Lambert and the bank, who saw Buffalo lawyer rates as a bargain. Not Jacobs. I was presented with a budget! That was bad enough—but when I learned that my fees (with other counsel) were being vetted by a social worker, I lodged emphatic protests with Ben Reisman. It wasn't the dollars; it was the indignity!

But I had other important clients, and I could not provide Jacobs with the concentration on Sportservice matters and the obedience to Jacobs's own laws that he wanted and needed. I would not sit waiting in the cubbyhole, waiting for my name to come up on the appointment pad. One day, while I was negotiating a major tax matter at Price Waterhouse, he tracked me down and insisted on pulling me out of a conference. "It'll only take a minute," he said. It was then about 9:15 AM. I protested, but agreed to listen to the problem. It turned out to be rather complicated, and—politely asking my permission at each point—he proceeded to bring in personnel— the accountants, the price people, the labor people, house counsel. It was like the Surprise Symphony, with the players entering and leaving the stage, enlarging, then reducing the crowd of contributors. I would ask for a recess, but no dice. "It'll just take a moment," Jacobs said. At several points, I pleaded, "Look, I'm only seven blocks away"—telling my PW colleagues their conference was blown—"it'll just take ten minutes. Let me come to your office and we can deal with this more effectively." No dice. Finally, around 2:45 PM, Jacobs announced they were calling for lunch. "Want some lunch, Bob?" asked Lou from seven blocks away. It was not long after that when Ben Reisman called, ruefully explaining that they couldn't use me anymore as counsel. "You're just like my son," Ben quoted Lou. "You have to do things your own way."

Yet in 1968, in our near win to get a National Baseball League franchise for Buffalo, Lou offered $1 million of the $5 million we needed. "It's a tribute to you," he told me.

Like the future wars of outlaw leagues—the ABA, the AFL, the WHA, the WFL—the Continental's intention was not in the long run to harm the establishment but to bring about a shotgun wedding—to join 'em. The most vulnerable part of the majors' backbone was the contract with individual players—the perpetual option clause that gave an owner a claim on the player's services for his entire career, thus setting up an impenetrable barricade against competitors seeking to sign the player away. The clause appeared innocent enough: the owner retained an option to sign the player to a contract for an additional year "on the same terms and conditions." The trouble was, those "terms and conditions" included the exclusive right to another option to sign the player for the next year, with such an option, and the next, and so on. Thus, in 1960 baseball, free agency did not exist and the players' union was neither strong nor sophisticated enough to force a reinterpretation of the clause or to get the courts to recognize that it aided and abetted the preservation of monopoly. In the later wars, the players' lawyers in the other professional sports would persuade the Supreme Court that the Holmes decision applied only to baseball as a historical aberration, and a succession of decisions held the perpetual option clause invalid as an antitrust violation in football, basketball, and hockey; hence, the fence it erected against invasion of the players in those three sports by an outlaw competing league was demolished. Finally, in 1975, even Major League Baseball lost this protection, when, pushed to arbitration by the players' union, MLB owners were confronted with the arbiter's decision in the Messersmith case, which reinterpreted the clause and held it wasn't really perpetual at all—it was an option for one year only.[1]

The ability to attack the standard player's contract and to sign away the player was an effective weapon in later league wars. The World Hockey Association captured Bobby Hull, Gerry Cheevers, and others in the early 1970s in an attempt to attain instant respectability, and the courts had no difficulty in holding invalid the NHL's version of the baseball "perpetual option" clause. But in 1960, in Major League Baseball, this weapon was not available because of the Holmes decision. Besides, thought the Continental League promoters, who wants to use it? The clause will protect us when we're in—not only against future outlaw league incursions, but against any partner who'd like to be a player pirate. In reducing the chances that a star can be signed away, the clause doubtless suppressed salaries. It was an economic asset to the business, and the Continental League promoters had no wish to destroy it.

As the battle to get a second New York club and the other cities into the majors went on, threats were made, but they were halfhearted and never made it into the courts. Shea's strategy was public and congressional pressure. He persuaded that senator with the coonskin cap, Estes Kefauver, to introduce a draconic bill: MLB teams, some of which had as many as five hundred players under contract, would be prohibited from controlling more than one hundred players each, and the "reserve clause" would be cut down with an annual draft within the leagues that would prevent the strong teams from monopolizing talent that wasn't on their playing rosters. (The NHL installed a similar procedure with its intraleague draft in 1967; it proved of marginal help to the new or nonplayoff teams, limited by a large, "untouchable" protected list for the established clubs and exemptions for one- or two-year professionals.)

So the Continental strategy was not to attack the provisions of the standard contracts, the relationship between the player and the club, but to cut into the clubs' overall control of player inventory. As part of organized baseball, the Continental teams would participate in the annual draft and stock their rosters accordingly from the more than thirty-six hundred players who would become available.

The "don't attack 'em—join 'em" approach had another peculiar impact that seemed to favor Buffalo. In what was largely a public relations response to the Continental demands, the majors announced a set of criteria for acceptance of a new league into the bosom of Major League Baseball, and the Continental gave lip service to those requirements. One of those was the minimum number of teams—eight. The organizers came up with New York City (of course), plus Toronto, Denver, Houston, Dallas–Fort Worth, Minneapolis–St. Paul, and Atlanta. An eighth team was needed—and logically the Continental turned to Western New York, where the International League Bisons had the best attendance record in minor-league baseball.

Reginald Taylor, a wealthy Buffalonian who had been president of the local Bisons and a friend of George Goodyear and the Schoellkopfs, was persuaded to make his debut as a major-league owner, and Buffalo as the eighth team seemed secure. The trouble was, Reg was a reluctant debutante: he was glad to be the pioneer—with someone else's money—at least until the prospects for major-league entry became concrete and clarified. How to accomplish this? We all viewed the major league for Buffalo project in part, at least, as a public objective for the benefit of the Western New York economy, and we had no desire to attempt to unseat the management or ownership of the Bisons—so why not get the Bisons to put up the $50,000 franchise fee? Reg's concept meant that the applicant for the Continental League franchise would be the minor-league club itself.

THE BASEBALL BISONS PROXY FIGHT

It was not so simple, as it turned out. The ownership profile of the Bisons was peculiar. In an episode, one of many, to "save baseball for Buffalo" some years earlier, shares of stock in Buffalo Bisons, Inc., had been sold to the public. Sportservice, the national concessionaire company owned by the Jacobs brothers, held the largest block of the shares; the minority was held in small lots by several thousand local citizens. Sportservice, sometimes supportive of local projects, had a basic conflict. It was the concessionaire for at least nine teams in the American and National leagues, and its clients were burning up the telephone lines demanding that the Buffalo entry into the Continental League be killed. (If they succeeded, that would leave the Continental, with fewer than eight teams, disqualified for the majors, under baseball's "guidelines.") I had to advise Reg that the only way funds of the Bisons could be used for the franchise fee was with a shareholder vote of approval—and Sportservice bloc held a veto. Moreover, the management of the club, led by local politicians John Stiglmeier and Harry Bisgeier, feared the intrusion of the Continental project would jeopardize their own positions, and were uncooperative.

The majors' criteria for a new league, and the Continental requirement as well, also required a stadium with a minimum capacity of twenty-five thousand. Offerman Stadium, the Bisons' park, could accommodate only ten to fifteen thousand with temporary seating. A new stadium, designed for Major League Baseball, might have made sense, but the parties were not thinking that big. In what turned out to be a monumental coincidence, on the same day that the formation of the Continental Baseball League was announced, the facing page of the *New York Times* carried a story describing the creation of a new major football league—the AFL—that promised serious competition for the NFL because, for the first time, a major TV network—CBS—would provide revenue and coverage to the new entry. And lo and behold, Buffalo was selected for a team in the new football league and needed a stadium. There was a football facility in Buffalo that could accommodate forty-five thousand—the ancient Civic Stadium, pejoratively described as the "Old Rockpile." Built under World War II WPA appropriations, it had lain fallow in recent years, used only for occasional high school football championships. The new Bills were willing to play in the Rockpile if it were refurbished and expanded. The cost? Three million dollars, to be paid by the city. The city's knowledgeable and intelligent mayor, Frank Sedita, was not so quick to take the bait. How could we justify, he asked, an expenditure of that size for a fledgling team in a rookie league, for only ten games a year?

Then came the creative response from the Bills: You've got the baseball Bisons, with the highest attendance in minor-league baseball; they are probably going to get a major-league franchise from the Continental League. How about persuading them to move from Offerman to Civic? That'll give you seventy more dates, give the Continentals a park to play in, and you'll have a major-league football team as well.

THE BILLS ENTER THE STADIUM MIX

The proposal posed two significant problems. First, Offerman Stadium was owned by the Jacobs brothers, operators of Sportservice, the leading concessionaire in the major baseball leagues; and Sportservice owned a veto bloc of the shares in the International League Bisons, Offerman's principal—if not only—tenant. Second, Civic was a football stadium, seating forty-five thousand people. The distance between third base and first base is 386 feet. The distance from football sideline to sideline was only 150. The only way the baseball diamond could be imposed on the football field would be to cut a triangular piece out of the football stands, and the resulting configuration would place the baseball fans, accustomed to close contact and communication with the infield, about as far from the pitcher and infielders as the football fans in the end zone. The confines of the football stands would mess up the outfield fences, producing a short right field that would plague Bison pitchers. By contrast, Offerman was a delightful little park, almost tailor-made for minor-league ball. Its ten to fifteen thousand seats could handle capacity dates and yet it was small enough so that the crowds of three to four thousand frequently present for many International League regular-season dates did not feel lonely.

The mayor and the Bills approached Lou Jacobs, president of Sportservice. Jacobs said no. The Bisons would not move; the club would not sign a lease to play in Civic Stadium, whatever the improvements. The mayor argued that this would expedite Major League Baseball—meeting the stadium requirement of the Continental League. Jacobs said no. The mayor offered to purchase Offerman, then threatened to take it by condemnation. The mayor offered to build a new high school on the Offerman site and name it the Louis M. Jacobs School. Jacobs still said no.

It was not just lack of confidence in the Continental League, or the urgent pleas of the Sportservice clients to kill its chances, or the possible loss of concession rights. Lou Jacobs told us all, over and over again, that the forty-five-thousand-seat football park was unsuitable for baseball, certainly for minor-league ball; that the Bison fans, used to an intimate venue in a small stadium frequently filled to capacity, would be uncomfortable and unenthusiastic rattling around in the ancient football edifice. He predicted that if, as might happen, the Continental League did not fly, the disappointment of the Bison fans, coupled with their discomfort in the new location, could lead to the destruction of the Bisons, which the public had fought so hard to keep alive only five years earlier. Events in later years proved him right: the Bills ultimately deserted the Rockpile for a new football-only stadium in the suburbs, and the Bisons fared poorly in the Rockpile, moving to Niagara Falls, and then into oblivion, until the Rich family revived the club with a brand-new baseball facility in 1983.

But in 1960 we were on a mission to get a Major League Baseball franchise for Buffalo, and we did not—could not—heed Jacobs's warnings. Shea and Rickey and Reg and I played the major-league tune to the full. The Continental League demanded that we have a lease for a suitable place to play, so the baseball club had to sign the lease and agree to move, whether as the minor-league Bisons or a major-league Continental franchise. And the media bought our pitch completely. For the newspapers and TV (our station, WGR-TV, was now a partner in the effort), the niceties of Jacobs's analysis were irrelevant. Buffalo wanted—*needed*—the major-league team, and Sportservice seemed to be in the way. I decided that we should force the issue with a stockholders meeting and vote, even if the concessionaire had the legal power, and the number of votes, to block approval of the lease and the entry into the Continental League. Perhaps the public pressure would compel the Jacobs family to change its position.

STADIUM POLITICS AND THE POWER OF THE PRESS

The meeting was called for a Saturday night in March in the Hotel Lafayette. The proxies assembled from the public shareholders amounted to about 40 percent, not enough to produce a quorum. We needed the Jacobses' proxies, not only to approve the plan and entry into the Continental, but to hold a meeting at all. Despite my attempts to persuade Jacobs and his counsel that it was not in the concessionaire's interest to oppose the plan, Sportservice hired a leading Buffalo trial lawyer, Frank Raichle—known as a tough cookie—to announce that they would not appear or file their proxies, so a legal meeting could not be held. They had ten objections to our papers, a litany of all the problems a Continental club would face: million-dollar demands for compensation from the International League, claimed breaches of the lease for Offerman Stadium held by a Sportservice subsidiary, failure to get approval from organized baseball, failure to include financials of the Bisons in the material sent to stockholders, and failure to spell out the financial plan in detail. Except for the last item, in my naive optimism, I was sure we could safely dispose of or ignore the objections. As to the financials, surely I had earned my spurs at enough public offerings to know the validity of Raichle's criticism on that score. The truth was, I didn't include the details of the plan because, absent specific commitments from my laconic client, Reg Taylor, I didn't really know what they were. In an analogy I used frequently in future battles, I said, "We're hopping from atoll to atoll trying to reach shore. Let's first make sure we don't fall in the water!" One leap at a time: if we could get approval of the $50,000 fee and the Continental entry, the sophisticated money raising could come later.

Fortunately—either because of some success in engendering doubt in the minds of Jacobs and his advisors as to the wisdom of their course or, as Raichle "confided" to me, because of his stated friendship with Reg Taylor—Raichle did not attack in court the validity of the notice to the shareholders, and we agreed to postpone the meeting. In the interim, Lou Jacobs took quite a beating in the press, and his negative stance began to weaken. The burden of seeming to obstruct both the coming of the Bills and the Continental League was too much. To free Jacobs to accept the Bills' move, the city had commenced condemnation proceedings to take Offerman Stadium—the appraisal price was $900,000, and there was no hope of preventing that—so the fight to preserve the Bisons in their delightful minor-league park was lost. At a meeting of the Continental key people in New York City, Jacobs's primary counsel, prominent Republican Ed Jaeckle, listened earnestly but painfully to the arguments of Shea, Rickey, and me; then, in my presence, he phoned and told Lou Jacobs he had to go along. Whether as a result of our effective suasion or Jacobs's own judgment that the Continental League would get nowhere, I do not know, Sportservice finally capitulated and voted its shares in favor of the Continental League plan. I do know that Jacobs did not welcome Jaeckle's advice. After the episode was over, he released the Jaeckle firm and, fortunately and ironically, hired me!

RICKEY AND SHEA'S BATTLE IN THE SENATE

On the national front, Shea and Rickey were not making much progress, but they had the attention of Congress. With the entry of the Buffalo group as the eighth team—Reg agreed to lend the $50,000 fee to the Bisons—and the signing of the lease to play in Civic Stadium, Rickey and Shea were able to claim compliance with MLB's key requirements for a "legitimate" third league. Shea persuaded Estes Kefauver, who was chairman of the Senate Subcommittee on Anti-Trust and Monopoly, to utter statements warning the establishment to accept the Continental League, with the underlying threat to remove baseball's exemption from antitrust. But the atmosphere elsewhere in the Senate was not conducive. The other major sports—football, baseball, and hockey—were horning in, lobbying to get similar exemptions for their sports, at least with regard to the option clause in player contracts and control of transfers of franchise location. MLB commissioner Ford Frick and his owners did not move. The hope to become part of the majors was fading, and the Continental promoters began to make sounds like an outlaw league.

As perhaps the most successful user of the farm system, Rickey nevertheless felt it had been abused and, with the raiding of players made difficult by the Holmes decision, sought a surgical attack on the bloated rosters of the two leagues. A survey showed that each major-league club owned or controlled an average of 370 players—quite a number for a sport that dressed nine players plus a bull pen, some utility infielders, and a few pinch hitters for each game. The system put the minor-league owners at the complete economic and competitive mercy of the majors. The surgical weapon: a bill introduced in the Senate by Kefauver that would have limited each major-league club to control of one hundred players and exposed all but forty of those players to an annual draft, in which the Continentals would be entitled to participate, and thus fill their rosters.

THE WESTERN CAROLINA "HOUSE" LEAGUE

In the nightly discussions of our Continental group, Rickey lectured Cooke and Shea and Reg and the rest of us on his unique plan for the Continental farm system. Instead of myriad cities of near-major status competing for young players at a high cost, and instead of the intense pressure on the rookies in those venues, Rickey proposed to substitute a single minor league, in which all Continental clubs would pool their rookies, who would be paid and assigned by the league itself. He chose the Western Carolina League, consisting of the typical small-town environments he considered the paradigm for training a young player. He proceeded to negotiate arrangements with that league and submitted the plan to Frick for approval. Frick's response was deadly: the Western Carolina League would not be accepted into organized baseball, pooling was a violation of baseball law, and trades or transactions with that league would not be recognized.

It was an ironic *renvoi*: Rickey, the founder of the farm system—the system that enabled major-league clubs to hunt, hide, and hold on to the players they developed—would endorse a bill and promote a practice that could destroy that system. In his bitter fight with Judge Landis in 1938, Landis had attacked the Cardinals, Dodgers, and Detroit farm tentacles, which then had contracts with more than five hundred players each, forcing Rickey to make hundreds of players free agents. It was Landis who demanded equality of player control for the clubs and a draconic draft—and here was Rickey, years later, espousing a Landis-like system! (I was to find similar developments in the NHL, when expansion produced the elimination of the vassal "sponsored" players and the freedom of the entry draft.

In discussions last year with Branch Rickey's grandson, Branch B. Rickey—now the president of baseball's Pacific Coast League—I raised the question of Rickey's motives. In those meetings of the new organization in 1960, I wondered why, at age seventy-eight, Rickey would undertake this confrontation with the fundamental structure and tenets of an organization he had spent his life promoting. The answers, as one would expect, range from the idealistic to the personal. Branch B. answered: "What he believed was that there were too many growing markets in the United States which could support big league teams and that they were being ignored." A recent panel on ESPN—participants included the legendary sports reporters Heywood Hale Broun and Jack Laing—suggested that Rickey was using the new league to force expansion. His grandson disagrees: "Expansion, in his estimation, was likely to be a disastrous route because the new teams would not be able to come in a par with the established franchises. The Continental League provided a solution where the entire League could play in competitive balance, and once its standards achieved a big league quality, playoffs could ensue between the new league and the other two."

Certainly the ability to get back at O'Malley—Rickey's firing by the Dodgers was too recent a memory to pass over—and the opportunity to try a new structure for baseball were too much to resist. Writing in the early twenty-first century, abiding a similar aging, I can perhaps better understand Rickey's 1960 adventure now. I tell my friends that after the sale of the Sabres in 2000, I'm not quite used to the silence of the cell phone. It's only partly a joke. After decades of control, of challenging the intellect, of dealing with the variegated media, of meeting problems of an industry with action and passion, the sedentary life is a reluctant option. Rickey must have been daring himself and Shea to affirm what we now know: that age sixty-five is just a pip on the chronological chart. This was his last chance to think, to create, to act. His concept of the house-development league—the Western Carolina—for all Continental teams may have been his practical way of achieving for the new owners what his original farm structure was intended to do: get to the young player first, with confidence that he could train them better and get them to the "big show" faster than anyone else. His impending diabetes may have slowed his body, but his brain, his analytical function, was still active and creative.

In a curious way, just as Cooke and Shea and DeWitt and O'Malley would appear in later episodes of my sporting life, Rickey's structural ideas caught hold in hockey. For many years NHL clubs used the Central League as an inexpensive training ground for young players, subsidized by the NHL itself. And in the first NHL expansion of 1967, the hockey moguls used the Rickey concept—all six new teams were placed in their own conference, so that their primary competition was against each other. It didn't last long: beginning with the Buffalo/Vancouver expansion in 1970, the NHL reverted to adding new teams by increments to the existing conferences and divisions. The Rickey scenario assumed parity at the point where interleague play was permitted. But in the NHL, with an honest universal draft, parity in play occurred soon enough—the Sabres made the playoffs in three years and the Stanley Cup Finals in five—but parity in gate attraction came too slowly. Soon, GMs from both old and new teams were impatient with the new team/separate conference structure. Los Angeles wanted more Montreal games; Montreal's Sam Pollock wanted less of the expansion clubs, who were initially poor draws; Toronto wanted none of the new teams in its building, while Buffalo's Punch Imlach wanted more—the rookie clubs were easier to conquer. "Realignment," as it was called, became the most predictable and most contentious issue at the governors' table regularly at expansion meetings.

So Rickey's structural concepts may not have inured the tests of practice in another league, but incorporated in the Kefauver bill—with an annual draft that would chop off the majors' player tentacles and feed them to the new league—they were a sufficient threat to energize the establishment into aggressive measures to delay, blunt, or destroy the new league. In throwing roadblocks against the Continental League, the majors did not neglect their colleagues in minor-league ball. Frank Shaughnessy, president of the International League, attacked the Continentals as outlaws, vowing not to deal with us—but did not hesitate to add that, if required to do so, the Internationals would demand $850,000 each for the Toronto and Buffalo territories. That was an unheard-of sum in those times, but the president of the American Association chimed in with a claim for $1 million for any of its territories that might be taken. In the undeveloped nature of the syndrome, no word was heard yet from the owners of the minor-league teams; the demands of the minor leagues alone were thought to be sufficient to discourage the Continentals. In Buffalo's case, we were sure that Stiglmeier and Bisgeier would claim damages for the Bisons—and our use of the Bisons as the applicant permitted avoidance of this demand, by a proposed plan to transfer the International League franchise to another minor-league city.

The Kefauver bill got the majors' attention, all right. Frick denounced it as the destroyer of the minor leagues, as the horrendous taking of the majors' property without compensation, and so on. The specific response of the majors, in a familiar pattern of establishment leagues, was dangerous: each of the American and National leagues would add two teams, either by expansion or from the members of the third league. The expansion alternative contained no commitment to choose from the Continentals first, although Shea received word that New York would surely get a nod. There was no assurance that the majors would not invade Continental territory and seat their own owners in the preempted cities. Shea uttered nice sounds like "nobody's defecting, we're continuing the fight," but the signs were ominous.

In the Senate, there was substantial support for the Kefauver bill, but the talk of expansion was troubling. Rickey and Shea offered to eliminate the hundred-player ceiling in return for an "unrestricted" annual draft, and the bill was amended accordingly. But in August 1960 the guillotine fell—the bill did not get enough votes to pass and Shea was forced to go along with a motion to recommit the legislation to committee, with the faint hope of revival in the next Congress.

THE DEATH BLOW TO THE CONTINENTAL LEAGUE

The vote to recommit was a death blow to the Continental League, but in a final meeting of Shea, Rickey, and Grant with Frick and the Senate committee—a meeting to which Buffalo was not invited—the announcement sounded like a partial victory. The commitment from the majors was, we thought, for four Continental League members to be chosen in the expansion. New York would get one slot, and the rest of us had a shot. Rickey made encouraging comments; John Stiglmeier claimed he had a credible source who assured him that Buffalo, with its stadium (forget the football configuration) and its financial plan (forget the unknown investors), would be "in." At the end of the episode, the expansion brought in three Continental cities: New York, Houston, and Minneapolis–St. Paul. The fourth, Los Angeles, went to the entertainer Gene Autry; neither city nor owner was a Continental. In Minneapolis–St. Paul, the Continental group headed by our friend Gordie Ritz was supplanted by the league's approval of a move to that city from Washington, DC, by Calvin Griffith, in a familiar decision by the league to satisfy an inside partner first. Toronto, Denver, Dallas, Atlanta, and Buffalo all lost out. Reg Taylor got his $50,000 back, Bill Shea had a stadium named after him, and I got a painful education in how *not* to get a major-league franchise![2]

Chapter 8

DOWN AND OUT IN O'MALLEY'S ALLEY

A call out of the blue from Bill DeWitt Sr. in early 1968 revived our group's hunger for a major-league franchise and gave me the chance to apply the lessons learned in the Continental and 1967 NHL disappointments. The baseball majors were about to expand, Bill said. It would cost between $5 and $10 million. Could I put a Buffalo group together? Bill would put up one-third of the cost. I checked with my key resources—the Schoellkopfs, George Goodyear, Bob Rich Jr., the Knoxes, and others—and the word was GO! The Knoxes were somewhat reluctant at first (saving themselves for hockey) but recognized the importance of keeping Buffalo in the major-league eye. Lou Jacobs confirmed that the majors would expand and was not very sanguine about our chances, but offered to help. From an unanticipated direction came an offer from Capital Cities Broadcasting, owner of Buffalo's Channel 7, to invest one-third of the equity. And Marine Midland Bank committed to finance any acquisition and working capital loans that might reasonably be required. So we were set and qualified financially, it seemed, very quickly. The group chose Jack Guthrie, a friend of my client Van DeVries (former president of Channel 2 in the Transcontinent regime) as its executive point man. My firm organized Major League for Buffalo, Inc., as the corporate entity that would technically file and pursue the application, and I got my familiar title—"vice president and counsel."

A ROUND ROBIN AT THE NATIONAL'S "COMMITTEE"

Sportservice's antennae indicated we were probably latecomers to the contest. The American League, the scoop said, had already informally picked its grantees; our best bet was to focus on the National—a "better," wealthier league, with larger cities and sounder ownership. I arranged for us to call or meet with every contact, strong or weak, that I could come up with, including Nelson Doubleday, part owner of the Mets; Bill Shea; Ed Williams of the Baltimore Orioles; the Cincinnati Reds, where Bill DeWitt would presumably have some influence; and Anheuser-Busch, owners of the St. Louis Cardinals. Sportservice introduced us to Dick Meyer, the Busch CEO. I even called Stan Kasten, GM of the Atlanta Braves, whom I'd come to know as a fellow board member of the Sports Lawyers Association. Word reached us that we must see in a personal interview every member of the National's committee—Walter O'Malley, Bob Carpenter, Walter Hofheinz, and August Busch.

Easier said than done. Weather, league politics, timing, and personalities—even racial crisis—would throw obstacles at us. But we put on a full-court press, to mix a sports metaphor. The first and most important at bat was O'Malley. He had led the successful move of his Dodgers from Brooklyn to the California coast, and he was reputed to be the most influential owner. But, like every member of the committee but Hofheinz, he was not where he was supposed to be. He was not in Brooklyn or Los Angeles, but was willing to meet with us in Vero Beach, Florida, site of the Dodgers' training camp. A time was set for an April Sunday morning in 1968.

Determined to get there well in advance, I boarded a US Air plane at the Buffalo airport at noon on Saturday. The plane taxied onto the runway—and stayed there for six hours! My pleas to return to the terminal, that I would miss a connection "vital" to the community, went unheeded, and I heard only the mistaken assurance from the pilot that the weather would clear "any minute." When the pilot final gave up, it was nearly 6 PM and the only available flight south was to Miami. There were no connecting flights from Miami to Vero Beach that would get me there in time for the meeting, and I wasn't about to seek a postponement from O'Malley in the middle of the night.

Desperate, I called the Florida long-distance operator, and together we searched the yellow pages for a charter from Miami to Vero (148 miles). I hit pay dirt on the third try, and the pilot on the other end sounded a little uncertain, but agreed to a rendezvous—assuming I got there—at the Miami field for private planes around 10:30 that night. A man—he said he was a pilot—in a leather jacket met me, named his price, and accepted my personal check. I'd had no time for cash and was glad to pay the $100, a price that seemed too reasonable, but I let it go. We took off, and as we gained altitude I heard him ask the control tower for directions to Vero. "About twenty minutes from now," said the ground, "you'll see a terminal on your left, with lights shaped in a 'U'—that'll be it." About five minutes into the flight, there was a U-shaped terminal in view, and my pilot started a sudden, deep-dive descent at a pretty hefty speed, and as the plane's fuselage began to scream, so did I, shouting, "THIS CAN'T BE IT—WE'RE ONLY FIVE MINUTES OUT OF MIAMI!" As the terminal name came into our sight, it was clear that our dive was a hundred miles off, and the pilot, determined to be an acrobat, pulled up sharply and got back on course. I don't know to this day whether he was a licensed pilot, or had stolen, rented, or misappropriated the plane—he never cashed the check—and I had visions of the aircraft being used in some drug operation, but he got me to O'Malley.

CONFRONTING O'MALLEY

At the meeting the next morning, my interrogation was cordial but sharp. What were the plans for a stadium? A temporary facility? A permanent ballpark? I responded that the Erie County authorities had announced plans for a two-stadium complex—one for the Bills, one a Major League Baseball stadium along the lines of the Kansas City development. The temporary facility would be Civic Stadium (the Rockpile, in which the Bills were now playing). But why, I asked, did we need a temporary facility? Bill DeWitt's description of the National League expansion plan called for a two-year postponement of entry, giving us time to erect an entirely new ballpark before we began operations. Oh no, said O'Malley, the American League is going to start play for the new teams immediately, and we'll have to do the same. That was the first time we heard this. I hoped our investors would hang in there, even if we had to play two years in the football Rockpile.

With some candor, O'Malley than asked me what I thought of San Diego as a leading candidate. Vamping for time, I made some learned but superficial remarks about our experience with that city in the Transcontinent Television business. "With the mountains and the sea," I observed, "there's really no room to grow." Walter O'Malley may have been impressed with my oral agility, but not with the substance of my answer—and, of course, the subsequent stats did not bear me out. I began to feel that the rumours about Buzzi Bavasi (the Dodgers GM) having an inside track as a San Diego owner had some reality.

O'Malley then hit us in the solar plexus with another comment. "I understand," he said, "you've got Bill DeWitt in your ownership group. I don't think you're helping your plans with Mr. DeWitt in there. He's made his money with two other baseball franchises [Cincinnati and Detroit], and there's a feeling on the part of some of the clubs that it should be someone else's turn now." DeWitt had brought the idea to us, and he was our major strategic resource; it would be impossible to cast him off. But how could we ignore the advice of the guy who had the power, we thought, to grant or deny the franchise?

THE LURE OF THE COVERED STADIUM

Then, after testing us with these negatives, the Dodgers' owner opened the door. "Mr. Swados," he asked, "this stadium that Erie County is planning— it wouldn't be covered, would it?"

Rarely at a loss for a response, even if it committed my clients to an issue never discussed before, I answered, "It's not in the plans, sir, but if the league required it, I'm sure the county would produce it!"

"Well," said O'Malley, "the league would never require it, but if you did cover it, it would be very favorable."

When I got back to our Buffalo base, we went into a quick huddle over the three issues raised at the O'Malley meeting: immediate play and the need for a temporary facility, DeWitt, and the cover or "dome." The county went for the domed concept immediately. Seth Abbott, chairman of the county legislature's committee, was enthusiastic and found the estimate of a $50 million bond issue to finance the construction "doable." My law firm's research showed that no referendum would be necessary, so we wouldn't have to face that frequent killer of stadium dreams. There was a burgeoning conflict over site, however—suburbs versus downtown—but I urged speed in getting back to the National League with a firm stadium plan and financing as quickly as possible. The fight over location, I said, could be settled later. I drafted the $50 million bond resolution so that it deferred the question of location but committed the dollars—and the county and the league bought it.

The other two issues were more difficult to solve. DeWitt was inaccessible—away on a long trip—and following O'Malley's suggestion on this deprived us not only of his judgment but of his one-third investment as well. The problem was compounded when the Watts interracial riots of that year were replicated in a small way on Jefferson Avenue—the street adjoining our temporary facility. O'Malley phoned me on it immediately, sounding grave and pessimistic. I furnished him with an affidavit from the Buffalo police commissioner stating that the riot had happened more than a mile from Civic Stadium and, further, that it had been much more limited than Watts, was quickly brought under control, and was an aberration that wouldn't occur again. But our own doubts about the old stadium as a baseball facility came back to haunt us, when our major investor, Capital

Cities, regretfully informed us that the threat of two years of losses in the Rockpile, together with the other financial changes proposed by the National League, were too much for them to swallow. The league had increased the price—it was a "better" league than the American—and, as a concession to the antiexpansionists, had denied or minimized the new clubs' share of national TV revenue for two years after the grant. Capital Cities cancelled its commitment.

There we were—with a $50 million bond resolution, but only one-third of the equity money we needed, and the league's deadline fast approaching. O'Malley said we had to meet with the other members of the league's committee. So I went back to the Buffalo airport, this time armed with the county domed stadium commitment, ready to fly to Bob Carpenter in Philadelphia, Hofheinz in Houston, and Busch in St. Louis. Weather, I thought, please stay away from my door. It was not to be. Unbelievably, the O'Malley trip repeated itself. The conference with Carpenter was scheduled for Sunday morning in Wilmington. I climbed into the aircraft at noon on Saturday, but the plane sat on the tarmac for five hours, blowing my connections. I never got to Wilmington before Carpenter politely excused himself and disappeared into his horse show or other pursuits. Guthrie, who had come down from New York City, reported that our reception was respectful but "routine and noncommittal."

AUGIE BUSCH AND HIS INTRACOASTAL LIVING ROOM

The meeting with Busch was well staged and prepared, and we were hopeful of a positive response. The site was the beautiful Busch winter home in Fort Lauderdale, Florida, in a part of the house that I swear straddled the intercoastal canal. We sat in Augie's den, and next to it was one of his small oceangoing yachts, afloat in the canal, and next to that, the kitchen. Sportservice had prepped Dick Meyer, the Anheuser-Busch CEO, who had come to the meeting ready, we believed, to recommend the Buffalo application to his boss. We started out well; Meyer's comments were favorable, Busch asked some questions about the market and the stadium that were now easy to answer, and our spirits began to rise, when Busch received a call from his boat mechanic across the state on the Sarasota coast. Some problem with his Sarasota engine, and Busch's gravelly voice began to rise in pitch and volume as he angrily argued with his west coast technician. It seemed as if Busch thought it necessary to reach his mechanic—four hours away—without benefit of the telephone! I saw Meyer shake his head, then spread his hands in frustration and resignation. That was our shot at Augie Busch. The interview was over, and our spirits dropped.

JUDGE HOFHEINZ AND HIS CIGARS

The Houston conference turned out to be more significant than anticipated. I had to make the trip alone. Hofheinz received me in the upper tier
of the Astrodome, equipped only with a small triangular cocktail table, on
which sat an ashtray, a telephone, and three cigars. The judge got right to
the point; confirmed his impressions (he was obviously prepared) as to
market, equity, and stadium; and then asked his key question: "And did
Erie County condition its approval of the $50 million bond issue on a lease
that would make the baseball club amortize the construction cost?"
Counsel in the crease again! But I had drafted the resolution, and I was able
to and resolved to answer, emphatically, "No."

For the first time I got the feeling that someone, other than O'Malley,
in the National League was listening to our pitch.

MRS. BUTLER COMES THROUGH . . . AND STEINBRENNER, TOO

I guess at that point you could call our chances at the committee plate one
strikeout (Carpenter), one single (Hofheinz), one rainout (Busch), and one
base on balls (O'Malley). But the interviews and county action had made
an impression. Word began to circulate that Buffalo had a real chance at
the franchise. Suddenly the equity investments began to reappear. We
needed, up front, $5 million in capital and $5 million in loans. The Major
League for Buffalo crowd would put up $1 million; Mrs. Edward H Butler,
widow of the founder of the leading newspaper, the *Buffalo Evening News*,
whose publisher son-in-law, Jim Righter, was in our corner, invited me up
to her cynosure office overlooking lower Main Street. Sitting ramrod-
straight at her desk, with my visitor's chair anchored to the floor so that I
could move no closer, she somberly complimented me on our campaign—
and offered an investment of $2 million by the *News*! She pointed out her
window at the scene below, lightly expressed her preference for the suburban site, but certainly aware of the sensitivity of the issue, did not condition her commitment on the choice of location. Lou Jacobs called me into
his office. He observed that he never thought I'd get as far as I had, but he
was getting good vibes about the Buffalo entry, and he would contribute $1
million to the equity.

But the best sign that the baseball gods might be with us came when
George Steinbrenner flew in from his Cleveland base and showed up at my
law office at 70 Niagara Street. Typically, he was prepared to move immediately—he had his lawyer and financial man with him, and was accompanied by his friend Max Margulis, proprietor and barkeep of the popular

Roundtable Restaurant in downtown Buffalo. George's staff, including Max's friend, Jimmy Naples, did a fast sweep through our documents and projections; George briefly commented that we were slightly optimistic, but then and there offered to take 20 percent of the equity—and thus fill in the final slot in our $5 million objective. I got a quick OK from Fred Schoellkopf and the *News* (although Fred had some concerns about control and Jim Righter had others about site); Lou Jacobs saw it as very good news, and we signed up the subscription papers that day.

Thus we were set, on the eve of the National League's decision, with a stronger balance sheet and wealthier partners than we had at the start of the expansion crusade. In the middle of our exhilaration, however, Bill DeWitt returned from Europe, called me to ask how things stood, and cast a cloud of misgivings in our direction. Bill seemed more upset over the two years of play in the Rockpile than he was at being "included out." He projected losses in the temporary facility far beyond our own estimates and feared a permanent turnoff by fans uncomfortable in the football stadium. "You've been led down a wrong road," he said in disgust and displeasure. We talked it over and made the judgment that we could control the losses and miti-gate the fan response. It might require additional capital down the road, but it was O'Malley's road, and we had to go down his alley.

In the next days we got encouraging words from Fred Fleig, assistant to Warren Giles, president of the National League, with directions and timing of the league meeting. John McHale, high brass in the commissioner's office and rumored to be one of O'Malley's pet choices to lead a new fran-chise, came by for a surprise visit.

The day of reckoning came, and we gathered in the hotel suite to hear the news. There were to be no further appearances of the candidates. We had a full slate of representatives on hand: in addition to Jack Guthrie and me, there were Seth Abbott, the chairman of the Erie County Legislature's committee; the print media (Cy Kritzer); and the Buffalo television anchors. We started early in the day, then waited, waited, waited. . . . The tension became palpable, and we attempted to calm the waters with any rumor that was edible: If they're taking so long, there must be a real con-test. If they're taking so long, we must be losing ground, it was supposed to be all set. Montreal can't be a serious candidate—they have no stadium and no stadium plan. But Montreal's mayor is here! A reporter calls in with great tidings! The headline in the *New York Daily News* makes San Diego and Buffalo the winners. . . .

At about 6 PM Fred Fleig called: "Get your group together, Bob—It looks like you're going to get it!" Fred would call to invite us in to the owners' meeting. Cheers, drinks, contingent congratulations, and thanks. . . . An hour went by . . . and another. Fred didn't answer his phone. Finally, nearly three hours after his first message, Fred called and dropped the guil-

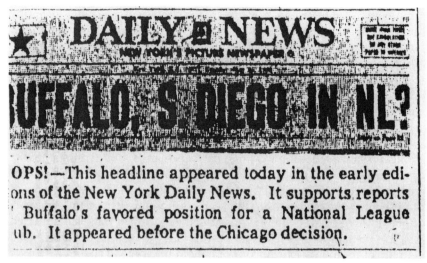

OPS!—This headline appeared today in the early editions of the New York Daily News. It supports reports Buffalo's favored position for a National League ub. It appeared before the Chicago decision.

The headline announcing that Buffalo would receive a Major League Baseball franchise appeared only in the paper's morning edition. This copy is courtesy of the author.

lotine: it's San Diego and Montreal, Bavasi and McHale. We were invited into the meeting all right, but only to hear the deadly verdict and make nice-nice to the owners. Montreal!? A Canadian venue with no stadium and no stadium plans except a hand-drawn map by latecomer mayor. We had a signed and sealed $50 million bond resolution! I could not bring myself to be pleasant and respectful. I talked of our disappointment and the big black blotch on the baseball map, with the thousands of Buffalo fans, the best minor-league market in the nation, deserting the sport. I resolved that this would be the last time we knocked at the door, like traveling salesmen. Bill Jennings, who preceeded me as NHL secretary, was right: your pitch has to be from inside the league.

Ten days later, our hopes got a temporary revival. McHale called. He could not seem to get funding and location for the kind of stadium he needed in Montreal. If it doesn't work out, he wanted to know, can he come to Buffalo? Sure, I said, our group is ready. I faintly hoped that the Montreal effort would collapse, but suspected that he was using me as a ploy. That's what it was, of course. The next day the national press in the United States and Canada quoted our telephone discourse, almost verbatim. McHale was being "driven out of Montreal to Buffalo" because of the intransigence of Montreal's authorities. The risk was too great for the the city's politicians, and they capitulated, giving McHale the site and funding he demanded. We got no commission and no consolation.

A column by Dick Young dated April 18, 1968, suggests O'Malley's excuse for turning us down: Young described an apparent conflict among the National League owners over whether to wait two years for construction of new stadia by the two most qualified applicants—Buffalo and Montreal—or take two that were immediately available—San Diego and Milwaukee—and thus stay even with the American League, which had scheduled two new teams to begin play in 1969. As to Buffalo, Young repeated damaging observations about the riots that occurred in the area of the existing Memorial Stadium (the Rockpile) several months before, which have an unpleasant echo of O'Malley's superficial response to the author at the time and which I suspect were dictated to Young by the Dodgers owner himself:

> The intolerable condition of Buffalo's Memorial Stadium is its insecurity. The International League club had to move out, had to move to Niagara Falls, because people were too frightened to go there at night. They were terrorized by the muggings and robberies.
>
> Buffalo authorities say their newball park will be built in a highly attractive locale, but what till then? Can they have a cop ride shotgun on every car that drives to the game? Can they post a cop in every rest room, at every concession stand?[1]

Years later, at a luncheon conference, former commissioner Bowie Kuhn (who had been acting as counsel for the National Baseball League at the time of our 1968 crusade) described to me in graphic language the efforts of our supporters in the league to get the unanimous vote needed for the Buffalo grant. We lost by one vote, he said. Whose vote? Horace Stoneham of the San Francisco Giants. Bowie described how they tried for three hours to eliminate his holdout—including rotating Buffalo sponsors, a full-court press, and frequent and generous application of alcoholic beverages—but Stoneham would not budge. In the end, they had to go to Montreal. Neither I nor any other member of the Buffalo entourage had ever met or talked to Mr. Stoneham. We had done nothing to incur his enmity or opposition. I have come to suspect that the Giants' owner was a shill for Walter O'Malley. The Dodgers owner was not willing to be tarred with his undisclosed opposition to the Buffalo cause, nor was he willing to desert his commitments to Bavasi and McHale, which we had been unable to unseat.

Part 3

THE HOCKEY WARS—
THE FACE-OFF

Chapter 9

SAVING OAKLAND, WINNING BUFFALO

THE KNOX-BUFFALO GROUP ON THE STAGE AT ST. REGIS

I had been a passionate fan of the theater and an active amateur actor all my life, so I knew what it meant to wait in the wings: to wait for your cue, to wait for your entrance, to wait for your line. But this was the first time I had to wait in the wings for the fate of my city. The scene was the cabaret of the St. Regis Hotel in New York City. The drama was the meeting of the Expansion Committee of the National Hockey League Board of Governors, at which the first six teams in the league's 1967 expansion, the first in its history, would be chosen. Seymour Knox III, Norty Knox, and I, representing the "Knox-Buffalo" group, had just completed our presentation for a franchise for Buffalo. The league was meeting on the floor of the hotel's nightclub; we were literally on the stage, behind the tall, gray flats and the curtain, waiting in the wings for the verdict.

The competition was, we thought, cities larger in size but lesser in the intensity of fan support. Certainly none were better in the thoroughness of preparation–purchase price, working capital, arena, hockey knowledge and plan, demographics, character, and influence of the applicant group—all had been covered in a whirlwind campaign. We'd undergone head-to-head, general and specific interviews with each of the existing owners: Harold Ballard and Stafford Smythe in Toronto; the Molsons in Montreal; the Wirtzes and Jim and Bruce Norris in Detroit and Chicago; Bill Jennings of the New York Rangers; Weston Adams Sr. and Weston Adams Jr. of the Boston Bruins. Remembering the painful loss in the baseball expansion competition, we had not neglected the associated forces: *Hockey Night in Canada* (Ted Hough); the president, doughty Clarence Campbell; Sportservice, the Buffalo concessionaire with considerable influence in certain quarters; the press; the politicians; and the hockey greats, including Toe Blake and Ned Harkness.

Of course we had filed an impeccable application, meeting each stipulated requirement of the league on the nose, on time, with style and substance—drawing compliments about our talent from the chairman of the committee, Bill Wirtz of the Blackhawks. We followed up with telephone contacts, intense and bizarre. Norty and Seymour did most of the selling; as graduates of Yale teams and world-class athletes themselves in polo and squash (Norty had just won the world championship in court tennis and had been captain of the US polo team), they had first-class contacts in almost every existing NHL franchise.

A typical scene: in the Boston airport, occupying three pay phones, we made the next appointment with an owner, reporting on the last meeting, seeking advice, adding to our complement of prospective owners. I joined in the strategy and tactics, but my principal assignment at that moment was running between the airport cashier and the telephone array, supplying the Knoxes with nickels, dimes, and quarters.

As we stood in the wings, we were apprehensive, but naively confident. On the merits, we thought we had it made. The competition included cities like Los Angeles and San Francisco—major in size, but with spotty hockey support and nonhockey climates; Baltimore and Cleveland, with solid attendance records in the minor American Hockey League but with arenas that, unlike ours, could not be expanded to meet the NHL minimum of fifteen thousand seats; and Canadian cities such as Ottawa and Vancouver, which stood little chance with a league that was primarily moved to expand by the need for more US television revenue. We had, we felt, one of the best cases, based on the quality of our group, its preparation and finances, the expandability of our building, the local political support, and the undoubted strength of our hockey audience.

THE OPPOSITION: JIM NORRIS, HAROLD BALLARD, AND STAFFORD SMYTHE

There were warnings, of course, but we tended to ignore them—or, more realistically, we were too determined to go forward anyway, notwithstanding the signs of negative votes. The owner of Channel 9 in Toronto, an associate of Ballard and Smythe, smiled at the Knoxes—his occasional squash buddies—but raised eyebrows at the thought of a competing hockey club and competing television station in the Toronto-Buffalo market, with the two cities only seventy miles apart, as the crow—or a VHF signal—flies. And Stafford Smythe, grumpy and intense, remarked: "Why should I give a franchise to you? I might as well give one to my friends down the street, who are always barking for a second franchise in this city." And there were rumors that the Norrises would vote no because of their losses in the grain business, with the Buffalo elevators now silent and vacant.

The warning from Jim Norris was mixed, but explicit: Our group had received suggestions that we could have a franchise in Los Angeles, Cleveland, or St. Louis, but not in Buffalo. We promptly declined. We're Buffalonians, we said, and our major objective is to provide an asset for our community. As I passed Norris in the hotel corridor on the previous day, he stopped me with a gruff "SWADOS!"

"Mr. Lawyer," he said, "you've made the best damn application, you've got the best group and you're the best damn lawyer here. BUT YOU'RE NOT GONNA GET IT!"

Jim Norris's oral punch went right to my solar plexus, but I tried to respond bravely through the nausea: "Well, Mr. Norris, thank you for your candor. But we're going to keep on trying. . . ." But as I stood there, waiting in the wings, I rode the mood swings between despair and determination. I began to face up to the reality: Despite the Knox friendships, our technical competence, and our hard work—despite the merits of our case—we were still outsiders; we were still salesmen, knocking at the door. We had only suspicions, no direct knowledge, of how the governors really viewed their own interests in the expansion, and we had no idea how the crosscurrents and conflicts among the owners would resolve and fall out.

BILL JENNINGS: DEFEAT AND HOPE

When the verdict came, Bill Jennings—the president of the New York Rangers, who turned out to be our most effective and practical friend on the board—came behind the curtain to give it to us. We didn't make it. The six new franchises went to Los Angeles, San Francisco–Oakland, our friends Gordie Ritz and Walter Bush in Minneapolis, Philadelphia, Pittsburgh, and, the unkindest cut of all, St. Louis. The last really stoked our anger—St. Louis had no owner! No application had been filed, no presentation had been made. All St. Louis had—with a minimal hockey history—was a building, owned by the Norrises, that needed a tenant. It was hardly due process. We were beaten by a ghost—a city with no hockey identity and no person we could attack. We were mad, and we lashed out: Did Stafford deliver the poison pill? Did the assurances of the Molsons and the Wirtzes count for nothing? How could our assets—owners, fans, building, capital— be ignored? At that moment if the founders of the outlaw WHA, which would come on the scene a few years later, had approached us, they would have found a willing target. Fortunately, Bill Jennings, a man of wisdom, power, and judgment, would not accept our anger. Bill grabbed me by the elbow and pulled me into the wings. "Hold on," he said. "Look . . . your group has really impressed us here. This isn't your last shot at a franchise. There'll be other opportunities. Tell your clients not to blow it!"

Seymour and Norty did not reconcile easily. They had wealth, power, and competence. Our case was among the best. The governors had shown themselves—at least some of them—to be political animals, and the Knoxes were not used to such treatment. Talk of threats, even litigation, bounced around like a minor storm, but fortunately Jennings's good sense prevailed.

Perhaps the Gods of Expansion were imposing punishment for our mistreatment of DeWitt. I tried to assuage my guilt in later years when I sought to help Bill's son obtain an NHL franchise for Cincinnati.

Certainly these experiences provided valuable coaching: get on the inside, line up your financing well in advance, get your building approved, set the timing so that you can use the new facility immediately on com-mencing operations, or as soon as possible . . . easier said than done!

JENNINGS MAKES THE CALL

It wasn't long before Bill Jennings pressed the Buffalo button. The Oakland Seals were in trouble and needed cash desperately. It had seemed like a well-constructed and financed franchise. The ownership included wealthy and notable partners like publisher Nelson Doubleday, who was a partner in the New York Mets, on the East Coast, and on the West, golfing buddies of Bing Crosby, like Barry van Gerbig. The National Hockey League had tried to make success easy for the new clubs by placing all six in their own division, with the winner of that division moving directly into the Stanley Cup Finals to face the champion of the "original six." But the team did not do very well, and the fans in San Francisco and San Jose, where the wealth was, did not care to make the twice-weekly trek to impoverished Oakland, where the building was. Charlie Finley's A's, with its array of star pitchers, could bring the fans across the Bay in summer, but the rookie hockey club failed to attract enough customers to produce any positive cash flow.

In its compelling appetite for the West Coast markets, the league had accepted an ownership profile of fifty-five partners for the Oakland Seals, organized in three partnerships, with none of the partnerships owning 51 percent, none having control, and no individual having enough of a stake in the venture to step up and solve the financial problem. It was January, and there was neither cash nor credit to finish the season. The league swept the likely investors—Seals partners, local people of note, Crosby, and Finley—without success. The league even approached Charles Schultz, an undoubted hockey fan with the financial capacity to handle the investment himself. But NHL play and prices in Oakland were obviously risky, and Snoopy stayed on his frozen birdbath.

Faced with the possible bankruptcy of the Seals in their second season— a devastating blow to the West Coast strategy—the league appealed to us for help. "The league would be very grateful . . . all we need is $1 million," said Jennings. "It's a major market, and if it doesn't work out, you might be able to move it to Buffalo. . . ." With the scars of our previous failures flashing, we bit, and bit hard. At the end of January 1968, I was promptly dispatched to New York and San Francisco to negotiate the deal.

SIGHTS ON BUFFALO: BECOMING "HOCKEY PEOPLE"

We had not been idle in the interim. It was clear to us that we had to establish a foothold, make ourselves "hockey people" somewhere. The Buffalo Bisons of the American Hockey League was a logical place to start. The team was owned by the three Pastor brothers, the local Pepsi Cola distributors, who would have a sharp interest in continuing Pepsi "pour rights" in the Aud. When the hockey Bisons played at home, there was no mistaking the bottle cap logo on the team uniforms. Ruby Pastor, the eldest brother, had already made a move toward obtaining an NHL franchise for his family, but he was a practical and genial soul, and he quickly recognized that if a major-league franchise were available, he would be better off being part of the group than going it alone. As it happened, the Pastors were unhappy with their minor-league working agreement with Detroit, and, with our good relations with Bill Jennings, we were able to offer Ruby and Fred Hunt—the club's general manager—a working agreement with the New York Rangers and general support in the club's operations. The only quid pro quo we requested was the addition of Seymour, Norty, and me to the Bisons' Board of Directors and an informal understanding that the Pastors would cooperate in and be part of our quest for an NHL franchise. Ruby had good relations with Buffalo mayor Frank Sedita and the local politicians, which could be important when we came to deal with the expected demand by the league for an increase in the Aud's capacity.

The original Knox-Buffalo Group. *From left*: Hazard Campbell, George Goodyear, Arthur Victor, Ruby Pastor, Norty Knox, Seymour Knox III (*in net*), Paul Schoellkopf, Fred Schoellkopf, Reg Taylor, and the author. Photo courtesy of the author.

THE KNOX-BUFFALO GROUP

Before we committed to the Jennings strategy for Oakland, it was essential to get our financing ducks in order. What had begun as a "loan" of about $900,000 to the Seals became, as it became clear how messy the Oakland situation was, a call to purchase the team outright. The fifty-five Seals partners had had enough of the Oakland losses, and none was willing to bet further on our ability to move the club to Buffalo. Fortunately, our original group, despite the failure in 1967 expansion, was strongly motivated by the opportunity to strengthen the city with a major-league asset. For the most part, they were citizens of Western New York who had already made significant contributions to the community and had an emotional investment in our pursuit. There was also some sense of loyalty and camaraderie, as they remembered their successful investment in Transcontinent Television, in which the Schoellkopfs, George Goodyear, Dave Forman, and I had provided much of the leadership. These were the pioneer owners, who provided the initial capital and faithfully responded to every call for additional investment over the years with almost no financial return.

Ed and Peter Andrews were former Buffalonians, Transcontinent TV investors, and principals in the *Buffalo Courier Express*, the morning newspaper that was ultimately absorbed by the *Buffalo Evening News*. Peter had been financial editor of the paper, an active supporter of the Studio Arena Theater, and, with my intense interest in that theater (I eventually became its vice chairman and president), an active supporter of my projects as well. Ed was a close friend of Seymour and proved to have very useful contacts for us among other league owners, particularly Chuck Dolan of Cablevision.

Hazard Campbell was Seymour's first cousin; George Collins, Seymour's doctor and a cousin of then governor Hugh Carey. George was a hockey enthusiast and a golfing buddy of Fred Hunt, the Bisons' GM, who first gave Seymour the news of the NHL expansion and planted the idea of an NHL club for Buffalo.

John Fisher was a principal in Fisher-Price Toys, a leading national toy manufacturer with its main plant in the Buffalo area. John had no previous commercial connection with our group, but he and his wife, Judy, became our good friends. Judy turned out to be a smart and effective politician, providing good input to the Sabres over the years as a member of the Buffalo Common Council and the Erie County Legislature.

Bob Rich Jr.'s family-owned business—Rich Products—was a very successful local company that grew in wealth and influence. The company had participated in our unsuccessful baseball ventures, and it later bought the Buffalo Bisons, generated a beautiful new stadium for that team with the city's help, and came close to acquiring a major-league franchise in that sport. The Rich family had also profited from our TV venture, but its loyalty to the Knoxes, particularly to Seymour and Norty's dad, doubtless strongly influenced their investment.

Richard Rupp was a prominent Buffalonian and operator of F. N. Burt Company, a leading paper box manufacturer. In the crisis years of the 1990s, he could always be counted on for substantial financial support.

Howie Saperston, another beneficiary of our television success, was a member of a leading real estate organization and, like Norty, a prep school and college hockey goalie. It was rumored that he sometimes practiced with the minor-league hockey Bisons and provided "semiexpert" comment.

Robert Schmon, and his company, Ontario Paper, gave us a solid Canadian identity. With his business located in nearby St. Catharines, he provided valuable insight and contact with our Canadian fans. When we finally received the NHL grant in 1969, the Sabres territory covered a fifty-mile radius from Buffalo, embracing St. Catharines, Welland, Fort Erie, and part of Hamilton—a population of more than half a million and more than three hundred thousand television homes. Over the years, the arena audience averaged 15 percent in Canadian fans and at times approached 30 percent.

Joe Stewart, a wealthy Buffalo investment banker, was a friend of the Knoxes and a prominent citizen. Joe served as treasurer of Buffalo General Hospital and held major posts in a number of the region's important charities.

George Strawbridge Jr. came to the Sabres by a remote connection (he lived in the Philadelphia area), but he was always a stalwart director and supporter of the franchise and the group. He was probably the wealthiest of the investors—a scion of the Dorrance family, principals in the Campbell Soup Company—but his connection came through his father-in-law, Dave Forman. Dave had been a vice president of Transcontinent Television, worked closely with me on its numerous acquisitions, and was a friend of the Schoellkopfs. We had him marked for the lead in the nonhockey, TV, and marketing phases of the team. In the crisis years of the late 1990s, George, along with Rich Products, made the largest single investments in the Sabres from our group.

The most loyal and quickest to respond to our plea for capital were the veterans of the Transcontinent Television crusade, Arthur Victor Jr. and Paul and Fred Schoellkopf. As detailed in chapter 6, the venture in the broadcasting industry had been exciting and profitable for all, and had given me and my firm a national stage on which we performed with luck and success. Artie Victor brought along his friends from the Democratic Party (also Transcontinent investors), such as Gene McMahon, Pat McGroder, and Peter Crotty (a former chairman of the party); and, with the strength of the Knoxes, Riches, and Schoellkopfs in the Republican Party, we had a power base on both sides of the aisle in the mayor's office, in the Buffalo Common Council, in the county legislature, and at the state level as well.

TAKING THE OAKLAND GAMBLE

With the Oakland franchise in peril, speed was essential. Bill Jennings had specified a needed investment of about $1 million, three thousand miles from home. But the money was needed almost overnight. In a theme that was to echo in my brain twenty-five years later in Buffalo, Bill Torrey (later of Islander and Panther fame), the Seals' assistant general manager, told me on my arrival at the arena in Oakland that the club was already late with the player payroll. If the team didn't get its checks by the following Friday, under the NHL rules the players would become free agents, and there'd be nothing to sell. In the instructions from Bill Jennings and the club attorneys, not only speed, but *secrecy*, was essential. The Seals were doing their best to keep the fans coming; if word got out that a group from Buffalo was on the scene, the season would be doomed.

I heeded the instructions. We worked around the clock negotiating the sale, stipulating in the contract that we had the right to walk away if the NHL Board of Governors didn't authorize a transfer to Buffalo. That right to terminate was somewhat theoretical, in the light of the state of the club's finances. If the transfer fell through, we would have to take our chances on recovering our money from another purchaser. I learned that Vancouver interests had already offered a deal for a move to that city. However, Jennings assured me that the league (meaning Toronto and Montreal) would never approve such a transaction and stressed that what was important was the help we were giving to the league, which would pay dividends down the road. His assurance that we "might" be able to work the transfer was more vague than we liked, but after a telephone conference with Seymour and Norty, we decided to go for it. Niagara Frontier Hockey, Inc., was the name of the company we had formed, and to save time and get the deal done, as the only officer on the scene, I signed the papers and dispatched them to Buffalo.

I soon learned, however, that in the world of professional sports, "secrecy" is a state devoutly wished for but rarely achieved. I asked the Seals group: There's a game in the Oakland arena Sunday night; can't I come and see "my team" play? A major issue! Arguments, consultations, and strong opinions followed. Finally, the verdict: I could attend the game, but only under restrictions. I had to come with a bodyguard, to keep me away from the press. I had to wear dark glasses as a semidisguise: "Everybody in hockey knows who you are," I was warned. I could not sit in the press box. I had to arrive late and leave early. I could not eat in the restaurant or at a hot dog stand. So I left the game ten minutes before the end of the third period, squired by my bodyguard, hungry—but still excited, and still silent.

The next morning, as I prepared to fly east, I opened the San Francisco newspaper to find the whole story emblazoned across its pages, in agonizing detail: Buffalo group, dollars, threat of transfer. Everyone was mildly upset—temporarily. Temporarily, because all knew that once our request to transfer the club was placed formally on the NHL governors' agenda, the "secret" would be out, anyway.

We had learned enough in our baseball projects and in the our failed attempt at entry into the NHL in 1967 to know we had work to do with the individual owners. Jennings made good on the first part of his commitment—the Board of Governors rejected the Vancouver application and recommended that ours be granted, subject to the consent of the clubs affected. That "consent" was a tough hurdle. Jim Norris, who had been so vocal and arbitrary on behalf of Chicago and Detroit in rejecting the expansion application for Buffalo in 1967, was out of the picture, and Bill Jennings suggested that the real opposition would come from Stafford Smythe, Harold Ballard, and their associates in Toronto. Buffalo's fifty-mile territorial circle, mandated by the NHL constitution, would overlap and invade the Toronto circle. The two cities were only seventy miles apart, and, clearly, Toronto had a legal and practical veto. We were seeking to be *admitted* to the monopolistic cartel—we were not about to raise the antitrust bogeyman. Seymour and I, supplemented by Norty on the phone, held intense in-person meetings with Smythe and John Bassett, principal owner of Toronto's Channel 9, and Ted Hough, representing *Hockey Night in Canada* on CBC, the principal Canadian network for NHL games. Bassett, a frequent squash competitor of Seymour's, was polite and urbane, allowing that it was Stafford's call; Hough was taciturn and unenthusiastic. I made what I thought was a moderately eloquent and factual presentation, based on history in other markets, showing that a grant to Buffalo would not invade or hurt the Maple Leafs' TV revenue—rather, it would lift the whole Buffalo-Toronto market, adding viewers, hockey interest, and income for both clubs. This ultimately turned out to be true, but Smythe would have none of it. As described in chapter 6, my "eloquence" produced only a profane "no" from Stafford. Even an on-the-spot offer of indemnification for the invasion of territory didn't budge the Toronto owners.

SLIDING THROUGH THE OAKLAND OPENING

Fate ultimately forced Smythe and Ballard to relent—their embezzlement charges weakened their position and forced them to accept, in 1970, expansion to Vancouver and Buffalo. That expansion was endorsed by all the other members of the league, induced largely by the $1 million payable to each of the existing clubs by the new franchises (at a price of $6 million per club, compared with the price in the first expansion of $2 million). But at the time of the Oakland effort, they were adamant: the move to Buffalo would not fly. Jennings called and asked me to persuade my clients to keep their money in. It would really sell us to the league, he said, and there was talk of further expansion. They had a potential buyer to fit with our investment.

The decision was not an easy one. If we had seats on the Board of Governors, I argued, for the first time we could press the Buffalo case from the *inside*. We could influence the expansion plans. Our money was already at risk, and the chances of recovery might be improved under new ownership. Admittedly, we couldn't run the franchise efficiently from three thousand miles away. The NHL board didn't help matters much. I suggested that since the Buffalo group's investment was the only cash then up front, we should have control and Seymour should be the governor. Not so fast, came the answer, as delivered by Bill Wirtz of Chicago: the Toronto hostility was still at work, there were no commitments for a transfer to Buffalo, and Vancouver, still in the picture, had sued the league. The NHL's decision: we would be restricted to 20 percent and Seymour would be the alternate governor. I would be just a vice president, without power. The new boys would have control.

IN BED WITH THE NEW BOYS

The "new boys" turned out to be an outfit, just formed, called TransNational Communications, headed by one Elwood "Woody" Erdman, a refugee from the broadcasting industry who agreed to take on Munson Campbell, a socialite drinking buddy of some of the NHL owners, as president. It was the habit of the governors to clothe any new owner who solved a league financial problem with glamorous status, whether he deserved it or not. A hard look at Erdman and his crew indicated that TransNational was about 10 percent money, 40 percent debt, and 50 percent bluff—or, to put it kindly, PR. The only deep pockets were the Buffalo investors. The only attractive assets presented by TransNational were three all-stars from football and baseball—Whitey Ford, a top pitcher of the New York Yankees; Pat Summerall, former Pro-Bowl place kicker for the New York Giants and announcer for the NFL; and Dick Lynch, popular linebacker from the Giants. The former players were described as investors. I never knew how much, if anything, they had put up as capital, but when calls for additional money arose, they were quick to retire to the locker room. Erdman's grand "strategy," we heard through the NHL grapevine, was to go public with the Seals, the star trio, and a minor-league baseball club; sell enough stock to recoup his debt; provide enough cash to keep the Seals going; and— maybe—pay us off.

For the Buffalo group, it was an outrageous gamble. It was not at all the type of stock Seymour the investment banker would recommend to his clients. But we could taste the heady brew of NHL ownership. Perhaps the

Buffalo, Vancouver Get NHL Franchises for 1970-71 Season

Bisons In Loop With Old Clubs

★ From Page 1

a lease satisfactory to the league must be signed with the city. These matters must be completed promptly so that the expanded Auditorium will be ready for next fall.

No Problem Anticipated

A number of organizational matters must be resolved in Vancouver, Campbell said, and the club must be wholly owned by Medicorp Corp., a Minneapolis-based concern which is buying the Vancouver Canucks of the Western Hockey League.

Knox, who will head the new Buffalo club, said he anticipated no problems in meeting the stipulations of the governors.

"Our first consideration now is to make Memorial Auditorium acceptable to the NHL," Knox said. "We submitted the Auditorium and the Domed Stadium to the league as home sites, and the league rejected the Domed Stadium.

"With regard to the modifications to Memorial Auditorium, we have supplied the league with letters of intent from Mayor Sedita; from 14 of the 15 councilmen, the 15th was out of town, and from members of the Board of Stadium.

Need Formal Resolution

"These letters were a tremendous help to us, and played a vital role in helping us get the franchise.

"Now, we must have the formal resolutions adopted approving the increase in the seating capacity, the other improvements, and the lease."

Knox, who headed the Buffalo group which made an abortive bid for a franchise when the NHL expanded from six to 12 teams, remained a minority stockholder in the Oakland Seals following an unsuccessful attempt to transfer the team to Buffalo.

"I was playing golf with Fred

Move Into NHL Delights Mayor

Mayor Frank A. Sedita's statement on the franchise was:

"I am, of course, delighted that we have received a National Hockey League franchise. This is, I think, an important forward step in Buffalo becoming a truly major league city in every respect. I am certain that we will all benefit.

"I want to extend my thanks and congratulations to Seymour H. Knox III, Northrup Knox,

Hunt (Bison's general manager) one day, and suggested an NHL team would go a long way in filling a void in Buffalo's sports picture, and would truly make the city a major-league city," Knox recalled.

Board Hears Knox, Swados

"Later, I talked about it with my brother, Northrup, and with my dad. Now, 4½ years later, we're in, and this is truly Hockey Day in Buffalo."

Robert O. Swados, attorney for the Knox group, and Seymour Knox III appeared before the Board of Governors Tuesday following lengthy appearances Monday before the finance and expansion committees. Dr. George Collins, a director of the club, and Henry M. Porter, assistant secretary of the club, also were here.

"We're dead tired, but we feel a great sense of exhilaration because we finally got Buffalo the recognition it deserves as a major league city," Swados said.

"No one will ever know how difficult, complex and, at times, discouraging a road we've had to travel. We're fortunate that the members of our group have hung in there, and helped us overcome each obstacle and disappointment.

"We've been helped tremendously by the Mayor, the council, including members of both political parties, who have backed us to the hilt. This impressed the league, and was a key factor in our success.

Oakland Share Helped

"We must all recognize that the decision to retain a share of the Oakland Franchise after our attempt to transfer it to Buffalo was frustrated, was an important factor in bringing the governors of the league to recognize the validity of Buffalo's case.

"There are still major problems to be solved in which we will need the help of the fans, the city fathers and everyone interested in our community."

Stafford Smythe, president of the Toronto Maple Leafs, warmly applauded the inclusion of Buffalo and Vancouver after being opposed to both cities in the initial expansion program.

TV Not a Factor Now

"It wasn't against Buffalo the first time," Smythe insisted. "I thought the six cities we took in then were better since increasing our potential television audience was the prime consideration," Smythe said.

"Television isn't a factor now, and Buffalo is a better hockey town that some we took in earlier. The football team there and the merger of the two pro football leagues have helped the image of the city."

Bill Wirtz, president of the Chicago Black Hawks and head of the NHL expansion committee, said, "you have to commend the Buffalo people for their perseverance. They certainly helped out a troubled situation at Oakland, and that helped them this time."

Buffalo and Vancouver will join Toronto, Montreal, New York, Detroit and Boston in the Eastern Division, with Chicago moving to the Western Division to join Oakland, Los Angeles, Pittsburgh, Minnesota, Philadelphia and St. Louis.

Four teams in each division will qualify for the Stanley Cup playoffs.

Seymour Knox III   Clarence Campbell   Robert Swados

National Hockey League president welcomes new members

Seymour Knox III and the author with Clarence Campbell, NHL president—announcing the grant of the NHL franchise for the Buffalo Sabres. Clipping courtesy of the author.

Chicago/Detroit/Toronto wall was crumbling? Our group made the million-dollar bet—and it paid off.

As alternate governor, Seymour had the right to attend all governors' meetings, and I could generally tag along as counsel. We determined that one of us—Seymour, Norty, or myself—would be present at every possible meeting of the league—board, committees, conference calls. We would act like good and resourceful partners. We couldn't cover every angle, for Erdman was the governor, and as president (and the league hierarchy) Clarence Campbell could call for "executive" sessions—one per team— whenever he wanted to consider a matter out of our presence. But now as club members of the NHL we learned some key facts: The pressure from western Canada was getting to the league, and an expansion plan was being prepared. The price was up for debate. The Vancouver interests were claiming that they should pay no more than the 1967 teams—$2 million. At that figure, Baltimore and Cleveland would probably put in a bid. Bill Wirtz called Seymour; Clarence Campbell called me: What would we offer? Norty, Seymour, and I met with our accountants and with Cy Siegfried and his son, our friends in the construction business. We knew from our previous investigation in the 1967 expansion that Buffalo's Memorial Auditorium could expand from ten to fifteen thousand seats and that the rinks in Baltimore and Cleveland probably could not.

The three of us agreed that the price had to be high enough to discourage, if not bar, the Baltimore and Cleveland applications. Six million dollars from each of two new clubs would produce $1 million for each of the existing twelve members, and we were pretty sure the other US cities could not justify that price—certainly not in their ten-thousand-seat buildings, and construction of new arenas was not in their cards. Norty, Seymour, and I surveyed the keys in our investment group, presented the projections at fifteen thousand seats, got confirmation from Mayor Sedita on the Aud expansion, and received unanimous approval. Seymour and I called Wirtz, Jennings, and Campbell: we would go for the six mil.

WE SCORE THE PRIZE GOAL

On December 2, 1969, Wirtz assembled his NHL Finance Committee in New York at the Ritz Carlton Hotel. Seymour and I paced the anteroom for an hour while the committee deliberated. I had recurring memories of our fruitless waits in the wings at the baseball meetings, but this time the result was different: Wirtz, Jennings, and Campbell emerged with congratulations. We would get the franchise, along with Vancouver; the price was $6 million and we had to add the five thousand seats and be ready for play by October 1970. It was a moment of joy![1]

FINESSING *HOCKEY NIGHT*

In a reminder that we still had word to do, Clarence Campbell whispered to me, "Make your deal with *Hockey Night in Canada!*" Clarence always had difficulty extracting himself from his longtime Canadian supporters, and a few days later I received a letter from Ted Hough demanding (1) that we stay out of Canada, even though our fifty-mile circle extended four miles into Hamilton and a healthy percentage of our American Hockey League fans came from Welland, St. Catharines, and Niagara Falls in southern Ontario; (2) gate protection—no Buffalo games on Wednesday or Saturday nights; (3) advertising protection—no TV advertisers competing with *Hockey Night in Canada* sponsors; and (4) indemnification. I thought Ted's letter was excessive chutzpah, and I appealed to Bill Wirtz. Bill's tone, now that we were "in"—and had demonstrated what he called our "talent and judgment"—was warm and supportive. Bill disagreed entirely with Hough. "You're paying the highest price in the history of the National Hockey League," he said. "You get the same territorial and other rights as anybody else. Toronto's getting its $1 million—you owe them nothing else."

The Knoxes and I saw this as a concrete, hearty welcome to the league. Yet I urged and was authorized some minor compromise. The final, formal vote by the Board of Governors had not yet occurred. So Ted and I worked out some adjustments. We did not budge on territory or on our right to exploit any and all fans in our Canadian area. Mayor Sedita wanted us to save Saturday dates for the Canisius College basketball program, so giving up that night was easy. We did agree to avoid sponsor conflict and mini-mize gate and TV interference by adopting what was basically a Thursday/Sunday schedule. All these adjustments were limited to the "development years."

On May 22, 1970, the governors granted our final NHL charter, and life was never the same.

Chapter 10

NORTY KNOX, SEYMOUR KNOX III, AND HENRY VIII

In early 1969, in the midst of our crusade for an NHL franchise, I saw Norty Knox become an international champion. It was in Manhattan, at the New York Racquet Club. The championship was none of your common varieties of sport, in many of which he had excelled: not hockey, in which he had been a Yale first-string goalie; not polo—he had been, or would be, the captain of the US team; not squash, for which he had won multiple trophies. It was fitting for Norty, for he was many things, but certainly elitist, that the championship he won that day was in the most royal of sports—court tennis. Not the sport of Flushing Meadows or Roland Garros or even Wimbledon. The contest I saw that day was tennis as played by Henry VIII at the edge of his castle, at Hampton Court Palace in 1530, according to legend, as he paid scant attention to word of the execution of Anne Boleyn; and by the Kings of France as *Jeu de Paume* at Versailles. I had never seen a court constructed for Real Tennis (as it's called in Britain) before, nor had I seen Norty so close for so long. He took the complexities of the royal game and the stress of competition with cool and competence.

It was a strange, vaguely familiar game in a space that seemed part tennis court, part medieval castle. There are only seven courts of this kind in the United States, seventeen in Great Britain, two in France, and three in Australia. The net and one end of the court look pretty much like they do in lawn tennis, although the net may vary in width or tension. In its early

Northrup & Seymour Knox

Northrup R.
Knox

Seymour H.
Knox

Founding Owners
Buffalo Sabres

days, the game was played against the castle wall, however, and the other end of the court is a three-dimensional picture of that wall: the player at the opposite end can aim at not only the floor or ground, as in lawn tennis, but the windows, the doors, and the roof of the shed that extends around three sides of the court (known as the "penthouse"). The player at the opposite end can score points by hitting these objects or openings before the defender intercepts or returns the ball.

A common serve is to slice the ball so as to give it a vertical spin, then hit the roof of the penthouse in such a way that it rolls and drops directly down, so close to the back wall as to send highly skilled wall scrapers like squash and racketball players into fibrillation. The ball itself is made of horsehide or tightly bound cloth, slightly smaller than a lawn tennis ball; its composition encourages slices, spins, and other odd strategies. The racket bears some resemblance to that used in lawn tennis, but its shape is slightly bent, as if designed for a painting by Picasso or Miro.

The scoring is similar to lawn tennis, but the rule that appeals to me is known as the "chase." When, at a certain stage of the match, one player gets ahead, he must give his opponent a short ball—hit the ball into the area nearest the net—so that the opponent has a chance to put the ball away with a kill shot and thus get back into the game.

Norty handled all these matters—slice, drive, spin, serve, overhead, lob, the castle, the penthouse, the tambour—with complete competence. I was impressed that I was working with a real champion. It gave us a confidence that served us well. Norty first won the world championship in 1959, the first amateur to do so in forty-five years, and held the title until 1969—the year we found our way from Oakland to the Sabres NHL franchise.

Seymour Knox III was no slouch as an athlete, either. He was nationally ranked in squash—as high as number nine; for three years, he was a US doubles champion in court tennis; and he was a five-goal handicap player on the Aurora Polo Team, which won a national championship in 1953 and reached the US Open Finals in 1956 and 1959.

In a bold script on a high beam above the bar at the Buffalo Saturn Club appears a quotation attributed to Herbert Spenser, the distinguished nineteenth-century philosopher of evolution who was widely known as the founding father of sociology and as the sorest loser at the pool table: "To play a good game of billiards is the mark of a well-rounded education; to play too good a game of billiards is the mark of a misspent youth."

I found no word of their record at billiards, but this quick survey of their triumphs in other sports suggests that in Spenser's view Seymour and Norty indeed must have had a prodigal adolescence. For example, I note for those among us who believe in sedentary sports that Seymour and Norty even left their mark on deep-sea fishing: both were at one time holders of the world record, at twenty-six pounds, for the Pacific big-eye tuna fifty-pound test.

Seymour and Norty were both Yalies: Seymour active in squash and swimming; Norty a varsity hockey goalie.

Their Yale and business contacts were widespread and high level; they were directors, sometimes officers, of national companies such as the Marine Midland Bank, Pratt & Lambert, and the Woolworth Corporation. The latter was the source of a substantial part of their fortune, arising out of an early partnership between Woolworth and their grandfather. Their athletic success and drive gave them unique favorable responses from coaches like Ned Harkness, GMs like Bill Torrey, and owners like Jennings and the Molsons and Bronfmans.

The Knox talent for sports had a mixed effect on me. At their insistence and example, I took up squash, and its demand for quickness and stamina put me in the best shape of my life. I'm sure the Knoxes would have liked to have a counsel who could compete as an athlete, but the special hand/eye coordination wasn't quite there. I won a tournament for "B" players at my own club, but after Boston's GM, Harry Sinden, invited me to play he reported to Seymour, with characteristic candor, that I should stick to lawyering. And when I bravely invited Seymour to play golf with me in an invitational tournament and failed to make a critical putt at the height of the match—despite Seymour's explicit instructions—the expression on his face strongly suggested I stay with books, swimming, and social tennis.

* * *

Fortunately for the citizens of Western New York, the athleticism and societal prominence of the Knoxes was accompanied by intelligence, social conscience, and a drive to make their community better. Seymour and Norty were born into wealth and influence, but not the kind that clips coupons and leaves the problems of the world to lesser beings. Their father, Seymour H. Knox Jr., had transformed the local art gallery—the Buffalo Fine Arts Academy, then known as the Albright Art Gallery—from a traditional house of ancient Greek sculpture and nineteenth-century landscapes and portraits into one of the most beautiful museums for modern art in the Western Hemisphere. To Gauguin, Matisse, Picasso, Van Gogh, Dufy, and Seurat were added Brill, Delawny, Motherwell, Chagall, Pollock, and Warhol—all introduced or made more prominent in the ancient edifice.

The contributions provided by Knox and his friends were so substantial and such a comprehensive departure from the historical works in the Albright that an entirely new building was called for. Knox produced a museum annex that was clean lined, open, and full of light. The architect of the structure was Gordon Bunshaft, a former Buffalonian who had planned the United Nations headquarters in New York. The architect of the new collection, hired by Knox, was the new curator, Gordon Smith. Seymour Jr. had to overcome the prejudices of the incumbent board, which had earlier wrinkled its collective nose at cubism and impressionism and now was skeptical of the abstract and pop art compositions promoted and purchased by Smith and Knox. That prejudice had discouraged A. Conger Goodyear (father of my friend George), also an early enthusiast of modern composition, to the point where he chose to donate some of the major works in his collection to the founding of the Museum of Modern Art in New York City. The Knox reputation and influence—as well the extent of the contributions—in the light of the transformation of the institution led to its new name: the Albright-*Knox*.

The new collection, the new building, and the national outlook required constant and skilled attention: to the choice of works to be acquired and promoted, to the generation of funding, to the financing of the structure, and to the operating budget. It was given full support by the elder Knox, and it was great on-the-job training for his sons. Seymour and Norty inherited from their father this discipline and ethic of skilled devotion to duty, and on his death the sons took over rigorously and vigorously the operation and continued vitality of the gallery.

The singular mark of Seymour and Norty as citizens was not only the breadth of their work in the community, but its intensity. I've seen plenty of "distinguished" directors on corporate or charitable boards that come to meetings, listen passively to the reports of the professional staff or executives, give a tacit blessing, then return exclusively to their own pursuits and concerns. With the Knoxes, there was always critical but appreciative evaluation and, if the organization needed it, a willingness to dig in and work—daily, if necessary—toward the solution of its problems. Norty could be seen doing this at the Marine Midland Bank (now HSBC), at the Niagara Share Investment Company, at the Buffalo Philharmonic, the Museum of Science, and the University at Buffalo. For Seymour it was the Smithsonian, the Woolworth board, the Buffalo General Hospital, and the Historical Society. Near the end of his life, Seymour even took on the chairmanship of funding campaigns for the regional YMCA.

Since the Knoxes played so important a part in my life and career, some attempt should be made at painting their looks, personality, and character. Like their father, they were both short—which facilitated mutual directness and candor. I respected them—but I didn't have to look up to them! They had receptive senses of humor; they enjoyed a laugh, but rarely told jokes, on- or off-color. They were thorough, but relied on their vast network of friends and supporters for information, strategy, and tactics—from Nelson Doubleday, the publisher/part owner of the Mets, to Amo Houghton, the Corning Glass heir and congressman from Wyoming County. They were loyal to staff and partners, so long as they delivered. The key word for Seymour was *warmth*; for Norty, it was *objective test*, but for those who passed, all-out support. If you were making a solid contribution to the organization and Seymour liked you, he would open up himself and his family and even some of his resources to you. My wife and I were invited frequently to the Seymour Knox homes in Buffalo, East Aurora, the Adirondacks, and Naples, Florida. Norty was more cautious, with a tougher mentality, but once he was convinced of merit, he generated energetic enthusiasm. He would attach his own nickname for key staffers (Dan DiPofi, the Sabres controller, was "DePuff"); but it was a sort of substitution for friendship. I never knew whether I had a Knox nickname (other than "Bob"). Perhaps age indicated more formality.

Like all of us, Norty and Seymour had their problems, and I've tried to describe the Knoxes with balance and candor in this book. But they were, for most of their thirty Sabres years, ideal owners—men of integrity and talent, and fun to be with.

On October 14, 1992, Seymour and Norty were inducted into the Greater Buffalo Sports Hall of Fame, and I was asked to give the introduction. Paul Maguire, the genial color commentator on NFL football telecasts and a former Buffalo Bill, was the master of ceremonies. Paul tried to limit me to one minute, the time allotted to introductions for the local high school coach or the Olympic speed skater. I argued that my friends were the most important sports figures, if not the most important citizens, of the community. I asked for five; Paul gave me three. I assured him I had never spoken for as little as one and would probably pay no attention to the cutoff, anyway. I did have enough time to say this:

> There is a popular perception of a professional sports owner as a *Guys and Dolls* character showing up once a blue moon, generally directing affairs with his cellular phone, cigar in mouth, flanked by at least two beautiful damsels, calling the plays from a Caribbean beach. Not Seymour and Norty! They mind the store, they demand, and closely monitor, class performance. Court tennis may be regarded as a metaphor for the Knoxes. Have the athletic skills, yes; reach the top, yes; but do not be content with ordinary victories; stretch the mind and the person in the pursuit of excellence. . . . Just as they could have been content with an elite player's skills, but wanted to achieve more, they could have been content with prestige and position—their custodianship of contributions like the Albright-Knox Gallery would have been sufficient for many. But Norty and Seymour wanted to make a *difference* in their community, to be leaders in their own right, to bring something of major value to the quality of life in Western New York, and they have certainly done so with the Sabres.

Chapter 11

GOIN' DAFT
WITH THE DRAFT

In chapter 7, I described Branch Rickey's vision, in 1960, of an outlaw league that would recruit, train, and allocate baseball's rookies. No vicious competition for teenagers, no secret sign-ups, no hiding talents, no under-the-table contracts. His solution was simple: All new players would be assigned to the Western Carolina League. There, in a small-town, no-pressure environment, with no pressure from the national sports pages, the managers could observe and judge the talent. The losers in the previous season would get first crack in some defined order, but the expense of the proliferated scouting system would be minimized. Emerging from the "sponsorship" era—when each of the six teams had searched for and signed its own rookies (sometimes with the advantage of territorial exclusivity)—the first NHL expansion in 1967 brought with it the first "amateur" draft. There was some temporary vestige of the old sponsorship system: until 1969 Montreal had the exclusive right to draft the first two French Canadian sons of French Canadian fathers. The Sabres would not have been able to acquire Gilbert Perreault but for the expiration of the Canadiens' prerogative prior to the 1970 draft. The intent was to give every club an equal crack, but there were holes: college players, European stars, Scandinavian, Czech, and Russian candidates, all emerging from different environments, had to be fit into the system. In the first decade after the league reached twelve teams, the main source of player supply was the Canadian junior leagues; and to protect the vitality of those leagues and that system, the rules precluded drafting a player until the year in which he reached age twenty. The sudden change in the market—there were twelve major-league clubs in 1967, fourteen in 1970, sixteen in 1972, eighteen in 1974, then (following the WHA merger in 1979) twenty-one competing for up-and-coming talent—meant more GMs, more player personnel directors, more scouts. The WHA forced the NHL to reduce its draft age to eighteen, producing more, if not better, targets for the scouting system. The growing international interest in the game and the willingness of the NHL owners to pay increasingly high salaries encouraged the European federations, especially the Swedes, to loosen the migration restrictions on their players. Ultimately, even the Czechs and the Russians, under "treaties" with the NHL, entered the market as suppliers of talent. This meant that it wasn't enough to sit in Toronto or Vancouver or Montreal and observe the juniors as they came to town. A careful club had to have an eastern scout, a western scout, a junior scout, a college scout, a European scout, and a representative who could get into—and out of—the Soviet Union.

The scouting numbers in club budgets began to swell. Two creative measures to save this growing expense were put in place. First, the Central Hockey League, a copycat of Rickey's Western Carolina League–wide training camp, was to be solely a development league, with modest salaries and limited promotion; and second, the NHL established Central Scouting, a bureau financed by the NHL clubs, either directly or as an allocation of the regular dues. The intent was that Central Scouting would investigate, scout, rate, and publish a list of the best players entering the draft. The information provided by Central Scouting, it was urged, would save each club a large percentage of the $300,000 to $400,000 or more consumed in its scouting department. It would also provide fairness: each club would start with the same amount and type of information about each player.

What does that miasma of organization, gossip, and judgment produce? It's obviously of great importance to teams, but also to the individual rookies—and their agents. Agents quickly attached themselves to the most likely and able prospects, to the point where the "market" in a new player's services began to be governed by his place in the draft. And from the interest of the owner and his tax adviser or accountant, the value of this group of assets—the entry draft choices—had a telling impact on the value of the team to a new purchaser and what he would pay for it.[1] In 1994, at the request of the team, I made a study of the San Jose Sharks' draft picks. I believe a study of this sort had never been done before—valuing the picks at their *statistical* probability of success. This is what I found, after examining Central Scouting's records to see how the players chosen in the entry draft between the years 1980 and 1987 could be counted as *successful*, based on their performance in the subsequent years. In defining "success," I rejected Central Scouting's concept that one game in one season in the NHL was enough; I wanted to focus on more important players who hung in there longer—those who truly became NHL veterans. So I came up with a definition of success as a rookie who played in not fewer than one hundred games within three seasons of being drafted. This is what I found:

OVERVIEW OF VALUE PLAYER ASSETS

For similar reasons, in analyzing the relative values and costs of players obtained by the Sharks in the various drafts, League statistics and general manager practice indicate that (i) much greater, even disproportionate, weight is given to picks in the early rounds (I and II); (ii) especially high picks (1 through 5) in those rounds. A measure of probability of success in the NHL, as related to the round in the Entry Draft in which the player was chosen is shown in the table below. For the years 1980 through 1987, NHL Central Scouting collected data listing all players in each of those Entry Drafts who had played at least one NHL game. I then analyzed to the NHL Central Scouting data, defining "success" for an Entry Draft pick as playing in no less than 100 NHL games within three seasons of the date of draft. On this basis, if we treat a first-round pick as having the relative value of 1, a second-round pick, for example, would have the relative probability of success and the relative value of .419, a sixth-round pick of .0769.

This analysis also indicated that the relative probability of success is disproportionately greater for the first five picks in the first round; is significant in the second round, but less than half of a first-round pick; and that after the fifth round, distinctions as to the pick's likelihood of success are problematical. This is consistent with the more intuitive views and practices of NHL general managers in drafting and trading.

A similar valuation approach—weighting the first *two* rounds heavily, and assigning much greater value to the first five picks—was adopted in a proposed agreement between the NHL and the Russian Hockey Federation of 1993. Hence, I made the judgment that this valuation approach should be applied to players chosen by the Sharks in the Expansion Draft, as well as the Entry Draft, and to the players selected by the Sharks in the Inter-Club Draft, except that in the Inter-Club Draft the weighting was applied to the early picks within the three categories (forwards, defensemen, and goaltenders).[2]

DRAFT PICKS

Ratios of Probability of "Success"
in NHL for Rounds Picked

Round	1980–1985%
Forwards and Defensemen:	
I	1.000
II	.419
III	.334
IV	.227
V	.120
VI	.0769
Goaltender (first round only)	.278

Ratios of probability of "success" in NHL based on round pick in Entry Draft.

The ratios are based upon data in NHL study of 1980–1985 Entry Drafts. ROS [the author] defined "success" as not less than 100 NHL games played within 3 years of draft.

It was clear that, to some extent, the tradesmen—the general managers—were working with an illusion: except for the first round, the chances that a draft pick would become a veteran were less than 40 percent, and after the fifth round it was just a roll of the dice.

Of course these dry statistics, as meaningful as they are, mean little to a young man seeking the NHL stage. For him, the word that he is being chosen by an NHL team is a life event in itself. His place in the draft may mark him forever, especially if he's a first-round pick. But even the lesser lights are given this boost to their careers. Punch Imlach asked me to call a player the Sabres had chosen in the fifth round. We couldn't find him in the building. He had no agent, thought he had only a faint hope of selection, and didn't have the money to make the trip to Montreal. When I gave him the news, I felt like Moses bringing him the promised land. I was sure he'd have an orgasm on the phone!

My friend John Anderson, Punch Imlach's assistant GM with the Sabres, retired in 2005 after many years as an official of the league's Central Scouting Department based in Toronto. He was a staunch defender and supporter of the program. In its early days under league president Clarence Campbell, he pointed out, it was not a competitive tool for the clubs; he used it to help the league as a whole. He had no compunction about calling a team to tell it whom to draft. John believes my analysis—the probability that a given rookie would become an NHL "regular"—would no longer be as accurate because of thirty teams compared to twenty-one in the 1980s, the influx of European players, and so forth. But Central Scouting is nevertheless a valuable asset. It has turned up a number of quality players regarded by the traditional GMs as late-round picks, for example, Craig Ramsay, Bill Hajt, and Peter McNab.

I asked John if Central Scouting performed its original conceived function of reducing the teams' budgets. "No," John answered. "Everybody kept the same number of scouts; we didn't save you a penny!"

Chapter 12

THE ROUND BALL AND THE SQUARE SHOOTER

I n the summer of 1969, shortly after we got the grant from the NHL and word that the city would fund the necessary increase in the capacity of the Aud, I received a call from Lou Jacobs's son, Jerry, asking for a breakfast meeting. It was the first of numerous key talks we had over the years—Jerry always seemed to be there for me, to help on key strategic judgments that affected the Sabres or the league. Jerry always had the facts—special insights or development that hadn't been articulated elsewhere. It seemed our success in getting the Sabres franchise had come to the attention of the NBA. There were moneyed people interested in investing in a Buffalo basketball team. Were we willing to accept one in the Aud? Were our people interested in making such an investment?

I was tempted—the thought of a second major-league tenant to share the cost of operating and the burden of the city rent was intriguing. But it could be a mixed blessing; sharing expenses might well be accompanied by a demand for sharing the revenue. We were so new at the business. I had trepidations about the implications. We needed maximum attention— from the city, from the sports fans, and from the media. Yet we could not be seen as blocking an NBA entry.

Financing the increase in the seating capacity of the Aud mandated by the league had not been easy. As part of our preparation for the franchise competition, we had produced an engineering survey that demonstrated

131

that the increase was physically possible. Mayor Frank Sedita and Common Council president Chet Gorski had given their enthusiastic assurances, but it soon became apparent that their enthusiasm would not be backed by municipal appropriations: the cost was ours. In a day of naïveté—and before the threat to move gambit became popular—we quickly assented. The city would advance the money, but the Sabres would amortize the cost through an increase in the rent. Dave Forman and I projected that the estimated $6 million price tag could be paid off over six years; the additional five thousand seats would produce enough additional revenue, we hoped, to pay the additional rent.

We duly and faithfully negotiated a new lease and agreement to cover the financing, with a condition that if the bids for the new seats came in at more than $6.2 million, either party could cancel the deal. We had confidence in the contractor, a public-spirited outfit that had helped to convert the Studio Arena's purchase of the city's leading nightclub, the Town Casino, into a thrust theater in forty days and forty nights. The plan was novel: lift the roof, pour the cement base for the new seats into the circular opening, construct the new seats, then lower the roof and close off the opening. It was imaginative and risky, but its possibility had enabled us to triumph over Baltimore and Cleveland, whose structures would not permit the increase and who could only qualify with entirely new buildings.

The day came for opening the bids. Seymour and I attended, excited and confident. When the contractor announced the low bid, it turned out to be $9.2 million—more than 50 percent above the estimate! My stomach caved, and Seymour and I turned absolutely green. But we recovered and consulted our colleagues, the mayor, the council president, and the league. In the blush of franchise ownership and the excitement in the city, there seemed to be no alternative except to increase the rent so as to amortize the increase. We put a sharper pencil to the cost estimate, eliminated some items, quickly reduced the cost to $8.2 million, and agreed with the city on a corresponding further increase in the appropriation and the rent we would have to pay.

The actual raising of the roof was a spectacular success. It was nearly unbelievable that this massive object could be lifted with such precision and care. There were measuring devices or meters to measure the levels of the roof at various points as it was raised and lowered. We walked round the Aud, fascinated by the process. It was exciting, but we worried that our expectations were too great, that the cost was too much.

It was in this atmosphere that I considered Jerry's news that an NBA franchise was available. I was sure that Seymour and Norty Knox would have little interest in investing in a basketball team. As they spoke emphatically when, in a later year, the Braves were up for grabs, they knew hockey, loved it, and had played it; they had no interest in the NBA. They regarded professional basketball as a sport dominated by vulgar types, sometimes involved in fistfights in the ownership rooms. It was a frequently heard, somewhat snide jape that NHL governors' events were socially positive, but the "thing to do" in the NBA was *not* to go to the governors' meetings. While the NBA ultimately became, under the first-rate stewardship of David Stern, a very successful league financially, in the early 1970s it was still a marginal, worrisome investment.

So I knew the Knoxes would not consent to a purchase of the NBA team by our group. This meant we'd have a competing major tenant not under our control grasping for concessions, advertising, parking, and preference on dates. NHL president Clarence Campbell was doubtful, even negative on an NBA partnership, commenting that NBA audiences would have entirely different demographics—forcing lower prices for tickets and concessions. However, as to dates, he was adamant: we must provide in the lease for absolute, permanent priority for the hockey club.

I believe I had none of these hang-ups. I had enjoyed playing basketball and being part of the intense and raucous fans in high school and the popular Little Three games between Canisius, Niagara, and St. Bonaventure in college. In the Oakland year, we had seen a popular and talented hockey player named Willie O'Ree, and I had visions of increasing the black participation on the ice and in the stands as high school and college hockey expanded in the new markets. But I made the decision to ask that they delay the NBA entry. I told Jerry Jacobs, "Give us some time to settle in." We had made major financial commitments to the league and the city, and our financial soundness came first. We needed to bind in the negotiations with the city on concessions and arena advertising, make our date priorities definite, try to get the city to put the parking lots under our control, and, most important, give us first crack at the sports fans and their discretionary spending, to lock in as many season tickets as we could before there was another major-league franchise competing for the Buffalo sports dollar. Jerry asked how much time we would need for this. He had concerns, as did I, that we would be painted as blocking basketball for Buffalo. After a thorough discussion, my "final answer" was at least a year. As it turned out, we didn't get the full year, but we got a head start.

As matters developed, that talk with Jerry was a great move. We got the good word from the NHL in the spring of 1969, and it took a whole year to get out of Oakland, move ahead with the raising of the roof, renegotiate the lease, get Common Council approval, and construct our advertising and TV revenue. I negotiated our first-ever TV deal with Larry Pollock at Channel 7. It was new ground for both of us, and it would certainly have been more difficult with another major-league team bidding for broadcast time and fees. We did pretty well on concessions, reaching agreement with Sportservice and the city: the "normal" commission for hockey events of 30 percent, plus—and this would exacerbate the basketball problem—a lesser percentage on concession, novelty, and advertising for *nonhockey events*. Our theory was that, as the principal tenant in the building, with forty-five or more dates, we would create traffic for all events and deserved compensation for increasing the value of the Aud as a whole. In general, the lease called for splitting the concession compensation payable by the concessionaire between the city and the Sabres. The raising of the roof and the construction of the five thousand additional seats could not take place until the hockey season was over, in the good weather of late spring and summer in 1971.

I tried hard, but I could not convince Mayor Sedita to do anything about parking. There was adequate parking in the numerous small lots around the periphery of the Aud, but the city had no legal rights in the parking lot revenues generated by Aud events. The lots were all owned by individuals or companies, many of whom contributed to the mayor's campaigns or to those of members of the Common Council. I tried to persuade Mayor Sedita and his counsel, Tony Manguso, that we would all be better off if the lots were appropriated and owned by the city—there could then be standard rates adjusted for the coming of a major-league hockey team under the city's or our control—but the city officials would have none of this, and we had neither the budget nor the room to build a ramp. Fortunately, the year's delay in installing the five thousand new seats worked well for us. To everyone's delight, the shortage of seats produced a major marketing bonus: season tickets became a necessity. Western New York fans moved quickly to season purchases to secure good locations, and the Canadian fans, used to cherry-picking games in a leisurely fashion, were compelled to buy season tickets for the current and *next* seasons to protect their locations and their Montreal and Toronto dates. The initial seat shortage and the consequent season ticket compulsion led, when the Sabres began to show a real competitive quality under Punch Imlach—going to the playoffs in the third year, the Finals in the fifth—to fifteen consecutive sold-out seasons.

The NBA team, named the Buffalo Braves, came on the horizon in the summer of 1970. We had pretty well settled in, preparing like mad for our first season in the Aud, when I received a call from Carl Scheer, a representative of Neuberger-Loeb, the investment bankers who had bought the NBA team. They were considering establishing a franchise in Buffalo but were somewhat concerned about the concession and advertising situation in the building. The Sabres seemed to have the lion's share locked up. NBA teams, he asserted, customarily shared those building revenues equally with the hockey teams. Would we be interested in working out such an arrangement? We were well-known citizens of the Buffalo community, and he was sure we did not wish to be perceived as blocking an NBA franchise for Buffalo. Forewarned and prepared, I responded firmly and courteously. I thought that we would welcome the Braves entry into the market and the arena, but we would not pay for that entry. We had worked long and hard to get the NHL for Buffalo—five years—and with a substantial investment in the franchise and major commitments in the lease, we would need all the revenue we could produce—and we would not, could not, hand over any of those dollars to basketball. I pointed out that, contrary to the basketball view, the NHL data showed that in every market in which both leagues operated, the NHL team produced the larger gate and the larger revenue. We expected and intended to be the dominant revenue producer in the Aud, and we were entitled to the advantages we had achieved. (In fact, while the Sabres gate rapidly reached the sellout level of more than fifteen thousand, the Braves attendance never got beyond eight thousand.)

I pointed out that the city of Buffalo had reserved for itself a substantial share of the concessions and advertising, and we would have no objection to the Braves hitting on the city to participate in or acquire the city's share of those revenues. The Braves' representative was, I am sure, somewhat shocked at the emotional content of my response, but he got the message. "Well," he said, "There's no harm in asking!"

I don't know how much this interlude contributed to subsequent events; the concession and advertising revenue (usually about 10 percent of total revenue for a club) should not have been important enough to control a decision as to whether or not to plant an NBA team in the Aud. There were other buildings, other venues, but the city ultimately did what I had suggested, agreeing to carve out a piece of its share of the in-house dollars for the Braves. In September 1970 word came that the investment banking house had sold the NBA club to Paul Snyder, a Buffalo businessman of some prominence.

Paul Snyder was an intelligent, hardworking, successful businessman, and had been a college athlete at the University at Buffalo—but he was not the equivalent to Seymour and Norty Knox. Wealth and social position had been largely inherited by the Knoxes; to Paul Snyder, it came tough. He was a fighter, not a lover; a competitor, not a problem solver; and the political and economic roadblocks in the sports world—superficially simple—proved tough for him to handle. The Knoxes could and did treat the Sabres as an institution invested with public responsibility, for the most part. We had turned down a Los Angeles, a Cleveland, and a St. Louis franchise. We wanted the Sabres for the Buffalo community. Tax and business considerations were secondary, except as they were essential to survival. For Paul Snyder—not so. He had created a very successful local company, Freezer Queen Foods, and survived difficult financing negotiations to build the Buffalo Hyatt Regency, but he never seemed comfortable with the Braves.

It wasn't long after the announcement of the sale that we began to receive calls from Snyder's organization. Paul finally worked out agreements that gave him part of the city's share of concessions and advertising, but he could never stomach the fact that the Braves percentage was less than ours. He would protest to the mayor, the Common Council, the county legislature, the press. Every difference became an issue. Paul bought the team for about $3.7 million in October 1970; less than four years later he was already flirting with the sale of the franchise and its possible move to another city.

The press recorded Snyder's frequent bouts with the sports and political world. We had ceded Saturday nights to Canisius and the Little Three, opting not to disturb that relationship. Paul felt it necessary to move in on that date reservation, generating a dispute with the popular local college. Switching dates to accommodate the conflicting demands of the two leagues should have been a no-brainer. Yet Paul ended up in a dispute with our usually genial general manager, Punch Imlach. As Steve Weller reported in the *Buffalo News*:

> Writing clear-headed, hard-hitting, straight from the shoulder, up-to-the-minute evaluations of the Buffalo Braves lease problems in Memorial Auditorium is tough because there are so many days in the week. Take care of Wednesday and all of a sudden Saturday becomes a headache. Iron out Tuesday and before you know it Monday afternoon rears its ugly head. And every time a new day starts causing trouble Paul Snyder decides to sell his basketball franchise. . . . When the Sabres gave up their claim to some dates Snyder wanted, most of the attention was paid to Wednesday. Which indicated Saturday was not all that important or that there was evidence Canisius College, which had first call on that day, would not be difficult to deal with. . . .

Everybody agreed a lease would be signed as soon as a Kelly girl showed up to type it. Life as the owner of a National Basketball Association franchise became fun-filled again and talk of selling the Braves to out-of-town interests died out. Briefly.

> Now we learn that Saturday remains a headache. Canisius has not agreed to fold up its Aud basketball program, that seven, count 'em, out-of-town groups want to buy the Braves and Snyder, once again fatigued, is eager to sell. . . . The Braves are an asset. I'd hate to see them leave. But it's tough getting up emotionally every time their owner cries out. . . . Who's to know if Snyder is serious? Maybe we've reached the point where the question should be—who's to care?[1]

The Braves produced a respectable team, made the playoffs three of the first four years, had a winning record and an authentic star in Bob McAdoo, but the fans did not gobble up the season tickets—the goal of five thousand was never met, and some losses were incurred. The press quoted Paul Snyder as claiming an aggregate loss as of 1976 for the six years of ownership. We had found out in Oakland that a bleeding sports franchise is no fun. But for a new business, get-going losses were not unexpected. It is unfortunate, but understandable, that Snyder did not foresee the financial successes of the David Stern era—after all, our group had made the same mistake with a premature sale of Transcontinent Television. But I suspect Paul Snyder's decision to sell—and move—the Braves did not arise because of the get-going losses. It starts with the fact that Snyder had only a marginal commitment to the sport and to the city, and ends with tax and other considerations. His repeated criticism of the Sabres suggests that he could not stand being second banana. I felt that if he spent as much time and resources promoting the Braves as he did lashing out like Don Quixote at the Sabres' agreements and dominance, he might have maintained a stable franchise that could have survived to reap the Stern rewards.

As the point man on the Sabres lease, television, league, and other negotiations, I received the brunt of the Snyder flack. Paul was not subtle. "Swados," he told me once, "you screwed me!" I would protest, in vain, that the Sabres agreements had been put in place well before he came on the scene and were fully justified. But the response was only a gentle smirk. Contact was essential—both franchises were living in the same building— and I tried to smooth the way. I was president of the local regional theater and invited Paul and his wife to our annual VIP dinner and special performance of a great show then playing. Paul accepted with alacrity and seeming enthusiasm—then never showed up. No notice, no call, no apology—just no show.

Strangely, there seemed to be some respect there, notwithstanding the flack. One day, out of the blue, Paul called and asked me to come out to his Freezer Queen offices. He was having some problems with his current lawyers. I spent the day there, he introduced me to his top executives, gave me two files to study, and asked my opinion. At the end of the day, he called me into his office, gave me two more files, and announced—in the presence of one of his minions—"This is Bob Swados, our new counsel. . . . I'll call you Monday, Bob." I was not surprised when the call never came: no apology, no communication whatsoever. So I returned to my Sabres and other legal pursuits, relieved of any conflict, busier than I needed to be, and wondering about the interpersonal relationships of this man in the sports business, where the ability to deal with a broad range of people—talent, players, media, and fans—is so important.

There is a strange dichotomy in sports ownership. The lure is the lure of Caesar: the speech from the Coliseum, the adulation of the mob. Yet the temptation to expose oneself to the constant pressures of the media can be a trap. Seymour Knox understood this; except in major crises, he kept himself in the background, delegating the confrontations to others. He had Dave Forman on business matters, the GM on players, the PR person on public relations, and me as a sort of utility infielder and outfielder on the league and everything else. We always tried to run our response through our director of communications. That provided management with time to think through what to say, who would say it, and whom to say it to. And that shielded Seymour and Norty, for the most part, from the daily pressures of the press and the tube, and saved their judgment for serious appeals. Early on, Bill Wirtz, principal owner of the Chicago Blackhawks and chairman of the league, advised me: "Bob, stop trying to get the fans to love the owners. . . . They want to *hate* the owners!"

I didn't entirely agree with Bill in our case—the Knoxes and our group had a semiheroic credit in the community that needed to be maintained. But I certainly agreed that the owners should not be out front daily or weekly, justifying a trade, arguing a salary, explaining a lease, protesting a penalty. The practice in professional sports is not uniform. Some owners, like Ed Snider of the Philadelphia Flyers, seem ready at any time to launch themselves into the fray, especially if a major asset is involved; Snider seems to like dealing with the press, and he has a blunt and effective style. Paul Snyder seemed unable or unwilling to delegate the PR matters and didn't seem to enjoy the interplay with the media, and the result was an appearance of discomfort and discontent. The Braves were doing well enough in the league and at the box office, though profits had not yet appeared, but in 1975—five years after the team came to Buffalo—Snyder had still not signed a long-term lease for the Aud, and rumors began that he might give up and sell—or move.

The year 1976 was critical. The Chamber of Commerce's attempt to boost season tickets for the coming season to the five thousand target was getting nowhere, average attendance had declined from twelve thousand to eight thousand, and Snyder's search for a local group to buy the team had been unsuccessful. In an unusually frank but pitiable press conference on June 15, 1976, Paul announced he was getting out of professional sports and was selling the team to Diplomat Hotel owner Irving Cowan, for relocation to Hollywood, Florida. He stated that he would recoup his $3 million loss—a price of $6 million, plus assumption of player obligations for another $2 million, was mentioned. Paul pointed to the drop in attendance, the heavy discounting of tickets, and so on. But "family considerations"—the constant pressure from the fans, the occasional boos—factored strongly in his decision.

Paul observed that the last couple of years have been very difficult experience for myself and my family. "It's been terrible. . . . I think I'm more affected by the problems I've had with the press and the media during the past year, maybe, than the bad way that the money part of the team has gone."[2]

The tangible threat of desertion to Florida may have been launched as a bargaining chip, an attempt to induce a better lease from the city and financial support—or purchase—from investors in the Buffalo community. (Sabres controller Bob Pickel and I had attempted to generate interest in our group, but the Knoxes were opposed, and Paul Snyder's efforts to expand local investment got nowhere.) Unfortunately, the venue chosen for the threat—the Sportatorium in Hollywood, Florida—was neither practical nor plausible. I had personally examined the site in 1972 as a possible venue for our minor-league hockey team. I remember vividly flying to Florida, being greeted courteously by pleasant gentlemen, driving for nearly an hour in the height of Florida summer heat, and arriving at a rectangle of impressive Roman columns forming the exterior of a building. The structure was a refurbished hangar. It was hot, and there seemed to be no air-conditioning.

"This is hockey we're talking about," I said. "How do we keep the ice from melting?"

"No problem," my host responded, directing my gaze to the roof. "You see, there's a space between the columns and the roof; the breezes are strong here, and we don't need air-conditioning!" I thanked my hosts, got back on the airplane, and duly filed my report—"Forget it!"

I don't know whether the space between the columns and the roof was ever filled—the city of Miami later built an arena for the NBA expansion Heat—but in the state of Snyder's ambivalence, the Hollywood site, which also had serious road access problems, was hardly appealing enough to drive him to move if there was a reasonable alternative. Paul's Florida adventure at least stirred up the animals. When Paul announced that he was moving the club to the Hollywood site because of the failure to sell the five thousand season tickets he had had set as the goal, the city of Buffalo, alleging breach of an agreement reached (but not signed) the previous year to sign a lease for fifteen years, sued in federal court for antitrust damages of $48 million, in state court for another $10 million, and obtained a show cause order or preliminary injunction preventing the sale and move. The federal suit named the NBA as a monopolist-defendant. In the face of the lawsuits, Snyder walked away from the Florida deal and signed what purported to be a fifteen-year lease, at rent similar to that of the Sabres. But the lease contained an escape clause: Snyder could terminate the lease in any year after a season in which the season ticket goal was not met. Irving Cowan, the owner of the Diplomat Hotel who was sponsoring the Hollywood move, threatened suit as well, but he ultimately gave up.

So the 1976–77 season began on a more hopeful note. But a renewed Chamber of Commerce initiative to achieve the season ticket requirement did not succeed, and Paul soon resumed his search for a buyer.

I do not know which of his seasons—and reasons—of discontent ultimately impelled Paul to sell. But one factor must have been important: the amortization of his player contracts had run out—*his income tax shelter had expired*. Unhappy with his status in the Aud, disappointed in the response of the fans, unable to meet his five-thousand season ticket goal, and no longer able to shelter his other income with noncash depreciation and amortization deductions from the Braves, Paul and his counsel engineered the Great Tax Escape.

There was a time when the purchase of a professional sports franchise was a tax bonanza. It worked like this: Suppose you bought an expansion team in the NHL for $3.1 million, paying $100,000 to the league for a fee and $3 million to the existing clubs for players acquired from those clubs in an expansion draft. Your tax adviser would set up the transaction on your books by allocating $100,000 to the franchise fee or goodwill and $3 million as the cost of the contracts or rights to the players you acquired in the expansion draft. Say the average playing life of a player is five years and your income tax bracket is 50 percent. You write off the player contracts at the rate of $600,000 per year, and this is a deduction against the salary or income from your nonhockey business, if, as may happen, the hockey club is not making money and can't use the deduction. At the end of the five years, you still own the franchise and the players, but the aggregate deductions for the amortization of the original player contracts have reduced your taxes by 50 percent of $3 million, or $1.5 million—so the team at that point has a net cost to you of $1.6 million.

Now you've had your flirtation with the sport, and you find a buyer who'll purchase at $3.1 million—your original purchase price. Your net cost or tax basis is $1.6 million, so you have a taxable profit of $1.5 million. Under the old tax regime, you'd treat that profit as capital gain, taxable at the lower rate for state and federal purposes, and your buyer would write up the purchased assets to $3.1 million and start his own amortization deductions all over again. There was an additional gimmick available: accelerated depreciation—instead of writing the player contracts off equally over five years (20 percent per year), you could, for example, deduct 40 percent the first year, 30 percent the second, 20 percent the third, and so on, loading the deductions in the earlier years and increasing the tax benefits in those years accordingly. The tax benefits made the purchase of a sports franchise more attractive and expanded the market for potential owners.

This bonanza obviously attracted its critics, but the impetus for reform came from a most unlikely, nonlogical source—the NBA Players' Association. When the NBA and ABA sought to merge, the players' association, headed by Bill Bradley, attacked the merger and the owners before the congressional committees, characterizing their tax schemes as immoral and unconscionable, and calling for elimination or severe cutbacks in the tax benefits. It was curious: here was an employees' union sponsoring measures that would *reduce* the dollars available to pay their salaries and *reduce* the market for their services. It was a function of the "owners as ogres" syndrome that the players unions in the other three sports have promoted as a means of polarizing issues and maintaining their control.

The tax benefits became a continuing source of trouble for the industry. I participated with Washington counsel in representing the NHL, in a joint effort with the other sports leagues, before Congress in the negotiation of the Tax Reform Acts of 1976, and we were constantly checked in our own end on the deductibility of tickets, skyboxes, amortization of player contracts, allocation of goodwill, and conversion of ordinary income to capital gain—all of which could be justifiably traced in part to the malice and vigor of Bradley's 1976 attack.

As Paul Snyder approached his decision on a sale of the Braves, he was confronted with the following reform developments that affected his plans:

1. If he sold his players, then liquidated the company, he would have to "recapture"—add back to income—all the amortization he had taken as deductions over the years of his ownership.
2. The recapture amount would be taxed as ordinary income, not capital gain.
3. If he distributed the cash he received for the players while he still controlled the company, it would be taxed as a dividend, as ordinary income, to him personally.
4. If he tried to sell the stock in the company that owned the Braves, the purchaser would be faced with the same tax problem, which could discourage the purchasers or reduce the price.
5. Under the new reform legislation, the purchaser could not write up the player contract assets again—he was stuck with the seller's own tax basis.
6. In the courts, the IRS was attacking the allocation of the purchase cost to player contracts and the deductibility of the amortization or write-off of player contracts. The new legislation set a cap of 50 percent on the amount of the purchase price of a professional sports franchise that could be allocated to player contracts.[3]

Meantime, with the collapse of the Florida initiative and the failure of Western New York investors to come forward, the Braves had to turn to out-of-town potentials—most of whom had but a marginal, temporary interest in Buffalo. As the events appeared in the press, the saga developed as follows. On November 5, 1976, Snyder persuaded John Y. Brown, former owner of the defunct ABA Kentucky Colonels—a franchise that had failed to make the "cut" in the merger of the two leagues—to make a partial investment in the Braves. (Brown's fortune was largely produced by Kentucky Fried Chicken.) The partial buy was 50 percent, though there was some talk that Brown had an option to buy 100 percent. Key players were sold or traded. Four months later, on March 25, 1977, Brown bought the remaining 50 percent of the Braves. Brown operated the team in Buffalo for a season, then announced, on June 25,1978, after a disappointing gate with a weakened roster, that "Buffalo is no fun," and proceeded to negotiate a double trade with the owner of the Boston Celtics. The Braves *franchise*—it's not clear with whose players—ended up in San Diego. Or was it Boston, and the Boston franchise became San Diego?

This is how a tax guru from Mars would imagine what actually happened: It was all part of one creative, inventive plan. Brown bought from Snyder 50 percent of the stock in the Braves. This meant Snyder was no longer "in control." The Braves sold the star, Bob McAdoo, and the other key players acquired in the amateur drafts for cash. There was no recapture tax on these players—they were not acquired in the expansion draft, and no depreciation or amortization was deducted on them (except possibly signing bonuses), so the cash received for them did not have to be added back to income. Four months later, in March 1977—a different tax year, so the transactions could not easily be tied together—the Braves company, using the cash generated by the sale of amateur draft or free agent players, redeemed the remaining stock in the Braves held by Snyder, and Snyder, free of the dividend and recapture taints, got his capital gain. Now Brown owned 100 percent of the company that owned the Braves, which still held the contracts of the remaining players, some of which were subject to recapture. But he didn't trade or sell those contracts. He traded the *franchise with its players* for Boston's franchise in an exchange of like kind for like kind— nontaxable under the Internal Revenue Code. Adjustments were made as to debts and player obligations, so the economic bargain made sense. Brown got an NBA franchise in Boston, a city he wanted; Snyder departed with a minimum tax cost; the Boston owner produced his trade, was relieved of his Boston player obligations without a tax consequence, and ended up in San Diego, near his desert home; and Buffalo lost its NBA basketball team.

It was really too bad. I didn't miss the Braves much, personally. Except for that episode in the sixties when Lou Jacobs dispatched me to evaluate the Cincinnati Royals, my contact with the game had been limited, and I still expect a ref to blow a whistle on a double dribble or a flagrant walk— but he doesn't. The changes wrought by the Stern era—with the benefit of Michael Jordan—have so far been marvelously successful. I felt bad for the community; basketball deserved a major role here. Now, across the lake, we have the Toronto Raptors, and Buffalo and the NBA may have missed their marriage.

Chapter 13

MARTIN AND MAYHEM

R ick Martin, left wing on the French Connection and first-string all-
star in 1974 and 1975, saw his career abruptly end when damage to
his knee shut down his performance. (Scotty Bowman traded Rick to Los
Angeles in March of 1981.) To Sabres management, the cause was arthritic
inflammation, aggravated at least as much by Rick's passion for golf as by
the demands of his hockey profession. But to Rick, the career-ending
damage was, he felt, produced by pressure from Bowman to play when he
had not fully recovered from a game injury to the knee. It was not entirely
clear that the team orthopedist, Peter Casagrande, had fully cleared Rick to
play. The ambiguity was typically created by the coach's attitude. Punch
Imlach once lectured me: "The doc can tell me what the condition is, but
not whether he's ready to go on the ice; I decide that!" Rick was no malin-
gerer and Scotty was too good a coach to endanger his star. But here was
Rick, attuned, if not permanently, to the high levels of salary in the NHL,
suddenly faced with an end to the life of a star, and it was natural to reach
for some way to perpetuate the income his knee could no longer provide
him. That reach produced one of the major victories of my career and saved
the Sabres a multimillion-dollar loss.

When Rick consulted his lawyer, he was confronted with trouble, big
time. If he claimed that the knee was an injury incurred on the ice, as an
employee he would be limited to workers' compensation. If he claimed

Rick Martin—All-Star and litigator. Copyright © Bill Wippert.

salary under his standard player's contract, if the injury did occur or arise from his play for the Sabres, the club was required to pay Rick's salary through the end of his contract (unlike NFL contracts, which at the time effectively limited liability to one year's compensation). The problem was Rick's salary under the contract continued when he was traded to the Kings, but it had only a few months to go, and the amount payable under a compensation claim was substantially less than even the truncated salary under the contract.

It wouldn't be enough to claim that Scotty or the team doctor had been negligent in getting Rick to play while not fully recovered. A claim against the employer (or a coemployee) for negligence (even gross negligence) is barred by the workers' compensation law, and the employee's claim is restricted to the low-level dollars fixed in the "comp" award. Research by Rick's counsel indicated that he would have to show that Bowman *intentionally* made Rick play while still injured, if he wanted the Sabres to pay one cent more than his remaining salary or the comp award. What about suing the doctor? Here, too, the compensation law intervened: if Casagrande were also an *employee* of the Sabres, Rick's recovery would be limited to the compensation award.

So how could he circumvent these restrictions? Sue the Sabres for intentional injury; sue the doctor for gross negligence in treatment and in permitting Martin to play; and seek to classify Casagrande as an independent contractor physician, who would not have the benefit of the compensation limit. The doctor would respond with his malpractice policy and the Sabres could respond with their general liability insurance. Right? Wrong! Rick demanded more than twice the doctor's coverage. Of greater threat, Karen Mathews, one of my close associates at the Cohen Swados firm, found a gaping hole in the Sabres' insurance contract. It turned out that after the team's original insurance structure was set, insurance agent Chuck Rice, a friend of Paul Schoellkopf from the Niagara Falls days, had received an endorsement that specifically excluded the kind of claim presented by Rick. The endorsement was never disclosed to me or vetted by other counsel, and it is unclear whether the agent failed to recognize its significance or was afraid to report it for fear of losing the premium or the account. A claim of malpractice against the carrier or the agent would seem to have been a no-brainer—the endorsement made the policy largely useless in this important area—but, doubtless because of the relationship and, ultimately, the successful defense, the claim was never pursued, even for the substantial expense incurred.

There were no funds, even in those halcyon days of the perpetual sellout, to pay a multimillion-dollar judgment. Rick had been a friend, a first-class Sabres player, and a supporter of the franchise. The owners had been fair and generous in salary and bonuses. When Rick had been seduced by the dishonest agent he had taken on without our advice or consent, he called me for help, with the cry, "Bob, you guys paid me a lot of money— *where is it?*" As one would expect, neither friendship nor past good faith discouraged Rick, now at the end of his hockey career, from commencing suit.

Our investigation of the facts was not comforting. Rick had returned to play a short time after the knee injury, and Scotty Bowman was certainly a tough taskmaster, not above viewing players, or at least some players, as malingerers—or at least in their later years as prone to take the extra day, week, or month when things were not going well on the ice. We were convinced that, as Casagrande believed, the ultimate injury to the knee was caused by arthritic deterioration, helped no doubt by hockey and golf over the years of Rick's athletic activity, but not by premature play following the injury. Nothing disclosed in the depositions or in our independent talks with the coach indicated to us that Scotty had "intentionally" put him back on the ice too soon. But there was enough to scare me. Scotty, in the pattern of some successful coaches, might have been too tough at times. It was conceivable that he, not fully sold on the team doctor, might have ignored or denigrated his advice. The line between gross negligence and intention might be clear enough to a sitting judge, but this would be jury judgment. All I could see was the destitute star against the rich Knoxes—no matter that it was the corporate club that would be the defendant. The jury would pay little attention to legal distinctions, and it would be a case of popular player against ogre owner. A major defeat was highly probable, and with insurance coverage in serious doubt, I could see us faced with raising substantial funds with a mediocre team and a financial statement that few self-respecting bankers would swallow.

So it was time for what Seymour called the "Swados home run." I was no trial lawyer. It was said around the firm—with some exaggeration—that if Bob had to go to court, a paralegal would need to lead the way. I had touched trial practice as a rookie lawyer, but I could never sleep the night before trial, and, thus, except for the most important cases—like the suit by the WHA in Philadelphia in which Judge Higginbothman labeled the NHL a monopoly— I had opted to the negotiating and problem-solving aspects of the business. I had not lost my Harvard Law arrogance, so I was sure I could do it if I had to, but my military years had also confirmed my sense of my own limitations.

The lawsuit was fraught with threats of injury to people important to me and the Sabres. First was Peter Casagrande—my *own* doctor. Faced with a claim that exceeded the amount of his malpractice insurance, and with the spotlight turned on by the sports world, he risked serious damage to his reputation. Second, there was Scotty Bowman, the coach and GM we had worked so hard to recruit, confronted with charges of overreaching, inconsideration, and harsh handling of a talented player. The prospect of a colossal judgment against the team was of serious concern for the NHL, with the ripple effect it would cause for every club that thought it had the protection of the limits on liability set by the workers' compensation laws. I was acutely conscious of my double role as league secretary and the need to perform well in that arena.

The knowledge that the team's insurance agent might have blown our coverage in failing to disclose the faulty indorsement certainly added to my discomfort.

Then there was Rick himself. I liked Rick, as a player and a person—and he had told me in confidence of the loss of his savings at the hands of a dishonest agent. I could understand his need to find some way to recoup the money he had earned with his talent and desire. I had to find a way, nevertheless, to defeat his threat to the Sabres financial health.

The circumstances called for prudent and aggressive management of the case. I remembered well the model given to me early in my career as law clerk to Calvert Magruder in Boston; the leading battle in the multimillion-dollar Chicago stockyards tax case, when what seemed a no-brainer for the US Treasury was overcome by a phalanx of skilled lawyers; the technician who was an expert in that provision of the Internal Revenue code; the skilled and urbane Joe Welch (of army/McCarthy fame); and the stentorian senator who nearly blasted the judge off his podium. I had three fields to conquer: the bureaucrats on the Workers' Compensation Board, who would decide whether Rick's claim entitled him or restricted him to a comp award; the trial judge on the Buffalo malpractice bench, who would decide if Rick's charge of "intentional injury" was valid and who would preside over the jury if he did not dismiss the suit against Scotty and the Sabres; and the Appellate Division, who would determine whether we could hold on if we won in the trial court. My phalanx would consist of Dan Roach, for the offense, tall, good-humoured, solid, and well known to the judges and juries in the Western New York courts; for our defense, my partner, Larry Kerman, canny and thorough, a former law clerk in the Appellate Division of New York's Supreme Court; and myself as coach, GM, language maven, and supervising owner. The three of us put the written presentation together, and, reading it today, I still get a charge remembering Justice Henry Gossel's comment: "It's the best brief I've seen in twenty-five years!" When we realized how important it was to manage the comp board case in Albany—a fumble of a normally routine award of an employee's claim could be disastrous—we added Gareth Williams, a local specialist in that field.

The brief had to be the best it could be. The odds were against us—star player against "rich" owner. We had a number of problems to surmount:

1. Get the Workers' Compensation Board in Albany to rule that Rick was entitled to a comp award—even if he didn't file a claim. The award would shut him out of a lawsuit based solely on *negligence*.

2. Get the trial court to hold that the comp board's ruling that Rick was an employee made the compensation award Rick's *exclusive* remedy, unless he could prove that Scotty or the team "intentionally" injured him by making him play hurt.
3. Hope that Peter Casagrande's lawyers could persuade the court that Peter was not an independent contractor but a coemployee of Rick, so Rick couldn't sue Peter, either.
4. Persuade Judge Gossel to throw out the case against the Sabres and Bowman by granting our motion for summary judgment on the ground there was no evidence of intentional injury.
5. If the judge wouldn't dismiss the case, persuade the jury to find no case against Scotty and the club.
6. If we won before Judge Gossel and Rick's lawyers appealed, convince the appellate court that the decisions in California, Ohio, and Illinois, which permit the player to sue the owner for negligence regardless of the comp board's award, should not apply in New York.

We were worried about this point. Although New York courts had seemed to adopt the majority rule—that the player was limited by the *exclusivity* of the comp board's finding—this was a Canadian sport. Mike Robitaille, a Canadian-born player and onetime teammate of Rick's, whom I had re-signed from the WHA, had won a judgment against the Vancouver Canucks in a comparable charge against the team's doctors when the British Columbia judges disregarded the claim for workers' compensation. We could distinguish the California rulings—the express language of their statute gave the player freedom to sue regardless of the comp award. But the facts often torment readers of a statute. It glared strongly from the record that four different doctors—Casagrande in Buffalo, Jackson in Toronto, Berens at the Buffalo General Hospital, and, after a trade to the Kings, the Los Angeles team orthopedist—had examined and treated Rick with varying degrees of care and had found varying conditions in the meniscus of his knee. But *all* cleared him to play.

The doctors were vulnerable, but we had convinced the trial judge that Bowman and the club were not, and our undisputed evidence was strong enough to justify taking the case away from a jury and granting summary judgment. The Appellate Division in Rochester stayed with majority rule, making the comp award binding and, on the facts, adopted the crucial finding set forth in my affidavit: "Rick Martin was a star and an acknowledged asset of the franchise. Any notion that a member of the Sabres organization would intentionally injure Mr. Martin is, therefore, simply preposterous."

Unfortunately, Peter Casagrande did not fare as well. The issue of negligence of the doctors was tried before a jury. The citizens who heard the testimony—who may or may not have been Sabres fans—did not ignore the emotional nature of the player's case. He had been subjected to numerous arthograms and arthroscopies, and while Casagrande's view insisted that no serious damage that would have produced a career-ending injury had been uncovered by any of the physicians, the defendants' lawyers could not clear away the impact—to a lay person—of the mere description of the Toronto doctor's (Dr. Donald Jackson) findings: ". . . a tear of the lateral meniscus, a large posterial horn fragment, a smaller anterial horn flap tear, fractured cartilage surface and separation with fragments of cartilage floating and other debris present, none of which was previously diagnosed."[1]

I am afraid that in one respect I did not help the doctor's defense. In one of those strange conflicts ("counsel in the crease" again), I found myself subpoenaed and required to testify for the plaintiff. The questions put to me were innocent enough and quite routine. Who was I? What was my position in the Sabres? Did I know Rick Martin? Was Rick an important player, a star? How long would his career have continued without the injury? All questions to which I could only in truth provide answers that were helpful to Martin. (In retrospect, I could have sent Don Luce or one of the staff—but it was I who was subpoenaed.) Yet my mere appearance on the witness stand upset Casagrande's wife. How could I testify against the family? My protests that I had no alternative, I'm sure, didn't help.

The jury brought in a judgment of $2 million against Peter. (If the Sabres were still in the case, it could have been four—with no insurance.) Casagrande had only $1 million in coverage, so the damage to his family was serious. An appeal was commenced, but Rick, consistent with his character, accepted a generous settlement. The lawsuit and the angst about doctors' insurance led Casagrande to retire from his profession. But Rick had retrieved some of the large sums he had earned, we had paid him, and he had lost.

Part 4

AT THE LEAGUE'S BLUE LINE

Chapter 14

ALL'S NOT WELL
WITH THE NHL

I don't know whether it's luck, genes, or workaholism, but I seemed during this period to have a talent for riding events to achieve personal goals. The $6 million price the Sabres and the Vancouver Canucks paid to enter the NHL—three times the expansion fee paid by the six new clubs in 1967, only three years earlier—did, as I recounted earlier, squeeze out Cleveland and Baltimore, but it did not still the plans or passions of the cities that were left out: Edmonton, Winnipeg, and Quebec on the Canadian side and Cincinnati and Hartford in the United States. Nor did it quiet New York City, where the Rangers prospered without competition. The situation looked like a fat target to California lawyers Gary Davidson and Denis Murphy, flush with their success in attacking the basketball establishment and forcing the NBA to take on the ABA teams in a merger, fast becoming the experts on the creation of an "outlaw" league—and its ultimate merger with the establishment. The NHL, they knew, was vulnerable: its player contracts still locked the players in with the ancient baseball "perpetual option," and its tight control agreements with the hockey minor leagues clearly raised the presumption that the NHL was a monopoly, without baseball's exemption from the US antitrust laws.

Vancouver and Buffalo began play in October 1970, and the NHL plans called for further expansion in 1972 (ultimately the New York Islanders and Washington) and 1974 (Atlanta—now Calgary—and Kansas City). The new league formed in January 1971, called the World Hockey Association (WHA) attacked immediately. All-star Bobby Hull, offered a million-dollar salary, signed with the Winnipeg Jets of the new league; John McKenzie and Gerry Cheevers of the Boston Bruins deserted shortly thereafter. Since the WHA did not require a $6 million entry fee, the new clubs could offer more money to key NHL players whose contracts were at the end of their fixed terms. To tap into the amateurs and junior leagues, the WHA adopted a rule permitting the signing of an amateur at age eighteen—and persuaded the courts that the NHL's attempt to restrict signing until age twenty was invalid—thus scooping the establishment on rookies like Wayne Gretzky and Mark Messier.

The new league did not limit its attack to players; it sought NHL venues as well. A fundamental rule of the outlaws was that the league must have a franchise in the New York market, and so arose the New York Raiders. The trouble was there was no suitable arena except Madison Square Garden, owned by the New York Rangers organization. The players, the markets, the expansion, the television rights—all were threatened. The logical move was to shut them out. But if the NHL was a monopoly, acts of that kind might be held in furtherance of the monopoly and subject all the clubs to substantial liability—the Sherman Act called for *treble* damages! Moreover, the Rangers had an acute problem: a doctrine had been developed by the courts in the football cases that if only one suitable facility was available in a market, the establishment club, as a member of the dominant league, could be required to give the new league dates in that facility.

The NHL's legal strategy was conflicted and slow in developing. This was partly because of an unrealistic reliance by Clarence Campbell and the Canadian clubs on the idea that the border provided a kind of wall protecting the NHL, as a Canadian organization, against the vagaries of US law. There were assertions by Canadian counsel that the US antitrust laws didn't apply and that the US courts couldn't reach Canadian persons or assets. The slow reaction was also, in part, because some of the NHL owners, conscious of the problems with aggressive defense—the Detroit and Chicago owners had faced the government assaults in the International Boxing case, which stuck the Norris/Wirtz group with the monopolist label and convicted them of a violation of the Sherman Antitrust Act—believed the best response was no response, that the new league would ultimately fail on its own. And partly, this was because some of the NHL owners believed that, while aggressive defense was essential—they'd sue individually to protect their own players—collective legal action ("conspiracy") might impose joint liability.

The legal tactics at first devolved upon Bill Jennings, a senior partner in the well-known New York City firm of Simpson, Thacher, and Bartlett that represented Madison Square Garden and the Rangers. Bill was brilliant, practical, and persuasive, and an officer of the league as well. He had

Bill Jennings, lawyer and president of the New York Rangers, got the author into league legal troubles. Photo courtesy of the author.

played an important role in the expansion, had advised us on the Oakland episode, and had been helpful in our gaining entrée to the league. He and his colleagues in the Garden had been very friendly to Seymour and Norty, and had expressed strong approval of the way we had handled our entry and the multiple tasks of establishing a new franchise.

The WHA presented its demand for dates in the Garden for the Raiders not to the league, but directly to the Rangers. Bill, doubtless conflicted by his multiple roles, lingered briefly over the demand, but in the end he decided that, in view of the single-facility doctrine, he had no choice but to grant the WHA demand. The treble damages claimed by the new league could encompass claims by all the WHA clubs, and the Rangers were not only sitting with the weakest case, but the deepest pockets. Under the circumstances, Bill did not want to risk a governors' vote, so the deal was made, unilaterally and secretly. When this was disclosed—as it had to be—at a governors' meeting, Bill sheepishly argued that the dates given had been set so they would not interfere with the NHL schedule (although he couldn't restrict them to breakfast), but the governors hit the ceiling. Charges of bad faith, conflict of interest, and violation of duty ensued. Bill argued the single-facility doctrine in vain—it was obvious, despite his magnificent track record, he could no longer represent the NHL in WHA matters. The solution was to set up a legal committee, and, to my great surprise and pleasure, I was named chairman. Thus began years of challenge and excitement—a lawyer's life in the major-league lane.

I was never sure why I got the nod as chairman. It may have been because I was from a rookie franchise, and thus couldn't be expected to do or control very much. It may have been because there was such conflict among the aggressive, the passive, and the litigatious wings, they couldn't agree on anybody else. Whatever the reason, I was determined to do the job well, as a lawyer and to protect the Sabres. I was acutely conscious of the economics and the erosion that the new league's pressure on salaries could produce.

The first assignment for the legal committee was to hire new outside counsel with a strong antitrust department. I proposed Covington & Burling, the firm of Dean Acheson, the distinguished secretary of state under President Harry S. Truman. Acheson was a law review classmate of Paul Cohen, the founder of my firm, and I had, in my close work with them as colleagues over varied issues and transactions of Transcontinent Television, found them excellent and with great depth. Dan Gribben and Harry Shniderman, classmates of mine at Harvard Law School, were partners in the firm, and Harry was a leading authority on the related Robinson Patman Act, which prevents stores from unfair competition by imposing unfair prices and discounts, and had steered a number of major companies through the perils of antitrust litigation. Harry was also one of the few members of my law school class who had slightly higher grades than I and, I might acknowledge in some circumstances, could produce a more skillful performance. To my surprise and pleasure, some of the members of my committee were thinking along similar lines, and when I heard this, I promptly flew to Washington, DC, met with Dan and Harry, and, after a conference call with my colleagues, set the retainer. I piled documents onto

Harry's desk and briefed him on the divergent views of the NHL owners on WHA strategy—so he had a jump start.

We were fortunate, because, as it happened, Harry was leaving the next day for a bar association trip to Russia, and Clarence Campbell, the president of the league, and Bill Wirtz, chairman of the finance committee, were already there, on hockey business. They met in Moscow, and Harry—always prudent, but never shy—told Clarence, straight out, "Mr. Campbell, your player contract is *worthless!*" Clarence was taken aback—competent Canadian counsel had reviewed the standard player's contract in the light of the WHA developments and had come up with only one suggestion: cut out the clause giving the club the right to terminate the contract for "lack of skill," which made the contract unbalanced and unfair. But, of course, the Canadian lawyers passed the buck on US antitrust issues. Harry stressed the latter—the NHL would probably be held by the courts to be a monopoly, and the "perpetual option" clause, if relied on to prevent raids by the competing league, would probably be condemned as in restraint of trade, and certainly attempts to enforce it would be treated as acts in furtherance of the monopoly. Harry persuaded his listeners, but in the politics of the Board of Governors, the factions holding to the status quo prevented, for the time being, any aggressive restructuring of the contract. The illusion of the Canada-US border wall persisted. According to Campbell, the league and the Canadian clubs were free to disregard any subpoena or subpoena duces tecum (demand for documents) issued by a US court. But at least the educational process had begun. Harry began to appear for privileged conferences with counsel at the governors' meetings.

The second task of the legal committee, as I saw it, was to coordinate the league's position in the diverse legal battles that had begun. The Boston Bruins had commenced litigation in the state courts in Massachusetts to enforce their rights under the standard player's contract to retain goaltender Gerry Cheevers and forward Derek Sanderson; Chicago had sued to prevent Bobby Hull from jumping to the new league; and, through another Bruin player, John McKenzie, the WHA had pressed a suit in the Philadelphia federal court to enjoin the NHL from attempting to enforce his contract. The coordination was important for two reasons: first, we wanted to make sure the individual club didn't take a position or make a statement that would hurt the league's strategy for all the clubs; and second, to the extent we could influence the developments, we wanted to control the choice of forum, seeking the best court and the best judge for the ultimate battle.

For the most part we got cooperation—slow down this case, accelerate that, and so on. But not from Boston, where the owners were difficult, and their counsel, more so. Charlie Mulcahy, the Bruins' lawyer, was a sometime golfing buddy of the Knoxes—always cryptic, always sitting with a magnificent meerschaum clamped between his teeth. I had used a tobacco pipe as a prop in my early days as a lawyer, pounding it on the table as an announcement that I was about to make a profound statement. I swear Charlie used the pipe as a prop for his silence. When I spoke of coordination with the league, I got raised eyebrows; when I pointed out that attempts to enforce the McKenzie and Cheevers contracts might be contraindicated as exertion of monopoly power, I got grunts emanating from the meerschaum. The local courts, friendly to the Bruins and unsophisticated in antitrust matters, gave a temporary victory to the club; but it soon became apparent that the Sherman Act had to be faced squarely, and the ultimate battle on that issue would be heard in Philadelphia federal court, before Judge A. Leon Higginbotham.

Harry Shniderman was logical, thorough, and understandable, and the legal committee had confidence in his ability to handle the Philadelphia case. But everyone—with the possible exception of the Canadiens—understood that sustaining the validity of the standard player's contract, with its perpetual option, was a long shot—and we needed a home run hitter. The able and powerful men around the governors' table had their own ideas about who could pull it off, not the least of which was my old colleague from the Continental Baseball League, Jack Kent Cooke, now the behind-the-scenes owner of the NFL's Washington Redskins and the owner absolute of the Los Angeles Kings in our league. Jack's candidate—and Jack had no difficulty being heard—was perhaps the most eminent, certainly the most publicized, trial lawyer on the national scene—Edward Bennett Williams.

It produced an interesting contrast: Harry was saturnine; Ed was genial. Harry was short and plain, spectacled, and bald; Ed was tall and handsome, athletic, and groomed in the fashion of the day. Harry looked for the devil in the details; Ed was broad brush. Each was persuasive in his own style. With my friendship with Harry, and the good word from my Continental colleague Jack Cooke, I was in a unique position to moderate their differences, and, with encouragement from John Ziegler and the other members of the committee, as the NHL person on the scene, I was able to do just that.

Some of my intellectual colleagues (including Harry himself) were put off by Ed's tendency to launch into flowery, emotional speeches. The case would be tried before Judge Higginbotham alone. But I had learned early in my career the value of oratory, even in a juryless courtroom. In my glory year as a young lawyer, member of the Harvard Law School faculty, and law clerk to Calvert Magruder, chief judge of the US Court of Appeals for the First Circuit, the judge asked me to monitor a major tax case, involving a taxpayer named Prince, the principal owner of the Chicago Stockyards Company. Prince was charged by the IRS with hoarding his company's earnings to avoid payment of the tax on dividends—unreasonable accumulation of surplus. The Treasury had presented Prince with a multimillion-dollar tax bill. The defense—which had to show a clear business purpose—

was creative, colorful, and dramatic. The fund had to be accumulated, said Prince, not to avoid the tax on dividends, but to set aside a fund to pay blackmail to his major packer customers. Periodically, the taxpayer reported, one or more of the packers would threaten to move—lock, stock, and barrel—to Indiana, and Prince would have to pay them off, or face disaster for the Chicago stockyards.

With the millions at stake, Prince's counsel had assembled an all-star team for the appeal from the tax court decision: first, a leading technician, a specialist in cases involving unreasonable accumulation of surplus; second, the renowned Joe Welch, defender of the army and destroyer of Joe McCarthy; and third, a politically adept US senator, George Horton Pepper, veteran of many speeches of public passion in the upper chamber. As the oral argument before the court developed, I was amused at the specialist tugging at the coattails of his distinguished colleagues in a vain attempt to prevent some technical gaffe, and I was shocked and impressed by the versatility of Joe Welch. In the McCarthy hearings he had played, with success, the role of the "country" lawyer—simple and naive, expressing homely truths in a country twang. Here, he was the ultimate sophisticate—urbane and polished, handling with ease the complex charts of the stockyards operations and financial transactions. As for the senator, he did not impress me at all. I had learned, and taught, the standard style of appellate argument—respectful, quiet, logical, and thorough, but unemotional. The senator paid no attention to these hoary guidelines. His tones were stentorian, his dialogue replete with disdain for the tax court; his pleas echoing like a filibuster demanding battle against an evil enemy. The IRS had it all wrong, he said. Prince was the fighter-founder of the stockyards; he should be treated "not as a robber baron, but as a hero!"

When I discussed the case with Judge Magruder, I flippantly characterized the senator's presentation as so much baloney, and I wrote a memorandum analyzing the financial statements, concluding that, even taking into account the threat of the packers' desertion, the surplus had been unreasonably accumulated, and the penalty tax should stand. At the time, the judge commented that "the senator knew what he was doing" and, to my great surprise, produced an opinion for the court that reversed the tax court and remanded the case for a new hearing, on the ground that the lower court had applied an improper standard in determining what was a "reasonable" accumulation. The Treasury officials exploded, appealed to the Supreme Court, and persuaded that court to reverse my boss and reinstate the multimillion-dollar tax bill by a vote of nine to zero. Judge Magruder joked—on the square, I hoped—that he would never ignore my advice again.

But I never forgot the Chicago stockyards, and the team that had managed, with oratory, to persuade three canny, experienced judges to beat the odds. So I was not only comfortable but glad to welcome Ed Williams into the NHL team for the critical WHA trial in Philadelphia.

In addition to my liaison duties in preparation for the trial, I was asked to produce an affidavit in support of the argument that the standard contract, with the option, was not illegal per se, but was a "reasonable" restraint, necessary for the conduct of the league's business. The Supreme Court and the federal courts for decades had engrafted a "rule of reason" on the draconian Sherman Act: not every contract in restraint of trade was illegal—in some situations, a showing could be made providing an economic or business justification for the restrictive practice.

The affidavit was also intended as an educational tool for Judge Higginbotham, to familiarize him with an affirmative touch, with the structure and requirements of the professional sport. Using my principle that my language as a lawyer should sound as little like a lawyer as possible, I produced what I thought was a pretty good explanation of NHL hockey. To justify the retention of the rights to the player after the expiration of the fixed term of his contract, I stressed the investment by the NHL owners in the minor professional, junior, and amateur leagues. We subsidized those leagues directly and indirectly, through appropriations, working agreements, direct ownership, and draft payments. This echoed the baseball argument, but of course we did not have the benefit of the federal baseball exemption. I pointed out, in what I hoped was an attractive and interesting way, the necessity of developing and holding on, for a reasonable period, to players at the various positions—forward, defense, and goaltender; the frequent trades; the intraleague draft; the opening of new jobs with expansion—whatever I could conjure up that would counter the impression of a restrictive, unreasonable system. Harry and Ed both liked the affidavit. Judge Higginbotham did not entirely agree. In his preliminary opinion, he commented upon the excellence of the work by counsel, but he observed that some of the arguments presented "belong more in *Sports Illustrated* than they do in this Court."[1]

It was a long, hot, hard summer, chained to Philadelphia, but I enjoyed the experience. Higginbotham had a solid reputation, and he lived up to it: black, Harvard Law School, tough, demanding, and fair. Antitrust cases in general, and this one in particular, produce massive records. The Brandeis tradition requires facts, facts, and more facts, and creates documents, documents, and more documents. Motions, subpoenas, discovery, challenges to relevance, briefs, and orders—all were plentiful. It takes an able and conscientious judge to keep the facts and documents moving, and to maintain a pace that produces a verdict in a reasonable time. Higginbotham worked hard, kept a tight schedule, and drove the lawyers to adhere to it. I got to know both sets of lawyers well. As always, Harry would challenge and lead the analysis, and stimulate the intellect; Ed was fully up to speed on the law, and was fun to be with. Both lead lawyers had able associates: Ed and Herb Dym from Covington & Burling and Bing Leverich and my Harvard classmate Harry Shniderman from the Williams firm. There were few conflicts on our side, and the division of labor seemed to go well.

Several years before, the Knoxes had got me into squash, and Ed played the game himself. I was hardly up to Ed's level, but I enjoyed the matches nevertheless. One day Ed asked me to play, and I had to beg off—a brief was due the following day, and I had to review it. Ed commented that he was sure he could get Otto Graham, once the Redskins coach, to substitute for me. The next day, I asked how the match went. Ed responded, and I got a glimpse of his owner's view of his football management: "Not very well. He's out of shape. I can't stand a coach who can't stay in shape—and I fired him!"

Despite Ed's oratory, Harry's sharp analysis, and the mountains of evidence (including my affidavit), the judge's ruling, in his 1972 opinion, turned out to be pretty much what Harry had predicted in Moscow: the NHL was a monopoly; the standard player contract with the "perpetual option" was a contract in restraint of trade; the NHL was not exempt from the antitrust laws; and our attempt to justify the contract under the "rule of reason" was insufficient. Enforcement of the existing contracts, so as to prevent the WHA from signing away players who had reached the end of the fixed term of their contracts, would be treated as attempts to prevent competition, would be illegal, and could be enjoined. The only good news in Higginbotham's opinion was that it took him forty-six pages to reach a decision, that he had employed the "rule of reason" and thus left the matter open, so that *some* restraints on the player could conceivably be developed that would be lawful.

The judge's verdict could perhaps have produced massive damage claims by the WHA clubs—to be trebled under the Sherman Act. It did not. With Bill Wirtz as the lead owner, Harry Shniderman in Washington, and me as the draftsman in the field, we worked out an agreement with the WHA that Wirtz later characterized as the "cheapest settlement in antitrust sports history." The outlaw league's legal expenses were paid, but we paid no damages. Both parties agreed not to appeal. The WHA had achieved its major objective—access to our veteran players—and since it had universally used large bumps in salaries to sign them away, its damage claims were probably not worth much. It was essentially a nolo contendere—live and let live—settlement, like a détente.

I would like to think the low cost of the settlement was attributable to the excellence of the lawyers, which I could not denigrate, but it really was influenced by the underlying and ultimate mood and purpose of the new league owner—"Don't fight 'em, join 'em!"

That had been the pattern in the Continental League, where Major League Baseball absorbed half of the new teams; in the NFL, with a merger of all the clubs in the American Football League; and in basketball, where the NBA and the ABA consolidated. The market entry of the WHA teams had nearly doubled the number of rosters to feed, producing a sharp upward shift in the demand for players. The escalation of salaries was already producing nightmares for owners in both leagues. Investors like Howard Baldwin in Hartford were not happy about maintaining a long economic struggle, and the escalation was already affecting the NHL's expansion plans. The new NHL teams in Long Island and Atlanta acquired their rosters and began play early enough (1972–73) that they were not immediately hit with the escalation. But the Washington Capitals and Kansas City Scouts—1974 entries—struggled financially, with the league forced to move the Kansas City team to Denver, Colorado, after two seasons produced near bankruptcy. The teams scheduled for the 1976 NHL expansion—Seattle and Denver—never made it to the ice at all, as the rising salaries made projections look worse and financing more and more difficult. (The Seattle owners ended up suing the NHL under the antitrust laws, in a futile effort to recover their application fee.)

On the WHA side, the withering of franchises and the substitution of new entrants was almost an annual event. The league started with twelve teams—Chicago Cougars, Los Angeles Sharks, New York Raiders, Minnesota Fighting Saints, Winnipeg Jets, Alberta Oilers, Calgary Broncos, Dayton Aeros, New England Whalers, Ottawa Nationals, Miami Screaming Eagles, and San Francisco. Before a game was ever played, San Francisco became the Quebec Nordiques, the Aeros moved from Dayton to Houston, Miami became the Philadelphia Blazers, and Calgary became the Cleveland Crusaders. The following year, Ottawa moved to Toronto; Philadelphia, the plaintiff in the suit before Judge Higginbotham, moved to Vancouver; and the New York Raiders changed to new ownership as the Golden Blades, then faded and failed. They were represented by another classmate of mine—Sy Kleinman, an able laywer affectionately known as the class comic, whose hockey demise at the hands of his NHL classmates was not funny to any of us at all. Teams in Indianapolis, Phoenix, Baltimore, Detroit, San Diego, and Birmingham appeared on the scene over the years; some stayed, some left.

There were, as usual, several schools of thought on the merging of the WHA. Montreal, faced now with an invasion of what it considered its market by Quebec City, was adamant; like its Toronto and Vancouver colleagues, the team stood firm: wait 'em out; there's no real money there, they'll die of economic attrition. On the other hand, some NHL owners, alarmed by the salary inflation, certainly gave signals to the WHA group that they would accept a consolidation. Clarence Campbell, as always influenced by the Canadiens, supported the "wait 'em out" school, but when John Ziegler became chairman of the Board of Governors in 1976, the open-minded Ziegler took a fresh look. The WHA was now down to eight clubs, and some accommo-

Gordie Howe, the all-time hockey great who jumped to the WHA, with Gerry Meehan, onetime Sabres captain and GM.

dation appeared to be possible—perhaps something less than eight clubs. A close look at each of them would be necessary.

While the franchises in both leagues shuffled, key players changed places as well. In addition to Hull and McKenzie, the list of jumpers to the WHA grew: Derek Sanderson, J. C. Tremblay, Gerry Cheevers, and Gordie Howe with his draft choice sons. A host of players who'd been buried in the depth charts in the NHL approached "stardom" in the new league. The Sabres roster didn't suffer very much. We were too new, and in the early 1970s there weren't very many valuable players on our list whose contracts were reaching the option stage. There was one, however—Mike Robitaille.

Mike was an experienced defenseman who had come to us from Detroit with Don Luce in a trade for goalie Joe Daley. In later years, as he became a Sabres color commentator, Mike would tend to overemphasize his role (as we all do), but was a good, solid fifth or sixth defenseman. He had been on several all-star teams in the minors and in junior; in the 1972–73 season he scored twenty-one points in sixty-five games; and as the WHA began to stretch the rosters, experienced NHL defensemen were hard to come by. Punch Imlach was ill and for the moment the tough player cases were referred to me. Word came that Mike had signed with the WHA, but I heard rumors that he was not entirely happy with his decision, and, fully sensitive to the effect the WHA demands were having on the player supply, I was determined to get him back. His lawyer, the brother of a player for the Buffalo Braves, was fortunately not opposed to a second look. He was persuaded, as ultimately was Mike, by my argument that he might destroy his career—poor coaching, uncertain financing, an employer that might not survive, and a reputation for disloyalty that would certainly hurt his future in the NHL. Mike's counsel showed me his WHA contract, and I concluded that it was defective. Mike had an out, since he had not yet played a game for the outlaws. Putting on my league hat for the moment, I called Harry to make sure I wasn't exposing us to antitrust claims. We concluded that there was a risk, but tactically the fact that an NHL club would fight back was more important. We negotiated in Seymour's lovely garden on Nottingham Terrace, across from Delaware Park—an atmosphere hardly conducive to warfare. After several days of intense talks we arranged for Mike to terminate the WHA deal and sign a new standard player's contract with the Sabres. We had recaptured a WHA player!

When Punch returned, he was sharply critical of the Robitaille move. He wanted little or nothing to do with disloyalty, and on October 14, 1974, Mike was traded to Vancouver with Gerry Meehan for Josh Guevremont and Bryan McSheffrey. So Mike missed our Stanley Cup Finals season. Punch had no interest in reclaiming a more important player—Rick Dudley, coming off a seventy-point season with the Sabres in 1974–75. Rick had been drafted by the WHA and flirted with the new league, and moved to the Cincinnati Stingers of the WHA at the close of the 1974–75 season.

Meanwhile, on the league front: With Higginbotham's decision having annulled the perpetual option, the NHL had to quickly come up with a new formula. Failing this, every player would become a completely free agent—and could sell his services to any club in either league—at the end of the fixed term of his contract. A longer fixed term was a possible solution, but that would lock the club into disagreeable situations if a player's skill declined, and impose difficult negotiation strategies on the general managers. The "Rozelle rule," in force for a time in the NFL, was considered, but it left the compensation for the club losing the player entirely uncertain—at the discretion of the commissioner or president—and might have a rocky time in the courts and in discussions with the players' union.

At a special meeting of the Board of Governors, Ed Williams and Jack Cooke placed a new proposal on the governors' table with the warning that it had to be adopted promptly or the NHL would have no defense against player raids and might face a revival of antitrust damage claims. The proposal had the gloss of arbitration, which helped on the issue of "reasonableness," but still left bargaining power in the clubs. For example: Gilbert Perreault reaches the end of his three-year contract and becomes a free agent, subject to "equalization." If Montreal offers him a new contract, and he accepts, Montreal is required to pay or deliver to Buffalo equalization. The signing club must offer cash, players, or draft picks in the entry draft, or any combination of these. The losing club makes a demand for cash, players, and/or draft picks. The arbitrator then chooses—without modifying either—which of the two will govern. The board approved immediately, and the crisis was abated.

There was no way to assure the validity of the equalization rule (which became known as Bylaw 9A) without one further, important step: approval by the players' association in collective bargaining. The initial plan, because of threats from the WHA, was to install the new system unilaterally. The outside lawyers, with whom I concurred, wanted to move to the new contract immediately. But there were other implications that had to be considered: What about existing contracts? What about the Robitaille syndrome—players who had defected but wanted to comeback once their WHA deals were over? Would we actually force a trade to comply with 9A if the player objected? Some of the leading agents held the view that if the player defected and played with the new league for more than a year, the old club lost its rights and the player could sign with *any NHL team*. I was asked to draft a bylaw to cover this problem, and the fruits of my labor—and that of Covington in review—produced Bylaw 9B, still in force, which preserves, within a specified time and under specified conditions, the old club's rights and preferences when the defected player wishes to return to the league.

The federal courts had developed a concept, called the nonstatutory labor exemption, under which a restriction that would otherwise violate the Sherman Act would be valid if it had been the subject of collective bargaining between the union and its employers. The principle was that if there were a conflict between the Sherman Act (which originated in 1890) and the policies of the Wagner Labor Relations Act, a product of the New Deal, which sought to encourage collective bargaining and the settlement of labor disputes, the more important labor policies should prevail. The new bylaws, which restricted player movement, clearly would have been banned by antitrust, and needed the blessing of union consent.

The decision, then, to seek players' association approval was certainly prudent, and with the union having just acquired some substance, I'm sure the thinking was that we could get it without opening up the issue completely—just a kiss, not a hug. With the market for the players booming from the WHA demand, Alan Eagleson and his player officers were willing, in consideration of other concessions by our owners, to accept 9A and 9B without change—and, really, without debate. As time went on, individual players objected to the new rule, especially where the arbitrator approved equalization that called for the forced move of a veteran player. Dale McCourt fought his forced transfer in the federal courts, arguing that the mere acceptance by the union did not constitute the collective "bargaining" demanded by the "nonstatutory labor exemption" from the antitrust laws; but the Court of Appeals held that the bylaw had in fact been "bargained." In a more recent attack on Bylaw 9B, Alexei Yashin sought to evade its provisions and put his services up for sale to the highest NHL bidder, again arguing that the provisions had not been collectively bargained; but the arbitrator ruled to the contrary, and the player, after a long holdout, signed with the Ottawa Senators, his old club.

But going to the union for its consent had opened scope for the union's power. As the years went by, and successive collective bargaining agreements were negotiated, Bylaw 9A changed substantially. The threat of win/lose arbitration did too good a job, the union complained, and there was too little player movement. GMs hesitated to sign away another team's player when the consequences were unknown. The first change was to eliminate existing players as equalization; then eliminate cash; then eliminate the arbitrator—create a table making the compensation to the old club fixed and certain. A GM considering a raid on another team's player knew, for example, that the team might have to give up three first-round draft picks if the salary offered was in excess of $1 million. As these changes took place, the owners sought to get back the right of first refusal, which had been omitted in the rush for 9A's enactment. The association's response was to insist that in some situations, the owner could have a right of first refusal *or* draft pick compensation, but not both. Finally, the players demanded that *they* be given the right to choose which form of compensation the losing club would receive.

Yet the principle that the old club retains rights at the end of the player's contract, and that it must be compensated when the player is signed away, remains in force, largely due to the quick and prudent response of the NHL leadership and their counsel in the face of the Higginbotham defeat.

The new bylaw protected the NHL team's roster from raids by its partners, but it had little braking effect on the constant escalation of player salaries produced by the WHA's demand for players. The peace faction began to gain ground, and it was encouraged and supported by John Ziegler, who became chairman and president of the league in 1976. A majority of the clubs actually voted for a plan of merger in 1978, but with Montreal and its cohorts standing fast, the resolution failed to get the supermajority vote required. Finally, in 1979, in a pattern that looked remarkably like the fate of the Continental Baseball League, four teams from the WHA were accepted into the NHL. The expansion fee was $6 million; but the actual cost, when the sums paid to departing clubs and creditors of the WHA were taken into account, was closer to $11 million for each WHA club.

The successful entrants were the Hartford Whalers and three Canadian teams—the Winnipeg Jets, Quebec Nordiques, and Edmonton Oilers. Gil Stein, then general counsel of the NHL, assigned the merger to his former Philadelphia firm, so I had little to do (except for review) with the expansion documents as such. My problems and assignment had to do with the clubs that didn't make it. The problems were both legal and personal. Ideally, we would have exacted from every former owner and executive of every team that failed to make the NHL cut, a full and complete release of liability from everything and everyone—from claims by shortstopped season ticket holders to charges that the merger violated the antitrust laws. The fact that the players' association gave its consent, with concessions, did not give us complete protection. The failed clubs were not even parties to the merger-expansion agreements. There was even a question as to whether a release of the antitrust claims was valid as a matter of public policy. To bring the merger-expansion about, we had to be satisfied with documents that rode on principles that sounded like quantum mechanics. We got the joining teams to indemnify us as to the known claims and we vetted the documents running between the successful clubs and the unsuccessful ones, pushing the releases into the antitrust area and hoping we had gone far enough and not too far. Neither an insurance company nor a surety company bond were available, so we had to just hope the size of the documents made the odds at least favorable. No lawsuit or injunction, private or governmental, appeared, so we relaxed.

Harry and I didn't care about the Miami Screaming Eagles, but the failure of the New York WHA club—withering and dying now in a town in New Jersey—troubled us. The failure of our friend Sy Kleinman's club, and the league, seemed to have hit him hard. As we negotiated the closing documents and releases, he seemed close to tears. Apparently he was afflicted with that discomfiting disease that hits lawyers involved with professional sports teams—overemotional commitment. You work harder, longer, under greater pressure, and receive less and less compensation. There was nothing we could do: the WHA owners had worked out the payments to the clubs that agreed to withdraw, and the provision for the New York Club, with its miserable record, was apparently minimal. We provided sympathy and flexibility wherever we could, but little else.

In the case of the Cincinnati Stingers, I felt a little like the parent whose child disobeyed his advice and ended up, as the parent predicted, in the stockade. A leader of the Cincinnati group was Bill DeWitt Jr. I had come to know his father in our 1978 pursuit of an expansion baseball franchise for Buffalo; the elder DeWitt had been very helpful in the process, offering to invest one-third of the equity. (As related in chapter 8, he remained a part of the Buffalo group until Walter O'Malley—perhaps to protect his protégé Buzzy Bavasi or John McHale—indicated our chances would be hurt by DeWitt's participation.) In the 1974 NHL expansion, the DeWitt group had made a fine presentation; the vote was close, but the nod went to Washington, largely because some governors felt it was important to have a franchise in the nation's capital. The governors and John Ziegler asked me to convey the message that they would receive the *next* NHL franchise in the next expansion. (There was no assurance as to when that expansion would take place, except the announced policy of the league to eventually reach thirty clubs). I did so, but brought the DeWitt representatives into the governors' meeting so they could hear the commitment directly, and on the record.

Unfortunately, I was not the only person giving advice to the DeWitt group. Billy was concerned about the window available for municipal support for a new arena. Cincinnati's mayor was on board, but the building would not be financed without a major-league hockey club, and no one could predict when the NHL would get around to granting a franchise to the Ohio city. Someone persuaded the DeWitt group that the WHA would merge with the NHL, and thus the cheapest way to become a member of the NHL was to join the WHA. So the Cincinnati group joined the outlaw league, built a new building, and stretched its financing—but didn't make the cut. I had worked hard to get them the NHL commitment, but the route the DeWitt group chose killed its chances.

The WHA experience was a difficult one for the NHL, of questionable value over time. The salary impact was a serious and persistent infection; yet, of the four teams admitted, only Edmonton survived in place. Quebec went to Denver, Winnipeg to Phoenix, and Hartford to North Carolina.

But for me personally, the WHA gave me a national stage in the NHL, an opportunity to show my competence and judgment. It led to my election as secretary of the Board of Governors and a greater role in league affairs.

My resulting friendship with Edward Bennett Williams was a gift that I treasured. It helped in the late 1990s when our colleague Bob Rich Jr. asked my assistance in his attempt to gain a major-league baseball franchise for his highly successful minor-league Bisons. I called Ed for his advice as the former owner of the Baltimore Orioles, and he spent two hours on the phone with me, analyzing the establishment owners—who would be on our side, who could be trusted, who could not, strategy and tactics. He sounded his usual good-humored enthusiastic self; I had no clue that he was ill with cancer. He died two weeks after our talk.

Chapter 15

ORR'S ORBIT AND THE LIMITS OF POWER

Bobby Orr—blond, handsome, with an appealing grin; flashy, but greatly talented—transformed the role of hundreds of defensemen, once resigned, and restricted, to the stay-at-home role of protectors, confined to the space behind the blue lines (hence "blueliners"). Orr changed all that, liberated some blueliners to join the play up ice, pitch in, become part of the offense. In many a hockey raconteur's galaxy, Orr was, without doubt, assigned the first star. Other defensemen had ventured occasionally into the offensive zone, but Orr did it with such dash and skill and success in his Boston Bruins uniform that he opened up the ice for talents like Ray Bourke and Paul Coffey, essentially creating a new position that in other eras might have seemed an oxymoron—offensive defenseman. Orr was named to the NHL All-Star first team eight times in the 1960s and 1970s.

Unfortunately, as an official of the Buffalo Sabres and the NHL, I didn't get to see Orr perform until he was near the end of his career. But I have a vivid recollection of one such event. The Bruins were in the Sabres' Aud and the game turned a little rough, with the Buffalo defense checking closely and ferociously. In an attempt to slow the Bruins attack, a Sabres check cracked a Bruin into the boards with such force that the plastic walls around the ice trembled. Orr led a charge of the entire Bruins team into the Buffalo players' bench. For fans of hockey fights (I am not among them) it was a beautiful brawl—staged directly in front of my seats, only four rows away. When the referee and linesmen managed to separate the combatants and send them off to the penalty box, I was shocked to see that the Bruins, who started the melee, received fewer penalties than the Sabres. In the ensuing power play, the Bruins scored the winning goal.

Incensed by what I saw as an unfair result, and perhaps overimpressed with my newly earned positions as alternate governor and chairman of the league's legal committee, after getting the OK from Punch Imlach (who was always glad to stir things up), I wrote what I thought was a cogent protest to President Clarence Campbell. I was not just writing as a lawyer, I said, I was a *witness*. The Bruins had started the brawl, eight feet away; they were the *instigators*. Campbell's reply was brief, but quite sufficient: "Swados," he said, "you're an excellent lawyer, but your qualifications as a referee are not equivalent. . . . Objection overruled."

Orr was only thirty years old when he was forced to retire because of a knee injury that could not, on the then state of surgical knowledge, be cured. Already, in the spring of 1975, the Boston Bruins knew that Orr's playing days were numbered. But he was still an icon, a force on the ice for as long as he could manage the pain and the offending knee would support his body. As it happened, the Weston Adams family, which had owned the Bruins for many years, decided to sell, and the proposed purchaser turned out to be the Jacobs brothers—founders of Sportservice, a leading conces-sionaire headquartered in Buffalo, with contractual ties to a number of NHL and Major League Baseball teams. As required by the NHL constitu-tion, the proposed transfer was submitted to the Board of Governors. After a substantial debate—the Bruins were a prize franchise—the board approved the transfer of ownership on August 28, 1975.

In the course of that debate, Bill Wirtz, principal owner of the Chicago Blackhawks and chairman of the Board of Governors, thought he had elicited from Jeremy Jacobs (who was to become the team's governor), a commitment to "take care of Bobby Orr." In Wirtz's view, this was not just kindness to a spectacular league star who was reaching the end of his career, but a tactic that was important to the league as well. Orr was then still a major client of lawyer/agent Alan Eagleson, who wore, as his other hat, that of executive director of the NHL Players' Association. Orr's playing contract with the Bruins would expire in 1976, and he would become a free agent—subject to "equalization" in the event another club signed him away from the Bruins. More important: the WHA was still in existence, com-peting, hungering for a talent of Orr's stature. Thus the re-signing of Orr was of importance to the whole league.

Equalization, at that stage of the collective bargaining agreement with the players' association, meant the new club must offer the old either cash, draft choices, or a player on the new club's roster. If the old club did not accept the new team's offer of equalization, the agreement and bylaw called

Bobby Orr—the great offensive defenseman.

for the old club to make a written demand, and an arbitrator would choose which of the two proposals would be approved. The arbitrator could not moderate between the two—he could only choose one or the other.

But to Bill Wirtz, the understanding did not contemplate a dispute or a proceeding: the Bruins were to "take care of Orr." That meant continuing his career and signing him to a reasonable renewal contract. Yet Orr's current performance was spotty, largely because of his knee, and the predictions of the team docs were increasingly pessimistic. A new contract could turn out to be largely a gift, with the club receiving little for the high salary to which the superstar had become accustomed—and which Orr seemed to expect would continue as long as he was on the ice. It became clear, as the 1975–76 season did little to reduce these concerns, that the Bruins were going to do very little to comply with their "commitment."

As the story is told, confirmed by Harry Sinden, but questioned by Bill Wirtz, the Bruins did offer Bobby a handsome contract, in writing, that included an 18.5 percent stake in the team. Harry says the offer was presented to Eagleson, who recorded his response on the offer itself, writing, "Received and rejected by me and my client, Bobby Orr." Orr, according to Sinden, says he never was informed of the offer. Somehow the reports of the inadequate results of the knee surgeries and the Eagleson response turned the Bruins off, and, says Wirtz, their offer was withdrawn. When Bill's father, Arthur Wirtz, heard this, he was outraged. Arthur had always had a warm, supportive relationship with Lou Jacobs and the Jacobs family, and he felt the Bruins' failure to perform its commitment was unacceptable, and he gave orders: if Boston won't sign him, we will! Chicago did, triggering the collective bargaining agreement—and further dispute.

In these events, both Clarence Campbell and John Ziegler, who succeeded him, had to recognize the "limits of power"; they could not press down their authority, whatever the documents, and only time cured the breach.

THE MAN IN THE STRIPED SHIRT

It was legend in NHL circles that, as a matter of principle and fairness, owners should exercise restraint in their dealings with referees. The owners had legal power, but the officials were employees, and the governors should turn the other cheek at the hold that was missed, the crosscheck that went unpenalized, the goal that never went in. Of course the principle was frequently mangled as the owner's anger flooded his judgment. I had my spells of rage, like any conscientious member of the brass, but nothing, I thought, like Bill Jennings. Jennings, in the 1970s president of the New York Rangers, is said to have broken down the door to the referees' room, furious at an egregious noncall by the guy in the striped shirt. The record

Andy Van Hellemond—
leading referee.

does not show the amount of Jennings's fine, but it is clear that he did not regard his dominant position in the league as an impediment to his freedom of speech. If you're part of this great game, an emotion eruption is bound to come.

I became secretary of the NHL Board of Governors in 1976. As I was only one of three officers elected by the board under the constitution, for a time some of the owners and a few of the appointed executives and hired hands thought I was some kind of ancient scribe whose duties were limited to rubber-stamping the minutes prepared by a vice president, Brian O'Neill. Of course, that concept didn't last long with me. I was determined to make the position meaningful and robust, consistent with its august description in the constitution. And before long, I was drafting my own minutes, in my own style—which tended to be more graphic and substantive than the bare and silent bones related above Brian had been creating in the past.

With the encouragement of John Ziegler as president and Bill Wirtz as chairman, I also began to be invited to cover the meetings of the principal committees of the board, like the advisory (executive) and finance committees and the Owner-Player Council—the outfit that negotiated with the players' union. And my role in those meetings moved over from secretary to special counsel and, with the players negotiations, to ex officio member of the negotiating group itself.

I never had much to do with the officials. That was handled by the hockey department (league and club), although I was very conscious, as an alternate governor, of the cost of the referees and linesmen, and the frequent variations in the policies and rules we promulgated from time to time, as the GMs battled with the owners on the fighting, crosschecking, goalie protections, and other on-ice conflicts that inflamed individual governors.

And, of course, as a hockey fan uninhibited by my guise as hockey mogul, I had my occasional sallies at the "unfair" judges on skates.

Still, I would insist from time to time that my duties and powers as a league officer were entitled to some weight even with the guys on the ice. I had always respected the referees and linesmen; our officials have the toughest job in professional sports: moving at thirty miles an hour, with minimal protection from a flying object that can penetrate the toughest jaw or the softest eye, and constant movement (until recently) to and fro the entire length of the rink. I voted in a special committee for cameras over the crease, to the dismay of some building owners, and the move to two referees—heeding the plea of the officials' union and our hockey department that the physical demands were wearing down the refs, causing retirement at an early age, and making the recruitment of rookie officials too difficult. Sure, I understood that the refs had their own union, but we still paid them, and their health and welfare was intimately important to the vitality of the game and the league. John McCauley, at the time the chief referee, understood this and on several occasions spoke with appreciation of my support of decisions and rule changes the officials were concerned about.

These notions were put severely to the test one night in the Sabres building. Orr's Bruins were in town when Andy Van Hellemond—later a chief referee himself—was hit by a stumbling defenseman and crashed to the ice. Our medical team and trainer saw the ref was in obvious pain— couldn't walk—and carried Van Hellemond from the arena. I didn't think as a Sabre or an owner, just that the ref was badly hurt, he was an employee of ours, and as a league officer I had to make sure he was given the best treatment available. I knew vaguely that the referees' room was off limits, but of course that didn't apply to the league secretary! So I opened the door and walked in. The ref had recovered rapidly, but he obviously was still in pain. I started to be solicitous, when Van Hellemond bellowed, "What the hell are you doing here?!"

John McCauley had run to the room as well, so I turned to John, asking, "Is he all right?"

John didn't hesitate: "Bob, get your *butt* out of here!" So I did.

And thus I learned the limits of power.

Chapter 16

THE OWNERS WHO
BAILED US OUT

D espite early efforts of some purists and monopolists to prevent companies or individuals from acquiring ownership in more than one sports league, there were some substantial relationships between hockey and the other sports, and they worked to our advantage. We'd worked with Jack Cooke of the Los Angeles Kings, Toronto Maple Leafs, and Washington Redskins; Bill Wirtz of the Chicago Blackhawks and Chicago Bulls; Bill Jennings of the Knicks and Rangers; Ed Williams of the Redskins and Baltimore Orioles; and Lou Jacobs of Sportservice, leading concessionaire to a number of the baseball and hockey teams. Nelson Doubleday, a principal owner of the New York Mets, had been one of the original partners in the Oakland Seals. Our forays into Major League Baseball in 1960 and 1968, though unsuccessful, had created goodwill across most of the MLB spectrum. The Knoxes' credentials were impeccable—as men of wealth, leading citizens of their community, and nationally recognized athletes in their own right, in polo, squash, and court tennis. When we combined this with a showing that we had know-how and drive, entrée to the corridors of power was easy, and we seemed to find owners happy to help us. After all, we did get Erie County to approve $50 million for the domed baseball stadium and the city of Buffalo to increase the seating capacity of Memorial Auditorium by five thousand seats, with a lease that was then quite favorable. We had assembled, almost overnight, in both the hockey and baseball crusades, a group of committed and well-funded investors, recruited primarily from the former shareholders in Transcontinent Television, whose loyalty and confidence in us had been fortified by the unexpected profits we had produced in that ten-year venture.

We even had a relationship with George Steinbrenner, who had made a commitment for 25 percent of the capital in our 1968 campaign for a National Baseball League franchise. We later offered Steinbrenner a position in the Sabres, but he declined, to "save himself for baseball." Steinbrenner later flirted with, and for a brief time actually held, a 5 percent position in the Tampa Bay Lightning.

Then there was Charles O. Finley: canny, gruff, earthy owner of the Oakland A's in the days of Rollie Fingers and Vida Blue; winner of five straight AL West titles and three straight World Series; veteran of numerous battles with the commissioner of Major League Baseball, the most egregious being his unsuccessful attempt to sell his three star pitchers for cash. I had first met Charley O. in 1968 in the course of our bid for a club in the baseball expansion. I was determined to talk to every owner who could help us, and when I heard that Finley would be available in Kansas City—I was in St. Louis in pursuit of the Cardinals' Augie Busch—I immediately headed for Finley's hotel. When I gave my name, the desk clerk said I could go right up. As I entered the corridor on Finley's floor, I nearly got hit by a fastball—or maybe it was a curve. Finley was throwing to Paul Richards—inventor of the oversized catcher's mitt, leading major-league manager, and onetime manager of the International League Buffalo Bisons—trying to learn what was wrong with the motion of one of his pitchers, whose record had suddenly gone into the tank. Finley apologized and invited me into his room. Then, as if to show that he really was a hands-on owner, he grabbed the telephone, called his manager in the dugout in Oakland, and, upon hearing the score, proceeded to dictate a pitching change!

Finley was baseball's pariah in some quarters (like the NFL's Al Davis), feared, respected for his know-how, but not loved as a partner or personality. He was strong in choosing talent, tough on salaries, and wicked in trades. But for some reason—intangible vibes that I can't analyze—from that day on he treated me with respect and a kind of laconic friendship. We discussed the baseball expansion, our group, the possibilities in the National League, the future of his team, the Bisons, his problems with the Oakland Coliseum, and so on. At the end he apologized for dragging me to Kansas City, but explained that the American League was determined to beat the National to the better venues and had already chosen its two new teams; my best bet was to pursue the other circuit.

Two years later, in the spring of 1970, Charley Finley became quite important to the Sabres. Our group had the informal nod from the NHL, but we were still hooked to the Oakland Seals—nearly a million dollars invested, three thousand miles from our Buffalo base, in a franchise that was still in trouble. We were the only deep pocket the Seals had; the former athletes—Whitey Ford, Pat Summerall, and Dick Lynch—were merely window dressing, and the principals in the entity that technically had majority control—"Transnational Corporation"—could not be found when a call for money went out. We could not own two NHL franchises. How could we extract the Buffalo group?

Luck was with us, together with Charley's competitive spirit, and it turned out to be—if it's not an oxymoron—a happy foreclosure. The bank holding the priority lien on the Seals assets began a court proceeding to seize the Oakland club, including its player contracts. The NHL intervened, and we stood nervously on the sidelines hoping for a sale that would return some of our money. The judge—unfamiliar with the workings of a professional sports franchise—was initially ready to declare the club bankrupt, dissolve it, and release the players as free agents. The league was largely helpless, not fitted—as it was in later years—with the Lender's Cooperation Agreement I subsequently developed, which gave the NHL control over the choice of buyer and method of sale. Fortunately, with the generation of interest from Charley Finley, we were able to present the court with two possible buyers for the franchise in whole, and the judge ordered an auction. The competing bidder's principal claim to fame was as the owner of a roller skating derby, and while his dollar offer was close to equivalent, the league and our group favored Charley. Charley was not about to let another owner dilute his Oakland domain, and Charley won.

Unfortunately, Finley's success in baseball did not carry over to hockey. The hockey fans were of a different demographic: baseball is a largely blue-collar sport in Oakland, while hockey appealed more to middle- and upper-class fans living in San Francisco and San Jose. The effort required to get to the Oakland Coliseum across the bay was apparently more than the hockey fans would commit, but Charley hung in there with the Seals for several years, hoping for the construction of a new arena, better located, which never materialized until the Gunds brought it about with the expansion San Jose Sharks in 1990. Charley incurred substantial criticism from the NHL hierarchy during his period of ownership. His reputation did not improve when he fired his old-line general manager without much notice and skimped on benefits to his players. But Charley foresaw more than most the overall financial difficulties of a league without major national television revenue and was playing his usual role of enthusiasm tempered by business sense.

The Seals adopted white skates, a new name (Golden Seals), and new personnel—all to no avail. A sale to Mel Swig, whose family owned the Fairmount Hotel, still did not produce the new arena at Urba Buena, and Swig, disappointed when the vote vetoed the new building, got permission in 1976 to move the franchise to Cleveland—itself without a satisfactory arena downtown. The move would not have been possible without cancellation of the long-term lease with the Oakland authorities, and I was able to use the goodwill we had created under our brief Oakland ownership, together with some technical arguments, to release the league and the franchise from their Oakland obligations. Throughout his participation in NHL Governors' meetings, Charley seemed to look to me, if not for help, at least for objectivity. He would seat himself directly across from me, lock on to my gaze, and speak at me while his strong bass voice spread his unpopular opinions around the room. For many years after he left the league and after his death, I handled the distribution of his share of NHL expansion revenues to his family, as he had directed me to do.

In 1977 came the blizzard of Buffalo—the worst snowstorm in the history of the city—and my wife, Bikki, frustrated by cancelled and delayed vacations—usually because of my NHL duties—persuaded me to buy a winter home in Boca Raton, Florida. The first call on the new phone was the booming bass of Charley O. We had not seen each other for several years, but Charley began without prelude: "Bob, this is Charles O. Finley. You got the NHL out of Oakland. How about helping me and my baseball team to get out, too?"

When Charley left the NHL, his counsel, John Paul Stevens (now a justice of the United States Supreme Court) and Frank Meyers reported, "Charley likes you, Bob. He says to tell you this league will be all right if they listen to you!" I laughed and wished them well.

Chapter 17

PUCKS, PRIDE, AND PREJUDICE

I t didn't take long to learn that NHL owners, like most of us, were not paradigms of intellect, courage, or virtue. I've dealt elsewhere with the Vancouver owner who tried to pass himself a major dividend without including the public shareholders in the distribution, the Pittsburgh banker who led his club straight to bankruptcy, the Hartford partner who defrauded the league and the lenders with forged balance sheets and income tax returns, the California chairman who pawned the same ancient coins with two different banks, and the Toronto hockey mogul who arranged for his personal home to be built with funds of the publicly held franchise. For the most part, however, NHL owners have been men of power and ability, with normal virtues but also normal faults—among the latter, the curse of prejudice.

It was June 1978, at the Montreal Forum. The scene: the draft table at the NHL Amateur Draft (later called the entry draft). The arena was packed: full of young players eighteen to twenty years old, their agents, lawyers, and parents—a high point in their lives. To be chosen by an NHL team in any round was like receiving a Phi Beta Kappa diploma from Harvard. With sixteen teams in the league, and twelve rounds, that meant fame and fortune—you were automatically one of the best two hundred players in that year's amateur class of more than five thousand. Every rookie who thought he had a chance was there, hoping to be picked in an early round, hoping

179

to be chosen by a famous team, hoping to be drafted by a club that needed his particular skills—defense, power forward, goaltender, forechecker, whatever—badly. Dreams of the Cup, the press, the salary.

It was a unique privilege to be at the drafting table. There were only ten or twelve chairs, and we needed to accommodate more than that. The GM, Punch Imlach, presided and performed. Then there was the assistant GM, John Anderson; the scouts—eastern, Canadian, western, Russian, European; the coaches; the PR guy; and the principal working owners, Seymour and Norty Knox. I earned a seat at the table, I guess, partly because of my work in creating the franchise, but also because we saw early on that legal interpretations of the rules and policy judgments were called for in the high-pressure, improvised nature of the draft. A highly talented, one-eyed player named Greg Neeld came up. Could we get him accepted by the league? Was the NHL rule requiring minimum sight constitutional? Could we, in our first year, have a pick in the interleague draft that could influence the pick coming up in the entry draft? Our European scout urged us to take a highly touted Russian player, Alexander Mogilny. Was it worthwhile wasting a late pick on him? The Soviets had refused to let their young players migrate to the NHL, even with an offered ransom. Could we get around the Russian rule?

These questions called for tough, extemporaneous answers, because you couldn't predict with any certainty—unless you had the number one overall pick (as we did with Perreault in our first draft in 1969)—whether or when a particular player would be available. I had earned Punch's satirical respect when, in that first draft, I had persuaded Clarence Campbell and the draft managers to give the new teams picks in the intraleague draft (from the minor leagues and from existing clubs). That gave us Joe Daley, who played goaltender without a mask, whom Punch immediately traded for goaltender Roger Crozier, who, along with Gilbert Perreault, gave us respectability and ultimately success in our first five years in the league.

The June 1978 draft returned to the Queen Elizabeth Hotel public format, much to the displeasure of Punch, and much to our entertainment. The draft by conference call, which had been in place for several years, had deprived the clubs and the fans of the theatrical atmosphere the draft could produce. Punch could once again use his wit, his perky hat, and his sense of theater to strut about the drafting floor, debate, declaim, horsetrade before the cameras. With his reputation, know-how, and results, he had brought our expansion team to the playoffs in three years and to the Stanley Cup Finals in five; the Knoxes, though world-class athletes themselves, for the most part withheld their veto powers.

We got Punch Imlach as our first, and probably best, general manager, through an accident of timing—he had just been fired by Harold Ballard from his post as GM of the Toronto Maple Leafs—and a sensitive and adroit call to me from NHL president Clarence Campbell. We had just been

Punch Imlach, the Sabres first GM. Copyright © Bill Wippert.

informed by the finance committee that we were getting the nod for an expansion franchise in the spring of 1969 when the call came in. "Bob," asked Clarence—it had been "Mr. Swados" or "Counsel" in Oakland; "Bob" was a recognition that we were at least junior partners now—"have you decided on a manager—who's going to run your club?" I responded that we had been so busy with getting the acceptance of the league, raising capital, and the like, we hadn't given it much thought.

"Well," he said, "That is the *first* thing you should be thinking about. There's a man available—and if you get him, it'd be a ten strike!" The man was George "Punch" Imlach, and it was a major seminal break for us. He taught us not only hockey strategy on and off the ice, the management of players, and the organization structure, but hockey economics as well. And he did it with humor, literate style, and mature confidence in his judgment. We got hold of him immediately, and after a few days of friendly, pro forma negotiations—he thoroughly enjoyed toying with these rookie owners—he condescended to sign up. It was really a no-brainer for Punch—it was almost the same market, only two hours from his home in Toronto, and a chance to crosscheck the scalawag who fired him.

(I'm reminded that, years later, when the NHL granted a franchise to Wayne Huizenga for the Florida Panthers in 1992, Wayne had his business vice president, Rich Rochon, ask me, "What should we do first, hire a president or a general manager?" I answered, remembering Punch, there's available one of the best guys in the business, who could handle both jobs. I recommended Bill Torrey, who had been our assistant GM in Oakland and helped create the five-Cup dynasty of the Islanders. Huizenga was on the phone, lining up Torrey, by three o'clock that afternoon.)

By 1978 Punch had gone through a heart attack, had been forced to give up coaching, and had suffered the disappointment of the loss by his strong team (even with the French Connection) to the Philadelphia Flyers in the 1975 Cup Finals. There were concerns that he was losing his drive. It wasn't long before I found out he still had guts.

As we approached the second round of the 1978 draft—our next pick was number thirty-two—there were a number of quality players still available: Stan Smyl, who would play 896 NHL games and score 673 points for the Vancouver Canucks; Rob McClanahan, a member of the 1980 Olympic team, who we drafted with one of our second-round picks; Curt Giles, who would be drafted by Minnesota; Craig McTavish, the Eastern Collegiate Conference rookie of the year, drafted later that day by the Boston Bruins; Anton Stastny; Russian star goaltender Viascheslav Fetisov; and Tony McKegney, a winger from Kingston in the OHA. After talking the situation over with his coach, Floyd Smith, and his scouts, Punch announced to the table his choice was McKegney. To our collective shock, Norty shouted, "No way!" McKegney was black.

The silence at the table was profound, with Punch staring boldly at the owner. Finally, Punch spoke: "Don't tell me I can't draft the best player available!" Norty backed off, and we drafted Tony.

This was Punch's last year with our team—it is possible that his departure was hastened by the McKegney confrontation. He renewed his love-hate relationship with Harold Ballard for a time, without success for the Leafs. Punch died in 1987.

McKegney proved to be a valuable asset of the Sabres for a number of years, from the 1978–79 through the 1982–83 seasons, scoring 268 points in 363 games, an average of nearly three-quarters of a point per game. In his last year with the Sabres, he produced nearly a point a game. He was personable and popular, and came back to live in Buffalo after his twelve-year career in the NHL was over.

McKegney did well under Scotty Bowman, Punch's ultimate successor as GM and coach, until, in the 1983 playoffs, he was caught napping (and yapping) at center ice and lost the faceoff, which led to the winning goal, ousting the Sabres from the series. Scotty merely expressed his "disappointment in Tony" to me; but Scotty's wrath was a formidable thing, and McKegney was traded that summer to Quebec in a deal for Real Cloutier and a first-round pick. Scotty called me at 5:00 AM to get legal approval, which I reluctantly gave. In Buffalo, Cloutier proved to be a complete over-the-hill bust.

Tony was a friend, fun to be with. For years my wife, Bikki, remembered the last four digits of our phone number by reciting, "Tony, Schony, Rene Robert": their uniform numbers—6 . . . 8 . . . 14.

PERREAULT THE NONPAREIL

From the drop of the first puck in October 1970, Gilbert Perreault *was* the Sabres franchise. In my judgment and recollection, until Dominik Hasek took over goal in the mid-1990s, no player so dominated play and popularity for the Buffalo club. He retired in 1986, after sixteen years in a Sabres uniform, and nearly twenty years later is still the team's all-time leader in almost every major category: regular-season games played, goals, assists, points, and game-winning goals. He had style and strength and skill. From the outset, he produced excitement; with his strong ankles and lower limbs, he cold pivot and deke and check and shoot and change speeds, frequently weaving his way through the entire opposition, leaving the forwards and defense looking weak and foolish. Unlike other great players who were net crashers or relied on "garbage goals"—standing in the slot, picking up loose pucks—Bert had a smooth, creative flow that was instantly visible and appealing to the sophisticated Sabres fans. For a rookie franchise, this was intoxicating. His defensive play might not match that of modern "two-

Gil Perreault. Copyright © Bill Wippert.

way" stars, but for the new franchise Punch was building, offense was the needed ingredient; and with the addition of Rick Martin as our number one pick in the 1971 draft (number five overall) and the trade for Rene Robert in 1972, came the French Connection, and the excitement and success continued. I've always had a very cordial relationship with Gilbert.

Bert had a boyish, playful personality. (He now regales the Sabre alumni events with very enthusiastic renditions of rock songs.) That, with his slow accommodation to English, obscured his intelligence. The knock on Bert among the professional hockey people in the organization, strangely enough, was that he was *too talented*. He could have been the greatest player in the business, they said, notwithstanding the Orrs and the LaFleurs and the Espositos, but he didn't work hard enough, he didn't have that drive to win at all costs. There was a certain amount of green monsterism, I think, especially among the grinders and defense, who had to work hard—and Bert made it look so easy! And, of course, he was well compensated, at early 1970s levels.

I had a quite different impression of Bert. In 1978, shortly before the end of Perreault's first contract, Punch Imlach suffered a heart attack, and the task of negotiating the renewal fell to me. I believe the negotiations were facilitated in part by my limited, but dramatic use of the French language. I appeared in a play in college—*Kind Lady*—in which the lady in question is kidnapped and imprisoned in her own home until a French man employed as an adviser rings the bell and the lady, under constant threat from the crooks, tries frantically to signal the true situation. My director had the discipline of a Scotty Bowman and in learning the part I had to spend weeks with the head of the French department, perfecting my spoken French. The result was an accent of quality—sounding authentic and close enough to Quebec French to give me an opening pleasant response. My vocabulary in the language was not equivalent and frequently got me into trouble in later years (as in army times in France and Alsace), when the authentic sounds of "Comment ça va" produced a stream of excited response with which I couldn't possibly keep up.

But the French was good enough for Bert and his agent. I had no difficulty hearing and understanding Bert's emphatic response to my first proposal: "Low pay," he whispered. We worked it out, and I acquired some respect for his acumen as well as his hockey skills.

My view of Bert was reinforced some years later when, at a game in the Canada Cup tournament in Hamilton, Bert, who had been invited to play on the Canadian team, was injured and sat in a box with me to view the game. It was a rare privilege: relaxed and under no pressure, his English became more fluent. His observations on the playoffs, the strategy, the plays—good and bad—were trenchant, witty, and perspicacious. I felt like a young student again and had a great time. I began to think: coach? Ever since my experience in the army in Europe in 1944 as a PFC and later as a second lieutenant, I had abandoned the notion that a graduate college education was a necessary ingredient of judgment or success. Some of the most effective managers in sports went directly from high school or junior into the sports franchise, and had remained there for most of their careers.

When it came time for Bert to retire in 1986, he expected, in view of his major contribution to the franchise, that he would be accorded treatment similar to that of Jean Beliveau, the great center for the Montreal Canadiens who had retired shortly after Bert came on the NHL scene. Beliveau, a handsome, urbane French Canadian, had been elected a vice president of the Montreal team and had been given respectable assignments, primarily of a public relations nature. Bert not only expected prestige, but a substantial salary, within a slapshot of his compensation as a player. In the eyes of his sometime teammate Gerry Meehan, however, the cases were not comparable. Gerry was now general manager of the Sabres, succeeding Scotty Bowman, and his view of Bert, supported by the Knoxes and influenced by budgetary pressures, gave no encouragement to Bert's desires, and he was left to his own devices. He served as a part-time scout for the team, then ended up coaching a club in the Quebec Major Junior Hockey League, with unsatisfactory results both on and off the ice. So we had, instead of a major public relations asset—Bert's popularity drew warm applause at every appearance—an embittered major star with a sense of a prejudiced, disinterested, and ungrateful ownership.

It took nearly ten years to return Bert to the Sabres fold. Some aggressive promotion and negotiations by a new agent, working with the French Connection as a group, finally persuaded Sabres management (primarily Larry Quinn, who believed in the threesome as a public relations asset) to make concrete arrangements for appearances and compensation, and the use of Bert in alumni events restored a positive relationship.

PETER GILBERT—THE "CABLE GUY"

Neither the McKegney incident, with its subsequent, if not related, departure of Punch, nor the severance or temporary disenchantment of Perreault had a permanent impact on the fortunes of the Sabres. But a major gaffe occurred with one Peter Gilbert, the owner of the principal cable systems in the Buffalo area.

Bill Wirtz, chairman of the Chicago Blackhawks, was an able leader—he was chairman of the NHL for most of my regime as secretary—and a committed and enthusiastic hockey man. But he had his prejudices, too—mostly against incompetence. One was a belief that *gate*, and not television, was the essential strength of the league. He did not discount the revenue from away games, but he refused to permit his Blackhawks to televise any hockey dates in his own arena. Sellouts were of paramount importance for the sale of season tickets, felt Bill, and he even cast a jaundiced eye on league playoff games when the Chicago team was involved. To this day, Blackhawk regular-season dates at home are broadcast on radio only. In the early days of the Sabres franchise, the "Wirtz doctrine" prevailed, and even with the onset of cable, few Buffalo home dates were televised. Preservation of the gate, Dave Forman agreed, was the governing rule. Then along came Peter Gilbert, former Israeli, builder and loser of two fortunes, aggressive, optimistic, and street smart—and knowledgeable and practical in the infant, but soon mushrooming, cable business.

Said Peter Gilbert to the Sabres: I understand your reluctance to televise your home dates; you're afraid you'll lose ticket sales. But suppose I can show you that you and I will make more money and expand your audience and my subscribers if we make the Sabres the most important product on cable television. Cable needs more patrons, and you need dollars beyond your gate. We'll pay you fees for your home game rights, and those fees will more than compensate you for any loss of ticket sales. Dave Forman, our vice president for television matters, liked Peter, and joined with me in working out our first cable arrangement. Dave did not go beyond a straight fixed-fee arrangement, but the fees were welcome dollars, and with the Sabres' record of sellouts and popularity, the risk that more fans would stay at home than buy tickets did not seem that great. The Sabres were at first sold only as a part of the standard cable fee, and the Gilbert idea worked well for the cable company; the right to see the games on basic cable was clearly a major factor in Gilbert's increased penetration of the cable market.

Of course, as the fans bought more seats, Dave Forman would demand and receive increased fees for the Sabres, but the contracts never shifted over to an equity participation. We received no percentage of Gilbert's profit. And the profits were substantial, as Peter acquired adjacent markets in the suburban areas. (He could not, at that time, acquire the customers in the inner city.)

By way of contrast, Ed Snider, the owner of the Philadelphia Flyers, adopted a different course—Ed insisted on full partnership participation on a percentage basis in cable growth, at least as to the part of the cable company's revenue attributable to the hockey nights. The owner of the New York Islanders went further, demanding and receiving a percentage of the *entire* revenue of its rights buyer, whether derived from hockey games, network programs, movies, or anything else. The Flyers and the Islanders took an equity risk, and the gambles paid handsomely.

In its deals with *Hockey Night in Canada*, because of the near monopoly by Molson in the Canadian market, the league had had to restrict itself to flat fees, and my friends around the governors' table continually chided me on our cable conservatism. But when I would raise the issue of an equity or percentage participation in overall cable revenue as a new contract came up, Dave and the Knoxes would not respond.

Peter was fun to be with, and as more Western New Yorkers leased his cable boxes to see the Sabres and he negotiated deals with the local officials, he became a popular figure. He joined the board of Studio Arena, making a substantial contribution; he became active in the United Way and the United Jewish Appeal, and the size of his gifts and his irrepressive energy gave him influence. I would tell with relish his encounter with Armand Hammer, the chairman of the board of General Dynamics. Peter was not shy, and before he left the chairman's office he departed with a signed check for a million dollars. He was an avid tennis player—doubles only. With stocky build and bald dome, he would poach like an ancient Judean tank.

It became clear that with his commercial success, he longed for social recognition. But his abrasive style and, I'm afraid, his religious persuasion were not social assets in some quarters. He applied for membership in the Buffalo Club (the city's primary private club) and was turned down. Too abrasive, too aggressive, too sharp, the word was. Peter did not consult me about these activities (except for the theater), and with the vivid memories of my own Niagara Falls experience, when it took my senior partner ten years to get into the exclusive Niagara Club, I was not about to volunteer advice. But I did at appropriate occasions describe his ventures to the Knoxes and keep alive his continued hints of the desire to trade a part of his company for part ownership of the Sabres. The issue boiled up when Peter offered the Sabres participation in a local UHF station, Channel 29. That owner needed money (Peter had supplied some), and the Buffalo VHF stations (Channels 2, 4, and 7) had lowballed the Sabres, claiming to have lost their appetite for the programming in view of the number of games on cable. It would, Peter argued, make a perfect fit. Channel 29 didn't barrel into Canada the way the major stations did, but it would reach the Canadian fans and give the team an exclusive over the air outlet to buttress the cable distribution.

Again reminding Seymour and Norty of the persistent advice from other owners in the NHL—"You should have a piece of the cable action"— I supported Peter's offer. The answer was abrupt and final: "You want to be partners with *that guy*?"

Peter was disappointed, as was I, but his desire for recognition and social stature was undiminished. A few months later the owner of the Colorado Rockies, a nice fellow named Arthur Imperatore, was in our Directors' Room for a game with the Sabres. He had important real estate holdings in the New Jersey area and had bought the Denver club with a view to moving it to the Meadowlands, near his property. Unfortunately, Arthur had run into one of those economic and political knots that sometimes drove strange decisions by the league. A few years later, the transfer to the Meadowlands would be sanctioned and the Quebec team would move to Denver, but at that juncture, Imperatore's move had failed to get Board of Governors approval. The Denver fans were not happy about a gypsy owner, and the losses were mounting.

Peter was in the Sabres' Directors' Room, mostly at the bar, and, as was his wont, had dipped deeply into the club's supply of Stolychnya vodka. Somehow, between periods, Imperatore and Gilbert had merged each other's troubles. After the game, Peter approached me, without ceremony, saying, "Bob, I've just *bought* the Colorado Rockies!"

Thinking, Do I respond as friend or league counsel? I replied, "Are you asking me or telling me?"

"I'M TELLING YOU!"

"Then, Peter," I said, "I have no responsibility."

With the width and breadth of my contacts and my knowledge of the financial problems of the Rockies, I could have alerted Peter to the dangers of the Colorado rapids; but I was acutely conscious of my role as league secretary, and I thought then that Peter was bailing my fellow owners out of a very uncomfortable situation. And, after all, Peter didn't ask for advice or information; he was hell-bent to show the Knox-Buffalo group that he could be a governor on his own.

The decision was bad news for all parties. Peter tried hard to be a generous and energetic owner. He tried all sorts of gimmicks to capture the fans, going so far on one game night as to auction off the sirloins, tenderloins, horns, and hooves of a prize bull. At one point I received a painful call. "You should have warned me," he said. "Not about the money, but about the *time* involved." But the Denver citizens still regarded the Buffalo cable impresario as a potential carpetbagger, and with the team giving only a journeyman performance, the gate never grew and the cash drain quickly became serious.

I had direct knowledge of how fast hockey losses could consume an owner's capital: it had happened in Oakland, St. Louis, Cleveland, and Kansas City. The league had refused to permit a move of the Blues from St. Louis to Saskatoon largely because the Saskatchewan applicant, who considered himself a wealthy man, showed assets that we judged clearly insufficient for the operating losses projected. I felt bad, though, when Peter called in distress; by the January of his second year as owner, he was ready to give up. The Rockies had drained so much cash it looked as if he couldn't finish the season. What could I do to help? "Look," I said, "you *must* finish the season. If you don't show up for your dates in the other teams' buildings and pay the players, nobody will give you a dollar, let alone a prayer, and it'll be lawsuit time." I called John Ziegler (then president), ran the

Oakland and Cleveland precedents by him, and assured him (with some trepidation) that Peter was not a deadbeat and would meet his responsibilities. Together, after consulting Bill Wirtz, we agreed that to protect the season, we could get enough teams to put a loan together. The move to the Meadowlands with an acceptable new owner was beginning to ripen, so Peter's departure might not be a permanent problem for the league.

At the board meeting we quickly convened, Peter's prayer was respectful but pitiful. "I've earned and lost two fortunes," he said. "I can't survive the loss of a third." We produced a loan of $1 million shared by some of the clubs (including the Sabres), enough to get the team to the end of the season. A group headed by John McMullen negotiated a purchase in a series of 2-to-5 AM conferences—with me as the league negotiator—involving some tough territorial and TV problems with the "corridor clubs" (Rangers, Islanders, and Philadelphia). Gilbert was partially bailed out with the funds from the McMullen group, and the Colorado Rockies were transmuted into the New Jersey Devils.

Meanwhile, the Sabres, faced with rising costs and having rejected Gilbert, his cable company, and Channel 29, embarked on its own television venture: the purchase of a new Buffalo UHF channel, 49. It consumed an additional investment by George Strawbridge, Rich Products, the Knoxes, and others in our group of more than $3.5 million. But its short and unhappy life, frustrated by the failure to get approval by television authorities to carry the Sabres games on Canadian cable, produced a near disaster.

Meanwhile, Peter found a measure of the recognition he sought so strongly in his personal life. As president of the city's regional theater, faced with the departure of our artistic director, I appointed Peter chairman of a committee to find a replacement. In the city of St. Louis he found not only the new theater head, but a charming lady with the strange first name Edes. Edes had credentials—she was headmistress of the leading damsels' private school in that city. She was gentle—and gentile—and qualified quickly in the right circles. They married, and I hope they did—I *believe* they did—live happily ever after.

Chapter 18

OWNERS I HAVE KNOWN AND HOPE NEVER TO SEE AGAIN

The Sabres' first season in the NHL was 1970–71. It was a time of excitement and joy as a new a member of the league, but it didn't take long to discover that all members of that elite club were not necessarily men of sterling character.

THE VANCOUVER SHELL GAME

Vancouver entered the National Hockey League in 1970, in tandem with Buffalo. There, the similarity ended. The Knox-Buffalo group had played the expansion game aggressively, forcing the price upward from $2 million to $6 million, as a means of sending its competition (Cleveland and Baltimore) to the dust heap. Yet the Canadians, who believed they were entitled to a franchise as a matter of right, balked at the new figure. (Punch Imlach told Seymour Knox we had paid "too much" for the Sabres!) Philadelphia, St. Louis, and Los Angeles—all questionable hockey markets—had got in for $2 million each; why should a traditional, hot hockey area such as Vancouver have to pay three times as much? British Columbia men of wealth stood on the sidelines, disdaining a "bad business deal." The league had to look to an American entrepreneur—some would say, adventurer—Tom Skallen, to accept the NHL's terms for the franchise.

Skallen was not a bad sort, just cash short. The league had opened the door, permitting the new clubs to pay for the franchise in installments, but that was not enough for Tom. He had to borrow even the cash portion. This required collateral, and the collateral was right in front of his nose—the assets and income of the Vancouver Canucks, the minor-league organization that had been a success in the Western Hockey League. But how to get at those assets? The shares in the minor-league company were owned by the public, who'd ended up with 20 percent of the equity in the combined major- and minor-league enterprise. Tom had decided not to dissolve the Canucks or buy the public shares—they were an important source of season ticket money—so he contrived the following "bootstrap" strategy: Tom's company, Northwest Sports, would borrow the money needed to pay the cash portion to the league, and give its note for the balance. Northwest Sports would buy 80 percent of the Canucks, leaving the public shares, representing the remaining 20 percent, in place. The Canucks would operate the NHL team and its earnings would be used to pay off the parent company's bank loan and debt to the league.

Under US tax law, as it was accepted at that time, the "bootstrap"—buying a company with its own assets—would be completed by *merging* the subsidiary (the Canucks) into the parent (Northwest), and the debt would end up in the same corporation as the earning assets. The merger technique would have been easy if Northwest were the only stockholder, but with the hundreds of public shareholders out there, the merger could not take place without risking costly demands by the public to be bought out—at the $6 million value. Moreover, there was no insurance that the Canadian authorities would not, as the US IRS ultimately did, disapprove the plan and tax the merger to death.

So when the time came to pay off the bank borrowings and the league note, Tom Skallen took the bull by the horns, taking what he thought was an equitable leap. After all, the debt had been incurred to buy the major-league franchise and the public shareholders in the Canucks would benefit proportionately with Tom's ownership—so why not have the Canucks pay off the debt? In the event, checks went from the Canucks directly to the league—or, rather, went from the Canucks to Northwest, from Northwest to the lending bank, and from the bank to the league. STOP! said the public shareholder dissenters—motivated no doubt for some by the opportunity for greenmail—forcing Skallen to pay them an inflated price, or perhaps resentment of others that the Americans had "stolen" the Canucks opportunity to go major league. "You paid yourself a dividend, and didn't pay anything to us!" they argued. And the Canadian courts held they were right.

Tom argued unsuccessfully that all he was doing was paying the hockey club's own debt. But he was undone by the form of the transaction he had created. Northwest, the 80 percent owner of the Canucks, owed the debt;

the Canucks did not. Thus, when he used Canucks money to pay off the loan or installment—without permission of the public shareholders—Tom had not only acted improperly, in the view of the British Columbia court, he had engaged in an act of grand larceny. A replenishment of the money "misappropriated" could probably have been arranged, but the passion and resentment of the Vancouver public could not and should not, in the eyes of the prosecutors, be curbed. And poor Tom Skallen, innovative planner but shoestring owner, went to jail.

The media attention given to Skallen's troubles did produce a sharper understanding of the value of the Vancouver NHL club, and with the purchase of two new franchises in 1972 (Atlanta and the Islanders)—again at $6 million—the expansion price seemed more acceptable, and the league was able to attract new owners of substance. Skallen was succeeded by Frank Griffith, owner of a burgeoning television and cable company covering most of western Canada, and his partner, Bill Hughes, a very popular radio commentator in Vancouver. Bill, who with his wife, Dorothy, became good friends of mine, served as president of the Canucks for several years, then sold out. Frank Griffith and his son Arthur remained as solid, intelligent owners and governors, supporters of league growth for many years.

Hockey ownership attracts people of drive, loyalty, and charm—as, for example, the first owner of the New York Islanders, Roy Boe. I would never put Roy in my Cabinet of NHL Rogues, although he, too, practiced prestidigitation with his bank collateral. (He apparently pledged the same TV rights with two different lenders.) But Roy had a winning smile, a showbiz approach to the game, and a kindness and sensitivity that was much appreciated. When my son, Lincoln, who was emotionally ill, needed a job to give him some sense of independence, Roy put him to work at the Islanders. Linc ultimately could not sustain the responsibility and had to withdraw and Roy later had to sell out. But I'll always be grateful for Roy's kindness. I much preferred his company to that of his successor, a wealthy Palm Beach socialite who was not above making secret deals under the governors' table.

Chances are that the financial difficulties of the Canucks and Islanders in those early years were exacerbated by the invasion of the WHA. The "outlaw" league began the salary escalation as it bid away stars such as Bobby Hull; and the sudden inflation of player budgets soured the financial projections.

THE HARTFORD DEBACLE

The Hartford Whalers were the only non-Canadian team to survive in the WHA and become an NHL club in the 1979 expansion. With the financial strength of Aetna and the other insurance companies headquartered in

Hartford, hopes were high for a successful life for NHL hockey in that city. The energy was provided by Howard Baldwin, an intelligent owner who would wrestle with a number of unstable franchise situations in the league over the years—from Hartford to Minnesota to Pittsburgh. The team was under the direction of Emile Francis, a once-great Ranger goaltender who served as general manager. I always liked Emile; he spoke with candor and relish, and a practical knowledge of the business. You might not agree with his judgments, but we always knew where he stood. Representing Aetna, the insurance giant, was Don Conrad, a very nice guy with a very attractive wife. Don ultimately became an owner, sharing his position with Richard Gordon, a pleasant but taciturn guy with a high net worth in Connecticut real estate. I handled the owner in and out transactions for the league, as its secretary and special counsel, and I enjoyed the occasional trips to Whalers headquarters to get the governors' requirements negotiated and executed.

Richard Gordon was a fine host and an enthusiastic tennis player—he had gone so far as to place Ivan Lendl, the once-dominant tennis champion, on the Whalers' board of directors. Ivan was a hockey fan as well—his father had been a hockey coach in Czechoslovakia. I had known Ivan from the days when he lived in my resort community of Boca West in Boca Raton, Florida. When Lendl was in residence, I would bike over to watch him practice—he'd hit those tremendous backhands down the line! The Sabres had chosen a talented Czech player, Jiri Dudachek, as their first pick in the entry draft. It was in the days before the treaty agreements between the NHL and the European countries, and we had a devil of a time getting him out. Defection would have been dangerous in those cold war times, as it was in 1989 for Alexander Mogilny. The Czechs were banning their top players from migrating to the United States. Ivan introduced me to the famous Czech Davis Cup tennis champion Nike Pillic, who promised to help. But we were never able to pierce the Czech hockey curtain, and Dudachek never reached the NHL and faded from view.

As salaries continued to escalate and his team did not produce any championship—even after giving up five first-round picks for defenseman Glen Wesley—Gordon became discouraged with the losses and asked to be bought out. The economy began to decline in Hartford; the staid fat cats in the insurance business didn't know how to compete, and their passion for Whalers season tickets began to fade. Even Aetna began to show signs of weakness. I was not surprised when President Bill Clinton's nominee for attorney general, Zoe Baird, an Aetna associate general counsel, turned out to be a mediocrity who failed to pay withholding taxes or report income of her domestic help. I liked and respected Don Conrad, but was not impressed with the other Aetna officers I met.

With the departure of Gordon, Conrad had to find a new partner. Don was a man of commitment, but he could not bear the fiscal burdens alone.

There then appeared on the scene one Ben Sisti, who offered to take over Gordon's position. His credentials looked fine. As was our practice, I requested recent tax returns and financial statements, as prepared by his CPA. The documents appeared, showing net worth and income in the millions—large enough to meet the NHL criteria and to satisfy Conrad that he would not be the only "deep pocket" in the picture. The certification on the financials bore the stamp and signature of one of the Big Eight national accounting firms.

It was a shock to discover, less than six months later, that the Sisti crowd were fakes; the financials were fiction, and the CPA signatures, even on the tax returns, were forged. Our friend Don Conrad was suddenly without a partner. But Sisti was still technically an owner, and the franchise was unbuyable in that state. The league had never had to oust one of several investors before. I had to craft a charge against the Whalers that would somehow exempt Conrad. I opted for a "magic bullet"—a charge of "involuntary termination" that would fit into the language of the constitution. This enabled the league to pull the franchise and sell a new one to Conrad and a new owner.

In the search for a new owner, there followed a period of reluctant courtship—reluctant because the Hartford market was now suspect—culminating in a purchase of Don's interest and the team's assets by Peter Karmanos, a very successful computer mogul who had flirted with NHL ownership for some years. Karmanos kept the team in place for a time, and Governor John Rowland made a feeble attempt to keep the team in Hartford; but the decline of the insurers and the Hartford economy had taken a severe toll, and ultimately the team was moved to Carolina, the Whale transmogrifying into the Hurricane.

To this day I don't know what motivated Sisti to become involved in the hockey team. Money laundering? A thirst for respectability? Or the hypnotic surge that comes with being part of the game?

A NEAR MISS

Then there were the cases where we were lucky and the scoundrel never made it to the governors' table. The Islanders had this experience in the late 1990s, after I had ceased to be secretary, when an applicant to purchase the franchise submitted his financials and his documents, got board approval, and the lawyers, accountants, owners, and league executives assembled for the closing. The problem? The buyer was absent, and, it appeared, absent without leave. Don't worry, came the word. Was the check in the mail? No, the *wire transfer* was on its way—from Great Britain. Amid rising anger, the assembled experts cooled their heels but not their blood pressure. Hours went by, and no wire transfer appeared. The funds never arrived, and the pretender disappeared from view. A further check with the "authentic" sources indicated that neither the applicant nor his fortune had ever existed.

THE STORM OVER THE LIGHTNING

I narrowly missed such a calamity in the course of negotiating the grant of a franchise to Tampa Bay in 1992. The group seeking the franchise were knowledgeable, experienced, and sophisticated. I liked them all: Phil Esposito, one of the greats of the game, a hero of the Canadian triumph over the Soviets in the 1972 Summit Series; his brother Tony, a record-holding goalie; and Mel Lowell, one of the smart financial guys in the Rangers organization. Both Tony and Phil had been active as officers of the NHL Players' Association, and my wife and I had had some good times with the Espositos at the owner-player meetings, where I had been an ex officio representative of the clubs on the negotiating committee. Phil was set to be the president and GM; Tony, the chief scout; and Mel, the controller. They had only one problem—their resources were far from adequate. They needed a money man badly.

The first meeting seemed to go well. George Steinbrenner, who had

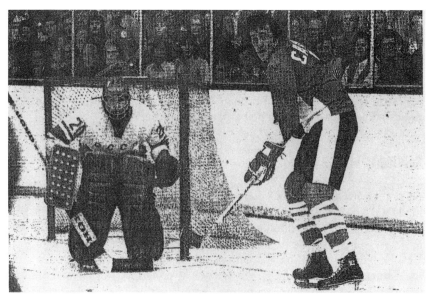

Phil Esposito and Soviet goaltender Vladislav Tretiak. Copyright © Bill Wippert.

substantial interests in the Tampa area, was present, recognized me from our Buffalo baseball crusading days—"I know the man!" he said—and seemed to help create an optimistic air. But George was only taking 5 percent, and he soon traded that off to another Tampa partner. For various reasons, the outside investors did not meld with the Esposito crew. Phil and Tony were determined to retain control disproportionate to their investment, and there was conflict over where the team should play while a new arena was being constructed. (The prospect of having to use as a temporary facility an indoor baseball stadium, an hour away from Tampa, seating twice the normal hockey capacity, was not very appealing.) There was a question as to whether the new hockey club would be entitled to Florida's $3 million subsidy for new professional sports venues. There was also a conflict over TV territory with the Miami club. I tried to help on every front I could, and we did resolve the TV dispute and clear the way for the subsidy, but the equity investment remained uncertain. Then word came to the league that the problem was solved. Phil had made a deal with—you guessed it!—British money. The "duke of Manchester" would provide the balance of the equity. The duke, we were told, had those resources typical of the English landed gentry—an impeccable historic dukedom and plenty of assets to go with it. The duke never appeared before the league in person, but Phil had met him and was appropriately impressed.

I ordered the usual due diligence, including financial and character investigations and references. Because of the off-shore funding, the investigation took longer than usual. We were well into negotiating the closing documents when the report came back from our British connections: the duke still had his title, all right, but little else. His record showed signs of insolvency, judgments, and charges of fraud—a nightmare. I called Phil with the bad news: the league would never accept the duke. Phil did not accept the news well. "Goddamn it!" he shouted. "You guys have never helped me at all!"

I felt bad—but it was not the league's job to raise the money for the Esposito group. But Phil, as dogged and determined in the financial arena as he always was in the crease, finally came up with his major investor: a Japanese company called Kokasai Green, owner and operator of numerous Japanese golf courses. It was a strange business, rarely a profitable one in the United States. The investment structure called for golfing members to invest in long-term, almost lifetime bonds, and the board of the golf course company had complete discretion as to how to reinvest the proceeds of the bond sales. In our anxiety to get the franchise secure—it was scheduled to enter the league with the Ottawa Senators, Disney's Mighty Ducks, and the Florida Panthers the next season—we tended to discount questions of board authority and rushed through the due diligence. I entertained the officers of the Kokasai board at a great dinner at Joe's Stone Crab—with an interpreter—and all the questions seemed to be answered with candor and satisfactory substance.

When the day came for Board of Governors' approval, an unexpected antagonist appeared. Stanley Jaffee, the newly appointed governor from the New York Rangers, was a representative of the Hollywood wing of Gulf & Western, the Rangers corporate ownership. He was a cranky critic. In a style more typical of Rodeo Drive than Thirty-third Street, Jaffee showed up with an ascot and a cane, and a demeanor that regarded most of the assembled governors, certainly the league staff, as beneath his purview. He did ask a seminal question, however: Where are the financials? I looked at Ken Sawyer, the NHL's financial vice president, and Ken looked at me. It would normally have been Ken's province, but as things had developed, John Ziegler was looking to me to close the expansion process. We had seen earlier, unaudited statements, but Jaffee was demanding audits. I asked for a time-out, frantically called my key numbers, and came back in the room, assuring the governors the audited statements were on the way. They were, but when I eagerly pulled the pages from the fax machine, I saw to my dismay that the statements were in *Japanese*! I asked for a few hours to get the translation, and my friends on the board acquiesced, but Jaffee would not: "Amateur night!" he shouted. We ultimately straightened it out: the audits were consistent with what had been represented, the Rangers were outvoted, and Phil and his friends got the franchise (with their equity positions diluted). But Stan Jaffee, the Rangers refugee from Hollywood, will forever be enshrined in my NHL Cabinet of Rogues.

THE BALLARD ENIGMA

Hockey people may fight like the devil, but they have one common interest: loyalty. We've all been part of the struggle to remain viable, to achieve recognition, to aspire for victory, or, if not, stability. This belief in loyalty as a major value may be the explanation for the kind treatment of one of the owners who strayed—Harold Ballard, who was in the 1980s and early 1990s the principal owner of the Toronto Maple Leafs. Ballard had been largely in the background in the 1967 to 1970 era, when the Knox-Buffalo group was striving to gain entry to the league. It was Stafford Smythe who seemed to be the guy who exercised the veto over Buffalo's plans, in a simplistic attempt to avoid Buffalo's TV and gate competition. And it may have been the Smythe and Ballard troubles with the Canadian tax authorities—and their minority shareholder and partners in Maple Leaf Gardens—that weakened the duo to the point that their opposition to the Sabres entry was no longer respected. I met Harold Ballard for lunch on the day the duo's indictment for theft was announced to the press. The governors had left the two of us alone—I as representing a rookie owner, but Harold seemed deserted as a disgraced governor. I tried to be kind and understanding, and offered my counselor's advice, but it was clear that I was too new; I was not a part of the Original Six, with its family-like traditions. I could see that Harold was, naturally, distracted, and consolation from this new kid on the block—a thorn in the Leafs' monopoly territory— was not worth much.

As the evidence rolled in, it appeared that Harold and Stafford—not the sole owners of the franchise at all—had played fast and loose with some of the assets of the Toronto team. The two lived in elaborate homes, built or improved, it was revealed, with funds and services provided by the Leafs at no cost to themselves. When the Gardens was engaged in a major refurbishing and expansion, Harold and Stafford had appropriated materials and services from the contractor. They were also accused of making unauthorized cash withdrawals from the Leafs' farm team. The prosecutor counted the misappropriations at about $500,000 for Harold, and some $700,000 for Stafford. Some dissident employee had spilled the beans to Revenue Canada, and the two were charged with the equivalent of grand larceny and income tax evasion—which precipitated a cleanup of the ownership house—and faced the threat of jail terms, reimbursement, and fines. Stafford, always a tense and nervous character and a candidate for serious illness, succumbed to severe bleeding ulcers and died before trial in 1971. But Harold somehow survived. He had bright and effective counsel, who, in the face of the evidence, could only postpone the trial until after the Soviet-Canada series of 1972. In October of that year the presiding judge excoriated Harold, convicted him, and sent him to the penitentiary for three years. (He served only one.) Stafford's death created the opportunity for Ballard to acquire Stafford's shares, and in the reorganization that resulted Harold emerged—with some brave borrowing—as the controlling shareholder, notwithstanding his defalcations.

I could never understand his continued acceptance by the league, and in a later era, it would not have been possible. But Clarence Campbell, the then president of the league, had loyalties to the old gang that had controlled the six-team NHL, and loyalty prevailed. Harold had shown himself to be a fighter: a canny, determined hockey man who had built or at least consolidated the Leafs' success. He was regarded with affection by these historical cronies (which included John Ziegler), but we were never part of it. While neither the Leafs nor *Hockey Night in Canada* (the team's alter ego in TV matters) could now prevent our entry or squeeze our territory—which extended into Canada as far as Hamilton—under Ballard the Leafs continued their hostility to any extension of the Sabres' Canadian activity.

I continuously tried to melt this hostility, preaching my theme that the Sabres were a half-Canadian franchise and that growth of our television presence would help both teams. To no avail: Harold had a pleasant, smiling exterior, but frequently invoked canny moves, and sometimes a rough crosscheck. In the seven years that Punch Imlach—a refugee from Ballard's autocracy—served as our general manager, he uttered few flattering phrases about Ballard. Yet Ballard had power—he owned one of the most successful franchises in the league, and even his former employees held a sort of reluctant respect and loyalty for the Toronto owner. I was shocked when, after his tour with us was over, Punch didn't hesitate to honor Harold's summons to return to the Leafs.

I did not come within Harold's orbit. Where others read benign, I saw malign. But I did seem to make some headway socially with Harold's family, especially his son Bill, who appreciated the value of my work as league secretary. The test came when the Board of Governors was to consider realignment of the teams into new divisions and conferences. I sat down with Harold before the vote, stressing the importance of getting Toronto and Buffalo into the same division: sellout games, minimum travel, high TV ratings, and so on.

Harold seemed for once to be on our side. "How do we do it, Bob?" he asked.

"Very simple," I answered. "We both vote *for* any resolution that puts us in the same division, and we both vote *against* every proposal that puts us in different divisions." He agreed.

The first proposal put Toronto with Boston, New York, and Montreal, our chief rivals; but sent Buffalo out west, with Vancouver, Edmonton, Calgary, and, I think, Minnesota. It would give us unattractive games and an impossible travel schedule. Buffalo voted first, and, as anticipated, I voted no. Did Harold perform according to our agreement? He did not: he voted a hearty yes! The opprobrious resolution passed, and the Sabres were exiled to the derriere of the Canadian clique. We would play Toronto only once a year in our building. It could have been a defeat of major proportions. Fortunately, John Ziegler and Bill Wirtz, who strongly supported a successful Buffalo franchise, realized what had happened and helped us get the resolution reversed. I asked for time-out. I sought out the mover and seconder of the resolution. Under the procedural rules under which the governors operated, I had to get both clubs to recant and move to recall the motion, plus a two-thirds vote. Fortunately, the movers were expansion franchises as well; their only interest was in the other realignments in the resolution, they didn't really care about the Toronto-Buffalo allocation, and they were glad to help rookie Buffalo instead of wealthy Toronto. Ziegler and Bill leaned on Harold, who abstained, and we got the resolution reversed, ending up with our natural and geographical rivals in the east—except for Toronto. It was only years later, after Steve Stavro took over ownership of the Leafs, that we could persuade Toronto (with the help of friends Ken

Dryden and Brian Bellmore) to join us in the same division—and that realignment has been a great success.

So while Harold would certainly be nominated, loyalty would save him from the NHL Cabinet of Rogues.

THE FALL OF McNALL

For my Cabinet of Rogues, I would initially have to nominate Bruce McNall, former president of the Los Angeles Kings and onetime chairman of the NHL Board of Governors. In chapter 24 I relate how Bruce purchased Wayne Gretzky from the Edmonton Oilers for a fancy sum, then gave Wayne a contract at a figure then unheard of in the National Hockey League. McNall's theory was that to be a success in Los Angeles, the team had to have "stars"—and, under the Hollywood definition of that term, a celebrity was not a "star" unless he received a Hollywood salary. I thought Bruce's moves were wrongheaded and gave a lethal burst to budget inflation, but that hardly qualifies him for the gallery.

The strategy seemed to work for a while with the Kings, and Bruce, having apparently converted a longtime box office loser to a winner, ascended to the post of chairman. He helped bring in Blockbuster's H. Wayne Huizenga and Disney's Michael Eisner (receiving, 'tis true, a $25 million "bonus" for the Ducks' invasion of Kings' territory). Bruce had a winning personality, with plenty of energy, and performed as an asset of the league on a number of fronts. I remember particularly when the lockout of 1993–94 had stalled, and we were getting nowhere in the bargaining with the union, Bruce flew in Gretzky to calm things down and melt the hostility. It did help, although the ultimate result of the bargaining proved inadequate. And I must record, in trying to be objective, his kind remarks about me at a governors' dinner in Buffalo. The expansions of the 1990s—Ducks, Sharks, Panthers, Senators, Lightning—would never have happened without me, he said. Nice to hear—but there were a few other characters involved, like Ziegler and Bettman and Wirtz and Krumpe and Stein and Gund.

As it happened, the Kings' "success" was more façade than fact. Financially, losses were severe, and Bruce had had to borrow extensively to keep afloat. When Bruce first applied for approval of his purchase of the Kings, I had to examine his financials. The numbers were adequate, and the guarantees of working capital were sufficient. However, as I commented to Ziegler, the assets in Bruce's balance sheet were certainly strange: instead of stocks and bonds, or land and buildings, the inventory consisted of *horses and rare coins*. But the sampling by our experts raised no questions about their true value, and I was under pressure, as always, to get the expansion done in time to meet the schedule and financing deadlines. As it turned out, there was nothing wrong with the assets—the ancient coins clearly had the values represented. The trouble was, Bruce (or his minions) had pledged the *same* coins to at least two different banks! The prestidigitation had been performed by having careful copies made, placing the copies in the safety deposit boxes of bank number one containing the collateral, then deftly moving the originals to the new lender's safe. The scheme was laid bare when Bruce ran out of cash and banks, followed by bankruptcy and jail. I liked Bruce; he was a sincere and valuable man. It was a tragedy, and I could not ignore the fact that Bruce was another victim of the league's economic incompetence combined with the hubris we all share. When Bruce's lawyer called the Sabres' chairman, Seymour Knox III, for a written recommendation to the sentencing judge, I did not hesitate to tell Seymour to sign the letter.

Loyalty, pity, friendship—whatever the reason, I cannot consign Bruce McNall to my Cabinet of Rogues. He is not one of those owners I hope never to see again.

THE GENTLEMAN GYPSY

Tom Cousins was a major bet for the NHL. In the 1972 expansion he was awarded Atlanta, which was to be the gateway to the South—with a strong economy, an established sports audience, and prospects for growth with development of its TV reach. Cousins was well connected socially, with an attractive wife, and had shown his business acumen and drive in the creation of the Omni, a massive complex built like a cathedral that included a large shopping mall, a convention center, and a fifteen-thousand-seat arena that would house the professional basketball team and the NHL hockey club, the Atlanta Flames. I never liked the Omni very much—it was too massive, with too much concrete, cold and unfriendly.

The league was still feeling its way with the ingredients for a new franchise: the conflict between the GMs who wanted to keep their assets and let the new clubs suffer with unproved draft choices and journeymen veterans; the "statesmen," who thought it was important to make the new teams competitive with some quality players (so the games against expansion clubs would sell some seats); and the new teams created by the 1967 and 1970 expansions, who were still having a tough time on the ice and resented the intrusion of yet more rookie clubs, even though they recognized the need to enlarge the league's TV footprint. So the debate always raged over whether the expansion clubs would pick first in the entry draft, how many players the existing teams could protect in the expansion draft, whether rookies on the old clubs' rosters—first- or second-year players—

would be exempt, which teams would have to accept the new clubs into their divisions, and how many games a team would have to play against them—at home or away. The price was still $6 million per expansion club payable by Cousins and by Roy Boe, the first owner of the New York Islanders. Like Vancouver and Buffalo in the 1970 expansion, the Flames and the Islanders were permitted to pay their entry fee in installments over five years, and each of the twelve teams emerging from the 1960s (the "original twelve") received "expansion notes" in the amount of about $400,000 each.

The Flames and the Islanders got some concessions on the drafts, exemptions, protected lists, and so forth, but a new factor had come into the picture: the WHA. The new league began rapidly to attack the existing clubs' rosters and preempt NHL draft choices with substantial salary increases. Moreover, the NHL had always protected the junior clubs in Canada and the amateur and college teams in the United States by prohibiting NHL teams from drafting or signing a player until age twenty. The WHA got a Canadian court to declare the restriction invalid, and the new league began signing eighteen-year-olds, including Wayne Gretzky and Mark Messier. The NHL had to follow suit, but it was too little, too late. In a number of instances, the new league scooped up talented young players, and when it didn't, it forced an auction that blasted holes in the budgets and expectations of the new NHL clubs. Both the Flames and the Islanders began to experience serious losses.

Cousins had sophisticated counsel, and, anticipating difficulties and possible inconstancy of his flirtation with hockey, they organized the Flames as a tiered subsidiary—Atlanta Flames, Inc. The organization gave its notes to Cousin's NHL partners, and the bank financing and Tom's equity dollars went to the parent company, Atlanta Hockey, Inc., which then loaned the funds to the Flames and took back a mortgage on the Flames assets.

Tom Cousins was popular with the other owners, and he was able to win his way in private sessions when formal maneuvers in the governors' meetings might have been frustrated. As the cash drain mounted, Tom began to lose his loyalty for Atlanta and his affection for hockey. The NHL constitution—and I believe also his franchise agreement—precluded a transfer of the location of the franchise without the unanimous consent of the governors. Tom's banks became restive, and his first move was to end-run the constitution. He argued that the Atlanta lenders would not continue to advance credit unless he could tell them that, in the event of default, he could sell the team and move it anywhere. Probably few owners could have achieved the escape clause, but Tom got it. His next move was to find a buyer, and the city of Calgary, Alberta, beckoned. A wealthy group headed by the Seamons and Harley Hotchkiss were eager for an NHL club.

A move would be a violation of Tom's representations to his friends at the governors' table, and the last thing the NHL needed was another Canadian franchise—it was *US* television markets that drove the expansion. But he had manipulated a right to escape.

One would have thought the ability to move to a good hockey market at a very fine price—$16 million—would have been enough. As Tom had played it, no new resolution or vote of the NHL board was necessary, and the Flames did move, without notice. It was only after they were ensconced in Calgary that we found out the greedy truth. Both Tom Cousins and the Calgary owners refused to pay the expansion notes. A normal move would doubtless have given the other owners a piece of the sale proceeds as payment for the new territory (as was later determined in the Al Davis litigation in the NFL). Yet Tom Cousins not only denied his partners that; he also attempted to finesse them out of the expansion debt he had incurred to buy the franchise.

How did he do it? The scheme was this: The notes were owed by the subsidiary, Atlanta Flames, Inc. The technique was to bankrupt the Flames and wipe out the notes, while the parent, Atlanta Hockey, merrily acquired the team's contracts and other assets in foreclosure of *its* mortgage, then sold the team to the Calgary crew and distributed the proceeds to its shareholders—that is, Tom Cousins. When the scheme was revealed, there was consternation and outrage. Tom's lawyers were snidely gleeful; Tom never showed his face at a league affair again.

I was given the unpleasant task of collecting on the notes. It was not a universal problem with the governors: some clubs had settled with Tom for less than face; the ones who were hurt were those who had indulged Cousins and had not forced payment. I analyzed the facts and concluded that there was a strong case for recovery, primarily because Cousins's lawyers had been too smart. The transactions had a strong odor of overreaching and deceit.

The suit had to be brought in Georgia, and I flew to Atlanta at the first opportunity. It was not easy to find high-quality local counsel willing to sue this distinguished citizen. Most of the high-profile firms I would ordinarily use had ties or relationships with Cousins's companies or the lending banks, but I did find an able lawyer I had known from my days in the TV business. When he heard the story, he had no compunction about suing Cousins. He had been out of Atlanta long enough that he had no Cousins dependency or conflict.

I wondered how it had been possible to do this without our learning about it—perhaps through some form of public notice? In New York, a foreclosure could not be accomplished without notifying the major creditors, and usually the notice was published in the newspapers for a specified length of time. Moreover, this involved a professional sports team, and the media usually jumped all over such a transaction. The answer was that Cousins's counsel had used an ancient Georgia procedure called "strict foreclosure." This required a notice, all right, but only a printed message pasted to the office door of the mortgagor. No mailing or publication of notice was necessary. And the size of the print on the message taped to the door was not regulated, nor was the amount of time it remained on the door!

To me, the use of this near-secret procedure itself justified the outrage of the noteholders, and when I reported this to John Ziegler and Bill Wirtz, and the New York Rangers—one of the clubs involved—they did not hesitate to tell us to proceed. Always one of my pet peeves, the attempted use of a wholly owned subsidiary to wall off a clear liability was another marker. The suggestion that the conduct of the Flames could be isolated from the conduct of its wholly owning parent—when there was an underlying obligation of partnership with the league—made no sense to me. Our local counsel went after Cousins and his cohorts hard, and the trickery, laid bare for a judge, was embarrassing. Cousins overruled his lawyers, and the settlement that ensued was happily received by the noteholders.

As for the Calgary owners—we decided to leave them alone. Hostile Canadian courts would not have been very receptive, and the Calgary group claimed innocence: if we knew nothing about the tainted transactions, they certainly didn't. As events developed, the Calgary group became a successful franchise and strong supporters of league initiatives. Harley Hotchkiss in later years became an effective chairman of the NHL's Board of Governors. So I certainly would not nominate him for my Cabinet of Rogues. But as for Tom Cousins . . .

Chapter 19

THE NHL
COMMISSIONERS

T he Black Sox scandal of 1920 produced the first sports monarch. "Shoeless Joe" Jackson and his cohorts would not leave the results of the World Series of 1919 to chance and had thrown the contest at the behest of the professional gamblers. The series, which appeared to have been won by the Cincinnati Reds five games to three, seemed irretrievably tainted when it was revealed in November of 1920 that eight players, including Jackson, had been offered bribes to lose the contest. The baseball moguls had little choice except to erect an executive who could erase the stench and give the sport immediate veracity. Their candidate, Judge Kenesaw Mountain Landis, defined the role of the professional sports commissioner for decades to come.

The business of baseball up to that time had been run by a three-man commission: one from the American League, one from the National, and a third—presumably neutral—elected by the two league representatives. When the Black Sox scandal broke, the two groups of owners could not agree on the third commissioner, or on how to deal with the gamblers' critical blow to the integrity of the game. The impasse led Landis, when he was approached for the position, to demand—and receive—unprecedented imperial powers. His dramatic, draconic response to the bribing of the Sox ballplayers was characteristic: the eight ballplayers (including one who only knew of the bribery) were acquitted in a jury trial, but that did not deter the judge, who immediately suspended all eight and banned them from baseball for life. This was done with no qualms about due process, no restrictions imposed by any collective bargaining agreement, no hearings, and no union interference. This czaristic response would probably be impossible for any league commissioner today. The power of the baseball commissioner to override owner or player, even union prerogatives, "in the best interests of Baseball" under the MLB agreement is a power devoutly wished for but seldom granted in the other major sports. Yet Landis and his successors intruded into these areas of "reserved powers" and made his intrusions stick. The farm system was attacked, players hidden from the draft or protected list system were freed, realignment of the teams into divisions against their will was enforced, sales of players for cash would be banned, and, in later years, baseball commissioners would even defy resolutions of their owners in triggering or terminating lockouts or strikes.

The owners did not always accept the imperial conduct with equanimity. Future commissioners, such as Albert B. "Happy" Chandler, General Eckert, and Bowie Kuhn, fought battles in the league councils when they attempted to exercise their "superpowers," and some did not survive because of it.

HIS HONOR, CLARENCE S. CAMPBELL

In contrast, the NHL began as an owner-operated league. Not only did it function with only six teams—Montreal, Toronto, Chicago, Detroit, Boston, and New York—early in the modern era, but for more than two decades, three of the six teams were owned by the same crowd: the Norris and Wirtz families. Hence the sports reporters' label for the NHL—the "Norris House League." In that era the president—as the office was titled until 1993—was largely a functionary, able to deal in rigorous fashion with the players, but virtually powerless in dealing with his owners. With the forced divestitures ordered by the Supreme Court in the International Boxing Club case—a business also controlled by the Norris crowd—and the doubling of the number of clubs in the 1967 expansion, new teams began to assert their views, and the president could find support for independence, when he had the guts to proclaim it.

Clarence Campbell, the first president I encountered in my NHL years, was a product of the "Norris House League," but he was also influenced in a major way by the looming presence of the Canadiens—the league's flagship franchise, operating in his headquarters city. Clarence fit the visual profile of a leader: a lawyer, a military history and a military bearing, a prosecutor at Nuremberg, and a onetime hockey referee. His voice was gruff and sinuous; he was tall, formal, and imposing. He had a sense of humor, but it rarely found its way into the governors' room. It was a common complaint when the Sabres entered the league that the Montreal team always got the edge, and Clarence did little to deflect the critics. For example, scheduling: it is important to get the league to give your club as many of your fans' favorite days of the week as possible and as many "fresh team at home" dates as possible. As to the latter, ideally you wanted your club sitting at home, rested after a day off, while the opponent arrived tired from travel and a game the night before. Somehow, the Canadiens seemed always to end up with the maximum number of Saturday nights (*Hockey Night in Canada*, of course!) in its building and more FTH dates than anybody else—usually at least twenty out of the forty home openings.

Clarence was comfortable with his role as chief referee, regulator of player transactions, disciplinarian, and model of justice from the Court of King's Bench. Clarence was less comfortable with the plethora of economic, legal, and political problems that came with expansion. He had relied on the dominance of the Canadiens as a club and the dominance of Canadian law and practice as a culture. He would not accept without a struggle that his standard player's contract—a clone of baseball's "perpetual option"—was worthless against the raids of the WHA, and he held out for the hope that the border was a wall the strange reach of US antitrust laws could not penetrate.

While aspiring to be a business-astute president, his experience was limited to the Original Six team owners: the Norrises, Bill Wirtz, the Molsons, Bill Jennings, Smythe and Ballard, and Weston Adams. All were monopolists, and only Wirtz had the scope and flexibility to handle competition and the rising strength of the players' union. Campbell's intelligence and dignity helped him stay afloat, but the complexities of the business of the new hockey environment were beyond him, and the owners' leaders began to take over.

Clarence was always fair and decent, sometimes respectful, with me and the Buffalo club. I've told earlier in these pages how he got us thinking about Punch Imlach, helped us deal with *Hockey Night in Canada*, and deftly rescued us from the domed stadium commitment. His attitude may have reflected the early support we got from Wirtz, Jennings, and, sometimes, Bruce Norris. He was direct and balanced in matters of player discipline and interclub disputes. He seemed to grow less competent, however, as the economic stress produced by the WHA competition compounded the league's problems. When Harry Shniderman of Covington & Burling pointed out the invalidity of the NHL's standard player contract under US antitrust laws, Clarence's first reaction was to go to *Canadian* outside counsel. The Canadian lawyer disclaimed any expertise in the Sherman Act, but this did not deter him from offering a remedy. As the contract stood in the early seventies, it was certainly unbalanced: the club had the right, at any time, to terminate the contract *for lack of skill*. This was an unfair provision and in effect gave the club an option on the player's services, with no corresponding right given to the player. Canadian counsel recommended we eliminate this provision, and we dutifully did so, but it was miles away from eliminating the real defect—the tainted "perpetual option." It was natural for Clarence to retreat to his Canadian turf, relying on the Montreal owners and staff. But as the Canadian membership in the league declined under the first three expansions (in 1967, 1970, and 1972–1976) from two in six to three in eighteen, his influence waned.

The Sabres were always respectful of the importance of the Montreal flagship and the Canadian character and appearance of the league. More than 70 percent of the team's players still came from Canada. But other American clubs were less respectful. The league needed a New York office—closer to the advertising and broadcast media centers—and we needed more emphasis and expertise in the commercial aspects of the business. The move by the new US franchises to seek a new league leader was accelerated when it was revealed that Clarence was facing serious charges of misconduct—really, abuse of his conflict of interest—arising out of his participation in the management of the Montreal airport concessions. I liked Clarence and found it tragic that a man of his authority and decency should have been trapped in an unethical transaction. All those years, I thought, of working next to men of high finance but little scruple, and this was his only chance to create an "estate" for himself.

JOHN ZIEGLER—"COUNSEL FOR THE SITUATION"

Campbell's personal problems precipitated the decision to replace him, a decision that was already under way because of the increased size of the league, the growing importance of the US clubs, and the drastic changes in the legal and economic environment that came with expansion on the one hand, and WHA competition on the other. Without the Clarence Campbell fall from grace, the league might have hired a headhunter, reached out to other sports, and chosen Clarence's successor in more deliberative fashion. But politics intervened. In 1976 my friend and supporter Seymour Knox III was approached by Ed Snider, the Flyers owner, to take the chairman's post—a move that was vetoed overnight by Bill Wirtz of Chicago. The old guard—the Original Six—were not about to cede control of the league to the expansion clubs—especially to an aggressive "nouveau riche" owner like Snider, whose "Broad Street Bullies" had, to the chagrin of the Rangers and the Canadiens, already won two Stanley Cups.

Ed Snider was and is an able, decent guy, but his tactics—as interpreted and implemented by his lawyer, Gil Stein (later general counsel and, for a

John A. Ziegler Jr., president of the NHL from 1976 to 1992.
Photo courtesy of the author.

brief episode, president of the league)—did not endear him to his fellow governors. When a series of motions and suggestions by Ed seemed to go nowhere, Ed expressed his displeasure by planting Gil at the midpoint of the owners' table. Gil would then turn on a large, ugly recording device, announcing to all present that their words were being cast in stone, and implying that litigation might proceed from those recordings.

The old-time owners had to come up quickly with a move that would block Snider and enssure control of the presidential office. Seymour Knox III, though well liked and respected (after all, the Sabres had made the play-offs within three years of entry, and the Finals within five), would not fit their bill: Seymour had already demonstrated his independence of the Original Six by agreeing to appoint Snider chairman of the Finance Committee. There wasn't time for a headhunter, and, anyway, bringing in an entirely new face was politically dangerous. Their choice was predictable but fortuitous: John A. Ziegler Jr., counsel for Bruce Norris, owner of the Detroit Red Wings.

John had served on my Legal Committee, and the experience was in every way pleasant and productive. He had a sense of humor; a quick grasp of issues; an articulate, simple manner of exposition; and a practical but ethical sensibility. From the Canadian view, he had handicaps. First, he was American, and that meant presumptively he was a rookie—his hockey impressions and experiences necessarily second echelon. Second, he was a lawyer, and while Clarence Campbell had been a member of the legal profession (and David Stern and Paul Tagliabue ultimately held sway, notwithstanding their barrister labels, in the NBA and the NFL), John's pronouncements on hockey matters—discipline, rule changes, and the like—were frequently met with doubt, sometimes derision. Third, he was short and light, lacking Campbell's judicial size and posture. He had some of the characteristics of perpetual youth, and when he would refer, as he frequently did—intending to be fatherly—to the "young men" on the ice, he seemed to be talking about his contemporaries.

But John had the intelligence and judgment to perform well in the job, notwithstanding these alleged handicaps. He had intellectual and emotional courage, and, while Campbell was largely a prisoner of his owners, John had the sophistication and selling ability to stand up to the governors and influence their direction. Of course I'm prejudiced, because I was the beneficiary of John's willingness to delegate and his trust in his delegatees. What began as a routine "minute taker" (I was frequently asked what the secretary of the Board of Governors did) expanded, with John's encouragement, into a full-fledged position as legal adviser to the main committees of the board and point man on expansion and many of the business issues of the league. John seemed to share my impatience with the traditional, limited role of business counsel—"Here are the alternatives, the choice is up to you"—and with the constant overhang of the press and the time pressures of the hockey season, and endorsed my desire and ability to move from recommendation to action. Eventually, once the board or the president approved a recommendation, I would be expected not only to draft the document but negotiate its terms, and, if time pressures called for it, even sign the instrument myself.

John was generally supported in his stance of independence by Bill

Bill Wirtz, Chicago Blackhawks chairman, later chairman of the NHL Board of Governors, was of much help in our battle to get into the league. Photo courtesy of the author.

Wirtz, the Chicago Blackhawks governor and for most of the 1970s and 1980s the leader of the owners as chairman of the board. John's view of the Board of Governors recognized the veto powers and special interests of the individual clubs—like the Continental Congress—and the necessity of *con-*

sensus. He would defer a move on a major issue until he had that consensus, and Bill would, more often than not, help him produce that agreement—either a majority or two-thirds or unanimity, whatever the issue required. But if the consensus didn't come quickly enough, John was perfectly capable of standing firm and using his powers as the unappealable arbiter and interpreter of the league constitution to maintain his policy.

When the 1970s began, the Canadian clubs still had the notion that there was an "electronic wall" at the border: the league could not force the Canadian clubs to participate in league television schedules, and an American club playing a Canadian team at a Canadian venue had no right, without the Canadian club's consent, to even carry a feed of the game back to the US market. This theoretical structure helped maintain the dominance of Molson's *Hockey Night in Canada* and brought some revenue to the clubs north of the border in the form of fees for the feed, but it was an impossible structure for a league desperate for additional national television revenue, which would have to come largely from the development of the US market. When the resistance of the Montreal team and its colleagues—which had been receiving reasonable fees from Molson for television rights—did not abate, John wrote a forceful opinion telling the clubs, Canadian and American, that they must participate in the US network and the Canadian national network chosen by the league and that the American clubs had a constitutional right to the feed, either to their home stations or the US NHL network. The opinions produced litigation, and the next step was to provide competition for Molson's *Hockey Night*. With the assistance of Quebec's Marcel Aubut, CTV, and Carlings-O'Keefe, a competing brewery, a competing network was formed and the Molson monopoly was penetrated. John's determined stance ultimately produced, for the first time in the league's history, a full sharing by the US clubs and the Canadian clubs in each other's national television revenue.

John had guts. One of the popular owners—a longtime governor from the Islanders—had a pet project for his club. He thought a league initiative looking toward a further sharing of advertising revenue would interfere with his plans. With his club producing surplus funds from its profitable cable contract, he offered one of the more impecunious Canadian owners an extra share of expansion revenue if he would vote against the league proposal. I don't know how, but John found out about the "bribe" and confronted the Islander owner in a special owners-only governors' meeting. The Islander owner, normally a decent guy, was abashed at his error and could not deny his conduct. John excoriated him, treating him like an altar boy caught with his hand in the till. The Islander left the conference room, never to be seen again at a governors' meeting for the remaining life of his ownership tenure.

Clarence Campbell had been wedded to the past, but for John Ziegler the goals of industry—growth, revenue, expansion, and increasing the footprint, image, and profitability of the league—were more appealing. He adopted one of the techniques of large business that provided an interesting episode but questionable results: the "retreat" to find the right "mission." There are organizations that specialize in this sort of brainstorming in search of the true grail. Everybody convenes at some out-of-the-way spa—usually a summer spot, vacant in the winter—and "facilitators" (part teacher, part salesman, part con-man) organize the agenda and lead the discussion. It makes sense for a conglomerate with numerous departments seeking its core business, but not for a league dedicated solely to providing good entertainment, filling the seats, attracting commercials, and finding good Nielsens. I went through this mission search in my years as a New York Commissioner of Probation, barely able to keep my temper as the facilitator took hours to lead us by the hand through elementary school on crime and punishment. The retreat was always a "production"—a full panoply of visual aids—charts and slides and projectors and statistical and anecdotal handbooks, tapes and microphones, maybe even a comedy "lecturer," set to music. I thought it a waste of time and money. Probation had a simple mission—control regression and recidivism—that was difficult to achieve with budgetary famine. We didn't need a "facilitator" to tell us what we had to do.

Yet the retreat at a private resort, notwithstanding its production baggage, made some sense for the NHL, and I went along willingly when John assigned me the task of researching potential hockey markets and appearing as a witness to get the talks started. The retreat was entitled "A Vision for the Nineties."

The focus was precipitated by the fact that we had made very little progress, despite the expansions of the 1970s—which brought the league to twenty-one clubs—US national TV ratings and revenue had increased very little. The notion that expansion would give the league a greater national stature—and thus better US ratings—had not proved true. The addition of another US club in Hartford, Connecticut, had not been helpful (it overlapped the Boston and New York City markets, anyway), and the league's acquisition of three Canadian clubs (Edmonton, Quebec, and Winnipeg) had done nothing for US revenue and had only redistributed Canadian TV dollars.[1]

The research we did as part of the "Vision" project confirmed that most of our clubs had high local TV ratings—both over the air and on cable—ranging from 10 (roughly 10 percent of the sets turned on) to over 30 in some cases, particularly important rivalries or key playoff games. But the *national* American audience, except for Canadian games on the Canadian network, remained low. This was largely a function of sheer mathematics: in 1989 we had only fifteen US franchises, and when one recognized the duplications (for example, the New York City market had three teams, the

Islanders, Rangers, and Devils), the true NHL footprint for a national net-work or advertiser was only 12/50, or 24 percent, perhaps a little more if one computes the ratio of the number of sets in our markets to the national total. The teachings of the "Vision" were clear but inconsistent: on the one hand, since we do well in our local markets, we should expand and nurture those, improve PR and marketing in nearby counties, and beef up our minor-league areas. On the other hand, if there was to be any hope for national TV ratings and income comparable to those of the other three major sports, creation of new hockey markets was a must. Out of the talks came the specific objective, announced in a Board of Governors resolution on November 13, 1990: expansion by nine teams to bring us to thirty by the close of the nineties.[2]

We also paid considerable attention to creating more high school and college hockey players in existing NHL markets. We heard a presentation from an enthusiastic manufacturer of plastic ice surfaces that could be sold and installed at high schools and universities at relatively little cost. I sug-gested subsidies by the league, but that suggestion, which would have involved large dollars on a nationwide basis, never got off the ground.

John maintained his regime as president as a leader, not an autocrat. It was *owners'* governance, and John did not attempt to acquire the overall control of a CEO. Basic economic decisions—such as expansion and over-time—were frequently generated by individual governors or their staffs, and the historic and constitutional powers of the individual clubs, and sometimes even their veto powers, meant that arriving at consensus before action was frequently not just good practice—it was essential. The key to consensus for John was Bill Wirtz, board chairman of the league and prin-cipal owner of the financially successful Chicago Blackhawks. Wirtz was no clinging vine—he had strong views; a powerful, deep voice; the respect of the other owners; and a drive toward getting problems solved and pro-ducing tangible results. But as John became more powerful himself, he could not move rapidly in any direction without Bill Wirtz. This may have been his undoing.

It became clear in the late 1980s that salary escalation was becoming a serious problem. In the Sabres organization, we tried to offset the problem by creating a financial cushion in 1988 with the acquisition of our own television station, Channel 49. (This move failed, and we barely escaped through a sale that retrieved most of our investment.) But the problem was leaguewide, and attempts to increase revenue, while worthwhile, fell short. Collective bargaining was the arena where the battle had to be fought—and here the president's powers were limited.

GIL STEIN—THE CONTROVERSIAL TRANSITIONER

When John Ziegler was ousted in 1991, the reason seemed to be his settlement of the strike in the face of opposition from owners who wanted to prolong the dispute and force tougher salary controls. I suspect political currents were at work. Ever since the confrontation in 1976, which denied Ed Snider the chairmanship of the Finance Committee and Seymour Knox the chairmanship of the league, tensions had continued between Ed and the Wirtz faction, which had maintained John in power. It was not a great surprise, then, that when an interim president was needed, the nod went to Gil Stein, the NHL general counsel, who had been Snider's lawyer. Gil's regime started well—he announced that he was going to "hit the ground running." As I've described elsewhere, he agreed to continue to use me and my firm on franchise, tax, and business matters for the league—provided I agreed not to run for reelection as secretary, so they could make that position a staff rather than a governors' post. I had no real choice but to accept the change, although I now think it was a means of clearing the way for franchise moves in which I might have been viewed as an obstruction. Gil spoke well—and wrote well—of my work, and for a time there was no friction between us. He tried to be innovative. For example, he announced that the league's practice of suspending disciplinary offenders from play made no sense: it deprived the fans of the performance of their stars, so he decreed that the offender would lose salary, but would be suspended on *nongame* days. It was a strange idea that didn't appeal very much to the team whose star was knocked out of the lineup by the two-hander committed by the "penalized" player. He negotiated short-term, marginal improvements in the national television revenue and moved us more toward the focus of the TV audience by moving the NHL from Sports-Channel, a largely regional network, to the more nationally recognized ESPN. But he ignored—or decided against—implementing the section in the 1992 collective bargaining agreement that contemplated a "study group" of players and owners, looking toward the negotiation of a cap or salary controls. Gil had a good sense of humor and a penchant for comic, but somewhat pedestrian, poetry that provided a spark for some of the governors' meetings. I'm sure he had a hope for a permanent presidency, but when the board went for a headhunter to find a permanent commissioner (as the post would henceforth be called), things turned sour for the Stein regime. Gil wrote his own book about this, called *Power Plays*,[3] which I won't attempt to critique here. Suffice it to say that he was perceived as having tried to get himself elected to the Hockey Hall of Fame by "packing" that institution's board. The ensuing brouhaha, exacerbated by friends of former NHL vice president Brian O'Neill in the Canadian press—angered by a response by Brian's friends to what seemed to be an injury to O'Neill's own future produced by the "packing" of the board—culminated in a critical report of an investigation into the episode ordered by the new commissioner, Gary Bettman. As demonstrated by the thirty-six pages in his book devoted to his justification, Gil stoutly defended his nomination, but in the end he felt compelled to decline the honor.

It was too bad. Gil was an intelligent, effective lawyer with creative ideas. I'm sure he had political ambitions for his return to Philadelphia. His connections with that city's notables, including a former mayor, were substantial. I had concrete evidence of this in the 1980s when I represented the NHL on a four-sport committee seeking to reverse the efforts of local governments to tax visiting teams and visiting players. Gil's leads into Philadelphia were the most useful to the committee, more effective than those we had in football, basketball, or baseball. He would certainly have liked, for his reentry into the Philadelphia political stage, a résumé that included the presidency of the league and a place in the Hockey Hall of Fame. But the former was foreshortened by the signing of Gary Bettman and the latter was denied by the unpleasant aftermath of the "packing" episode. Politics, which had been a large part of Gil's life and power, failed him. Perhaps he, too, should have remembered that he was a "counsel in the crease"; in the end, he was regarded as lawyer, not an executive, and with the limitations ascribed to his profession, he needed help to score.

GARY BETTMAN—THE "IMPERIAL" COMMISSIONER

As former general counsel of the NBA, Gary Bettman came to the NHL well versed in the issues of leagues and players, but he knew little about hockey. He had worked closely with David Stern, commissioner of the NBA. Stern was regarded as perhaps the most successful of the four heads of major professional sports: he had converted a losing, litigious league into a financially successful organization with a growing audience and high Nielsen ratings that produced multimillion-dollar TV revenues for each of its clubs in a relatively peaceful union relationship. John Y. Brown had sold the Buffalo Braves for $3 million in 1978. Under the Stern leadership, an NBA club in a similar market years later sold for fifty times that amount. Stern got most of the credit, but his former law partner could easily be associated with the success.

My first contact with Gary Bettman came when the NBA, approaching the grant of its first Canadian expansion franchises to Vancouver and Toronto, asked for advice from the NHL on whatever special problems it might encounter in Canadian ownership and operation. John Ziegler asked me to respond, and I crafted a memorandum outlining the peculiar aspects of the problems we had had to deal with across the border. I described the

Gary B. Bettman, NHL commissioner from 1993 to the present.
Copyright © Bill Wippert.

initial fantasies supported by NHL president Clarence Campbell: that there was an "electronic wall" at the border; that US clubs could not broadcast into Canada without permission of the Canadian team involved; and that the US club playing in Canada had no right to take a television feed back home without the Canadian club's consent, for which it could, and frequently did, charge a substantial fee. I noted also a similar fortress scenario in Campbell's attitude toward US antitrust law and other attempts of US courts to reach Canadian assets or persons: the local Canadian teams, Clarence thought, could ignore any subpoena issued by an American judge; the Sherman Act was inapplicable to Canadian conduct, even though every Canadian team played—and thus did business in—the United States. John Ziegler had pretty much torpedoed the first fantasy with his ruling in the 1980s giving US clubs the right to a feed of their away games, and Judge Higginbotham had exploded the second with his grip on teams of both countries in his decisions in the WHA antitrust litigation of the 1970s. But the notion of the wall persists, whether born of sovereignty or ethnocentrocism.

I listed other special views and practical issues arising in Canadian operations. Gary apparently liked the memo and appreciated the character of Sabres ownership and management, because one of the first things he did on becoming commissioner was to invite Seymour Knox III and me for a confidential assessment of the state of the league. The discussion was wide ranging—covering TV, Canada, the governors, the referees, expansion, discipline, free agency, the union, products and promotion, the Olympics, salaries, and playing rules. At various stages, Gary brought in NHL officers with special expertise: Jeff Pash, the new general counsel; Brian Burke, then in charge of hockey operations; and Michael Cardozo of New York City's Proskauer Rose firm, whom I noted with approval was acting as the commissioner's counsel.

Gary seemed dispassionate and objective, probing with energy and enthusiasm. Some questions went to the heart of the Sabres' near-private concerns, and I was hesitant at first, but I remembered John Ziegler's observation to me about Gary: "You'll have no trouble with him, Bob, he's a square shooter." So I laid the facts and my judgments on the table as best I knew them. Seymour was impressed with the discussion. "You can feel the respect for you in that room," he said. "It's tangible."

The new commissioner and I did not agree on everything. In the NBA, when a player reached the end of the fixed term of his contract, he was a free agent. In our league, although the collective bargaining agreement might not spell it out, there was still a vestige of priority for the original team. I supported this, citing the history—the option clauses, the WHA litigation, and so forth. Gary was skeptical. The issue was still important, for example, in situations where the player would defect to Europe, sit out his contract years, then try to sign with a different club. Our most serious divergence, however, was on Bylaw 36—which I had helped draft—the rule that announced the policy of the league on transfers of franchise location. Our bylaw said that the governors could refuse a transfer to a new city if the league found that there was adequate financial, fan, and local government support in the existing location—even if the bid of the proposed transferor was higher. We had adopted that policy in 1976 when we refused to permit Ralston Purina to move the St. Louis team to Saskatoon, Saskatchewan, and reinforced it in 1990 when we thwarted a move of the Minnesota North Stars to San Jose. (See chapter 21.)

"This league is *crazy*!" said Gary. The NBA had not been so fortunate in its litigation—it had bowed to the Davis case, in which the federal court in California had held the NFL liable for damages in obstructing Al Davis's attempt to transfer the Raiders from Oakland to Los Angeles, and had been hit by the California courts in the San Diego litigation, rebuffing the NBA's attempt to block that club's move into Los Angeles territory. But we had a judge's decision on our side, and I mildly defended the policy to protect the local market, especially where the local government had invested in the franchise facilities. (Someday, I sensed, that might be important to keep the Sabres in town.)

As it happened, Gary arrived on the scene just as I was completing the latest change in the Islanders' ownership. The ultimate investors were led by the Entenmanns—the cookie people—but their counsel insisted on a layer of intermediate partnerships and trusts to protect their position as "silent" partners. The complex structure led to a complex document, to which we seemed to add pages every time I heard from the buyers' lawyer, and when he finally presented me with the signed agreement one night at a governors' dinner—in front of the new commissioner—I was somewhat embarrassed to see how fat it was. Gary's eyebrows peaked when he saw it, and I hastily muttered a brief explanation that didn't do justice to the months of hairy negotiations.

That was probably the last official act on my part as outside counsel to the league. I saw it coming, for from the start of his reign it was clear that Gary was going to take over the administration of the NHL as a CEO, with all the powers and subordinate staff that implies. John Ziegler's view of the office—perhaps necessitated by his dependence on and loyalty to Bill Wirtz, Bruce Norris, and the Original Six—was as counsel and agent of the Board of Governors. He would rarely move without a consensus of the owners. Not so for Gary; he would *lead* and *rule*. I had been a governor—I was beholden and loyal to a particular club, although I believe I was always objective and fair to all—but in the configuration Gary envisioned, the lawyers for the league would be beholden to no particular owner, and if they were to be beholden to anybody, it would be to Gary—the appointing power. Gary initiated a series of amendments to the constitution that weakened—in some cases, eliminated—the ability of individual clubs to veto governors' actions and strengthened the commissioner's authority. The Advisory Committee—the group of governors that had in reality run the league, and for which I had been de facto counsel—was abolished. In its place was an executive committee whose primary function was as a sounding board and consultative body. The league's policy and practice would be created and implemented by the professional staff. My role as counsel to the league on business and tax matters—confirmed only a year earlier in the press release negotiated with Gil Stein when I agreed not to stand for reelection as secretary—was to disappear, unnoticed, in the rush of events with the ascension of the new NHL commissioner.

The change was serious for me. The league fees had been important; in the constant and pervasive pressure of NHL business, I had turned over many of my client contacts to other lawyers in my firm. As events transpired—with Seymour's illness, the need for new capital, and the project for a new arena—there were more than enough Sabres problems to capture my attention and concentration. And I could not quarrel, as a representative of the Sabres, with Gary's choice of counsel. He had touched all the bases: primary reliance on Michael Cardozo from his old firm, Proskauer, with a strong supporting cast on the outside, consisting of Jeff Pash, an able émigré from Covington & Burling; and, at a later point, Bill Daly from the Skadden Arps organization. Both Pash and Daly had participated in the NFL struggles with its union, and the campaign for a salary cap or other cost controls was to be a major objective of the Bettman administration.

I continued to be the Sabres' representative on the Board of Governors, and since there was still a hint of respect for and interest in my activities, I was still able to get the ears of Gary and his house counsel and to help the league from time to time. Gary tended to be laconic and semiautocratic, but he was always confident in his responses, except when on stage. He had his enthusiasms, and I was sometimes able to evoke a quiet cheer. He surprised me once. Like most of the clubs in the league, we were apprehensive of the inroads of "superstations" on our TV markets. TBS in Atlanta, WGN in Chicago, Molson in its control of *Hockey Night in Canada*—all were threats to the local clubs' local revenue. The Islanders had attempted to penetrate our Rochester, New York, market, and I had fought them off with the help of a thorough presentation of the history of the NHL regulations. Gary, with an assist from my friend Joel Nixon (who had been in charge of broadcasting during my regime as secretary), held a hearing and ruled for the Sabres' exclusivity in that city. It was a sensitive antitrust issue, but as far back as the period when Bill Jennings ran Madison Square Garden Corporation for Gulf and Western, the Rangers had operated their network so as to minimize impact on a local NHL broadcast. When the Board of Governors received a request for change of ownership of the Rangers to a new entity with national broadcast facilities, I challenged the new owners for their stance on national telecasts of Rangers games in the territories of other member clubs. In the context of their request for the governors' approval, the Rangers rep had to make a commitment to staying out of the clubs' markets, and Gary came by, put his arm around me, and whispered that "this was the best question you've asked in all your years at these meetings."

As described elsewhere in this tale, sometimes the commissioner's curtain was drawn and Gary's position was not precisely what the Sabres would want. But, as John Ziegler had predicted, he was a straight shooter, and if I could put my league hat on, I would recognize the value of his objectivity. As the Sabres' financial troubles mounted in the interregnum years—1997 to 2000—when our group still owned the team but had turned over operating control to the Rigas family and their company, Adelphia, while we waited for a closing of the Funding and Purchase Agreement, Gary was helpful but hardly partisan. I have no doubt that our friends still around the governors' table—Wirtz of Chicago, Jacobs of the Bruins, and the Gunds of the Sharks—encouraged his support. After all, we had been first-class citizens of the NHL for more than twenty-five years. But when a specific issue came up and financing was necessary—and our group was reluctant to make any further investment—candor ruled. Gary told me, "Frankly, Bob, I must tilt toward the money."

The money in this case, of course, was Rigas money. Even though our group invested half the amount required to cover the operating loss in the first year of the interregnum—to protect against a takeover by Adelphia—since we had signed an agreement to sell and our investment coffers were depleted, it was clear that ultimately the league would have to look to the Rigases or Adelphia for long-term capital. The conflict—between loyalty to the owners departing and good relations with the owners staying—appeared several times. The first arose when the Rigas group sought to bargain down the financing arrangements with the public sector and the banks for the new arena. We thought we had negotiated pretty good financing and lease deals. After all, we had produced $55 million from the city, county, and state toward the $130 million construction cost, without incurring any substantial financing cost. Except for the annual ground rent of $500,000 payable to the city, the public sector entities received only an "equity" position for their money—a right to participate in the profits or positive cash flow of the arena (in increasing percentages—starting at 33 percent and ending at 49 percent). We objected to the Rigases' attempts to cut even this down—it could endanger our relations with the governments—and that relationship would be important if, as was certainly possible, the Rigases' purchase failed to close. While we did not exclude a later modification—it seemed to us that the timing was bad—we had been in the new building less than three years. Yet Gary sided with Adelphia. "You've created a 1990s building with a 1970s lease," he argued with me, citing the much more favorable terms recently exacted by other NHL franchises. In Miami, for example, the Florida Panthers had acquired a brand-new arena with government capital at a cost of $30 million more than ours, with a lease that gave the public sector no rent in any year until the Panthers' profits on the arena exceeded $13 million in that year.

Then came the controversy over naming rights. HSBC had acquired the rights when the bank's name was Marine Midland. When Marine Midland made substantial acquisitions, increasing it size and worldwide operations, it decided to take the name of HSBC Bank, the British-owned, China-based company that was the major source of its capital. Quite reasonably, I thought, the bank sought to change the arena name to HSBC as well. To our surprise, Adelphia refused to permit the change. They had no legal authority, but were the incumbent owners. Obviously the company had another agenda—that is, cash, or the ability to later change the name—but the company's officers argued aesthetics. There was some ambiguity in the rights agreement, but it was certainly reasonable to read the document as permitting the change in view of the change in the parent company's name.

Gary, again, sided with Adelphia: "Who wants a Chinese name for a hockey rink?" I would not quit on this one. I trotted out a list of recent stadium and arena names, many of which made no sense and gave the TV announcers fits. "It's HSBC," I said, "not Hong Kong and Shanghai!" It was a test of my interpretation of the Funding and Purchase Agreement—this was not an issue arising in the ordinary course of business—and I insisted that we had a say in this and that Adelphia's obstruction was not in the club's interest. (I don't think I was really influenced by the fact that my law firm's office in Niagara Falls had represented Marine Midland Bank and it predecessors in that city for many years.)

When Adelphia refused to move on its opposition, I received a call from London. It was the bank's CEO, Sir John Bond. "What are we going to do, Bob? The season's about to open, we want to change the signs so we'll get the publicity on the new name, but Adelphia won't move. . . ." Now, how, and in what capacity, should I answer this? As lawyer for the Sabres sellers? Going along with Adelphia might help us get to a closing. As onetime lawyer for the bank? As an officer of the Sabres, looking out for the club's long-term interests? I decided to go for the merits. "Hang tough," I said. "The Rigases are always looking for cash. Offer them some substantial dollars for an extension of the rights agreement." I called Adelphia's Ed Hartman to lend my support. The proposal worked, and the signs got changed before the opening face-off.

But whatever the minor differences I had with Gary Bettman, he certainly earned my everlasting homage with his management of the messy Sabres crisis created by the bankruptcy of Adelphia and the abandonment of the team by the Rigas family in the face of their indictment and arrest.

(More on this in chapter 36). He showed patience, fortitude, and loyalty to the Buffalo NHL franchise. It would have been an easy out to shop the team to Paul Allen in Portland, Oregon, or a similar carpetbagger. (Although, in such a case, I would have launched Bylaw 36—the policy against franchise moves when there is local money and fan support, of which I was a partial author—as a missile into the fracas.) But Gary announced at the outset of the crisis that he was not interested in moving the team, arranged for temporary financing, maintained his position through exhaustion of the NHL's team operating fund, endured bankruptcy of the club, and shrugged off the collapse of the early bids, the initial misgivings of the eventual owner, and the frustrated response of the fans to the stymied hockey department's missed playoffs and nonexistent moves. The closing of the purchase by Tom Golisano, retaining the team in Western New York, was a triumph for Gary and his counsel, Dave Zimmerman and Bill Daly, and great good fortune for the city of Buffalo and the Niagara Frontier.

Chapter 20

THE ARENA ILLUSION

I n the interregnum—the period between our turndown by the National Hockey League and the National Baseball League in 1966 and 1968 and the Oakland opportunity in 1969—a dangerous situation arose for which I was at least partially responsible. In the pursuit of the baseball franchise, I and my colleagues had persuaded the Erie County Legislature to pass a $50 million bond resolution to construct a domed stadium for a Major League Baseball team. After the turndown by O'Malley in 1968, our pursuit of the expansion baseball franchise was dead, but the bonds were not. The thought of a $50 million fund sitting there, unspent, was more than the politicians could bear. Even the normally conservative *Buffalo News*, bitten by the sports bug and smarting from the defeat, wanted the project to continue. I received a call from Paul Neville, the paper's editor. A new group was interested; with a new covered stadium authorized, wouldn't Buffalo be the logical place for baseball's next move? After all, we had been told that all but one of the owners were in favor of Buffalo. What were my recommendations?

I took the call in a phone booth at the airport, about to board the plane on a client's mission. Nothing Neville said indicated I would have any role in the baseball project, but I answered with as much candor and judgment as I could muster at the moment. I responded: first, get yourself someone on the *inside* of the majors, who can push your case with the other owners; second, create a financial incentive for the insider in the development of the stadium and the club. I observed that one of the ways to do this that seemed to be in fashion was to place the stadium in an undeveloped area, where the peripheral land could be purchased and made valuable by the stadium development. I pointed out that I had deliberately drafted the bond resolution so as to leave the building location open. My purpose was to avoid a delaying fight over a downtown versus suburban site. This point went over well with Neville, for his boss, publisher Kate Butler, had been a strong advocate of the suburban location, no doubt desirous of keeping the crowds away from the *News* building operation, which was close to the proposed downtown site.

The trouble was, the county politicians acted on my recommendation, and soon what had been a vague vision began to seem real. A local automobile dealer named Ed Cottrell, with an able lawyer named Vic Fusak, appeared to present the franchise capital; began to acquire a suburban site; persuaded Judge Roy Hofheinz, principal owner of the Houston Astros franchise in the National League, to be his sponsor; and pushed the Erie County Legislature into signing a contract that bound the county, it was believed, to construct the stadium.

My recommendation in the phone booth had come back to bite us. Caught up in the city's enthusiasm for the domed stadium, and desperate for anything that would give the city credibility with the hockey league, in a weak moment we let it be known by letter that if the domed stadium were actually built, and we got an NHL franchise, we would be glad to add NHL hockey to the stadium's program and revenue.

Little thought was given at that moment to the design and construction problems such a venture would produce. It's 386 feet from first base to third base; it's only 85 feet from one side of an NHL hockey rink to the other. The optimum seating for an NHL game then was thought to be fifteen thousand, while the domed stadium would seat forty-five thousand. How to sell season tickets for hockey when a plethora of seats would always be available? When the Oakland opportunity arose, and we began to be serious about the NHL, our sponsors in the NHL were dead set against the dome. We were then confronted with our naive offer to help the Cottrell project. Ruby Pastor, the AHL Bisons owner and a potential partner in the hockey effort, began to make threatening noises at NHL headquarters. We were damaging the hockey standing, he said, by even toying with play in the dome. Of course, his desire for the pouring rights for his Pepsi Cola business would have little chance with the Cottrell dome.

As written elsewhere in this account, as soon as the league finance committee told us we were going to get the franchise, Campbell, Wirtz, and other NHL friends began to rain advice upon us: managers, coaches, concessionaires, architects, contractors, players—all were nominated. If we got Perreault, don't trade him to Montreal. Make a deal with *Hockey Night in Canada*. Hire Imlach; don't hire Joe Crozier. Get Steinbrenner for your investment group. Don't get Steinbrenner for your investment group. And so on. But the most serious, objective advice was, *don't play in the domed stadium!* This advice ran smack into the desires of the Cottrell dome group. We were accused of welching and worse. We called on the president of the league, Clarence Campbell, to be the Solomon, and Clarence duly convened a hearing in Buffalo to resolve the dispute.

The proponents of the dome put up a good fight, but their case—which was probably hopeless anyway—was destroyed by their hastily constructed plan as to how to change the stadium configuration from baseball to hockey, and back. The conflict between the hockey and baseball seasons would conceivably require this switch about fourteen times, in the months of September, October, April, and, in playoff years, May and June. The change from the baseball diamond seating to the hockey rectangle would, in the Cottrell plan, be accomplished with movable sections on one side of the stadium—leaving seats on the other side a substantial distance from the hockey boards. The excessive number of seats available for hockey was clearly a problem for season ticket sales, even though some sections would be curtained off, but the most telling blow came when it was revealed that the dome plan provided no restrooms in the movable sections and patrons in those sections would be required to go around to the other side of the stadium to relieve themselves of the beer it was hoped they would be consuming.

"Have you ever been in an NHL arena?" asked the exasperated Campbell. "With the crowds in the corridors between periods, it would take the entire intermission—they'd never make it!"

It was a narrow escape. As the demise of the minor-league baseball Bisons in the forty-five-thousand-seat football stadium had shown, the dome stadium's size would have been fatal to the Sabres. The dome never was built, Buffalo never got a Major League Baseball franchise, and the contract to construct it produced nothing but ten years of litigation.[1]

As for the Sabres, as described earlier, we did get the city to agree to add five thousand seats to the venerable Aud—after facing a taxpayers' suit that, fortunately, delayed the construction a year.

I suspect that the taxpayers' suit was encouraged, if not financed, by the dome stadium crowd. In every public project, especially one involving sports, it's rather easy to find a "naysayer"—an organization that feeds its sponsors and contributors on the doctrine that government is corrupt, and governments that increase taxes are absolutely corrupt. I had learned early on, in the pursuit of a Major League Baseball franchise, that public votes on a new stadium should be avoided wherever possible. The Oakland NHL club never emerged from deficits because the arena was in the wrong place, and every attempt to get public financing for new building across the bay in San Francisco—where the hockey fans lived—was defeated in the taxpayer ballot. New York State, except, unfortunately, in the case of school board budgets, was still wedded to the notion that leaders should be able to lead, even when the issuance of bonds means a rise in tax rates. This provided some openings. In fashioning the dome stadium bond resolution itself, I was careful to prepare it and have it approved by the county legislature in such a way that no referendum would be required.

I had thought the financing of the Aud expansion would be an easy route, for, in the good citizen tradition of the Knox group, in essence the Sabres were going to pay off the $8.2 million bonds for the addition of the five thousand new seats with an increase in the rent, and this would amortize the cost completely in seven years. When we were served with the complaint, it was clear that the "irate taxpayer" was claiming only technical errors in the Common Council's legislative proceedings, easily curable with time. But seats unsold are lost forever, and I asked my partner, Hilary Bradford, to press the court for immediate action, so we could expand before the start of the new season. I was sure the action was a "strike" suit, designed to foul up the Aud financing and give the dome time to take over.

Of course I had to admit that non-Harvard law schools produce good lawyers, too, and Hilary was convincing proof of this. He had established some kind of record for grades at the University at Buffalo Law School, had served as law clerk to the justices of the Appellate Division of the New York Supreme Court, had a solid reputation among the trial bar and bench, and had an urbane, literate, but aggressive style that I liked. He began his oral argument before the judge, "Every time a good citizen like Bob Swados tries to do something good for this community, some cranky nay-sayer throws in a monkey wrench. . . ."

Opening a major-league hockey arena with only ten thousand seats forced a shortage, and as the town began to fall in love with NHL hockey, with good marketing we were able to move into a sellout mode that lasted nearly fifteen years.

We began the Sabres era as the dominant occupant of the Aud, content to be a tenant with a decent long-term lease and some of the sweeteners— advertising, concessions, and so forth. But no parking revenue and the few skyboxes were just under the roof and produced no dollars of any consequence. As the payroll pressure began to mount in later years, however, the club, like other ownership in the league, looked to the prospect of a new arena—with parking and luxury box revenue, and with the club participating in management and landlord profits—as the solution for its economic ills. Was the new building indeed the Holy Grail—or an illusion?

Chapter 21

SINGIN' AND SAVIN' THE BLUES

LOOKING FOR MR. SOLOMON

T he NHL gave birth to the Blues all right, but it was nearly stillborn. The franchise began as a building looking for an owner. In the 1967 expansion, the league reawakened the charge that it was the "Norris House League" when it announced that the last of six expansion grants would go to St. Louis—even though no purchaser of the franchise had yet been found.

The St. Louis arena was then owned by the Jim Norris and Arthur Wirtz families, still involved in the Detroit Red Wings and the Chicago Blackhawks, and, not so long ago—until the antitrust courts intervened—investors in the New York Rangers as well. The Buffalo group, rejected along with Cleveland, Baltimore, and Vancouver, resented the NHL announcement, felt their cases as popular minor-league clubs in good hockey markets were much stronger, and viewed the St. Louis grant, with no one coming forward as owner or operator, as exposing a weakness the NHL should not have to accept. For many years the Buffalo complaint on the selection of St. Louis seemed justified, as the St. Louis club went from owner to owner, teetering on the edge of viability, and the league struggled to maintain its presence in the heart of the Midwest.

When we heard the announcement of our rejection in 1967, Jim Norris's defiant prediction in the corridors of New York's St. Regis Hotel hit hard: "You're the best applicants here, Swados, but you're not gonna get it!" But the Norrises did get it—an NHL tenant for their largely vacant building. They were major partners in the six-team league, and few NHL governors were to complain in later years about the principle that, in expansion, you take care of your partners first.

It took some time, but the league did come up with a St. Louis owner: Sidney Solomon Jr., a pleasant, canny businessman who made a real college try. Sid was well connected in Missouri politics—he had been a friend and supporter of Harry Truman, and he believed that effective promotion and good business judgment could make a success of the Blues even in that warm climate market dominated by the Major League Baseball team and its owner-sponsor, Anheuser-Busch. When the Sabres finally were accepted into the NHL, Seymour Knox and I did a tour of key clubs with city of Buffalo officials to learn as much as we could about major-league hockey operations on site. Montreal was the flagship franchise, of course, but we chose Minnesota as a new building and St. Louis as an older arena for the study. I was impressed with the St. Louis club's vehicles and Directors' Room. We were met at the airport by a sharp, spanking-new blue Pontiac, emblazoned with the club's colors and logo, soon to be overwhelmed by the fact that there were more than *forty* similar Pontiacs constantly on the road for the organization! GMs, coaches, players, owners, scouts, ticket managers—all drove the blue Blues' sedans. It was a great promotion, and it cost plenty.

Another great promotion was the club's Directors' Room. Most original NHL clubs (with the exception of the Canadiens) seemed to treat visiting fans as lucky to be in the building in the first place—the game was the only entertainment offered. Not so the Blues. The Solomons recognized early on the virtues of an elitist milieu for the visiting advertisers and other VIPs. Their Directors' Room was beautifully decorated in a modern style that appealed to women as well as men, with a comfortable, smart bar and gourmet hors d'oeuvres and generous buffet dinners. Local politicians, frequent guests, loved it. When I returned between periods of the Blues game to find that one of our councilmen had not moved from his seat at the bar, I asked, "Jerry, aren't you going to watch the game?" "No, thanks, Bob," he responded in his Irish brogue. "I'm stayin' here—this sure beats the Fourth Ward!" We persuaded the city of Buffalo to let us build our Directors' Room and our season ticket–holders' Aud Club after the Solomon model.

I was less impressed with the Norris building. It was a big, high-ceilinged barn with spartan decor. In the fashion of the postwar era, its "boxes" were at the top of the arena, hardly the "premium" loges that were the major targets of arena revenue in the 1990s. When I had to visit the Blues on Sabres or league matters, I did my best to avoid being invited to sit in the Solomons' box. The seats were so far away from the ice, it was like watching a football game with a ten-inch TV set in the end zone. The twenty thousand seats—now an achievable capacity with the growth of the NHL footprint and TV coverage—were probably too much for a fledgling franchise trying to promote hockey in a warm climate. With so many seats available, season tickets, essential for cash flow, were a hard sell.

The Solomons did their utmost to encourage a family-like relationship with the players. (In contrast, I was once warned by a league executive: "Bob, don't get too close, don't make heroes out of these guys. One day you may have to drop the guillotine!") Sid Jr. owned the Golden Strand, a pleasant hotel on the Hollywood Strip in Florida, and the players and key staff ended their seasons with free vacations at the Solomons' resort.

The Blues performed well on the ice, in the regular season. The league structured the schedule so that all six new teams were in the same conference, and competed essentially only against each other, and with Scotty Bowman as the coach, the St. Louis club proved to be the best of the expansion teams, winning the conference title three years in a row. But the playoffs—which turned out to be a contest against the best of the Original Six—were a different matter. The Blues lost every final round in those three seasons and didn't win a game against the Original Six in the Finals. The protected lists of the older clubs in the expansion draft and the priority rights of the Canadiens to the top French Canadian players in the amateur drafts (a provision not eliminated until 1969) were too much for the new clubs to overcome.

As the expansion clubs were integrated into the realigned league schedule, wins became more difficult and the heady fan enthusiasm of the early years, fed on expansion wins, began to dissipate. Sid III took over, installing a harsher regime, and Scotty Bowman left the team in 1971. Sid III may have established a record as he set about to prove that an NHL coach has the most perilous job in professional sports. In the six years after Scotty's departure, the Blues players and fans had to deal with *eight* different coaches!

CHECKIN' WITH RALSTON

The situation worsened with the appearance of the WHA in the early 1970s, which put severe pressure on salaries, and the Blues, despite a determined and temporarily successful reorganization by Emile Francis, struggled on the ice and at the gate. A white knight appeared in 1977 in the form of Ralston Purina and its chairman, the engaging and enthusiastic Hal Dean, and Emile and the Solomons persuaded the company to purchase the team and the building. Ralston began to tie in promotions, renamed the arena the Checkerdome, and, under Red Berenson, the team responded with a high of 107 points in the 1980–81 season.

I suspect that it was Emile Francis, the "Cat," in the goal net, who pulled off the Ralston Purina purchase. I liked Emile. He was not large and rangy, like the current elite goaltenders. He was short and quick, like Roger Crozier. He had energy, an air of authority as a hockey veteran, and a plain-speaking technique that I admired. At league and franchise meetings, he had a way of making his gravel-voiced views simple and unchallengeable—maybe too simple. Perhaps I was influenced by Seymour Knox, who had known Emile in his days as a Rangers fan and had come under his spell. I had assumed in the early years, listening to him as rookie owner/brass, that he was one of the greats of the game. It was something of a shock to find, in my research for this book, that Emile spent most of his career in the minors (in the heyday of the six-team league) and had produced a goals-against average that, in the two-plus days of Dominik Hasek, Patrick Roy, and Martin Brodeur, would never win a Vezina: 3.76. But Emile could sell himself, and he sold Hal Dean, with some strategic help from John Ziegler and Bill Wirtz.

I remember Hal Dean vividly because of his tennis technique. In place of the Florida hotel owned by the Solomons, Ralston Purina provided vacations at its Breckenridge, Colorado, resort, and league meetings were held there. Dean was an enthusiastic tennis player, but he is the only one I have ever seen play with a sliced backhand and a lit cigar in his mouth, on the forehand side. Unfortunately, and I hope it was not because of the performance of the Blues, Dean retired in 1983, and William Stiritz, a tough CEO with little enthusiasm for hockey and less for a red bottom line, took over. Stiritz did not care at all to explain to Ralston Purina stockholders why the company continued to hold this "asset" that performed poorly on the ice, was losing more than $1.8 million a year, and provided little useful PR for its animal feed. The team was for sale, he announced, and proceeded to enter into an agreement to transfer and sell the franchise to interests in Saskatoon, Saskatchewan.

What then transpired led Commissioner Bettman in later years to say, "The NHL is crazy!" But for me, it may have been the league's finest hour.

Our investigation showed several factors unfavorable to the proposed move. The fan base in St. Louis was still strong, though somewhat disillusioned by the team's inability to get to—or out of—the first round of the playoffs. The Saskatoon market was probably too small—it took the somewhat arbitrary inclusion of fans 150 miles away in Regina to build its numbers up to a satisfactory level. From the point of view of the league's future, the move would be devastating—depriving the NHL of a major TV and gate market in the United States and substituting a Canadian city that would add absolutely nothing to the league's US TV ratings or income. With the network of Molson's *Hockey Night in Canada* already feeding the Saskatchewan fans with the preferred diet of Canadiens, Leafs, and Oilers, the transfer would force a reduction and redistribution of the Molson revenue among the other Canadian clubs, already struggling to meet escalating payrolls. There were doubts that Ralston had really searched the St. Louis or national market to find a buyer who would keep the team in St. Louis. And the proposed Saskatoon purchaser, though stoutly defended by Bill Hunter—a well-known hockey character and owner-refugee from the WHA—had capital that would only marginally qualify him for membership.

The last factor emerged at a hearing held by the NHL Finance Committee in Saskatoon, at which, as was frequently the case, I was designated to ask the "bad-cop" questions. The applicant seemed a nice guy, but lacking great enthusiasm or confidence. It soon became clear that the payments demanded by Ralston plus the need for immediate working capital could well exhaust his entire net worth. One season of substantial red ink, and we could be back in the soup, again. We did not want to repeat the Kansas City experience, when the near bankruptcy of the owner had forced a midsummer transfer to Denver.

The league decided to reject the Ralston proposal. It was a courageous decision by John Ziegler and the governors' leadership. We had the cautious blessing of antitrust counsel, but it was 1986, and Al Davis, football's notorious renegade, had just opened the era of "franchise free agency" with a multimillion-dollar judgment against the NFL owners for their refusal to permit him to move from Oakland to Los Angeles. The ruling by the Ninth Circuit Court of Appeals in 1984—in what has become labeled as "Raiders I"—held that the NFL rule, requiring a three-quarters vote of the owners to approve such a transfer, was a violation of the federal antitrust laws, as applied to the Raiders/Oakland/Los Angeles set of facts. Raiders I was later modified by Raiders II and Raiders III, and we thought our set of facts was different; but in the meantime the San Diego basketball team had migrated without NBA approval, and we had seen the NFL's Baltimore Colts steal away to Indiana.

Stiritz was a fighter, but he had not previously encountered anything like the media attacks he received for his attempt to rip the Blues from his headquarters city. The attacks increased in pitch and volume when he took steps that seemed sheer mindless anger: he padlocked the arena and announced that, in effect, the Blues were dead. If Ralston Purina couldn't sell the club to its chosen buyer, nobody could have the Blues. He instructed the staff not to participate or even appear in the June entry draft, and on top of its other woes, the franchise forfeited all ten of its 1983 picks—in a draft that presented ultimate all-stars Pat LaFontaine, Steve Yzerman, Tom Barasso, and Cam Neely. That omission, and the attempt to move the franchise without Board of Governors' consent, exposed Ralston to the charge that it had intentionally violated the league's constitution and bylaws—a violation that enabled the league to *terminate* the Ralston ownership, without compensation. And we did so, quickly, and sold a *new* franchise to one Harry Ornest, a Toronto character of means who had been waiting in the wings for a franchise bargain.

SURVIVING WITH HARRY

I remember very little of Harry, except that he seemed to think he was doing the NHL such a favor he should have been able to buy the club for a song (which he did) and without restrictions (which he did not). As empowered and instructed by the Board of Governors and its committee, I insisted on representations and covenants that he was buying the club to operate in St. Louis only, and he had to acknowledge that he had been given no authority or promise or exemption from the constitutional restrictions against moving the franchise out of that city. We demanded security for working capital up front and full payment of certain outstanding debts and salaries then left in limbo by the checkered Ralston. Harry tried to resist these measures, and he brought in a Hollywood lawyer to negotiate with this "country" counsel. Harry thought I should have been dazzled by his lawyer's reputation, but I was impressed only by his cowboy boots, which were yellow, pointed, and prominent. We managed to work out a complex but satisfactory consent agreement in record time, however—training camp was less than two months away. I like to think I was cooperative: I gave in on some of the dollar points, but stood firm on the league issues.

The instruments proved to be several inches thick. As various governors proffered their ideas at the meeting—ranging from anger to trepidation—the board resolution approving the sale to Ornest itself was six long, single-spaced pages. Ralston had commenced a suit against the league, and we had to eliminate that. The land and building was in one ownership, the Blues equipment and tangible assets in another; the player contracts were in the hands of the NHL, and we had to make sure they were paid so they wouldn't become free agents. Harry was paying only part of the price in cash, the balance over time, partly in orthodox debt obligations, partly in notes—payable only when, as, and if the club produced a specified profit, or when, as, and if it received expansion fees. The latter came to be used in other NHL transactions and became known in league circles, appropriately enough, as "blue notes" or "soft notes."

On the litigation front, the antitrust phalanx from Covington & Burling —able lawyers Harry Shniderman, Herb Dym, and Bing Leverich—supported the view of John Ziegler, Gil Stein, and myself that we could effectively distinguish our case from the Raiders decision. We had a better bylaw—a lower vote requirement—and standards that assured a thorough search of the market in St. Louis and of the financial qualifications of the new buyer and the new area proposed. The policy of the league—as it should be now—was to discourage transfers of location, and to support commitments to a local community that supported us. In addition, we had a unique legal precedent—probably a naive interpretation of the antitrust laws, and no longer valid, but still on the books: a federal court in California had approved the league's refusal, in 1968, to permit a transfer of the Oakland Seals to Vancouver. There were some rumbling threats from the Canadian Combines Commission on the rejection of Saskatoon, but for once our Canadian brethren were not quick to defend any Canadian demand, and that proceeding never got off the ground.

The Board of Governors chose to endorse our refusal to permit the transfer and sale, invoked the "involuntary termination" provisions of the NHL constitution, canceled the Ralston franchise, and seized the player contracts and other hockey assets.

Fortunately Stiritz, faced with our media pressure and our surgical response, chose not to pursue the litigation, and, with some minor payments, Ralston capitulated. At a TV news conference on July 27, 1983, we announced that the club would stay in St. Louis. An excited reporter introduced me as the "savior" of the Blues, and an NHL official asked me to say something nice about Ralston Purina. I demurred at the garland of roses and gave credit to the league and Harry, but somehow I didn't quite get to any praise for Ralston.

In his three years in the NHL, Harry proved to be a decent, but temporary, owner. He took control of the budget and kept the club afloat. He hired a competent GM in Ron Caron and a fine coach in Jacques Demers, who took the team to an exciting comeback win in the conference finals in 1986—the "Monday Night Miracle."

In his relations with the league, however, Harry established a record for complaints, some justifiably critical, some cranky. He must have resented my powers and attitude. As a fellow member of the Jewish faith and practically a Canadian neighbor in Buffalo, I guess he thought I should have been more complaisant and supportive of his views, instead of adhering to my establishment NHL and Sabres stance. Shortly after he sold the club, Harry let it be known to Al Strachan, the *Globe and Mail*'s acidic man on the hockey beat—or at least I'm sure Harry was the source of the story—that "everybody knows how to get what you want in the National Hockey League: just see Bob Swados. He's been charging those exorbitant fees for that service for years."

I was irate over the slander and its implications in the Board of Governors, denigrating my motives and ethics, and called my friend Brian Bellmore, counsel for the Toronto Maple Leafs, asking him to consider an action for libel. I gave him my fee scale. "Why those are 1950 fees!" he said. "I thought you'd been paid a living wage!" Brian talked me out of a lawsuit. "Besides," he said, "it's *good* publicity."

FINDING AN EVEN KIEL

Harry sold the club to the Mike Shanahan group on December 12, 1986, and Shanahan finally moved the franchise into stable ownership in 1991 in a sale to Kiel Center Corporation, a syndicate of twenty leading St. Louis companies and interests that had built a new arena—originally called the Kiel Center—a syndicate that included, surprisingly, Ralston Purina.

In the second round of the Western Conference playoffs in the spring of 2001, the NHL fans were entertained on national television by a great series—it went to seven games—between the Blues and the ultimate winner of the Stanley Cup, the Colorado Avalanche. It was fast, skillful, crunching hockey at its best. Pierre Turgeon, originally drafted by the Sabres, was a star performer for the St. Louis team. With the Buffalo club already out, I could cheer unequivocally for St. Louis and thrill at the twenty thousand ecstatic fans with their beautiful arena and their new, solid owner—remembering with a glow the day we saved the Blues.

Chapter 22

THE VIEW FROM BOWMAN'S BENCH

I have always had a special regard for William Scott Bowman, the winningest coach in the modern history of the NHL. This is perhaps because, of all the general managers and coaches on the Sabres roster over the years, he was the most direct with me, and the least political. I knew his talent and his limitations, and he knew mine in the hockey world, but he respected my position and my judgment. In the six-year term of his tour as Sabres coach and GM, we developed a friendly and mutually supportive relationship: not just colleagues—more like professor and pupil, though sometimes it was difficult to tell who was which. He taught me hockey; I tried to teach him people and finance. At lunch recently I asked Scotty, "We had you under contract. Why did we lose you?"

The Sabres had a spectacular birth for an expansion club: Under Punch Imlach's direction, the team made the playoffs in its third year and the Stanley Cup Finals in its fifth. They played before sellout crowds almost from the first game. The team, solid down the middle with Gil Perreault and the French Connection, seemed ready to take on the league and establish a dynasty. But after the near championship in 1975, it didn't happen. Bernie Parent, the Flyers goalie who stiffed us in the last game of the Finals, remarked to me, "Oh, Mr. Swados, you had *such* a strong team. . . ." The Sabres were competitive, amassing more than one hundred points (the equivalent of fifty wins) in four straight seasons, but after 1975 they could not do better than win the preliminary, three-game round in the playoffs—losing the quarterfinal series to the Islanders in 1976 and 1977 and to Philadelphia in 1978. When the point total dropped to eighty-eight in 1978–79 and the team was knocked out of the playoffs in the preliminary round, I had to tell our friend John Anderson—Punch's principal assistant who had been acting as general manager—that his job was at risk. When they took over following Punch's heart attack, I had liked the low-key performance by Anderson and Billy Inglis (as rookie coach), but it was clear that the Knoxes wanted an experienced GM with a record of success, and I agreed. When word came that Scotty was not going to be re-signed as coach of the Montreal Canadiens, and that he wanted to become a general manager, Bowman became our immediate target.

There was strong competition for the star coach of the league's flagship franchise, and we had been told that Bowman wanted no pressure from publicity, so it was important that negotiations go forward immediately and be kept from the press—so far as that was possible in the fishbowl of NHL hockey. I got Scotty's whereabouts from the Canadiens' Sam Pollock. Scotty was vacationing with his family at the Colony Club, the tennis resort operated by Nick Bolliteri and owned by Murph Klauber, a onetime Buffalo dentist, on Long Boat Key on Florida's west coast. I was at my winter place on the east coast—but it was only about a four-hour drive from Boca Raton, so I called Seymour Knox and arranged to pick him up at the Sarasota airport. I took great pains to mask our intentions: I had a friend call and make the reservations in his name, let it be known that we were going to New York City, hired a rental car with Florida plates, and talked to no one at the resort except Klauber, swearing him to secrecy.

Things seemed to go according to plan. Word came that Scotty was interested, and the newspapers contained no story about our activities. We arrived at the resort on time—even a little early—and drove to our suite without incident. However, as I began to unpack the trunk, I felt a friendly hand on my shoulder. "Nice to see you, Bob!" . . . It was Jim Peters, the *Buffalo Courier Express* reporter on the hockey beat. Thus, I learned again that *nothing* stays confidential in the hockey world.

Fortunately, Scotty was not put off, largely amused by the leak, and we moved immediately into friendly discussions of details. I reminded Scotty and Seymour of our first contact, in our first season at a game in St. Louis. We were all in the press box, and, as we watched the Sabres struggle, Scotty picked up our roster and, without hesitation, gave the word on each of our players: re-sign this one, terminate these, send these to the minors, and so on—a complete roster cleansing, a road map for converting our expansion team of castoffs and rookies into a competitive club. I'm sure our then manager-coach, Punch Imlach, would have dissented from some of Scotty's judgements, but it was still an impressive performance.

The money we offered, the term of the contract, and other aspects were competitive with the proposals Scotty had already received, but, as often happens, it was personal insights that turned the trick. We had done our homework, and we had two important facts: Scotty wanted, and felt he was entitled, to be the head man in the hockey department. He also indicated a desire to get away from the compulsory coach's travel. We agreed that he would begin as both general manager and coach, then relinquish the coaching duties when, in his judgement, he had brought in a first-class man to assume those duties. Scotty needed no sales pitch for the Niagara Frontier. Like most experienced hockey men in those days, he viewed Buffalo, with its Canadian adjacency, as a first-rate hockey market. Seymour's generous and sincere manner appealed to Scotty, but it was not until we mentioned St. Rita's that we knew from Bowman's reaction that the deal could be done. We had learned that Scotty and his wife, Suella, were most concerned about finding an institution for their mentally handicapped son, who was prone to illness. I had investigated the Western New York facilities and had determined that St. Rita's, in a northern suburb of Buffalo, had a fine reputation and excellent staff, and could provide a practical solution for the Bowmans' child. When I gave Scotty the details, which were, I hoped, thoroughly and sensitively presented, I knew we had scored. The signing was easy.

Scotty chose Roger Neilson as his first assistant coach, to succeed Scotty when he chose to restrict himself to management duties. As Montreal's Sam Pollock would remark later, we all thought this was a "marriage made in heaven": Scotty was a hunch player, manipulating rosters and game tactics and gambles like nobody else in the business; Roger was logical and well organized, analyzing game films with a precision and thoroughness not seen elsewhere in the league until the advent of the computer. But what seemed like complement turned to conflict.

Roger, viewing the game from his press box seat, complained to me: "Scotty and I go through this joint analysis and come up with a game plan. On a power play against, say, Boston, X is to handle the right point, Y the left face-off circle, on the first line change. We agreed on that before the face-off. Then the power play comes, and I look down from on high—and Z is at the point and Y is not on the ice at all!" Scotty had a hunch.

As the season developed, the conflicts between their disparate personalities and practices became disruptive. I tried to mediate and ameliorate the schism, but Roger was unhappy and Scotty was unmoved, and the team results were not what we had hoped. The club under Scotty made no conference finals and went from 110 points in 1979–80 to 64 in 1986–87. In an attempt to get at the root of the problem, I called Sam Pollock and arranged to discuss the situation with him in Montreal.

I asked Sam, "Why didn't you promote Scotty to general manager of

Scotty Bowman, the most successful coach in the history
of the modern NHL. Copyright © Bill Wippert.

the Canadiens? He certainly performed well for you, and he deserved a reward!"

Sam's answer: "If you're looking for someone who's great at putting the right players on the ice, at matching lines, at judging when a rookie is ready to play NHL hockey or a veteran should retire—fine. . . . But we never let him near the team management. If you're looking for business judgment in a time of crisis, *forget it!*"

When I asked Scotty, "We had you under contract. Why did we lose you?" he seemed to acknowledge that there was some validity to Sam's comment. In the days of Scotty's greatest successes—with the Red Wings and the Canadiens—he had finally understood that his métier, his talent, was *coaching*. In his time with the Sabres, he still sought the "top" hockey job, which custom in the trade—sometimes erroneously, I think—assigns to the GM. "In Buffalo," said Scotty, "I was distracted by my GM duties, and didn't do as good a job as I might have as coach."

I would have to agree with Scotty's latter-day judgment. Roger Neilson may have undervalued the importance and validity of Scotty's hunches, gambles, and emotional calls, but they did not fit the normal pattern of the GM-trader. I have a memory of Scotty calling me at 5 AM in Montreal, asking for my approval of a "major" development—the trade of Tony McKegney, J. F. Sauve, and Andre Savard for a once-prominent refugee from the WHA—Real Cloutier. The Sabres lost two effective young second-line players for a reputation that proved a complete bust. It may have been the worst trade in Sabres history. On the other hand, I remember ruefully watching with Scotty the performance of my friend Danny Gare, the hero manqué of the famous "finals in the fog," who had been traded to Detroit. Scotty accurately predicted the end of Danny's playing career. "He's a nice kid," said Scotty, "but his knees are gone."

How important is the coach? By the time a rookie reaches the NHL, he has been educated and trained to a fare-thee-well in the basic hockey skills, usually in thorough and competent coaching, for as many as ten years, an apprenticeship that covered midget; amateur (in the United States), junior (in Canada), or college (in both countries); elite (in Russia, Eastern Europe, and Scandinavia); and sometimes even professional (in the minor leagues). The new player has had his fill of drills: pregame warm-up, back-check, breakout, feet and puck, forecheck, goalie, passing, power plays, penalty killing, shooting, skating, stick handling, offense, left-wing lock, penalty shots, on-ice awareness and reaction, changing lines, and so on. For these players, honing and fine-tuning skills, producing and dealing with major-league speed and strength, coordination with linemates, position and angles are all a part of the responsibilities of the major-league mentor. For veteran players, who may know it all and may hate drills and practice, the head coach must provide pregame preparation and in-game strategy and tactics that enable the team to compete effectively on the ice. For all players, old or young, the coach must provide *motivation*—energy and desire to reinforce the player's own drive, without which he should not be in the NHL in the first place. But ultimately, the team's success over time will depend on the "horses" management has provided the coach. How did they draft? How did they trade? How did they manage the compensation? For many years, I have felt that the success of the Sabres—success in all but the final Stanley Cup rounds—has been largely attributable to the moves of the hockey department as a whole—the GMs' trades, of course, but of vital importance are the drafts, in Canada, the United States, and Europe—largely engineered by Don Luce and the excellent North American, European, and Russian scouting staffs.

There are a number of fine hockey organizations around the league that have produced winning records consistently over time: Lou Lamoriello in New Jersey, Bobby Clarke's Flyers, Glen Sather and John Muckler wherever they are, Jim Devellano in Detroit, Pierre Lacrox in Colorado, Harry Sinden in Boston, and Ken Dryden and Pat Quinn in Toronto. And when these teams meet, it is often the coach who makes the difference. Scotty Bowman may have definitively underscored the coach's value in the 2002 and 2003 playoff seasons. In 2002, with Scotty at the bench, the Detroit Red Wings won the Stanley Cup. In 2003, with Scotty in retirement but essentially the same team except for a change in goal in place of the retired Dominik Hasek, Dave Lewis, who had been Bowman's first assistant coach, could not prevent a four-game sweep by the Mighty Ducks of Anaheim, who ousted the rueful Wings from the playoffs in the first round. Of course, there were other factors at play: although a first-class goaltender, Curtis Joseph may not have equaled the world-class Hasek; and the team's stars were all a year older. But one senses that these overage, overpaid stars needed the hard and expert hand of Bowman. Did Scotty sense that the knees of his stellar aggregation, like those of Danny Gare in Buffalo a decade earlier, had started to go?

The Red Wings' experience in the 2003 NHL playoffs did little to answer the question of the coach's importance, but it did provide evidence for the proposition that the "top" stars are overpaid, and the high player budget may be a road of no return. Loading up a team with VIP players may not be the greatest gift to a hard-working coach. Let's look at the performance of the ten highest-paid players in the league for the 2003 season. Each had a contract for $9 million or more for that year, compared with the NHL average salary of $1.6 million.

Of course, there are other factors at work in each case, but it is significant that eight of the ten top-salaried players either failed to make the playoffs or were knocked out in the first round. In a discussion of the rating of coaches in the NHL with Scotty Bowman, he warned, "You have to distin-

Player	Team	Team Playoff Achievement	2003 Player Playoff Pts.
Peter Forsberg	Colorado	Lost in first round to Minnesota	8
Mario Lemieux	Pittsburgh	Missed playoffs	0
Jaromir Jagr	Washington	Lost in first round to Tampa Bay	7
Paul Kariya	Anaheim	Lost in Stanley Cup Finals to New Jersey	12
Pavel Bure	New York Rangers	Missed playoffs	0
Joe Sakic	Colorado	Lost in first round to Minnesota	9
Teemu Selanne	San Jose	Missed playoffs	0
Chris Pronger	St. Louis	Lost in first round to Vancouver	4
John LeClair	Philadelphia	Lost in second round to Ottawa	5
Doug Weight	St. Louis	Lost in first round to Vancouver	13

guish between those that have money [i.e., large payroll budgets] and those who don't." These figures may well weaken that distinction.

My observation over the thirty-five years I've focused on NHL games is that a key to the quality of a coach is not so much how he handles the stars, but how he brings out the talent in the rookie, or in the journeyman who wants to get better. One could argue that Gilbert Perreault, for example, needed no coaching. He had physical strength, speed, quickness, a great shot, and a complete understanding of the tactics and play of the game. The Knoxes and our successive general managers in Gilbert's era always seemed to be put off by the language difference, and denigrate Bert's intelligence. He was genial, could be comic (as he is today when he sings rock music), and never seemed to work as hard as the coach would like—he didn't need to. To me, he surpasses Gretzky and Lemieux in the excitement he created. In the old Aud, he would spurt and wheel, do a 180-degree turn, burst through a check—skate through the whole opposing team to score. One night, while Gilbert was out of the lineup with a broken tibia, we watched a Canada Cup game in Hamilton together, in the press box. It was a revelation: not only how much he knew about the game, but how sharp his analysis was and how articulate his discussion of it. When I asked Bowman about Perreault, he agreed with my judgment as to the excitement he created, but he felt Bert was handicapped by the small size of the arena. (In those days the Aud, like the Boston Garden and the Chicago Stadium, was short in length and width, and did not meet the ultimate standard of 85 by 200 feet. This gave a slower defense an advantage in the smaller and sharper corners.) "In a larger arena," Scotty said, "Perreault would have been recognized as a great player." Sorry, Scotty—in the Niagara Frontier he certainly had that recognition!

Even after he left the Sabres organization, Scotty continued to make his home in Buffalo, retained his interest, and from time to time chimed in with comments about what we were doing. In 1987, when the Sabres had the first pick in the entry draft for the first time since we took Gilbert Perreault, the focus was on Pierre Turgeon, a handsome, skillful offensive center. Scotty was quick to advise us—"Don't draft Turgeon; he's too soft!" (The next player touted in the draft was Brendan Shanahan, a fine two-way player, who went to the Detroit Red Wings.) Scotty's judgment was probably correct; our new coach, Ted Sator, observed that Pierre, a very likeable kid, was pretty much a one-way player. Sator did not give up on Pierre, however—he devoted hours on and off the bench, pressing Pierre to acquire defensive skills and the appetite to use them. A less sensitive coach would have restricted him to the power play or sent him down to the minors for further training. Scotty's current take on Turgeon: "He's an example of a player who performs well if he's not asked to lead."

I have great respect for the Sabres' current coach, Lindy Ruff, but I wonder if he is willing to take the time and effort to convert a talented skater into a two-way player. Maxim Afinogenov, a young player from Russia drafted in 1997, obviously has special speed and talent, but he contributes little on the back-check or forecheck. I see Max use his speed to penetrate time after time, but little happens, and he becomes vulnerable in the transition game. Lindy's judgment—Max's value is restricted—may be correct, but I had hoped to see more development. Would Scotty have developed him more?

Who are Bowman's ranking coaches? He named Ken Hitchcock, who coached Dallas to victory over the Sabres in the 1999 Stanley Cup Finals, then got a pink slip and went on to lead the Flyers in a fantastic run in the 2004 playoffs; Jacques Martin of Ottawa; Joel Quenneville, then of St. Louis; and Brian Sutter, then with Chicago. Notably, Scotty did not name Mike Keenan, once an assistant coach in the Sabres organization, then head coach for Chicago, the New York Rangers, and the Florida Panthers. Mike is certainly knowledgeable and carries great PR. Yet I would hesitate quite a bit before hiring him, especially for a young team.

In my Boca Raton home, I read the *Sun Sentinel* sports pages and, with my friends Bill Torrey (a principal officer) and Wayne Huizenga (still a part owner), I follow the fortunes of the Panthers religiously. After a surprisingly quick start—reaching the Finals in their third year—the team put together by Torrey hasn't had much success, and Keenan (now GM) hasn't helped much. The players are professionals, certainly, despite their youth, and should be able to take constructive criticism in the dressing room, even on the ice. But in the press? From their coach? I have never, in my thirty-five years in the business, observed a coach who excoriates his team and individual players day after day, *in public*! It may get rid of Mike's frustration, but it's hard to believe that it has anything but a negative effect. Results would justify—but the Panthers missed the playoffs again in 2003, despite the coach's public anger.

I decided to test Scotty's dictum—that in assessing a coach or a GM, you must distinguish between those who have money to spend and those who don't. The usual approach is to add up the salaries—say, for the twenty-three players on the official roster. That gives you a comparison of the aggregate wage bill, but I tried a different formula: let's see who goes after the high-priced players. I used two lists: (1) how many players on the team roster ranked in the top thirty in the league in salary, and (2) how many players on the club's roster earned $3 million or more. Three million dollars is slightly more than 200 percent of the NHL's average salary. On this basis, the most "greedy" were Dallas, Philadelphia, New York Rangers, Detroit, and New Jersey, followed by Colorado, San Jose, St. Louis, Los Angeles, and Washington.

How did these big spenders fare in the 2002–2003 season? Three—Rangers, San Jose, and Los Angeles—missed the playoffs altogether. Four—Detroit, Washington, Colorado, and St. Louis—were knocked out in the first round. Dallas and Philadelphia made it as far as the second round. New Jersey went on to win the Stanley Cup.

How about the clubs at the conservative end of the pay scale? Five made the playoffs: Ottawa, Minnesota, Anaheim, Vancouver, and Tampa Bay. In the first round, Anaheim swept Detroit; Minnesota defeated Colorado; Vancouver ousted St. Louis; and Tampa Bay shocked Washington—in each case, the smaller salary team ousted the big spender. In the end, only one big spender—New Jersey—made it to the conference finals.

Scotty's list of leading coaches did pretty well: Brian Sutter's Blackhawks missed the playoffs, but Ken Hitchcock's Flyers made it to the quarterfinals, as did Jacques Martin's Senators, and Joel Quenneville's Blues lost a tough series to Vancouver. I would add some names to the list, considering the 2002–2003 season's results and historical data.

Scotty's record, the best in history, shows a win percentage of .654 in the regular season and .633 in the playoffs.

Jacques Lemaire produced a startlingly successful season for his expansion club, the Minnesota Wild, in its third year in the league, knocking off the high-powered Colorado Avalanche in the first round and the Vancouver Canucks in the second. Lemaire's record (through 2000) was .593/.590.

Ken Hitchcock, leading Philadelphia into the semifinal round, had the second-best record: .625/.614.

Jacques Martin improved his rating this year with a third-round appearance. The Senators' lack of progress in the playoffs accounts for a playoff percentage of only .386, as compared to his regular-season performance of .510.

Pat Burns demonstrated again with the Devils—the eventual Stanley Cup champions—that despite the change of team, he is a quality coach, with a .562/.508 record.

Marc Crawford, having moved north to Vancouver, proved his value, at least temporarily, before losing to Minnesota in the second round. Crawford (.576/.596), along with Glen Sather (.616/ .705), is in that very small group of coaches in modern times whose playoff win percentage exceeds their performance in the regular season.

I asked Scotty about Sather. Glen spent most of his career in Edmonton, operating with great success (four Stanley Cups) despite the handicaps of small budgets and Canadian dollars. Then he moved to the New York Rangers, and fiscal discipline disappeared. Glenn seemed to have been infected with the same unbridled passion for costly free agents and $70 million budgets that drove his predecessors—and produced, in large measure, only futility. "Why?" I asked Scotty.

"The low-budget scenario is too hard," he said. "Drafting, trading, building a team player by player, then selling 'em off when their salaries get too high, then starting over. . . . That takes time and skill and patience. For some, that's too tough."

Maybe Lemaire with the Wild, John Tortorella with the Lightning, and Martin with the Senators will change that thinking. Maybe a welcome change in the crazy economics of the National Hockey League is on the way.

Chapter 23

THE MOGILNY
NIGHTMARE

As I wrote this chapter—playoff time 2001—Alexander Mogilny, the Sabres' fourth-round pick in the 1988 NHL Entry Draft, refugee, or, if you will, AWOL from the Soviet army, had scored more than a point a game in the 2000–2001 season and had emerged as a resurrected star in the playoffs. In an overtime win over the Toronto Maple Leafs, Mogilny had two goals and three assists. He was tied with Mario Lemieux for the most points in the playoffs. Unfortunately for the Sabres, Alex was traded away in 1995, and the New Jersey Devils had the benefit of his extraordinary talent.[1] The Sabres "captured" Alex from the Soviets in 1989, and the story of his reign in the Sabres organization is one of luck, determination, intrigue, and disappointment.

For a snapshot in time, Alexander Mogilny and Pat LaFontaine formed one of the most exciting and dangerous duos in the history of the sport. In the 1992–93 Sabres season, Alex produced seventy-six goals— nearly a goal a game—and was tied for the league lead. Pat came up with 148 points, still a Sabres record. Together, they gave the Buffalo fans a diet of ecstatic tension unseen since the French Connection and the Stanley Cup Finals in 1975. The saga began in the spring of 1989 when Phil Esposito, then the Rangers general manager, received word through the grapevine that Mogilny, a star forward on the Moscow and Soviet Olympic teams, was ready to defect. Mogilny had called the New York club's European scout. Alex had heard of the Rangers, but he knew very little about the other NHL teams and had no idea that one of the other clubs might hold his rights. Phil Esposito knew: in the 1988 draft list in the *NHL Guide*, the name MOGILNY appeared opposite BUFFALO, loud and clear. Phil made his call to the Sabres' Don Luce (a former teammate) seem casual: "The player believes he belongs to New York, wants to play here. . . . The Soviets won't like it. They'll fight against any of their young players going to North America. We'll be glad to take the problem off your hands."

But Don did not bite. He knew, as Calgary GM Cliff Fletcher remarked on hearing of Mogilny's defection, that "this could change the league around!"

Mogilny was sitting with his companion, who acted as a temporary interpreter and adviser, in Sweden, and in the utmost secrecy—it was still the cold war—Don and Gerry Meehan (then the Sabres GM) arranged immediately to get Alex on a plane and get him in to Buffalo, creating whatever minimal documents they needed to run him past US customs and immigration.

So we had Alex, but could we keep him? He was in the United States on the skimpiest legality—a visitor's permit—limited in scope and time, and we were sure the Russians were already bellowing for his return. In the NHL, the immigration worry for a US club was not just the initial entry of the foreign player. In 1989 there were seven Canadian clubs (Montreal, Toronto, Vancouver, Winnipeg, Edmonton, Calgary, and Quebec City). The Sabres played them all at least once in Canadian arenas, and in some cases three or more games. That meant that Mogilny would have to go into Canada and return to the United States at least foureen times a season. That meant fourteen times every year that conscientious and aggressive immigration inspectors for both countries would be examining the papers of this "man without a country."

I had confronted the immigration problem early in the history of the Sabres when a Canadian player named Tracy Pratt, carrying a standard H-1 US visitor's visa, was stopped at the border near Vancouver by US officials and sent back to Canada. Never mind that he had been previously issued the normal immigration papers for a hockey player by the US immigration department, the local officials were entitled to take another look every time Tracy crossed the border. The gung ho inspector in Seattle searched the record anew and found that Tracy had been involved as a young adult in an escapade unjustly described, according to the player, as statutory rape. The charges had been dismissed, but the local inspector would not yield. Dave Forman had from the start established good relations for the Sabres with the immigration officers at the Buffalo–Fort Erie Peace Bridge. We moved Tracy across Canada to Fort Erie and, after appropriate education of the local officials, got the player through immigration there. But the necessity of continual border crossing hung over the player as long as he was in the Buffalo organization, and we kept our border contacts fine-tuned from then on.

With Mogilny, a Russian citizen, the problem could occur both ways: Canadian inspectors, even at the Peace Bridge, had hockey loyalties, of course, but the loyalties were without question to the Canadiens or the Maple Leafs; they might not be willing to stretch the rules enough to help a US club. So entry to Canada, on any Canadian road trip, might be barred. Adjustments over the decades enabled Canadian players under contract to US clubs to cross and recross the border without much difficulty. The H-1 usually committed the player to return to the country of his nationality, but in Mogilny's case, this would be disaster—both for the Sabres and for Alex personally. We had to get him some permanent status in the United States that would permit him to travel with the team without impediment or threat.

The first step was to sign Mogilny to a contract. I had unexpected problems with my GM, Gerry Meehan, with the language—and with providing Alex with adequate independent legal protection. The dollars were the least of it. But how could we come up with a document that Alex understood and we felt was fair? Mogilny's companion/interpreter seemed to have the player's confidence, but his English vocabulary was limited, and his business acumen was doubtful. We insisted that Alex have a local lawyer, but the gentleman chosen by the companion was prepared only to rubber-stamp whatever we came up with. I had always managed the communication well with other foreign players we had signed: my French was good enough to deal with the Quebec picks, the Scandinavian players generally either understood English or could handle French, and my army German got me by, with help from my old friend Julius Pick; but Russian was on another planet. We found an émigré doctor in the Southtowns of Erie County who could converse fluently with Alex and his companion, and had a degree of sophistication that made us more comfortable.

In discussions with Gerry Meehan, I suggested that we stick as closely as possible to the preprinted NHL standard player's contract. That would limit the possibilities of misunderstanding and claims of overreaching. But Gerry was a very conscientious and ethical lawyer, and his first draft had so many outs for Alex—Gerry was nearly paranoid about being unfair—that I sent it back to Meehan with a comment that it wasn't a contract at all! The draft reminded me of the small print on commercial sale forms that give the buyer the right to walk away from the deal for three days or for three weeks, whatever. For the trouble and expense we incurred to get Alex, I didn't want just a piece of paper that the Soviets—or Alex—could tear up in a second. Gerry and I resolved our differences, and I met directly with Alex and his companion, fortified by the additional interpreter, went painstakingly over every aspect of the contract, and was satisfied that we had done our utmost to be fair and open, but prudent.

In the talks with Alex and his representatives, it was important to overcome what I could see as fear and hostility. I was an authority figure—a lawyer, an owner, and officer of the league—and we knew from our investigation that Alex, if not a revolutionary, had shown resistance to authority—to his coaches, his Soviet army superiors, and the Russian Hockey Federation. And I tried very hard—as much as I could, working through an interpreter—to get his confidence, to change that rigid stare to a relaxed smile. It was important not only for the contract, but to prepare him for appearance and testimony in the immigration proceedings I had in mind.

How could we get Alex protected status? A talk with the local immigration inspectors produced sympathy, but no help. They had no power to grant anything more than the visitor's permit, and that could not be extended beyond the end of the current season. We had no idea what the Canadian authorities would do if Alex were apprehended in Canada and the Soviets put pressure on a government less critical of the Russian regime. After research, I concluded that the only possible solution was to have Alex declared a political refugee. There was a federal statute, ancient in origin, designed to help immigrants who had fled their native lands in fear for their lives because of religious or political persecution. If Alex could be classified as a refugee within the meaning of the statute, he would have the status and papers equivalent to those of a permanent resident of the United States.

There were two problems: one administrative, one substantive. Inquiry at the Peace Bridge immigration office indicated the refugee status had to come directly from Washington and that we needed an OK from a very high level in the State Department. I concluded that intervention by a congressman or senator with clout would be necessary. Henry Nowak and John LaFalce, representatives from Western New York who had been helpful to the Sabres, either had no jurisdiction or were not available. There was little time—the status had to be solved before the end of the season, when Mogilny's visitor's permit would expire. The list of congressional committees showed Amo Houghton, of the Corning Glass family, as a member of the key committee; his district included part of Monroe and Wyoming counties, the territory of our minor-league farm club, the Rochester Americans. I went to Seymour. Did he know Houghton? He certainly did—they had been contemporaries at Yale—and with that wonderful way he had of reaching out and energizing friends to help, he had Amo and me working together on the Mogilny project in a matter of hours.

Houghton immediately ordered and produced direct contact with Raymond Seitz, the assistant secretary of state in charge of refugee issues, and there began a double-barreled pressure the unsuspecting assistant secretary rarely encountered. Amo Houghton grasped the legal, hockey, and political issues immediately and made it his personal project. The assistant secretary was buffeted with calls, faxes, telegrams, letters, and petitions from both of us until the job was done.

So the procedural play was set. With Dave Forman's help, we overcame continuing resistance from the local office—some jurisdictional jealousy, some mere inertia, some skepticism. The prime difficulty was that the refugee statute was created for the benefit of persons threatened with imprisonment or death for their beliefs—a Russian pogrom, an ethnic cleansing, a German Holocaust. But could it be used by a hockey player to escape from his Soviet team?

Then the Soviets, in their ineffable intransigence, played into our hands. Alex, as a star of the Soviet Olympic team and as a means of providing him with a salary, had been appointed a nominal captain in the Soviet army. When Mogilny's defection became known, the Russian Hockey Federation, angered at losing a star player without compensation (unlike the Swedes, they had refused to enter into an agreement with the NHL to cover such situations), proceeded to attack Mogilny in every way they could. It was announced that Mogilny was a deserter and faced court-martial for "treason," the punishment for which could be death. His mother was fired from her department store job; his father's home was trashed. I received a call from the league: "Bob, counsel for the Russian Hockey Federation wants to see you, we think you should at least meet with him."

I asked, "Am I under any compulsion to respond? Because we're not going to let him go, and we're not going to pay blackmail."

We met at the league conference room in New York City. The Soviets' lawyer had a longish gray beard; he looked to me like a combination of Burl Ives and Zero Mostel. His demeanor was surprisingly mild, even semiapologetic. I assume he had been advised of our position. But the mildness did not cancel the message he had been directed to convey: Alex had committed a serious offense; he was a deserter from the Russian army; his loss to the Soviet hockey program was most damaging; and the Soviets would not rest until Alex returned to his team and/or the Russian federation received appropriate compensation. I answered that the Soviet treatment of Mogilny was repugnant to the American system of values; that Alex should be free to pursue his career wherever he wished; that the Soviets had had every opportunity to negotiate an agreement for compensating the Russian federation when a player moved to the NHL (as Sweden had done), but had refused to do so; and that Alex was a hockey player, not a soldier, his "captaincy" was a sham and the charge of desertion and treason was an unconscionable threat. We were not going to take our protection away from Alex, we were not going to let the Soviets take him back, and we were not going to pay blackmail. The Soviets' lawyer then thanked me for meeting with him and left, commenting that "this matter is not over; you will be hearing from us."

Of course, we were quick to tell the assistant secretary of state that the conduct of the Soviets read right on the refugee statute. There was no way of knowing how real the Soviet threats were, but the sounds of "treason," the damage to his father's home and the firing of his mother, coupled with

Alex Mogilny, as "refugee." Copyright © Bill Wippert.

the language of their counsel, were enough to enable the State Department to heed the irrepressible push from Amo. We got the refugee certificate, served it on the local office, and Alex was a free resident of the United States and a portable player in the National Hockey League.

I took the words of the Soviets' lawyer seriously enough. When Alex played his first game for the Sabres in Canada—against the Montreal Canadiens—I retained Jacques Courtois, former counsel for the Montreal team when it was owned by the Bronfmans, and instructed him to be prepared for any move the Soviets might make on Mogilny or on the Sabres. An attack with an injunction was a distinct possibility, with a claim that we had interfered with the player's "contractual" relationship with the Soviet team. Nothing developed, and I know not whether this was the result of my forceful oratory, the support of the Department of State and the league, or conciliatory moves made by Alex himself.

When the refugee status was set, my wife, Bikki, and I took off on a cruise planned for the Mediterranean Greek Islands, Turkey and the Hellespont, and the Black Sea. When Norty Knox heard that we would touch two ports in Russia, he instructed me, "Bob, those Soviets don't like you. When you get to Russia, *don't get off the boat!*" Thirteen thousand miles away from the NHL, the controversy seemed remote and I didn't heed Norty's warning. We debarked for short tours of Yalta and Odessa, the regions of Russia where my mother's ancestors had lived generations ago. Bikki asked me why the streets of Yalta were so clean? I responded—only half kidding—"Because they've been washed with *blood!*"

On the return trip, as we passed through the Hellespont, I began to feel ill, strange spots appeared on my palms, and my tongue seemed to thicken. I went to see the ship's doctor, resplendent in his white uniform with the gold buttons. He was a German on a Swedish ship, and his English was fragmentary. He heard the description of my ailment, looked in a large, thick tome, didn't touch or examine me, but did not hesitate to make a judgment. "Mr. Schwaadoss," he intoned. "Your voyage is destroyed! Unless . . . unless you will permit me to give you something to knock it out." I agreed, and swallowed the pills he proffered (later determined to be tetracycline). Within twenty-four hours I was in danger, near delirium, and Bikki, in a marvelous display of guts, got me off the ship and flew me home to Buffalo via Frankfurt and Paris under emergency orders from the two airlines that probably saved my life—Lufthansa and US Air. It was a great stroke of luck; none of the doctors on the ship, in Frankfurt, or in the airports had been able to diagnose the illness. In the emergency room at Buffalo General Hospital, the specialist in infectious diseases, Dr. Brass, and the head of dermatology, Dr. Stephanie Pincus, recognized the rare disease: it was Stephens-Johnson Syndrome, the most serious and critical phase of erythema multiformes. It is an autoimmunological reaction of the skin; in fighting off what it perceives as an allergen, the immune system attacks every mucous membrane in the body—eyes, mouth, groin, throat. With their experience in the hospital's burn treatment center and the actual Stephens-Johnson cases they had seen in children overreacting to sulfa, the Buffalo doctors knew what it was and what to do. I was in intensive care for three weeks, often delirious, sometimes unconscious, and without the skillful treatment I received, my career and my life would have been over.

The disease was so rare—the blotches looked like little targets with bull's-eyes in the center—there was a constant stream of residents, interns, doctors, and nurses into my room to view this strange phenomenon. My own internist, a fine physician named Bob Kohn, visited every day, taking notes while I came in and out of consciousness. Seymour and Norty, hearing that I was in trouble, were shocked at my appearance. When I finally had enough strength to look in the mirror, I could see why: My skin—which I learned was the largest organ in the body—had changed in color as it was being replaced, much like the result of a burn. I looked like the Creature from the Green Lagoon.

The doctors never announced with great certainty what caused the Stephens-Johnson. Perhaps it was an infection—the swallowing of some unclean water while I tried to swim in the pitching shipboard pool—or the tetracycline the ship's doctor had thrust down my unsuspecting throat. My daughter, Liz, in her book *The Four of Us*,[2] portrays me as talking, lecturing, singing through my delirium. There were strange dreams, whose shape is vague now; one was inspired no doubt by the guilt for having disobeyed Norty's instructions. A Russian with a Stalin-like mustache appears and denounces me. "Swados," he says. "You son of a bitch; you kidnapper. How dare you, how dare you return to the land from which your ancestors fled! You're not only a Jew, you're a *Sabre*!"

Chapter 24

GRETZKY THE GREAT

The Star None of Us Could Afford

Any hockey fan knows that Wayne Gretzky was probably the greatest forward in the modern history of the NHL. Few know that his purchase (disguised as a "trade") by the Los Angeles Kings from the Edmonton Oilers in 1988 was the "big bang" that accelerated the salary inflation virus, that destroyed the Winnipeg and Quebec franchises and drove them into the United States, and that even today threatens the viability of the league. The seller was Peter Pocklington, urbane owner of the Oilers—likeable, politically connected in provincial and national politics, who had assembled somethiing of a dynasty with Gretzky, Jari Kurri, Mark Messier, Grant Fuhr, and other highly talented players drafted when the team was a member of the WHA and shortly after its entry into the NHL. The buyer was Bruce McNall, a newcomer to hockey, who had just bought the Los Angeles team, a constant disappointment at the box office. McNall saw the success of the Los Angeles Lakers in the same building and was determined to achieve "success" with the fans and a positive bottom line for the Kings.

Both men needed money: McNall, to recoup the hockey losses; Pocklington, to restore the cash he had taken out of Oilers profits to fund losses and pay debts incurred in his meat business and other unfortunate commercial ventures. As special counsel for the league, I had recently negotiated a consent agreement with Peter that restricted his borrowing (from the

Alberta Provincial Treasury) to $40 million and prohibited commingling of hockey assets or income with other business operations.

It didn't take long for the meat company to reach bankruptcy, and Peter faced a default to the banks and a breach of his obligations to the league—a breach that could trigger termination of his ownership of the franchise. The solution? Sell some of his key players for cash. The problem? The NHL had in place a policy against selling player contracts for cash. At a time when there were still substantial restrictions on raids by one team on the players of another and free agency was a rare gift, no owner wanted a league like the old American Baseball League, where the rich Yankees could pick off stars from the hapless small markets with cash offers and no replacement players—where Kansas City, for example, was regarded as a farm team of the big New York club. In the years between 1976 and 1992 when I served on the Owner-Player Council, the negotiation team on union matters, we successively pruned cash from the compensation for "forced" trades. Baseball confronted this issue when Charley Finley in 1974 tried to sell Catfish Hunter and two other star pitchers from his champion Oakland A's, and the league's commissioner successfully nullified the deal. The owners on the NHL negotiating committee limited the circumstances in which, in a "forced" trade, a club signing away another team's player could compensate the old club with cash. For a number of years, the compensation was another player or draft picks; today, it's generally draft picks or the right to match. Cash was poison.

On a number of occasions, I was asked to produce a valuation of a club's roster and its other assets, usually for tax purposes, and it was very difficult to find a concrete example of a simple sale of a player contract for cash. About the only one I found was a purchase in the 1970s by an NHL team of the contract of Anders Hedberg from Winnipeg, then a WHA club, for $500,000—and later developments made that transaction of little relevance. I'm sure the Hedberg deal didn't help McNall and Pocklington arrive at a price for Gretzky. That price turned out to be $15 million—a price unheard of in the history of the league, nearly three times the $6 million Pocklington paid for his entire NHL franchise. Sure, to avoid the appearance of violating the NHL policy against cash purchases of players, it was tacked on to a "trade"—but there was no doubt in NHL councils that it was the cash that was the substance of the deal. But with the recurring gate and financial problems of the Los Angeles club, Mr. McNall's move to make the Kings successful in this major market was welcomed, and league authorities looked the other way.

So the inflationary poison—cash—was injected into the NHL system. But it didn't stop with the purchase price, none of which went directly to Wayne Gretzky. The owner of the Lakers, Jerry Buss, who sold the Kings to McNall in 1989, had made the NBA team the rage of Hollywood, the place

Wayne Gretzky. Copyright © Bill Wippert.

In the Sabres' Directors' Room—Phil Esposito (*right*) with friends
(*from left to right*) Glen Sather, Wayne Gretzky, Goldie Hawn,
and Burt Reynolds. Copyright © Bill Wippert.

to go, the thing to do: movie stars held seats in the elite circle on the floor, mingling and socializing with the basketball stars, whose salaries made them eligible and acceptable. It was McNall's view that if the hockey stars were to succeed at the gate in Los Angeles in the same building and market, they had to have salaries that labeled them "major league." This view may have been influenced by the New York Rangers, a team that has tradition-ally held that position, no matter who is GM. The Rangers would say at league meetings: "We're the number one market, what's good for us is good for the league. We need major stars and must pay them accordingly, even if it seems to hurt the smaller markets."

So McNall, on top of the $15 million he paid Pocklington to acquire the player, increased Gretzky's salary to $2 million per year, a quantum leap over his Edmonton pay, a drastic shock to the league scale, and a burst to salary escalation from which the league never has recovered.[1]

There were at least three problems with McNall's decision to emulate the Lakers: first, the income of the Kings and of NHL clubs generally, espe-cially the television income, was only a fraction of that of the NBA team; second, the NBA had its salary levels under control (ultimately through a negotiated salary cap), whereas the NHL did not; and third, he was using other people's money—ultimately, it turned out, stolen money—to pay Wayne's salary.

At the time of the deal, the average salary in the league was about

$223,000 per year. Gretzky was paid $2 million per year by McNall. That projected to a club payroll for the normal playing roster of twenty-six "big club" players of about $26 million per season—more than most clubs' gate, and more than most NHL teams could afford.

McNall doubtless believed, with justification, that the doleful history of the Kings called for drastic measures. The franchise had initially gone begging in the first expansion in 1967. Climate, minor-league history, and distance from the core NHL cities were of major concern. Jim Norris, the Detroit owner and a power in the league then, articulated his prejudice against Buffalo when he told me "You're the best group, with the best preparation and the best financing, but if you insist on Buffalo, you're not gonna get it." The league offered us our choice of Los Angeles, Cleveland, or St. Louis; but we were Buffalo people, and we wanted not just a hockey franchise, but a major-league asset for our community. Jack Kent Cooke finally agreed to purchase the expansion franchise for $2 million and build the new arena, the Forum. Cooke's decision was premised on the report that there were more than three hundred thousand Canadians in the Los Angeles area, only to state, after losing the quarterfinals and semifinals in the first two years and being out of the playoffs in the next four consecutive seasons—with poor gate and low revenue—uttered, no doubt in his normal, stentorian tone, "I found out why they moved . . . they hated hockey!"[2]

Jack Cooke was succeeded by Jerry Buss as the Kings' owner. Jerry bought the Lakers, the Kings, and the Forum in 1979. He was a PhD, psychologist, real estate entrepreneur, and cultural sophisticate, but he didn't have much success with the Kings. His reign as an NHL governor was distinguished, in my memory, by his showing up late for his own party for the governors, flanked by two gorgeous demimondaines, one blonde, one brunette. He didn't seem to have much interest in the Kings or the league, although he was a fan of his profitable basketball team. As NHL secretary and special counsel, I had the responsibility for the league documents on his entry and departure. I remember trying for weeks to reach him by phone, without response. Then I went to the opening of my daughter's show at the Mark Taper Forum in Los Angeles, and there was Jerry—knowledgeable, affable, supportive, flanked again by two delightful damsels, one blonde, one brunette.

Bruce McNall was affable, too—more outgoing, more expansive, definitely involved in league affairs, and committed to improving the NHL in its economic and other components. At the time of the players' strike in 1992, when we seemed to be at impasse, he brought Wayne Gretzky to the negotiating table, and it seemed to get things moving toward an ultimate settlement. His salesmanship and energy, together with the importance of the NHL market to the league, led to his election as chairman of the Board of Governors.

In those days, the league took considerable pains to assure working capital, adequate financing, and control on the entry of a new owner, but it did little monitoring of the club's financial affairs after that, until a crisis arose. I recall that both the Buss and the McNall balance sheets were unusual—indeed, strange. Instead of business assets, cash, or marketable securities, there were real estate interests, horses, and, in McNall's case, rare and ancient coins. I asked John Ziegler if we should make some independent investigation of the values, but in view of the importance of the market and the urgency of the matter, the league elected to follow its usual procedures, and the verifications by the owner and his accountants were accepted.

I had no clue as to trouble in the Kings' coffers. In December 1992, with me representing the league in legal matters, the NHL awarded expansion franchises in Florida and Anaheim to Wayne Huizenga and Disney, respectively, with play to begin in the 1993–94 season. The fifty-mile territorial radius of the Anaheim franchise overlapped the territory of the Kings, and this produced a payment of $25 million as compensation from Disney out of the expansion proceeds. McNall gave a gracious speech at a league dinner in Buffalo later that year, thanking me for the Florida/Tampa/Ottawa/Anaheim expansion in 1992 and 1993, which, he said, would not have occurred without my efforts. I saw no irony in this, although when Bruce was indicted in 1996, I recalled the strange call I received from Gil Stein (then acting president of the league). "To whom is the $25 million check payable?" he asked. I responded, "It's payable to the Kings; it'll require an endorsement by the company itself." What happened to the proceeds of the check, I know not—there were apparently plenty of creditors waiting in line.

Did the drastic Gretzky transaction accomplish its goals for anybody? Certainly Wayne's presence in the United States and his outstanding individual performance contributed to increased NHL promotion and acceptance. Yet the results for his team on the ice did not improve even with Wayne on the roster, and McNall and successive owners of the Kings piled up a deficit of over $100 million, forcing the club to go through bankruptcy proceedings to find stabilized ownership. Pocklington's $15 million sale of Gretzky was not enough to solve his nonhockey problems, and he was ultimately forced to sell. McNall, desperately recycling the same rare coins as collateral to two different lenders, ended up in jail.

The Gretzky transaction level certainly contributed to the $18 million price paid by the Flyers in the auction in December 1989 for the rights to Eric Lindros—hotly contested by the Rangers. A glance at the table on page 304 shows the abrupt escalation of the average salary following the Gretzky transaction: from $188,000 in 1988, it rose at a rate of more than $100,000 per year. Applying that to the major-league roster of twenty-four per team, that's $2.4 million per team per year. It is hardly a coincidence that the new Gretzky level was followed closely by multimillion-dollar salaries never seen before in the league—some achieved by his old teammates in the Edmonton dynasty, like Mark Messier, in his move to the Rangers, and others by free agent signings or acquisitions in trades of Pat LaFontaine by Buffalo, John LeClair by Philadelphia, and Brendan Shanahan by Detroit. The most shocking was the Lindros matter—a year after the Gretzky signing, when my friend Marcel Aubut got the Rangers and Flyers into an auction for Eric Lindros (who had never played a game in the NHL) and produced a trade that loaded $18 million into the Quebec coffers; and the uncharacteristic offer sheet shortly thereafter by Bill Wirtz of Chicago for Keith Tkachuk of Winnipeg—forcing the Canadian club to pay the theretofore unheard of salary of $6 million to exercise its right of first refusal and forcing the American clubs, under the "Canadian assistance plan," to subsidize the exchange differential between the US and Canadian currency.

The league average salary is now more than $1.8 million, producing an average annual roster cost for twenty-four players of nearly $36 million; superstars like Jaromir Jagr, Dominik Hasek, and Paul Kariya are earning $8 to $10 million a year; and nearly half the teams in the NHL are losing substantial money. The Gretzky transaction was, of course, not the sole cause—but it accelerated the potential disaster.

Chapter 25

"HEAD" NOTES

Eric Lindros, the talented "big man" and leading scorer whose baggage includes seven concussions in less than four years and an aggressive father-agent, finally ended up with the club with the largest budget—the New York Rangers. But no one—not Glen Sather, nor Herr Lindros, nor the Flyers who traded him, nor Lindros himself—knows whether or how long or how well he'll be able to play. Moreover, no one knows who, if anybody, is going to end up paying his $9 million salary. It could be the Flyers, the Rangers, or the insurance company.

Multiple concussions, as I learned from our episode with Pat LaFontaine, are a perplexing problem. There is some disagreement in the medical profession, at this stage of its knowledge, as to the impact of the word "multiple." You break your arm; it heals. You break it again. Is the second break automatically more serious? Or does the first healing strengthen the arm? Does each injury have to be considered separately, or is there a tendency that must be taken into account? At multimillion-dollar salary levels, the possibilities have major consequences. The NHL standard player's contract contemplates liability on the part of the team, in the event of injury on the ice, for the full salary for the full fixed term of the contract, excluding option years. Insurance, which has become more and more expensive, ordinarily covers only 80 percent of the potential liability, even for a top-five player. So the club may not be able to pass off the liability completely, even if it can find an insurance company willing to underwrite the contract in the face of the injury record.

Entirely apart from the serious legal and financial issues, the club faces human and ethical concerns. Should a player who seems to have a concussion weakness be permitted to go out on the ice again—risking his health, his career, and maybe his life—even if the player and the underwriter are willing to take the gamble? The doctors may not be of much help in making the judgment. In Pat LaFontaine's case, a fifth—maybe a sixth—concussion led the Sabres doctors to tell the team, and the Sabres to tell Pat, that he should never play again. Yet Pat found two physicians with reputations in the field who, after looking at the same tapes and the same x-rays, advised Pat that resuming play was an acceptable risk—or, alternatively, it was up to him.

The problem is exacerbated when you read the clauses in the standard contract that relieve the club of responsibility if the player is "unable" to perform and yet require the judgment to be made first by the player (or his doctor), then by arbitration in the event the doctors disagree. You search for an insurer—it's unlikely the player or his agent will solve this—and you find there's really only one place to go: Lloyd's of London or one of its affiliates. And you may need the league's help to get there at all. You would love to unload the problem on another club through a trade, but disclosure must be total. And the new organization will have the same doubts and concerns.

I first had to face up to the concussion "syndrome" when LaFontaine's contract came up for renewal or renegotiation in 1994. We did not make much of an issue of the size of his salary ($4.5 million) or the duration of his contract. While it was not true—as asserted by Devils owner John McMullen—that we had borrowed $15 million from John Rigas so we could sign Pat LaFontaine, we certainly were counting on him as a top-twenty-five scorer, the captain of the team, and a major selling point for the new arena. And, up to that point, Pat had delivered. We had acquired Pat from the Islanders, trading away the talented Pierre Turgeon (our number one first-round pick in 1987), perhaps in belated response to Scotty Bowman's comment when we drafted Pierre that he was "too soft." Pat had scored more than a point and a half a game in the two years thus far spent with us; produced a phenomenal season with Alexander Mogilny—148 points in ninety-four games (including the playoffs); captained the team and made himself known as a charitable citizen of the community; and even signed up for two of the most expensive luxury suites in the new arena. He had demonstrated leadership on the ice and in the locker room, sometimes acting more like an owner than an employee.

Pat asked for more communication and input from the players to management, leading us to set up a regular meeting with Pat and his agent, Don Meehan, to talk about overall concerns. At the first meeting I was the owner

Pat LaFontaine. Copyright © Bill Wippert.

representative, and it was friendly and productive. Pat asked why the owners (Seymour, Norty, and me) only came into the dressing room after we had won the game. It would make more sense, Pat argued, for us to come in after a loss, when the players needed support. I gave the answer I'd received when I asked the same question of Punch Imlach: "These guys don't like to lose," he said. "I'm afraid to go near them after a loss!"

The investment in Pat seemed like a good one, and when Gerry Meehan (then our general manager) presented the proposed new contract, I didn't argue very much, even though some members of the Board of Governors criticized us later for "breaching the market" with the $4.5 million. I even went along with a no-trade clause yet to be approved in the collective bargaining negotiations. As always, I had a tendency, when an important player was involved, to make the deal and fix the technical problems later. One problem, however, could not be deferred: career-ending insurance and Pat's concussion record. With a fixed term of at least three years and a standard, guaranteed contract that made us liable for the full salary over that term, an injury to Pat early in the contract could make us liable for $13.5 million, and insurance was imperative. And I felt it essential to have that insurance in hand before we signed the new deal. The numbers made the underwriters skittish with Pat's record. It was not clear how many or how extensive his concussions had been. Incidents had taken place when Pat had struck his head in a collision or fall to the ice; sometimes the trainer or physician put a full report in the record (as mandated by league rules or practice), and sometimes the injury was regarded as minor—not serious enough to call it a concussion—and there was no report except a trainer's note or a newspaper story.

There was no concrete definition of a "concussion," although in practice the doctors would focus on the circumstances of the injury and the time the player was unconscious. One online encyclopedia describes a concussion as an "injury to the brain from a fall or blow to the head, usually with loss of consciousness, *the reason for which is not entirely understood."*

The description continues: "After effects such as dizziness, headaches and nervousness may continue for several days, weeks, or even years after the initial injury. A concussion may temporarily or permanently damage nerve tissue, producing amnesia, irritability, and fatigue; memory is often impaired. Recovery from a concussion is generally complete and prompt after less severe injuries."[1]

If the recovery from a single "less severe" injury may be complete, surely the probability that one in six or one in seven may be career and life threatening would lead an intelligent fan to accept a ban on further participation in the sport. Yet Pat, and now Eric Lindros, pushed the odds to the limit. Why? I have often wondered at the capacity of the professional athlete, especially the hockey athlete, to play in pain. The cuts to the face, the hits to the head, the crashes into the boards—padding and helmets notwithstanding—would send most of us to the comfort of the nearest Barcalounger. Hockey players will play with severe cuts to the face, sutured on the spot, and will put themselves at risk of major damage to their health and their future. Perhaps the most egregious examples are the players who are half blind and risk losing their sight forever. We had Greg Neeld, who never did get to play for the Sabres and was ruled ineligible by Clarence Campbell. (A ruling under the NHL bylaw sustained by the federal courts after ten years of litigation.) The New York Rangers now have Bryan Berard, who technically has marginal vision in the injured eye, but would be effectively blind if he lost vision in the eye that escaped injury.

I believe this bizarre adhesion to the game is not just financial. Certainly neither Roger Crozier, playing with a diseased pancreas; nor Mario Lemieux, with his life-threatening cancer; nor Eric Lindros and Pat LaFontaine, with their concussion syndromes, had financial concerns. Mario, like the NBA's Michael Jordan, may have motivations dictated by his role as owner, but it is hard to believe that his years of multimillion-dollar earnings have gone up in smoke. It's the *life* they won't give up: the game, the camaraderie, the bus and airplane rides, the excitement, the being *somebody* before eighteen thousand fans—the daily mesmerization of the hockey life.[2]

For Pat LaFontaine, these concussion problems were routine, and he had little patience with the "paperwork." But for the Sabres, protection of the club (and the player) demanded insurance coverage, against loss of games and a career-ending injury. In making the application for the insurance in 1994, we had to disclose the record of injuries—and a misstatement could void the coverage. The local insurance salesmen were of no help. Some competition for the coverage would have been useful, but I soon found that all roads led to London, ultimately Lloyds. Fortunately, Jeff Pash, the NHL general counsel, gave us a big boost, entered the negotiations, and helped us arrive at a compromise. It took many calls even to find the guy in England who had the authority and the independence to make the commitment. It was important to the league as a whole—if we couldn't produce the coverage, nobody else could, and the salary structure and relations with the union would be affected. (In retrospect, maybe we should have relied on the insurance difficulties to halt the salary escalation.)

The Knoxes had invited us for a much-needed vacation at their place on Tupper Lake in the Adirondacks, and after hearing the anguished cries from my wife, Bikki, at the threat of another cancelled vacation, I set out for Tupper Lake, even though agreement had not been reached on the LaFontaine insurance. Jeff Pash caught up with me on a lonely road north of Albany. I found a pay phone in a gas station, and with my cell phone in one hand and the proprietor's instrument in the other, managed to hook up Don Meehan in Canada, Jeff in New York, and the underwriter in London. The compromise, which formed a pattern for other player transactions, called for a short period of testing. If the player did not incur a serious injury during the test period—say, thirty games—the insurance locked in for a season; further injury-free periods earned further coverage. We were at grave risk for thirty or forty games, but the deal was made, and an important asset was secured. Hockey is no business for people who are afraid to take risks.

I noted in the 2002 brouhaha involving Eric Lindros that the Rangers and the player were faced with the same issues: How many of the incidents involved "real" concussions? Is there a cumulative effect? Does extensive rehab reduce the risk of another major injury? I saw that Lindros tended to minimize, the club was not so sure, and the doctor said "Wait!" When Lindros returned to play on January 12, 2002, the *New York Times* reported that "Lindros was credited with no hits, no goals and no assists. He skated much of yesterday afternoon as if avoiding contact. He stayed away from the scenes that make hockey so competitive at its best."[3]

At that juncture, Rangers GM Glen Sather was confronted with the same possibility we feared in Buffalo with Pat LaFontaine—the worst of all possible worlds: you have to pay the player $9 or $10 million for a performance that's 10 percent of his normal hard-hitting, high-flying output; you have no insurance to cover the loss of value; you're using up dollars that could buy you substitute talent; and in every game, the player risks his career and maybe his life.

Thus our caution with Pat certainly made sense. Pat was hexed by injuries, played no more than half of the scheduled games over the next three years, and a horrendous fall to the ice in the last season of his contract posed the issue again. In the game against the Boston Bruins on October 17, 1996, Pat was blindsided, received a hard blow to the head, fell to the ice surface, and hit his head again against the ice. (The tape shows his skull making a three- or four-inch bounce before he settled to the ice, unconscious for some moments, then groggy and dazed.) The fact that Pat remained unconscious for several moments was a bad sign under any doctor's criteria. After a few days of recovery, we expected that Pat would be back to normal, but we received reports that after months Pat was still experiencing headaches, dizziness, and other symptoms that were signs that the recovery was slow and the concussion had been severe and dangerous. Under the circumstances—Pat was well-off—we thought he'd want to retire; but word came back that this talented, financially set player wanted to go back into the fray again. Under the NHL standard contract, the player is examined by his own doctor, then declares himself ready to play, and, if the club had no objection, things resume as they were before the injury. If the club disagrees, it can call for examination by its own doctor, and if the doctors do not agree, the matter goes to arbitration, with the two physicians choosing a third, whose decision would be binding. Overlooking the debate, the insurance carrier has a lot to say. If the contract does not exclude or limit the coverage for concussions, the carrier might still assert as a defense—to this injury or the next—failure to disclose prior injuries.

John Butsch, the nice guy and competent emergency physician who administered the Sabres medical section, made it clear at the outset that in his view Pat should never play again. The risk of permanent damage to his health and brain was too great. However, under the circumstances—and John often had to hand over the case to a specialist, in view of Pat's attitude—we had to bring in a doctor whose judgment we respected but who also had reputation and experience in the field of brain damage. The doctor chosen by John Butsch and Larry Quinn (then president of the Sabres) was "Nicky" Hopkins, a close friend of John's and a leading Western New York brain surgeon. For purely emotional reasons, I would not have made that choice. My only contact with Hopkins occurred when Al Baker, a young associate of mine, of whom I was very fond and for whom I had high hopes, was diagnosed with brain cancer. Al had difficult family circumstances, and he seemed to rely on me for judgment and comfort. I spent hours at the hospital trying to keep up his spirits and help him ventilate his frustrations and fears. Hopkins was his surgeon, and, as the disease began to eat away at his brain and his psyche, the drugs and the pain seemed to make me his father and the good doctor his enemy. He lashed out at Hopkins—"Bob, keep him away from me!"—on my every visit, until death mercifully intervened.

The memory of that episode of futile expertise remained sharply in my subconscious, so much so that when in the spring of 1998 Bikki's lung tumor migrated to her brain, I could not, despite his undoubted competence, ask Hopkins to perform the operation. But when it came to a major Sabres player, I did not object to John Butsch's choice. I must have reviewed the tape a dozen times: the hit, the snap of the head, the bounce of the skull on the ice. How could Pat want to risk himself and his family again, for the sixth time? I asked Hopkins, "Did the helmet not provide protection?" "Not much," he responded. He pointed out that the brain in effect floats in the skull, and the helmet doesn't prevent the brain, given momentum by the crash or the hit, from smashing against the inside of the skull.

As to the existence of a tendency, or the cumulative effect of a series of concussions, Hopkins was not willing to eliminate this as a further risk. Should the decision be up to the player, as suggested by the "specialists" Pat's agent had recruited? Not according to Hopkins. It was case-by-case—but in this case, with this history and the severity of the hit and the crash, only one result was rational.

I felt a special concern and loyalty to Pat. He was not only an exciting player, he was articulate (always a plus with me), kind, considerate and a character with charisma, a "mensch," who had contributed to our efforts to solve the arena problems. I did not entirely feel that way about our brilliant but sometimes quixotic president, Larry Quinn. One of the perks of sports management is control of the tickets, especially the limited supply of good ones when the team is on the road. I had always been annoyed at having to wait until the "priorities" were taken care of before I got my seats, but Quinn took the practice to an extreme in the first game of the first round of the 1997 playoffs at Ottawa. My tickets were usually hand delivered to me by the PR guy or by Seymour H. Knox IV well before face-off. In this instance, I arrived separately from New York, where I had been involved in a league matter. When I got to the hotel—no tickets. I called the PR guy, who had no idea of their whereabouts; same with the controller, the assistant GM, and so on. I finally tracked down Larry. He had "no idea" where I was, and he had left the tickets at the Ottawa will-call.

This was the first Ottawa playoff game in its modern history. The facility staff had no comprehension of the crowds to expect, nor how to handle them. The will-call windows were utter chaos: lines stretching out into the street, inexperienced operators, an angry mob shouting for service as we approached within minutes of the face-off. And there I was, voting trustee, vice chairman, general counsel, embarrassed big shot—struggling with the rest of them to get to the window. I was angry. With the excitement of the game, the anger disappeared (we won), but the adrenaline continued to flow. In the Sabres dressing room after the game, the adrenaline surge finally left me and I suddenly felt faint and started to fall. Pat LaFontaine was standing next to me, saw my pale face, grabbed me, and called the Ottawa doctor. They laid me out on the nearest table, and out came the stethoscope, which showed nothing serious. I recovered promptly. But the crash of Swados could not have been more center stage and was known instantly throughout the Sabres hierarchy.

Subsequent diagnosis back in Buffalo pegged a heart arrhythmia as the cause of the episode, and medication has kept it under control ever since. But the myth of my invulnerability was no more. Those who wished to boot me to the sidelines joined those who sincerely felt I should go into retirement, with the Ottawa incident as evidence, and with Seymour gone and Norty dying, it was harder than ever to keep control over the diverse elements in the Sabres picture. But I was determined to see the matters through to fruition, and I was still, certainly after Norty's death a few months later, the guy with the major responsibilities, along with Bob Rich, who preferred a silent role, except on the performance of the agreement to sell to the Rigases.

After his next serious head injury occurred in October 1996, Pat had to undergo thorough rehabilitation. His postconcussion symptoms were troubling, and the remainder of the 1996–97 season passed without Pat's return to the ice. When we heard the full extent of Pat's difficult recovery and the concussion history, we concluded that Pat should retire. Larry Quinn, temporarily president of the team, took the lead and announced, perhaps prematurely, that Pat could not play again for the Buffalo Sabres. This was the kind of situation that would have been solved best in a quiet conference with Pat and his agent, but Larry seemed unable—the media would not let the issue alone—to solve the matter quietly. As he would in the Nolan/Muckler/Regier controversy, Larry heated up the dispute—involving medical judgment and Pat's life and career—until it became the picture of a heartless franchise abusing a brave and determined star. I had to educate and mediate among Larry, the GM and the coach, the Knox-Buffalo members of the board, and John Rigas, who was now "interim" chairman of the board under the 1997 agreement. I insisted on meeting head to head, so to speak, with Dr. Hopkins, and I sat in his office while he prepared his opinion. I told him that in the face of the letters from Pat's doctors, we needed an unvarnished, clear judgment that would guide us. And Hopkins gave it to us straight: the injury was serious; the hit and the fall produced a substantial period of unconsciousness; the indicators showed serious trauma; and the concussion history was relevant and significant. Based on all the factors, in Hopkins's judgment, Pat should never play hockey again. I reran the tape, saw that awful bounce of his skull, and was satisfied that our position was right for Pat and right for the club. Larry and I agreed that we could not risk a career-ending, maybe life-ending, injury the next time.

I never got to talk to Pat personally about it. Pat was adamant, and his agent, ever the adversary, soon converted the matter into an owner versus player issue. I had hoped that Don Meehan would convince Pat to hang up his skates; instead, he strengthened Pat's opposition by recruiting liberal "experts," who really passed the buck by saying the decision was up to the player. In a strange legal dance, neither side asked for arbitration. Neither wanted to preclude any option. Perhaps each was afraid the other was right. We were reluctant to publish the Hopkins letter—it might knock out any possible trade—and the press took the line that our stance that Pat was no longer able to play was designed to make the insurance carrier, rather than the club, pay his salary.

The loss of Pat's skill and his position as Sabres citizen and promoter of the new arena would be a blow to our plans, but a trade was the only viable solution. (John Muckler did not dissent. Pat, Muckler told me, had been playing before his injury "like an ordinary hockey player.") The Rangers were interested, and with complex disclaimers and delicate negotiations with the insurer, the hockey department managed to get the problem, in large part, off our backs. The trade took place just before the start of the new season, on September 29, 1997, and the Sabres received only a third-round draft pick and "future considerations," neither of which ever produced anything of value for the Buffalo club. Pat did contribute to the Rangers, with sixty-two points in sixty-seven games in the ensuing season. But the "saving" of the LaFontaine career was only temporary. On March 16, 1998, Pat suffered another serious concussion. Fortunately, the injury did not destroy his life; but this time no doctor would pass the buck, and Pat hung up his skates.

Chapter 26

CANADIAN SUNSETS

*A Peck of Peter Pocklington,
a Slice of Barry Shenkarow,
and Adieu, Marcel Aubut*

The owners in the triumvirate of refugees from the World Hockey Association were distinguished by more than their Canadian heritage—their wives were all beautiful women. Francine Aubut of Quebec, Eva Pocklington of Edmonton, and Rena Shenkarow of Winnipeg all contributed grace and fun to the occasional soirees that surrounded the NHL governors' meetings—meetings that were, more often then not, hard working, sometimes contentious, sometimes futile.

Until her illness, my wife, Bikki, was a major participant in the good times, as a lady of fashion and charm in her own right. (I have a fetching picture of her winning the league croquet tournament with the Washington Capitals' Dick Patrick.) I had always claimed, since the start of the Sabres, that the franchise was half Canadian—with Ontario Paper Company as one of the important investors, my years as US counsel for Moore Corporation of Toronto (once the world's leading producer of business forms), the five thousand or more Canadian fans that regularly filled our seats in the sellout days, and the predominance of Gil Perreault, Rick Martin, and other Canadian draft picks on our roster. But it was not until Evelyn Lerner consented to move to the big city from Rochester, New York, and marry me in 1975 that I gained some sort of equitable entitlement to the character "Canadian." Bikki was born a Canadian citizen in Ottawa, the country's capital, and her mother, Elsa, was a staunch alumna of the Ottawa government, having served as private secretary to a leading Canadian statesman—or bureaucrat, as the case may be. Elsa, until her death in 1999, could and would quote Shakespeare at the drop of a hat and sing naughty Restoration rhymes on call.

Of course Bikki had to be a hockey fan—there was no escaping it. But I'm afraid she was spoiled early on: the season of our marriage was 1975—the Stanley Cup—with intoxicating victories in Chicago and Montreal, until the final round with the famous "fog" game and the ultimate triumph by the big, bad Broad Street Bullies led by Bobby Clarke. We happened to play against the most hospitable owners in the league, so Bikki got the impression that the NHL was a series of magnificent parties interrupted by an occasional hockey game.

I've never felt that strongly about the connection, but I've never gotten over the feeling that that line on the map that purports to divide Ontario from New York is not really real. Sure, I know all about the Fenians, who tried to invade Canada in some comic crossing of the Niagara River, and mad King George III, and the British Columbians who wanted to join America and the Quebecois who want to merge with the Parisians, and, of course the ugly things the British did to Washington in the War of 1812. I respect our neighbors' independence, but Western New Yorkers have lived with them too long and too intimately to give it too much weight. After a lifetime of taking the kids to Canadian camps, of fishing in the Georgian Bay, of shopping in the Toronto shops, of summering on the northern shore, let us not speak much of separation or schism. We do speak the same language, close, even, to the same accent. And even as to the Quebecois, I prided myself on and worked diligently at maintaining my status as a Francophile. Said the female diplomat at the NHL summer meeting on the Canadian warship in Quebec City, "Oh, Mr. Swados, your French accent is so *classique*!" Not so great, I must report, on the vocabulary end.

So I always felt, rightly or wrongly, a special kinship with my Canadian colleagues. I didn't think Canadian and didn't think American; I thought NHL, in that special country in which we spent so much of our nights and days. And those were heady and busy days in that decade after 1979, when the three Canadian teams and the Hartford Whalers entered the league. It's hard to accept now that, except for what stood strongly for years as Peter Pocklington's Oilers, the others are all gone. Quebec moved to Colorado, Hartford to Carolina, and Winnipeg to Phoenix—to better economics, perhaps, but the major-league dreams of three good hockey towns went up in smoke.

The league tried to protect them, but the economics were too tough. They weren't at first. We attacked, for example, the disparities between the US and Canadian currency and the US and Canadian tax impact, both of which translated into wide disparity in salary levels between US and Canadian clubs. My good friend and strong supporter George Strawbridge, a major Sabres investor, gave me a stiff jab for my league vote in favor of sub-sidizing Canadian club losses on the border disparities. But I stoutly main-tained, as I did throughout my NHL career, that the health of the Canadian clubs was essential to the vitality of the league.

A SLICE OF BARRY SHENKAROW

With the support of my co-officers, Chairman Bill Wirtz and President John Ziegler, I tried to help, and *did* help in various ways. Barry Shenkarow, whose family owned the Jets, called, extremely concerned that the club was in trouble with the city of Winnipeg. The city had invested heavily—according to their perceptions—in the effort to bring the Jets first into the "outlaw" league and then into the NHL, and its politicians were demanding control of the franchise. Of course, that was the last thing the governors would want. Imagine having to trade for a star with a politico from the Third Ward, or carry a resolution in the city council to approve the league's entry into the World Cup!

Barry and I had not had much contact (the 1979 expansion had largely been handled by Gil Stein's Philadelphia firm), but Barry expressed confi-dence in me and implored me to come out to do battle. The trick was to bring on my actor's guise and be the embodiment of league power. It worked. I suspect I looked more like Sam Pollock than Clarence Campbell, but the local politico had never seen either one of us, and my stern but helpful demeanor helped. I started with the position that the city's demand for control of the franchise was outrageous and intolerable, and the munic-ipality could not be permitted by the NHL to own any part of the club. The city would have to sell out. (Of course, the Jets didn't want to pay for it—and neither did we.)

The discussion continued for some bitter hours, until I pulled out my hole card. The city could continue to hold some interest, if it were a min-imal, advisory interest only. We finally settled on an equitable stock interest of 20 percent, nonvoting (later increased by my successors to 30 percent, nonvoting). Barry rapidly took me to my plane back east, content that I per-formed with the dignity and authority consistent with my august title of sec-retary—or at least with enough to get the job done and get out of town, fast!

A PECK OF PETER POCKLINGTON

The problems of Peter Pocklington were more complicated. If one looked at his initial balance sheet and profit and loss statement in 1979 when he entered the NHL, Peter probably had the strongest franchise of all four

Peter Pocklington (*left*) and friends (*from left to right*) Seymour Knox III, Goldie Hawn, Mark Messier, and Burt Reynolds.
Copyright © Bill Wippert.

newcomers. He was a savvy and popular politician, with cross-Canada connections, and soldout houses in a strong regional economy. What caused him trouble, however, was not his hockey team, but his extracurricular adventures. I found early on, and reported to John Ziegler, that if we weren't careful, we would be in a peck of trouble with Peter.

The first sign of this was the meat company. While Peter was a successful hockey mogul, his qualifications as a businessman were not, apparently, equivalent. His meat debts were eating up his hockey profit, and when the lenders complained, the league had to get involved—especially when the principal lender was the province of Alberta. I established two controls I thought might work, based on my experience with other franchises. First, it was agreed that there could be no commingling. In other words, the Oilers could not use the cash or the earnings of the hockey club to pay for other Pocklington operations or loans. Second, we put a cap on the amount of debt the Oilers itself could incur. (This was for the protection of the NHL as well; we didn't want to face the end of the season with no funds to pay the players' salaries.) The cap was initially set at $40 million, but soon that fund was exhausted. Peter's troubles continued, and, at the end of my regime as secretary in 1993, the Alberta Treasury Branches were directing a good part of their professional attention to the Edmonton Oilers and their popular owner.

Yet Peter was a colleague—intelligent, driven, like many of us, and fun to be with. He was not above a prank or two. The post-WHA days were busy and productive, and, always a gadgeteer, I quickly appropriated a new business toy, the cellular phone. A fancy plaque in my office shows that Cellular One awarded me a new cell and twelve-inch ad as second-largest individual user in Western New York. With my workload in my law office, my travel to Bikki's widespread eye clinics, and the increasing pressures of league matters, that cell phone was really in demand. It frequently penetrated governors' meetings. Calls were frequent. I never realized how frequent until a few months ago, when my friend Bob Rich reported that on a fishing trip in the Caribbean, Peter admitted that he and some of the other guys were the source. Discombobulation was the intent.

I'm sorry that Peter, harassed by his mounting debt in nonhockey ventures, ultimately had to give up control. But the Oilers are still alive and in Edmonton, and doing their usual professional and prudent job—as they did with Glen Sather and John Muckler—discombobulating every NHL club that comes into their building.

ADIEU, MARCEL AUBUT

Barry and Peter were colleagues, but Marcel Aubut was a comrade, and my favorite governor.

Barry was somewhat saturnine, Peter was ebullient; but Marcel had girth as well as worth. He was a bright and charming man, in a constant struggle to keep his weight from turning gargantuan. Aubut and I had good mutual vibes almost from the beginning. In his *accent Quebecois*, he quite naturally called me "Bobby"—a diminutive I hadn't heard since eighth grade. Marcel came to me, as league secretary and special counsel, for help on his financial arrangements. As had happened elsewhere, the demands for working capital had outstripped the resources and the investment enthusiasm of the original Nordiques. Marcel had found a new principal investor in the Carling-O'Keefe Breweries—at the time a principal competitor of Molson's. We had to find a way, and we did find the formula for bringing Carling into a league dominated for years by its competition. The legal arrangements with the league, which were largely in my charge, were relatively easy, and we installed Marcel in control as governor of the Nordiques without much difficulty. Molson could hardly oppose the move.

However, the league analysis showed that Molson not only owned the Montreal Canadiens (directly or, at times, indirectly) and the cross-Canada

Hockey Night in Canada, but also had a hook in the local TV contracts of every Canadian club except Vancouver.

That continuing monopoly could be largely attributed to the diligence of my friend Ted Hough—head of Molson's broadcast enterprise—with a major assist from the Toronto Maple Leafs. But another charmer closer to home was complicit: Dave Forman, the Sabres' vice president, as league negotiator. Not intentionally—Dave was too nice a guy for that. But over a series of contracts between the NHL and Molson, the increase in the sums we received for Canadian rights was viewed as inadequate, if not minuscule; and Marcel, with his client and colleague Carling goosing him vigorously, was determined to break the Molson's TV monopoly—not just for the sake of Carling, but to create a competitive market for the league itself. Notwithstanding the delightful years spent negotiating with Hough at Dave's beautiful Eagle Island in the Georgian Bay, the league took over Dave's negotiating power and handed it to Marcel, Gil Stein, and John Ziegler himself.

Marcel and Gil worked the connections to set up a competing network based on the CBC's competitor, CTV's Toronto outlet, and John wrote and ordered the opinions that gave all the clubs the right to a Canadian "feed," so they could bring their away games back to their home arenas, and resolutions that enabled the league to compete for, even to buy, the local TV rights for the Canadian markets. Marcel did most of the selling and the negotiating, and ultimately produced a major triumph: competition that pushed the Molson offers to a market level, a genuine equal sharing by all clubs of national TV rights on both sides of the border, and an overall modest improvement of the league's participation in the TV revenues of the national networks of both countries.

Marcel had the intellect and drive of the quality lawyer; he could see the substance, make the fair judgment, and deliver. He demonstrated that again in 1983–84, only four years after he entered the league, when he persuaded some of the stodgy owners to adopt the five-minute overtime period for ties in the regular season—certainly a major contributor to fan excitement and variety and vitality of the game.

* * *

Peter Pocklington had enough stamina and support to keep his fans in the league; but Barry and Marcel could not. The salary cancer did them in. I have a vivid memory of our last owners' caucus during the union negotiations following the strike of 1991–92. All three of us—Barry, Marcel, and I—were distraught over what seemed to be a premature end of the strike and the failure to achieve a salary cap. Gary Bettman had just come on board as commissioner and had yet to face his first battle with Goodenow. Both Marcel and Barry were deeply concerned about the future of the

Nordiques and the Jets. But Barry said, with more hope than conviction, "I know Gary Bettman will protect us."

Gary Bettman did not, could not protect them—except, or course, for any losses they could recoup on sale to the new franchises in Denver and Phoenix. The failure to achieve a cap for veteran players in the 1994 lockout, I knew, was the end of the line for Barry and Marcel. And by July 1995 the Quebec Nordiques, and by the summer of 1996 the Winnipeg Jets, had both passed to the Hot Stove League in the sky.

Chapter 27

THE SIAMESE
FRANCHISE

My friends George and Gordon Gund are as fine a pair of owners as you could wish for: wealthy, experienced, usually reasonable, determined, indefatigable lovers of sports. Gordon was made blind at age twenty-nine by the same disease that afflicted my wife, Bikki—retinitis pigmentosa—but it never dimmed his intelligence or his enthusiasm for hockey. The Gunds tried to resurrect the NHL in their native Cleveland area in the late 1980s—unfortunately in an inadequate building situated in Richford, too far from the Ohio metropolis—then merged their Cleveland club (itself a refugee from Oakland, California) into the Minnesota North Stars, which had been abandoned by the Gordon Ritz/Walter Bush crowd when they ran out of capital in the face of losses induced by the WHA. After a five-year try at turning the Minnesota club to a profit, the Gunds proposed to transfer the team to San Jose, back to its Bay Area origins. The league now viewed San Jose as expansion territory but opposed the desertion of the Minnesota fans. A row ensued at the Board of Governors table. The solution adopted at the end of the 1989–90 season treated the North Stars as Siamese twins, carving the club into two franchises—one in San Jose, one remaining (at least temporarily) in Minneapolis.

Technically, the Gunds received an expansion franchise for San Jose named the Sharks, and Howard Baldwin and Morris Belzberg, former Hartford Whalers investors, purchased the ownership of the continuing Min-

**The Convoluted Travels of One Hockey Club through
Oakland, Cleveland, Minneapolis–St. Paul, San Jose, and Dallas**

Phase 1
The Oakland Seals are sold by Charles Finley to the NHL, and by the NHL to
Mel Swig, in 1974.

Phase 2
Swig moves the Seals to Cleveland, where they play as the Cleveland Barons,
and sells the team to the Gunds in 1976.

Phase 3
The Gunds merge the Barons with the Minnesota North Stars in 1978.

Phase 4
The NHL splits the North Stars roster (veterans and draft picks) between
Minnesota (owned by Harold Baldwin and Morris Belzberg) and a new franchise in San Jose (owned by the Gunds) in 1990. The Minnesota franchise is
sold by Baldwin to Norman Green in 1991.

Phase 5
Green moves the North Stars to Dallas, renaming the team the Dallas Stars,
in 1993.

---

nesota franchise. But the league forced surgery on both teams: the Minnesota club in effect gave the Gunds half of its experienced players through
an interclub draft, and the Minnesota club exercised half of San Jose's picks
in the next entry draft and in the expansion draft from the other NHL clubs.

The Gunds paid the $50 million expansion fee fixed for the next expan-
sion, partly with the proceeds of the sale of the Minnesota team to the
Baldwin/Belzberg syndicate. In the course of the proceedings in 1991,
Norman Green, another NHL "trader," took over the Baldwin/Belzberg position. Norm had been an investor in Calgary, then in Hartford, before he
acquired the North Stars residuary franchise. Not long after the severance,
that attempt to save NHL hockey in Minnesota proved futile. The Minneapolis and St. Paul fans were unhappy about the maneuvering with their
hockey team, and the hoped-for rise in attendance did not occur. The hockey
rinks in the Twin Cities were no longer financially acceptable, and no new
building for the NHL franchise was likely to be on stream. When attempts to
make a favorable deal with the new NBA Target Center failed, Green moved
the Stars to Dallas—which may have been his intention all along—in 1993.

What about NHL Bylaw 36 and the strong policy against "portable"
franchises? Presumably Green satisfied the conditions precedent; certainly

bona fide attempts had been made to find a local buyer in Minneapolis–St. Paul, without success in the light of the continuous losses. But Norm Green no longer had the primary exponents of that policy to contend with: John Ziegler was no longer president; I was no longer secretary; Gil Stein, the temporary president, would be inclined to help Green; and the incoming commissioner, Gary Bettman, thought our policy, in the face of the Davis and NBA court decisions, was "crazy." Thus, Green had a relatively easy time in transferring the location of his franchise to the unknown—as to hockey—but booming Texas market.

The rosters of Green's team and the Gunds' team were still governed by the agreements as to expansion and dispersal drafts negotiated in the dark hours of June 1991. This after-midnight syndrome seemed to be a Gund pattern.

I remember the first transaction in the track of the movable franchise in 1976—my first year as league secretary. Nick Mileti, a prosecutor/politician from Ohio, had constructed a fine $25,000 three-dimensional model for a new arena in an attempt to persuade the NHL Board of Governors to grant an expansion franchise for the Cleveland area. I liked the idea of the model, but the board was not impressed with Mileti's financing, and with the WHA hovering as an alternative, Mileti got the building built, anyway— but in Richfield, Ohio, not in Cleveland, in an attempt to attract a wider Ohio market and to build on cheaper farmland.

As the Cleveland WHA team did poorly at the gate and the Oakland Seals' owner—Mel Swig of the Fairmont Hotel—desperately sought escape to Ohio, a transaction appeared possible between the Gunds and Sandy Greenberg, who had become the owner of the Richfield building. As I sat there in the negotiations in the wee hours, I was tempted to call this a case of the blind *really* leading the blind. Gordon Gund, one of the brothers who were the principal buyers, had lost his sight to retinitis pigmentosa. Greenberg, the principal seller, had been blinded at an early age as well. I was humbled by the depth, intelligence, and negotiating smarts of the combatants. The other senses proved entirely satisfactory and a deal was made.

Despite the Gunds' resources and efforts, the quick move and the arena location were too much for the survival of the Cleveland club, and two years later, in 1978, again in the wee hours, we worked out a merger of the Cleveland franchise into the Minnesota club, with the Gunds ending up as the owners of the North Stars. The merger was possible because the Gordie Ritz/Walter Bush crowd, to whom the Sabres had looked for guidance when we entered the league, had become "tapped out" and were looking for financial rescue. It was a hairy transaction, requiring the players' association's OK of the termination of half the Cleveland roster, as well as a dispersal draft. But the guts of the deal were worked out in a 4 AM negotiation—again in darkness. I prize the document; it was a complex matter, recorded on one and a half sheets of paper. With no secretary available at that hour, I had scribbled the changes in the draft in my handwriting (initialed, of course), which had been illegible since my tour at Harvard Law in the 1940s.

When the Board of Governors did its Siamese act in 1990, the dispersal of the players again was negotiated in the wee hours—to meet a board deadline the following morning—and the curious outcome may have been a function of the negotiators' sleepless nights.

San Jose, an expansion franchise, was giving up half its prized draft picks to the old Minnesota club. The North Stars, needing continued credibility with the Minnesota fans, nevertheless sent half its playing roster to San Jose. The mechanism was an interclub draft of the veterans and a participation by the North Stars in the Sharks' entry draft.

In the drafts of players under contract, the Gunds seemed to emphasize younger players already in the North Stars system, while the Green/Baldwin group opted more for veterans. It is revealing to compare the record of the two clubs in the ten years since the bifurcation. In an appraisal I produced for the Gunds as of the acquisition date, June 14, 1990, I valued the top twenty-six players on the Minnesota North Stars roster at $25.2 million.

The comparison of the development of the two clubs spawned by the split is interesting, not only for the different approach to the player roster, but for the innovative structure of management adopted by the Gunds in San Jose. To a rookie expansion owner, the utterances by the general manager had a magical authority. If the investor had to hear a lecture by his GM on the definition of "icing," he was at least more reluctant to interfere with his employee's judgment on whom to sign and how much he should be paid. Frequently, the GM was the only guy around who had been exposed to the business pressures of an NHL club. This led to a tendency of new owners to make the GM a CEO—even a president, and frequently a governor—a tendency that longtime owners like Bill Wirtz of Chicago despised. The GM was not necessarily a businessman, and his presence at the governors' table for important owner decisions was sometimes an annoyance, if not an embarrassment.

The Gunds were not rookie owners, and they decided to carve up the GM responsibility and power into three compartments. Instead of one omnipotent executive, they assigned a triumvirate: George Kingston as the head coach; Chuck Grillo in charge financial aspects, such as negotiation of contracts and player budget; and Dean Lombardi in charge of the drafting and recruitment of player personnel. Supervising them all was a bright and resourceful executive, whom I'd found to be first rate in my valuation process, Art Savage. (Unfortunately he was released later by the Gunds when the franchise did not achieve rapid success.)

The Green, and later Tom Hicks, ownership in Dallas adopted a more traditional structure. Bob Gainey, the former Canadien who had been the league's top defensive forward for many years, ultimately became the Stars' general manager, with the usual panoply of powers in the player sector. The owner-executive financial monitoring was supplied by Jim Lites, an intelligent, articulate, and forceful character who had been prominent in the Detroit organization. I had always admired Gainey, who had spent several years coaching in Epinal, France—the site of my miraculous survival in World War II.

The table compares the playoff records of the Sharks and the Stars on the ice. How to make a judgment? What are the criteria? Gary Bettman, in his attempts to educate the owners, has pointed to the "bang for the buck" formula. He calls it, under the more polite nomenclature "efficiency," but it is basically player payroll (or payroll in excess of a league norm or average) divided by the number of points achieved by the team.

The 620-page tome *The Business of Hockey 2001*, applies the "bang for your buck" formula to hockey. On the basis of its calculations—which are at least sophisticated hearsay—the winner of the cost-per-point trophy for the year 1999–2000 was the Ottawa Senators, at $234,737 per point. Its team payroll for that season was $22.3 million, as against a league average of $31.2 million.[1] Yet without additional evidence, one would be hard-pressed to crown Ottawa as the best-managed team in the NHL. With a peak of 103 points in 1998–99, the team averaged 80 points over the five-year period (1995–96 through 1999–2000), made the playoffs four years in a row, but lost in the first round in each of those four years, except for 1997–98, when it was knocked out in the conference semifinal.

When I was asked a number of years ago, in the course of making personnel decisions at the Sabres, to come up with a rating of other GMs, I used a more sophisticated—or, at least, different!—

The Siamese Franchise:
Split of Stars into Dallas and San Jose

Year	Points	Playoffs	GM
		Dallas	
91–92*	70	L conf F	Bob Gainey
92–93*	82	out of POs	"
93–94*	97	L conf SF	"
94–95	42	L conf QF	"
95–96	66	out of POs	"
96–97	104	L conf F	"
97–98	109	L conf F	"
98–99	114	W Cup	"
99–00	102	L Final	"
Avg.	87.3		
		San Jose	
91–92	39	out of POs	Jack Fenneira
92–93	24	out of POs	Chuck Grillo
93–94	82	L conf SF	"
94–95	42	L conf SF	"
95–96	47	out of POs	"
96–97	62	out of POs	Dean Lombardi
97–98	78	L conf QF	"
98–99	80	L conf QF	"
99–00	87	L conf SF	"
Avg.	60		

* at Minnesota

formula, ranking the organizations on the basis of four factors: aggregate player payroll, points, gate, and participation in the playoffs. I gave the organization a bonus for making the playoffs and a higher bonus for penetration in the playoffs—division championship, conference championship, Stanley Cup. The analysis covered five successive years. Of course, the weight I gave to each of the factors was judgmental and arbitrary. Suffice it say that the clear winner in the late 1980s and early 1990s was the Boston Bruins, managed by the veteran Harry Sinden.[2]

Now that we have more data publicly available, I suggest we use net income or loss, rather than gate, as the financial factor, and use local TV ratings as a further measure of success. (The two markets—Dallas and San Jose/San Francisco/Oakland—are comparable in size.) Let's apply these factors to the twin franchises, Dallas and San Jose. Perhaps it will give us a clue to the importance of the managerial approach, and, more important, the ability of agile and intelligent management to avoid the salary cancer.

Using estimated revenue for 2000–2001, both clubs are making a profit, and the Dallas payroll is 58.6 percent of estimated total income as compared to 55 percent for San Jose. If a salary cap for veterans were attained, neither club would be subject to a possible rollback that might emerge from the next CBA (collective bargaining agreement) negotiations. (I say this with some trepidation, remembering that the Dallas owner, Tom Hicks, is the same character who gave the astronomical $250 million contract to his baseball star, Alex "A-Rod" Rodriguez, and didn't make the playoffs.) At that time it was hard to conceive of an agreement by the players' association that would fix the veteran cap at less than 58.6 percent.

On my grading system, if we weight all factors equally, Dallas management did the better job, even though the Stars moved to Dallas three years after the Sharks opened in a new, modern building in San Jose, and the Stars operated in Reunion Arena, an older edifice built by the municipality, with no luxury boxes or suites. The Dallas points, total revenue, profit, TV ratings, and playoff success are all greater. Yet the "bang for the buck" standard—which focuses on regular-season points and player payroll—would make the comparison pretty even ($403,922 for Dallas per point; $421,839 for the Sharks.) I suppose Gary Bettman would argue that San Jose is better prepared for the hoped-for CBA salary rollback because of its substantially lower payroll.

I think the San Jose experience was not a fair test of the "triumvirate" hockey management structure. Within five years, frequent turnovers in the head coach slot, the departure of Art Savage as principal executive, and the failure of the team to make the playoffs apparently led George Gund to abandon the experiment. In 1996 Dean Lombardi became general manager, with the full panoply of powers. *The NHL 2001 Guidebook* describes Lombardi as the "top hockey executive" who negotiates player contracts, makes player personnel decisions, and coordinates scouting and player evaluation. It cannot be gainsaid that Lites and Gainey—with Ken Hitch-cock as coach—did a much better job on the ice. Whether it was the Gunds overinfatuation with their minor-league roster or the Stars' luck in drafting and keeping, in the intraclub draft, that excellent two-way player Mike Modano, it is tough to argue with a Stanley Cup and two visits to the Finals in the five years under examination.

Chapter 28

OH-OH ONTARIO!

T he "vision of the nineties," John Ziegler's 1990 plan to move the footprint of the league up to those of the other major professional sports, called for an expansion of the NHL to thirty teams, up nine from its complement of twenty-one. The first phase was to be the addition of four new franchises. While the objective was to increase US television revenue, there was no way John could get the votes for expansion unless at least one Canadian club was included. In the league Board of Governors, the issue came down to a battle between our neighbor, Hamilton, Ontario—only fifty miles up the "Queen E" from Buffalo or down the Queen E" from Toronto—and Ottawa, Ontario, the capital of Canada and well within the reach of the Montreal market.

The first time the Sabres played in the Montreal Forum in the fall of 1969 was a mesmerizing and magical night. It was the holy house of hockey, and we were its anointed worshippers: the excitement, the sellout crowd, Jean Beliveau, and the ten-time champions; the colors, the flashing skates, the grace and speed of the skaters. I don't remember whether we won or lost, and it really was irrelevant: we had made it. They were the paradigm, and for years would dominate the league as a model for skill and success, not only in play, but in draft and trade, in revenue and profit, and in the gracious hospitality we tried to emulate. Whether it was the Bronfmans or the Molsons, who were enthroned as the owners of the Montreal club, we were always treated as partners, and in the early years we didn't hesitate to tap their resources for advice. As our input into league affairs grew—in part with my role on behalf of all the clubs as chair of the legal committee and as secretary of the Board of Governors—the relationship became more reciprocal, and we arrived at our own judgments on league club matters, but the Canadiens were still the fount of wisdom and experience, just as the hockey youth across Canada were our ultimate resource. For the Sabres ownership, there was still more than a vestige of the view that the continued success of the Canadiens was important to every member club.

Other NHL owners had a less worshipful view of the Canadiens. In the first expansion of 1967, the Montreal club was hit with the loss of its long-time preference in the draft. For years the Habs were entitled, regardless of their order of finish, to seize the "first two French sons of French fathers." This special rule—with limited intraleague draft and limited waiver provisions—and the astute use by Pollock and his predecessors of a Rickey-like farm system, had enabled the club to build up a massive inventory of French players in junior hockey and in the minor professional leagues. In the first expansion, the new clubs demanded and succeeded in eliminating the "French sons" rule as of the 1969–70 season. Faced with this loss of first-round picks, Pollock had persuaded a number of the new clubs—some of which, typical of expansion teams, were frantic for immediate credibility on the ice—to hand Pollock their first-round choices to come up in later years for an immediate transfer of current players not needed by Montreal in its well-stocked rosters. Ed Snider, the Flyers' owner, once warned me, "Don't give the Canadiens anything—it'll be ten years before they exhaust their inventory!" (And we can really compete.)

In pursuit of the Sabres franchise, I had tried—with the Knoxes' support—to stay very close to every major decision. It was something of a shock to my ego, therefore, when I discovered that my privity was not necessarily pervasive. As the finance committee announced on 1969 in New York's St. Regis that Buffalo and Vancouver were to get the expansion nod, Bill Jennings of the Rangers and Bill Wirtz of the Blackhawks grabbed Seymour's arm and swept him into the next room, behind a closed door. I was concerned—the Board of Governors still had to vote, and I had stark memories of the Norris and Smythe opposition that did us in in 1967. When Seymour emerged after nearly thirty minutes, I plunged to ask, "What was that all about?" "Perreault," said Seymour. "He's a French son of a French father. He'll certainly be the number one pick in the amateur draft. They wanted me to promise that if we got the first pick we wouldn't trade him to Montreal—and I agreed!"

As related elsewhere in these pages, Gilbert Perreault was the first overall pick in the entry draft in June of 1969, and it was the spin of the wheel that gave us number 11 and a jump-start to a successful franchise. He was the most exciting player the Sabres—or any other team in the NHL—ever had. Wayne Gretzky had outstanding ice vision, Mario Lemieux had power, Bobby Orr had drive, Mike Bossy produced goals, but no other player could produce the singlehanded excitement Bert gave our fans in those years. Sure, he was a French son of a French father—but we never traded him to Montreal or anybody else. Bert gave us sixteen great seasons.

Situated at the border, we were always conscious of the ambience and the importance of the fans across Lakes Erie and Ontario and the Niagara River. In the pre-NHL days, the American Hockey League Bisons drew large segments of their audience for particular games from Canada, and we wanted to cultivate that audience with vigor. I would regularly describe the Sabres, in dealing with the league and local contacts, as "half-Canadian"—it wasn't much of an exaggeration. Under the NHL constitution, our territory embraced everything (including parts of Lakes Ontario and Erie) within fifty miles of the Buffalo city limits. That meant our theoretical reach extended through St. Catharines, Welland, and Fort Erie and four miles into Hamilton. The Sabres circle overlapped with the Toronto territorial circle, so there was an area both teams could claim, but at the outset we sought in various ways to make the adjacent communities part of our fan base. We made a prominent St. Catharines citizen—Bob Schmon, head of Ontario Paper Company—part of our investment group and a member of our Board of Directors. We set our training camp in southern Ontario—first in Peterborough, then in St. Catharines. We even installed the practice—which persists to this day—of playing the Canadian national anthem just before the "Star Spangled Banner" at the beginning of each home game.

My wife, Bikki, was born in Ottawa. It was a family legend that her mother, Elsa, insisted on returning to Ottawa from Vermont for her lying in, so that her daughter could be a citizen. I tended to discount this—and the story that "Bikki" was a legitimate name—until I saw the play *The Dresser*. The lead character, the actor—called "Sir"—mounts a temperamental rampage, and his dresser calms him down with the promise of a spot of tea and a "bikki"—which turned out to be for a biscuit, or, Americanized, a cookie. I used this account to some advantage in selling the Sabres as a part-Canadian franchise, along with my tales of annual fishing trips to Muskoka and French River, depositing my children in Ontario camps in summer, and the lovely island home of our great Sabres friend and vice president, Dave Forman, on Eagle Lake at the edge of Georgian Bay.

Dave had been a close associate in the ten-year history of Transcontinent Television. He was tall, good-looking, likeable, and, generally, pretty tough. His wife, Libby, was attractive and personable, and they both had authentic credentials, as well as highly useful social relationships in the Buffalo community as close friends of the Schoellkopfs. Dave was a cousin of George Goodyear. He had been brought in to the Sabres to run the in-house matters—the arena, television, and so on. As our appearances at league meetings began to show our competence and success as a franchise and I became more and more involved in league legal matters, Dave also appealed to the NHL hierarchy as a negotiator in TV contact negotiations. The drive from Buffalo to Eagle Lake was about three and a half hours—on the "Queen E" north. We became familiar to customs, as Sabres, and as friends of Dave Forman. (For a brief period, Dave even persuaded the bina-tional commission for the Peace Bridge to name me as their counsel.) Dave was a world-class host. You knew this as soon as you reached the dock at Eagle Lake. As if to denote your importance, he would greet you in the most magnificent boat in his flotilla—a champion mahogany inboard, waxed and shined to perfection. I called it the "Tuxedo." Or, in a sporting mood, he'd arrive in a terrific flat-hulled speedboat, the original and only asset of a company I'd organized for him and Paul Schoellkopf called Ontario Marine. Even the tennis court was special: set in the middle of the island forest and composed of the kind of red brick clay dust I'd played on in Brazil. Libby was a joyful tennis player, and we had the kind of noncom-petitive, socially fun games I miss very much, with my recalcitrant knees.

The Eagle Island house was a natural for meeting with the Molson and *Hockey Night in Canada* brass, and Dave soon became the league's point man on negotiations over what was called the Border Television Agree-ment. The border agreement and related contracts defined the rights fees paid to the US clubs for their participation in the venue games and con-firmed the powers of the US teams to telecast the games back to the visiting teams' markets. Of particular importance to the Sabres, the border agree-ment contained clauses protecting the US border clubs—Detroit and Buf-falo—against invasion of their TV schedules, or provided some compensa-tion for preemption by a network. It was not easy to achieve this: the Maple Leafs and the Molsons for years assumed or maintained that the border constituted an electronic wall—American clubs could not take feeds out of Canada for local broadcasts of away games—without the permission of the club; and for years, conversely argued that network or local club telecasts of the games in cities against both US teams and Canadian teams belonged, both as to control and compensation, to the clubs. Clarence Campbell, until he was educated otherwise, had difficulty understanding or accepting the other view; for him, it was Canada's game, and the peculiarities of US antitrust law were of little concern to him. These assumptions and practices were not eliminated until John Ziegler's ruling of 1988 and the litigation arising out of the league's attempt to establish a second TV network with Carling-O'Keefe and CTV, to compete with the venerated Molson/CBC/ *Hockey Night in Canada* combine. It was only after those events—and the modest growth of national US TV revenue—that US clubs gained the absolute right (subject to camera location priorities) to take a feed to their home markets, and national TV revenue, along with US network revenue, began to be shared by all NHL clubs.

It was during these developing years that Dave Forman negotiated for the NHL with Ted Hough, the primary representative of the Molson and *Hockey Night* interests. Dave had limited scope, since there was no competition for *Hockey Night*, and in later years other American clubs would second-guess the modest increases he achieved. I had met Hough briefly in the late sixties when we were pressing for the franchise, and Campbell had strongly advised us to make a deal with *Hockey Night in Canada*. This advice had been countermanded in part by Bill Wirtz's protective comment: "You've paid the highest price in the history of the league—$6 million— you don't have to make a deal. Toronto got its $1 million in the expansion; your rights are the same as those of any club in the league." In what seemed somewhat unfriendly negotiations with a new partner, Hough had attempted to treat us as "invaders" in the overlapping Toronto-Buffalo market and had demanded a wall against our advertising and promotion in Canada, an agreement not to play or televise on Saturday nights, an agreement not to use conflicting sponsors, and so on. Campbell, on his own, suggested a solution that reminded me of attempts to resolve the Israeli-Arab disputes: a territorial line would be drawn, north to south, bisecting southern Ontario, giving the Maple Leafs Hamilton and its environs (the largest city after Toronto), and giving us our neighbor, Fort Erie, Niagara Falls, and the smaller communities to the south and east.

Not fewer than three hundred thousand TV homes were at stake. Many of these were hockey Bisons customers. Yet I did not wish us to start out in the league as a partner of controversy. Ted presented a friendly demeanor, but his real face was that of Stafford Smythe. After consulting Seymour and Norty, and emboldened by the words of Wirtz, we took a tough stance: no bisecting map; no agreement on advertisers. However, we would, as a matter of courtesy, "in the development years"—on a voluntary basis—stay away from Saturday nights. That was easy: the Little Three college basketball teams—Canisius, Niagara, and St. Bonaventure—were a hot entertainment item in Western New York at the time. Saturdays were their main night, and we had already made a commitment to Buffalo mayor Frank Sedita that we would protect Canisius in our schedule.

Used to the Molson role of autocrat at the television table, Ted Hough protested, but had no choice, and he initially regarded me as some kind of unruly alien. However, the Formans liked the Houghs as a couple, as did I, and we began to see them regularly at Eagle Lake, and Ted and I at least became tentative, if not contingent, friends.

Ted's wife, Jean, was from Hamilton, and from time to time the conversation would turn to a lament that the city deserved a franchise in the

NHL, had never received one in the recent expansions—even though it had had an NHL club (the Hamilton Tigers) in the early days. I would respond that it would be difficult to fit Hamilton in: it was less than fifty miles from Buffalo and less than fifty miles from Toronto, and it would add no new customers or television ratings or revenue to the league. But I certainly wished them luck in their ongoing quest for a franchise.

The view of Hamilton as a threat to the Sabres was not unanimously held in our councils. As the heady days of sellout seasons began to erode for Buffalo, and the need for additional revenue and capital for the Sabres began to be serious, Norty would speak of Hamilton as a probable source of major funding for our club. The practice had grown up, enabled by the constitution and bylaws of the league, and confirmed in spades when the Denver, Colorado, club was moved to the Meadowlands in New Jersey, to have the league and the adjacent or overlapping teams exact "indemnification" for the loss of territory or goodwill. With Ontario fans contributing 15 to 20 percent (for some games, 30 percent) of our gate, a case could be made for compensation on the order of $5 to $10 million, payable over time. Norty, making the judgment that capital could not be raised easily to cover our impending losses—the Knoxes were apparently not ready or able to supply the needed funds—was salivating over the prospects of Hamilton indemnification. In the Meadowlands transfer, John McMullen and associates had agreed to pay an aggregate of $21 million to the clubs that claimed their territories or revenues would be invaded: $10 million to the Rangers, whose territory was almost completely overlapped by the area awarded to the new Devils; $6 million to the league; $5 million to the Islanders, whose territory was equivalent to the Rangers; and even $5 million to the Philadelphia Flyers, whose overlap was minimal and whose claim was almost entirely rooted in television and cable impact.

I was strongly opposed to a Hamilton invasion. I had negotiated the Meadowlands transfer on behalf of the NHL, and I knew the problems as well as anybody else. I knew that John McMullen, notwithstanding the indemnification agreements I had negotiated, had refused and/or delayed making substantial payments to either the Flyers or the Islanders (he later brought an arbitration suit against the Meadowlands club). I knew that John Pickett, the principal Islanders owner, had told me and the finance committee on several occasions that consenting to the Devils invasion was the "worst mistake" he had ever made. I knew, further, that whatever the bylaws might say, backed by Montreal and Vancouver and the other clubs, the Hamilton owners, with a claim of "historic" rights to the franchise and the territory, would demand the most minimal compensation. Seymour concurred in my view, and I suspected that the Toronto Maple Leafs—although they would be faced with a difficult choice in the event it was put to a vote—were basically opposed to a Hamilton grant. With the financial problems already erupting, I could not see how the Sabres club could stand the loss of 15 to 20 percent of its revenue. I was sure our neighbors, now regularly coming to Sabres games, would promptly move their loyalties to Hamilton. I confirmed this when, at an exhibition game celebrating the opening of a new arena across the river in Fort Erie, notwithstanding our years of promotion of the fans, I saw not a single Sabres symbol—only jackets and T-shirts with the crest or logo of the Maple Leafs or the Canadiens.

The issue came to crisis in the 1992 expansion. No Canadian club had been added to the league since Vancouver had been admitted with Buffalo in 1970 and Quebec, Winnipeg, and Edmonton (with Hartford) produced the WHA merger in 1979. An attempt by Ralston Purina to move its St. Louis club, the Blues, to Saskatoon, Saskatchewan, had been frustrated by the NHL in a gutsy counterattack in 1976, maintaining the governors' veto over inadvisable franchise transfers. Gary Bettman reviewed the league history on his appointment as commissioner in 1992, contrasting our stance with the court decisions creating "franchise free agency" in the NFL Davis case and basketball's San Diego transfer, and recalled the Baltimore Colts' stealing silently away, with impunity, in the middle of the night to Indianapolis. Gary said to me, "Your league is crazy!" Restraint on undesirable moves was the NHL law. Yet Hamilton was determined to find some way to achieve its self-appointed destiny.

The Canadian government, pressured by the hockey cities' complaint about subsidies for a new building in Vancouver in 1970, the WHA teams that gained entry to the NHL in 1979, and the prospects of further NHL expansion, heard the pleas of the Hamilton promoters and provided a grant of $3 million to finance the construction of the eighteen-thousand-seat Copps Coliseum in the 1990s. The erection of the new arena emboldened Ted Hough and *Hockey Night in Canada,* and in one spirited conversation on Eagle Island, Ted defiantly announced: "Bob, you're not going to be able to keep 'em out! Don't you realize they built Copps just outside your fifty-mile circle?" Ted—and the Hamilton promoters—were reading the NHL constitution, which prohibited the grant of a franchise that invaded another team's territory without that team's consent, as giving the neighbor club a veto only if the new team's arena invaded the old team's fifty-mile circle. It was an unfortunate, naive decision.

As matters turned out, the spot chosen for the rink didn't affect the league's franchise decision at all, but led the Hamilton fathers to place the arena in an undesirable location, where parking and egress and ingress were wholly inadequate. Dave Forman and I attended a Canada Cup finals at Copps in 1981. The game was sold out, but it took us a solid hour to get out of the parking lot. The parking and exit problems could be cured with the expenditure of large sums, but in the haste to build the arena and be ready for expansion, the builders had also opted for a minimal, Spartan

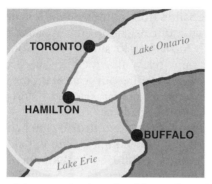

This map depicts the fifty-mile radius of the city of Hamilton.
It is only forty-six miles from the corporate limits of Buffalo,
thus showing that a Hamilton franchise would encroach four miles
into the Sabres territory.

arena, typical of the 1970s construction, with no luxury boxes or other rev-enue-enhancing features.

The legal situation in the event of an attempt to place an NHL franchise in Hamilton was, to put it mildly, mixed. I had participated in the drafting of the constitution and bylaw provisions involved, and I was confident that the Sabres' right to protest—or to claim indemnification—did not turn on the location of the Hamilton building. In my thinking, based on prece-dents in other sports, nothing required a member club to accept a demand by a new city to become a partner so it could steal the old club's revenues, and it was the economic impact, not the geography, that counted. But it was important to have clear standing to protest. The Sabres' territory was defined by the league constitution and our franchise agreement as the areas within fifty miles of the legal limits of the city of Buffalo. In the 1990s—well before Copps Coliseum actually appeared—I had hired an engineer with access to aeronautical data to prepare and certify a map, showing (1) the point on the Buffalo city limits nearest of Hamilton (it turned out to be what used to be known in early America as Black Rock); (2) a circle, con-structed in accordance with the definition of a team's "home territory" in Article 4.1 of the NHL constitution, with a radius of fifty miles extending from that point on the city limits—that would be the Sabres home terri-tory; (3) a similar circle for the Toronto Maple Leafs; and (4) a similar circle for the city of Hamilton.

The map showed the substantial overlap of the territories of the three cities. But most important, the map showed that the Buffalo Sabres' terri-tory extended four miles into the city of Hamilton. Copps, built later, was within Toronto's fifty-mile territory, but outside ours.

To set the legal stage: the key provisions in the constitution—which would apply both to an expansion franchise and to a transfer of an existing club to the Hamilton location—are these: "No other member of the League shall be permitted to play games (except regularly scheduled League games with the home club) in the home territory of a member without the latter member's consent," and, most important, "No franchise shall be granted for a home territory within the home territory of a member without the written consent of such member."

Both of these provisions were (and are) in Article 4.2, and could and cannot under Article 12 be amended without the unanimous consent of all members present and voting or by an instrument signed by every member club.

I was convinced that, bearing in mind the purpose of these provisions—which was to protect the economic health of the existing partners first—we could not be denied standing to protest when our territory and area of permitted operations overlapped most of the proposed Hamilton grant, embraced more than three hundred thousand potential customers in the southern Ontario portions of the Hamilton circle, and penetrated four miles into that city itself. Moreover, in any proposed transfer or expansion grant, we were entitled to invoke the provisions of Bylaw 36 (partially drafted by me), which recognize that each club, voting on such a transaction, was entitled to take into account the viability of the franchise in the proposed location, the impact on neighboring clubs, and the impact on the welfare of the league. I felt strongly that a policy or practice that permitted a new or old club to move into another's territory without compensation for lost customers and goodwill would certainly produce a "disincentive to participation in the League," as described in Bylaw 36.5(1).

There were other practical considerations. Toronto was clearly involved and had a veto. But it could not, as one of the most financially successful in the NHL, play the invaded pauper, and the political pressure from its partner clubs would be difficult for the Leafs to withstand. So we would have to do our own exploration and defense. First, we needed a hook, to get us firmly into the league judgment process. After clearing with the Knoxes and the board, I filed a letter with President John Ziegler, asking him to rule on our veto rights, arguing that, regardless of the geographical situation, the impact on us of a grant to Hamilton was so great that our views, if not our veto, were essential for any league decision on the matter. The ruling was a pleasant surprise, if not a total victory. John ruled that, since Copps was outside our fifty-mile circle, we could not prevent the playing of games in that building, but our four-mile overlap into the city of Hamilton meant that a grant to Hamilton of a franchise could not be made or transferred without our consent.

So we had the hook. But could we use it? The antitrust laws of the United States and the Combines Act of Canada were foreboding. I was concerned, as was the league, that if we exercised our right or power to veto a Hamilton franchise—either in an expansion context or in a proposed transfer of location by another club—our conduct would be attacked in either the US or Canadian courts as restraint of trade, exercise of monopoly power, or violation of the Combines Act. There were arguments that the risk was minimal—the NHL had in 1970 refused to transfer the Oakland club to Vancouver, and the federal district court had thrown out the Vancouver complaint without so much as a mention of the antitrust laws. The NHL had also rejected the attempt by Ralston Purina to move the Blues to Saskatoon, without successful judicial intervention. We thought we would have a good defense, also, under the "failing company" exemption: we'd have a pretty good case, now that the salary escalation had become so great and the complete sellout seasons had disappeared, that three NHL teams could not exist in the Toronto-Buffalo market, and the likely victim would be Buffalo.

But the cases in other sports were red flags. Al Davis, in his first lawsuit, successfully blasted the NFL's attempt to block his move from Oakland to the Los Angeles territory then occupied by the Rams. The NBA had come a cropper in trying to prevent a move by one of its franchises. And with the NFL forced to declare open season for a time on franchise transfers, the owner of the Baltimore Colts had moved his players, equipment, and franchise to Indianapolis in the middle of the night, without a squawk or a protest, except from the Baltimore fans. The second Davis case had somewhat weakened the Raiders' victory, for the appellate court had revealed that the NFL decision to bar the transfer was not absolutely illegal—it was too restrictive, and the requirement of a supermajority vote was unreasonable—but this could perhaps be corrected with bylaw or constitution amendments. The Davis case also took away some of the invader's benefits from the "franchise free agency" concept, since it held the league had a stake in the territory and a demand by the NHL for payment of compensation for that stake in reasonable terms would not violate the antitrust laws.

But the Davis fears were unsettling, and the NHL Board of Governors, listening to its antitrust counsel, modified its bylaws to make the task of the proposed new club or new location somewhat easier (Article 4.2 and by Bylaw 36.4) by changing the vote requirements from unanimous to a three-quarters vote. That meant, as things stood after the absorption of the WHA in 1979, that six out of the twenty-one clubs could block an expansion or a transfer. The Davis case raised the question as to whether even a three-quarters vote was too tough: in antitrust language, whether it was "more restrictive than reasonably necessary" to protect the legitimate business goals of the league without adversely affecting competition. These fears led to an amendment of Bylaw 36, in the 1980s, which would change the vote to a mere majority and would, inferentially, bar the adjacent or overlapping club's veto, "in the event that the prohibition on transfers recited in Section

4.2 of the constitution is determined by counsel to the League specifically retained for this purpose, based on all relevant factors, to be unlawful with respect to the proposed transfer."

With the admission of Ottawa in 1992, there were eight Canadian members of the league: Toronto and Montreal, of the Original Six; Vancouver, admitted with Buffalo in 1970; Winnipeg, Edmonton, and Quebec, entries from the WHA merger in 1979; Calgary, a transfer from Atlanta; and Ottawa. The Canadian phalanx (with the possible exception of Toronto, which could abstain) would doubtless feel compelled to vote in favor of any legitimate applicant from across the border. So, assuming unity under the "majority" rule, all a Hamilton applicant needed was three additional votes. The situation was, to put it mildly, disquieting for the Sabres.

The entry of Ottawa was not without birth pains, and I was in the middle, as a reluctant midwife. John Ziegler and the expansion committee (headed by Bill Wirtz as league chairman) had assigned me to the development of the expansion agreements and to the negotiation of those agreements with the chosen applicants; and as secretary of the Board of Governors, I would be expected to attend most major committee meetings. So I knew pretty well who was getting where in the expansion scramble. It soon became apparent that the league could not, this time, avoid the designation of a venue for one of the four new cities to be admitted, even though the new club could not contribute a single TV set to the enhanced national audience sought by the expansion. The contenders would be Saskatoon, a long shot, in view of its earlier rejection by the Board of Governors; Ottawa, the nation's capital at the center of the intense Ontario-Quebec hockey market; and Hamilton. In their natural response to the momentary successes of Edmonton, Calgary, Vancouver, Winnipeg, and Quebec in acquiring NHL recognition, and in their pressure to seize the national government subsidy while it was still available, the Hamilton promoters had committed a major-league error: they had built the building without a franchise, and without a franchise owner!

As the league had expanded, so had the owners' view of the value of their franchises. The first expansion cost $2 million per team; the Buffalo/Vancouver grants cost $6 million each—with Vancouver paying in Canadian dollars, then at a premium. The 1972 and 1974 expansion teams also came in for $6 million, and that figure was the nominal price for the WHA merger of four teams, including the three Canadian entries. But the actual cost for each WHA entrant, including debts, liabilities assumed, and "cleanup costs," was in excess of $11 million each. When the league moved the grant of San Jose to the Gunds (then owners of the Minnesota team), the price for that grant and for the applicants for expansion in 1992 became $50 million.

Hamilton had trouble finding an owner. The promoters could not find investors who could rid themselves of the notion that an NHL franchise wasn't really worth $50 million—the six-team league was still their model. Six million dollars was bad enough; $11 million was highway robbery—why should Hamilton have to pay more than their sister cities?

Ottawa found an owner, of sorts. A handsome, affable real estate promoter named Bruce Firestone contrived a plan to pay the $50 million—it was to be financed by the presumptive value of the land peripheral to the presumptive arena. Thus the stage was set for the contest in the Board of Governors: a city with an arena and no owner versus a city with an owner and no arena.

The stage itself had been affected by the multiple expansions of the league. When we first applied for Buffalo in the first expansion, the meetings were held in a small, informal room in a high-quality New York or Montreal hotel. As the league expanded to twenty-one—more than three times its original composition—so did the meeting room and the governors' table, to the point where intimate conferences sometimes turned into public brawls. The demand for seats at the governors' table became inflated as well: if a team had multiple owners, each wanted a seat; the owner needed his GM for player and hockey problems, his finance man for budget, his lawyer for comfort, and so on. John Ziegler ultimately, as permitted by the constitution and bylaws, began to restrict each club to two representatives; sometimes to one, in "executive session," leading to difficult choices for the owner, and forcing the owner to cover many bases, with the league's staff and counsel ready to provide support. It became incumbent on each club to arrive early and claim a good position for its seats, as the meetings grew to League of Nations (if not United Nations) proportions, and the oblong table formation pushed some clubs a considerable distance from the management end. (I once suggested "arena seating"—used frequently in modern law school and science classrooms—to John, but the problems of who got the first row apparently negated the benefits of the configuration). John and his staff—vice presidents for hockey operations, general counsel, finance vice president, outside counsel, and so on—lined up at one side, generally the far right, with owners disposed around the periphery. I was both an owner representative and a league officer, so I set Buffalo's place at the right corner, next to the other officers, so that I could hear well and take notes, I hoped, both faithful and accurate. While the Knox meeting philosophy was, at the outset of our ownership, to minimize participation and let the old clubs run things, my role as secretary and sometimes league counsel, combined with John Ziegler's frequent and confident calls for my comment or assignment, required more active participation. As the league's use of technology increased—the meetings now employ microphones and TV monitors at each governor's position—participation became easier.

When it came to the choice among the applicants, however, I chose silence. The conflict of interest, for both Toronto and Buffalo, was painfully apparent. We declined to participate in decisions of the committees on the subject, and, when it came to the governors' vote, abstained. Legal advice for the governors was placed in the capable hands of John Ziegler himself, Gil Stein as general counsel, and the very astute outside firms.

The price fixed by the Board of Governors and set forth in the expansion agreements I had drafted was $50 million cash, payable in part on signing, half the balance six months later, and the remainder before the June draft preceding the first season of play. Word was still fragmented and uncertain from the Hamilton camp as to whether anyone qualified would come forward to invest. As for Ottawa, its plans were a paradox of contingency. Firestone and his family had a reputation for substance and respectability, but the picture did not show the capacity to finance a $50 million franchise fee plus the working capital to cover start-up expense or loss. The financing plan was utterly dependent on the land. The land on which the putative arena was to be located, the presentation said, was owned or would be owned by the Firestone group. If the NHL franchise was granted, the plan contemplated that this land—and its periphery—would become very valuable. The banks would lend against the real property and the franchise, and, as the peripheral lots were sold, this would generate the cash flow to pay off the loans incurred to pay the franchise fee. It was a superb bootstrap. The first owner of the Kansas City franchise in 1974 had tried a similar ploy, never realized the financing, and defaulted on the league notes. I had my first experience in saving an insolvent franchise with the transfer of the Kansas City Scouts to Colorado, and the committee had a reminder of this as it deliberated. The building would be located in suburban Kanata, Ontario, not in downtown Ottawa, and the suburban location would require the construction of access roads and infrastructure, demanding the financial support of the municipal and regional governments, described in the Ottawa presentation only in the most general terms. As the committee sought firmer details and commitments for the Firestone plans, delays threatened the expansion timetable.

Meanwhile, the Hamilton promoters, doubtless emboldened by Ottawa's troubles, found an owner. He turned out to be a substantial and decent guy we knew fairly well—Ron Joyce, principal in the doughnut chain founded by Ron and the late, great Sabre and Maple Leaf defenseman Tim Horton. Ron was a Sabres season ticket holder. It was ironic that the threat to the Sabres should come from the former partner of the team's all-star. I had come to know Joyce and Tim's widow, Lori, in 1972 when I went to St. Catharines to investigate the circumstances of Tim's death. Joyce had taken the Horton idea and logo, a minimal operation at the time of Tim's death, and developed it into an international chain of doughnut shops.

The shops were, for the most part, privately owned, franchised by Joyce's company, and the franchisees were in effect to be investors in the NHL team, and provide the lending base for the NHL franchise fee.

Word came to me about Joyce and Hamilton during a governors' meeting. I was told that Peter Pocklington, the Edmonton owner, was secretly lobbying and trying to lock up votes for Hamilton. Even more threatening was the report that a deal was in the works under which, as a matter of equity, Hamilton would be admitted without requiring any compensation to Buffalo. I repeated to myself my own legal advice—to stay neutral, to stay out of the contest—but I was furious. As I looked around the governors' room, there was hardly a club that I had not helped in some way—nursing a new owner or solving a financing or a legal problem. For a number, in my own lights, I had been the godfather of the franchise or the implementing agent for the league. Seymour wasn't on hand to help, and things were moving swiftly toward a vote. As soon as we adjourned to the corridors, I made no bones about my displeasure. I repeated to Bill Wirtz and all within hearing distance John Pickett's often-repeated statement that the acceptance of the Devils into Islander territory was the worst mistake he and the league had ever made; that the $5 million indemnity—not yet paid—didn't put a dent into his loss; that the league should never do that to a partner again; that at the very least this should be discussed in open session, not secretly; that the notion of no compensation was outrageous. I was emphatic that the Sabres would abstain in any vote, but we were entitled to full, fair, and open discussion and judgment.

When the vote was taken and announced—and Ottawa was awarded the franchise—I knew that I was Hamilton's bête noir. There were rumors of antitrust suits, Combines Act investigations against the Leafs and the Sabres. But as the facts developed, it turned out Ron Joyce did not agree to pay the price fixed by the plan of expansion, Ottawa did, and there was no contest. At the end, Hamilton failed to qualify, and the league had no alternative except to accept Firestone's agreement—there was no other qualified applicant. Ron Joyce and the Hamilton promoters were trapped by their own pejorative view of the league: the NHL was asking too much, Hamilton should not be asked to pay more than their sister cities had committed in 1979, and so forth. At the last moment, under prodding from Pocklington, the Hamilton group did offer $50 million, but not in cash: $25 million up front, the balance over time, with essentially unsecured notes. Toronto and Buffalo listened silently—but anxiously—to the debate. Pocklington asked for more time; one club—the Flyers—believed to have an understanding for management of Copps Coliseum, argued for a grant to Hamilton. But the league lawyers indicated time had run out. Any further delays would jeopardize the Tampa grant and the plan of expansion itself; Firestone had indicated he needed an immediate go-ahead. Hamilton had not complied with the plan within the time fixed by the board. If the league tried to change the plan at this last minute to accommodate Hamilton, the lawyers warned the board, it could face a lawsuit from Ottawa, which was offering the $50 million in cash. In the end, the vote was overwhelming for Ottawa, with Buffalo and Toronto not participating.

So Toronto and Buffalo could relax. Or could they? The first sign of unease came with the bizarre conduct of Firestone and the lawyers for the Ottawa group. The expansion agreement between the league and the Ottawa applicants called for a down payment on signing in June, and half of the balance by December. Ottawa managed the down payment—late—but as we approached the second date, we began to hear sounds of difficulty. Could they borrow the payment? After consulting Bill Wirtz and Jack Krumpe, a member of the board committee monitoring the closing, I gave the response required by the league documents and policies: no, the league would not accept a note; cash was required. The plan of expansion limited the amount and percentage of the franchise value that could be financed or provided as security for a bank loan. Each of these rules and limits had been fully disclosed and explained to the Ottawa applicants and their Ottawa lawyers. I reported my concern to Jack, but we all hoped the problem would disappear. We heard nothing concrete further until a Friday night in December, a few days before the first balance payment was due. Out of the blue came a call from Toronto, from Bruce Firestone himself.

"Bob," he said, "where are you?"

"I'm here at my office, about to go home to dinner. What can I do for you?"

"Why aren't you here?" he asked. "We're at the Bank of Commerce in Toronto, ready to put the financing to bed so we can pay our installment to the league. We need your OK of the documents and signature of the league. Everybody's upset because you're not here and we can't close—"

I interrupted him. "Sorry, but that's impossible. Nobody, no one gave us notice of any kind of this meeting. No one sent us a draft of the documents you want us to sign—not to me, not to my juniors, not to Ziegler or Krumpe. I'd like to cooperate, but I can't review, clear, and sign the documents in these circumstances."

"Well, it's the league's fault, then, that we can't close and make the payment," Firestone said.

"Bruce, please get off the line and let me talk to your lawyer."

Bruce's lawyer then picked up the phone and, after an inept apology, agreed to get drafts to me over the weekend. After the drafts arrived and we had a chance to read them, it was regrettable—but understandable—why no advance call was made. The documents were a sixty-page shell game.

Twenty-five million dollars was due the league and its owners by December 15 of the year prior to entry. Somewhere, someone in the NHL hierarchy had been asked, despite my clear admonition, if a collateralized bank credit would be sufficient. I am sure that if the question had been put to John Ziegler, Jack Krumpe, Bill Wirtz, or me, the answer would have been no. Even an irrevocable, unconditional letter of credit, with interest accruing to the league, would have been a hard sell. A letter of credit that is both irrevocable and unconditional is close to cash, since the entity in whose favor the instrument is written has the power to draw on it—cash it in—at any time.

I imagine the next step in the Ottawa group's attempt to meet the cash requirement of the expansion agreement without putting up the cash went something like this: *Look, NHL, you don't want to burden your new partner unnecessarily. We shouldn't have to pay the banks that "stiff" fee for a letter of credit (say 1 percent on $25 million, which would have been $250,000). Couldn't we just establish an escrow account for the $25 million?*

For the most part, with John's cooperation, I was able to keep the channel of communications through me. But occasionally—and this could have been one of those misses—an applicant or supplicant would shop and scroll the league owners or staff to find someone with a more accept-able answer. So what we were presented with was not an irrevocable letter of credit, but a form of "trust" or escrow. The document looked impressive, full of boilerplate. But when one read the not-so-fine print, the near scam emerged. The league couldn't draw on the trust fund, so we were not able to make a partial distribution to the existing clubs. That was bad enough. But the clause that was the killer provided that the Ottawa applicant could terminate the escrow or "trust" at any time, without any duty even to put up substitute collateral. The termination didn't even require our consent or the bank's. Hence the "trust" or escrow was worthless. This was the piece of paper I was asked to approve for the league without prior notice at mid-night on that Friday.

I was furious—so furious that I wrote a letter to Ottawa's counsel charging them with gross misconduct. The killer document was an outright evasion of the plan of expansion, of the expansion agreement, and of direct representations made to John Ziegler, the committee, and me. When the applicant's lawyer called me on my cell during a governors' meeting a few days later to apologize, I was still so fired up I let him have it over the phone, giving him notice that if the Firestone group didn't come forward with the real dollars required, tout de suite, the franchise was doomed. (I didn't have the "vibrator" option on my cell phone in those days, so the bell jangled right through some hot discussion on a hockey issue, and John, not fully aware of the subject of the call or the identity of the caller, sardonically apologized on behalf of the governors for interrupting me!)

Gil Stein, league general counsel, thought I had overreacted with my letter, but I didn't want to deal with an applicant or its counsel that couldn't be trusted; moreover, the episode was a clear signal that the Firestone group didn't have the financial resources, and going down their iffy road would take the league to a dead end.

It was not lost on me that Hamilton might be waiting in the wings, especially if the league weakened the financial requirements in any respect. And Tampa Bay, having its own fiscal troubles, would certainly demand a revision of its own financial requirements. As the days went by without any concrete move by the Ottawa group to avoid a coming default, I decided that the whole, sorry mess should be spread before the governors. At the next meeting, when called upon for my report on closing the expansion agreements, I gave the governors a full account—what Jack Krumpe later described as my "litany of troubles"—of what the Ottawa group had put me through: the highly speculative projected source of cash flow for capital, the periphery sales of real property, the continuous failure to meet deadlines, the uncertainty as to infrastructure and access for a new building, and the specious "escrow." I concluded with the flat statement that, in view of this record, the league might be better off to start over and cancel the Ottawa grant—even if it meant inviting new applicants.

My report was greeted with dead silence. No one had the appetite to start over. We had to do our best to keep the fish on the line, keep it from drowning.

Fortunately—at least for a time—the Ottawa group found some financial and political help. Rod Bryden, through a series of swaps, took over the Firestone position and managed to acquire or produce enough credit and capital to pay the league the $50 million franchise fee. The closing, too, had its bizarre aspects. When the first signs arose of the way in which the Firestone group planned to finance the purchase of the franchise—through sale of the lots surrounding the building—I had retained Gowling, a well-known Montreal and Ottawa law firm, to monitor the local matters for the league.

When I appeared at the closing, prepared to read the final documents, there seemed to be extra people around. The extras, it turned out, were partners in the Gowling firm—not representing the league. I had little use for them for the closing, since it was my document that needed to be signed— but Gowling was representing its long-term client, a leading concessionaire, Ogden Corporation. I was greeted cordially by our mutual counselors. But after the introductions, and once we found out who was who, there occurred some whispered conferences in the corner, not including me. A few minutes later, as I was checking the signatures on my NHL Consent Agreement, one of the Gowling lawyers appeared and said—handing me a thick file—"Mr. Swados, perhaps you'd like to look at this?"

At this juncture, almost nothing surprised me, but I was in for another shock. Bryden was still $3 million short! Ogden was there to negotiate a loan in that amount, with the concession contract to be the security. No proof was offered that the loan didn't push the franchise debt over the 50 percent limit. In some past franchise transactions, like Peter Pocklington's $40 million loan from the Alberta Treasury Branches, we had insisted that the 50 percent cap be spelled out in fixed dollars in the consent agreement. I was concerned, again, about the lack of candor. It was only the coincidence of our retaining the Gowling firm, and that firm's ethical sense, that informed us what was going on. I called Ziegler before I signed the closing documents. John was concerned, as well—but remembering the view of the governors, as expressed in their silent reaction to my report at the last meeting, we mutually agreed that the best course was to get the fish on the boat, and deal with any anomalies or defaults later on.

The Ottawa Senators thus began to live a life of sellout houses, deeply in debt, capital poor, constantly scrambling for subsidy. They are still scrambling. Gary Bettman made an inscrutable remark to me not long ago. "The Ottawa franchise," he said, "has never been paid for."

In the 2002–2003 season, at the new year the performance of the Ottawa Senators under coach Jacques Martin was excellent. Its twenty-three wins and fifty-one points led the Eastern Conference. Yet its economic agony continued. On January 2, 2003, the club announced that some of the team's major creditors—the Imperial Bank of Commerce, Fleet Bank, and Covanta Energy Corporation—had rejected the financing plan sought by the Senators' principal equity investor, Rod Bryden. The team was out of cash and out of options, and, for the first time in the history of the league since the demise of the Cleveland franchise, the players did not receive their checks on payday. The words of Gary Bettman echoed: "The Ottawa franchise has never been paid for." The memory of that strange Ottawa closing in 1992 was vivid: the excessive borrowing; the $3 million loan from Ogden Corporation that was secret until the last-minute disclosure by our local counsel; the "bootstrap" financing with prospective land sales; and my recommendation—disregarded by the Board of Governors—that the proposals were unacceptable and either the applicants or Ottawa itself should be abandoned. Apparently the acquisition debt was never paid off, the monies to pay losses were borrowed, and the unpaid debt service accumulated to an estimated $160 million, a point where the interested banks had had their fill.

The unease of the lenders was compounded when Covanta—the successor of the Ogden Corporation, which made the covert loan in 1992—went into bankruptcy itself. The financial façade was over when, in January 2003, the league reached the end of its rope—a rope of $10 million advanced to the team—and the Senators went into bankruptcy. The next step is uncertain, but Rod Bryden is still hoping somehow, despite the financial failure, to emerge from "reorganization" (comparable to Chapter 11 in the United States) with some equity interest in the team.

The failure to pay the players' salaries really threw me. Even in the tension-filled Sabres days of 1996 and 1997, when Larry Quinn and the general managers were screaming for funds, there was no way we were going to let that default come about. I knew that the collective bargaining agreement would set the players free to sign with any other club if the default continued for ten days. The league might well pay the players itself to avoid such a catastrophe, even a "dispersal" draft, but there was no assurance, and with the league already into the Ottawa club for more than $9 million, that default was dangerous, indeed. The mark of failure and insolvency it would produce was the last thing the Sabres wanted in our critical negotiations with the public sector to finance our new arena. I used the threat of that potential disaster as a tool to bring about additional investments by Adelphia and our own group to avoid the crisis. The contracts with valuable players were Ottawa's principal asset, and it needed protection at all cost.

I note that the players' association is going to be "patient" with Bryden and his successors who emerge from the inevitable bankruptcy. I hope it will be more than "patient"; I hope—with faint expectation—that Bob Goodenow will permit his constituents to recognize the true nature of the crisis: here is a highly and regularly competitive team in a fine hockey market, in the capital of Canada; selling out, the only game in town, and it can't make it. It's the salary cancer.

Chapter 29

THE SALARY CANCER

Flying High with the Eagle, No Go with Goodenow

In 1976, with the complex pressures of the WHA competition, the antitrust threats, the problems of the new franchises, the death of Bill Jennings, and Clarence Campbell's discomfort with the increasing US business issues, there arose a movement among the governors—a movement for a changing of the guard. The movement was accelerated when Campbell was hit with charges of misconduct in his post as a director of a Montreal Airport affiliate. Clarence was a man of integrity and honor in his dealings with me and the Sabres, and I don't know how he got involved in the somewhat tasteless transaction, but he did take a position in and income from a company that provided service to the airport, without disclosure, and, it was claimed, in violation of his fiduciary duty as an officer of a public institution. He'd been around people of wealth all his life without acquiring wealth himself, and perhaps influenced by the rapacity of the Ballards and Smythes and Norrises, he could not resist the temptation to reach some real dollars on his own, after a life of modest lawyer's compensation. When the transaction was revealed, there was talk of criminal charges, which were later dismissed with the help of some of the governors, but Clarence's resignation as NHL president was mandated. Seymour called me, said he had been asked to be league chairman, and announced that he was going to accept at the governor's meeting the following day.

As I've indicated throughout these pages, I tried throughout my legal and hockey careers to keep carefully and closely in touch with my clients' moves, and the Knoxes responded and approved of this for the most part. But Seymour was ultimately his own man, and there were some elements of his personality and drives to which I could not penetrate. He did not tell me who had offered him the chairmanship, so my political sensors were useless. I congratulated him and said it was great for the Sabres.

It turned out that the offer had come from a faction headed by Ed Snider, principal owner of the Philadelphia Flyers, and Ed had conditioned the offer on the understanding that he would be named chairman of the finance committee, then the most important owner's post in an owner-operated league. Later that night, when Seymour innocently revealed the offer to Bill Wirtz—definitely *not* a cohort of Snider—the plan produced a cyclone. Bill called Seymour back and pronounced his verdict: the plan would not fly, Seymour would not have the votes for chairman, and there was opposition to the choice of Ed Snider as finance chairman—strong enough to beat Ed and deny Seymour position or influence on the board. I was not made privy to the negotiations, but what emerged profoundly affected the league and me personally. The new plan called for John Ziegler to be chairman and president (the chair ultimately went to Bill Wirtz, who first became finance chairman) and for me, the rookie alternate governor from the expansion franchise, to be secretary. The election produced a negative view of the Sabres emanating from the Flyers that took me years to ameliorate.

Secretary was one of only three offices elected by the board, by the owners—chairman and president were the others. Fortunately, John Ziegler and Bill Wirtz trusted me and trusted my judgment. The result was that I made much more of the position of secretary than that of taker of the minutes, a function to which the office had largely been confined in recent years. John assigned me as a member of most of the major committees—finance, expansion, legal, National Hockey League Services (the NHL product and endorsement operation), advisory, and labor (the last known as the "executive committee of the Owner-Player Council"). My firm and I were retained to deal with a wide range of league matters—expansion, taxes (I focused and lobbied for the NHL positions in the Tax Reform Act of 1976), transfers of franchises to new owners and new locations, negotiations with the clubs and providers on market territory, intellectual rights, bylaw changes, and so on. It was exciting and profitable, and it rapidly consumed so much of my time and effort that, with the Sabres still a major responsibility, my attention to other law firm clients began to fade. But I had my national stage!

Was there a conflict of interest? I thought not. Every issue affected my Sabres client, but the interests of the league and the Sabres were nearly always congruent, and on the rare occasions when they differed, there was always Gil Stein, as league general counsel, and independent lawyers, such as those at Covington & Burling, for added protection. From the point of view of the Sabres, there isn't the slightest doubt that my election to the post of secretary was highly beneficial; the Sabres had early information and frequent input on most major issues. I have never had trouble drawing the confidentiality or conflict of interest line. In the spirit of Justice Brandeis, I have always known when the wall must go up and when I could act objectively. And my multiple hats—as league officer and Sabres owner—strengthened my scope, authority, and impact.

Perhaps the most important ex officio assignment was the Owner-Player Council. This was the committee designated by the collective bargaining agreement to negotiate contracts with the NHL Players' Association and other player matters, including salaries, arbitration, discipline, playing conditions, and tournaments like the World Cup and the Olympics. The first players' union negotiation I was involved in took place at the airport in St. Louis in 1976, and I remember it as a slapdash rubber stamp of approval, as the player reps were on their way to their respective out-of-town games. As matters developed in later years, the agenda and the negotiations—and the venues—became more elaborate. The structure called for the president (John Ziegler) and chairman (Bill Wirtz) of the NHL and five appointed owners of the NHL, plus officers of the league designated by the president (usually Stein and me). That constituted the owners' executive committee. On the players' side, the documents provided for the executive director (Alan Eagleson; later, Bob Goodenow) plus the officers of the players' association—the professional advisers, plus five players, usually chosen intentionally from the players with star reputations and financial clout. Both sides had outside counsel—during Ziegler's regime, Covington & Burling for us; Weil, Gottschal, and Manges for the union. Behind the scenes, in every major negotiation, were the players' agents, more involved in Goodenow's regime than in that of Eagleson. (Alan behaved as if he represented everybody, anyway.)

I had certain advantages that led John to use me directly in the negotiations. I was not a labor relations specialist, but I knew the field. I was part of the ownership of a small-market franchise, and thus my views might be more creditable—or, at least, more so than they would be launched by a major-market club like Chicago or New York. I was a league officer, so I could serve on the committee ex officio without using up a slot. That meant another club would be participating in, and bound by, the negotiating strategy. Finally, I had been active on the board of the Sports Lawyers Association (in the early days, I was the only management representative), so I had, at least at the start, some credibility with Goodenow and a few other important player agents.

The original philosophy of the Owner-Player Council was to avoid the polarization that had taken place in the other professional sports. It was a ploy frequently used by other player unions to paint the owners as ogres, to promote solidarity in general, and to gain support for particular issues. The NHL idea was that, within limits, the players and owners were partners in hockey, and the negotiations should take place in a comfortable atmosphere, with mutual respect. And Eagleson—whatever else one must say about him—promoted and performed under the umbrella of this philosophy. I remember vividly hearing the "hate the owners" creed at a seminar conducted by leading NFL agents, and I have already remarked how Bill Bradley assaulted the basketball owners and hurt them financially before the congressional tax committees. As part of the research for this book, I dug up a 1981 volume written by hockey enforcer Dave Schultz. The word "owner" appears numerous times, but *never* unaccompanied by the word "greed."[1] And at sessions of the Sports Lawyers Association, Dick Moss, assistant general counsel of the baseball players' union, another Harvard Law graduate—though bedecked in a neck chain instead of a tie—would look at me as if I were an unwelcome encounter from another planet when I described the Sabres as reasonable owners, sensitive to the needs and rights of the players.

The "partner" philosophy worked for a time, aided by Eagleson's sophisticated attention to venue.

Eagleson didn't hesitate to hold the owner-player meetings at pleasant vacation resorts and to ply the union's providers with subsidies or discount arrangements for the meetings. We met in Bermuda, Nassau, Florida, Cape Cod, even London—the latter, financed or arranged by the insurance agents and underwriters who dealt with the association's pension, life, and liability coverage. The venue was the association's call, and it would have been foolish to object. Who wanted to irritate or affront Lloyd's of London?

The negotiations in the 1970s and 1980s seemed generally successful and friendly. I got to know and like the union player leaders—like Mike Milbury, Bryan Trottier, and Bobby Smith, all of whom are in management today and who justified the comment by one Buffalo reporter to me that NHL players were the most reasonable and articulate and cooperative, in contrast to the multimillionaire reps in the other leagues, who were frequently unmitigated pains in the neck.

When I first began attending the owner-player meetings, I was really nothing more that a sideline auditor, but it was not my nature to sit silent, and, with John Ziegler's encouragement, I gradually moved to the front row, especially when Bob Goodenow came on the scene as the new executive director of the players' association and the negotiations moved from time to time to broader economic issues. I was never very comfortable in these negotiations, perhaps again because of my tendency to seek control of the flow of any meeting, and I certainly *didn't* control the Owner-Player Council!

Wirtz and Ziegler were usually in command for our side, and Eagleson did more than enough talking for the players. If the discussion focused on technical matters—waivers, drafts, training camp, and so on—it was better to let the GMs do the talking. The best of the GM group—like Bill Torrey, Harry Sinden, and Lou Lamoriello—were usually present to provide concrete and intelligent input. My discomfort was partly because of my problems with the union executive directors: I was offended by Eagleson's profanity and by Goodenow's duplicity. I had been a rookie private in the infantry in World War II and had lived with former residents of the stockade, awaiting assignment to the front, so I was fully familiar with a variety of curses. But with Eagleson the f-word supplanted the definite article for frequency in the English language!

With Goodenow the objection was more serious. He had ousted Eagleson on the wave of a protest movement from some of the player reps and their lawyers, claiming that Eagleson had abused his powers, with occasional dips into the union's and the players' till through corruptive arrangements and contracts. The leaders of the reform movement were litigious, seemed to echo the untrammeled critiques observed in the baseball and football owner/player battles, and threatened action against the NHL itself. The choice of Goodenow presented, at first, some hope. There should have been rapport between Goodenow and me: both Harvard Law School; both active in the Sports Lawyers Association; both with an intellectual bent. I had stressed, in my discussions in the Sports Lawyers Association, that polarization was not necessary—the union and ownership-management were both dependent on the economic health of the business. Accommodation, not polarized conflict, was what was called for in an environment such as the NHL, where losses were pervasive and growth was mandatory. But it didn't take long for Goodenow's mask to disappear. He gave a speech at an SLA meeting (I attended, and Gil Stein had it taped) that had ominous undertones and overtones. We began to find in Goodenow's regime the same rigidity, the same distrust of the owners, the same use of distortion and denial observed in the other sports.

The worst episode occurred during the 1991–92 negotiations. The escalation of salaries had reached the point where few franchises were making a profit, there were frequent multimillion-dollar losses, it was becoming difficult to raise additional capital, and the lives of a number of clubs, especially those in small Canadian markets like Winnipeg, Quebec City, and Edmonton, were threatened. Some teams were paying out nearly 70 percent of their revenues in player payroll—meaning ultimate franchise suicide. We asked the union representatives to recognize this, moderate their demands, and begin serious negotiations toward a cap, greater club compensation, and other efforts to prevent or slow salary inflation—or tie it into or make it dependent on increases in league revenue. Goodenow refused to listen, citing the expansions and the increase in franchise prices, asserting that the clubs "must be" making large profits, at player expense. We offered to give the players' association an opportunity to examine (using as much time as they wished, and their own auditors) the books of four different clubs. Buffalo volunteered, as did Detroit. The audits took place.

At the next meeting of the Owner-Player Council during the 1991–92 season, the colloquy went something like this:

Swados: Did you examine the four teams' financial records? Did you have enough time? Did you get full cooperation?
Goodenow: Yes.
Mike Illitch (Detroit owner): Did you find anything inconsistent with what we've been telling you about our losses?
Goodenow: No
Swados: Well, Bob, are you ready to acknowledge the seriousness of the situation, and work toward a solution?
Goodenow: No, we are not.
Illitch: I took four days of my time to meet with your people—why not?
Goodenow: We believe you're using two sets of books.

In the owners' caucus following this episode, Mike Illitch stated he would not deal with Goodenow again, *ever.*

I must acknowledge that as an ex officio member of the Owner-Player Council, I was not aware or informed of everything. It took a while for me to be admitted to the inner councils. At one session in the early 1970s, I had to break into the caucus, uninvited. Marcel Aubut (the Nordiques governor) apologized for the lapse, noting that he didn't know I was not "just a lawyer" but an owner as well. The practice was to have a caucus of the owners' side, and then a caucus within the caucus. If the issue was an important one and closure was near, John Ziegler would often meet one-on-one with Eagleson, frequently with Bill Wirtz tripping along, to provide clout or emphasis. This was especially true of international hockey matters, like the Canada Cup. Under the collective bargaining agreement (CBA), these issues were expressly confined to the international committee, which, as a practical matter, consisted of Wirtz, Ziegler, and Eagleson.

The commercial activities of Eagleson with his player clients and the union have been excoriated in the Canadian press and the courts. I have no independent knowledge of them and will not comment here. But as to the union/league negotiations in the seven years I was on the committee (1976–1993), I believe he did a very effective job for the players. Average salary went from $86,000 to $562,000, and the number of major-league jobs went from 360 to 880. And he did so with some sensitivity for the underlying principle that the players' financial success was dependent on the economic health of the league. At one meeting—I think it was in Nassau—John Ziegler asked me to give a speech at dinner and to say something nice about Eagleson. "Coming from you and the Sabres," John said, "it'll be more meaningful than if it comes again from Bill or me." I complied, and I said, with some conviction, "Alan has done a good job for the players, but he's always acted in the broad interests of hockey."

However, with the unfortunate concurrence of our negotiators, Eagleson may have planted the seeds of our salary cancer. I have described elsewhere how, when told by Judge Higginbotham that our standard player contract, with its perpetual option, was worthless, we sought the union's help to ensure the validity of the "equalization" system. This produced a pattern: if we wanted postcontract player rights, we had to pay for them, and the payment was not just in fewer restrictions on movement or accelerated free agency, but, in effect, mandated increases in salary. At one point in the negotiations with Goodenow in 1992, the players demanded that, before a club could have a right of first refusal or compensatory draft picks, we had to make a "qualifying offer" to the player of *200 percent* of his current salary. I exploded, in what must have been forceful language—though not Eagleson language—which led to Jack Krumpe's recommendation that I continue in the lineup, as "one of the toughest" of the negotiators. The percentage went away, but the notion did not; and the CBA signed required a club to offer to a player reaching restricted free agency an automatic 15 percent bump in salary to preserve its rights to equalization and club compensation.

In the caucus preceding the agreement, I argued that even 15 percent was too much—since it would become the point from which the GM would start, it would be offered automatically to all players approaching restrictive free agency, and we would be faced with a *minimum* 15 percent inflationary increase every year. The 15 percent would become the general manager's yardstick. On a cumulative basis, it would make every other anti-inflationary measure ineffective. John Pickett, the Islanders owner—rushing, as we always seemed to be, to conclude the negotiations—responded that I "didn't know when to make a deal." I was outvoted, and this—which I believe was the most invidious clause in the agreement—became a permanent feature. It remained unchanged until 1993 when, after protests by me to Ed Snider and Bill Wirtz, which may have had some influence, the minimum bump was changed to 10 percent.

This concept—that we had to *pay* for a provision that was designed to promote parity, designed to discourage the rich teams from invading the rosters of the smaller markets—I believe, hurt us badly. *Yet we persisted in paying for the concept.* I suppose we did so, first, because our GMs wanted it, but also because we thought it would have an anti-inflationary effect—in other words, the threat of having to give up three (later five, for top-salaried players) first-round draft picks would discourage offer sheets from other

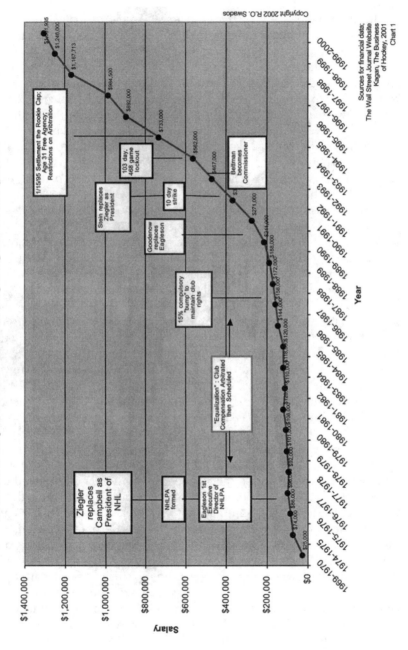

Economic History of the NHL - Collective Bargaining and the Salary Cancer

Sources for financial data;
The Wall Street Journal Website
Kagan, The Business
of Hockey, 2001
Chart 1

teams, reduce the number of buyers, and thus slow salary increases for restricted free agents.

It didn't happen. An owner desperate for help to make the playoffs would not be deterred by the draft choice penalty. When Hartford (now Carolina) sought a strong, two-way defenseman in Glen Wesley, it did not hesitate very much, it was not deterred, and it gave to Boston its first-round entry draft picks in 1995, 1996, and 1997. When Chicago, perhaps miffed by the failure to close a player deal with Winnipeg (now Phoenix), sought a star forward in Keith Tkachuk, it was not deterred by the draft pick penalty, nor even by the Canadian club subsidy; the Blackhawks gave a "through the roof" offer to Tkachuk, of more than $6 million, forcing Winnipeg to exercise its right to match and imposing on the other US NHL clubs (with few exceptions) the obligation to pay for the 33 percent difference in the exchange rate value of Canadian and US dollars.

Instead of attacking the *level* of salaries, the backbone of the system, the Owner-Player Council negotiations in the late 1970s and 1980s seemed, in retrospect, only to fiddle with the spare ribs—equalization, waivers, training camp, arbitration. The general managers seemed obsessed with arbitration. I remember one of the leading manager's comment that permitting someone else to fix the salary of his player was an abomination. I felt this issue was not critical. Experience in the other leagues suggested that changes in the arbitrator, changes in the arbitration criteria, elimination of totally free agents from the comparison data, and so forth presented much better targets than attempts to bar arbitration entirely. The players considered arbitration like a constitutional right, akin to free speech. There were valid points the GMs made—such as limiting the number of times arbitration was available—but the issue did not go to the guts of the problem.

Of more importance was the age at which the player became a totally free agent. In CBA after CBA (usually a new negotiation every four or five years) we lost ground on this. The cutoff of owner rights was originally at age thirty-three; it was reduced to thirty-two, then to thirty-one, and it was expected that a concession in the 2005 negotiations might further reduce it to age thirty. The change exposed more than fifty players each year to the free market, and as top players continued to perform in their mid- and late thirties, the release of this group deprived the owners of control of a large segment of their most valuable players. Even the right to match disappeared. Only a modest "commissioner's draft pick," inserted after the first round in the entry draft, provided some compensation for the player's departure.

The piecemeal defense against salary inflation did not work, but we continued to go through the motions in the 1970s and 1980s. It takes two to bargain, and Eagleson and, later, Goodenow were intransigent, refused to recognize the economic realities or refused to enter substantive discussions of a cap on salaries, even though that concept had made headway in the NFL and the NBA. No doubt the players' association's resistance was strengthened by the opposition of the agents. Particularly during Goodenow's regime, we knew that he was constantly talking to the leading agents during negotiations. They were unanimously opposed to a cap—it severely limits their scope—and we began to feel that the agents' interference was so gross that a case might be made that the negotiations were not bona fide and that the union, in conspiracy with the agents, had violated the National Labor Relations Act. But a lawsuit would not have accomplished much and would have destroyed the illusion that the players and owners were partners trying to solve a mutual industry problem.

Of course, there were other factors that prevented our coming to grips with a salary ceiling. With each mention of a salary cap, the players would retort with a demand for revenue sharing. That was a tough sell in our league. The Original Six continued to insist on maintaining their separate islands of revenue—they had made early investments in their buildings, built largely with private funds, and were not ready to share those revenues with their later-arriving partners. There were arguments about the components or formula for determining what revenue would be shared. The original NBA cap had excluded arena revenue, but we were not very sanguine about keeping our players away from it once the revenue-sharing principle was accepted. However, revenue sharing was making some inroads—for example, without much difficulty, since it owned the playoffs, the NHL began to take over more and more of the postseason revenue—both gate and TV—and this had the effect of spreading some of the playoff benefits among all of the NHL clubs. When the US national television revenue became much larger than that received from *Hockey Night in Canada*, the Canadian clubs stopped arguing against full sharing of national television dollars from both Canadian and American sources, and that is now in effect.

As the NHL clubs had to be educated to revenue sharing, so did our players have to become amenable to the salary cap, and the timing was not good. When we began serious negotiations of the concept in the Owner-Player Council in 1991, the NFL had not yet adopted it, but would within a year. The cap forces hard choices on management in dealing with the older, high-priced players. While the cap may be in the interests of the team and the industry as a whole, it also may bring about an earlier termination of a player's career with his traditional team. In the last few years, the cap has compelled the Buffalo Bills to give up on Bruce Smith and Doug Flutie, both all-stars. It sets up a conflict—inevitable but troublesome nevertheless—between the young veteran and the old star. As the cap negotiations in our league continued, I began to hear reports (never verified) that if the Sabres players voted for a cap, the Bills would come over and "beat 'em up."

In the course of the 1991–1993 negotiations I had several substantive talks with our player representative, Craig Simpson, an educated and well-balanced guy. Craig downplayed the football players' comments and even went so far as to indicate that, in the Sabres' thinking, there was no permanent hostility to the cap—it was not a "big deal." And, of course, the NFL players learned to like it. With modifications and differences, the cap concept has been retained in the current collective bargaining agreements of both the NBA and the NFL. Major League Baseball, after some very difficult strike and lockout months, adopted a "luxury tax," designed to be a substi-

Bob Goodenow—executive director of the NHL Players' Union. AP Photo.

tute for the cap: a club that pays more than the stated average or defined goal gets fined a substantial amount, the fine increasing geometrically the more the club exceeds the defined goal. We attempted this idea in the early 1990s negotiations, but Goodenow was intransigent. Perhaps we were lucky he was so stubborn—the system seems to have been a total failure in Major League Baseball. The New York Yankees have a payroll of $200 million, two or three times the average, pay the fine without difficulty, and continue to dominate the league. In the 2002 negotiations for baseball, that sport ended up with recommendations for a salary cap *and* a luxury tax—the latter designed to enforce the former.

The uncompromising opposition of the NHL Players' Association to any salary regulation produced its bitter harvest in the players' strike of 1991–92 and the owners' lockout of 1994–95—and in the ouster of John Ziegler from the presidency in 1993.

The 1990–91 owner-player negotiations resonated as if the two parties were speaking two different languages from two different planets. Bob Goodenow was new to the meetings—he had just taken over as executive director of the union and was loath to be seen as finding anything good in the owners' proposals. John Ziegler was under pressure to bury his normal instincts for reason and accommodation; as Marcel Aubut, the Nordiques' governor expressed it, "our mandate is to give them nothing!" The result was almost no movement on either side, and with the players' executive director refusing to acknowledge the financial facts, the negotiating sessions were consumed by arguments about side issues—pensions, allocation of product, and promotional revenue. The two sides met several times without progress, and most of the 1991–92 season passed, without a new contract.

Under Goodenow, an atmosphere of distrust of the owners was encouraged, and with the frustration of our every attempt to deal with the level of salaries, the willingness to continue operations without a new CBA eroded and Goodenow—perhaps to show his toughness and promote solidarity—called a strike. The job action, called in April 1992, lasted ten days. Bruce McNall brought Wayne Gretzky and other stars to the negotiating room to demonstrate that within the union there were differing views on the strike. The timing of the strike was probably better for the union: the players receive only awards for the playoffs, and their regular salaries are normally fully paid at the end of the regular season. The loss of the playoffs would hit primarily at the owners—most count on playoff revenues for profit, or at least to reduce operational deficits. There appeared to be, moreover, some slight recognition by some of the player reps and some of the union officers—but not Goodenow—that we should come to grips with salary escalation. I hammered at this in my own brief talks with the Sabres reps. To John Ziegler, it made sense to cut and run, and come back for a more fruitful day. I agreed.

There was some paranoia in our ownership group. I arrived for a session one day to find that the owners were in a secret room, and I was told I was not authorized to enter. I paged Marcel Aubut, the owner who was most active in leadership. I had gotten to know Marcel well when I had represented the league in dealing with some of his financing and ownership problems. I challenged him: What the devil was he doing, excluding me from the caucus? Marcel apologized; they hadn't intended to exclude me. They were trying to keep the "staff" out, I had those multiple hats—"counsel in the crease" again—and Marcel didn't realize, or had forgotten, that I was not just league secretary, I was a co-owner of the Sabres, though with a modest share. John Ziegler was not his usual, unflappable self; he seemed overly tense, distracted. When I sensed this and asked him what was wrong, he whispered in my ear that he had received a call from an owner—he would not tell me his name—who told him that, if John settled the strike, his job might not be protected.

In Gil Stein's book *Power Plays*, he tags the warning call to Bill Wirtz, with Barry Shenkarow of Winnipeg and Marcel Aubut on the line, and describes a movement of other owners to unseat John that had been gaining strength. (Not including the Sabres—too close to John, we were kept out of the loop on this one.) Stein attributes the trigger of John's emotional reaction to Wirtz's high-volume criticism on the call. Wirtz, according to Stein, objected to John's arranging a further meeting with the players without a fax confirming Goodenow's commitments.[2]

John remembers it differently: the Board of Governors had instructed the committee to continue negotiations, to try to work something out and settle the strike. Although Wirtz was chairman of the board, those instructions were still in effect. John believed that the group seeking his ouster—and opposing strike settlement—was a minority. At most, seven or eight clubs, with three or four on the fence. John argued that it would be impossible to make the kind of long-term deal we wanted with Goodenow; we had to get to the players, get them to trust us and our position—and for that we needed another year. The three owners listened, but in a later call with Wirtz—not in the inflamed atmosphere described by Stein—Bill did not threaten John with the loss of his job, but warned John that if he did not keep the labor dispute broiling, as requested by Aubut and Shenkarow, Bill did not know if he could protect John from further attack. Neither John nor I knew that the ouster crew had coalesced.

When, in the following days, John asked whether there was a consensus for his ouster, he was told that Bruce McNall had polled the western clubs and reported that those clubs were unanimous for a change. It turned out that McNall—the temporary chairman of the league who later was convicted of fraud—never made calls to the western clubs at all. John, still under the board mandate, decided to proceed with the settlement. Not missed by the media, and important in all of our thinking, was the fact that the settlement would save the playoffs and avoid the negative blows baseball was threatened with and later encountered.

I reported to John that Craig Simpson, the Sabres' player rep, had given me the impression that, for them, the cap was no longer just a hate object and that, if other issues could be worked out, there was a good chance that, without the pressure of the playoffs and with more time, some progress on salary control—either with a cap or a luxury tax—might be possible in the following season. John asked what I thought of a one-year deal. I said I would not object to it, if we got a firm commitment on cap negotiation. John felt that, notwithstanding the warning call, we should settle in the long-term interests of the league, and our negotiating lawyers went back to the table on this basis.

Compromises were worked out on the side issues, and, most important to me, the CBA was extended only one year, and the extension agreement contained an express commitment by the union for a study group to begin work immediately and enter into bona fide negotiations looking toward a cap similar to that in force in the NBA. In the executive committee meetings and in the governors' sessions, I voted for the extension solely because of this commitment.

What happened to the commitment? Political events in the league intervened, and it disappeared into thin air. In the course of eighteen months, the actors at the bargaining table changed radically. Goodenow had ousted Eagleson, Gil Stein had moved in with the ouster of John Ziegler, and Stein was in turn shunted aside with the election of Gary Bettman. And, in what I considered an unfortunate fallout of the changes— but others may have treated as a dividend—the post of secretary was downgraded to staff, and I no longer served as a league officer or as a member of the Owner-Player Council.

I have recounted these events in some detail because I believe that the failure to move on that commitment to negotiate a cap was a major failure: it wasted the one-year window of opportunity we had created, suppressing the cap negotiations, and the salary cancer worsened.

The ouster of John Ziegler fulfilled Wirtz's threat. When word came around that John would not be reelected, I was still league secretary, and I felt a duty to the league to assist in the transition while doing what I could to protect John's interests. Certainly John had been a strong supporter of mine, and I had agreed with his decision to settle the strike as a temporary measure, but I thought I still had independent views and other supporters. I was still a voting trustee of the Sabres franchise and its alternate governor. I tried to help on John's termination contract, but in a few days I could see that I—and the Sabres—would be treated as part of the outs, not the ins. When I set up a conference call among key owners on a special committee to deal with John's matter, I was asked, for the first time since my election in 1976, to get off the line.

The probabilities were that the "revolution" came about because of the conviction of some owners that the strike should not have been settled, and John and the rest of our committee should have continued to say no to any and all of the players' association's demands. The hope of the anti-Ziegler faction was that "hanging on to the negative" would ultimately break the back of the players' resistance to salary regulation. I thought differently. With the conditions that then prevailed, it would have taken from April to October—eight months—before the players would have felt any money pinch or pressure, and our committee had never articulated what we really wanted. I'm not sure we even knew. A salary cap without revenue sharing? That would have been impossible to achieve.

When the governors who assumed power reported that Gil Stein was their choice for interim, if not permanent, president, it was tempting to connect the dots—and the arrow pointed straight to Ed Snider, starting with the selection of his lawyer as president. I had mixed reactions. I had always admired Ed as an intelligent, aggressive businessman who had done a great job with the Flyers; he was a hands-on owner, with the judgment to make it work. If the league affairs were more influenced by Ed's views from now on, it might not be so good for Bob Swados, but it might give the league a boost of energy.

I was not so sure about Gil Stein. He had demonstrated over the years that he was a brainy, politically savvy lawyer. He and I had clashed occasionally; he was a league officer who was clearly partisan to his club's separate interests—and I thought I was not. I had memories of his conduct in the mid-1970s when Ed failed to get his way on some matters before the governors—he was determined to break the lock of the Canadians' influence, while we were inclined to live with it. In the period before his designation as general counsel, Gil showed his and Ed's displeasure by placing a recording device on the governors' table, in full view—as if he were prepared to sue each of us if we disagreed with the Flyers on any issue.

As soon as he got the nod for president, Gil approached me. It was just before the June meeting of the governors, at which league and Board of Governors officers would be elected. They were going to downgrade the secretary, Gil said, make it a staff office, rather than a governors' post. This would require an amendment to the constitution, and "the fellas" didn't think I should oppose it—or run for reelection. If I didn't oppose the change, and I didn't stand for reelection, he would continue to use me (and my law firm) as special counsel. If I didn't agree, the "fellas" wouldn't like it; I would have to take my chances, probably didn't have the votes, and Gil wouldn't be able to use me on league legal matters.

It was not the first time I had felt the unkind cut of politics—I remembered 1942, when the local Democrats had tried to block my transfer from Washington to Buffalo to be with my ailing wife by holding up my paychecks! I consulted Seymour, some of my friends around the table, like Dick Patrick of the Capitals, and Bill Wirtz. In my work as secretary and special counsel, I had helped most of the owners. I hoped they'd give me a clear signal to fight it out—but they didn't, although some suggested that the votes might still be there if I insisted on reelection. I was "counsel in the crease" again—it was a blow to my personal prestige, and the Sabres could lose influence, but a run and a defeat could mean my firm would lose an important client and the franchise would be part of an isolated minority.

I didn't like the result, but in the end I heeded Bill Wirtz's advice: get it in writing! I drafted a release that spelled out my continued role on behalf of the league as special counsel in franchise, tax, and business matters; Gil approved it and read it to the governors. It was greeted with a kind of strained silence, then issued to the press. So ended my reign as a league officer and my participation as a member of the Owner-Player Council. Gil did make good on his promise of continued employment, for as long as he continued in office himself. I was assigned the Anaheim, Tampa, Florida, and Ottawa expansion transactions, as related elsewhere. When Gary Bettman came on board as commissioner, he restructured the governance of the league so as to reduce the administrative role of the owners and increase the role of the staff and general managers, and I was not reappointed to the negotiating committee.

At the time of these events, I believed that my withdrawal as secretary was largely engineered as a by-product of John Ziegler's problems, politics, and disappointment with the outcome of the 1992 strike. However, there may have been special interests at work. One of the owners on the conference call when I was asked to hang up was Norm Green. Green had originally been a partner in the Calgary franchise, then was involved in Hartford with Howard Baldwin. He stepped up to take over the Minnesota North Stars in the complex transactions of 1990, when the league refused to allow the Gunds to transfer the club to San Jose, instead insisting on the purchase of an expansion franchise for the California city, coupled with an interclub draft to maintain a player presence in Minnesota. It became evident in the 1992 player negotiations that Barry Shenkarow of Winnipeg and Marcel Aubut of Quebec viewed the attempt to get control of salaries as critical to their survival as Canadian franchises. Norm Green had intervened in an attempt to save a venue that the Gunds had found unsupportable, and it was apparent that he, too, was a potential carpetbagger. There were territories in the Southwest that could be fertile franchises.

John Ziegler, with Bill Wirtz's support, had maintained a policy that discouraged the portability of NHL franchises, and I had been the primary executor of that policy. Gary Bettman had remarked to me that our league was "crazy," but we had successfully prevented the transfer of Oakland to Vancouver, of St. Louis to Saskatoon, and of Minnesota to San Jose. I, with Covington & Burling input, had drafted Bylaw 36, which sets forth twenty-four strict conditions and standards that must be considered by the member clubs before a transfer of location will be approved. The transfer from Denver to New Jersey occurred only after years of opposition and delay, after local capital had been exhausted, and after very substantial compensation to the league and the neighboring franchises had been agreed upon. I suspect that Norm welcomed, if indeed he did not encourage, elimination of a possible roadblock by moving me out of the way and substituting a staff employee who would obey the junta's orders on transfers. Actually, the transfers to Phoenix, Colorado, and Dallas would have been acceptable to me, because the conditions of the bylaw would have been met, but approval by the league of those transactions was certainly facilitated without the presence of a league officer with the power to prevent or delay the transactions. A proposed transfer of Quebec or Winnipeg to Hamilton might also have easier going if I were not in office. I have no proof, however, and the bottom line is that our failure to solve the salary problem lost two franchises for Canada and deprived central Connecticut of NHL hockey.

Gil Stein, as John Ziegler's interim successor, apparently had no appetite for the difficult, irritative proceedings that negotiation of a cap with Goodenow would require. Gil had too full a personal plate. First, he had to explore the possibilities that his temporary presidency could be converted into a permanent post as "commissioner." He tried to be innovative, and I, after consulting Seymour, tried to help him. It was the general response of the governors to respect the office, even if one did not agree with everything he suggested. For example, Gil's policy on suspensions seems bizarre, in retrospect: his view was that we should keep our stars on the ice—so if Jaromir Jagr received a match penalty for intentional injury, for example, in the past he would have received a suspension, effective immediately, barred from play, say, for six games. Under Gil's diktat, the suspension was imposed for six *nongame days*. The fine might be the same, even larger (subject to the ceiling on player fines under the CBA), but the fans could still see Jagr perform without interruption. The change was not viewed favorably by the victim, however—usually confined to the press box until his injury had healed, watching his tormentor perform. So the change did not last, but you can't blame Gil for trying.

Gil made good on his commitments to me: kept me in the expansion legal process on the grants to Disney and Wayne Huizenga, and appointed me to a committee to study the powers of the commissioners in the NFL, NBA, and Major League Baseball and compare them to the NHL provisions. Gil showed some reluctance to give me any title, however; the committee had no chairman, but when my colleagues showed as reluctant debutantes, Gil acquiesced in my coordinating the project and writing the final report. I was quite proud of my essay on commissioner powers, but, so far as I knew, it was never acted on by the governors. When Gary Bettman came on as commissioner, he and his counsel, Michael Cardozo, must have read it, but Gary brought along his own menu of constitutional changes in the powers and procedures of the league' s chief executive officer.

But Gil did not appoint me to the negotiating committee, and there was, as I recall it, little activity in the Owner-Player Council during his brief reign. Once the governors hired a headhunter, it was apparent that Gil was not to continue as president or commissioner, and he was significantly distracted by the problems of the pay and perks of a departing chief executive, including an unfortunate foray into the Hockey Hall of Fame, in which, like an FDR, he sought to reorganize and "pack" the hall's board of directors to facilitate his induction.

It was natural, when Gary Bettman came on board, for the new commissioner (the title did, indeed, change) to seek a period of peace and orientation, and it was not until the fall of 1994 that the league again took up the central issue of salary escalation. Bettman faced the issue head on, armed with very able lieutenants. Jeff Pash, formerly of Covington, as general counsel, was flanked by Jerry Ackerman of that firm—both of whom had had significant experience in the NFL player wars, Michael Cardozo of the Proskauer Rose firm that represented the NBA in its negotiations toward a cap, and Frank Rothman of Skadden Arps. Rothman had been the lead litigator in the legal battles of the NFL that had forged the rulings of the Supreme Court and other federal courts on impasse and other issues in collective bargaining. It was an all-star cast, and there was no doubt in anyone's mind at the governors' table that we were, this time, inexorably out to capture the cap—or something like it.

When the players' association showed no disposition to move on the issue, the commissioner, without difficulty, achieved a Board of Governors' vote in favor of a lockout in 1994. This time, unlike the strike of 1992, the conditions seemed more propitious for the owners. It was the regular season, and, notwithstanding some warnings from labor counsel, the owners held their course and withheld the players' compensation through the fall and winter. The lockout was harassed from time to time by perplexing legal questions and minor contests in the courts, but it was largely static: Could we refuse to pay salaries under the individual player contracts? Were the clubs liable on their various rental arrangements? What would happen to the television agreements—local and national? What about deferred compensation due from prior years? Would the players become free agents because their salaries were not being paid?

The hard economic fact determined the practical answer: if the clubs could withhold salaries in the lockout—and the legal advice favored the affirmative—most of the clubs, like the Sabres, would *save money by shutting down*. So the economic pressure was on the players: once into the lockout, there was little incentive for the owners to resume the season without major concessions from the association, and the lockout—accompanied by difficult, frustrating negotiations—continued through the fall and winter.

The most difficult and critical legal question was whether the owners, having bargained in good faith to "impasse," could unilaterally install a reasonable salary control system—a cap or a luxury tax—on excessive pay-rolls. The NFL was struggling through this issue in the Brown case and would receive a very favorable ruling in the opinion of Justice Stephen G. Breyer in the Supreme Court of the United States. When the NFL owners, after exhaustive but futile negotiations on the salaries of their reserve players, called the "taxi squad," set their own salary scale, the players contended that this was a violation of the antitrust laws—that once "impasse" had been reached, the "nonstatutory labor exemption" disappeared. That exemption clothed with immunity from antitrust claim provisions unilaterally installed by the owners, if they had been the subject of collective bargaining. By a majority vote, the Supreme Court held that the immunity continued as long as the subject matter had been dealt with in collective bargaining, even if not resolved, and there was still something left to the bargaining process.

It was a tempting idea. The NHL Players' Association had been arbitrary, failed to face the facts, and refused to deal with the most important issue—the salaries of veteran players. So put the salary controls discussed in the bargaining—similar to those accepted in the NBA and NFL—directly into our system, order the players back to work, and resume the season. Even the millionaire stars were beginning to feel the pinch of zero income. But another development would blow this chance.

The projections for most teams in the league were miserable. Despite the restrictions on free agency, the losses continued to mount. The results of a collective bargaining were a gamble. Player salaries were taking too much of the teams' revenue. The future worried me so that, in the middle of what should have been a delightful cruise on the four-master *Windsong* in the Mediterranean, I sent a handwritten note to Gary Bettman, pleading for a vigorous campaign for a salary cap. The existing caps in the NBA were from 56 to 57 percent. When I returned, Gary asked if I would accept a 60 percent ceiling, implying that this might be achievable—or at least would be a practical target. The Sabres were already approaching 65 percent, and I said that if we had to, I thought we could live with it. When I reviewed the hockey department's projections for the years 1995 and 1996, I reported my discussions with the commissioner to the Knoxes, and, over the protest of General Manager Gerry Meehan, we cut the projection for major-league salaries so that it would fit within the 60 percent of revenue ceiling. To the argument that the assumption of a 60 percent cap was mere speculation, I responded, "We need to survive—if we don't get a cap from the league, we're going to impose it on our own budget, ourselves."

The Sabres' need for a drastic cut in salaries or a major new source of revenue had veered into close-up in 1988. The automatic sellouts had disappeared, and along with them disappeared the appetite of our principal investors for the funding of the hockey team as a stand-alone business. As described in chapter 6, in 1988 we attempted to build a major leap in income with the acquisition of a new UHF station, Channel 49. That adventure got us nowhere, except deeper in debt, as the purchase and ultimate bailout required borrowing—through the issuance of $3.7 million in subordinated debentures to our key partners—money that might otherwise have strengthened our hand in future negotiations with the Rigas family and other potential investors in the team. Except for the increased debt, we managed to escape from Channel 49 without major damage, recouping the station's cash losses in a resale. Yet the need for new revenue persisted. The port in the salary storm? The arena. The "solution" was to construct a new building, with larger capacity than the Aud, include a slew of well-placed luxury boxes that would generate $5 million more in income, and arrange it so that the Sabres were the owner and operator of the arena. As our own landlord, we could tap the box, concessions, advertising, parking, and other in-house revenue, without having to hand over any substantial part of this revenue to the city or county.

Of course, this "solution" had occurred to other NHL clubs. At the time of the 1994 lockout, as many as eight NHL owners were planning, designing, financing, or already constructing new arenas. That a new arena might produce greater expense, as well as income, was not fully apparent at the time, nor did it come home to the Sabres planners that operation of the building was a *new business*, for which the small staff of the hockey club might not be trained, equipped, or experienced. The NHL season and playoffs used, at the most—even with a Stanley Cup Final round and exhibition games—only sixty-two dates. Management would have to promote and sell, at fees that would contribute to cash flow, concerts, marginally profitable sports such as indoor soccer and lacrosse, college basketball, and other events for the remaining 303 dates. The attractiveness of an NBA franchise, even if one could be had, was diminished by the high purchase cost (upward of $150 million) and the certainty that the NBA team would dip sharply into the concessions, advertising, and other revenue from nonhockey events. The economics and financing would vary all over the market—as would the probability of success. But in 1994, it was clear that a substantial number of NHL member clubs were determined to build new buildings.

The move to build a major structure like a new arena, with its economic implications for the team and the community, soon takes on a life of its own. Gary Bettman was to remark to me in later years, in the course of a plea by the Sabres for league help, "You didn't ask our permission to build that building!" My response, in the spirit of that desperate time, was, "Ask your permission to *survive*?"

In a scenario that was, I suspect, typical of the arena efforts of other NHL clubs, the Buffalo building project, called "the Crossroads," involved political gambits, executive changes, outside "experts," hockey star promotion, media massage, fiscal fortune-telling, and new investors. As the lockout continued through the winter of the 1994–95 season, most of the steps in the building of the Crossroads Arena, some involving real commitments, were already under way. We had already hired, and fired, Sam Katz, a Philadelphia expert who was negative on the project; incurred the wrath of Buffalo mayor Jimmy Griffin by persuading the Common Council to override his veto of $2.5 million in seed money; issued projections to the banks that foresaw a substantial building profit—not interrupted by continued labor strife; signed Pat LaFontaine, who, coming off a points-record season, was to be the star of the new arena, to a new contract, with a salary in the upper reaches of the league hierarchy; and welcomed, in the light of the desperate need for cash to cover the losses in the interim, John J. Rigas and Adelphia Communications Corporation as new owners of 34 percent of the Sabres equity, for an investment of $15 million.

Meanwhile, on the labor relations front, Gary Bettman and his colleagues were grinding out substantial progress on the flanks of the battle, but getting nowhere on the main issue—the control of veterans' salaries. The commissioner produced valuable movement in two areas that were of concern to the general managers—the restriction of arbitration and the regulation of entry-level contracts. What emerged over the long months of negotiation was a system under which the salary of a first-round draft choice was capped at a figure moving up from ($800,000 to $1 million), and the draft pick was bound to that contract for three years and was denied arbitration for two additional years. Thus the GM had a cap on his offer and the rookie's demand, and retained control of the salary for a total of five years. At the end of the fifth year, the rookie became a restricted free agent; he could, theoretically, receive an offer sheet from any club, subject to the provisions for a right of first refusal or compensation for his old club, in the event he was signed away. There were other "goodies" for management—for example, a limited right to walk away from an arbitration award deemed too high. Naturally, the grants to the owners were accompanied by gifts to the players: the age for absolute free agency would be reduced from thirty-two to thirty-one, and a player who failed to attain the league average salary after ten years could opt for free agency then.

But with no salary cap for veterans, both restricted and unrestricted free agents—usually the most experienced and valuable players—could shoot for the moon. And there would be no luxury tax on overspending owners.

The lockout was not a pleasant experience for anybody. The media varied from superficial economic analysis to partisan charges of ownership "greed." In what was otherwise a friendly discussion between the owner-managers of the two teams in Toronto's Hot Stove Club, Cliff Fletcher, a general manager with an old-line reputation, looking straight at me, blamed the whole messy situation on "the American owners."

The negotiations hopped from venue to venue, and the governors were brought into the developments in great detail, sometimes on very short notice. I remember vividly one marathon session that arose in a conference call while my Rochester, New York, ophthalmologist, Hobie Lerner, was giving me a vision test. Lerner, a good friend and a staff doctor for our farm team, the Amerks, surrendered one of his phone lines for a full day while I participated in a debate on the merits of the latest proposals. The good doctor's own staff—all hockey fans—reveled in their propinquity to the mysterious NHL goings-on. As the days wore on, Bettman sought to put a cosmetic spin on the situation: we were not engaged in a lockout—he was merely postponing the start of the season.

But as more and more game days passed by—and nearly half the season had melted away—Bettman had to tell the governors that the prospects for a global, surgical solution of the salary problem were melting away as well. The willingness of Goodenow to grant the concessions on rookie players was certainly motivated by the pressure we had on the players: no games and no compensation. But the commissioner also had to report that there was no further give; he presented a Hobson's choice: We could get a cap, he said, but only if we were willing to sacrifice the remainder of the season and the playoffs. For a continuance of the lockout, he felt, there must be unanimity. If the players were to face another year without compensation, Bettman sounded confident that their opposition to a cap would collapse. But he was not willing to recommend canceling the season unless he had 100 percent support. We would face a cannonade from the media and the fans—and it would be intolerable if there were dissenters among the owners.

But we did not have unanimity. The partial achievements of the negotiations—a rookie cap and restricted arbitration—had an appeal to some of the owners, especially those who were in midstream on their building plans. The rookie cap put a brake on the cost of new players, and if you managed well, did not break ranks, said no to veterans making unreasonable demands, and walked away from outrageous arbitration awards, why couldn't you maintain a viable franchise? Saying yes to the negotiations and no to the continued lockout would get the press off our backs, avoid the alienation of our fans, and give the banks a seminormal season and labor environment on which to base critical projections. The crucial league conference call came into the Sabres board meeting I convened. The debate showed clearly that there were six clubs (not counting the Sabres) that would not agree to continue the lockout. Gary Bettman had become adamant: no unanimity, no further lockout. The negotiations had produced a system that, Gary argued, while falling short of our hopes, with prudent implementation, could work.

Abe Pollin, principal owner of the Washington Capitals and a veteran of the basketball wars with his NBA team, pleaded—even begged—that the decision be deferred to a full, face-to-face meeting of the governors. Gary responded that there was no time left for a further delay; the season, half gone, would be destroyed without our control, and the gains achieved in the negotiations could well be retracted by the players' association and lost. The proposed five-year contract did not preclude us from a cap forever, and we would be better prepared next time, financially and otherwise. The vote was to accept the players' proposals and begin what was left of the season.

It was a fatal mistake. The new collective bargaining agreement did not put a real brake on salaries. There were too many holes in the net. The initial pleasure at the rookie cap and the restrictions on arbitration soon dissipated, as second- and third-round picks sought to approach the first-round cap (there was no "slotting," increments governing the fixing of salaries below the cap), and players dissatisfied with the prospects in arbitration began to use long holdouts as a technique for bludgeoning management into larger increases. The escape into free agency at age thirty-one, once thought to be of minor importance, proved to be a serious lapse as the ablest of the players turned out to have the most chronological stamina. Steve Yzerman, Mario Lemieux, Wayne Gretzky, Dominik Hasek, Ray Bourque, Mark Messier—all were maintaining their careers—and their demand for multimillion-dollar salaries—well into their late thirties, even forties. And the owners, driven by fears of fan turnoff, did not act prudently or responsibly: club compensation proved no impediment to signing free agents. Salaries continued to escalate, though at a slower rate, starting from a level that was too high in the first place.

As I could predict from the negotiations surrounding the 1992 strike and the 1998–99 lockout, the first to desert were the two Canadian franchises in the small markets—Winnipeg and Quebec. As the teams settled into the uncertain, up-and-down cycles of the new system, other agenda interfered with the hope that we could get back soon to negotiating the cap. The CBA, originally providing for a termination in 1998, was extended twice—once to get the players' consent to expansion and a second time to get players' consent to participation in the Olympics. It was September 15, 2004 (see chapter 40), before any basic revision of the system was possible. In the absence of a revelation by Goodenow and his cohorts, that might never come—unless more NHL clubs end up prostrate and with no where to go—but bankruptcy court.

Part 5

COUNSEL IN THE CREASE

Chapter 30

MINDING THE STORE

S everal weeks before his death from cancer in May 1996, I met Seymour at the family estate, Ess Kay Farms, in East Aurora. Seymour was very down, looking pale, thin, and weak. I tried to cheer him up, telling him he'd won many a fight before. "I need a miracle," he said. When Norty arrived a few minutes later, I stressed that, with Seymour ill and Norty still involved with the bank, it was necessary for someone to be designated head of the Sabres, governor at NHL meetings, principal spokesman, and so on. Seymour responded, "I have no problem with Bob minding the store."

Norty did not object—he stayed silent—and for nearly a year I did mind the store, without publicity or formal confirmation. As vice chairman of the board and voting trustee, I was the "senior" officer, and Bob Rich, the other vice chairman, and the other members of the board accepted, or at least acquiesced in, my role. With the ongoing negotiations to sell our interests to Adelphia or the Rigas family, and John Rigas serving as chairman of the "emergency executive committee," a formal resolution ratifying my role would have been awkward.

I had no clue as to Norty's discontent. Through the years, Norty and I had had some disagreements, but those were always resolved and his support and confidence in me seemed unshakeable—as demonstrated when he seconded my election to the Sabres Hall of Fame in 1995 and when, on June 6, 1996, he was inducted into the highly prestigious Cult of the Buffalo, a ceremony that honors the most distinguished citizens of the community. The inductee is permitted to have five of his closest friends and associates sit at a separate table at the front of the assemblage. Norty chose me to be one of the five.

The episode of May 9, 1997, described in the memorandum that follows, was a shock.

MEMORANDUM

TO: File

FROM: Bob Swados

DATE: May 27, 1997 (dictated May 23, 1997)

RE: Board of Directors Seat NFHMC—Circumstances of NRK Coming on the Board and Election as Chairman

On Friday, May 9, NRK asked ROS to be in his office in the Marine Midland Center at 9:30 a.m. to discuss ROS matters, future of the club and "other things." I had no clue or intimation of what NRK had in mind, although I was certainly aware of his very strong belief that continued pressure must be put on John Rigas to make good on the general understanding we have had since Seymour III became ill that Adelphia would somehow bring about the purchase of the interest held by those investors who wanted to get out. I appeared promptly at 9:30 and was told, without warning, that NRK felt he should be Chairman of the Board as part of the strategy, that so far as he had been able to figure out (he hadn't discussed it with me to see if there were alternatives), the only way that it could be done was for me to resign from the Board, and that this was going to happen at 3:30 that afternoon and stated, quite unequivocally, that what would happen to me as a consequence of that depended upon how I responded. I did not respond affirmatively. I said that this is not the way you treat an asset of the organization and it would be viewed as a demotion, a reduction in responsibility, and already there was 180 degrees away from what I was entitled to. Norty answered that I would still be General Counsel, I would still be aware of what was going on and as to my compensation—that depended on my reaction. I answered that he was "cutting me in half" and I could not acquiesce in that although I fully understood his strategy vis-à-vis Adelphia. While I was not enthusiastic about the idea, I pointed out that the way to resolve this problem without cutting an asset in half was to add a seat to the Board. Maybe Adelphia would be willing to go along with that, although it would change the percentage of seats on the Board which they held from three out of eight to three out of nine. Norty was willing to consider this and suggested that we make a "joint call" to John Rigas immediately because this was going to happen at 3:30 regardless of the outcome of any such call.

Norty then called John Rigas in my presence, told him I was on the line, told him that I had offered to resign from the Board (I had not yet done so) unless a way could be found to continue me on the Board and still add Norty and elect him Chairman. I had advised Norty that any such change under the documents required Adelphia's consent. John Rigas responded immediately to the effect, "Well, for God sakes, keep Bob on the Board . . ." and proceeded to agree to whatever changes in the documents had to be made to add the ninth seat and accomplish the election of Norty to the Board and to the chairmanship.

Norty later added in private conversation with me that he was glad it had worked out that way.

As the above indicates, I did not solicit John Rigas' position on this issue—his response was as objective and positive as one could ask, without a moment of preparation or persuasion.

RS.eb

Norty had been such a supportive colleague and friend, but the "Big C" brings strange twists to personality and judgment. I now know that, around the time Norty assumed the Sabres chair, he learned for the first time that he had incurable bone cancer and his time was running out. I now believe that, as suggested by Bob Rich, Norty's fight with his own cancer was taking its toll.[1] He was undergoing both radiation and chemotherapy. He no longer had his best friend and partner—his brother, Seymour—for a resource. It did not affect his intelligence—I remember his speech at the Society of the Buffalo ceremony as brilliant, witty, and literate, in imagery and substance. But it seemed to exacerbate his critical demands on himself and others, and destroy his patience.

As many of us will, he was hanging on for dear life, and with the issues still troubling his days he was determined to accomplish certain goals, stripped of the niceties. Using his intelligence and grit, but giving no quarter to softness or indecision, and "suffering no fools gladly," he made the sale of the Sabres one of those goals, important to his family and our friends. As the Rigas crowd and Adelphia delayed month after month in closing their contract to buy us out, I'm afraid even my loyalty and commitment seemed to strain in Norty's vision. John's response for a new director's seat, so Norty could become chairman without bumping me, had been so quick and positive—"By all means, keep Bob on the board!" Had my loyalty shifted? Could he no longer count, as he had for thirty years, on my primary focus and commitment to the Knox Group?

I began to find matters referred to Rich Products or its counsel, instead of to me; Quinn's judgment was sometimes preferred to mine—at least temporarily. When it came time to adjust my compensation, instead of giving me the unqualified support I thought I deserved at board meetings,

Norty would refrain from comment. In my thinking, my loyalty was unswerving, but I made the judgment, in the interests of all of our seventy-seven partners, that maintaining a good, candid, and mutually respectful relationship with John was an important asset for all of us. No one had such a relationship with anybody else in the Rigas spectrum. And events proved me correct—it certainly was a principal force in bringing about the final closing in July 2000 that overcame serious risks and roadblocks.

For some time I could not make sense of Norty's treatment of me in those two years before his death. Was I being too harsh in this book? Norty had been too important in my life and career to leave the question unanswered. So, before I committed this text to the record, I went back to Jim Wendel. Except for his family, Jim had been Norty's closest associate in-house—calm, stable, intelligent, professional, and loyal. He saw Norty in his humor, his toughness, his drive, his impatience. I explained my doubts and concerns.

"Bob," Jim said, "Norty wouldn't have kept you in the organization for five minutes, instead of thirty years, except that he believed in you and respected you. It was the cancer, Bob. . . . He loved you. . . ."

Chapter 31

THE COACH AND
AUNTIE MAME

Most amateurs who become involved in the management of professional sports become infected with what I call the "GM syndrome": whatever business issues there are—advertising, taxation, sales, power costs, revenue, even legal problems—sooner or later, knowledgeable or not, they are drawn by a powerful magnet to getting involved with the management of the action on the ice. Sure, the business problems need attention—but, after all, the players are our major asset, aren't they? And the CEO can't neglect them! The Knoxes used to kid even this high-flying counsel that he really wanted to take over for Punch Imlach or Scotty Bowman. At least in my case, I recognized that my hockey-playing experience was limited to games of shinny on the lake in Delaware Park. But in Larry Quinn's case the syndrome was worse: he was a regular participant in amateur leagues, with some hockey talent. So, like the Knoxes, Larry's political appetite was fortified by his inward suspicion that maybe he could have been taking the face-off himself and, perhaps, the sense that the failing revenues of the building he built were more difficult than could be solved by a successful team afflicted by personal conflicts. Whatever the reason, Larry Quinn, like Doug Moss before him, plunged into the management control of the team on the ice.

It didn't take long in this chaotic state of things for Larry Quinn to make his move, and, unfortunately, to tip his hand.

The first step—the appointment of a new general manager—was relatively easy and, within the Sabres ownership, relatively noncontroversial. John Muckler was, in my opinion, a first-rate hockey man—experienced, successful—although his Stanley Cup win for Edmonton had come as coach, with a team largely assembled by Glen Sather. Muckler was well organized and intelligent enough to deal with rookies as well as veterans, including our Czech superstar, Dominik Hasek. The Mogilny transaction—a transfer of a star who had lost his sparkle for two first-round picks and Michael Peca, all of whom became major contributors to the team—seemed strong evidence of John's ability as a trader and judge of talent. I had some reservations, because I had watched Don Luce, the director of player personnel, and the scouts perform at a number of yearly drafts, and I wasn't at all sure that the accolades for the Sabres' younger players in the *Hockey News* weren't in large measure attributable to Don and his staff.

If John had any weakness, it was in his treatment of people, the press and public relations. I suspect that as his conflict with coach Ted Nolan developed, and he did not receive absolute support from the board, and the tiff with the fans caught very negative press (especially from *Buffalo News* hockey beat reporter Jim Kelley), John's public persona—and his valuation by a public relations–conscious board—went downhill. A naturally taciturn man, his public responses became more abrupt, and the continued popularity and positive treatment in the media of Nolan—who should have been under John's control—created a difficult environment. I became concerned myself about his growing disaffection when Hasek was threatened by the league, on the eve of the 1997 playoffs, with suspension for twenty games, over a tussle with Kelley. Larry Quinn, Kevin Billet, and I argued the appeal before Commissioner Gary Bettman and got the suspension reduced to three games, but I was disturbed by what seemed like a "couldn't care less" lack of support from John.

Under the circumstances, as a new CEO with a disaffected GM, it made sense for Larry to get the board to approve—or at least acquiesce in—the appointment of a new GM. As was my routine role, I supervised the termination arrangements and agreements and assured John he would have no difficulty finding a new place in hockey, while he enjoyed the fruits of his continuing salary payments from the Sabres. (He still had a year to go on his contract.) Larry gave some lip service to my twenty-five years as league governor and counsel and secretary by briefly asking for suggestions—to which he paid very little attention.

I have had a pet analysis that the general manager is not necessarily a talent and that the job might better be broken down into its principal duties, with specialists assigned to its components: you could have someone like Luce assigned to picking new players or new trades, a lawyer assigned to negotiate the contracts, an accountant to handle the hockey budget, and so on. This would simplify the recruiting process, probably reduce the cost, and retain better control by senior business management. My friends George and Gordon Gund instituted this kind of a regime for their San Jose Sharks, but so far this system had not produced any startling results for their team. Larry opted for the traditional general manager setup—subject, however, to his own hockey hands-on control.

The traditional NHL GM sees himself as the most important club officer, destined, like Pat Quinn, Cliff Fletcher, Lou Lamoriollo, and Harry Sinden, to be president of the organization. With such presumed importance, they get paid accordingly, and John Muckler was in the highest third of NHL GM salaries. I gave Larry some specific names—including former players who had shown business judgment, as I had observed as talent in the negotiations with the players' union (like Mike Milbury, Brian Trottier, Bobby Smith, and even Mike Liut)—but Larry elected to go his own way and chose Darcy Regier out of the Islanders' organization. The other members of the board from the Knox-Buffalo group had no difficulty going along with Larry the CEO. John Rigas demurred some (perhaps with notions of Nolan), but when I reported good recommendations on Darcy from Bill Torrey (Florida Panthers) and Jimmy Devellano (Detroit Red Wings), two GM-executives in whom I had confidence, John did not object to Larry's choice and the board unanimously concurred, doubtless content with the news that Regier's compensation would be less than half of John's.

The Regier/Muckler switch came on June 4, 1997. Did a new GM mean

Larry Quinn, John Muckler, and Ted Nolan. Copyright © Bill Wippert.

a new head coach, or would Regier dissolve the conflict? To the insiders, it was pretty clear that one of the silent conditions of Regier's employment was that he dispose of Nolan. As early as February of the 1996–97 season, I was sitting with Quinn watching practice when Larry—unaware of our mutual history—introduced me to Terry O'Reilly, the onetime Boston Bruin who had been our nemesis in the 1970s and 1980s. I had no idea what he was doing in the Sabres building, but his presence with Larry could hardly be a coincidence. Terry had been out of hockey for some time, but I remembered him as the kind of provocative, feisty, aggressive, and winning player you hate in the opposition but would love to have on your own team.

My reaction to Larry's presumed attempt at recruitment was amused but positive, except for one thing: the last time I had seen Terry, he was testifying in his own defense, in a hearing on charges that (like John Muckler earlier that season) he had gone into the stands after a profane and offensive critic and had taken a poke at the fan. I was a member of the governors' panel that heard his appeal, and we unanimously dismissed the appeal and approved Brian O'Neill's suspension decision. I had a conflicted reaction to Larry's introduction—he was making a move without consultation—but O'Reilly could be a great choice. Would we end up with another Muckler?

I muttered, "You look good, Terry . . . certainly better than you did the last time I saw you, when we suspended you for six games!" Quinn looked shocked, and O'Reilly produced an embarrassed laugh. "It's OK," I said. "Glad to have you here. I remember your final statement very well—'I'm not a monster!'"

Larry's O'Reilly idea was a good one, assuming Terry could, after ten years out of the business, recoup his hockey know-how and drive. The trouble was that Larry had forgotten, if he ever knew, that *nothing* stays secret for more than a moment in the hockey business. (I had learned this early on, in our first venture with the Oakland Seals in 1968, when, despite every corporate precaution I knew and despite the sellers' efforts to hustle me in and out of the arena incognito, the fans had the whole story on our purchase of the Seals twenty-four hours later.) It didn't take long for the organization and the media to learn of O'Reilly's visit, and the speculation about Nolan—who had not yet been offered a new contract—began to boil into anger.

The press and radio critics began to zero in with their blunderbuss assaults. How could the Sabres so mistreat their Coach of the Year? How could the club alienate the large First Nations population in southern Ontario? How could the Sabres turn their back on a coach who had given them such an exciting season? Protests appeared in the press that assumed that Nolan would not be offered a new contract—or, if he were offered one, it would be an unfair lowball offer—too little, too short. The *Buffalo News* gave sympathetic support to Nolan, and cancellations by season ticket holders began to grow, beyond the normal attrition. Norty and I asked for

Ted Nolan—controversial coach. Copyright © Bill Wippert.

a private meeting with the *News* executives and staff. Whatever qualms we had about the coaching change proposed by Quinn and Regier (I had more concerns than Norty), we felt the need to support management and to take the bile out of the press commentary. The *News* brass had been strong supporters of the Sabres over the years, and these policy tête-á-têtes had always been helpful. But this time we were confronted with sharp criticism of our new president. Quinn was too arbitrary, they said, too arrogant, not respectful of the journalists, sometimes obscuring the facts. When Norty's plea for support on the Nolan issue seemed to be getting nowhere, I asked if the vice chairman could have a shot. Why didn't the *News* respect *our* judgment? I asked. We were the same people, Buffalo citizens, not trying to feather our own nests, but seeking the best result for the community. The newspaper had always recognized our good faith and expertise in the past—why not now?

The meeting did lower the temperature of the debate for a few days. But Nolan was too heroic a victim for the media to leave it alone. The ticket cancellations had reached $200,000. A large protest crowd assembled in Niagara Square. And who was on the podium, who led the protest march? None other than that glamorous socialite widow of the founder—Jean Read Knox. When I heard the report, I laughed in appreciation. Here was the founder's wife picketing the decision of the august board her husband had created. It fitted juicily into my sense of theater. I called Jean and told her she was right on; she was our joyful Carrie Nation, our own Auntie Mame. I expressed my own frustration at the impending loss of revenue and goodwill—losses that should never occur over such an issue. Ted deserved another shot, and, if not, there were plenty of other good young coaches tuning up every year. Jean agreed, however, that with my recently fragile relationship with Norty, I'd better keep a low profile.

From private talks with John Muckler and associate coach Don Lever, I was well aware of the poor relationship between Nolan and goalie Dominik Hasek, on the one hand, and, on the other, the failure to get Nolan and Muckler to cooperate. I had Norty's admonition well in mind: "Bob, you keep your coach, you lose your goaltender."

Ted Nolan was an attractive man who looked and acted like a fighter, and his First Nations status gave him a special glamour that was good PR. But I could not see the sense of a brouhaha that could lose us major dollars over a *coach*, especially *this* coach.

But Quinn was determined to terminate Ted; Regier was uncomfortable with the idea of Ted still around, acting as if he had power; and Norty—a veteran of many disputes with his widow sister-in-law—was determined to back up his CEO. I was directed to call a meeting of the board to resolve the issue. Jean wrote a letter to Norty, charging that management was grievously mishandling the Nolan matter and threatened to destroy "all the work my husband had done to make the Sabres a major asset of the community." Norty refused to read the letter to the board. He took umbrage at Jean's conduct—he regarded it as disloyal to the franchise, confirming his judgment in anger: "Well, Jean's an Indian, anyway!"

At the board meeting, I asked for the latest number on the cancellations—$250,000. The consensus was obviously ready to back Regier and Quinn. "Suppose it becomes four hundred thousand?" I asked. "Are we still ready to take that hit—over a *coach*?" Silence. It was clear that the board had already passed the question of whether to fire Nolan; it was concerned only with how to bring it about with minimum cost and maximum closure. On the trip home from an NHL meeting later that week, the strategy proposed by Quinn and Regier called for an offer of a contract, for PR purposes, but (hopefully) one Ted would certainly refuse. Sensing my disapproval— "You're the only one, Bob"—Norty assigned the drafting of the offer to Kevin Billet, the Sabres' in-house counsel. I was asked to run the concept by John Rigas. I tracked him down in a nearby hotel and persuaded him to go along with a one-year renewal, in the interests of peace in the Sabres family. John reluctantly agreed. When we reached the Buffalo airport, I was given a copy of the draft. It was a one-year offer, but it named no salary. I immediately said to the group: "This won't fly. It's not a genuine offer. It's a fake, and the press will label it as such and stomp all over us." Norty showed his exasperation. "You're the only one," he said again. But he accepted my judgment as a lawyer, and the draft was amended to insert a dollar figure not far from Ted's previous compensation.

At the board meeting, Regier was instructed to charter a plane and present the offer to Ted personally, giving him only until midnight the next day to accept. John Rigas called me. He had received a call from Ted. What should Nolan do? I was in the crease, again. John was an officer of the company, a major investor. Norty was the chairman, a cofounder. There was no time to consult. I could only utter as objective a call as I could come up with. I told John that Nolan should make a counteroffer, immediately. For reasons never given to me, Ted—perhaps out of pride, perhaps out of confusion, perhaps because he was given no assurance he could break through the Knox/Quinn/Regier phalanx—never made a counteroffer. His chance with the Sabres having evaporated, Nolan tried to find employment with other NHL clubs, without success.

The rage of the Nolan fans ultimately cost the Sabres, according to former controller Dan DiPofi, nearly $3.2 million, never recovered. The new, popular coach, Lindy Ruff—a choice I thoroughly approved—produced a good rapport with Dominik Hasek and exciting seasons that brought most of those fans back in later years.

Ted Nolan's career as an NHL coach was aborted—perhaps unfairly. But in hockey luck plays a major role. In 2003 Mike Milbury, a decent and reasonable hockey man, chose not to hire Ted to rebuild the Islanders. I hope Ted can find a way to prove himself again. He deserves an NHL role. Perhaps someday he'll find a GM strong enough—and secure enough—to take him on.[1]

Chapter 32

WHAT'S IT ALL WORTH?

Like the "dot-coms" of the 2000 bull market, the price of an NHL franchise seems to have no relationship to earnings, losses, cost of assets, or book value. Beginning with our entry into the league in 1970 down to the present, most franchises barely break even, and many have substantial deficits. Yet, looking at the expansion fee alone, the "value" of a rookie NHL club went from $2 million in 1967 to $6 million in 1970 to $50 million in 1990 to $80 million in 1997, when Atlanta, Nashville, Minnesota, and Columbus entered the league. In the same thirty-year period, the consumer price index went from 116.3 to 535.8. I had to face the problem of how to value an NHL club at both the local and national levels. From time to time individual Sabres holders would seek to sell their shares—usually because of a death or move from the area. We paid no dividends—all potential profits, if any, went into the player payroll—and had no established market. The only purchaser available was the company itself. The standard practice was what I call "cramp down": we were in control, and the financial statement showed no substantial earnings, so, the practice dictated, we could force the departing minority shareholder to pay the minimum price, even if it was less than the "true" value. I took a different view, and Seymour went along. This is a semicivic enterprise, I said: we hold control only through the voting trust, and no dividends are foreseeable—why shouldn't all of our shareholders participate, at least to some extent, in the appreciation of franchise values?

Karl Hepp, the partner in the CPA firm Price Waterhouse on the Sabres accounts, protested we were making unnecessary gifts to the selling shareholders; but I persisted, working out a formula that averaged the original cost to the shareholder ($10 per share) with a value based on the most recent expansion fee or selling price of a franchise in a comparable market, and we paid the fairer price. But only small holdings were involved.

When I became secretary of the Board of Governors, and began to monitor franchise sales on behalf of the league, selling owners would sometimes ask me for input on a proposed selling price, or purchasing owners would ask me to appraise the club's assets for tax purposes. The tax deductions for depreciation of physical assets and the amortization of the cost of player contracts were still important. If the buyer of the Hartford Whalers, for example, paid $36 million, what was the real value? How much of that price was for goodwill—which couldn't be written off—and how much for the player contracts, which could, over the projected playing life of the player. And what was that playing life? Was it different for goaltenders, forwards, and defensemen? What was the value of the club's major-league roster and draft picks compared to those of other clubs? This led to all kinds of fascinating, juicy judgments. With the aid of able hockey men like Jim Gregory of the league and Jim Devellano of the Detroit Red Wings, I developed a kind of special expertise in the field.

But the bottom line was, What is it all worth? I couldn't just roll the dice or throw darts against the wall—though the data on sale prices seemed that crazy. I took my clue from the sales of television stations, which seemed to lay down a pattern—adhered to in sale negotiations—of a revenue/price ratio. The value was uncertain, but the dollars that came in the till were not. I found that the NHL clubs, whether they made money or lost money, seemed to sell at about 2.2 times revenue. For example, if you added up the gate, local TV, concessions, parking, and league-generated revenue (which was pretty much the same for every club) and it came to $25 million, that would justify a price of about $55 million. That would be your starting point. Then you could adjust for intangible factors, like the rank of the ADI (TV area of dominant influence), the number and character of the stars on the roster, and so on. Howard Baldwin, sometime owner of three clubs in the league (the Whalers, North Stars, and Penguins), thought my formula was too simplistic and conservative, but it was accepted in the limited NHL market, and I think it influenced the economic history of the league.

I was hoist on my own petard in 1996–97 when we were attempting to sell the Sabres to Adelphia and the Rigas family. Their financial vice president, Jim Brown, began to attack my formula with a sort of genial ferocity. And with the salary cancer, the recent bankruptcies, and the 2005 lockout, my valuation formula may go up in smoke.

Chapter 33

DALLAS AND THE NO-GOAL CUP

It was Dallas: June 8, 1999, the Stanley Cup Finals. The Sabres, on the strong back and magic reflexes of Dominik Hasek, had made it to the big show and had even stolen the first game, in overtime, no less, three to two, in the Dallas building. As had been the custom for thirty years in Buffalo, I was on my way to the Sabres dressing room to congratulate our coaches and players. The walk to the players' room in Reunion Arena was through a long, brown corridor, crowded with characters, it seemed, who had consumed a good part of my life and career for nearly thirty years: Jean Knox, perky widow of Sabres founder Seymour Knox III; John Rigas, head of the debt-ridden, highly successful cable TV company that was in the process of buying the franchise; the owners of the Dallas Stars, new at the game and new in the league, and not very friendly; my former colleagues and fellow officers of the NHL—Jim Gregory and Coley Campbell, in charge of hockey operations; Steve Solomon, then CEO of the NHL, a nice guy, but never a Buffalo booster; and Commissioner Gary Bettman himself.

We (the Sabres people) were high and rolling—we'd taken the first Stanley Cup game, and in the opposition's building—a big leap toward victory in a seven-game series. We expected—and got—reluctant cordiality from the losers. From the league? Of course neutrality must be maintained, but when I reached for a handshake from the NHL brass all I got was stony silence. The game had been chippy, loaded with penalties, most of which hit the Sabres. At one point seven straight Buffalo players were sent to the box. Naturally, that seemed a little disproportionate to us. When I saw the commissioner, I was prepared for a measure of congratulations, but heard none.

Groping in the silence, I said to Gary, "Well, I guess justice triumphed over adversity?"

Not a smile. Gary responded like a stern judge: "Adversity justified."

Said I, "That depends on your point of view, Commissioner!"

"Well, I'm objective . . . ," said Bettman.

"Well," I replied, seeing the grim faces of Solomon, Campbell, and Gregory, "I'm not!"

It was clear that the Sabres' win in the Stars' arena had injected an unpleasant ghost into the league's TV plans and projected ratings. If the Dominator and friends could take the first game in the Dallas building, a Buffalo sweep was possible. The Sabres had knocked Boston out of the playoffs with four straight wins. The Texas TV market was much larger than Buffalo. The acceptance of major-league hockey in the Southwest was still in question. (A few months later candidate and Governor George W. Bush commented to me—at my expression of pleasure at our time in Dallas— "Oh, that hockey thing . . . a lot of Texans still don't understand it!")

It was not the first or last time economics intruded on the sport. Two nights later it was reported to me that two NHL officials had been heard to predict in an elevator that "Buffalo can't win tonight." And we didn't.

An NHL Stanley Cup game between highly skilled, driven teams is one of the wonders of the world. The intensity, the color, the danger, the speed, strength, and resilience of the players are unmatched in spectator sport. In the first NHL playoff game I saw—the Sabres against the Montreal Canadiens—a 1973 overtime win by the new franchise, the tension was so great I was actually in delirious pain. It's been that way for me for thirty years, and the Sabres-Stars series was a continuation of that syndrome. When you have an interest or commitment to the team, the intensity and pleasure/pain are magnified. You're pumped up, not only by the action on the ice, but by the response of the fans, the media, and the community. The reverberations in the arena are like the *1812 Overture*. In the Sabres building, my pride in having had a part in producing it reached the roof, at a sellout crowd having a great time, and I imagine the walls of the arena bursting from the joyful noise within.

THE NO-GOAL GAME

The Stanley Cup series between the Dallas Stars and the Buffalo Sabres was hard-fought, exciting hockey, with the bigger, flashier Dallas team circling the puck in the Sabres zone, and the Buffalo team holding them off with a quick transition game, forechecking effectively, and ultimately protected by the fantastic efforts of Dominik Hasek, acknowledged to be the world's best goaltender. Dom had won the Vezina and Jennings trophies in the NHL, had been honored as the league's most valuable player, and had led the Czech team to the gold medal in the 1998 Olympics. The Stars had offensive "stars" in Mike Modano, Joe Nieuwyndyk, and Brett Hull. The Sabres had young, skilled players in Miroslav Satan, Curtis Brown, and a fine two-way center named Mike Peca; effective defensemen like Alexei Zhitnik, but no forwards of the quality and reputation on the Dallas roster.

Each team won a game in the other team's building; Dallas defeated Buffalo in the fifth game on Dallas home ice, and the climactic struggle was staged in the Sabres' Marine Midland Arena in Game 6. It was a tough, physical contest; neither team could break through, and Ed Belfour of the Stars met the Dominator's challenge save for save. At the end of regulation play—three periods of intense struggle—the game went into overtime. In NHL playoffs there is no limit to the sudden-death overtime, and nearly three hours later, in the wee hours of the morning, the score was still tied, when, in a scramble in front of the net, Sabres defenseman Jay McKee fell,

Dominik Hasek as goaltender with Brett Hull in the crease.
Copyright © Bill Wippert.

and sharpshooter Brett Hull fired the puck past Hasek into the net. Hull's foot was planted firmly, clearly, and indubitably in the crease.

As the league rules and procedures then stood, what should have happened, and what Sabres coach Lindy Ruff expected to happen, was this: The Sabres would request review; the referee would call upstairs to the video judge; that judge, applying the normal "man in the crease" prohibition, would disallow the goal; and play would continue. Accounts of league, Sabres, and building officials differ, but what actually took place was quite different from normal expectations. Literally hundreds of goals had been disallowed (including one by the Sabres earlier in the playoffs) because a man on the offensive team was in the crease, even if his position did not interfere with the goaltender; and the basic rule—72 (b)—made no distinction between the shooter and any of his teammates.

Rule 72: Protection of Goalkeeper

Unless the puck is in the goal crease area, a player of the attacking side may not stand in the goal crease. If the puck should enter the net while such conditions prevail the goal shall not be allowed. . . .

In the tense and flamboyant atmosphere of the Stanley Cup Finals, at 2:00 AM, with nineteen-thousand screaming fans (no one had left the rink) ready to pounce, it was no time for fine distinctions or objective delibera-

Pandemonium on the Sabres' ice. Copyright © Bill Wippert.

tions. Within thirty seconds the Zamboni gate was opened, the ice was flooded with press, media, players, hangers-on, league officials, hysterical fans—if the replay judge ever uttered a judgment, no one heard it, and the attempt by Ruff to get a reversal of the referee's call was rebuffed.

It is unclear whether procedures were followed. Did the referee ask for review? Was Ruff prevented from seeking it? Did Bettman turn his back on the coach? Did the gatekeeper open the Zamboni entrance prematurely? Did a league official order him to do so?

The confusion was such that I was unaware of the dispute until just as I was about to enter the Stars dressing room. As was our custom, I had gone down to congratulate the victors, and I particularly wanted to see Jim Lites, the Stars president, and Bob Gainey, the team's general manager—friends from my days as league secretary. There was a TV monitor in the area, and I was confronted with Brian Lewis, the NHL chief referee, attempting to justify the failure to disallow the goal, parrying hostile question after hostile question from the media with reference to an obscure interpretation of a memo circulated to the GMs in March 1999 to the effect that the prohibition of the man in the crease did not apply if the shooter "had control of the puck." It did not take an experienced trial lawyer to tell that poor Lewis was straining to defend the event. He sounded neither confident nor secure, and I immediately recalled the incident after Game 1 when the NHL brass looked and sounded so grim over Buffalo's temporary victory.

But I knew from thirty years' experience that appeal was futile; the game was over, Dallas had won, and that was history. I went through the dressing room door to shake the hands of my friends Jim Lites and Bob Gainey, the victors. Did they seem slightly abashed, or was it my imagination?

At the meeting of the Board of Governors on the Monday following the game, Gary Bettman made no comment on the matter—except to note that the staff was working on changes in the rule that would "clear up the misunderstanding." But there was, until the meeting actually began, a stream of commiseration showered on me from the other club representatives. The Dallas ruling was certainly contrary to the general understanding of the NHL cadre and the Hot Stove League. However, Coley Campbell, in charge of the referees, and then Jim Gregory, in charge of hockey operations, each came up to me with a pitch for the party line: Brett Hull was in "control of the puck," so he was properly in the crease. Suppose the player deked the goaltender, they argued, and in the course of the deke entered the crease—such a goal would certainly be allowed.

I prefer to remember the judgment on the scene of the tainted game of Pat Quinn, Toronto coach and veteran of Vancouver and Los Angeles years. Coming down the stairs at the hotel, he said to me, "You got screwed, Bob."

AND ON GOES THE BATTLE OFF THE ICE

At the time of the Stanley Cup Finals in Dallas, the Funding and Purchase Agreement (FPA) called for John Rigas to be named interim chairman of the Sabres; John, in turn, named his son Tim—who was chief financial officer of Adelphia—CEO of the Sabres, and placed the Adelphia ownership in charge of all "operating matters." Nonoperating matters—major transactions like naming rights, sale of the farm team, building loans, and trades involving salaries of more than a million dollars—were subject to the control and veto of the management oversight committee, consisting of two from Adelphia—John and Tim Rigas—and two from our group—Bob Rich and Norty Knox Jr. The board of the Sabres general partner, on which we held a majority, was not modified in any way. Bob continued as vice chairman, and I continued to hold my multiple positions—voting trustee, vice chairman, general counsel, and so on. And the ownership profile was—with no closing ever having taken place—unchanged: Adelphia and the Rigases held only 34 percent (their options to convert the notes to units had never been exercised), we had legal control, and the longer the delay, the more realistic was the possibility we'd take back operating control—with its financial headache. The Knoxes still had the largest segment of ownership paper and voting rights; the Rigas parties had invested the most money since 1994, and with PIKS, options, and conversion rights could approach more than 50 percent of the equity; but the voting trustees—Seymour Knox IV and I could outvote John Rigas—controlled the general partner, which, except for FPA agreement, controlled and ran the partnership. The Rigases could still not reach the magic 67 percent needed to throw us out and obtain permanent control unless they consummated the purchase agreement.

So who owned the Sabres? The philosophy of the FPA was that we couldn't get the Rigas family to buy us out when they thought they'd ultimately get control without paying for it, so we'd give them operating control now, on condition they agree to buy us out. The Rigases didn't respond, except slowly and reluctantly, to the promises of payment—but they eagerly swallowed the powers and perks of franchise ownership. John was not content with being "interim chairman," and Tim and his associates were not content with limiting themselves to "operating" matters. Their highly efficient public relations people, supported by the Empire Sports Network—of which Sabres games and shows were the backbone of their programming—soon began to title John as chairman, and Sabres game programs repeated photographs of John and Tim describing them as if they were the "owners of the Sabres"—as if the deal had been consummated.

The Rigases also began negotiations with the banks and the public sector as if they were in charge of everything and owned every partnership unit. Board meetings and partnership meetings—unknown to or disregard by the press—continued to reflect the real legal situation. Ever hopeful of the deal coming to fruition, our protests were kept private, and we insisted on being consulted on major transactions and trades. As for the National Hockey League, Seymour and I continued to be present at governors' meetings. John was never elected governor—that would have required board action—and I, as technically the first alternate governor, continued to represent the club in those meetings. John sought and listened to my advice; we had a good relationship and, except where issues involving the deal were presented, I tried to act and advise in the interests of the Sabres franchise and owners as a whole. Tim was also named alternate governor and began to come to the meetings and, to some extent, tried to bypass me on league matters. He never articulated any protest at my continued representation but sort of disowned me at league meetings by sitting on the opposite side of the conference room with Darcy Regier, while John and I had adjoining chairs and shared a microphone.

So who owned the Sabres? The issue was comically posed on the second day of the Dallas series. Jean Knox, Seymour IV, and I decided, in accordance with honored custom of our ownership, to go to the team's practice. As we reached the tunnel entrance for Reunion Arena, we were confronted by a female guard, dressed military police style, who demanded our credentials. "They are the owners of the Sabres," said our limo driver.

Responded the lady, "Oh no they're not. I know the owner of the Sabres—and it's not these people!" She refused to admit us. With one coordinated move, Jean, Seymour, and I leaped from the car in anger. "I'm the founder's wife!" said Jean. "I'm vice president," said Seymour IV. "I'm vice chairman of the board," intoned I.

Our protests did not move the steadfast guard, but she did call for her supervisor, in the face of our coordinated attack. "Look," I told the supervisor, in quieter, if not kinder, tones, "there are seventy-six owners of the Sabres."

The strength of numbers, if not the quality of the protest, prevailed. We were finally admitted to Reunion Arena.

THE VOTING TRUST—THEORETICAL POWER

The question posed by the guard at the entrance to Reunion Arena—Who owned the Sabres?—required a complex answer. Perhaps we deserve a brief detour, a flashback, to explain. The question could also be modified: Who *controlled* the Sabres?

The operations of the Sabres were, under the partnership agreement, vested in the Niagara Frontier Hockey Management Corporation, the general partner. There were initially three stockholders in NFHMC—Seymour,

Norty, and me. All the stock was placed in a voting trust; at the start, the three stockholders were the three trustees. While Norty had a major position with the bank, he stepped out of the voting trustee role, retaining the right to reassume the post at any time; but, although he took over the chairmanship for some time after Seymour's death, Norty never reassumed the voting trustee position. On Seymour's death in 1996, his son, Seymour H. Knox IV, took his place, and when Adelphia made its initial investment of $15 million in 1994, the voting trust had been revised to make John Rigas the third trustee. So at the time of the Stanley Cup Finals in June of 1999, the trustee lineup was Seymour IV, John Rigas, and me.

Under the Voting Trust Agreement and the Partnership Agreement, a majority of the trustees had the power to manage and to elect the board of directors of the general partner. The trustees' powers were not absolute, however—decisions as to sale of the franchise, for example, required a vote of two-thirds of the limited partner units. Moreover, beginning with the Memorandum of Agreement of December 31, 1997, power over operations were granted—temporarily, pending sale—to John Rigas as interim chairman. (For more on this, see chapter 35.)

As the issues of management, ownership, and sale became so very difficult to solve, John Rigas looked at the voting trust. "Bob," he said, "you have the power. You're the 'swing vote' as the third trustee. Why don't you exercise your powers and bring about what you feel is the right thing to do?"

Was I tempted, even for a moment? I don't think so. I responded, "I can't, John. I'm a fiduciary!" In my conception of my office as voting trustee, I was the fiduciary assigned to resolve disputes between Seymour and Norty (and, now, their estates) and I was the fiduciary assigned to represent the interests of all of the seventy-seven limited partners.

THE NO-DEAL DEAL

While the battle on the ice flourished, that fortnight in June 1999, with Dominik holding off the continued assault by a tough and talented Dallas team, the fight to get the Rigases to make good on their promises to buy the Knox-Buffalo interest in the Sabres was getting nowhere. After months of unpleasant negotiations (Jim Brown's words echoed in my memory: "Nobody wants to do the deal, Bob")—with me benched by Norty because I was "too tough" or "too friendly with John Rigas" (the crosscheck varied from day to day)—the parties finally produced a monstrosity of an agreement. It reached conception on New Year's Eve, December 31, 1997, after months of foreplay, in the form of a letter of intent (called a Memorandum of Understanding, or MOU). Typically, my benching was only temporary—until a crisis occurred—and then it fell upon me to solve it. What was produced by the negotiating team nearly fell apart and nearly destroyed our plans to celebrate or commiserate that evening; but I was able to patch up the document in part and defray the cyclical anger of the purchaser principals—and, as always necessary, sign the document. I was prepared to play the role of the rejected Moses, who never sees the promised land, but instead had to assume the part of the ancient quarterback thrust into the game to save the coach's derriere.

Here it was, nearly eighteen months after the MOU was signed, and no closing. The agreement, negotiated with very little bargaining power in our corner, had at least three major defects: first, it had no cutoff or "drop-dead date"; second, it gave the sellers notes—for two-thirds of the purchase price—that might never pay off; and third, it made the deal conditional on the consent of the banks and the league, but told the buyers they didn't have to make any financial commitment, or "assume any burden," to get those consents. It was clear that a faction in Adelphia's cadre in Coudersport, Pennsylvania, focusing primarily on Adelphia's rapidly expanding cable TV empire, didn't want to do the deal at all. To that faction, hockey, with its slowly growing revenue, its high cost of operation in the new arena, and its punishing escalation of player salaries, was a "black hole." Adelphia, always cash hungry because of its constantly increasing debt, had little use for an operation that produced no cash, but instead created a cash drain the Rigases would describe as much as $10 million a season.

This faction did not change its position—"no deal"—much. The real defect in the New Year's Eve deal is that it gave the faction the ability to say, "All right, John Rigas and colleagues, who are so infatuated with owning a sports franchise—we'll change the 'no deal' to no deal unless we drastically reduce the losses and cut the purchase and financing costs." That meant no deal unless everybody on the seller side took a "haircut." The banks would have to wipe out part of their loans on the building; the league would have to accept a lower guarantee of working capital, or none at all; and the public sector—the state, county, and city—would have to improve the lease, take on some of the building expense, and give the Sabres a deal more like that granted the Buffalo Bills, in which, it is said, the county gave the Bills the store.

Now none of these conditions, mind you, can be found anywhere in the New Year's Eve agreement or in its formal successor, the Funding and Purchase Agreement of March 20, 1998. But these were Adelphia's and the Rigases' true conditions, their real intentions, as I began to understand them between face-offs in Dallas, pondering the long, frustrating series of episodes, of nonclosings, with meetings missed, drafts delayed, and deadlines ignored. Members of the group had become angrier and angrier, and I was forced to resort to painful analogies in my attempts to pacify the irate partners. "Will you, won't you join the dance?" "You can lead a horse to water . . ." "It's like trying to wrestle a three-legged alligator." "Just as we're bringing the ship into port, an ill wind blows us out to sea!"

So the "no-deal deal," despite our march to the Finals, hung on—unresolved.

THE STEINBRENNER DREAM

It was in Dallas in 1999 that my concept of independence and fiduciary responsibility as the "third," or "swing," voting trustee began to encounter some tough crosschecks. Our ownership group had managed to survive the disputes over the failure to close the Rigases' New Year's Eve agreement without disintegration, so far. But it was at a pleasant Mexican lunch near Reunion Arena that I realized for the first time how far my friend and supporter Jean Knox had wandered from the view, endorsed for more than twenty-five years by her husband, that I was not just a Knox lawyer, I did—and had to—represent all of the members of the board, and, in a sense, all seventy-seven partners.

Almost from the start of the franchise, I had had a recurring dream—or nightmare—that George Steinbrenner, now the principal owner of the New York Yankees, accepted our offer to become a 25 percent partner in the Sabres. (We had made the offer in recognition of his participation in our 1968 effort to acquire a Major League Baseball franchise for Buffalo). We needed a third trustee, and I sensed that the aggressive and knowledgeable Steinbrenner would not have been content with a nonvoting position. But George had declined the Sabres investment, and principal investors like George Strawbridge (Philadelphia son-in-law of our close associate, Dave Forman) and Bob Rich Jr. had other pursuits; my clients Paul and Fred Schoellkopf, who had made major contributions in the baseball and TV projects, chose to take minor roles in the Sabres. So I was picked as the third trustee.

I had the confidence of Seymour and Norty and of Paul and Fred, but I never knew precisely why I was chosen. I suspect the rule that movement is more important than logic came into play. I had worked side by side with Norty and Seymour with the achievement of the franchise; helped Seymour in the solicitation of the investors, some of whom were my clients—and, after all, I still had my reputation as the greatest living expert on how *not* to get a major-league sports franchise!

Whatever the reasons for my appointment, I adopted my own rationales and operating principles:

1. I was going to try to act in the interest of all the investors.
2. Since I had been given business responsibilities, I was not going to be just a "one-armed" lawyer ("on the one hand . . .").

3. If Seymour and Norty disagreed on a major issue, I was going to have to settle it. (And Paul Schoellkopf warned me, they had been known to battle ferociously at times in disagreement.)

So long as things went well—and they did go well for many years—the other principals suppressed any resentment at the voting trust, and let the Knoxes (and me, in a lesser role) run the franchise. When the Sabres converted to a partnership in 1988, the concept of management centralized in the three of us was carried over into the voting trust of the stock in the general partner. Its presence gave me a legal and practical strength that helped in the difficult years after Seymour's death—years that seemed to darken that day in Dallas.

It was June 18, 1999. My report to the "Non-Adelphia Members of the Closing Committee," in my primitive computer capital letters, began:

RE: BOB'S BAD DAY IN BIG "D"

The commissioner had begun to show his predicted "tilt" against us, and toward the "money" (i.e., Adelphia): the Rigases would get that tilt as long as they were doing the financing; we had put too much of our resources into the new building; the Rigases' attempts to lower debt and increase cash flow were reasonable; we should have gotten the public sector to pay for the building itself; our monitoring rights under the New Year's Eve agreement were minimal; and the Rigases had driven the value of the franchise down so low, other buyers might be interested. I made it clear, in a calm way, that Gary Bettman's "tilt" was off the track and that he and our partners in the league would have to remember, and my friends around the table *would* remember, that we were their partners and the Rigases were the applicants. We would have to become aggressive, in some way.

The quesidilla at the Mexican restaurant, normally a favorite, was quite unappetizing, especially after Jean dropped the gloves. She rapidly began an assault of her own: her interests were not being protected; she wanted to explore everything that happened since her husband died. As to the deal, she was not interested in it at the present price—to which we had all signed an agreement—the value had gone up (compare Gerry Bettman's judgment!), and we should find another buyer. Besides, it turned out, continually frazzled by the continuing dispute with Norty and then Norty's executors over Ess Kay Farms (the Knox estate), she was hiring her own lawyer.

Thus, up in smoke went my vision of myself as trustee for everybody, solving everybody's problems.

Chapter 34

"NO GOAL II"

In the second game of their 2000 first-round playoff series, Buffalo at Philadelphia, on April 14, 2000, the Flyers' John LeClair apparently scored a goal, and the Flyers went on to win that crucial game 2 to 1. Sabres goalkeeper Dominik Hasek had no idea how the puck got past him, and within two minutes after the referee's call the Sabres' GM, Darcy Regier, received a message from one of our scouts that the ESPN telecast showed clearly that the puck had not crossed the goal line—it had entered through the side of the net, and thus was "no goal."

A frantic, apoplectic Regier broke into the supervising referee's booth, and his anger produced an immediate inspection by the on-ice officials, who found the culprit: a hole in the side of the net. But, despite the bitter memory of the illegal overtime goal by Brett Hull that gave the 1999 Stanley Cup to Dallas, the officials would not cancel the LeClair goal. Once play had resumed after the goal, the referee ruled, the Sabres' protest was too late. It was the worst hosing I had ever experienced, and in a conference after the game with Lindy Ruff, Darcy, and John Rigas, I urged an immediate appeal to Commissioner Gary Bettman. It had always been my view over the years—in law as well as in hockey—that when you've been hurt badly, but unfairly, by a judge, an arbitrator, or a referee—*you let them know it*—you appeal, even if your chances are negligible.

You may lose the appeal, but you may be treated differently the next time around. The Buffalo-Philadelphia series wasn't over, even with the tainted loss. There was some concern, I pointed out, about a possible negative reaction and fine from Bettman—he didn't like public criticism of league officials, and we had ownership fish to fry with him. John asked me to draft the protest, to see what it would look like before the decision was made.

This is my draft:

CONFIDENTIAL DRAFT

Saturday, April 15, 2000

Hon. Gary B. Bettman
Commissioner, National Hockey League
Re Game 2, Philadelphia at Buffalo, 4/14/00

PROTEST AND PETITION FOR HEARING

Dear Commissioner:

As acknowledged by the series supervisor in the press conference last night, on review the evidence showed clearly that the shot by Philadelphia player LeClair at 04:53 of the second period of last night's game never crossed the goal line, entered the net through a hole in the mesh at the side, and thus was no goal at all. As a result, the power play goal by Desjardins at 04:53 of the third period did not produce a "win" at all; at most a tie, and the game should have continued into overtime. This horrendous error in a game of great importance must be corrected.

In the interests of the Buffalo Sabres players, fans, organization, and of the League itself, the Buffalo Sabres hereby PROTEST the award of a win to the Philadelphia Flyers in last night's game and request that the Commissioner—recognizing that the outcome was produced by a clearly illegal goal—order a replay of Game 2 from the point at which the LeClair shot took place, with the score Sabres 1, Flyers 0; or at the point where Desjardins scored his goal, with the score Sabres 1, Flyers 1; or at the end of regulation, with the teams tied and playing into overtime.

Such a replay, or continuation of Game 2, could take place before or after Game 3 or 4 in Buffalo, or if the Sabres win either game, before or after the next game in Philadelphia.

In the alternative, we ask that a hearing be held forthwith, to investigate the matter and determine whether such a replay should be ordered.

The essential facts are not in dispute. Supervisor D'Amico at his press conference following the game confirmed that (1) reexamination of the NHL tapes and review of the ESPN film showed unequivocally that the puck on LeClair's shot never crossed the goal line, but entered the goal area through a hole in the mesh on the side of the net; (2) that if this had been known at the time of the event the goal would have been disallowed; (3) with the Sabres leading at the time 1 to 0, and the final "score" 2 to 1, the error clearly damaged the game and unfairly affected the outcome. While the error was discovered by League officials and the Sabres general manager within five minutes of the event—ample time for a correction, with nearly a full two periods left to play—the League officials refused to accept the Sabres protest, reverse the initial judgment, and disallow the goal.

The rebuffs by the officials were doubtless made in good faith, in reliance on the "rule" that corrections cannot be made once the puck is dropped for the next face-off. But this is merely a League practice, designed to discourage pro forma or dilatory complaints. There is no such "rule." We believe there have been a number of instances in recent years when similar judgments have been reversed, some minutes after the puck was dropped. In an important close playoff game between contending teams, we believe the "rule" should be—and is—patience, care, and prudence.

This is the second time within a year the Sabres have been damaged by a controversial goal. This time, however, it was not a question of judgment. The "goal last night" was unequivocally and absolutely *never scored*. It is important not only for the Sabres but for maintenance of confidence in League processes that this injustice be repaired immediately.

The Commissioner has broad powers, and could and should order a replay or continuation of Game 2, "in the interests of justice." At the very least the Commissioner should order an immediate hearing to investigate the matter and determine whether such a continuation or reply should be ordered.

Such a hearing could provide answers to questions like the following, which have erupted and should be answered with clarity and candor:

(1) Did the puck ever cross the goal line? (Clearly no, but public acknowledgment would be helpful)
(2) Did the tapes available to the replay officials show that the puck did not make the required entry across the goal line?
(3) Did the required review by off-ice officials take place before the "goal" was announced and the face-off commenced?
(4) Was the puck dropped prematurely, so that an adequate review did not or could not take place?
(5) Was the replay equipment available to the replay officials properly positioned or angled and otherwise adequate to enable them to see the error and correct it? Should the ESPN or other television replays be available to the officials?
(6) Even though the puck had already been dropped, are League officials *prohibited* from correcting a manifest, egregious error in allowing the goal—within five minutes of the event?

We emphasize that we are not criticizing the League or any individual. The judgments to allow the goal and to refuse to correct the error, though deplorable and harmful, were made sincerely by experienced men of integrity. But "a goal is a very serious matter," one of them said, and the error, inadvertent or not, must be explained and corrected.

Respectfully submitted,

John J. Rigas
Interim Chairman and Alternate Governor
Buffalo Sabres

John never issued the protest and we lost the series. With our group's need to keep the support of the commissioner in the ongoing struggle to close our sale to the Rigas family, it was probably just as well that the protest never reached Gary Bettman—or the press.

Chapter 35

OVERTIME

The Saga of the Sale of the Sabres

THE SHORT, UNHAPPY LIFE OF CHANNEL 49

With the ouster of my friend and supporter, John Ziegler as the president of the NHL in 1992 and the sudden departure of Gil Stein as his successor, the Board of Governors turned in 1993 to Gary Bettman, former general counsel of the NBA, as its new commissioner. I had first met Gary several years earlier, when he was still with the basketball league, and the NBA was considering expansion grants to two Canadian cities, Toronto and Vancouver. Gary had asked for a memo analyzing the special problems of operating north of the border, and I had plenty of material. I pointed to such factors as the rate of exchange; the Canadian insistence that a player was entitled to enter the draft, with full rights, at age eighteen; the peculiarities of the Canadian Combines (monopoly) Act; the view by some that the border formed a "wall" behind which Canadian clubs could ignore US laws and subpoenas; problems of xenophobia; the differences in the pension laws; and the problem of integrating social security credits under the two economies when a player played in one country and performed mostly in another. I concluded that these were interesting issues, but most were solvable or could be lived with, and nothing that should discourage expansion to our neighbor to the north. Gary had seemed to appreciate the analysis, so I did not come cold to his orbit when he assumed leadership of our league.

357

When John Ziegler heard of Gary's election his comment to me was, "Gary's a straight shooter. You'll have no trouble with him." Over the years from 1993 until the sale of the Sabres in 2000, I had a good relationship, somewhat closer than arm's length, with Gary and the excellent staff he brought in—David Zimmerman (a Proskauer lawyer retained by Stein) continued as corporate counsel, and first Jeff Pash of Covington & Burling, then Bill Daly of Skadden Arps, served as general counsel. All were encouraged to consult me on significant matters. But Gary was a full-control executive, a CEO-like commissioner; the owner committees that had handled so much of the league planning and franchise transactions under John Ziegler—and had employed me as their lawyer—were abandoned or deprived of their power, and league legal issues were either kept in-house or referred to excellent outside counsel, mostly through Gary's former firm, Proskauer. Some assignments went to my old friends at Covington & Burling, some to the nationally prominent firm Skadden Arps.

I could not object to Gary's choices—I had employed each of them from time to time for my firm's other clients. The Proskauer firm relationship went back to my uncle/partner, Paul Cohen, who had been Judge Joseph Proskauer's son-in-law. Covington was our outside resource in the Transcontinent Television years and as NHL counsel in the WHA and players' association battles, and I had used Skadden Arps to assist me in a number of cases of tender offer defense. So I shifted gears as rapidly as I could. I had to educate the new commissioner and the new staff on the special Sabres problems—including the Canadian territorial and Rochester TV issues—and I was especially pleased when Gary asked me to run my position papers by Michael Cardozo of the Proskauer firm, whom I'd admired for a long time for his successful forays into NBA antitrust and labor issues. But I was no longer secretary and I was no longer league special counsel. It meant a loss of income for me, but I was free to engage myself fully in Sabres matters. That was perhaps fortunate for the Sabres, because their problems were mounting.

IN AND OUT OF CHANNEL 49

Norty Knox, as the watchdog of the Sabres "treasury," had foreseen as early as 1987 that the combination of the inflation in player salaries and the disappearance of automatic sellouts required a radical infusion of income—and of more capital as well. The first attempt to bolster revenue was the purchase of a new UHF television station for the Buffalo area, Channel 49. The idea was triggered when we found that the local VHF stations—2, 4, and 7—were lowballing their offers for the right to broadcast Sabres games. We were used to a full schedule of over-the-air telecasts of away Sabres games, supplemented by cable deliveries of the home schedule. But the growth of the cable program had somewhat turned off the VHF stations. Channel 4, the CBS outlet, had never had much interest in hockey—it promoted the NFL Bills—Channel 7 (ABC), our original station, and Channel 2 (NBC), our rights holder in the 1980s, were interested, but at less than half the current fee. There were suggestions by Peter Gilbert, then the dominant cable owner in the area, that we either make cable our exclusive telecaster or join him in a purchase or investment in UHF Channel 29, a moderately successful, nonnetwork operation. The Knoxes were not enthusiastic about partnership with either Peter or the Channel 29 ownership, and I had serious concerns about reaching our Canadians fans: the US cable company couldn't get into Canada; the Ontario cable systems would be loaded up with Toronto Maple Leafs and Montreal Canadiens games; and the Channel 29 signal had minimal viewership across the border.

The founder's son, Seymour Knox IV, and I went up to Toronto to explore the possibilities of pay-per-view telecasts by a fledgling network created there. The network representatives were enthusiastic, but their footprint was rather small, as was the number of Sabres games they would consider incorporating into their programs. I called the league for help and got very little, despite my position as a league officer. Steve Solomon, a refugee from NBC in charge of NHL broadcast matters, seemed to have an anti-Buffalo complex. Despite our high ratings in the network and local broadcasts, Steve seemed to regard Buffalo as an embarrassment. We impinged the southern Ontario market, and our presence made league negotiations with the Canadian networks and clubs more sensitive, if not more difficult. I tried several times to have Buffalo, along with Detroit (as the other "border club"), included in the league's plans for a Canadian cable or satellite network—without success.

In the familiar Sabres "crisis" atmosphere, the solution, we thought, was to buy our own TV station: Channel 49. After all, our group had ten years of television experience, and the idea of a Sabres-owned station could attract capital. The Channel 49 construction permit had just been authorized by the FCC, and the Act III executive, a good technician—but a better salesman—sold us on the acquisition. The new business made for exciting days for the organization—we were not just sportsmen, we were broadcasters! At the board meeting in the Sabres Directors' Room to approve the station purchase, the debate was intense and high pressure. I had called Cliff Kirtland, former financial vice president of Transcontinent Television who had taken the same post with Cox Broadcasting, a chain over-the-air and cable company, to get his views. I reported Cliff's comment: "Hockey games can only cover six to nine hours of the broadcast week. What are you going to do for the other seventy-five?" It should have been a sobering brake, but the gambling spirit was aroused, and with the urgent need for increased revenue, the references to Ed Snider in Philadelphia and John Pickett in Long Island had the greatest weight. Both had leveraged their hockey success into ownership of the broadcast and cable entities who rode that success. Even the ever-so-prudent Norty was mesmerized by the hope that here, at last, was a growth investment that would fuel the voracious hockey franchise.

It *was* a good idea. But then occurred the kind of mixed-motive, soft-hearted decision that sometimes afflicted the club over the years. Obviously, we needed an experienced broadcast executive. We had the choice of several, but the need for a careful "chancellor of the exchequer" was very important. While we had raised $3.2 million in new capital from our existing investors, there was not much more readily available, and we could not afford or manage extravagant expenditures. So instead of hiring the broadcast executive first, we went to the money/budget man. The Knoxes' choice was Paul Mooney, well thought of by Sportservice and onetime president of the Boston Bruins. Paul was a friend of ours and had the reputation of a tough controller. But his experience with broadcasting had been limited to selling the Bruins' rights. I liked Paul, as did Seymour and Norty, but he was not the right choice for a business where promotion is all and where advertising competition is brutal. I acquiesced, and I blame myself for not fighting harder for a young broadcaster with creative energy.

The problem was compounded when Paul, operating under the "CEO is king" syndrome that brooked no interference, did not hire an experienced broadcaster as executive, but retained the part-time advisory services of the elderly former head of Channel 38 in Boston—the Bruins' rights holder. But the Channel 38 veteran, a nice guy, had never had to face the price and advertising competition, had never endured the pain and frustration of creating a new broadcast entity from scratch. The Sabres telecasts on our Channel 49, WNYB-TV, were successful in the US market, but the non-hockey programming, advertising, and ratings were slow in coming on stream, and, instead of cash support, the station produced a heavy drain on the Sabres' revenue.

The most important disappointment was the failure to get the Ontario cable systems to carry the Sabres games. We were aware of a rule issued by the Canadian regulatory commission limiting entry of US broadcasters into the Canadian cable programming to stations that were on the air in 1985, but our confidence—*over*confidence—in our Canadian relationships led us to believe we could get an exception to the freeze. After all, our players were more than 70 percent Canadian, we had an important Canadian investor (Ontario Paper Company of St. Catharines, Ontario), 30 percent of our fans were Canadian, our territory reached fifty miles into Canada, and we were the only NHL club that played the Canadian national anthem along with the "Star Spangled Banner" before every home game! The owners of the cable systems operating in our Canadian territory (St. Catharines, Welland, Niagara Falls, and parts of Hamilton) assured us they wanted and would carry the Sabres games, but the regulators in Montreal would not budge. Our neighbors to the north might speak positively of free trade, but when it came to books, magazines, television, and cable, protectionism was rampant.

We joined forces for a time with Act III Broadcasting Company, a new multiple-station company specializing in UHF channels. The top executive was a young, aggressive operator whom we liked very much. He was a fine tennis player, usually my tennis partner at the summer Sabres outings, and he carried me to several modest doubles "championships." But even his organization couldn't open the Canadian cable doors. So our Channel 49 had little penetration—our fans across the border didn't take kindly to conversion boxes for UHF, and without the boxes the high-frequency channel didn't produce picture quality at that distance, anyway.

For a brief time, things were nevertheless upbeat. One of the principal investors in the UHF chain broadcasting company was Norman Lear, the creator of the TV show *All in the Family*. Lear knew my daughter, Liz, admired her work, and made friendly noises. I thought, Aha! Here is the deep pocket we need! But then it turned out Lear was having financial problems himself; he was in no position to fund the Sabres' station losses.

The Channel 49 deficits were not appealing to either our new or our old partners. Financial staying power was needed, and we didn't have it— or those who had it were unwilling to take the gamble. When the chance came to sell the station to a religious group, I was ordered to grab it. We did manage to bail the Sabres out at no additional cost, but the hockey partners who invested $3.2 million in new convertible debentures to handle the station had to leave their money in the hockey club. It was a major disappointment, but the search for new operating capital and additional income had to go on.

In 1988, when we bought the station, we switched the Sabres entity to a partnership, so that the investors who put new money into the venture could offset other income with their shares of the losses, subject to some rather complex tax rules. The franchise structure remained substantially the same. We had a corporate general partner with power to manage and operate—Niagara Frontier Hockey Management Corporation (NFHMC)— and the other investors received "limited partner" interests in Niagara Frontier Hockey, L.P. (NFHLP), with liability limited to investment and, as required by the state partnership law and IRS regulations, no vote on or participation in operating matters. To meet the concentration of power required by the league, the voting trust continued. Norty, Seymour, and I owned all the stock in the general partner, and the three of us were the voting trustees who elected the board of directors. I persuaded my fellow voting trustees that the selection of board members should be absolutely objective; the directors would be selected in the order of their aggregate investment in the Sabres, including the recent debentures purchased to fund the Channel 49 transaction. The directors with the largest investments would be members of the "management board." That turned out to be, in addition to the voting trustees, George Strawbridge, Bob Rich (representing Rich Products), and Joe Stewart. The remaining directors were assigned to the "partnership board," whose functions were advisory only, but whose members over the years proved to be among our most loyal and effective supporters.

At no time did the Knoxes own more than 25 percent of the franchise, but the voting trust and general partner structure maintained their legal and practical control. When Norty had to resign as director because of possible conflicts with his position as chairman of our principal lender— Marine Midland Bank (later HSBC)—a special provision gave him the power to step back in at any time. Seymour continued as chairman of the board, with Bob Rich as vice chairman and me as vice chairman and counsel. The lot of us could be thrown out, however, by a vote of 67 percent of the limited partnership interests to remove the general partner. As I describe the events later on, that provision proved a headache as the search for new capital continued.

Meanwhile, as described in chapter 29, the league tried, but accomplished little, to relieve the red ink generated by escalating player salaries. It began to be clear that the Knox families would contribute, but they either could not or would not lead the way with major new investments. At the same time, the notion began to circulate around the league that the solution was in a new eighteen- to twenty-thousand-seat hockey building, to be owned by the hockey club, with all the revenue goodies flowing to the hockey club as well—luxury suites, concessions, in-house advertising, food courts, novelty, clothing and equipment store, parking, and so on. If we had to go to outside investors, the financial projections had to be carefully prepared. Two major problems immediately surfaced. First, Bob Pickel, our financial vice president, came to me, complaining that the "figures don't work out." Second, Sam Katz, a Philadelphia expert employed on the Flyers' building plan, gave a very discouraging report: "You'd be better off," he said, "trying to improve the present Aud. It'll require a tremendous financial and political effort, and what you get won't really be worth it."

My analysis indicated that the vice was in the salary projections. Based on budgets prepared by GM Gerry Meehan and his hockey department, the recent average salary increases, if continued, would push the player bill beyond 70 percent of revenue. I proposed to cut the salary costs back to 60 percent. The cap in the other major sports was around 53 percent at that time. Meehan objected—it would force unwise hockey decisions, he said, and we'd negotiated no salary cap with the players' association. I responded that if we couldn't get a CBA with a cap, we'd have to impose it on ourselves. Pickel agreed, and the projections were revised accordingly.

Katz's comments were more serious, but their validity really turned on how well we could negotiate with the public sector. If we could receive *grants*, instead of loans, the debt service burden would be much less. If we could hand off some of the operating costs, perhaps even the Katz figures could be accepted. My gastric juices really took a beating when I learned that the financial plan called for a pledge of concessions—operating income—to provide part of the construction cost of the new arena. In the franchise projections, concessions were an important part of the revenue— perhaps 10 to 15 percent. My brief discussions with possible investors in the franchise made this an absolute no-no. "Your concessions," this potential bidder said, "are the profile of your growth." He flatly refused to consider an investment if the concessions were pledged.

I insisted on further analysis. I hired Dave Andrews, then controller of the Hartford Whalers, to go over the data to see if the pledge of concessions made sense. His report, perhaps intimidated by its importance, marginally approved the pledge. I protested to Seymour and Norty that we were scraping away too much of the club's revenue to finance the arena: "What are we building here," I asked, "a business or a monument?"

At that moment (late 1993 and early 1994), we were too early in the arena project to foresee all of its complex, tension-filled issues. The immediate need was to cover the current cash losses and to provide a financial bridge into the day when we'd have a spanking-new house to cure our ills. We had to survive until that day. There was then no focus on the sale of the club itself; we sought *investors*. In fact, since the $130 million financing of the new building would depend in large part on the goodwill and trust of the local politicos, any suggestion of new ownership—especially out-of-town ownership—was verboten. The internal sources of capital, I saw, were drying up, so we had to go outside our partnership list, but keep our group in control. Keeping the Knox "control" was a key decision; without the presence, prestige, and drive of Seymour and his marvelous ability to attract talent and power to his project team—from banker to architect to mayor to governor—the HSBC Arena would never have been built.

Seymour and I surveyed the local financial landscape. The candidate had to be one with financial stamina, a passion for sports, a cooperative spirit, and a vested, strong economic interest in the vitality of Western New York. There weren't many that would meet those qualifications. Almost all of them were already on our partner list, and we were afraid they'd be tapped out. We did some tentative talking in New York to John Rigas of Adelphia Communications—the company that had succeeded Peter Gilbert as our cable rights buyer—and to our very pleasant surprise, he was interested. He certainly met the test: with over five hundred thousand cable subscribers in the market, most of whom had been induced to sign up for cable to get the Sabres games, Adelphia would be concerned about the success and survival of the team.

THE FIRST $15 MILLION

We needed $15 million to cover the red ink until we opened the new building. I was a little hesitant to give a single new owner so large a piece of the equity—we couldn't just add more debt—but Seymour wanted to go for it. (I think the changes in the family fortunes and the beginnings of illness were forcing the tough decision.) For the first time, he began to talk of a possible sale of the entire franchise. The critical meeting took place in a beautiful spring setting—the Knox estate in suburban East Aurora, Ess Kay Farms—out on the patio, with Jean Knox, the verdure, the grazing horses, the hummingbirds, the handsome dogs, the Canada geese, everything in full bloom. It was a scene that always softened the style of the toughest negotiator. And it turned out—or so it seemed—John was a softy. Adelphia had just lost out on its bid to buy the Pittsburgh Pirates baseball team, and our timing was right on.

The talks progressed. We stressed the star power of Pat LaFontaine, the prospects of league expansion, the income boost that would come from the new building. We seemed to be getting somewhere—John was obviously disappointed in the Pirates episode and was hungry for a professional sports connection, even though we had to be explain offsides, the number of players on the ice, and the meaning of the crease. We did well until we got to the player payroll. Gerry Meehan presented his player budget, projecting the average salary escalation over the last several years, and I, somewhat to Norty's initial displeasure, had to interrupt with my collectively bargained or management-imposed cap. (The previous year's lockout had ended with a commitment—not followed through—to negotiate such a cap.) John caught on immediately, but he indicated for the first time that he was not wholly in charge. "Can't you make those projections better?" he asked.

We went back to the drawing board. My mandated cap and other adjustments produced projections that were acceptable to John and apparently satisfactory to his Adelphia colleagues—on certain conditions. And here, we became more than a little bit pregnant. The key condition was that Adelphia (or the Rigas family) acquire 34 percent of the equity—and 34 percent of the vote. That would keep our group in control of day-to-day operations, Board of Directors, and league relationships, through continuation of the voting trust, but at the cost of a Rigas veto over certain major transactions, such as a sale of assets or a change of the managing partner. Those transactions required a vote of 67 percent of the limited partner units, and with a 34 percent holding, Adelphia could set up a roadblock. I pointed out to Seymour and Norty that this could make a sale of the franchise in the future more difficult. Theoretically, we could sell the controlling interest in the Sabres *partnership units* to a third person, but if the Rigases would not go along with the sale, the buyer would have to be content with Adelphia as a partner.

It was a major decision. At this point, in 1994, the Knoxes were not concerned about the veto or the restrictions on a subsequent sale to an outsider—their concerns were in keeping the franchise in Buffalo, and their expectation was that the Rigas family would purchase the whole thing anyway. Seymour was convinced that John Rigas had given him such a commitment, and continued to resist any moves toward competing purchasers. "John is an honest man," he said. "He'll make good on his promise. Don't irritate him with outsiders." From my point of view, there was really no alternative, in that pressured time. The payroll needed to be paid; the arena project would die if we couldn't demonstrate immediate viability. If we didn't have the cash to make a binding deal with our star forward, Pat LaFontaine, successful marketing of the move from a sixteen-thousand- to a nineteen-thousand-seat arena might be impossible.

In retrospect, if we could have divined what our real intentions were—or would be—perhaps we would have refused the Rigas offer and launched a campaign to find a buyer at a top price, at a time when the accumulated losses had not yet wiped out our equity. But we had created the franchise to be an asset of the Buffalo community, and that idealistic motive was still predominant in 1994. We did not yet regard our investment as at risk—not with *expansion* franchises fetching a $50 million price! And the new building conceivably could solve our problems.

So we accepted John's offer of $15 million for 34 percent, and there began six years of exciting hockey—but, off the ice, continued crisis. It should have been six years of prosperity and ease. It started out pleasantly for me. Apparently delighted at my negotiation of the critical "save," Seymour and Norty nominated me, and on January 1, 1995, I was inducted into the Buffalo Sabres Hall of Fame. The corridors of the new HSBC Arena bear a staged photograph of me—typical of the counsel in the crease—holding not a goalie stick, but a tennis racket.

I am sure that, on my induction, the Knoxes had in mind a peaceful retirement for their counsel. It was not to be. Seymour's illness suddenly began to look serious. We needed a new president, in a hurry: the management of the team, the planning for the new building, the relations with the league, the press, and the Rigases—all demanded a new CEO. I was seventy-six years old—though, I maintained, still vertical and vigorous. With Norty still tied up as Marine Midland Bank's US chairman, the task of reorganization fell to me. I hired a headhunter, the same outfit I'd seen perform well for the NHL in the shift from Ziegler to Stein to Bettman. The in-house candidates were Gerry Meehan and (at my urging) Larry Quinn, who seemed to be doing a superb job in bringing the construction of the new arena in under budget. The headhunter came up with the head of women's tennis, the CEO of the World Wrestling Federation, and two executives of Madison Square Garden. The reorganization committee consisted of George Strawbridge, Bob Rich, Norty, Seymour, and me. Larry Quinn produced a great interview, but Seymour was adamant: "Larry should stay where he is. The building project isn't finished." Of the remaining candidates, the consensus was Doug Moss, then in charge of television at Madison Square Garden. Moss was certainly familiar with professional sports operations, and he assured us he could adjust down from the Rangers' big budgets to our strong need for financial discipline. He made a good first impression, and I went along—with some doubts about whether his experience was broad enough and whether a New York market man really could stay within our budget.

I was not ready to retire, and I was beginning to feel some angst about my own position. Moss didn't help much when he brought in his own lawyer from the Garden—with Knox approval—at a salary nearly double what I had earned and far above the league average. (Norty's comment: "Well, you're not going to live forever, Bob.") But my league, board, and other powers didn't seem to be affected.

THE $9.7 MILLION ARENA SHORTFALL

The insertion of the new house lawyer did not help or affect my evident responsibility to raise the money. With Pat LaFontaine leading the charge up the salary scale and the losses continuing, Adelphia's $15 million didn't last very long. The anxiety was compounded when it was revealed that the financing of the new arena was short—by about $6 million, and then short again, by about $3.7 million. In these episodes, the Knoxes were relatively nonparticipant—both because of Seymour's illness and because, I believe, their private fortunes were under assault with the decline and fall of Woolworth's, the source of a substantial portion of their net worth. The first shortfall was met by Adelphia in a convoluted transaction involving a difficult pledge of the company's interest in the Sabres that called upon all of my experience as a league lawyer. The second shortfall was met by Rich Products and George Strawbridge—a transaction that really caused problems. I was sensitive to the growing position of the Rigases in the ownership picture and the danger of loss of control, and I was counting on George and Bob Rich (who had always come through for me) to lead a fundraising project to maintain the Knox-Buffalo group's control position in the club. Under pressure, Dan DiPofi, the Sabres controller, and Greg Ivancic of my law firm, jumped the gun on this, and the priority lien given to the $3.7 million—George and Bob would get their money out first when the arena financing was completed—produced significant trouble in later negotiations with Adelphia.

Bob Rich Jr., vice chairman of the Sabres
and president of Rich Products, Inc.

THE MAYOR'S VETO AND THE BOOMERANG OVERRIDE

As described in chapter 20, the Knoxes—or the Fates, as the case may be—seemed determined to erode my position at the center of the Sabres legal/economic strategy. As house counsel, Kevin Billet, the refugee from the Rangers, had taken over much of the routine legal matters. Yet Seymour, sounding desperate at the stalling of Mayor Jimmy Griffin, had appealed to me to get the city's $2.5 million in seed money for the arena out of the mayor's hands. Griffin, a baseball fan but no friend of hockey—or of the Establishment—had vetoed the grant by the Common Council. The motion to override failed by one vote when Rosemary LoTempio, on whom we had counted, voted with the mayor's bloc, against the grant.

I received the news in the morning when I returned from a league meeting. Seymour was depressed. "What are we going to do?" he asked. "The whole project will fail if we don't get going now." I told Seymour: "I'm going right to the council chamber from the airport. I'm going to sit in that meeting and stare at LoTempio until she changes her vote. She's going to see in my face the full wrath of the Sabres." LoTempio did change her vote.

Gratitude? Yes. Empowerment? No. Word spread that my action in getting the council to override had angered the mayor; he was threatening to block the project unless he was allowed to be fully involved. I was remembering Griffin's overly modest acceptance speech on his election: "I appreciate your voting for a guy who really doesn't have very much on the ball!!" Despite our baseball affinity—Griffin had always expressed warm approval of my efforts to get a major-league franchise in that sport—and his respect for my Studio Arena work, it was reported to Seymour and Norty that Griffin's anger focused on me. The next thing I knew, Gerry Lippes, a wealthy lawyer who had made significant recent contributions to the Albright-Knox Art Gallery, was hired to run the arena-financing campaign.

Some of my friends expressed sympathy—I had "lost the Sabres." In private meetings, Seymour was quick to assure me that was not the case. Lippes had been hired because of his political acumen and connections. My job was to make sure there were no "legal mistakes"—"counsel in the crease" again! I was also to keep Dennis Gorski, the Erie County executive, strongly on our side. The county's share of the cost was to be $20 million. The county task was relatively easy. Dennis and his family had been friends of my family for generations. His father, Chester, a former congressman, and a key member of the Common Council in 1970 when we received the NHL franchise, had worked as a young man in my grandfather's department store on the East Side. And Dennis did not need to be proselytized or converted; he believed in the Sabres and the arena project—as he did with the Bills and their stadium—as essential to the vitality of Western New York.

The financing of the Crossroads Arena was something else. The plan called for a total of about $130 million—$20 million from the county; $10 million from the city; $25 million from the state; $32.5 million from the concessions lender; $35 million from a second lender, secured by the new building; and the balance of about $23 million in equity investment. It was, to put it mildly, highly leveraged. Yet Seymour and Gerry Lippes, with Larry Quinn joining in the tough negotiating and lobbying, did a marvelous job of getting it done.

FINANCING THE ARENA "ON THE COME"

But it was complicated, and it took more time than ever anticipated. The task of monitoring the multiple resolutions, special laws, documents, loan agreements, league consents, and multiple parties was tough enough. But the delay and complexity put almost unbearable burdens on the Sabres and on me, as still the club's principal fund-raiser. It was like the military campaigns of World War II: the airplanes, the artillery, the missiles, and the tanks made glamorous forays, yet in the end it was the foot soldier who had to protect the flank and take the hill.

The major purpose of the new arena was to help the Sabres' cash flow, but the delays and complexities of the financing of the building stood that on its head. In the rush to get the building built, the lenders and the governments wouldn't commit and it was the *Sabres'* revenue that had to provide the money to pay the architects, the engineers, the carpenters, the suppliers, and the laborers. Quinn, with the Knoxes' acquiescence, just strong-armed the dollars from the Sabres till. It was a brave but outrageous gamble—as the lawyers would say, probably ultra vires, that is, without legal support. In 1996, when the building was finally completed and the financing closed, the arena owed the hockey club nearly $30 million.

The road to the arena closing was rocky, indeed. The city was difficult, reluctantly giving up its role as owner of the facility. The banks were skeptical of the projections. Marine Midland Bank (now HSBC) stayed rather loyal and supportive, but M&T, the second-largest bank in the community, targeted as the lead lender, walked away. I was informed of this by Larry Quinn in a 7 AM conference call, reporting that he had retaliated by pulling all of the Sabres and arena M&T accounts. (I thought to myself: Another hostility created, when we need all the friends we can get.)

One important contributor stayed steadfast—Jerry Jacobs of the Boston Bruins and Sportservice. The Sportservice guarantee of concession income secured the loan from that source. But the banking group on the $35 million loan took more than a year to form and solidify. The size of the debt made the league wary; and the NHL consent agreement and lender's cooperation agreement did not come easily. I was called upon to resolve the issues and finalize the documents. Even the state grant, despite the effective Lippes/Quinn lobbying, ran into trouble. With the governor's wand passing from Cuomo to Pataki, there were some anxious months while we waited for the new governor to give his approval.

I have described elsewhere the painful pressure and tension created by my efforts to obtain additional cash from Adelphia or other sources. My arms still ache with that painful memory. The losses were continuing, and with the demands of arena construction, the calls from the staff for funds to meet the player payroll were now exacerbated by threats from arena head Larry Quinn that if we didn't supply *their* payroll funds, the carpenters, ironworkers, bricklayers, cement workers, and others would walk off the job. The delay and negative publicity would kill the project.

Seymour's illness was close to terminal; Norty was still involved with his bank chairmanship. I could not go back to George Strawbridge or Bob Rich—they had already gone beyond the call of duty with their $3.7 million commitment. I tried the league. Jeff Pash, NHL general counsel, was sympathetic. After checking with Gary Bettman, he offered a loan of $1 million—only one-sixth of what we needed. Moreover, the collateral the league requested—TV revenue—was already pledged to the working capital lenders. I considered a public offering. How could I prepare and ask the directors and officers to sign an SEC registration statement or prospectus "selling" the investment to individuals? The prospectus would have to state accurately the salary escalation and the other negatives of which I was aware. Maybe the crazy hockey enthusiasts would buy into it nevertheless, but the inevitable negative publicity would be damaging to our negotiations with the banks and the local governments. A private offering to a sophisticated investor like Adelphia, which could realize and digest the negatives, was safer. But there was no time for a public offering—such an undertaking would take months—and Adelphia, as the holder of 34 percent, would be required to approve it, anyway. We needed $6 million. A telephone survey of our key partners showed no more than $600,000 would come from them. Seymour and Norty and the board agreed—I had no choice. It was back to John Rigas.

IN THE MOUTH OF A CANNON

I had very little leverage. As George Strawbridge assessed the situation: "Bob, you were negotiating in the mouth of a cannon, with a cap pistol!!"

Between 1994 and 1997, I was able to persuade John Rigas and his Adelphia colleagues to invest $31.5 million in the Sabres: $15 million in 1994; another $6 million in 1995, in connection with the arena; $6.5 million in 1996; and, with our group investing an equal amount, $3.6 million in 1997.

It was not easy. As described earlier in these pages, there were key people in the Adelphia setup who, as financial officer Jim Brown expressed it to me, "don't want to do the deal at all." Another characterized the Sabres as a "black hole." Adelphia itself was highly leveraged. Its annual report and prospectus showed that, while it was making impressive acquisitions to become the fifth-largest cable system in the country, those acquisitions were largely financed with debt, and the company regularly borrowed each year to pay interest and debt service on the previous year's acquisition debt. Thus, the presence on the Adelphia balance sheet of a sports franchise dripping red ink was not a welcome sight—especially for a financial vice president bent on making positive waves for his company with the investment bankers.

THE JAWS OF THE LENDER BEGIN TO CLOSE

So it was not surprising that, with each request by us for funding, the Adelphia/Rigas term sheets became tougher. The 34 percent veto of major transactions was just a start. Restrictions on borrowing, rights of conversion and first refusal, and participation in the board and voting trust were added. The interest rate rose to 14 and 15 percent. We preserved a right to redeem Adelphia out, under certain restrictions, and at a predetermined price. But Adelphia rejected provisions that would have required them to join in a sale. Perhaps the toughest clause, and the one that caused the greatest concern, was the provision for paid-in-kind units (PIKs). In other words, if the Sabres did not have the cash to pay interest on the Adelphia notes, the noteholders could require the franchise to issue additional ownership units to Adelphia. At the rate the Sabres losses were continuing, and the Adelphia investment was increasing, the Rigases' potential ownership could in a few years approach 51 percent, and even—with some adroit purchases from existing unit holders—aspire to the 67 percent trigger that would enable them to oust our general partner and take control. It would not come automatically—the Adelphia noteholders would have to give up their priority claims and their right to interest payments, and the league Board of Governors would have to approve the change in control. With a large sum of money—$8 to $10 million—we could redeem Adelphia out or force them to convert their notes and preferred units into a minority position in common units. So we had strategic defenses, but the growing PIKs were a serious threat.

In my thinking, it was not the threat to control as such; it was the threat to the *ability to sell*. With Seymour's illness and ultimate death, followed by Norty's, and the substantial increase in investment made by Rich Products, George Strawbridge, and others in our group, a change took place in the motives of our partners. It was still important to keep the franchise in Buffalo, but the recovery of our partners' investment became of prime importance, and without control we had nothing to sell and no way to sell it.

ATTEMPTS TO SELL TO OUTSIDERS

Men of wealth asked to make a multimillion-dollar investment in a sports franchise almost always want control. They usually desire the hands-on feel of power and the public prestige that comes with ownership. This was demonstrated on the two occasions when I was able to shake free of Seymour's injunctions against consideration of outside offers. He was insistent, right up to the end, that John Rigas would make good on his commitment and buy us out. He agreed to let me talk to third parties only on the condition that I was using them to get movement out of John. The first offer was a written, one-sheet letter proposal from an investor in a minorleague hockey franchise. His net worth, according to our investigation, was in excess of $200 million, and he had interests in Western New York, so he would probably meet our special specifications. The price offered was near the ballpark. However, he was interested only if he could obtain majority control—though he might consider retaining Adelphia as a minority partner. I forwarded the letter to Adelphia. No response. I called John and other Adelphia officers. Not interested.

Next I appealed to the commissioner. Gary expressed some surprise that we had not come to him earlier, but he had a candidate: the owner of an important Pepsi Cola regional franchise in the Hudson Valley. We set up a meeting with the Pepsi Cola mogul in New York City. Bob Rich came to the meeting with me, and there seemed to be some real interest. But the soda man wanted control, without any minority veto—and Adelphia didn't show up.

I went back to John Rigas. The losses were accumulating, the cash was disappearing, and the PIKs were mounting up. The "commitment" relied upon by Seymour produced only general expressions of interest from John and his associates. In raising the series of investments and loans made by Adelphia between 1994 and 1996, I had literally stayed on top of John, to compel or persuade, to cajole or argue, incessantly, if necessary, to produce the dollars—even if only to avoid another call from me! John had a simple but effective procedure to handle his many telephone calls—take off! He would rise early, shower, work out with his trainer, then take his car to one of several restaurants in his company town of Coudersport, Pennsylvania, for breakfast. He would answer only those calls that interested him, or where the caller was indefatigable (like me) on his cell phone, then embark on tour of the town's activities pursuant to a spontaneous schedule that even his special secretary did not know or could not predict. John did not seem to resent my calls—we continue to have good rapport—and, in fact, he would instruct me to call at home, between his shower and his workout. If I did, I usually had the pleasure of a lively discourse on the current hockey team problems and some substantive response to my request. If I didn't call at the appointed moment, he was gone, "out on the farm," usually unreachable, and it was a lost day. As for approaches to the other Adelphia officers—like John's son Tim, the able executive vice president, or Jim Brown, a very smart and cautious financial officer—they were usually futile. The Sabres were "Dad's deal"; hockey matters were neither their priority nor their preference, and only orders from John (sometimes not obeyed) would produce the movement we wanted.

THE RIGAS PRELIMINARIES

The new building—renamed Marine Midland Arena—opened in the spring of 1997, and it was an immediate box office success. The fans delighted in the lively atrium entrance, the new seats, the great Jumbotron, and the easy flow into and out of the arena. The fresh start (and the growing PIKs) led us to press for a head-to-head meeting with the Adelphia brass, and we met in Coudersport to see if we could find common ground for a transaction. Bob Rich and I headed the Sabres delegation; Tim Rigas and Jim Brown, the Adelphia group. Significantly, John Rigas was not present. Unfortunately, Jim Brown led off with a presentation of figures that showed that "the Sabres [had] so much debt, they [were] under water." Why should they offer *anything* for the Knox-Buffalo group's equity?

We had not planned who would say what, but when Bob Rich gave me a sharp poke in the ribs, I sprang to the attack. That kind of approach, I said, did not advance the cause whatsoever. Jim's math might be accurate, but he had ignored the recent rise in franchise values—sales and expansion fees. His math also ignored the impact of the new arena, which certainly increased the value of the Sabres far above the chalk figure on Brown's blackboard.

Jim had always been skeptical about the relationship, and the dialogue became rather heated. We adjourned to a small, private meeting of the principals, and out of that came the plan to hire an independent intermediary—who could, hopefully, create a transaction that would be acceptable to both sides.

While I had participated in the negotiations for the 1997 investment, and had to make urgent calls to our limited partners, John Rigas, and Adelphia personnel in aid of the transaction, new characters were added to the scenario. The episode began when Bob Rich asked me to prepare a memorandum on what we had to sell, in which I pointed out that in each of the previous Adelphia investment deals, our group had been given rights to participate and maintain its percentage ownership, but relatively few had

In happier times—John Rigas with Seymour Knox III.
Copyright © Bill Wippert.

responded; and with the accumulation of the Adelphia PIKs, if our group did not join in the investment in a substantial way, the voting trust and the control by our general partner could be overturned, and we'd have nothing to sell: the Rigases would have all the voting and management power they needed *without having to pay us anything for our interests*. Bob Rich, George, and Norty heard the warning, and they agreed to support a transaction in which our group would put up 50 percent of the amount needed, with Adelphia supplying the balance. (The investment turned out to be $7.2 million in the aggregate; the Knox-Buffalo share, $3.6 million.) This time, however, it was determined that the Sabres budget had to be approved by the holders of the new notes—it was to be annexed in some form to the notes—and sanctions were to be imposed if the budget was busted. The watchdog chosen was James Haddad, the vice president of finance at Rich Products.

James was a firebrand—quick, bright, full of energy and drive. It was a brave effort, but the economics of the league and of the Sabres were tough to handle, even with a prickly document. The Pittsburgh Penguins were in bankruptcy—as I reminded our board—and while Mario Lemieux emerged with a chance to have his deferred compensation paid, the equity owners, Howard Baldwin and Roger Marino, were entirely wiped out. In the frustrating two and a half years that followed, as we struggled to close a sale,

James and I got to know and like each other, though our differences on tactics were sometimes sharp. I particularly admired his technique as a word processor. He had his computer set up on a waist-high stand at which he stood; and as he typed at the keyboard, his office rattled with the sound and speed of his attack. At first hearing I thought someone had let loose with an Uzi machine gun!

The second new character was from my own law firm—Ray McCabe, the tax partner who had been assigned to handle some of my client problems. He was thorough and fast—one of my first contacts with a computer-integrated lawyer. The technology sped up the draftsmanship; but it's a lonely technique, and sometimes I think it sacrifices the interplay of ideas and critiques that partner-to-partner relationships should and do produce. I saw this in our first contact. Ray did an analysis of a Sabres problem on his computer that read well, but it was prepared without discussion with me, or any other Sabre officer, and without taking into account certain agreements, the existence of which he could not have known without asking. Nevertheless, Ray's opinion sounded as if he were Chief Justice William H. Rehnquist of the United States Supreme Court pronouncing the unassailable law.

We held a spirited critique, which he did not seem to resent, and he became part of my regular Sabres legal team.

SWADOS IS BENCHED—OR IS HE?

That is, as long as the team was a *team*. The independent negotiator chosen (after the failure of the Rigases to show up for meetings I had set up with Thomas Tenney Jr., owner of the Albany-area Pepsi Cola franchise, and Frank B. DuRoss, a Utica investor already involved in minor-league hockey) to craft the Sabres/Adelphia deal was Ted Behringer, a former Buffalonian, a member of the Buffalo Country Club, the head of an outfit called Mid-Atlantic, and a sometime friend of Bob Rich Jr. He seemed able, practical, and friendly. As the new man in the picture, he was determined to start clean, and I was the guy (never mind the $36 million I'd elicited from Adelphia) who had done most of the negotiating—but hadn't produced the sale. Suddenly, I was benched. With Seymour gone, Norty listened to the critical gossip wafted by "wannabe" counsel and the Adelphia cohorts who didn't want the deal anyway: I was too tough. No, I was too easy. I was too friendly with John. The voting trust was an irritation. I shouldn't be calling John so often, especially at home. I should stay out of it. I didn't get along with Jim Brown. The Adelphia crew was not interested at all in the price I had proposed (which was 25 percent less than Seymour's number). It was determined that the negotiations on behalf of Knox-Buffalo would be conducted by James Haddad and Ray McCabe.

But of course I wasn't really benched—not entirely. The talks were conducted in person or by conference call on the fourth-floor of my law firm's building in Buffalo, an imposing edifice that once housed the Schoellkopf corporate clients, Niagara Share and Crescent Tool; the "war room" in the baseball crusades, and, in the early days, the Buffalo Sabres. My office was on the first floor, but I had no difficulty hearing the hot sounds of the conferences as Haddad and McCabe fought with Brown and Ed Hartman (the point man for Adelphia). I would go up to the fourth floor to see if I could help as the days dragged on without fruition. James Haddad would silently take my arm, lead me out into the corridor, vent his exasperation at the lack of progress, and ask for my brief advice. And of course, notwithstanding the negative gossip, I was expected to and did stay in touch with John Rigas; any major policy decision still needed his concurrence.

The deal constructed by the intermediary and negotiated by Haddad and McCabe was a strange but creative gamble. The Rigas family, with its PIKs, wanted control—so we'd give it to them, provided they agreed to buy us out. We'd put them in the saddle, so they got a taste of the bliss of running a major-league sports franchise, got hooked, and paid us off. The total size of the deal was not very attractive, but considering the alternative—a Pittsburgh-like bankruptcy—it would have to do. After all the debt and the Adelphia notes were subtracted from the appraised value of $92 million, about $16 million was left for the Knox-Buffalo group of fifteen directors, seventy-seven limited partners with common units, and ten holders of preferred units and subordinated notes—barely enough to get back their investment.

Although James Haddad, once he got to know me firsthand, was willing to consult me and involve me to a limited extent in the negotiating process, my colleague at the law firm, Ray McCabe, was not. It was a new experience for me; I was used to command and to have my commands obeyed. McCabe resisted my input, going so far as to hang up on my calls—pleading the constant pressure from James. At this writing I do not know what really caused this nonsensical arrangement: the man with the most experience, the most contact with and confidence of the partners, the strongest relationship with the league, and the legal responsibility as a senior officer of the client was being shut out of the negotiations. Was it Norty's instructions, Haddad's demands, the paranoid view of Adelphia's desires, McCabe's ego (he argued that I could contribute nothing new), or my own failure to mend fences so I could control matters at Cohen Swados?

Since the mid-1980s I had really not been legally or financially part of my law firm's power structure. The hockey matters, at both the franchise and the league levels, had so dominated my time, my interest—and my compensation—that I had no time or appetite for law firm politics. In the twenty-five years after Paul Cohen's death, when I was running the firm, most of the junior lawyers (now partners) who worked with me were recruited by me and trained by me, and they were, I like to think, loyal and supportive of my projects. Ray McCabe was an import; he may have had an acceptable intellectual record, but we had neither the emotional nor the professional relationship I had created with the associates I had chosen in the past. He was able, but he was not *my* man. In the selection of Ray as the negotiating companion for James Haddad, I was not consulted. I might have chosen one of several lawyers in the firm with more negotiating experience: Ray had never, so far as I knew, negotiated a major corporate transaction. (His forte was federal taxation.) Other lawyers in the firm saw this and complained. Somehow, Jane Clemens, whom I'd appointed assistant secretary of the Sabres, ended up as Ray's backstop; but with the crush and pressure of the negotiations, I got the impression that Jane, though an able lawyer, never really caught up. She, too, was forechecked into Band-aid contributions.

I had participated to some extent in the drafting and negotiating of the letter of intent—the nonbinding Memorandum of Understanding (MOU) of December 31, 1997, that basically outlined the main features of the deal. I regarded the MOU as a simple, understandable document. It was to be followed by the negotiation of the formal Funding and Purchase Agreement (FPA). In the proverbial pattern—benched or not—I had been called on New Year's Eve by the Adelphia crew to correct an obvious hiatus in the document; and, with no one else available, I had closed the gap and started the deal on its way—or so I thought. As I reread the MOU, I think my major focus was in the clauses reserving the corporate powers of our board and our group. The day-to-day operations were to be handed over immediately to John and his financial appointee. (I was expected to finesse any league objections to this partial transfer of control without Board of Governors' consent). John could not engage in major corporate transactions, sign or make a player trade involving a salary of more than a million dollars, or change the managing partner or the league governors (including Bob Rich and me) without the consent of our members of the designated committees. My strong construction of that veto power was never entirely accepted by the Adelphia crew, but it enabled us to stick our fist—or at least our finger—into sensitive Rigas proposals and proceedings, such as bank loan payments (or nonpayments), arena naming rights, major player signings and trades, and so forth. It also permitted me to continue to represent the club (along with John Rigas) at NHL governors' meetings, and, as we shall see, that was of considerable practical importance.

TROUBLE, TROUBLE AT COHEN SWADOS

I did not realize how much my absorption in NHL matters had separated, if not alienated, me from the core of my law firm. During the sixteen years of my tenure as a league officer, I had contributed substantially to the firm's revenue with Sabres and NHL fees, as well as fees from my work with the firm's corporate clients, both those I had brought to the firm—like the paint manufacturer Pratt & Lambert and the NHL—and those that represented the traditional, long-term customers like Moore Corporation. But I was just "of counsel" or "special counsel"; I did not sign the checks for the other lawyers, and I eschewed the administrative decisions such as recruiting new associates. I had no desire—and was not invited—to involve myself in the decisions of the firm as a business. After the merger of Pratt & Lambert into Sherwin-Williams in 1995, and the death of some of my principal individual clients, except for the Sabres and occasional league matters, I ceased to be an important factor in the firm's revenue. I had permitted or acquiesced in the assignment of Moore matters to other partners in the firm. As for the Sabres account, the proposed transactions with Adelphia and the Rigas family were apparently viewed by some members of the firm hierarchy, with some justification, as a painful burden on the firm's cash flow. From the time of the signing of the MOU in December 1997 to the ultimate closing on July 16, 2000, the firm accrued nearly $600,000 in time charges, with no payments on account. As John Rigas and associates ascended to "interim" management, with the Sabres' multimillion-dollar losses continuing, I had no power to bring about payment of the firm's bills—although my Sabres salary was paid until Norty's death in July 1998. Thereafter, I, too, had to work without compensation until the July 2000 closing.

I also did not realize the deterioration in the firm's client revenue—I received no financial data—or in its morale. Without strong leadership, significant rainmaking, and continued growth, and with the withering away of its major account—Moore Corporation and its US main subsidiary, Moore Business Forms—fissures began to develop. Jealousies translated into scrambles for position. I did not then understand why, but the schisms seriously affected the performance of the organization. In the negotiation of the Funding and Purchase Agreement, the thrust of the firm's reaction was not to support my efforts to improve the document and the deal, but to attack Ray McCabe's performance and insert themselves into the negotiation process. As for me, a founder of the firm and the source of the Sabres billings—which aggregated millions of dollars of cash and prestige over thirty years—the firm's object (or the object of the desperately aggressive faction) seemed to be to unseat me as quickly as possible. After all, I was in my seventies, wouldn't last forever, and under some law firms' policies would long ago have been put out to pasture.

From my vantage point, the conduct of the firm during the three years of frustration was bizarre and wrongheaded. Paul Schoellkopf once remarked to me that he was surprised, could not understand, how I kept the job of Sabres counsel for so long. "They were always bringing in their cronies," he said. I responded that I hoped it was because I delivered the goods. But was it the voting trust? It was probably a factor—though the Knoxes never hesitated to call in the "gray ghost," usually me, to drop the guillotine for failure to perform. (There's quite a list of departed "cronies": Joe Crozier, Punch Imlach, Paul Wieland, Bob Pickel, Doug Moss, Bob Chambers, Craig Ramsay, and others) As I sat down to write this chapter, I received a call announcing the termination of the life of the firm. The organization I helped to create, and of which I was so proud, was about to dissolve. Could I have done anything to avoid its demise?

In the light of the firm's conduct in the Sabres negotiations, I certainly had no motive (except pride) to invest my remaining life in resuscitation, even if I had the client muscle to do so. The deal as outlined in the MOU contemplated a sale of all the interests of the Knox-Buffalo group in the Sabres for about $16 million—payable about one-third in cash at closing, another 20 percent ($3 million) in one-year notes to be signed by John Rigas personally, and the balance in five-year subordinated capital funding notes to be issued by the Sabres, at 14 percent, with the interest payable only if the franchise had positive cash flow. Theoretically, we could "put" (force a purchase of) the notes or force a sale of the franchise at the end of the five years if the notes weren't paid at maturity, if the franchise had the cash to make the payment. As pointed out above, John Rigas could, and did, step in as interim chairman, and Tim Rigas could—and did—take over as interim CEO for daily operations. It was my position that our board and league powers remain largely intact—as they had to be under the NHL constitution, until the league approved the deal and the deal was consummated.

Not too difficult to describe. But as the formal contract of sale emerged from the negotiations, it was a *monstrosity.* The powers retained by our board and officers were imprecise; the league requirements were either ignored or inaccurately described; the Adelphia parties were given uncertain "outs" if the banks didn't come through with cancellations or modification of the franchise and arena loans; and Adelphia could offset, maybe even wipe out, the Rigas notes if the Sabres' "liabilities" turned out to be more than shown on an unaudited and ill-defined balance sheet. Under the buyer's naturally partisan analysis of "liabilities," the $3 million in Rigas notes would be largely wiped out, but our negotiators felt comfortable with this clause because the Sabres held an interest in Tickets.com, which was expected to rise in value in a public offering, to the point where its appreciation would offset the Adelphia offset. (In fact, the stock in Tickets.com "tanked"—fortunately, after the July 2000 closing under a revised agreement.) The problem of paying the bills shifted, at least while the FPA was in force, to the Rigas parties; but their obligation to finance the team was not fixed in amount or in duration. They could conceivably walk away and leave the franchise to the bankruptcy courts.

The most important vice of the Purchase and Funding Agreement was that it had no closing date. The closing would take place only after the key consents had been obtained. The major consents involved the Sabres banks, the arena lenders, the public authorities, and the league. Each of those approvals required negotiation and execution of documents by the Rigas parties—meaning that, provided that the buyers could show good faith, the timing of any closing was almost completely in Adelphia's unilateral hands. It soon became clear that, with the club approaching insolvency and the cash drain increasing, the buyers were in no hurry to obtain the consents.

The PIKs were mounting up, so Adelphia had an alternative to buying us out, and the agreement did not even contain a "standstill," preventing the group from increasing its ownership. It took thirty-one months—more than two and a half years—from the signing of the MOU to produce a closing, and then only after drastic changes were made to the form, price, and substance of the deal.

Why did the FPA turn out to be so defective? Primarily because, despite John Rigas's goodwill and respectable intentions, the "black hole" faction in the Adelphia hierarchy "didn't want the deal at all." Their views were changed only in small measure by the signing of the FPA. "No deal" became "no closing" unless the key agreements—loans and leases and government grants—were changed to make the losses disappear, or at least reduce in size, so that ownership of the Sabres would become more palatable.

Certainly the weakness in the FPA was permitted because our negotiators had very little leverage. In part, however, the document that permitted this egregious delay and uncertainty could perhaps have been cured of some of its defects if the law firm had used the fifty years of experience available to it. Tim Rigas, Ed Hartman, and Jim Brown were able, tough negotiators working for a debt-constricted company, but their strategies might have been turned toward more creative and fruitful roads if the Sabres negotiators had not barred their key players from leaving the dressing room.

PUSHING AT THE ADELPHIA ROPE— "IMPLEMENTING" THE FPA

Norty, in pain and nausea with his cancer therapy, questioned my strategy. But I felt that, in trying to implement the FPA and get to a closing, it was imperative to clear away the roadblocks over which we had control or influence. That way it would be clear that any failure to close was solely the buyers' responsibility, and we would be in the best position to invoke league help. We could not persuade, nor could we attempt to influence, the banks (even our own client, HSBC) to modify their loans or continue the present debt without protections they thought were necessary. They knew of the Sabres' financial condition, but some of the banks were just being introduced to the proposed new ownership. But we could influence the city and the league. Mike McCarthy, an old friend and onetime associate who had worked under me at the law firm, was in charge of the city agency that issued certificates of occupancy (COs). Strangely, though the new building was in full operation, no CO had ever been granted. It was politically dangerous for him to bypass channels—the chairman of the council finance committee, James Pitts, was still resentful of the loss of the city's operating role and was looking for any city benefits he could pick up. But Mike was a fan of the Sabres, and, I guess, a fan of mine, and I was able to persuade him that no further council action was required, and he issued the CO.

The league consent was more complex and more difficult. The most important issues were the guaranty of working capital, the ability of the owner to walk away, and the consequences of bankruptcy—bankruptcy of the club and bankruptcy or foreclosure of the arena. The documents were more sophisticated versions of the consent and lenders cooperation agreements I had developed for the NHL in the expansions and sales in the 1980s and 1990s. The basic financial ideas: (1) commit the owner to maintaining a guaranteed and secured working capital in a fixed amount, so the club can always finish the season; (2) limit the amount of debt secured by the franchise, generally a ceiling of 50 percent of asset value; and (3) if the club or building runs into trouble and a bank tries to foreclose, make sure the league has time to find a purchaser, its claims against the club are paid, and it continues to control or approve the identity, acceptability, and financing of the new owner. As the experiences in St. Louis, Minnesota, Hartford, and Pittsburgh demonstrated, the league must be in a position to deal effectively with attempts by the owner or a foreclosing creditor to move the franchise to another city, and the agreements required of a new owner try to protect the NHL's power to regulate such attempts.

I pushed as hard as I could. When Adelphia delayed in filing its application with the league, I filed ours immediately, instead of waiting for a joint petition. With John Rigas's encouragement, I participated in a conference call with Adelphia and Dave Zimmerman of the NHL, helping them arrive at an acceptable formula for the guaranty. I pushed Covington & Burling, the NHL outside counsel on transfers, and helped resolve the impasse between Rigas and NHL language. All through this, I believed that my presence and participation at league meetings was vital. I wanted my friends around the governors' table, most of whom I'd helped over the years, to know this was an important issue for us, and, in a dispute, *we* were the longtime partners who should be supported.

The bifurcated management of the Sabres during this period created a practical problem: seats at the governors' table. As the league expanded, the number of representatives frequently exceeded the number of chairs at the table. I would get down early and plant my documents at my usual territory—near the commissioner's and staff section, to the commissioner's left. I would save three seats—more would have been overreaching—one for John Rigas, one for me, and one for Tim Rigas, if he showed up, or for Seymour Knox IV, if he did not. John invariably sat next to me, and our hushed dialogue at the governors' table provided the valuable communication between us the early morning telephones could not. Tim, on the other hand, would always wave off my offer of a seat and place himself with Darcy Regier (our GM) on the opposite side of the room. That meant that when an issue came up on which I felt Tim should have input, and I was required to vote as the "senior" governor, Tim and I had to communicate practically by hand signals, or I would dash around the big oblong table, get Tim's reaction, then dash back to my seat to vote. As the months went by, John wished to vote himself, and I acquiesced.

And what was my authority to continue to function as a club officer, as a league governor, and as inside counsel? We had conducted no new elections—that would have been controversial, and a sign of weakness. I was still in office, and I was still the swing voting trustee. So what did my distinguished law firm do to support my efforts? I heard a casual remark from an outside source—"That voting trust doesn't amount to much"—and as I left my office at night a few days later, I found on the floor, partially obscured by the couch, a memorandum signed by a new associate (prepared or inspired by whom, I still don't know) finding that the voting trust had expired—because we had failed to refile it after ten years. The writer had not consulted me and had completely failed to take into account the John Rigas and Adelphia documents that had recast the trust—in effect, created a new trust—and had made John Rigas a third trustee. I was sure, based on the remark I had overheard, that this half-baked memo had already been circulated. I had never had such a crude, destructive, and incompetent experience in my life. I was owed consultation and loyalty, either as the senior lawyer in the firm or as the vice chairman of the client—and this behavior was off the wall.

SPREADING THE "GOODIES" AROUND

Once the FPA was ready for signature, it became essential to decide how the proceeds of that agreement, if any, would be allocated among the diverse interests of the Knox/Buffalo partners. Most held common units; some held preferred units, convertible debentures, and subordinated convertible notes—or all of the above. The notes and units were purchased at different times and under different conditions; some provided PIKs and high interest rates. Some partners held securities in two or more categories. There was an issue as to the priority of the special notes held by George Strawbridge and Rich Products, representing the $3.7 million they had advanced to close the gap in the arena financing. The holders of the Class C debentures—$2 million worth—had put up this money in 1988 to fund the Channel 49 transaction. Their debentures were due in 1998—and under the language of their instruments, they seemed entitled to priority. But would that be fair to the partners who had converted their Class A and B debentures a year earlier into voting common units, as a means of helping to buttress the Knox-Buffalo ownership to slow the "creep" of the Rigas parties toward control?

At a board conference call, a number of possible approaches to allocation were discussed, including:

1. All the "preferred interests"—the notes and debentures—get paid 100 percent, principal plus accrued interest, before the common gets anything. That would essentially wipe out the common, including those partners who had converted their debentures at $38 per common unit, just a year before.
2. First, the common gets paid a fair figure—presumably the conversion price of somewhere between $30 to $38 per unit. That would have cut substantially into the claims of the note holders and debenture holders, whose documents spoke of priority.
3. The holders of the C debentures—including the $750,000 debenture held by the general partner—get paid first. That would probably inure to the benefit of the Seymour H. Knox III estate, of which his widow, Jean Knox, was the principal beneficiary. That would create a conflict with other holders.
4. Pay off first the most recent investments—the 1996 and 1997 notes. That could violate the priority clauses in the debentures.
5. Convert everybody's holdings to common units, based on the conversion price in their instruments, then pay out according to their proportionate interest in the common after such conversion. That would have demanded a substantial discount from Rich Products, George Strawbridge, and the other note and debenture holders.

There was not enough available in the $15.6 million of cash and notes to pay the common anything like what they had come to expect from the news of franchise sales and still pay off 100 percent of the interest and principal due or ultimately payable under the notes and debentures. Some of the notes were accompanied by "bonus" preferred units that really had no cost basis. Should these participate at all, or at a discount?

There was another issue in the allocation formula. Once we determined who should get what percentage of the total proceeds—who gets the cash, who gets the Rigas one-year notes—who was left with the subordinated notes of the Sabres "on the come"? Here, too, an assertion by the note holders of their full-priority claims could leave the equity holders with nothing but the subordinated notes, highly contingent and of questionable value.

I was convinced that approval of the seventy-seven common unit holders who had stayed with us for nearly thirty years was legally, practically, and ethically necessary. I felt that a proposal that wiped them out, or gave them substantially less than their cost, would not fly. A compromise of the claims of *all* the investment categories had to be worked out, if we were ever to produce a closing for anybody. A bankruptcy-type allocation would produce controversy and possible litigation, and play right into the hands of the Adelphia faction that would be delighted at delay and frustration of the deal. The FPA called for a schedule to be attached to the agreement setting out the specific allocation to each partner and security holder, so there was no time for any detour.

We were asked to prepare a list and compute possible allocation formulas to be considered. This is where I made a tactical mistake. I had always prided myself on the ability, as John Ziegler would say, to go right to the core of a problem and its solution. This time I went too far, too fast. At the next conference call, I had my associates submit a list that showed various approaches, all of which provided something for the common. I gave preference to the "conversion" formula, because that was the simplest and easiest to understand—of importance in selling the deal to the multiple partners. All the note holders held common units as well, so what they lost on the "apples" they would probably gain on the "bananas." But I did not submit the approach at the opposite end of the spectrum—the "bankruptcy" formula, under which the preferred interests got 100 percent of principal and accrued interest before the common participated at all. As I've said above, I was convinced that this would get us nowhere but trouble.

I had underestimated the tensions that were boiling beneath the surface and overestimated the confidence the soon-to-be-warring parties had in my judgment and fairness to settle the matter. I had had such confidence for nearly thirty years, and I was shocked when George Strawbridge, then Bob Rich, then Norty Knox, upbraided me for not giving proper weight to the priority claims of the notes and debentures.

I held to my position, but retreated, revised our memorandum, and, with Norty participating directly, the board finally approved an allocation that provided for adjustments throughout the investment spectrum, slashed the "bonus" preferred, and gave the notes and debentures a high priority while limiting interest accruals and leaving something for the common. The settlement of the issue left undisturbed the preferential payouts received by George and Rich Products on their arena notes. The approved allocation also divided each of the elements of the consideration across the board: for example, if a partner was entitled to 5 percent of the deal, he would receive 5 percent of the cash, 5 percent of the Rigas notes, and 5 percent of the Sabres subordinated five-year notes. But the deal went over with irritation, conflict, and concern, and suddenly lawyers appeared all over the place: Bill Grieshober, a tough but nice guy in the Rich Products legal crew, took over as the lead lawyer; Jim Locke, a talented but taciturn counsel for Norty, then Norty's estate, began to do some of the drafting; George Strawbridge called upon his Philadelphia lawyer, Richard Wild, with whom I had had a mutually respectful relationship, and I took care to keep him informed of developments. Then, when it transpired that there were serious issues between Jean Knox and Norty, issues that began with territorial claims over the Knox Estate in East Aurora (Ess Kay Farms), Jean Knox hired her own counsel, a tax lawyer whose contribution to solutions was quite limited, but whose voice was always heard.

And there was Swados—in the crease, trying to get to the slot, trying to score, with his "teammates" . . .

NONSUPPORT II—"CONFLICTS OF INTEREST"

With the sudden hands-on attention of other counsel, Jane Clemens asked me, "Whom do we represent?" My immediate response was: "You go with the guys who brought you to the dance"—the Knoxes and the other members of the board who were the principal investors. "But each has his own lawyer," she demurred. "No matter," I said. "We're still 'counsel for the situation'—we have to do the best job we can, to get this done for everybody: the general partners, the note holders, and the seventy-seven limited partners who've been with us for thirty years." Jane, still perturbed by the sounds of conflict she'd heard on the conference calls dealing with allocation, was not at ease: "Can't we just represent the *company*?" she asked, as she went out the door.

I confess I've never paid much attention to "conflicts of interest." I have tried to be fair, accurate, thorough, and reasonable. I've gone through many situations where members of a family or a corporate group with differing, even opposing, interests invest in my judgment and belief that "what's fair works; what's not, does not." I'm not adversarial by nature, but I tend to react and move strongly in support of what I judge to be a fair compromise. I intended to act no differently now. I had friends and present and former clients all over the Sabres spectrum. Jean Knox may have been looking for special treatment because her late husband was a hardworking Sabres leader and never was compensated for it, but I had to be sensitive to the interests of her brothers and her children, who had substantial investments, primarily in the common. I felt I had to be sensitive to Jean's needs as well, even though I did not represent her officially. I had to give weight to providing protection for limited partners such as Peter and Ed Andrews, good friends of Seymour's and of mine who had come through with purchases of the subordinated notes when we needed the dollars badly. I could not desert the longtime Sabres partners who converted their debentures at maturity into voting common units to help us maintain control. Bob Rich's company and Norty and George were well represented by able counsel who were participating in the negotiation process, but the directors with the third- and fourth-largest investments, Joe Stewart and Dick Rupp, clearly had their counsel rely on my judgment. I was still vice chairman and counsel and voting trustee. I was still the guy with the greatest league experience and contacts, and the *only* friendly, positive relationship with the Rigas family. Nobody had unelected me; I could not step back into the safe, neutral, nonactive closet.

To be charitable, I will assume that the apparent conflict between the principals, including George Strawbridge and the holders of equity units, rattled one or more of the senior partners in my firm. The ghosts of litigation and malpractice began to haunt them. They feared I was leading them into a lawsuit, so their distinguished strategy was to dissociate themselves from me as much as possible. I had not renewed my contract with the firm as counsel, so there was no legal relationship. But that did not satisfy the paranoid faction. When James Haddad of Rich Products, feeling his way into the complex situation, asked if the firm represented Bob Swados, Jane Clemens was persuaded to write a letter to Haddad stating that, of course they didn't; moreover, she gratuitously added, Haddad didn't have to worry about conflict, because, unlike me, they wouldn't be influenced by an investment in the club! I thought the letter was outrageous, even libelous. I had brought the firm to the dance; I was a senior officer of the client, the hockey partnership, so they certainly owed me consideration, if not loyalty. Moreover, the senior partners in the firm—Thomas J. Hanifin, Hilary Bradford, Jay Brett, and Harry Nichols—owned common units in the partnership, obtained from me. My shares in the general partner, common units and notes, amounted to about 1 percent of the ownership, and this had been disclosed time after time in the prospectuses issued to the partners in connection with each offering in the raising of Sabres capital. This ownership, together with the position as voting trustee and my active participation in management, had helped maintain the firm's position and revenue as outside counsel to the Sabres for thirty years. It was ironic that the paranoid faction in the law firm should seek to undermine the relationship at the same time that other elements in the Sabres—who would later fail to continue to retain the firm as their lawyers—were seeking to destroy it in order to eradicate or minimize my influence. I was ready to blow the place apart, but with some urging from McCabe, I settled down to the real issue: getting the FPA closed. This dissension in the firm, which resulted in what I called a "constipated" reaction to pressure, doubtless contributed to the decline and fall of the firm in 2001.

SWADOS AS THE FINANCIAL KIBITZER

The coterie of lawyers, along with James Haddad, agreed, or at least acquiesced, that we should stick our nose into every transaction proposed by the buyers that was not "in ordinary course." That meant that when Adelphia or the Rigas family tried to renegotiate the Sabres' bank loans, or refused to make a payment due the arena lenders, or objected to the attempt by HSBC to rename the building HSBC Arena, we had to be present and respond, or at least observe. In case the FPA failed to close, and we had to take back management of the club, we could not permit the buyers to poison our banking or governmental relationships. On the other hand, we could not really interfere with or prejudice the buyers' attempts to reduce the burdens of the obligations we were trying to get them to assume. Such interference might be a breach of good faith, violating our covenants under the agreement. So, with such a Hobson's choice, we usually ended up just observing; and I felt just like a lonely kibitzer.

It was comical, sometimes. At one point, Ed Hartman, the Adelphia point man, asked for a substantial discount from HSBC on its portion of the bank loans—accompanied by a proposal to permit the change of name of the arena the bank wanted, for an additional consideration. I believed, on the merits, that the bank—my firm's long-term client in Niagara Falls—had the right to change the name unilaterally, but I certainly wanted the buyers to achieve the discount, hoping that they would move on to closing. Hartman agreed that I could be present, but only after he finished talking to the bank's representative, Bob Engel. (I had known Engel well from the time he represented Scotty Bowman in the negotiation of his contract). I had to come to TGIFriday's—a strange place to renegotiate a $35 million loan—and sit at a separate booth, out of Engel's sight. I tried to be helpful, and I thought we'd achieved a good resolution. But when weeks went by without movement by Adelphia, I was really put on the spot: John Bond, the British head of the bank, called me. What should they do? If they didn't reach an agreement soon, they would lose a whole season on the promotion of the new name. I hesitated, then answered as objectively as I could. "Hang tough," I said. "It's really a no-brainer. Adelphia needs cash, and if you offer it to them, they'll move favorably. The new name is no worse than the jawbreakers adorning the walls of ten other arenas." That's the way it worked out.

The delays in closing the FPA that resulted from the buyers' attempts to reduce the club's obligations and expenses, and the delays that resulted from whatever other reason, rankled Haddad and Rich, frustrated me, and led to multiple calls daily from the seventy-seven partners. When were they going to get the proceeds? What was holding it up? I cautioned patience as long as I could, but Haddad had a list of failed meetings, missed deadlines, and no-shows that looked like a telephone book. I finally proposed that we call a partnership meeting, so that the buyers could tell their story directly to the investors. The meeting, extremely well attended, was held in the large room in the dressing room area of the arena usually reserved for press conferences. As I look back upon it, the atmosphere produced a dramatic flair that was inappropriate for a negotiation, and I'm not particularly proud of the way it came off. I asked Bob Rich if he wanted to chair the meeting, but he passed off to me, and he and James Haddad disappeared into the crowd. I set up a chair for myself and one for Tim Rigas, but Tim moved it to the other side of the stage, as if we were about to begin a debate. Tim made no opening remarks, so I had to plunge in with some questions, which I asked politely but with a somewhat sharp edge, reflecting the frustration felt by the audience.

When would the agreement be closed? I asked. There had been all kinds of delays. More than fifteen months had passed since the signing of the MOU, a year since the FPA. The partners would really like to have some date when they can count on the closing.

Tim's answer was cautious and limiting. He described the obstacles that had to be overcome. The bank loans had to be modified; the losses were too great; the lease arrangements had to be improved. One of the banks (he did not say which) was being very difficult. It might take a long time to get that bank to move. He could not give any date.

I then asked a second question, much in the minds of the partners. The newspapers had reported, over the last few months, a series of acquisitions by Adelphia involving billions of dollars in stock and cash. We congratulated Adelphia on moving up from the eighth- to the fifth-largest cable system. But if Adelphia could find the capital to make those acquisitions, why couldn't this one be closed? It only involved $5 million in cash.

Again, Tim's answer was cautious and limiting, and not very reassuring: "Each deal is different. We can't close until the conditions are right. This deal, for the reasons I've just stated, is not ready."

Bob Rich and James Haddad offered to help with the banks, and I was instructed later to resume my kibitzing role.

But Tim's cautious responses and John Rigas's absence did not sit well with the partners. Yet the meeting did at least educate the partnership; they knew what we were up against.

Tim obviously sensed the criticism and even hostility, but the limited partners were for the most part people who had not participated in the recent funding and—though season ticket holders—did not seem important enough in Adelphia's strategy to affect its deliberate, contingent timetable. The delays, unproductive conferences, and missed deadlines continued.

At a board meeting months later, after we had finally closed under a new agreement, as Bob Rich and I did our postmortem, he remarked that "it probably would have been better if they'd told us their plans and brought us in to the negotiations on their side." My recollection was that they almost did that. Ed Hartman arrived at the meeting with a series of computations showing the cash losses and the burden of the debt service for the Sabres and the arena. A slide machine was set up for the presentation, but neither the computations nor the projector was ever used. Perhaps the atmosphere at the meeting turned Tim off, and changed his mind.

PUSHING AT THE RIGAS ROPE AGAIN . . . AND AGAIN

James Haddad and I faithfully attended the meetings of the buyers with the syndicate of banks. The lenders included HSBC, Fleet, and others. We listened painfully while Ed Hartman detailed the Adelphia analysis that the arena was a loss operation; that the expenses had turned out to be much more, and the arena income much less, than projected. We had difficulty remaining in our seats while the lease arrangements (which the Knoxes had thought a highly favorable deal) were denigrated and the out-of-town banks responded with delightful suggestions such as going back to the American Hockey League or adopting a lowball salary budget and roster like that of the expansion teams. All these negotiations were conducted in a crisis atmosphere because Adelphia, as part of its strategy, had refused to pay the arena loans when due—raising the threat of foreclosure or bankruptcy of the building, perhaps of the franchise, and triggering the possible intervention of the league.

The FPA called for a good-faith effort by the buyers to obtain the bank consents. Was this good faith? The Adelphia posture was that the buyers were not required to assume any "burden" in order to obtain the consents. The arena had failed to generate its own cash to pay its bank debt, and thus Adelphia, it argued—or the Sabres managed by Adelphia—was not required to pick up the arena burden.

We wondered if we should ask the NHL commissioner to intervene. Bob Rich and I independently called Gary Bettman to get a preliminary reaction. The answers didn't justify any hurrahs. Gary had a skeptical, even critical view of our arena arrangements. "You didn't ask our permission to build that building," he said. "Ask permission to survive?" I responded. Gary said, "No. I mean you have a '90s building with a '70s lease." More serious was his comment that he wanted to help, but I should know that he had to "tilt" toward the money to keep the club alive, and since Adelphia was financing the club and we were not, we had better make our judgments accordingly. Of course, if Bob Rich or any of our group were prepared to go forward with capital for the future, he would certainly tilt our way. And he wanted to help us, as longtime, good partners in the league.

THE "SPECIAL AUDIT"—HELP FROM THE NHL

No one in our group was ready to reassume the financial burden of operating the club. Frustration continued, and demands for litigation penetrated our councils. It was agreed that litigation counsel should be retained, at least to explore the possibilities of forcing the buyers to close. It had to be a non-Buffalo firm, with clout. I recommended my friend Mel Weiss of Milberg Weiss, the noted—and notorious—national leader in stockholder litigation who had helped the Sabres in threatening a suit against M&T Bank for its refusal to participate in the arena financing, but Bill Grieshober came up with an even more creative suggestion: Weil, Gotschal & Manges, the firm that represents the NHL Players' Association. Bruce Meyer, the partner assigned to our matter, turned out to be a first-class ally—quiet, thorough, firm, and practical.

Litigation was not so easy. The language of the FPA—what was a "burden"?—the vagueness of the "good faith" standard, and the lack of a closing date all made a lawsuit a questionable course. (To say nothing about what it might do to John Rigas's goodwill, which I, at least, regarded as a real asset.) There was a major question as to whether any court would take the case. The NHL constitution appears to give *exclusive* jurisdiction to the commissioner in a dispute between owners. I pointed out that there was an issue as to whether Adelphia was an "owner"—the company had never converted its notes into voting units—but I concurred that Gary Bettman would probably assert jurisdiction. The puzzle was, how to get before Bettman, get his help, without waiving the right to go to court if we lost.

The Adelphia crew, aggressive businessmen, had been quite brazen in taking over the advertising space and opportunities in the arena. The building featured a special area devoted not to the Sabres, but to Adelphia activities. The relationship between the Sabres and Adelphia's Empire Sports Network was murky; we had little idea of who was paying who for what. The financial results of the playoffs seemed low, especially compared to the results furnished me by my friends in Dallas and Pittsburgh.

Adelphia had systematically eliminated accounting personnel at the arena office and moved the accounting procedures and records to Coudersport. Bank accounts, including those on which Bob Rich, James Haddad, or I were supposed to be cosignatories, were ignored and made the subject of end runs so payments could be made without checking with us. They did continue to check with us on player signings and trades involving more than a million dollars—as required by the FPA—but Haddad had genuine concerns about "leakages"—moneys, credits, or benefits flowing to Adelphia that may have belonged to the Sabres—and the occasional financial statements we were furnished did not reflect this. These conflict situations presented a genuine legal issue, and, after consulting with Bruce Meyer, we seized upon this as a means of getting a toe in the commissioner's door. I drafted, with the input of Bob Rich, James Haddad, Bill Grieshober, and Bruce Meyer, and signed and filed a petition to the commissioner asking him to order a special audit. I did not deal with the FPA directly, but of course if and when the commissioner ordered a hearing on the petition, we had hopes that, with the parties in front of him, he would encourage, maybe even force, the buyers toward a closing.

The audit strategy did not come about without a little intellectual internecine fisticuffs. Some of our group wanted to go to court, really wanted the audit, and felt the commissioner, "tilting toward the money," would not really help us. I strongly opposed that route. Mindful of the accretion of the PIKs, the weakness of the agreement, and the years it would take for a final result in the courts, I felt we'd get nowhere useful in the time available, and the public embarrassment these charges would produce might alienate Tim Rigas, John Rigas, and Adelphia permanently. Meyer supported me, and we opted for the hearing, which could be kept confidential.

The hearing was practically a shutout. We had the materials, the witnesses, and the better of the argument. By the end of the morning, Ed Hartman and Adelphia's new counsel, Mike Snyder, were ready to settle, when the commissioner stated that his object was to get the parties to close the deal, that in his opinion we had the right to the special audit, and that if we didn't reach an agreement to consummate the sale by the end of the day, he would order the special audit forthwith. Meyer, Adelphia's counsel, and Dave Zimmerman of the league prepared an agreement to that effect and we signed it on the spot. We then proceeded to the real issue—a new deal that had been surfacing in the discussions with the commissioner.

THE "FINAL" AGREEMENT

The FPA, a product of so many months of fractious negotiations and eternal frustrations, lay there unapproved by the banks, disrespected by the lawyers, and unperformed by everybody. It did produce one thing for the parties, however: a mutual desire to get rid of each other. The 1998 agreement contemplated that we would all stay in for half the deal—holding speculative notes that depended on the ability of the Sabres to survive, protected only by a "put" right, whose value depended on the market value of the franchise five to seven years down the road and the ability and willingness of the league to respect our "put," find a well-financed purchaser, and maybe even extract our rights from a bankruptcy court. The 1998 deal also was vulnerable to the claims by Hartman and Brown that our "liabilities" exceeded the amounts shown on an interim balance sheet and thus, according to Hartman's calculations, should largely eat up the $3 million of Rigas notes. Out of the negotiations under the auspices of the commissioner came a new proposal, generated by Bob Rich: Forget the Rigas notes, forget the liabilities, forget the $8 million of Sabres subordinated paper, and forget the $16 million of contingent consideration—give us $10 million in cash, and we'll say good-bye. The concept seemed to appeal to all. Hartman called Tim, and we seemed to be in general accord.

In the private discussions before Bettman, Adelphia had still sung its "liability" dirge, and Bob Rich had countered with our stock in Tickets.com, which he expected to reach the market in an initial public offering at a value of $5 million—more than enough to eliminate any excess liability. When Bob came up to report the proposal to us in our caucus, we were hit, for the first time, with the unfortunate fact that there were *liabilities* of the joint venture that held the Tickets.com stock amounting to $1.5 million dollars—liabilities to Rich Products, which had financed the ticket equipment. It also was revealed that the stock was frozen for six months under an agreement not to resell during that period. While Bob's wife, Mindy, who had been our representative on the Tickets.com board, felt bound by the commitment, I felt the underwriter might well give us a release. Bob was ready to leave the negotiations in frustration, but I said he should go back in, lay out the facts, and argue that there would still be a surplus, based on the expected opening price and projected increase. I felt strongly that it was important to reach a definitive deal in the commissioner's presence. After consulting his colleagues, Bob did go back in and work it out. The deal was to be $9.65 million in cash, to reflect our share of the ticket company's debt, but the difference would be made up by the grant of two season tickets to each 100 percent seller for two years. (I inserted the phrases "at the 200 level" and "including playoffs.") We left the league office believing the deal was done.

Bob assured me he would get George's OK. Bob had been the reluctant but steadfast voice of reason throughout these difficult days.

Two days later I received a call from Adelphia: they would only go forward if Bob Rich would guarantee that the Tickets.com stock would have a value of $5 million. Concurrently, I ran into HSBC counsel in the US Air Club, and he reported that Adelphia had not accepted the most recent offer from the lenders, and the meeting had gone badly. When I reported these developments to Bill Grieshober of Rich Products, I could hear the gnashing of teeth and the splat of the phone against the wall. A few minutes later, Bill called me back. He spoke in tones reminiscent of Rush Limbaugh in his most

The closing, at long last—the author and his associate, Greg Ivancic.
Photo courtesy of the author.

foul of moods: "Bob has had it. He says, 'If Mister Swados thinks he can get
John Rigas to come up with the $10 million, let him do it. But I'm through!
I'm instructing you now, Bill, to stop working on this matter. I want Haddad
to stop working on this matter, I want not one cent more of Rich Products
funds to be spent on this. I'm through!'"

That was a lovely message. I felt naked and alone.

I had no other resources except my own voice, and whatever credit I
had with John—if I could reach him—and Gary Bettman. I plied them
both with threat, oratory, and plea, in equal parts, and miraculously word
came that the Rigas crowd had softened on the Tickets.com stock. We proceeded to closing, at long last, on July 16, 2000. I have no illusion about
what produced the change. The threat to move on the special audit was still
there—we had hired Ernst and Young and its litigation specialist to move
on the audit. But I now believe it was the portents of things to come that
caused Adelphia to capitulate. As Bill Grieshober reminds me, there were
already questions in the financial press about the number of subscribers
portrayed in the SEC documents. Enron's scandal was exposed in the fall of
2001, leading to the disclosures of April 2002 by Adelphia and what I call
"Enronitis" that hit the cable company, indicted the Rigases, and nearly
destroyed the Sabres franchise.

Chapter 36

ENRONITIS ON ICE

THE ENRONITIS PLAGUE

John Rigas, a scoundrel? It was hard to accept, hard to swallow. He was a man of gentle, kindly demeanor, a problem solver for so many. It was hard to imagine this community leader, pulled from his daughter's Manhattan home at 6 AM, arrested like a common thug, and dragged in plastic handcuffs before the cameras on every TV and cable news channel in the land. It was a display of the Bush administration's parade of determination to "get" the financial scoundrels. But where were the bozos who let forth the deluge, who bailed out and produced riches for themselves while the common stockholders lost their savings? Where were Ken Lay of Enron, Dennis Kozlowski of Tyco, Bernie Ebbers of WorldCom, and Gary Winnick of Global Crossing? Comfortable in their lawyers' suites, constructing intricate and technical defenses?

It was inevitable, with the search for owners with the resources—or apparent resources—needed to absorb the spreading losses, that the NHL governors' profile would include significant émigrés from the communications and dot-com worlds. There was Chuck Dolan of Cablevision with the Rangers, Philip Anschutz of Qwest with the Kings, John McCaw of McCaw Communications with the Canucks, Ted Leonsis of AmericaOnline with the Capitals, Computer Associates principals as the new owners of the

Islanders, and Comcast with the Flyers. It was also not surprising—in the light of a history that embraced such pleasant scoundrels as Bruce McNall of the Kings and Tom Skallen, the first owner of the Canucks—that some NHL owner would be entangled in the implosion of the stock market and the accounting scandals of 2002. Yet I never anticipated that these shocks to the financial world would ensnare my own former franchise, the Buffalo Sabres, endangering the institution that had been created and maintained with nearly thirty-five years of work, worry, and gastric juices by the Knox-Buffalo group, led by Seymour Knox III, Norty Knox, and me. After nearly three years of intense, sometimes unpleasant, negotiations, with the help of Commissioner Gary Bettman, we had finally produced a closing of the Rigas agreement to buy us out in July 2000. It was a great shock just two years later to see on TV the seventy-seven-year-old chairman of Adelphia Communications arrested. The charges made by the SEC and the federal prosecutors—levied against John's sons Tim and Mike as well—were mail fraud, lying in the company's SEC documents and representations to Adelphia stockholders, and plundering of the company's assets through fake transactions and misappropriation of corporate funds for the private benefit of the Rigas family. But the worry to us was the possibility that the Rigases would go broke and the Sabres would be shorn of finances, possibly dying in the process.

John Rigas, a scoundrel? I could not accept it.

But the events were inescapable: in four short months, John had gone from respected billionaire, a hero in the Buffalo community as owner of the Buffalo Sabres and the hope of its future growth, to an indicted felon ousted from control of his company. The company itself had been thrust into Chapter 11 bankruptcy, its stock thrown off the NASDAQ Exchange and selling for peanuts. I felt bad for John. We were out of the Sabres financially—but we had sold to the Rigas family, as the Western New York cable owners who would have a continuing interest in keeping the team in Buffalo. We could not ignore the danger that the survival of the Sabres in Western New York would be threatened by the destruction of the Rigas/Adelphia anchor.

Like the citizens of Coudersport, the small town in northwestern Pennsylvania where Adelphia was headquartered, I had experienced numerous signs of John's considerate kindness, perhaps dispensed in the miasma of Adelphia's billion-dollar revenues that made the cost of almost any gift seem insignificant, but kind and thoughtful nevertheless. I invited John to the first public performance of my daughter's choral cantata, *Bible Women*, in New York City in 1997, never expecting him to show. He certainly did (a little late, as usual)—the whole family did. I saw it as a sign of loyalty and support that has always been an important value to me. Even after July 2000, when I ceased to have any financial interest or power in the Sabres, he had made sure my office in the arena and my perks (tickets were part of the agreement) were still available. For years I had paid out of my own pocket for satellite TV service so that I could watch Sabres games in the winter months in Florida. When my condo association in Boca Raton decreed that, as part of a renovation plan, I had to remove my DirecTV dish from the roof, John ordered his Boca Raton people to install the NHL game program on my TV set, with special Adelphia connections, so I could watch Sabres games.

Yet I had been part of the opposition, and I had no illusions that the relationship was a close one. When the news of the Enron-like charges destroyed the market in Adelphia shares in May 2002—and ousted the Rigas family from control—my first reaction was that an avalanche had swept them into a strange ravine. Enron, Tyco, Global Crossing, WorldCom —the fraud and the plunder by those executives dwarfed the stupid offenses of John and his sons. And they hadn't bailed out. Their fortunes disappeared along with those of their investors. I sent messages to John of condolence and comfort. I called at the usual time—between his workout and his shower. My calls were never returned. On TV he looked drawn and uncertain. At his arraignment, the *Wall Street Journal* reported that when the judge asked for his plea, his counsel had to tap him on the shoulder to get him to answer, "Not guilty."[1]

GAMBLING WITH EBITDA

Year after year between 1996 and 1999, Adelphia's annual report disclosed the gambling nature of the business. Any intelligent and thorough investment banker, broker, analyst, or sophisticated investor should have been well aware of the dangers. As we would find after we signed the MOU in 1997, Adelphia was widely known as the most highly leveraged cable system in the industry. The portion of its capital derived from equity investment (stock or its equivalent) was the worst, as was the ratio of its debt to its cash flow (technically described as earnings before interest, taxes and depreciation, amortization, and debt service, or EBITDA). Moreover, the company's SEC filings showed that it was robbing Peter to pay Paul. Adelphia produced a cash flow in the billions, but it was not enough to pay the prior year's debt service, so the company had to borrow more this year to meet last year's payments on principal and interest. The survival religion was that, so long as the underlying assets—the contracts with the cable subscribers—increased in value, the debt was irrelevant. The market value per subscriber did increase from $3,000 to, at one point, $5,000 per subscriber. This meant Adelphia had assets of $5 billion. Someday, the number of subscribers and the monthly revenue per customer should increase to the point where the debt could be reduced or even paid off, and the owners would end up with a billion-dollar equity. This was not a philosophy peculiar to Adelphia: Cablevision in New York City, Charter Communications on the West Coast, Comcast in Colorado, and Cox in Atlanta all trusted the concept, to a greater or lesser degree.

It worked pretty well while the cable companies were closely held and the determination of market value was made by the owners and their bankers. But when they sought capital from the public for upgrades of lines or for the purpose of expanding their markets, the game went out of their control, into the hands of the investment bankers, analysts, and brokers who govern the vagaries of the stock market. In normal years, the value of a company's shares over time is usually determined by its earnings per share, to which the market applies a multiple (the "price/earnings" ratio)—say, ten to twenty times earnings per share. But these cable companies had no earnings. Because of their debt burden, interest and principal payments produced just losses. So, to give these shares a market value, the securities industry bought into the cable industry's philosophy that it was the generation of cash that determined value—the debt would be paid off ultimately, so it could be ignored unless it got too high or went into default. Certainly this philosophy was influenced by the concurrent rise of the dot-coms, whose assets were largely intangible and many of which had no earnings whatsoever but somehow flew high on the stock market scale. Those companies, despite their losses, secured large loans from prestigious lenders.

The tumescent bull market of the 1990s was exciting. Adelphia's A shares, held by the public, went from $7 to a high of $70 per share. During the same period the company, through acquisitions funded with its now valuable stock, had grown from the tenth-largest cable system (measured by the number of subscribers) to the sixth-largest in North America. At the time of the May 24, 2002, disclosure filing by the company's new management that burst the bubble, the market price was about $25 per share.

ENRON POISONS THE MARKET

A few months earlier, Enron executives, in a panic, had been forced to disclose conduct that appeared to be colossal fraud, on three counts:

1. Since they were not in the cable business, and had originated as a public utility that traditionally held plants and other tangible, hard assets (mostly sold or mortgaged to the hilt), they could not sell the investment bankers just on "cash flow" (EBITDA), and had to create traditional "earnings." They used their position in the energy industry to trade contract rights and treat the rights going out (the purchase) at cost and the rights coming in

(the sale price) at market value—producing a "gain," thus "earnings." Unfortunately, with a highly criticized series of "trades"—some say manipulations—particularly in California, they ran out of real companies to trade with. So what did they do? They created their own buyers. They formed partnerships into which the Enron crew put some assets, some Enron stock. The owners of the shares in a partnership would be 99 percent Enron, but 1 percent would be given or sold to Enron executives or their families or friends. That 1 percent outsider ownership, in the view of the organizers of the scheme, their counsel, and their accountants, was enough to make the transaction a bona fide sale, and the parent company, Enron, could report the transaction as a "gain," which could wipe out or offset its actual operating losses and justify a high market price for the stock, which had no real earnings to support it. More than eight hundred of these fraudulent partnership scenarios were created.

2. The executives who concocted this scheme received, as a reward, options to buy stock at the current price or a discounted price, exercise the options, then sell—even after the schemes were exposed within the company. The true bankrupt state of Enron affairs should have been revealed, and the Enron public shareholders, including the millions in 401(k)s and other pension plans, took disastrous losses.

3. Transactions that would ordinarily be accounted for as expense—thus reducing "earnings"—were converted into capital "investment," which had little effect on current earnings. In some cases this was converted into a "sale" of assets, producing a fictitious gain that added to earnings or masked a loss.

In comparing the charges of invidious conduct of the Rigases with that of Ken Lay and his cronies at Enron, it is clear that the Adelphia owners did not, as the Enronites did, bail out through profitable stock sales in the face of insider portents of doom. They, and others involved in the fiscal swindles of the time, realized, in the aggregate, billions of dollars from sales of their shares while their companies were known in the inner sanctums to be on the precipice, and their outside investors were left to disaster. This, the Rigases did not do: when the price of Adelphia shares went from double-digit dollars to single cents, the family went down with its ship. Nor, until late in 2000 and early 2001, did the Rigases attempt to boost earnings by illusory sales of assets to affiliated corporate or partnership entities that had no substance and were created just to stage fictitious transactions. The exception, which must have been grabbed in a panicky imitation of Arthur Andersen (the CPA firm which was the conspiring culprit in Enron) was the "converter box" episode. The boxes, which sit on top of TVs, converting the

sets for cable reception, especially digital reception, were normally purchased by Adelphia from Scientific Atlanta. Some inventory was maintained at Adelphia, but the purchases were usually tied to customer orders
and shipped by the manufacturers as needed. Toward the end of 2001 and
in the first quarter of 2002—after Enron had collapsed—the Rigases or
their associates began to see that maintaining earnings, or at least EBITDA,
was critical to avoid violating the covenants in the major loan agreements.
In the same crisis, maintaining the stock market price had become urgent,
indeed. The instruments granting the billion-dollar loans contained
covenants that would permit the banks to "call" the loans—require repay-
ment of the debt in full—if EBITDA, earnings, or the Adelphia share price
on the NASDAQ dropped below a certain level. To meet this crisis, the
Adelphia executives apparently produced book entries showing a transfer
of the inventory of the boxes to a wholly owned subsidiary or affiliate, for
notes, and reported the transfer as a "gain" that offset the expense incurred
in buying the cable boxes in the first place. (The subsidiary had no need for
the boxes, and it was not even in the cable business.)

While members of the Rigas family did not profit, so far as we know at
this writing, from the sale of their shares in the company—and indeed, the
drop in market value and delisting led to margin calls on the stock they had
pledged, which the family had to cover or get Adelphia to cover—there is
little doubt that the disclosures in the company's SEC filings and proxy
statements in the public offerings of Adelphia shares were not fully forth-
right. In managing the public offerings, Adelphia's investment bankers regularly advised that if the Rigases wanted the sale of the shares to go well
and the market in the stock to stay strong, they should demonstrate their
confidence in the company by investing in the new shares along with the
public. This was especially appropriate, and perhaps necessary, because the
class of stock owned by the Rigases—the B shares—had ten votes per share,
versus one vote per share in the class owned by the public. The supervote B
stock thus assured that, for the foreseeable future, the family would retain
control. And the Rigases did invest along with the outside investors. The
trouble was, they invested with money loaned to them by a subsidiary, and
the parent company was on the hook as guarantor of the loans. Anyone
reading the SEC documents at first blush would be given the impression
that the investments came out of the pockets of John and Tim and Mike,
but, so the charges go, since the company was on the hook, it really wasn't
their personal money that was paid for the stock, it was company debt. This
should have been clearly revealed in the reports to the SEC and the shareholders. Failure to reveal it was material—and even though the proceeds of
the borrowings went into the company till (or into the central cash management system—itself a questionable practice), conceivably some
investors would never have bought the stock or merged their own cable

companies with Adelphia if they had known the full facts on these arrangements. There were references to "coborrowings" in the proxy statements and annual reports, but no red flags.

It is possible that support for the public offerings and mergers was the real motive for the stock/loan transactions. The prosecutors claimed in the federal indictment that the reporting of those transactions was a misleading attempt to reduce the appearance of debt. That claim may not have support.

I must sound a cautionary note here. I have never seen an accounting or bookkeeping record of Adelphia or the Rigases, internal or external, except for the published SEC documents and annual reports. The indictments and complaints in the civil actions suggest, even allege, that the accounting records of the stock/loan transactions were ephemeral—that the company described what should have happened, not what did. That the Rigases did not borrow to invest in the company; no cash flowed into Adelphia from their stock purchase—just a memorandum telling that tale. I prefer to believe, pending proof that the small-town, close-to-the-vest, frugal history of the family persisted; and the bookkeeping never rose in sophistication with the growth of the company into a national, billionaire enterprise. The debt, I believe, consisted only of a bookkeeping transaction: the equivalent of notes from the Rigases to the company and stock out to the Rigases from the company.

The Rigases had lived with debt almost from the beginning. John relished his role as spokesman/mogul for the Sabres, and he was much in demand in Buffalo—especially with the arts institutions seeking his largesse. If, as frequently happened, he couldn't come up with a theme for his speech on the spur of the moment, he would trot out the story of how he came to purchase his first cable franchise, in Coudersport, Pennsylvania, for $500. He was persuaded by a movie salesman named "Sam" (no last name ever given), after several futile attempts, to spend the $500. John finally agreed that buying the "community television" franchise was a good thing, but he didn't have the $500, so, of course, he borrowed it. When the opportunity came later to expand his cable domain for $50,000, he borrowed that, too, from a sympathetic secretary who wanted him to succeed. John's story cast him well as modest, charming, and lucky.

If the Rigases did not line their pockets with insider trading of Adelphia shares, they nevertheless did use some Adelphia revenues in ways that gave rise to the charge that they had "looted" Adelphia's coffers. The 8-K filed with the SEC on May 24, 2002, by the company's new management (after the Rigas family was asked to leave the board) described a "cash management system" labeled "CMS" under which all cash received—whether generated by Adelphia, the entities owned by the Rigas family alone, or subsidiaries or affiliates like the Sabres—was pooled. Then, in a practice doubtless begun when Adelphia was just a family business, John and his sons would meet with Jim Brown—usually for breakfast—needs and requests for funds would be presented, and John—and later, Tim—would decide whose demands would be met, and, whether it was cable, telephone, Sabres, or personal, the cash would be allocated "to each according to its needs" and disbursed from the same pool, sometimes from the same bank account. This commingling is a no-no under normal accounting standards and corporate procedures designed to identify profit and loss and distinguish between parent and subsidiary, insiders and outsiders. It should have been abandoned once the company had issued a substantial number of shares to the public. But in an atmosphere where losses were continuous, cash was the only true legal tender, and control seemed invulnerable, inertia prevailed and the "family practice" continued.

According to the May 2002 SEC filing and the allegations in the SEC suit against the company and the criminal charges against the family, among the cash distributions allocated from the CMS pool were funds for recreational facilities in Cancun, Mexico; Ellen Rigas's apartment in New York City; funding for Ellen's movie company in the production of the film *Songcatcher*; funding for the investment business of Ellen's husband, Peter Venetis; $16 million for the construction of a golf course in Coudersport; and possible funding of other ventures, including, perhaps, the Buffalo Sabres. As for the latter, the charges publicized in May 2002 asserted that the Rigases had "loaned" $150 million to the Sabres, some of which, it was claimed, came out of the CMS pool.

THE INTERREGNUM, 1997 TO 2000: OWNERS ON THE SIDELINES

As month after month passed without a closing before the sale in 2000, I pressed John for movement. He would frequently come into the Directors' Room and, after greeting everyone in the place, sit down for a chat and put questions to me. What did I think about the coach? Should Pat LaFontaine's number be retired? What about arbitration? Player salaries? The league? (I was still going to all the meetings as alternate governor.) John's responses to my questions about our deal were usually punctuated with the comment that the decision was "up to Tim." I appreciated John's coming frequently down to sit with me during the first period before he went up to the Rigas box. (Adelphia owned Empire, the regional TV sports network. It was later pointed out to me that my seats, in the second row of the 200 level, were ideally situated for Empire's TV cameras. The TV shots frequently showed John, it was said, but never the vice chairman in the seat next to him!)

On one of those occasions in the 1999–2000 season, I got what I now realize was my first hint of the cash management system described in the

SEC filing, and the pool thinking behind it. As part of its effort to be a major player in Buffalo's economy and politics, Adelphia had floated a proposal to build, with government aid, a new building on the waterfront, near the HSBC Arena. The building would be an imposing structure, a catalyst for long-awaited waterfront development, and would house a new headquarters for Adelphia—which, as a large national company, could no longer be based in Coudersport—and create more than one thousand new jobs for Western New York. Anticipating my usual comment and complaint, John started the conversation with the observation, "There's good news for the Sabres! That is, for your group."

"What's that?" I asked, wary but hopeful.

"Governor Pataki has approved the waterfront deal, and the state will make a substantial contribution to the project," he replied.

"Congratulations," I said. "But how does that help us?"

"Look—the state will provide cash," he explained. "At least $25 million. That'll make it easier to close your deal!"

Cash for the waterfront. Cash for the Sabres. In John's thinking, it was all the same: in and out of the CMS pool![2]

As described in chapter 35, Gary Bettman's order eventually triggered action toward closing of the Rigas/Adelphia purchase of our interest in the Sabres, but we were never sure whether our suspicions of Adelphia's conduct had any substance. Whether because of the threat of what the special audit would expose or the rumbling of events that would ultimately trigger the Adelphia collapse, the Rigases finally, more than three years after the original agreement, consented to close. The shocks that imperiled their company and ousted the Rigases from ownership and control could have been of just academic or emotional concern to the Knox-Buffalo group; but that collapse threatened the very existence of the Buffalo Sabres—the institution to which Seymour and Norty and I and our colleagues had devoted more than thirty years.

All this became just history, I thought, when we finally, exhausted and unbelieving, consummated the sale of our interests in the Sabres on July 10, in the year of the end of our reign, 2000. I had to wrestle with my corporate lawyer's prudence (part paranoia), so I retained five hundred shares of Adelphia stock of the block George Gregory had bought for my retirement plan. I had the faint idea that, if anything went wrong with Adelphia, or with their maintenance of the Sabres—if, say, an overaggressive trustee in bankruptcy tried to reverse our transaction—I would have some standing in the courts as a shareholder of Adelphia. For what purpose? Why, of course, to play the role of the Dutch boy with his finger in the dike—or, more likely, Don Quixote, charging at the bankruptcy windmills. I have yet to use those five hundred shares, but I'm ready!

THE RIGASES—
CAUGHT IN THE ENRON AVALANCHE

I was shocked when, two years later, in the spring of 2002, the Rigas/Adelphia disaster loomed, and the very future of the Sabres in Buffalo was imperiled. The Enron/Arthur Andersen "plague" began in October 2001, when the fake partnerships, manipulation of expenses, and horrendous stock bailouts by Enron executives were first revealed. As the other "major" accounting firms began to face the ugly truths of the Enron collapse, Enronitis spread like a malignant flood: the CPAs demanded "cure or cover," and a flood of SEC filings and complex press releases disclosed that Tyco, Global Crossing, and WorldCom, among others, had been infected by Enronitis and had suffered the consequent crash of their shares. The plague did not reach Adelphia until the following March, when its CPA firm, Deloitte, demanded an acknowledgment of loans, cash withdrawals, and purported illicit expenditures that the Rigases could not agree were improper. On May 24, 2002, doubtless at the insistence of counsel, an 8-K filed with the SEC drew back the curtain, and the ugly portrait of conflict and chaos was displayed. It appeared that in the five months following the Enron revelations, the cadre at Adelphia had tried desperately to somehow inflate the company's revenues and cloak its expenses in an attempt to avoid a collapse of its share price.

It was unfortunate. The late measures were futile, and they succeeded only in tarring the Adelphia and Rigas operations with the Enron brush. In rapid succession, the Deloitte firm resigned, the stock crashed from around $25 to less than $1 per share, multiple lawsuits were filed against the company and the family, John and his sons resigned from the board, the stock was delisted by NASDAQ, and the new Adelphia board turned into an apparent enemy of the Rigases—joining with what seemed like inappropriate enthusiasm in the attacks on the family by the SEC and the US Department of Justice.

Bankruptcy of Adelphia and its subsidiaries in June 2002 was followed quickly by the arrest, staged for the cameras of CNN and the broadcast networks, and culminating in indictment on September 23, accompanied by some gustatory phrases from the US attorney:

> The scheme charged in the Indictment is one of the most elaborate and extensive corporate frauds in United States history. The Rigas defendants and their co-conspirators exploited Adelphia's byzantine corporate and financial structure to create a towering façade of false success, even as Adelphia was collapsing under the weight of its staggering debt burden and the defendants' failing management of the company, and the Rigas family lined their pockets with shareholder dollars.[3]

Did the US attorney's diatribe—scoundrel, trickster, and thief—fit the case? I saw no signs, in the eight years of our association with Adelphia, of perfidy. Tough business practices, yes, but sophistication and intelligence, sometimes accompanied by what I considered bad judgment. The company's debt burden and absence of true "earnings" was typical of the cable industry—although near the precipice—and the disaster was precipitated by the stock market's reaction to Enron's flagrant cancerous conduct—a sudden flight from the world of EBITDA—of no earnings, stratospheric share prices, and outrageous executive compensation.

"ERKIE"—SAVIOR OR JUDAS?

One of the uglier aspects of the tragedy is the role that Erland "Erkie" Kailbourne, John Rigas's friend and neighbor, played—or was forced to play—as the drama unfolded. Erkie, originally an officer of one of Adelphia's lead banks, had gained notoriety and respect in the Buffalo community for his successful leadership in the drive to sell the boxes and club seats required by the NFL Bills to keep that team in Buffalo. Kailbourne came from northwestern Pennsylvania, the area graced by Adelphia's headquarters at Coudersport. John placed him on the Adelphia board, and when events forced the family to resign, he was elected chairman—doubtless with the expectation that he would protect the family's interest (although his previous connection with the lenders was certainly important). But the charges, whether or not provable or just, were too serious. Kailbourne had to act objectively, in the interests of all the shareholders, including those like Leonard Tow, who were out to skin the Rigases alive for the disaster that had befallen the Adelphia shares they had taken as the price, or part of the price, in mergers with Adelphia. Thus the new board sued the Rigases and all their family-owned affiliates (initially including the Sabres), cooperated with the SEC and the Justice Department in developing the charges against them, and generally behaved in a hostile manner. Perhaps they went too far in hitting back at the Rigases, however: when the indictment of John, Tim, and Michael was announced on September 23, 2002, the Adelphia release recorded the board as "applauding" the indictment—it helped "distance" the company from the Rigas family.

The slings and arrows of the Rigases' "outrageous fortune" continued at an unrelenting pace, and the Kailbourne board did nothing to stay their impact. The board opposed the payment of the family's legal fees by the company, and the bankruptcy court initially sided with the board. The company announced that it would not make the salary payments called for under John Rigas's termination contract. The carriers who'd issued the Adelphia officers and directors liability insurance policies disclaimed and threatened cancellation. Bankruptcy had so far proved as much of a weapon against the family as a protection of the creditors.

As for the fate of the Rigas family and of Adelphia itself, I had no special talent for prognostication. With the universal anger at Enron and its coterie, the abominable performance and corruption of the investment banking industry—analysts and brokers alike—and the natural pressure from the president to punish the violators, this would be a dangerous era for the family from Coudersport. I believe the attention on the Rigases has been disproportionate to their offenses, and I could envision defenses for the major claims, defenses that could conceivably produce a chance of escape.

On the main charge—misrepresentation and failure to disclose in the filings with the SEC and the statements and reports sent to the shareholders—the government's case was not without weakness. As I pointed out above in this chapter, the lenders, investment bankers, brokers, and cable system owners all knew that Adelphia was a high-risk, speculative investment. They knew, and the written reports disclosed, that Adelphia had a high-debt burden, was the most highly leveraged of the leading cable systems, had no earnings, just EBITDA, and that the company did not generate enough cash flow to pay last year's debt service, let alone this year's principal and interest on its multibillion-dollar obligations. Thus, as the reports spelled out quite clearly, Adelphia had borrowed more and more each year to cover the cash shortage. As to the "coborrowing"—the $2 billion plus of loans obtained by the Rigases with the guarantee of Adelphia: the coborrowing was disclosed—in a footnote; and even the amount of that "coborrowing" was indicated in the statement in the documents that the two parties (Adelphia and the Rigas family or their family-owned company) could "each" borrow "up to" $4 billion. The government had to persuade the fact finder (judge or jury) that "up to" was misleading or insufficient. In a criminal case, the burden of proof beyond a reasonable doubt (applicable in securities cases?) is on the government. Why a parenthetical note? When a company has a negative issue or episode, and is seeking to sell its shares to the public, it is the common policy of securities lawyers (with SEC acquiescence) to disclose enough, but not too much, and never, except where SEC regulations require otherwise, emblazon the negative reference across the pages of the annual report or proxy statement, so it cannot be missed. "Up to" in a note—was it enough?

On the charge of "looting" the company by using the CMS cash management system—the pooled cash—for personal benefits: the aggregate amount of these withdrawals veers toward insignificance, when compared to the aggregate revenues produced by the company—more than a billion dollars annually. There is no way that these withdrawals undermined the financial status of the company or were responsible for the crash of its shares. Some of the individual components of the "looting" may indeed be justified. As a multibillion-dollar company with cable systems that operated in localities spread across the United States, the use of company planes and a base in New York City may be shown to be necessary and appropriate. The fact that the Rigases, as officers of the company, used daughter Ellen's Manhattan apartment rather than a separate, expensive headquarters, may have been evidence of the Rigases' small-town frugality, rather than the reverse, Cancun—a luxury vacation spot for John and his family? John's lawyers argued that it was obtained and used as a major entertainment resource for conventions and meetings of its myriad lenders, investment bankers, cable suppliers, management, and affiliates. I gave a lecture at one such meeting myself, shortly after Adelphia made its first investment in the Sabres. Much ado about the golf course in Coudersport, being constructed at a cost of $18 million. Before 9/11, and until the decline of the industry, the Lackawanna suburb of Buffalo was known as a company town, run by one of the titans of steel—Bethlehem; Bethlehem constructed its own golf course—largely restricted to company management—as a means of keeping good executives in that ugly suburb. John Rigas had the same conception: Coudersport was a small town, off the beaten track; yet it was to continue to be Adelphia's principal headquarters. A golf course might well be an inducement for staff of ability to remain in that small-town environment. And since golf courses rarely produce cash flow, it made sense for the family to make the investment, instead of the company.

Muriel Siebert, former New York State superintendent of banking and the first woman to buy a seat on the New York Stock Exchange, in a 2002 interview in the *New York Times*, was asked, What was the worst single excess of the 1990s? Her answer:

> I basically feel that Enron was a case of total moral bankruptcy. It was not just the company and its executives. It was not just the accountants. They had to get legal opinions from a law firm. They had to get the derivatives [stock options, participations in subsidiary transactions, and "hot" initial offerings, et al.] from the banks and Wall Street firms. One group alone could not have done it. The money was vast and the money was fast. . . . [4]

The Rigases' conduct, however deficient or reprehensible, was not of the same character. The family had no "derivatives." Unlike the principals in Enron, Global Crossing, Tyco, and WorldCom, they did not bail out. They took the shellacking along with the public shareholders. They did not sell their shares with insider knowledge of the financial failures. They did not receive magnificent stock options. And they did not destroy the company they had built. A report on September 13, 2002, just before their indictment issued by the company's new auditors, Price Waterhouse Coopers, declared that, as of July 31, 2002, "the company and its sub-

sidiaries had $52.8 billion in consolidated assets and 48.8 billion in con-
solidated liabilities."[5]

I don't know by what method PWC valued the assets—market, I hope;
book, I hope not; but the net of $4 billion produces a hope, however computed.

Of course, although I thought I knew John well, and our contact on
Sabres matters was intense and thorough, I was still on the periphery of
Adelphia's own matters: I was just an interested observer. Certainly I didn't
know everything, or everybody. For example, among the five Adelphia officers charged was one Michael Mulcahey, described in the indictment as the
company's director of internal reporting. I had never seen or heard of Mulcahey in the eight years of the team's relationship with the Rigas family.
John's son James, who was not indicted, always gave a pleasant smile, but
he never participated in the business or legal meetings when I was present.
He always seemed to be leaving for some conference on fiber optics or
some other technical or scientific aspect of the telecommunications business. Mike's indictment must have flowed solely from his position as a
principal company officer. I never heard a sharp or unkind or slippery word
from Mike. My principal contact in the later years were with Ed Hartman,
who served as the major financial contact on Sabres issues. Ed always
seemed to me to be tough, knowledgeable, and, within the partisan instructions placed on him by Adelphia, fair. As for Tim, Adelphia's CEO, I've
described the bizarre scenes in the Board of Governors' meetings, in which
he seemed to wish to distance himself as much as possible from me. We
began on quite friendly terms, but as the financial troubles of the Sabres
came front and center, he seemed to blame me for getting his father into
the morass in the first place. He was taller and more handsome than his
brothers, with a pleasant countenance, and the reserved, careful intelligence of a poker player. Our relationship in the later years can best be
described as ambivalent and prickly. In the interregnum—the three years
when we granted operating control to the Rigases but retained ownership
and board control while awaiting a closing of the Funding and Purchase
Agreement—I remember vividly two scenes. The first was in the 1999 conference finals in Toronto. We were in the Rigas box. To the surprise of
everyone but Lindy Ruff and the team, we won the deciding game of the
series against the Leafs, which meant we were in the Stanley Cup Finals. My
gal, Frances, and I were ecstatic. I turned to look at Tim and saw no ecstasy
there—just a frown and a grimace. Were they counting on failure, so they
could press the lenders for greater bargains?

The second scene was in my seats in our arena during a Sabres game.
The hot issue of the moment was the attempt of the Marine Midland Bank
to change the building's signs to reflect the new name of the banking institution—HSBC—and the attempt by the Rigases to get concessions on the
public sector "loans" and the arena lease. Rich Tobe, Erie County Executive

Dennis Gorski's principal business counsel, came up to ask me about it. My response was restrained and factual, I thought, but when I looked up, Tim was staring at me; his façade had disappeared and the smile became a snarl. This seemed to be more evidence that Tim regarded me as an obstruction to his plans and the spider who dragged the Rigases into the Sabres' web, as perhaps I was. But until we began the proceeding before Gary Bettman for a special audit, I saw tough, sharp business postures in Tim's positions, but none that foretold the conduct alleged in the criminal and civil charges that surfaced against him in the summer of 2002. Some of my colleagues did not agree, but despite Tim's obvious displeasure at my ubiquitous presence, I judged my positive relationship with John an asset that, in the fight to bring our ship into port, we could not pitch overboard.

As for John, whom I still regard as a friend (although I have had no contact with him personally for several years), I must acknowledge that my view was not unanimously accepted in the Sabres organization. He was many-sided, and it is certainly possible that my sighting was limited. I remember Larry Quinn, our brilliant arena builder and temporary president, coming back from a session with John in Coudersport. Larry was ordinarily confident, judgmental, and sometimes arrogant: no stranger to hidden agendas of his own creation. He was discussing his future, assuming the Rigases ever closed our agreement. He was strongly opposed to reintroducing Ted Nolan to the franchise, and other matters that seemed important to John. Larry came back red-faced, flustered, and beaten. He had seen a side of John Rigas he had never anticipated—confronted with opposition, John had lowered the guillotine. It was left to me to work out his termination.

"FLIPPING" BROWN AND "ROLLING UP" RIGAS

As fans of the TV show *Law and Order* know well, it is a common strategy of prosecutors to hit hard at an underling involved in a corporate crime, to persuade him—perhaps with offers of a lighter sentence—to provide evidence for the prosecution of the boss above him. Since the underling normally has some vestige of loyalty to his superiors that must be overcome, the tactic is known as "flipping" the employee. The district attorney uses this evidence to trap the bosses, echelon by echelon, in similar flipping, until the principal executives are "rolled up"—damned for conviction with the underling's evidence. On November 15, 2002, it became clear that the Adelphia "flippee" was former vice president of finance Jim Brown and the "rollee" was John or Tim Rigas, perhaps both. On that day Jim Brown pleaded guilty in Manhattan federal court before Judge Leonard B. Sand. In his plea, Brown admitted that he had misrepresented the state of the company's finances, the pace of the growth in the company's earnings (or cash flow), and the number of its cable subscribers. The misrepresentations had apparently occurred in key meetings or conference calls with investment bankers and Moody's (the leading corporate credit rating agency) in January 2002. The *Wall Street Journal* reported that in his appearance before the judge, Brown acknowledged that "with the assistance and agreement of others, [he] helped to manipulate and overstate earnings"; admitted that he knew the misstatements would mislead lenders and investors; named the "others" as including John, Tim, and Michael Rigas; and agreed to cooperate in the government investigation and to testify at any trial, if necessary. Sentencing was scheduled for April 13, 2003—doubtless to provide time for a full probation report and evaluation, recording, and, perhaps, fine-tuning Brown's prospective testimony. The admission of guilt includes three counts of conspiracy, bank, and securities fraud—which could theoretically produce a sentence of as much as forty-five years in prison. But Jim Brown's testimony could perhaps cut his sentence to only a small fraction of that. One notes that, against the malign background of the billions appropriated by the scoundrels in Enron, Tyco, and Global Crossing, Brown was forced to surrender $85,000 and his BMW.

Brown and I crossed swords a number of times in the Sabres negotiations through 1997 (when the MOU was signed). We disagreed, and I sometimes went over his head, but we ultimately resolved the issues and moved on. I had difficulty reading some of the Adelphia crew, especially Tim. But Jim Brown seemed the most genuine. He had candor and enthusiasm. There was tension in our contacts, but at times we would even give each other high fives at a Sabres playoff victory, while the others stayed silent. The confrontations we had, sometimes nasty in temporary tone, led some of my owner colleagues to believe I was too tough for the negotiations of the 1998 agreement formalizing the MOU, and I was temporarily "benched." But the negotiations, which lasted more than six months before a formal agreement was reached to cover a good-faith handshake, proved that Jim Brown did not reserve his ornery style just for me. Ray McCabe, the younger lawyer in my firm sent into the fray as my backup, described the negotiations with Brown as "the most unpleasant experience of my life." My characterization would be somewhat milder. Tension and desperation rout polite discourse, and I now see—as I suspected in 1997—that Jim Brown was desperate in his attempts, on which the Rigases were depending, to keep the overloaded Adelphia ship afloat. He was opposed to the Sabres deal, considering it the buyout of owners he thought were "under the water" and investing more in a franchise that was already losing large sums, and he fought hard to cut it off—or least to make the contract so full of holes it might never reach fruition.

The situation turned really ugly when Erkie Kailbourne morphed from friend to foe. Leonard Tow, a former cable owner who sold his busines to Adelphia for stock, began an assault on control, the Deloitte accounting firm deserted, and the SEC and various stockholder groups hit the Rigas family with countless lawsuits. Now Jim Brown turned Judas. And his admissions were apparently accepted by the jury in the later conviction of Tim and John. Knowledgeable and distinguished law firms—Buchanan Ingersoll, for example (once headed by my Harvard Law School classmate John Buchanan)—apparently gave some of the transactions their legal imprimatur. But the civil liability—financial responsibility for damages and losses—may be insurmountable in some cases, because liability under the federal Securities Acts does not necessarily require a showing of intent. If a company makes a material misstatement in a proxy paper or report and an investor relies upon it, a director may be liable even if he didn't participate in preparing or know about the document. Jim Brown's "flip" may not technically affect the civil liability of his superiors—which arises from the mistakes and missteps in the documents given the public—but it puts him against John and Tim in the criminal trial, where the question of who knew what was exceedingly relevant in determining who had the criminal "intent" and engaged in the criminal acts which would fix the label "felon."

What about the bankers, lawyers, and accountants who gave advice that resulted in the misleading misstatements? Until the Supreme Court of the United States 1994 decision in the *Central Bank of Denver* case,[6] the securities industry believed that anyone who aided or abetted the fraud on the issuance or sale of securities could be liable as "directly or indirectly" producing the fraud. That decision, in a 5–4 vote, held that Congress had failed specifically to nail the "abettors," and set free a bank that had knowingly let a stale appraisal of the property securing the bond issue go unmodified when the property declined in value. In reading the decision years later, it seems unreal—written from another planet. I favor the dissenting opinion of John Paul Stevens, defining the "abettor" to include those who are *indirectly* involved, and not only because he was always very friendly to me in the days when he represented Charley O. Finley at NHL governors' meetings. I remember vividly the views of my first boss, Jim Landis, a major player in the development of the Securities Acts of 1933 and 1934 and the SEC. Landis would have tied his prominent eyebrows in knots at the thought that the legislation that he had helped create in the destruction of values following the 1929 stock market crash did not hit a professional or a banker who'd helped foist a fraud on the public, even though he did not "participate" in the transaction. The whole culture, focus, and hopes of Washington in those days—disregarded by Kennedy—was to rein in not only the rascals who brought about the debacle but their crew as well. "Directly or indirectly" should have been good enough to hang the contributing professionals.

Eight years later, in 2002, we saw what *Central Bank* had wrought. An accounting firm, acting as a "consultant," approves (or maybe even creates) an "independent partnership" with assets of the company and gives an opinion that a sale to the "partnership" produces a "gain" that can be added to the company's "earnings." The facts show that the partnership is not really independent and the transaction was a fake. The effect of the *Central Bank* ruling is that the executives may escape liability if (as they will testify) they relied on the accountant's advice, and the accountant escapes because the Securities Act of 1934, in the Court's view, does not apply to an "abettor."

Fortunately, a courageous judge in Houston recognized the defect and dangerous consequences of the *Central Bank* opinion and chose not to be bound by it. On December 20, 2002, US District Judge Melinda Harmon ruled that bankers, law firms, and investment houses involved in the Enron catastrophe could be held accountable if it could be proved that they acted with "intent to deceive." The opinion is long and complex, and appeals are certain. So the distinguished law firms and CPAs who produced the approvals of the Adelphia transactions have some anxious days ahead.

THIEVES OR VICTIMS?

The prosecutors and plaintiffs in the Adelphia criminal and civil proceedings, notwithstanding *Central Bank*, claim intentional misstatements by the principals, abetted by their professionals. I was appalled to read of the cable box transaction with a subsidiary that was not even in the cable business, and the backdating of documents. But I have difficulty fitting that conduct into the characters of the Rigas family I knew—particularly not John. I suspect what happened—in the face of the stock market avalanche that nearly destroyed the company and the family—is more appropriately described in the words of Michael Jensen, quoted by John Cassidy in his perceptive piece in the *New Yorker*:

> It is important to recognize that this doesn't come about as the result of crooks. This comes about as a result of honest people being subjected to forces that they don't understand. The forces are very strong, and this evolves over a period of time. You end up with highly moral, honest people doing dishonest things. It wasn't as if the Mafia had taken over corporate America. We are too quick to say—and the media feed this—that if a bad thing happens it's because a bad person did it, and that person had evil intentions. It is much more likely that there were some bad systems in place.[7]

When the disclosures of April and May 2002 by the Kailbourne Adelphia board reached the press, multiple lawsuits were launched, by the SEC and in class actions by stockholder groups, claiming losses aggregating as much as $2.5 billion. On September 28, 2002, those actions were stayed by the Pennsylvania federal judge, pending the outcome of the SEC and Department of Justice proceedings. Of course, as pointed out above, there probably are technical, and more than technical, violations of the security laws and regulations—at least those arising from the quick-fix attempts to maintain EBITDA, the appearance of growth and of cash flow—following the Enron collapse. But I question whether the equities justify the harsh language and conduct in the government's treatment of the Rigases. And the presence of equity, that is, net worth—apparently as much as $4 billion—in the company's balance sheet, creates the possibility of mitigating the damages and a decent chance that the company will emerge from Chapter 11 and preserve some value for its investors, maybe including the Rigas family, after all. I wish them luck! Let the nightmare be over.

As the government's trial against John, Tim, and Michael Rigas unfolded in Manhattan federal court in the Spring of 2004, the courtroom displayed the expected ugly spectacle of the prosecution's attempt at "rolling up" the Rigases by "turning" Adelphia's vice president of finance, Jim Brown. As the defendants' lawyers counterattacked with charges of lying and betrayal, my concern was for John, who over the six years of our contact had given me, as the Sabres' vice chairman and, I thought, as a friend, tokens of respect and good intentions. But Brown's testimony began to unmask—or at least cast substantial doubt on—the belief about John's innocence I preferred to cherish.

During the long three years (1997 to 2000) when we were unable to force Adelphia to close our sale of the Sabres, I had repeatedly challenged John on the delay—it was bad faith and bad policy, I said. John's response was: "I hear what you're saying, Bob. But I've turned the business over to my sons, and I can't control them. . . ." Yet according to the testimony of Jim Brown on May 16, 2004, when Jim urged Tim Rigas to stop his father from repeating his tales of "virtue"—John didn't sell Adelphia shares, he didn't take stock options, he didn't receive outrageous salaries—Tim's response echoed through the courtroom: "I can't control my father. . . ."[8]

The revelations—or assertions—by Brown were clearly influenced by his hope for favored treatment as a prosecution witness. But they troubled me. Concerns about John's intentions had been raised by my colleagues when we still owned the team. So I was not totally surprised as the trial lifted the curtain from the primitive notes and books that the Rigas crowd had used for "accounting." In my days as a corporate counsel, an acquisition or a stock purchase, even if within the corporate family, would be dressed with all the paraphernalia of the investment banker, the corporate draftsman, and the certified accountant—designed, of course, to protect its tax and business legality. Journal entries were preceded or followed by documents and board resolutions, SEC filings, and even press releases. But the Rigas family apparently never adjusted to their public robes and roles, and, except where their advisers insisted otherwise, stayed with their primitive notes and sometimes ambiguous entries in Brown's journals.

But I had thought, or hoped, as indicated in the previous section, that these primitive bogus accounts, describing transactions like the sale of the cable boxes to entities that had no use for the cable business, were limited in scope and borne by the desperation following the collapse that hit Adelphia's stock in 2002 in the wake of the Enron plague. Yet Brown's testimony tells us that the manipulative accounting began as early as 1997, the year the Knox-Buffalo group signed the Memorandum of Understanding, designed to sell our ownership of the Sabres to the Rigas family, and turned over the operating control. It was in place during the years when, as John described the event to me and to the community in a large public gathering in front of the arena, the family or the company was going to fund the construction of a major new thousand-employee plant on Buffalo's waterfront that would revive the local economy, a bit of legerdemain that evaporated with Adelphia's bankruptcy and the move of its headquarters to Denver.

Was it all a big con?

Was it all just a reflection of the corporate immorality that became the accepted conduct of a company grown too big and too reckless for its financial breeches?

In the fall of 2003, Medaille College asked me to lecture in a course in sports management. I asked the students, who seemed a bright and energetic lot, "How would you compare the moral conduct of the investment banking business with that of professional sports?" The class wasn't sure how to answer this philosophical question from this stranger from the sports world. I said sports would win hands down. (No repetition for three generations of the Chicago Black Sox scandal.) There are few secret transactions. You can't draft or sign a player or buy a franchise without a media broadcast within twenty-four hours. Salaries, some subject to caps, are determined transactions that are always spread promptly and prominently on the sports pages. Insiders' tricks would fail, as the league or the players' association came down upon them. And the tests of success and hard work and skill are "transparent"—as the politicians like to describe it—last night's stats are there for all the fans in the Hot Stove League to see.

RESTITUTION AND RETRIBUTION; PAYBACK AND VENGEANCE

On June 20, 2005, the guillotine fell. The federal judge spoke his words of doom. With their heritage, some may see the marks of Greek tragedy for John and Tim. But I am reminded more of the last line of Leoncavallo's opera *Pagliacci*: "La Commedia e' finite!" For John Rigas the magnificent play and ploy he created with billions of Adelphia dollars is ended. The sentences: fifteen years in prison for John; twenty years for Tim.

In convicting, the jury was not impresed—nor was I—by the puerile efforts of John's counsel, which consisted largely of an attack on "turncoat" Jim Brown. Nor was the sentencing judge, Leonard B. Sand, much impressed by arguments of John's supporters, which consisted largely of references of good character and a plea for John's age and infirmity, nor of John's own plea—after sentencing—of remorse coupled with a belief that he did good, not wrong. The prodigious efforts of the family to restore the investors' losses—more than 90 percent of the Rigases' assets were surrendered—did not seem to be considered; nor was the fact that the Rigases, unlike so many of their concurrent offenders, did not bail out, but took their shellacking along with the other stockholders. There was no recognition of the view that the collapse of Adelphia shares was not caused by technical violation of the security laws. Judge Sand had the opportunity to show mercy on the wings of a recent decision of the Supreme Court freeing the federal judiciary from the compulsory draconian sentences in the federal guidelines. But the judge would have none of this. Except for a curious "option" giving John the possibility of parole in the event he were ninety days from *death*, the judge spoke not at all of justice, little of the issues, but more of vengeance:

> The man I have to sentence is the man reflected in the evidence, a man who long ago sent Adelphia on a track of lying and cheating and defrauding. . . . Regretfully for everyone, this was not stopped over ten years ago, but continued and got more brazen and culminated in one of the largest frauds in corporate history.[9]

The federal prosecutors demanded 215 years' punishment for Tim and John. The Rigases were not the worst of the offenders, although they may have been the first. Perhaps the federal lawyers in the Manhattan court, loyal to the Bush administration that appointed them, were influenced by the competition from their Democratic rival, New York State attorney general Elliott Spitzer, whose litigators really struck terror into the investment crowd.

The fates, or the works of negotiation, left the family—presumably Ellen and Doris and James and, hopefully, Michael—two small cable systems in western Pennsylvania, so returning the Rigases to the origin of their grand escapade, the $500 drive-in theater in Coudersport. I still have difficulty squaring the judge's judgment with the man I knew. Appeals are still possible, but since John did not take the stand, the "know nothing" defense, which produced an acquittal for former CEO Richard M. Scrushy in the Health South case,[10] may not be available for John. Unless his lawyers have some miraculous legal escape,[11] more than they have shown so far, the odds are remote. So the "commedia" is really "finite."

Chapter 37

THE ENRON PLAGUE, CONTINUED

THE BANKRUPT SABRES IN INTENSIVE CARE

It was the fall of Enron that foisted the plague on the telecommunications industry and the dot-coms, and ultimately on the broad securities market. The debacle would have been an event of solely intellectual significance for me but for the sudden threat to the Sabres. After the closing of July 2000, I no longer had any financial interest in the team. Thanks to John's generosity, I was allowed to keep my office in the arena, where I could work on my book, and, as a member of the Hall of Fame, I was occasionally invited to Sabres dinners and outings. At one, after the team's failure to make the playoffs in 2002, John asked me to warm up the proceedings with a "positive" pep talk. I responded with the hope the players weren't "mad" at the loss and that they have provided exciting hockey. I recounted the time Pat LaFontaine asked me why the Knoxes and I, as owners, always came into the dressing room after a win, but never after a loss. That was on the advice of our first GM, Punch Imlach, I said. When I had asked the same question of Punch, he replied, "I'd never go in after the team gets beat—it's too dangerous—they're too mad!" I was still a hockey fan, but, after the closing of our deal, I had no access to or appetite for the financials, except a raising of the eyebrows at the talk in the press about losses of $20 million per year.

Then came the flood: Chapter 11 bankruptcy for Adelphia, disaster for its stock, the televised arrest of the Rigases and their ouster from management, and, finally, the family's abandonment of the Sabres, with the league taking over operating control. There was immediate talk of gloom and doom. The team owed, it was said, $150 million to Adelphia, and the ubiquitous Paul Allen, a cofounder of Microsoft, was rumored to be ready to buy the team and move it to Portland, Oregon. The bankruptcy court, the experts proclaimed, would be sure to take the highest bid, and the Sabres would be gone.

Thirty-five years of work and worry by Seymour, Norty, and me; thirty-five years of support, of hanging in there by Bob Rich and George Strawbridge and Joe Stewart and George Gregory and John Fisher and the Andrews and our clients and friends and colleagues; thirty-five years of investment by the city and county and state; thirty-five years of loyalty and support from the hundreds of thousands of fans—up in smoke, destroyed by Enronitis?

I had to abandon my semiretired routine. I had to do something.

MINISTER WITHOUT PORTFOLIO

The *Sports Business Journal* published a punishing, negative "scoop" on the Sabres, reporting that the club had lost $20 million a year for years, the Rigases (or Adelphia) were owed more than $150 million, the team was mediocre, the fans had been turned off, and the franchise was headed for the scrap heap, in bankruptcy. I called Gary Bettman and said no one would buy the Sabres if they believed that article. Gary called back a few minutes later, asking me to help him "persuade Bob Rich to buy the team." I told the commissioner I was not Bob's counsel; Bob and I talked frequently, and I believed there was a measure of mutual respect there, but Bob was an independent thinker and I certainly had no control over Rich or his company, Rich Products. However, I would do my best. The only way I could do what the commissioner asked, I said, was to keep Bob currently and expertly informed, and provide him with factual data and analysis that would counter the hearsay, negative information being circulated by the media.

Then began months of painstaking effort. I tracked everything I could find about Adelphia on the Internet, read the SEC documents as they were filed, and made frequent calls to the NHL's able David Zimmerman, who seemed to be my designated responder and who continued to treat me, with discretion, as still a part of the NHL family. I reported fully to Bob Rich, and, as several of the candidates approached me for help, I made it clear that my input was available, without discrimination, to any and all candidates who sought to buy the club for continued operation in Buffalo. To someone seeking to move the franchise, I had no such obligation. Such a move, where a qualified local buyer was present, would violate the policy against "gypsy franchises" embraced in the NHL constitution and Bylaw 36, which I had helped create in the 1970s during my tour of duty as league secretary.

SWADOS AS THE ANTI-CASSANDRA

I had no illusions about the efficacy of my efforts. It would have been nice to win a global lottery and buy the team myself, but I had to adjust, again, to being "counsel in the crease." I needed help to score. If Bob Rich wouldn't do it, I hoped someone else would. It was too good a franchise, too fine a hockey market. Bob had other interests: he had his baseball team, the minor-league Buffalo Bisons; he was an active CEO of a major company; he was an avid deep-sea fisherman; and he had just published a fine book, *Fish Fights*, and was at work on another. He, his family, and his company had shown a tendency to be quixotic in the sports arena. I remembered, vividly, the Riches' sudden premonition about Major League Baseball finances and their abrupt termination in the 1990s of the last effort to acquire a franchise for Buffalo.

But Bob did not completely dash our hockey hopes. He repeatedly asked me to keep him "in the loop," and to me and others he at times stated that, so long as others could swing it, he needn't participate, but if things developed toward a threat to move the franchise, he might well step in and help to keep it here. So I had the opportunity (without compensation), and I was not completely without resource. One of the painful problems of age and retirement, for one who thinks of himself as a "mover and shaker," is the passing of power. Except for Bob, most of the clients, colleagues, and friends who had employed positions as leaders of the community on behalf of my projects were gone: Seymour and Norty Knox, George Goodyear, Paul and Fred Schoellkopf, Franz Stone, Burt Wilkinson. I did have the respect and the ear of Gary Bettman and his lawyers, and a residue of goodwill in the league and its territories and in the Western New York political scene. But I was not a man of wealth—I'd lived too well without any capital gain bonanzas—I was in my eighties, a stage, in the eyes of most beholders, of irrelevance. So the only power I had left was the power of reason, of fact, of good intentions, and of speech.

The chance to speak out came from an unlikely source. Milous Hairston, one of the anchors on the CBS station in Buffalo, Channel 4, called, asking for comment on the Sabres situation. Someone had suggested I might have a different point of view. Over the years, Channel 4 had never shown any special interest in the Sabres. The channel's sports guy, Van Miller, was the Bills' play-by-play man, and the football team absorbed their support. However, I checked with the league, got clearance, and agreed to an interview. I wasn't sure whether I was Don Quixote and I was certain I wasn't Moses or Jeremiah, but I was determined to penetrate the fear and paranoia with which the Rigas catastrophe had engulfed the media. As I view the tape today, I looked like some ancient crone. I had emerged the previous day from the hospital, and it showed. I was afraid to smile: in the course of a series of ailments I had been hit with Bell's palsy, a temporary partial paralysis of the face that turned my smile into a snarl. (Some friendly critics said, "So what else is new?") But I spoke with a decent measure of candor and vehemence.

"There's too much gloom and doom," I said. "The Buffalo Sabres are not a black hole."

The gloomy mood adopted by the press arose from the Adelphia bankruptcy. The Sabres were not yet in bankruptcy, but the press assumed it was inevitable. I did not agree. At that point, early in the summer of 2002, the league was paying the bills, and the crisis had come on at a time when the finances were easiest to handle: the team was out of the playoffs, most of the players had been paid in full for the 2001–2002 season, and their salaries for the next season would not be due for five months (October). The station treated the interview as a substantial one, extending it from the five o'clock into the six o'clock news, so I had enough time to get some good strokes in. The media were frightened by the losses, described as $20 million per year by the Adelphia crew, and the debt owed to the Rigases. Since the company had guaranteed the loans to the club, the debt was actually owed to Adelphia—and now to its creditors. That debt, according to the May 24, 2002, filing with the SEC, amounted to more than $150 million. Of further concern was the rumored presence of Paul Allen as a potential buyer with no interest in keeping the franchise in Buffalo; the expectation that Allen—working from a new, growing market in Portland—would outbid any local group, and the bankruptcy court would take the highest bidder; and the fear that no local buyers with sufficient capital and staying power would surface. These fears were underscored by a feeble season ticket response from the fans, who were looking back on the missed playoffs and the failure to sign favorite Michael Peca; and speeches by GM Darcy Regier—the only executive dealing with the press—whose lame duck limitations seemed to lead him to predict only minimal budgets for this "small market" and mediocre, soft teams in the foreseeable future.

I tried to deal with each of these "songs of Cassandra." As to the first cry, I was convinced that the cash losses were nowhere near $20 million per year. They were $6 million in 1997, the last year in which we had control, and I had seen Ed Hartman, Adelphia's able point man, strain to denigrate the numbers in his search for concessions from the lending banks. I checked with Dan DiPofi, the financial vice president in our administration, and he opined that there was no way, contrary to Adelphia's claim, that the new arena could produce a loss. Its positive cash flow was at least $3 million per year. As to the "mountainous" debt, the league agreed with me that it was a mixed bag. I knew that as of the 1997–98 season, Adelphia had invested a total of $31.5 million. How did that get to $150 million in less than five years, even if the losses were $10 million a year? It was obvious from the May 2002 filing that to reach the $150 million figure, the Kailbourne crew had added in the $31.5 million (which was equity, not loan); the money invested up to the sale in 2000, which the NHL had insisted be represented by subordinated notes (again, really equity, not debt); and what was left of the construction loan and concession loan— both debt of the arena, not obligations of the Sabres. Moreover, the concession loan was fully secured by the concession contract, under which Sportservice was required to pay $4.2 million per year to the Sabres, more than enough to pay debt service (interest and principal) on that loan.

Of course I could not spell this out in detail in a fifteen-minute television interview. But I did say, with emphasis, that "the financial problems of the Sabres are much easier to solve than those of Adelphia."

Not only was the "debt," for the most part, not really debt at all, but it was owed to the Rigas family, not Adelphia, and it was a serious legal step to give the Adelphia corporation ownership of the claims. If the claims really were equity, the Rigases, as holders of the notes, faced a fate like that of the former Penguin owners, Howard Baldwin and Roger Marino, in the Pittsburgh bankruptcy. That bankruptcy ended up with the ownership of the team awarded to a group formed by superstar Mario Lemieux. Lemieux's status as a creditor for his unpaid deferred compensation got him the team, but the Baldwin and Marino notes and securities ended up at the bottom of the pile—their investment pulverized and wiped out.

The Rigas family could no longer fund the team's operation or pay its bills or its players. This meant that without league intervention, insolvency would become bankruptcy. Thus, the Rigas family, as a practical matter, had no further financial interest in the Sabres. Whatever the team would sell for, after the NHL claims were satisfied and the payment of the $35 million portion of the team loans secured by the franchise, the Adelphia and Rigas creditors could fight over what was left—but the Rigas family would get nothing.

In these circumstances, then, it was not difficult for the league to persuade the family (and Adelphia) to turn over operating control to the NHL. If the league chose to use its constitution and bylaws as a weapon, it had ample leverage. Bankruptcy of the team, if forced by some creditor, enabled the league to terminate the franchise and, even without bankruptcy, breaches by the club of its league obligations would also permit a termination. The league could then issue a new franchise to the new buyer, sell it for a price determined by the league, and take over the player contracts and arena lease, and the team's creditors could be left holding a miserable bag of furniture and hockey sticks. While this procedure might be more difficult under the current version of the documents, there was a precedent: in an earlier Pittsburgh Penguins bankruptcy in 1974, that is precisely what happened. The other teams in the league, as they would in the case of an expansion franchise, claimed and received most of the sale price for the "new" franchise. The creditors of the old franchise had to accept a relative pittance—an allocation of a part of the sale proceeds—what was left after the other NHL owners received their shares.[1]

As to the fear that Allen or some other non-Buffalonian would steal the team with a preemptive bid and move it: this should have been a no-brainer. Under NHL Bylaw 36, which I had a hand in drafting in the mid-1970s, the policy of the league clearly calls for any qualified local group (or a nonlocal group intending to keep the team in town), to have first crack at the franchise—even if a carpetbagger puts in a higher bid. The Board of Governors adopted the bylaw in 1976 in the course of rejecting and defeating the attempt by Ralston Purina to move the Blues from St. Louis to Saskatoon, Saskatchewan. Of course, the governors could elect to "end run" the bylaw, or they may find that there is no financially qualified local group, or that the franchise was no longer viable in that market. That's how the Quebec Nordiques were permitted to move to Colorado, the Winnipeg Jets to Phoenix, and the Hartford Whalers to North Carolina. But even a quick glance at the long list of requirements for such a move would give the carpetbagger pause and the locals encouragement. If the board stuck to its guns—and my friends within the league assured me that they would—the outsider would have to show there was no money available for the team to stay in place.

I could not, in good conscience, dispel all doubts about the Sabres future. The seminal cause of the financial problems, I am convinced, was the outlandish level of player salaries. No business can survive if it has to pay 70 percent of its revenue for labor alone. And, notwithstanding the comments of the sportswriter "gurus," there is very little an owner can do to fight the escalation on his own. If he insists on staying at the bottom of the payroll list, and rejecting every opportunity to invest in a star, his fans will desert to some other pastime, and the red ink will fill his account books. Yet the salary level is rooted in the collective bargaining agreement, and that is a leaguewide problem. A way must be found for an owner of reasonable wealth and intelligence in a 2.5-million-person NHL market to at least break even. Otherwise, our Canadian friends (except for the Leafs) and some of their American colleagues, can kiss their franchises au revoir.

Chapter 38

THE CURE AND
THE RESURRECTION

How will this all turn out? The Kailbourne board took a careless step in including the Sabres in its omnibus suit against the Rigas affiliates. Fortunately, an irate Gary Bettman and his counsel, Dave Zimmerman and Bill Daly, persuaded Adelphia, its bankruptcy court, and the Rigas family that the only way the Rigas/Adelphia creditors could collect on their claims against the Sabres was through a prudent, fair, unfettered sale of the team—and that was a transaction that must be left to the league's control and management. The Manhattan federal court handling Adelphia's Chapter 11 bankruptcy quickly acceded to the motion to dismiss the suit as against Niagara Frontier Hockey, LP (the Sabres).

I had predicted that the financial problems of the Sabres would be much easier to solve than those of Adelphia or the Rigas family and that Western New York was too good a hockey market to let go down the drain. This would certainly have been true if a qualified buyer had moved in quickly to take charge and "make like an owner." Unfortunately, this did not happen: uncertainty, overlawyering, and political conflicts prevailed. Pulling out at the loss of their courage or their backers, white knights became black nightmares.

TWO FROM THE SOO

In the midst of this citadel of uncertainty I got a call from Scotty Bowman. Scotty's friend Alan Maislin, of the Canadian family that once had a major trucking empire, was interested in buying the Sabres. Could he bring him to see me? I was inclined to say yes: first, because I respect Scotty and as a friend I'd be inclined to see if I could help; and second, because of a faint glimmer of loyalty to the Maislin family. I had once represented their Buffalo cousins, and Sam Maislin was now a judge in the Buffalo area. I told Scotty that I had to clear the interview first (I didn't say with whom). I called Gary Bettman and Dave Zimmerman at the NHL offices; they had no objection, and would be interested in what I could report. Maislin and Scotty came out to my house in Williamsville immediately that afternoon. Maislin said he had a group ready to file with the league, but he wanted to add "a few" local investors—say, at $10 million each. Whom should they contact? I responded by describing the two main groups of financial interests in the Buffalo market: those represented by HSBC (the former Marine Midland Bank) and those represented by M&T (particularly its principal, Bob Wilmers) and, even though he had never shown much enthusiasm for the Sabres, Andy Rudnick, president of the Buffalo Niagara Partnership. Maislin demurred at the latter: "He's too close to Mark Hamister; Hamister's his boss as head of the partnership." "That makes no difference," I insisted. "M&T are important players in this city. They'll have to be objective to some extent, and you can't neglect a major segment of the community." I called Jim Locke of the Phillips Lytle firm for the appropriate HSBC contact. He suggested the bank's in-house counsel. I relayed that to Maislin.

The meeting then proceeded to other matters. "How much are you putting in, Alan?" I asked. "Oh, nothing," he responded. "I'm just organizing things for Sherry Bassin." (Negative number one, I thought. The league will want to see the color of the real money.)

Sherry Bassin? He'd been knocking around hockey for some time, running the Erie, Pennsylvania, minor-league team, but he's never been regarded as a man of wealth. "Do you have the resources for this project?" I asked. "You'll need at least $50 or $60 million to cover the initial losses, to pay the purchase price, and to give the league a working capital guarantee, so the players'll get paid if things go badly and you try to walk away."

"Oh, we've got it; dollars are no problem," Maislin assured me.

Already an expert on the Buffalo hockey situation, he then announced: "The first thing we're going to do is hire Ted Nolan as the coach."

"That," I said, "might be your first mistake." It wasn't that Ted wasn't a capable and popular coach—he was. But I thought potential ownership ought to hold off on that kind of a decision until they knew more about the organization, had made decisions about a president, a general manager, and so on.

There were many young and experienced coaches available. And Ted could come with a two-edged sword. By contrast, I related how Wayne Huizenga had approached the problem when he acquired the Florida Panthers, and he had come up with the excellent choice of Bill Torrey as president.

Scotty joined in: "I agree. You certainly should go slow on the choice of a coach."

It was apparent that Maislin envisaged Bassin as the GM and himself in the business role. That was their privilege. He promised to make the contacts I suggested, but I was still uneasy. "Who is your main money source?" I asked.

"Oh, a doctor in Sault St. Marie."

What are his assets? "Billions."

What's his name? The response was unrecognizable. "How do you spell it?" I asked. Said Maislin: "I've forgotten how—I've got it written down, somewhere."

Hardly a response productive of confidence in the financial staying power of the Maislin group. When I reported the conversation to Bettman and Zimmerman, the answering silence was painful.

Weeks went by, and we began to hear that Maislin was soliciting investors all over Western New York, and not just for $10 million. For a time, things seemed to take hold when Maislin and his new associate held a very optimistic press conference in front of the arena. A Utica investor, Frank DuRoss, had been interested in buying the Sabres while Seymour Knox III was still alive. I had liked him and thought he was a man of substance, though perhaps not substantial enough to swing the deal alone. More weeks went by with no concrete progress. In a pattern that was to repeat itself several times, the delay was attributed on any given day to the banks, the league, the public sector, or Adelphia creditors—until one day Seymour IV called me with the unpleasant development: Maislin's money man, the unknown Sault St. Marie billionaire, had been hit with a heart attack and had canceled his commitment. So the Maislin/Bassin/Soo "bid" collapsed in parturition.

HAMISTER AND THE PUBLIC SECTOR

Meanwhile, rumors about Paul Allen and Portland, Oregon, continued to float, but Gary Bettman made it very clear that the league was looking only for parties who would keep the team in Buffalo, and ultimately two offers were presented: one by Mark Hamister, a Buffalo businessman who owned the Destroyers arena football team, and one by Tom Golisano, a Rochester billionaire who was making his second try as an independent candidate for governor of New York. Hamister was thought to be unable to handle the financial demands of the franchise—operating loss as well as purchase—on his own. Golisano had no such problem, but the knock on him was the question: Does he really want to buy, or is this just a political ploy to help his campaign? From my point of view, there is no surer way for a wealthy man to gain public prominence and prestige: a major-league franchise owner has all of that, and his team gives him almost daily press.

For a while it seemed Hamister had found his wealthy partner (Todd Berman, a former Buffalonian and head of the New York private equity investment group Charter Investment), got the approval of Adelphia, and the nod from the league. Golisano not only refused the chance to increase or modify his bid, but in fact he decreased his bid at the end and succeeded only in raising questions about his bona fides. Some of Golisano's friends (which included one of my former colleagues) were mortified when he attacked the Hamister bid, claiming that it was asking too much help from the public sector, as compared with the Golisano proposal, which he claimed was mostly cash. I read the Golisano bid, and it was so marred by ifs, conditions, delays, and difficult or irrelevant demands that it did not pass even the "smell" test. If it had been presented in my time as point man for the league on transactions of this kind, it would have been rapidly consigned to the round file. And, as Gary Bettman stated in his long press conference on the day of the Sabres bankruptcy filing, the requests for help from the state, county, and city governments in the two bids were "comparable." In early January 2003 serious technical and legal steps still remained to be taken, but hopes were high that Hamister and Berman would restore the stability and vitality of the franchise. Their speeches to the media were first rate. But Gary Bettman still had to say, "Show me the money!"

The fears returned on January 14, 2003. The NHL suddenly had to face not only the Sabres' problems, but the collapse of Rod Bryden's attempted bailout of the debt-ridden Ottawa Senators. The league had invested more than $10 million to keep the Senators afloat, but when his proposed "sale" to a company Bryden would control failed, the governors and commissioner determined that the league's "save the franchise" funds were exhausted. No bank would lend any further monies if its loan had to compete for collateral with the myriad other creditors—so the only alternative was DIP financing: the team would file a petition for "reorganization" in bankruptcy court, and the bankruptcy judge would permit the team to borrow as a debtor in possession and give the new lender a priority over all other creditors that would permit the loan to be made. Faced with a similar financial situation with the Sabres—even though the Hamister bid had been accepted informally and was undergoing the usual contractual negotiations—the league decided it had no more monies for the Sabres, either, and a petition for reorganization and DIP financing of $10 million were approved by the federal bankruptcy court in the Western District of New York during third week in February 2003.

I was not surprised or downcast, but disappointed. I had felt that the bankruptcy filing would give the team and the market a "damaged goods" label they neither needed nor deserved. To those who had sought my help, I had recommended a different strategy: tell the lawyers to get the deal done, and as rapidly as possible, so you can move into management at the first opportunity. The league had sufficient powers that new ownership wouldn't need a Sabres bankruptcy to protect itself against Adelphia/Rigas claims that were, except for the $33 to $35 million secured by the franchise, essentially worthless. Whatever additional expense was incurred to put the acquisition on a fast track would be dwarfed by the losses incurred if the deterioration of ticket response and fan morale was allowed to continue.

Unfortunately, the Hamister group did not or could not opt for the fast track, and I could not quarrel with the league's decision to spend no more of its own money and choose DIP financing instead.

Throughout these unfortunate events, I carried on as "minister without portfolio," maintained my office in the Sabres suite at the arena, kept in touch with the local scene, reported to Bettman and Zimmerman, and kept Bob Rich informed of developments and insights, both of us hoping that the faltering "applicants" would turn out to be heroes after all.

GOLISANO—GOVERNOR OR BOARD OF GOVERNORS, KNIGHT OR KNAVE?

The Hamister bid, which needed solid financial underpinning, took an unfortunate turn when it was conditioned on various grants or concessions from the public sector, focused primarily on the financing of the arena. The press totaled these at $40 million. Apparently Hamister's theory was that the state, county, and city had offered substantial adjustments to Adelphia as part of its project to save the Buffalo waterfront—maybe as much as $25 million—and therefore Hamister was entitled to just as much for saving the Sabres. But the times were out of joint. Governor George Pataki was facing a multibillion-dollar deficit with the additional obligations of the protection of the state's citizens against terrorism. His commitment was nebulous, and Golisano, whose bid had been rejected by the league, didn't help matters by attacking the Hamister proposal in the press, asserting that he would save the Sabres without going to the public trough. The polls, naturally, showed a populace wanting to keep the Sabres, all right—but without public subsidy. The Hamister requests were, in the view of the league, not much different from those of Golisano on this point, but the dispute became temporarily academic when Hamister's partner, Todd Berman—no doubt frustrated by the delays, the inadequate response of the state to the financing and of the fans to the season-ticket campaign, coupled with the woeful performance of the team, mired in last place—withdrew his support. In a whimper, poor Hamister "suspended" his bid.

Would governor wannabe Golisano step up and save the Sabres for the city of Buffalo? I hoped so. I was in favor of anybody who'd keep the team in Western New York. The proposals so far advanced by the Golisano camp looked overlawyered. The first had so many conditions it would not have received serious consideration. The second, in a brief letter to Bettman, was analyzed as follows by someone in the know: "Golisano is not offering enough money. Under his proposal, Adelphia would have to write Golisano a check!"

When the Hamister bid failed and the Golisano letter was rejected by the league, I received an e-mail from one of my friends at the *Buffalo News* who'd appreciated my off-the-record insights on the developing situation. "Bob," he said. "You must be feeling very badly to see all that you've put into it over all those years go down the drain. . . ." "No, I'm not," I replied. "I'm still optimistic!"

There were some solid signs that my optimism was justified. Not at first: Golisano acquired some questionable baggage with Steve Pigeon, the ousted former head of the Erie County Democratic Party, who didn't seem to be a happy choice to create a good relationship with either the Republican governor Pataki or his associates, the Republican county executive Joe Giambra or the Democratic mayor, Tony Masiello, all of whom supported the governor. But then Golisano added to his team both Larry Quinn, a former Sabres president, and Dan DiPofi, a former Sabres chief financial officer, both intelligent, able men with the requisite experience and emotional attachment to the game.

The delays caused by the Maislin, Hamister, and Golisano false starts made the solution more complicated and risky than it should have been. A formula had to be found to satisfy the league (to pay back the operating capital it had provided, and a guaranty to assure the financial stamina to endure expected losses), the Sabres lenders, the Adelphia creditors, and the bankruptcy court. But guts and know-how, sparked by the magnetism of a major-league franchise, paid off. On March 14, 2003, in a joint press conference at HSBC Arena, Gary Bettman, flanked by Golisano and—lo and behold—Erkie Kailbourne, acting as chairman of Adelphia, announced that an agreement had been reached for Golisano to acquire the Sabres.

Later that day, I called Larry Quinn with congratulations. "Be sure to tell Tom Golisano," I said, "that his life will never be the same!"

QUINN THE CONUNDRUM

As reported elsewhere in this tale, I'd had some difficulties with Larry Quinn, but I never doubted or denigrated his ability and drive. When Larry called late in 2003 to ask for my help on his application for retainer on the construction and financing of a new Pittsburgh arena, I had no hesitation in recommending him to my friend Ken Sawyer, the Penguins CFO. (Ken served as chief financial officer to the NHL while I was the league's secretary and special counsel.) And Larry got the job.

I was sure he'd be helpful to Golisano. Yet I had lingering concerns.

When Seymour Knox III had become ill in 1996 and a headhunter was collecting candidates to succeed him as president, I talked Seymour—and Larry—into putting Quinn's name on the candidate list. Seymour was reluctant—"Larry should stay where he is," he said. "The arena job [construction and financing] isn't finished. And we don't know how Larry would function at the head of the whole operation." But I felt Larry's performance was so good—in the construction, financing, and political management of the new arena—he deserved to be in line for the top job down the road.

When we later decided that our first choice, Doug Moss, had to be terminated, I pushed for Larry. And the board went along with me, appointing Larry president of the Sabres. But the resolution I suggested, which was adopted by the board, contained an oversight provision—a committee of three with which he had to confer on any major policy issue. Bearing in mind Seymour's cautionary view, I was not yet ready to give Larry unrestricted CEO powers. However, when Norty assumed the chairmanship after Seymour's death in July 1997, he rejected the resolution. It was unthinkable to him, in his conceptualist, sometimes arbitrary, approach, that you appoint someone a head man and then put restraints on his judgment and performance. (You could always fire him, subject to his contract.) In my view, Larry was a rookie hockey president, notwithstanding his passionate performance in amateur hockey and his success in building the arena; and ceding major policy decisions to him should await his actual results in the top job.

Recent disasters produced by CEOs in Tyco, Enron, Global Crossing, Arthur Andersen, and others suggest that, in the Sabres situation, my approach may have been the right one. Of course each situation, each company, each crisis is different. It is to be recognized that I was seeking to protect not only the board's powers but my own as well (as vice chairman, voting trustee, etc.). After all, my own executive, league, and hockey experience was significant, and I was not about to cast it to the winds.

Our relationship had its ups and downs. Larry would call on me to address the staff from time to time, and when pictures of Buffalo notables were shown on the Jumbotron at the opening of the new arena, he included a photo of my composer daughter, Elizabeth. But then he would attempt to end run my judgment on legal matters by allocating major issues to the staff or by intervening in league transactions that were clearly my bailiwick. Doubtless he was uncomfortable with the fact that he could not, because of my position, enjoy the privilege many CEOs have of hiring their own counsel to be the company's lawyer.

Yet we worked well as a team on important matters. As Gary Bettman confirmed after the hearing on Dominik Hasek was over, when our world-class goaltender was charged with assaulting reporter Jim Kelley, the presentation by Larry and me succeeded in reducing his suspension from twenty to three games. And our joint negotiations with my friends Brian Bellmore and Ken Dryden brought about the good relationship with the Toronto Maple Leafs we'd been trying to achieve for years. We finally put Toronto and Buffalo in the same division, and that gave us Toronto-Buffalo sellouts every year.

The relationship was prickly at times, but I would still recommend Larry for any job in the field (except player)—provided a gentle but firm hand is kept on his belt!

In the spring of 2003, Larry had been acting as Golisano's representative and ended up as managing partner of the Golisano Sabres. That was fine with me; I was sure he'd do a superior job. He had a major conflict at the outset: he rehired Darcy Regier, who has, justifiably or not, become the symbol of a frozen GM in a season of futility. But there are, as there must be, limits on Larry's loyalty—so presumably he'll be surgical, if necessary.

Tom Golisano and Gary Bettman. Copyright © Bill Wippert.

* * *

Despite the Rigases, this chapter has (at least temporarily) a happy ending for the fans of the Niagara Frontier. The abandonment of the club by the Adelphia crowd did not destroy the Sabres or bring permanent damage to the club. My prediction on Channel 4, that the Sabres were too good a franchise in too good a hockey market to disappear, turned out to be true. On April 10, 2003, Commissioner Gary Bettman announced that both the bankruptcy court and the NHL Board of Governors had approved the sale to Tom Golisano. Golisano is committed, both publicly and in written agreements, to keeping the team in Buffalo. The patience and judgment of Gary Bettman, his counsel, and the Board of Governors had triumphed. I could not have faced Seymour and Norty Knox in the hereafter if we had failed.

Chapter 39

THE FUTURE OF
THE NHL

W e saw in chapter 29 the history of the "salary cancer" and the stark economic fact that NHL clubs are paying average salaries higher than the NFL clubs, but with less than 6 percent of their television income. The hockey league must expand its income base. Is expanded revenue from a program of national network games on the tube the future of the NHL?

THE MAJOR NETWORKS

After more than thirty years of battling to improve the NHL's TV audience and increase its penetration of the telecasts of the other three major sports, the annual "television pies" looked like this, in the periods just before the 2004–2005 lockout:

	Per League	Approx. Per 30 Clubs
NFL	$2.26 billion	75 million
NBA	660 million	22 million
MLB	417 million	14 million
NHL	120 million	4 million

I'm certainly biased, but I think NHL hockey is the most exciting spectator sport in the world: it has speed, danger, color, skill, physical combat, a magnificent stage, and continuous, largely uninterrupted action. The rhythm of professional football is start and stop, start and stop. The mood of baseball is slow and relaxed, with moments of tension. The NBA seems to go through three periods of relatively meaningless displays of skill and static foul shots, with the thrills usually concentrated in the final minutes—interrupted frequently by the numerous "time-outs" called at the whim of the well-dressed coach, seated comfortably on the sideline. For me and for the hundreds of thousands of hockey fans, the tension of play is continuous. Even with the game one-sided, the attack on the goalkeeper is a thrill: the 3 on 2s, the 2 on 1s, the breakaway, the pass, the check, the deke, the hold, the slash, the trap, the block, the slap shot, the wrist shot, the save or the score—all are there with every change of possession. It is easy for the fan to lock on with the emotion, identification, and worship that are so essential to the success of any spectator sport.

Why, then, doesn't NHL hockey produce revenue and profit that will attract investment and stability?

Over the decades I've been involved in the NHL, the league has strived mightily to become the Queenly Bride of TV stardom—without success. In the early 1970s the league left ABC, CBS, and NBC to establish its own network—under the guidance of a nice guy who sponsored the creation of "Peter Puck" and whose name, appropriately enough, was Donald Ruck. The cartoon character was designed to educate consumers to the rules and joys of hockey; but Peter produced neither ratings nor revenue enough to keep it on the TV screen. Then the league attacked the Molson/*Hockey Night in Canada*, to force higher earnings. Through the glowing salesmanship of Marcel Aubut, it persuaded the NHL to mount a competitor across Canada with a partnership of the Carling-O'Keefe Brewery and CTV—the "other" Canada network. That got the NHL owners nowhere, except some favorable rulings by then NHL president John Ziegler that confirmed the American clubs' right to take a free "feed" of the TV broadcast in Canada back to their home US venues. The league's contract with Fox in the 1990s I remember well as the governors heard glowing predictions of growth, but that network's "glowing" puck brought only a glimmer, as purists attacked it as a gimmick and Fox faded away to Nascar and other more profitable pursuits.

ALONE WITH PETER PUCK

A similar venture sought to improve on the national TV network revenue with the appearance, for a while, of a cable chain called Sports Channel. The Sabres tried for three years to establish their own TV station (WNYB), but the start-up losses were too much for the Buffalo/Knox Group. The last decade of the twentieth century produced a flirtation with NBC, Fox, and ESPN (owned by ABC/Disney), with some marginal improvement, but the disappearance of NHL hockey during the lockout of 2004–2005 (see chapter 40) administered the near fatal "coup" without much "gras," when ESPN announced it would not pick up its $60 million a year option and would not extend its TV rights agreement. As reported by Michael Hiestand in the *USA Today* of August 17, 2005: ". . . Based on recent years, it's possible to project the NHL national ratings could hit zero in the not-too-distant future."[1]

CABLE THE SAVIOR?

Then on August 17, 2005, riding out of the near sunset comes the Outdoor Living Network (OLN)—on the heels of the successful promotion of Lance Armstrong's win in the Tour de France—to present the NHL with fifty-eight games at a cost of $135 million for two years with renewal options (an offer that ESPN refused to match)—not exactly a rescue; but at least it let the NHL in out of the cold! The new network has the potential to reach millions, through systems owned by its parent, Comcast, about sixty-two million subscribers; about 60 percent of the potential reach by the major principal over the air networks (ABC, CBS, NBC, and Fox).

The regular-season games will be played on Mondays and Tuesdays (hardly the most desirable TV nights) on Comcast systems and affiliates. They'll be supplemented by some playoff and Stanley Cup games—on NBC—but with no fixed rights fee, the league's compensation is dependent on earnings of a partnership arrangement. When you add up the cable nights and the NBC days and the local TV of the individual clubs, the NHL TV take will still be far, far away from the NFL television revenue—a revenue needed to support a salary structure that is now comparable for the two leagues.

Of interest: Comcast, owner of OLN, once tried earlier in 2005 to take over Disney, owner of ESPN. Could the move on a major sport like hockey be a prelude to Comcast moving toward becoming a major cable network? That could help the NHL, if the league could extend its own reach.

THE EXPANSION MARKET

In the "Vision of the Nineties," the NHL expansion plan in which I played an active role as planner and negotiator, the road map was: more franchises. Maybe what we need is more fans! But let's look at the expansion possibilities.

Advertisers, networks, and sponsors have a tendency to look first at the top ten, then twenty, then fifty markets. The football, basketball, and baseball major leagues all operate franchises in the top thirty markets; only the NHL fails to cover six franchise slots in the United States, where one or more of the other three sports operate; those slots being occupied, of course, by the six Canadian NHL clubs. The result is that the hockey league "misses," for example, the following markets:

City*	Rank	TV Homes (in millions)
Houston	11	1.902
Seattle	12	1.690
Cleveland	16	1.556
Sacramento	19	1.315
Orlando	20	1.303
Baltimore	23	1.087
	Total	8.853

*Note: Other top fifty markets of lower rank not included in the NHL include Portland, San Diego, Indianapolis, Hartford, Nashville, Kansas City, and Milwaukee.

THE "RATINGS"

Thus kept out of the counting are the TV homes in those six markets that would bring the NHL lineup to thirty US venues. Nine million homes—that's quite a bundle to miss. Sports fans understand that a "rating" is a fraction or percentage of which the numerator is the number of TV homes in the market and the denominator is the universe of TV homes in the United States. So the NHL takes a bad rap every time the calculation is made because Nielsen and other rating systems cover only American markets, and the Canadian homes reached by the league are kept out of the numerator and the denominator. Result: the NHL's rating record looks worse than it should be. I found myself continuously battling with league brass to count in the Canadian viewership, and particularly to include the adjacent Ontario homes—conservatively three hundred thousand—as part of the Buffalo market.

Here are some comparisons—in 2002, a more normal period two years prior to the lockout:

	Average Regular Season Rating
NFL	11.0
Nascar	6.0
MLB and NBA	2.5–3.0
NHL	1.8

Source: Nielsen as reported by Angelique S. Chengelis, *Detroit News*, June 2, 2002.

Even if we make an adjustment for the "missed markets," and add in the Canadian homes, the NHL rating still looks pretty puny!

THE CANADIAN AUDIENCE

Of course, we should fully count the impact of the intense interest in the game from our cousins across the northern border. According to the Kagan Organization, using the 1995 to 2000 averages, and treating *Hockey Night in Canada* and its affiliates as the equivalent of the US networks, the data show this:

Average TV homes /NHL
(Reg. season)

US over-the-air networks	1,789,000
ESPN	503,999
Total US	2,292,999
Canadian, *Hockey Night in Canada* average viewers	746,280
Total	3,039,279

Source: Kagan's *The Business of Hockey*, 2001, pp. 456, 458.

The ratio of Canadian hockey homes tuned in total 24.5 percent. Suppose we adjust the US average rating of 1.8 by adding in the Canadian percentage: 1.8 x 1.245 = 2.24. That's a far cry from those other sports ratings shown above. Of course, we must recognize that spectacular events, like the surprise victory of the United States over the Russians in the Olympics, can spike the rating to NFL levels. But it looks as if even the expansion growth of the league from 1979 to the present, from twenty-one to thirty teams, did not improve its ratings by any satisfactory standard.

SOUND AND SIGHT IN THE PLAY-BY-PLAY

Most hockey jockeys—play-by-play or color—are still haunted by their radio origins. Canadian fans' ears are tuned to the sonorous tones and deliberate detailed rhythms of the Foster Hewitts and Danny Galivans or the modern-day Harry Neales and Brian McFarlanes. I know that as late as the mid-1990s some owners, like Bill Wirtz of the Blackhawks, still had a prejudice against the tube, at least for home games (it could hurt the gate!); and Total Hockey tells us that in the early days of network television the CBC would not show the game until after the first period. Those early play-by-play fellows were radio announcers, and they felt compelled to tell the listener—even after he became a viewer—every detail, every movement, check, back check, forecheck, shot, score, nonscore, penalty, deke, roundabout, whose line is on, whose line is not, whatever happened when it happened, in a torrent of words that never stopped. I have some prejudices myself, and I'm not shy (a-ha!). Here's one: let the camera speak for the game!

Gary Thorne, a favorite of hockey networks in seasons past, drones out a torrent of information; but he seems to forget that the star is not his voice, but the camera jockeys whose lenses and lights and angles give us the direct excitement never available before. Let's minimize those far shots from the arena ceiling that make the players unrecognizable dwarfs. (My dislike of those camera positions began with the away games in St. Louis, when the Solomons would insist that we sit in the attic at the top of that big barn, which served as the owners' box.) Let's move in with plenty of close-ups, with shots that under the new technology can move quickly and still have clarity. Go for frequent in-game replays of what just happened. Let's give some play-by-play to the ladies, in recognition of the growing importance of their success and their strong showing as fans in the demographics. With the coming of the shoot out to NHL hockey, there's an opportunity to give the gals a chance to show their emotion and know-how in situations that are great for variety, simplicity, and drama (as a contrast to the orations of the Bonnie Bernsteins at the NFL telecasts that usually end up as uttered gossip, delivered at a frantic pace to fit into the thirty seconds allotted). The announcements of the plans for the OLN network promise "enhance-ments." I hope they're along these lines. Bring back the lessons of Peter Puck for the uninitiated—between periods. But when the camera and the crease are at center stage—silence is golden!

OTHER SOURCES OF INCOME

In 2002 I made a study, based in part on figures employed by the Kagan organization, that showed that eighteen of thirty NHL teams were in "peril"—hit with substantial cash losses, on the verge, in some cases, of bankruptcy or insolvency (a prediction verified by the bankruptcies in the last five years of Buffalo, Ottawa, and Pittsburgh). Resolution of the lockout and salary controversies may ameliorate the expense side of the situation. Depending on how hard or loose the cap turns out to be, it still behooves us, in the pursuit of truth or its equivalent, to make sure the impoverished state of the NHL is not caused by a dearth of income from other sources.

"LOCAL" REVENUE

There is not, except for national TV rights, much of a divergence between the streams of income of an NHL club as compared with an NFL team. Here's a capsule profile for 2002 of the Bills and the Sabres, operating in the same local market:

	Bills	Sabres
Annual profit and loss	$11.5 million Profit	$10 to 20 million Loss
Regular season attendance	506,465	731,418
Concessions	$1.3 million	2.9 million
Average ticket price	$45.45	$37.07
Share of national TV	$75.3 million	$4 million

Source: *Buffalo News*, May 15, 2002.

In the long battle nearing a climax over player salaries, a side war was over the share—actual or constructive—of the owner in the profits of the arena, if any. We have seen that the ownership or rental of an arena, even if dominated by the hockey club, is not an automatic picnic (see chapters 20 and 25). The financing and participation in revenue of those structures are all over the lot. In his presentation to the NHL and the players' association, Arthur Levitt attempted, with some degree of success, to find a formula for assigning a fair share of the financial benefits of the arena to the participating franchise (see chapter 40). Yet sports franchises continue to build them, often with imposing a major financial charge on the city or county or province involved. No matter how romantic or revered the old edifice may be (like Buffalo's "Aud"), the owner cannot ignore the multiple pressures of the fans, the press, and the financial statement, so they build more expensive arenas. Witness the hubbub over the more than $750 million taxpayers of New York State are being asked to pay for a new stadium in Manhattan.

The pressure for a new arena comes partly from the fear that, as economists would describe it, the demand curve for the local club's seats, local TV, and advertising is highly inelastic: a modest drop in the performance of a high-profile team—especially if it misses the playoffs—can produce a major decline in attendance, season tickets, and revenue. The club may be "high profile" because it's a new or expansion franchise—or because its building is new, built partly or wholly with public funds, its newness promising excitement and success. A look at the NHL landscape demonstrates that at least 40 percent of the NHL teams fit one category or the other: Minnesota, Columbus, Atlanta, and Nashville are products of the last (2001) expansion plan. Arenas built within the last six years in other NHL cities include Los Angeles, Denver, Miami, Washington, DC, Dallas, Tampa, Philadelphia, Ottawa, Montreal, and Buffalo. That's fourteen out of thirty—nearly half of the member clubs. When we built HSBC Arena in Buffalo in 1996, John McMullen attacked my presentation to the Board of Governors with the charge that we were "building the arena so the Sabres could pay Pat LaFontaine's excessive salary" (then 4.5 million per year). I was reminded that, during the strike and lockout of 1992–93, one prominent owner, Ed Snider, from Philadelphia, in debating whether to continue the lockout of the players, remarked that he'd rather kill his building project than "give it to them!" The owner built his modern arena, but his instincts were correct: as I pointed out in chapter 20, the new-arena craze became an illusion—it didn't cure the salary cancer.

MERCHANDISE SALES

I am afraid that the pattern seen in the TV ratings is echoed in the merchandise market. The press reported in 2002 that the scale of sales of licensed merchandise looks like this, in billions of dollars:

NFL	$3 billion
College sports	2.7
MLB	2.4
NBA	1.4
Nascar (big jump)	1.2
NHL	1

* * *

I hope with all my brain and heart that the new CBA and the new rules, which eliminate the red line and put new restrictions on the goaltenders, will take hold and really bring the NHL into a new era, free to create enjoyment for its public and its participants. But I've seen too many turnabouts in the obstructions rules, too many outrageous leaks in the salary dike, not to be wary. Yet I'll put my money on those hardworking parents getting up at dawn to take their passionate kids to the rink. We need more support for them. Consider some of the possibilities.

CROSS-ICE AND GRASS ROOTS

As I've said, expansion has certainly been a good thing from almost every point of view; but what we need, more than more franchises, are more fans. For years I sat at the NHL governors' table voting for continual subsidies to Canadian Junior Hockey and US amateur, national, and Olympic teams. With my absorption in my assigned duties in the league and with the Sabres, I never paid much attention to the amount or the direction of those subsidies. But with the professional salary cancer hopefully to be cured in some way, attention must be paid to the six-year-old and the ten-year-old and the high school freshman—in existing or new hockey markets. Ways must be found to reduce or cover the minimum start-up cost for a kid of $300 for equipment growing to more than $1000 when you add ice time and coaching and transportation. A youngster choosing (or his parent's choosing) his first experience in organized sport has a much easier time for lacrosse or soccer, where all he needs is a pair of sneakers. His or her mother will find her schedule for soccer much more flexible with the number of fields available, especially when she's consigned to 5 AM in one of the few rinks in her city that will accommodate her six-year-old's early passion for hockey. Where do all the NHL dollars go in the structured organization of US and Canadian hockey? It's pretty clear it's gone to the elite clubs—to the Memorial Cup teams in Canada and the national and Olympic teams in the United States. It never dribbles down to the grass roots. I asked a friend David Braunstein, head of the Western Division of New York State in US Hockey, who's been involved in every level of non-pro hockey all his life about this. David replied: "In all those years, we never saw a check!"

We have to face up to the fact that hockey is, relatively speaking, an elitist sport, even at the public school level. Braunstein tells me that the median annual income for the typical two-income-earning parents who bring their children into the organized clubs is $138,000. They can afford their juveniles' passion. But must it be limited to that income class?

One obvious measure: more rinks, so the cost of ice time ($10 or more per player per hour for a six-year-old) is more acceptable. A project that seemed hopeful in the 1980s—in which the classy all-star and recent coach Bryan Trottier was involved for a time—was the construction of artificial rinks made of a rigid, ice-like material. The project died partly because the artificial surface didn't seem enough like "ice," and capital for further research disappeared. This idea should certainly be investigated again.

The concept of "cross-ice," recently initiated by US Hockey, is a base for optimism. Instead of a two-hundred-foot surface with only two goal nets, the rink is divided into three areas (could be four), with nets at each end of each segment, separated by portable dividers or "bumpers"—to keep the puck out of the adjacent area. Presto change-o you have three rinks instead of one, thirty-six players on the ice instead of twelve, and a distance for a breakaway, sideboards to sideboards, of eighty-five feet, that's much easier for the six-year-old to handle and to learn from. The cross-ice system has been adopted with success by organizations in Wisconsin, Michigan, Mass-achusetts, and Georgia, among others.[2] Of course, the purists will say it's not "real" hockey; but we're talking about creating training and enjoyment for the kid who's just entering school, and we want him (or his parent) to choose the sport on ice.

All these measures—more rinks, cheaper equipment for the juvenile player, coaching (even with the many enthusiastic volunteers)—cost money. I'm suggesting that, with the new era that we hope comes with the cure of the "salary cancer," the NHL and its players' association should take a good hard look at the structure and financing of amateur hockey and find ways to collect and invest substantial sums—not just for championships and honors for the elite players at the top but to encourage that six-year-old kid and his passionate mom and dad to enter our game.

Chapter 40

THE LOCKOUT AND THE END GAME

CRISIS IN 2004

In a pattern defined clearly when Bob Goodenow succeeded Alan Eagleson as director of the NHL Players' Association in the early 1990s—a less kindly relater would call the pattern Goodenow's "modus operandi"—Bob again in 2004 refused the owners' tentative groping for negotiations and effectively did nothing until the crisis was upon us, with the expiration of the CBA on September 15, 2004. In an attempt to avert the inevitable futile dispute over the *facts*, the owners, at the cost of over a million dollars in fees, retained the distinguished Arthur Levitt Jr., former chairman of the Securities and Exchange Commission and former president of the American Stock Exchange, to do a thoroughgoing audit of the finances and operations of the thirty NHL clubs. Levitt's conclusions, in his report of February 5, 2004, after many pages and many interviews, starkly records an NHL flood of red ink that, if unchecked, will become a tsunami. His findings are of critical importance:

NHL Summary Statement of Operations
Combined Leaguewide URO
2002–2003 Season
(Millions of US Dollars)

	Regular Season	Playoffs	Total
Revenues			
Gate Receipts	$886	$111	$997
Pre-Season & Special Games	50	—	50
Broadcasting and			
New Media Revenues	432	17	449
In Arena Revenues	401	14	415
Other Hockey Revenues	82	3	85
Total Revenues	**1,851**	**145**	**1,996**
Player Costs			
Salaries and Bonuses	1,415	14	1,429
Benefits	64	1	65
Total Player Costs	**1,479**	**15**	**1,494**
Other Operating Costs			
Other Player Costs	28	28	
Team Operating Costs	259	23	282
Team Development Costs	69	2	71
Arena & Building Costs	138	7	145
General & Administration	116	1	117
Adv. Mkt., PR. & Tickets	126	6	132
Total Operating Costs	**736**	**39**	**775**
Total Costs	**2,215**	**54**	**2,269**
Operating Loss (excluding Depreciation, amortization, Interest and taxes	($364)	$91	($273)

In the 2002–2003 season, 19 teams reported operating losses and 11 teams reported operating profits. The largest profit reported in its URO by a team was $14.6 million and the largest loss was $40.9 million. The average profit of the 11 teams reporting a profit on the URO was $6.4 million. The average loss of the 19 teams reporting losses was $18.0 million. The average loss reported on the combined Leaguewide URO for the 30 teams was $9.1 million.

Below the number of teams are segmented by size of operating loss/profit. In reviewing the underlying data, there appears to be no clear relationship between the size of the loss and revenue ranking or market size as measured by a relative DMA ranking. All amounts reported below include operating profits earned in playoffs.

	Number of Teams	Average (Loss) /Profit	Highest (Loss) /Profit	Combined (Loss) /Profit
Teams Reporting Operating Losses:				
Over $30 Million	4	($35.5)	($40.9)	($142.0)
$20–$29.9 Million	2	(23.2)	(26.2)	(46.4)
$10–$19.9 Million	6	(16.9)	(19.0)	(101.5)
$5–$9.9 Million	6	(8.2)	(9.9)	(49.4)
Under $5 Million	1	(3.1)	(3.1)	(3.1)
Totals for Teams				
Reporting Operating Losses	19	(18.0)	(40.9)	(342.4)
Teams Report Operating Profits				
Over $10 Million	2	$12.7	$14.6	$25.3
$5.0–$9.9 Million	4	8.1	9.4	32.4
Under $5 Million	5	2.4	4.3	12.1
Total for Teams Reporting Operating Profits	11	6.4		14.6 69.8
Overall Combined Operating Loss				($272.6)

It is my opinion, based on all our work, that the combined URO operating loss for the fiscal year-ended June 30, 2003 of $273 million is a comprehensive and accurate statement, in all material respects, of the results of operating the 30 NHL hockey franchise during the 2002–2003 season and includes all revenue and expenses attributable to the hockey business whether recorded by the team or in an affiliated or related entity.

"This business (and its system) is sick," wrote Levitt, "and anybody who puts any money in it is crazy."

It was an impressive document, promulgated by an impressive leading figure in the financial world. The clear signal was that the system must be changed to halt—and reverse—the destructive escalation. The salary cap, which had proved successful in the NFL and the NBA, beckoned. Yet Bob Goodenow refused to change his tactics or his position.

For his players, Bob insisted, the cap was anathema. Exactly why, was never made apparent. So he attacked the Levitt report. It was "pure PR," he said. That didn't sell. Levitt didn't include "related or affiliated" income that the clubs have. Trouble was, his examples didn't fly. He picked the Islanders, which had historically—and I knew this as the league's negotiator—as a result of the investment acumen of the team's previous owners, acquired not just the *hockey* TV rights but an ownership interest in the entire Long Island cable system. (The Sabres had failed at a similar investment in Western New York.) But treating nonhockey cable income as offsetting the club's operating losses was highly inappropriate. It's as if Peter Pocklington was required to use his meat company revenue—if he'd made any money at it—to reduce his Oilers' red ink.

Levitt's figures pretty much supported the historical analysis of team "peril." But Levitt's magnificent million-dollar data produced no budge in the union's position—until the fans, particularly the Canadian ones, began to weigh in. My friend Gene Warner and his boss, editorial chief Gerry Goldberg of the *Buffalo News*, asked for comment. Gerry persuaded me to condense the comment from 1,600 to about 870 words—nearly breaking my artistic arm—but here you're privileged to read the uncut version:

HEY, MR. SANTAYANA—Déjà Vu!

It's September 25, 2004. The NHL's CBA has expired. Gary Bettman proclaims the Governors' decision to lock out the players—and probably tank the season. My memory jumps to that brittle window in the 1991–1992 negotiations when we had a chance to work out something like a salary cap—before the unmanageable escalation began. Craig Simpson, an ex-Edmonton star acquired by John Muckler, was the Sabres player rep. The NHLPA (the Players' Association) was sticking to its rigid position—still its party line—that a salary cap was poison. At the end of the '91–'92 season, the hockey league had threatened to cancel the playoffs. The Buffalo Bills were battling with the NFL owners, and word came that if the Sabres players voted for a cap, the Bills would come over and "beat them up!" I got hold of Simpson—I wasn't shy about talking to our own team. I spoke strongly: the stance that the cap was a poison pill was nonsense; the cap was a way to share income on reasonable terms but stop ruinous inflation that could destroy their jobs. The average had already more than doubled in five years; the restraints on free agency hadn't worked to control salaries. I argued, with a rational division of income, the players could preserve all their meaningful rights—options, arbitration, free agency, fixed contracts, and their agents could still be well paid. Craig seemed to listen, and later in the day it was on Buffalo TV. "The salary cap is not such a big deal," he said. "I talked to Bob Swados, and I'm glad to know he agrees."

Encouraged, I voted on April 12, 1992, to restore the '92 playoffs, with a clause calling for a joint committee to negotiate a new system "along the lines of the *NBA's cap*." The Bills' threat never materialized; but within less than a year after we signed off—on May 6, 1993—the NFL players agreed to their own salary cap—still in effect 11 years later. In 1994–95 Bettman tried again, but was forced to terminate the lockout—without control of veterans' salaries—when six clubs, primarily those constructing new arenas—wouldn't support continuation of the work stoppage.

That was costly. In two four-year extensions for the Olympics and expansion, the league tried to compensate. It didn't work. The bumps in revenue never caught up with the escalation of salaries. Average, '91–'92: $361,000. Today: $1,800,000.

The poet-philosopher George Santayana many years ago warned us all: *"Those who forget their history are bound to repeat it!!"* Little has changed since '91–'92. Once at less than 50 percent, the players are eating up 75 percent of the revenue. Look at this:

- The gamble of '95—the $1 million rookie cap—didn't work, the veterans' pay, uncontrolled.

- The principal battlers still the same: urbane Bettman, relying on "jawboning" and logic; the Harvard Canadian Goodenow, still sticking to the stone wall.

- The powerful agents, like Don Meehan and IMGI, doubtless protecting their superstars with Goodenow behind the scenes—even though their commissions would be largely unaffected by a salary cap.

- Player leaders of the union, ignoring or carping at the facts. In 1992–93, they ignored their own audits of the four clubs offered by the league (including the Sabres and the Red Wings). The reply to me and to Mike Illitch of Detroit was: "We think you're using two sets of books," an insult that still rankles. This year, they disregard as "PR baloney" figures showing 18 clubs of 30 had losses of aggregating nearly $300 million—figures produced by former SEC Chairman Arthur Levitt, whose reputation is nearly unimpeachable.

Noting this and the recent (hopefully not temporary) escape from bankruptcy of Buffalo, Ottawa, Los Angeles, and Mr. Lemieux's Pittsburgh—said Mr. Levitt to Mr. Bettman and his 30 owners and 700 players—your industry is sick. *Anybody who invests any money in it is crazy!*

Perhaps one should assemble the 30 guys, once stars on the ice, now a part of ownership or management, who know how tough it is to make black ink out of a *red* franchise financial. Paying NFL salaries with less than 5 percent of an NFL team's TV revenue. Ask Phil Esposito how hard it is to raise capital. Ask Mario Lemieux! Ask the former player representatives or officers of the union, like Bob Clarke or Mike Milbury or Bob Gainey. Little help from superstar, now part owner, Wayne Gretzky. Says Wayne: "This is way over my head!"

I'm fond and supportive of our talented, gutsy, hardworking performers, deserving of the highest compensation our sport can afford. But they cannot continue to take so much of the income that they threaten the life of the business, their own jobs, and the fans who sustain all of us.

Goodenow and his agent cohorts must open up their prejudices and face the problem. The usual attempt to produce antiowner animus won't work in the face of an average salary offer of over $1.3 million; fans, two-thirds of whom think the players are overpaid; and players who want to end up with careers in hockey management anyway. I'm afraid we're in for a long winter. . . . Hey, Mr. Santayana!!![1]

I'm sure it wasn't my *Buffalo News* piece that did it, but the pressure in the press, and the painful cries from many of the players at their loss of income, and the hot dog vendors, the novelty sellers, the TV advertisers, the silent sports pages, particularly in the United States, had their effect. At the meeting of the negotiators on December 9, 2004, came a major surprise: The players offered a 24 percent *rollback* in salaries—across the board! It seemed a very significant move by the players, but this time the *owners* balked. As the schedule began to disappear into the graveyard, this deadlock really got me talking to myself. Fortunately, the editors of the *Sports Business Journal* overheard this conversation and were nice enough to print it:

NO LIGHT AT THE END OF THE TUNNEL VISION

Bob Swados, former Special Counsel and Secretary of the NHL Board of Governors and Member of the Owner-Player Council interviews Bob Swados, former Vice Chairman and part owner of the Buffalo Sabres

The Special Counsel: What did you think of the players' offer of a 24% rollback?

Bob: It was a logical, statesman-like move. My newspaper friends used to tell me "your hockey players are the best guys in the sports business," and this proposal proves they were right.

The Special Counsel: Then why wasn't it enough to solve the lockout?

Bob: A great judge (Benjamin Cardozo of the U.S. Supreme Court) once proclaimed that "an ounce of history is worth a pound of logic." The PA proposal does not go far enough; it would perpetuate the existing system, and that has produced four bankruptcies in recent years, a loss of two good cities, one-third of the Canadian clubs, endangered a flagship franchise in Montreal that could not find a Canadian buyer. It's brought financial peril for more than half of the U.S. teams in the NHL.

The Special Counsel: Did anything good come out of the negotiations so far?

Bob: Yes. Both sides are apart on their predictions, but it's important they now have agreed on the financial facts, on the reality, and the magnitude of the losses and the dire threat to the franchise and the players' jobs.

The Special Counsel: Are you sure? I've heard a lot of harsh language from Messrs. Goodenow and Bettman.

Bob: The facts are there. You can't sneeze away $230 to $270 million in losses. Maybe the parties get irritated when the dialogue gets too complicated. "Fatally flawed," from the Commissioner, maybe was too strong; and the charge of "made-up numbers" from Bob Goodenow was certainly out of line. But the use of an arcane, fancy economist's word like "deflator" didn't help; it sounds like a bad pun from John Maynard Keynes.

The Special Counsel: As I understand the goods on the table, if there were a split of the net revenues the League produces, the players would receive 56.6% under the players' proposal and 54% under the owners plan. Why can't they bridge the gap?

Bob: So near and yet so far? The difficulty is not in the size of the rollback, or in what would turn out to be a sharing of revenue *now*—but in the League's concern, based on salary history, as to what would happen in 2 or 3 years. The owners strongly believe that if the *system* isn't changed, the same forces and conduct that produced the inflation sickness would blow the salary levels to smithereens again.

The Special Counsel: Isn't this all about the "salary cap"? Why is the union so obsessed that the "cap" is "poison"? Weren't they willing to consider such a sharing of revenue at one time?

Bob: The problem really goes back to 1992, when I was a member of the Owner-Player Council, and the president, John Ziegler, settled the strike and saved the playoffs that year. As Alternate Governor that year I voted for the settlement on the basis of a side agreement that called for a committee to be appointed by the two sides to negotiate a new deal "along the lines of the NBA cap." But the NFL players, who had opposed the concept, agreed to the cap a few months later, and political changes in our League and union ignored the informal agreement, then signed the CBA after the 1995 lockout that placed us in our dire trouble today. There was no historic view or policy that the cap is "poison."

The Special Counsel: The union argues that (1) the fact that the cap has been successful in the two major leagues that are financially sound is not relevant—all leagues are different; (2) it is entitled as a matter of right to a "market" mechanism that lets salaries float; and (3) the problems would disappear if the clubs had something called "responsible management."

Bob: Point 3 is nonsense. It is the essential nature of the old system that it mandates irresponsible business decisions that escalate salaries above a reasonable level. Time after time we see intelligent owners breaking through the market in the name of fan support, or building promotion, or star retention. The Buffalo Sabres were as prudently managed as any in the League. We had continuous sellouts for the first 15 years in the League; we had two League-leading seasons; two Stanley Cup appearances, a continually competitive team. Every dollar generated—no dividends to the owners—was plowed back into the players' salaries. We had careful budgets and local TV revenue in the higher range of the NHL. Yet when a new arena became essential, we broke the barrier too: one of the first $5 million salaries. I remember Devils owner John McMullen objecting, "Mr. Knox built a new building so he could pay for Mr. LaFontaine." And of course we all remember the Los Angeles deal for

Wayne Gretzky—purchased for a large cash amount for the first time in the history of the League, to be followed by a salary twice what anyone else had paid at that time. And did Wayne Gretzky, despite his greatness, or Mario Lemieux, make his team a power in the League?

As to the notion that the PA has some constitutional or ethical right to a "market system," that's baloney. Regulation is the rule rather than the exception, for an industry affected with the public interest. Look at the Canadian and U.S. airlines—and the difficulties of Chrysler—calling on their employees for rollbacks to permit survival.

I would ask my GMs—there's a star player we need to sign, what are you waiting for? Answer—which would regularly spike my blood pressure: "The market." Whose market, I would ask—and it was always some *other* GM at a price higher than we should pay.

The Special Counsel: Aren't there player advantages with a cap?

Bob: Of course, it's easier to see them, with a business like the NBA and the NFL that have such plush TV revenues. But the advantages are still there for a League like the NHL. The cap system makes all the other problems less important, or even dispensable. Guaranteed contracts, as Bettman has said, would fit in easily, only the overall level would be affected. Options could be variable. Trades and free agencies could be loosened. Commissions payable to agents would be largely unaffected—as the success of reps for NFL and NBA players, who are subject to the caps, has shown. Arbitration— a cause célèbre—though I have always that more trouble than it's worth, to player or owner—could be eliminated or confined by the cap levels or limited to adjustments for inequitable disparities.

The Special Counsel: The League suggested modifying the 24% rollback, so that the lower paid players got hit less, the top salaries got hit more. Sort of like an income tax. I understand it was described by the players as an "insult to the stars."

Bob: Certainly we make a large part of our sales pitch based on the great players who break records and move their teams to leadership on the ice. We certainly don't want to change that. But in a time of crisis, you have to take a good hard look at who and how much is contributed to success on the ice, and who can best contribute to the cost of survival. It's not irrelevant that in the 2003 playoffs not *one* of the top 25 salaried players made it to the quarterfinals (except Paul Kariya, who was traded the following season); and the success of Tampa Bay and Calgary in the 2004 Cup argues more for team equity, rather than maintaining the stars' share of the revenue pie.

The Special Counsel: So what's the answer?

Bob: Bob and Gary: Keep talkin' the talk! Maybe then you'll be able to walk the walk! Maybe even a "trigger" should be considered. So we start with the PA proposal—for five years, not one or two, with a contingent cap system that automatically locks in, if the PA proposal doesn't do the job. Say the average escalation is 12% per year, the PA system must beat that figure by at least 2/3 down to 4%, a normal inflation range. An escrow could be established so that modest departures of the system from the inflation standard could be corrected, on an across the board basis.[2]

* * *

On July 13, 2005, 301 days after Commissioner Gary Bettman canceled the 2004–2005 NHL season, the players and owners announced the settlement of their dispute over salaries and the salary cap, crowned in six hundred pages of high expectations and legal dexterity: a brand-new collective bargaining agreement. Ratification by owners and union came on July 21 and 22. The major issue—control of salary escalation—could probably have been settled without the "burning of a year," but for the intransigence of NHLPA executive director Bob Goodenow, whose stubborn treatment of a salary cap as "poison" obstructed the settlement. Goodenow, his main man, Ted Saskin, and the NHLPA executive committee appear to be the culprits of this near disaster. I suspect other villains, however. It has been said, without much evidence, that Bob Goodenow fell under the spell of Don Fehr, the baseball union's head, who has been bitterly opposed to a salary cap for baseball, notwithstanding the successes produced by that system in the NFL and the NBA. Fortunately, the fans, the owners, the media, and, ultimately, the knowledgeable players and agents persevered and, after a year of futility, forced the right course. The awakening came when the player representatives finally came to grips with the Levitt report, which predicted disaster if drastic changes in the salary system were not made.

The settlement contained the core elements: a salary cap—"hard," but subject to adjustments—starting at a maximum of $39 million and a minimum of $21.5 million per team tied to a percentage of leaguewide revenue ("LGR"), initially 54 percent, coupled with revenue sharing, with the top ten teams, measured by revenue, contributing to the lowest ten. The 24 percent salary rollback offered by the players as their initial response to the crisis is now in place.

The year's frustration led Eric Dubacheck, sports editor of the *Globe and Mail*, appraising the performance of Bettman and Goodenow, to conclude, "Fire them both!" I think that may be unfair to the principals and neglectful of the history. "Collective bargaining" is a misnomer for power on power, in which forces, rather than people, prevail. Hockey fans have seen instead controlled jubilation by the owners, resignation by the players, followed by a growing excitement and enthusiasm, now that we're all back at the ice.

An important feature of the new CBA, suggested by the NBA experience and by my *Sports Business Journal* piece of January 17, 2005, is an escrow of revenue dollars, which provides security for both players and owners: if the players get paid too much, the owners tap into escrow; if the revenue stream is more than predicted, the players get the adjustment, within the limits of the escrow. The concept was diluted somewhat in the final drafting, substituting a pay-as-you-go principle for a fixed percentage and looking more like a corporate dividend program.

Thus we have to catch up and start from scratch. Let's hope the long hours and anxious nights bear perennial, if not permanent, fruit. I would like to have seen some commitment to the *future* of the league, by owners or players or both: measures such as investment focused on the basic problem of a lack of fans in important markets. For example, during my regime as secretary, we heard a presentation of manufacturers of artificial ice surfaces. The utopian objective was to make sure every high school and college in possible expansion markets had an ice rink.

These measures might include contracts with research teams to improve cameras and lenses to increase the viewability of the game—close-ups of action, instead of distance shots from the arena ceiling; reexamining the structure of amateur and minor-league hockey to concentrate on the development of new fans, new kids that play, instead of the historically useful but limited work of the American and Western hockey leagues and the Canadian Major junior teams. The NHL could subsidize these—either directly through grants or indirectly through salary payments. Maybe these could be increased and extended to new markets as the seeds of growth.

Meanwhile, we have peace and partnership, for at least six years. The new era started with a bang, with a raft of changes to the playing rules that will drive coaches like Lindy Ruff back to school with new plays designed to take advantage of the opening up of the ice for long passes that can bypass the red line, and intense enforcement of the prohibitions against the clutch-and-grab and left-wing lock. I see the warning in the NHL announcement: "Zero tolerance on interference, hooking and holding obstruction." I saw that pendulum swing many times in my thirty years on the Board of Governors.

The new rules grant the offense more leverage and make the goaltender more vulnerable, with skinnier pads and with his wanderings back of the net, limited to a twenty-eight-foot area described, in a reversion to high school plane geometry, as a "trapezoid."

But they haven't changed the size of the "crease": you still have to fight like hell to get there, and you need help to score!

WHAT HAVE YOU DONE FOR ME, LATELY?

On July 29, 2005, three days after the ratification of the new CBA, the players' association announced that Bob Goodenow—fifteen-year leader who had moved the average salary to six times its 1994 level—would step down as its executive director and general counsel. He was succeeded by Ted Saskin, the PA's senior director of business affairs, who apparently took over the reins toward the end of the negotiations.

Epilogue

"I'M STILL VERTICAL"

The Future of ROS

Methuselah lived nine hundred years. Armand Hammer ran the multibillion-dollar conglomerate General Dynamics at age ninety-five. I'm just eighty-six, in reasonably good health, determinedly *unretired*. So, with luck, I have a decade of years to fill. Retirement would be easy—I have my books, including several volumes of Kissinger and Stephen Hawking, looking handsome in my bookcase, but unread. I have my music—a hacker at the keyboard, an easy mark for a piano pedagogue, and tapes of Mozart and Kurt Weill and Poulenc, some unheard. I have my gal, Frances—and, as Ogden Nash found, "There's something about Frances"— like me, a hockey and opera nut. I have oceans of knowledge I don't fully understand and want to know more about: from the black holes of the cosmos to the thirty thousand genes—or is it forty?—in the human genome to the "infidels" of Islam. I have enough to live on, and winter reasonably well in my condo in Boca Raton (home of graceful golf and gourmet guffaws). I have my daughter, Elizabeth—brilliant, creative, idealistic; planning as I write to go to the Middle East to create and produce a new musical work in a Christian town with Palestinian and Israeli teenagers in the joint cast.

With the sale of the Sabres and the end of my role as league governor and counsel, the core of my past professional life is no more. Its last vestige disappeared with the announcement in September 2001 that the Cohen

Swados law firm, which I'd helped create, was closing its doors. I'd with-drawn from its financial and legal concerns years ago, so it did not impact my income, but the disappearance of an institution that encompassed so much of my life and effort and memory was hard to take. The firm had sur-vived the Gluck Building fire that had destroyed its records, had blossomed in its move from Niagara Falls to the commercial market of the larger city, and had changed its focus from a litigator on behalf of rapacious chemical companies to an adviser and companion in growth in a wide range and national territory of business, tax, and financial sectors. Yet it could not sur-vive, in the hands of men of limited scope, passion, and power, the decline and sale of its principal clients. This account tells of my encounters: the loss of the "corsetieres" of Spirella in a bumbling proxy fight; the improvident but multimillion-dollar sale of the national TV chain Transcontinent; the ultimate absorption of the Pratt & Lambert paint company by Sherwin Williams, after three decades of battles to keep the business independent; and my thirty-year move into success—or escape—in professional sports. With my concentration in hockey, the firm needed rainmakers—lawyers who could attract new business—but those it had were unable to counter the contraction of the Buffalo population and economy, and the remaining partners were caught in a vise of untidy competition for the existing clien-tele. The final blow apparently occurred when the firm's principal client, Moore Corporation, the Canadian parent of Moore Business Forms, the leading international manufacturer of paper forms, fell on hard times. A confidential Moore study I saw long ago had predicted a seminal threat to the forms business from optical character recognition (OCR) but had failed, like most of us, to foresee the impact of the personal and office com-puter. Unlike Philip Morris, which used its cigarette revenue to purchase new business and change its character, the Moore Company could not overcome its natural Canadian conservatism and cultural lag, and could not find and finance, in time, a new product line to fit with the irrepress-ible dot-coms or the giant Microsoft. It is ironic to recall that I had fought so hard with the distinguished Board of Directors of Moore to establish a "poison pill" to protect its high income, broad distribution, and low stock price from the inevitable voracious raider. At the board meeting in Toronto when the pill was adopted, the chairman remarked, "I knew, Bob, that sooner or later you'd get this company into trouble!" It is ironic because, when a new Moore management sought to acquire a new business by way of a hostile merger, it was met with—what else?—a poison pill.

I like to think that ten or fifteen years ago, at the apogee of my power and influence as a corporate and sports lawyer, I would not have permitted the Cohen Swados debacle to happen. I can hear Paul Cohen now, fulmi-nating from above: "I left you a gem of a business, wealthy and prominent clients like the Schoellkopfs, strong local corporations like Moore, able lieutenants like Wright and Hanifin and Bradford. What happened?" Look, I would say, I went my own way; I created more than I lost; I found a challenging, profitable stage in hockey that contributed greatly to my community. I'm sorry that my absorption in sports may have weakened the firm. I'm sorry if I didn't fight harder to retain and compensate the able young lawyers who could not break through the seniors' glass ceiling and defected over the years to other law firms. I no longer have the power to save the institution, even if the present company of lawyers had the guts to desire it.

So the last excuse for a Swados law practice seemed to disappear. I had no place to hang my legal hat. But I would not become an intellectual dodderer. Some firms have a rule—especially if they provide a substantial pension (which mine did not)—that at age sixty-five a partner must surrender, completely and forever: withdraw from the firm, turn over his clients, and put himself out for his personal pasture. I find such a rule preposterous and wasteful for society. A retirement for me at age sixty-five would have meant that I would have missed the growth of the Studio Arena Theater; half my tour as secretary of the league; the expansions to San Jose, Tampa, Miami, Anaheim, and Ottawa; the critical owner-player negotiations of 1992 and 1993 and the strike holdout of 1995; the financing and building of HSBC Arena; and the Sabres Hall of Fame. I feel today the adrenaline of challenge when I'm presented with a tough problem or project. I feel the backbone of confidence and competence, still. And I demand the right to meet challenge, to live!

Of course there are dissenters: "Get that old guy out of the way so the young lions—or lawyers—can feast on the firm income." But in respect of the old firm's revenue, in this case, I've been out of the way for years, and with the old firm's passing, the revenue's irrelevant.

When people ask this eighty-six-year old how I am—expecting a litany of the vexing ailments of aging—I respond, "I'm still vertical!" By that I mean not just my geometric relationship to the earth, but my overall grasp and drive are still alive. I question, I analyze, I research, I draft, I argue, I negotiate, I solve, I produce. In a touching display of respect and affection, two friends at the Bar invited me into their respective organizations—two of the leading firms in Western New York. I had some sleepless nights in making the happy choice, but I did choose one. I'm "of counsel," and proud to be there, with first-class associates, a magnificent library, and a fine office on the walls of which I can mount the trophies of my past career, and hopefully some sanguine signs of the present, if not the future.

And I wrote this book.

So I'm still vertical!

THE COUNSEL'S CORNER

Cases That Formed the Backbone and Background of
Some of the Key Events and Issues in This Book

CHAPTER 1

Chicago Stockyards Co. v. Commissioner of Internal Revenue, 129 F.2d 937
(July 24, 1942), US Court of Appeals, 1st Circuit, Calvert Magruder, Chief
Judge; reversed unan. 318 US 693 Supreme Court (April 12, 1943). The
technical argument under Section 102 of the Internal Revenue Code, which
imposed a penalty tax for unreasonable accumulation of surplus, was pre-
sented in the Court of Appeals by Joe Welch (the "stinger" of Joe
McCarthy); the oratory that captured Judge Magruder, but not the Supreme
Court, was provided by former senator George Wharton Pepper of Georgia.

CHAPTER 14

WHA v. NHL. Remarks from the bench by Federal District Judge A. Leon
Higginbotham. In the course of his opinion holding that the NHL had violated the antitrust laws as a monopoly under Section 2 of the Sherman Act,
the judge cited at numerous points the Swados affidavit filed on behalf of
the NHL, but ruled against the hockey league, commenting: "Despite the
thousands of words uttered on this record by all parties about the glory of
the sport of hockey and the grandeur of its superstars, the basic factors here

are not the sheer exhilaration from observing the speeding puck but rather tom maximize the available buck." *Philadelphia World Hockey Club, Inc., et al. v. National Hockey League et al*, 351 F. Supp. 462 (November 8,1972) at 4, 9–10.

CHAPTER 21

Davis I, II and III. The forbears and progeny of *Los Angeles Memorial Coliseum [and the Oakland Raiders] v. National Football League* 468 F. Supp. 154 (1979), 519 F. Supp 581 (1981), 726 F.2d 1381 (1984), and 791 F.2d 1356 (1986)—the disputes between the NFL and Al Davis over his attempts to move the Raiders to Los Angeles without league approval had an important influence on all major sports, including the events described in chapters 7, 8, 9, and 21. In a series of battles over many years, the California federal courts held that (1) the NFL rule requiring a three-quarters vote for franchise transfer was an unreasonable restraint of trade under the Sherman Act; (2) after a modification of the NFL documents, the demand of a majority vote was not unreasonable; and (3) damages to the Raider owner would be limited or offset by the principle that the territory to which the Raiders sought to move was owned by the league, and the NFL or its clubs were entitled to appropriate "compensation" (thus reducing the award for damages in the Raiders case). In the interregnum, while the NFL restriction was deemed invalid, the Baltimore football team became the Indianapolis Colts and the NBA franchise moved from San Diego to LA. The NHL responded more cautiously, with the standards in Bylaw 36, ultimately setting the stage for its own loosening of the restriction after 1986 in the light of the Davis cases. Compare *San Francisco Seals, Ltd v. NHL*, US Dist. Cal., 379 Fed. Supp. 966 (July 18, 1974).

CHAPTER 27

Mid-South Grizzlies v. NFL, US D.C. Eastern District of Pa., 550 F. Supp. 558 (1982). The federal court relieved the NFL from liability under the antitrust laws when it refused to grant an NFL expansion franchise for Memphis. The court reasoned that the refusal had no anticompetitive effect, since the market remained available to a competing professional football league (at 570).

CHAPTER 29

During the late 1970s after the Higginbotham decision (*WHA v. NHL*) in 1972 the hockey league adopted its own version of the football "Rozelle rule," which awarded compensation determined by the commissioner to the club losing the player at the end of his contract. Under NHL bylaw (9A), the compensation was fixed by an arbitration process, with the losing club making an offer, the signing club making its offer, and an arbitrator choosing which prevailed. Dale McCourt was forced under the arbitration to be moved from the Detroit Red Wings to the Los Angeles Kings as "equalization." The federal court of appeals found the bylaw had been collectively bargained and withstood antitrust attack. A later modification of the bylaw restricted the "equalization" currency to cash and draft picks. *McCourt v. California Sports, Inc.* 600 F.2d 1193 (1979).

CHAPTER 40

For the long months of the 2004–2005 lockout, the underlying threat was—if the parties couldn't agree, and reached "impasse," would the owners install a salary cap on their own? The principles of the answer would come from *Brown v. Pro Football, Inc., d.b.a. Washington Redskins, et al.*, US Supreme Court, case no. 95388, decided June 20, 1006; opinion by Justice Breyer, in which the US Supreme Court held that "after impasse in collective bargaining, the federal labor laws shielded from antitrust attack the NFL's action in putting into effect a low paid 'taxi squad'—their last best good faith offer" made in the course of the bargaining (at 3–4).

NOTES

INTRODUCTION: THE AUTHOR—AS FAN, COUNSEL, MOVER, AND HOCKEY MOGUL

1. Twenty-six years later, on October 1, 2004, Major League Baseball announced that it could no longer support a team in Montreal and would move the franchise. The Quebecois separatists and the departure of many English-oriented businesses from Montreal had not helped the Expos. The club would be transferred not to Buffalo, but to Washington, DC.

CHAPTER 1: WASHINGTON, DC: THE LAWYER AS PUBLIC SERVANT

1. See, for example, Timothy Noah, "Alger Hiss Innocent, Anticommunists Declare!" *Slate*, March 22, 2001, http://slate.msn.com/id/1007346.

2. The Buffalo doctors could not diagnose the malady, either, and the fevers ultimately went away. Years later, an unrelated operation disclosed a cyst on her ovarian vein.

CHAPTER 2: IT ISN'T RAINING VIOLETS

1. I found that Epinal was the point where Gen. George Patton's tank forces joined the line established north and south by US and French armies to form a straight line from the Mediterranean to the North Sea.

CHAPTER 3: DEATH AT DACHAU

1. Felix L. Sparks, "Dachau and Its Liberation," June 15, 1989, http://www .45thinfantrydivision.com/new_page_6.htm.

2. Ibid.

3. There is a suggestion in the literature that the shipments to Dachau were a part of a desperate act by the Waffen SS to send the horrible mess back to the camp where it all began—"the model for the Kingdom of Death." Leni Yahil, *The Holocaust: The Fate of European Jewry, 1932–1945*, trans. Ina Friedman and Haya Galai (New York: Oxford University Press, 1990), p. 537.

4. United States Holocaust Memorial Museum, *Historical Atlas of the Holocaust* (New York: Macmillan, 1996), p. 208.

5. Ibid., p. 209.

6. Michael Berenbaum, *The World Must Know: The History of the Holocaust as Told in the United States Holocaust Museum* (Boston: Little, Brown, 1993), p. 189.

7. Sparks, "Dachau and Its Liberation."

8. Berenbaum, *The World Must Know*, p. 189.

See account of Lieutenant Colonel Felix Sparks, commanding the battalion that liberated the camp: "As I turned to look over the prison yard with unbelieving eyes, I saw a large number of dead inmates, lying where they had fallen in the last few hours or days before our arrival. Since all the many bodies were in various stages of decomposition, the stench of death was overpowering." See generally as background for this chapter, particularly at p. 64, "Dachau and Its Liberation," by Felix L. Sparks, included in *Dachau, the Hour of the Avenger*, a compilation by Colonel Howard A. Buechner, 45th Infantry Division, Thunderbird Press, 1986; see also 45th Division News, May 2005, p. 9; and *Concentration Camp Dachau 1933–1945*, visitor's catalogue, published by Bavarian State Government; chart of arrivals and deaths, with US Army photograph, pp. 212–13.

CHAPTER 4: THE ROOKIE MILITARY JUDGE

1. Robert L. Hilliard, *Surviving the Americans: The Continued Struggle of the Jews after Liberation* (New York: Seven Stories Press, 1997).

CHAPTER 5: THE COUNTRY LAWYER IN THE CORPORATE BOARDROOM

1. Note that William and Mary claimed power over France, as well as England.

CHAPTER 6: TV OR NOT TV

1. In fact the Channel 7 fight was not resolved until November 30, 1958, four years after we got Channel 2 on the air.

2. The fortunes of our NFAC group (later Transcontinent) owners received a major boost when the Federal Communications Commission generated a bitter four-year battle for Buffalo's Channel 7 by refusing to permit the morning newspaper, the *Courier Express*, to acquire a TV station in the same city, while the *Buffalo News* continued to own Channel 4 (which was ultimately sold). The failure to acquire the TV station doubtless contributed to the decision by the Connors and Andrews families to liquidate the *Courier Express*, but the delay the battle caused enabled our group to leverage the ABC network and bring NBC back; it lit the spark that produced Transcontinent. Fifty years later, with a changing broadcast "landscape," the FCC reversed the policy that defeated the Andrews and Connors families. On June 3, 2003, by a vote of three Republicans to two Democrats, the commission announced that newspapers were no longer barred from owning broadcast stations in the same community, and networks or others could own multiple stations reaching as much as 45 percent of the national market. The FCC chairman, Michael Powell (son of the secretary of state) stressed that competition from satellite dish and cable system programming and distribution would assure competition and that viewers would hear and see all points of view, and the antitrust views of earlier commissions did not deter him. I think Powell has made a major mistake. The control of monopolies is not antithetical to conservative economics. The philosophy of the Sherman Act is an inviolable part of our constitutional culture. Justice Brandeis's "The Curse of Bigness" should not be ignored, especially in a field where so fundamental a right and value as freedom of speech must be protected and nurtured.

CHAPTER 7: DOIN' THE CONTINENTAL

1. Messersmith was an interpretive decision by a Major League Baseball arbitrator. Earlier US and Canadian antitrust decisions had already opened up the other three sports.

2. The Continental League had a short life, less than a year. But its short life—with intense but naive effort—carried within it most of the major problems in any fight for an expansion franchise, either within an established league or through an outlaw coalition—problems that, beginning in 1967, gave me full wrestling time in the National Hockey League for the twenty-five years I served as secretary of the league and as its special counsel on expansion matters. If you asked me for a schedule of expansion issues, my memo would look something like this:

1. Persuade the existing owners that expansion is a good thing. The obvious inducement is a fee, for a share of the league's monopoly on territory, players, and TV revenue. The Continentals offered no fee and the majors, pressured by the threat to their player system, demanded none.

2. Persuade the general managers. General managers usually resist expansion. The expansion teams will be poor draws for existing teams, as a number of games will replace traditional rivals that bring good crowds. If the establishment club is playing well, near the top of its division or conference, the GMs cry that their competitive position will be hurt by the players that will be taken from them to stock the expansion rosters. Cries of anguish from the GMs will usually be accompanied by charges that there is not enough talent, and the quality of play will be diluted. Rickey's plan did not originally contemplate taking established players away from the existing teams: he proposed to use his in-house pool of rookies in the Western Carolina League to grow his own players. As the Kefauver bill developed, however, the scheme began to look more like the expansion draft and intraleague draft later used by the NHL. The old club sets a "protected list"—the number, positions, and experience to be defined in variegated ways—while the new clubs draft a limited number of players from those not on the protected list or otherwise not exempt from the draft. Kefauver's proposal would have protected forty per club; the NHL drafts protected between fifteen and twenty players, exempting one- or two-year rookies.

3. Persuade the financial officers. In the NHL, the expansion fee increased from $2 million in 1967 (the first expansion, six teams) to $6 million per team in 1970 (the year the Sabres entered), to $50 million in 1991 and 1992, and to $80 million in the late 1990s. Financial analysis would point out the loss of gate, the usual necessity of giving the new teams a part of the national TV and advertising pie, and, perhaps most important of all, the increase in operating costs that would come from the upward pressure on salaries generated by the additional demand for players from the new teams' rosters. I remember vividly a lively argument I had in 1996 with Wayne Huizenga and Bill Torrey (the principal owner and president-GM of the Florida Panthers). The four new NHL teams (Columbus, Nashville, Minnesota, and Atlanta) would pay a total of $320 million to the existing twenty-six clubs over a three-year period—approximately $12 million per club. Wayne Huizenga insisted that the $12 million wasn't worth it, because the expansion income would be rapidly eaten up in salary escalation. The cost of the Panthers' or Sabres' roster would easily be pushed up by $4 million per year as the four new teams bid up the price of free agents and (subject to the cap imposed by the CBA) rookies, as well. The willingness of the union to accept the expansion was pretty good evidence of the validity of the Huizenga analysis.

4. Persuade the league of the benefits of expansion and the financial com-

mitment and stamina of the proposed new owners. In 1960 the majors had no compelling economic reason to expand. Baseball was played in every city in the country. Its heroes were national heroes; its televised games were national programs. The National League, as the stronger league with the largest cities and more established organizations, was always a reluctant partner in expansion. Over the years, it was slower to respond and demanded more for sharing its territorial TV and player rights. For the NHL, however, there was a clear objective that overruled the concerns about gate and payroll: TV ratings and national TV revenue. For most of the last half of the twentieth century, the NHL labored under relatively minuscule ratings and TV revenue. As of this writing, each NHL club receives about $4 million a year from national TV. The other major sports receive from ten to forty times that amount. The base of ratings is determined essentially by the number of major markets in which the sport is played, specifically by the number of markets in the top fifty in which the league's franchises have actual operation.

CHAPTER 8: DOWN AND OUT IN O'MALLEY'S ALLEY

1. Dick Young, "Neither Buffalo or Montreal Are Ready," *New York Daily News*, April 18, 1969, p. 85.

CHAPTER 9: SAVING OAKLAND, WINNING BUFFALO

1. Grant of NHL Franchise to Niagara Frontier Hockey Corporation: Conditional Grant Board of Governors meeting, Warwick Hotel, New York, December 2, 1969 (Minutes, Resolution, p. 239). Final Grant, Governors meeting, Waldorf Astoria Hotel, New York, May 19, 1970 (Minutes, p. 2).

CHAPTER 11: GOIN' DAFT WITH THE DRAFT

1. A new tax bill adopted by Congress in October 2004 may simplify the valuation of player assets such as draft picks and increase the marketability of some franchises slightly in facilitating the write-off of those assets.
2. Robert O. Swados, July 15, 1994, pp. 14–16.

CHAPTER 12: THE ROUND BALL AND THE SQUARE SHOOTER

1. Steve Weller, *Buffalo News*, February 25, 1976.
2. Paul Snyder, press conference, June 15, 1976.

3. For the history of owners' efforts to produce a quick tax write-off (deduction) by allocating and amortizing the cost of player contracts—whether acquired in an acquisition or expansion—see *Laird v. United States*, 391 F. Supp. 656, Nor. Dist. Ga. (1975) and statement of the author's friend and then commissioner of Internal Revenue, Donald C. Alexander (see chapter 6) in hearings before the House Select Committee on Professional Sports, 94th Congress, 2nd Sess., Pt. 2, 1976, p. 268; Internal Revenue Code, Section 1245.

CHAPTER 13: MARTIN AND MAYHEM

1. Appellate Division Brief filed by my firm with the New York State Appellate Division, 4th Dept., p. 7.

CHAPTER 14: ALL'S NOT WELL WITH THE NHL

1. *WHA v. NHL*. Remarks from the bench by Federal District Judge A. Leon Higginbotham. In the course of his opinion holding that the NHL had violated the antitrust laws as a monopoly under Section 2 of the Sherman Act, the judge cited at numerous points the Swados affidavit filed on behalf of the NHL, but ruled against the hockey league, commenting: "Despite the thousands of words uttered on this report by all parties about the glory of the sport of hockey and the grandeur of its superstars, the basic factors here are not the sheer exhilaration from observing the speeding puck but rather to maximize the available buck." *Philadelphia World Hockey Club, Inc., et al. v. National Hockey League et al.*, 351 F. Supp. 462 (November 8, 1972) at 4, 9–10, 29.

CHAPTER 19: THE NHL COMMISSIONERS

1. It is interesting to note that the 1979 expansion was the least successful of any of the growth plans. The disappearance of the WHA did not put the brakes on salary escalation, and only one of the WHA clubs we absorbed, Edmonton, made it into the twenty-first century: Winnipeg fled to Phoenix, Quebec to Colorado, and Hartford to North Carolina.

2. Report to the Board of Governors by the Franchise and Market Analysis Committee, November 13, 1990. The "Vision of the Nineties" was announced during the 1989–90 season and included in the report to the Board of Governors. I had a major hand in drafting the report, which analyzed applications from Tampa, Miami, Anaheim, and Ottawa, which were subsequently approved, and Houston, St. Petersburg, Seattle, Hamilton, and San Diego, which were rejected. The governors had previously approved the expansion grant to San Jose, coupled with the "Siamese" transfer of ownership in Minneapolis.

3. Gil Stein, *Power Plays: An Inside Look at the Big Business of the National Hockey League* (Secaucus, NJ: Carol Publishing, 1997).

CHAPTER 20: THE ARENA ILLUSION

1. Our friend and colleague Bob Rich, with help from the city of Buffalo, county of Erie, and New York State, revived the Bisons in 1983 and built a beautiful park downtown, designed specifically for minor-league baseball and expandable for major-league ball.

CHAPTER 23: THE MOGILNY NIGHTMARE

1. Alex had great stats, more than a point a game, in each of the next five seasons at Buffalo, but despite the efforts of player Pat LaFontaine and GM and coaches Gerry Meehan, Rick Dudley, and John Muckler, the team could not get beyond the first round of the playoffs year after year. Finally, on July 8, 1995, John Muckler—egged on by the new CEO, Doug Moss—persuaded the Knoxes and me to go along with a trade

Perhaps influenced by the time and effort I had invested in Alex, I demurred at first, arguing that we were giving up excitement for defense—the very concept espoused by Roger Neilson, which had led to his dismissal as Sabres coach. I felt that the good relationship with Alex that had come out of the fight to keep him from the Soviets had been allowed to erode. But I could not ignore my own disappointment as I watched Mogilny in the 1995 playoffs—as he got breakaway after breakaway, only to fire the puck over the crossbar. I went along to the 1995 entry draft in Vancouver, as had been the custom, as the representative of ownership to approve whatever transaction might ultimately be proposed. John Muckler was a good hockey man and he made a good deal. Ultimately, the Mogilny trade produced three fine players: Michael Peca, Jay McKee, and Rhett Warrener (acquired by a trade of Mike Wilson). But some of the magic was gone, and it would be four years before the skills of the Dominator (goaltender Dominik Hasek) would bring us again to the Stanley Cup Finals.

Alex is now a star forward with the Toronto Maple Leafs.

2. Elizabeth Swados, *The Four of Us: A Family Memoir* (New York: Plume, 1993).

CHAPTER 24: GRETZKY THE GREAT: THE STAR NONE OF US COULD AFFORD

1. In Bruce McNall's book *Fun While It Lasted*, he recalls that in 1988 he paid $15 million to Pocklington for Gretzky and considered making his first offer to the star to equal basketball great Magic Johnson's salary—$3 million a year. He settled on $2 million, "which was less than I thought he deserved, but still the highest salary of any player in the game. I also guaranteed him that if at any time another player's contract surpassed his, I would increase his pay beyond that point." Bruce McNall, with Michael D'Antonio, *Fun While It Lasted: My Rise and Fall in the Land of Fame and Fortune* (New York: Hyperion, 2003), p. 141.

CHAPTER 25: "HEAD" NOTES

1. "Concussion of the Brain," Microsoft Encarta, http://encarta.msn.com/encyclopedia_761573917/Concussion_of_the_Brain.html (italics mine).

2. In a 2002 interview in the *New York Times*, NFL great Jim Brown had these comments on why "some stars don't know how to quit": "When athletes haven't taken any time to develop any kind of life for themselves—true life, with real value—they can't leave the field. . . . Because that's it, that's their life, that's their thing. To move away from that, not to feel that crowd, not to be able to perform, that's like death." Rhoden, *New York Times*, February 2, 2002, p. B17.

3. Joe Lapointe, *New York Times*, January 13, 2002.

CHAPTER 27: THE SIAMESE FRANCHISE

1. *The Business of Hockey 2001* (Carmel, CA: Paul Kagan Associates, 2001), pp. 394–95.

2. In the year 2003, a strong competitor would be Lou Lamoriello of the New Jersey Devils.

CHAPTER 29: THE SALARY CANCER: FLYING HIGH WITH THE EAGLE, NO GO WITH GOODENOW

1. Dave Schultz, *The Hammer: Confessions of a Hockey Enforcer* (New York: Summit Books, 1981).

2. Gil Stein, *Power Plays: An Inside Look at the Big Business of the National Hockey League* (Secaucus, NJ: Carol Publishing, 1997), pp. 210ff.

CHAPTER 30: MINDING THE STORE

1. The disease brought about his death on July 24, 1998.

CHAPTER 31: THE COACH AND AUNTIE MAME

1. Ted at long last reentered the hockey world in April 2005 when he was named coach and director of hockey operations of the Moncton Wildcats of the Quebec Major Junior Hockey League.

CHAPTER 36: ENRONITIS ON ICE

1. "Key Events in the Adelphia Saga," *Wall Street Journal*, September 23, 2002, http://online.wsj.com/article.

2. The Adelphia waterfront project never got off the ground, and it's prospects never moved Tim to close "John's" Sabres deal. Our partners were getting angry and fed up, and we had to find other measures to consummate the sale or get Adelphia off our backs.

3. Indictment and arrest of John and Tim Rigas, July 24, 2002. They were convicted on July 18, 2004. Compare, R. Lowenstein, "The Fall of the House of Rigas," *New York Times Magazine*, February 1, 2004, p. 27.

4. *New York Times*, November 24, 2002.

5. Dow Jones Newswires, September 14, 2002.

6. *Central Bank of Denver v. First Interstate Bank*, 511 US 164 (1994).

7. John Cassidy, *New Yorker*, September 23, 2004.

8. *New York Times*, May 11, 2004, p. C10.

9. Comments from the bench quoted in Jerry Zremski, *Buffalo News*, June 21, 2005.

10. The intensity of the administration's drive against these offenders is highlighted by the news that, at this writing, Mr. Scrushy, despite his acquittal, is still being pursued with both civil and criminal charges by the SEC.

11. On July 14, 2005, Judge Sand at least temporarily accepted their pleas in part permitting John and Tim Rigas to remain free while appealing their convictions. He also gave notice that he was assigning son Michael's retrial to a different judge, citing opinions about the fraud he expressed during the sentencing.

CHAPTER 37: THE ENRON PLAGUE, CONTINUED

1. The "supremacy" of the league constitution has not been precisely tested in court, but I believe the bankruptcy judge would respect these provisions. See chapter 21.

CHAPTER 39: THE FUTURE OF THE NHL

1. Michael Hiestand, *USA Today*, August 17, 2005, p. 2C.

2. See Harry Thompson, "Cross Ice Converts," and Joe Gustafson, "The First Step in the Right Direction," at http://usahockey.com.

CHAPTER 40: THE LOCKOUT AND THE END GAME

1. Robert O. Swados, *Buffalo News*, October 17, 2004.

2. A good summary of the CBA can be found at the league's Web site, http://www.nhl.com.

THE FANS' INDEX
Page numbers in *italic* indicate illustrations

**GOVERNMENT, POLITICS, AND
POLITICIANS**

THE AUTHOR'S THUMBNAIL

A Biographical Index

American Stock Exchange, 46
Ames Competition, 18
Anacostia, 21
Angostora bitters, 47
Arnie (army handyman), 29
Aschaffenburg, Germany, 32–33
Auschwitz (concentration camp), 36

Bains Les Bains (hotel), 30
Barrett, Sergeant, 34–35, 36
"Bathless Baths." *See* Bains Les Bains (hotel)
Battle of the Bulge, 31
Bell's palsy, 418
Berg, Sandy, 47
Berg, Steven, 46–51
Bergen-Belsen (concentration camp), 35, 36
Bible Women (Swados), 395
Block, Sam, 20, 21
Boca Raton home, 178, 194, 238, 244, 396, 451
Bolling Field (airport), 21
Bradford, Hilary, 452

Brass, Dr., 253
bridge (game), 80
British Spirella Company, 45
Buchenwald (concentration camp), 36
Buffalo General Hospital, 253–54
Buffalo Regional Office of OPA, 21
buyouts and corporate trading, 43–51

Camp Croft (SC), 26
Carpentras, France, 27
Castiglia, Jerry, 51
Chambers, Whittaker, 19
Channel 7 (Buffalo), 24
Chicago Stockyards Company, 158–59
children
  Elizabeth, 47, 254, 361, 395, 427, 451
  Lincoln, 21, 47, 193
Churchill, Clinton H., 22–24
Churchill, Winston, 27
Cohen, Paul Pincus, 19, 23, 44, 156, 452
Cohen Swados (law firm), 451–53
Cohn, Morris, 44
Company C, 28, 33